"This book will help anyone who wishes to develop the skills of communication coaching and Dr Dennis Becker has the experience and personal style to guide that development. Dr Dennis is a witty, intelligent, kind, and a very personable leader in the field of human communication. He is a veteran coach whose talents have given solace and strength to men and women throughout the world. I have no hesitation witnessing his professionalism in this important field of human growth."

Majed Salem Al Romaithi, *Senior Executive,*
Mid-East Investment Firm

"This is a must-have resource for any communication trainer. *The Handbook of Communication Training* is indispensable for all communication trainers or educators who seek real-world, research-based best practices for designing and delivering communication training. Organized around the best training practices of the National Communication Association Training and Development Division, this masterfully crafted book offers a comprehensive compendium of practical tips, strategies, and techniques to make communication training successful."

Steven A. Beebe, *PhD, Regents' and University Distinguished*
Professor, Texas State University, Past President,
National Communication Association

"Drawing on a broad array of professional expertise, Wallace and Becker have compiled a truly excellent training resource. From proposal development to managing institutional culture to multimedia design, this volume delightfully intersects the theory and practice of training, presenting useful techniques with solid contextual background. If you are interested in making the most of a training initiative, in ramping up the quality of existing processes, or in educating new practitioners, this is an invaluable resource."

Star A. Muir, *Associate Professor, George Mason University,*
First Vice President of National Communication Association

T0299314

The Handbook of Communication Training

Communication remains a significant topic for job acquisition, development, and advancement. As such, there are no shortage of classes, seminars, and books written on the subject. However, there are few designed for the corporate consultant that are not aligned with some proprietary system, traditional academic classrooms, or author's speculation. These tend to be either inaccessible, questionable in their content, or specifically aligned with the producers' interests. So where can the communication trainers and consultants go to focus on fundamental touchstone research and practices?

The Handbook of Communication Training is a powerful template, and first of its kind, for communication practitioners and academicians who wish to strengthen their professional capabilities. It also acts as a guide and standard for consumers and clients of these services.

The chapters within are an outgrowth of the National Communication Association's Training & Development Division's desire to provide guidance, structure, and support for members and non-members alike. It is specifically targeted at those pursuing best practices regarding communication consulting, coaching, teaching, and training. The 7 Best Practices presented in this book represent capabilities that are foundational to the effective transfer of communication promotion and skill enhancement. As such, these practices, and supporting chapters, should appeal to novice and experts alike.

J. D. Wallace, PhD, is a Professor of Communication at Abilene Christian University. Past works include over 100 national/international presentations and publications with a special emphasis on training and development. Professionally, he is an award-winning scholar and teacher with numerous consultations in profit and non-profit organizations.

Dennis Becker, PhD, founded The Speech Improvement Company, the nation's oldest Speech Coaching firm. In addition to having taught at Harvard and MIT, Dennis consults and coaches worldwide. This book is his sixth on communication and represents his continuing effort to strengthen the quality of communication training.

The Handbook of Communication Training

A Best Practices Framework for Assessing and Developing Competence

Edited by
J.D. Wallace and Dennis Becker

Routledge
Taylor & Francis Group

LONDON AND NEW YORK

First published 2019
by Routledge
2 Park Square, Milton Park, Abingdon, Oxon OX14 4RN

and by Routledge
605 Third Avenue, New York, NY 10017

Routledge is an imprint of the Taylor & Francis Group, an informa business

British Library Cataloguing-in-Publication Data
A catalogue record for this book is available from the British Library

Library of Congress Cataloguing-in-Publication Data
Names: Wallace, J. D., 1958– editor. | Becker, Dennis, 1942– editor.
Title: The handbook of communication training: a best practices
framework for assessing and developing competence / edited by
J.D. Wallace and Dennis Becker.
Description: Abingdon, Oxon; New York, NY: Routledge, 2018. |
Includes bibliographical references and index.
Identifiers: LCCN 2018014825 (print) | LCCN 2018018180 (ebook) |
ISBN 9781315185859 (eBook) | ISBN 9781138736528 (hardback: alk. paper)
Subjects: LCSH: Communication in organizations. | Business communication.
Classification: LCC HD30.3 (ebook) |
LCC HD30.3 .H3539 2018 (print) | DDC 658.3/124—dc23
LC record available at https://lccn.loc.gov/2018014825

ISBN 13: 978-1-138-73652-8 (hbk)

Typeset in Bembo
by codeMantra

Contents

Acknowledgements

As with many projects, especially ones with the importance and magnitude of this undertaking, there are a variety of hands that have made it possible, and we want to acknowledge a few of those whose shoulders this volume stands upon. At the top of the list is Taylor & Francis on their support for the creation of this long needed volume. Alexandra Atkinson and Amy Laurens were there to answer questions and provide insights as we moved toward publication. Also thanks to Jonathan Norman for his understanding of the value of this project and supporting it from the very start. He has moved on to other opportunities and we wish him much success.

Most appropriately, we want to thank the National Communication Association's Training & Development Division (NCA's T & D division) for providing support, promotion, guidance, and an ongoing vision in the development of resources. The origins of this project began in late May in 2007 when Christina Bates headed up an exploratory committee of 20 communication training and development professionals. Findings of this committee revealed the complexity both in terms of depth and breadth of communication consultants, coaches, trainers, and teachers. Interests ranged from applied to theoretical, with two major mandates established moving forward. First, and most importantly, some sort of standards, or touchstone points, needed to be established to distinguish competent communication training and consultation from inadequate or counterfeit. Second, such touchstone points were necessary to provide visibility to those already practicing against a field of academicians and practitioners that might need further development.

This culminated in the 2010 Blue Ribbon Communication Training and Development Best Practices Task Force. We would like to especially thank our fellow Blue Ribbon Task Force members Robert C. Chandler and Timothy Mottet. Additionally, we would like to thank the 100+ professionals who served as reviewers. We were highly encouraged by a survey given to the membership of NCA's Training & Development Division. These respondents represented a reach to over a million potential trainees, clients, practitioners, and students. Both of these groups helped provide prima fascia validity and vet content after extensive research established initial topics and categories. This research and evaluation of the findings evolved into 7 Best Practices that communication consultants, coaches, teachers, and trainers should possess and utilize. President of NCA, Steven Beebe, deserves special recognition for his encouragement and help in promoting the NCA's T & D Best Practices to a national audience and beyond. Additionally, we would like to thank current and past leadership of NCA's

T & D Division for their support since the establishment of The Blue Ribbon Task Force. Included in this list are Ross Brinkert, Joe Cardot, "Pui" Charoensap-Kelly, Lori Charron, Laurie Diles, Craig Engstrom, Seth Frei, Liane Gray-Starner, Peter Jorgensen, Paul Lakey, Nicole Laster, Jeffrey Martin, Robin Golinski, Greg Patton, Mary Pilgrim, "Dee" Priddis, DeeDee Smartt, Jayne Violette, and Caleb Williams.

No volume could come to fruition without the scores of submissions that were received and we appreciate the overwhelming patience and diligence of all our submitters and we authors as we worked through the process. Authors names are recorded in the table of contents but many others had high quality submissions that ultimately did not fit this volume. We are hopeful they will be published in other venues as their quality and diligence was evident.

Lastly as co-editors, we have had a great deal of support from a variety sources. For J D Wallace this includes both Abilene Christian University and Pepperdine University, without whose support my participation in this project and the research required would not have been possible. I especially appreciate my chair Joe Cardot as sounding board, support, and friend. My family endured innumerable unattended activities in deference to this volume. Without their understanding and patience, my contributions would not be possible. Both my wife and daughter are graduated English majors whom I inflicted materials upon on numerous occasions. Merrill Wallace, my wife of 30 years, my best friend and companion, provided indefatigable support and encouragement throughout this process. I am not sure why, but she continues to be my biggest cheerleader without whom my life would not be the joy that it is. Finally, and certainly not least, I credit my faith in God as causal in the pursuit of excellence and the patience necessary for such an authoritarian multi-authored volume as this.

For Dennis Becker the completion of this volume and the development of the 7 Best Practices represents a multi-decade effort to establish a set of criteria which help to differentiate those of us for whom human communication is a professional passion from those for whom it is a profit seeking pastime. My deepest gratitude goes to my wife, best friend, coach and muse of 52 years, Paula Borkum Becker. She left this earthly sphere before the completion of this volume but continues to inspire and guide me in every way. My colleagues at The Speech Improvement Company, Inc., who endured by constant questioning and challenging for guidance were a significant support for which I am grateful. They continue to be the standing example of the best we bring to others. It was a privilege to work closely with so many carefully selected, insightful, and patient professional communication contributors who brought their unique talents to this volume. Special recognition must go to NCA and The Training & Development Division for their recognition and acceptance of the value and role that practitioners, academicians, and scholars play in helping humankind become wiser and more peaceful inhabitants of our mother earth.

List of contributors

Elissa A. Adame, Ph.D., is an assistant research professor in the Hugh Downs School of Human Communication at Arizona State University. Her research interests involve leadership communication, organizational training and development, and organizational learning processes. Her work is published in journals such as *Communication Research Reports*, *Management Communication Quarterly*, *Health Communication*, and *International Journal of Business Communication*. Currently, she is working on research to investigate communication strategies to maximize feedback effectiveness and learning outcomes.

Jay Baldwin, Ph.D., is an assistant professor of communication at Abraham Baldwin Agricultural College in southwest Georgia. Prior to entering the academy, he enjoyed a successful career in real estate development, sales and marketing management, and media relations. He is also the former director of Idaho's higher education consortium.

Amber Barnes, MA, is the founder and CLO of StartHuman, a leadership development practice based in Reno, Nevada. She brings over 15 years of training and organizational diagnostics experience, both as an internal and external consultant. Amber's experience includes Fortune 500 companies, start-ups, non-profits, government entities, and higher education.

Steven A. Beebe, Ph.D., is Regents' and University Distinguished Professor Emeritus of Communication Studies at Texas State University. He is the author and co-author of 12 books (with most books in multiple editions) and numerous articles about communication focusing on communication skill development. He has served as President of the National Communication Association.

Thomas A. Birk (Ph.D., Southern Illinois University, 1997) served as an organizational consultant for educational institutions and businesses for over 20 years. He was a faculty member at Southern Illinois University and adjunct faculty for the University of Nebraska, University of Nebraska Medical Center, Dana College, and the University of Phoenix Online.

Ross Brinkert (Ph.D., Temple University, 2006) is chair and associate professor of Corporate Communication at Penn State Abington, past co-chair of the NCA Training and Development Division, and co-leader of the Division's Mentoring Program. Ross is also a consultant with more than 20 years of experience across sectors.

Lacey Corey Brown, M.A., is a doctoral candidate and instructor of communication at Southern Illinois University Carbondale. She teaches courses in business communication, organizational communication, and fundamentals of public speaking.

Marjorie M. Buckner, Ph.D., is an assistant professor in the Department of Communication Studies at Texas Tech University. Marjorie's research examines expressed dissent in organizations as well as instructor and student communication behaviors related to learning. She has created and facilitated trainings for academic and professional audiences.

Barton Buechner, Ph.D., is a professor with the Adler University Masters in Psychology with Emphasis in Military Psychology (MAMP) program, where he supervises student capstone projects and teaches a variety of courses. Dr. Buechner retired from the Navy at the rank of Captain after 30 years of military service.

John E. Burk, Ph.D., is an organizational development consultant at Intel Corporation focused on aligning talent, teams, leaders, and organizations to execute business strategies. John has been an internal and external consultant in previous organizations and a faculty member at Arizona State University.

Piyawan Charoensap-Kelly, MA, is Piyawan Charoensap-Kelly is a lecturer of organizational communication at the University of Alabama in Huntsville and a doctoral candidate at the University of Southern Mississippi. a doctoral candidate at the University of Southern Mississippi. She received the 2016 Rising Star Award from the National Communication Association's Training and Development Division and is co-chair of the Division. Her recent work can be found in the *Business and Professional Communication Quarterly* and the *Journal of Education Advancement & Marketing*.

Cody M. Clemens (M.A., Duquesne University) is currently a Doctoral Candidate at Bowling Green State University (Bowling Green, OH). Also, he is a visiting assistant professor of Communication at Marietta College (Marietta, OH) and an associate consultant for Smartt Strategies, LLC. His research focuses on health, organizational, and relational communication.

Sara DeTurk, Ph.D., is a former training consultant and currently professor of Communication at the University of Texas at San Antonio. Her teaching and research interests include intercultural communication, training and group facilitation, intergroup dialogue, and alliances for social justice activism.

Belynda Dix, MA, is a research assistant for the RED Early Childhood Mental Health Studies and does training development for Project Play at the University of Arkansas for Medical Sciences. Her research interests include investigating communication strategies that promote learning in young children and adults. Her co-authored work has been submitted to Public Health Nutrition.

Donna M. Elkins, PH.D., Professor, School of Communication, Spalding University, holds a Ph.D. in Communication from the University of Kentucky. She previously provided corporate training in Personal and Organizational Leadership to several industries. In the past, she also spearheaded the development of a comprehensive distance learning quality process for her higher education institution.

Craig Engstrom, Ph.D., is an assistant professor of organizational communication at Southern Illinois University Carbondale. He teaches training, consulting, social media, and business communication courses. He is lead consultant and owner of Sophisticated Communication Consulting. He has served on NCA's Training and Development Division leadership team. More information: www.craigengstrom. ninja.

Amber N. Finn, Ph.D., is an associate professor at Texas Christian University, where she teaches courses in training and development. Her research examines how teacher/ trainer communication behaviors and methods of instruction impact instructional outcomes. Amber has designed and facilitated communication skills-training for public and non-profit organizations.

Michael Forst, MA, is a doctoral candidate and instructor of communication at Southern Illinois University Carbondale. He teaches courses in intercultural communication, research methods, and fundamentals of public speaking. He is the 2017 chairperson of the annual training institute for HOBY, an international youth leadership non-profit.

Seth S. Frei (Ph.D., University of Texas at Austin) is a lecturer in the Department of Management at Texas State University. He teaches various courses in management, business communication, and instructional communication. His research has appeared in various communication journals and focuses on the use and development of communication skills in professional and instructional contexts.

Ralph A. Gigliotti, Ph.D., is director of leadership development and research in the Center for Leadership at Rutgers University. Ralph is the co-author of A Guide for Leaders in Higher Education: Core Concepts, Competencies, and Tools and Leadership: Communication and Social Influence in Personal and Professional Contexts.

Robin Golinski, BS, founded a successful company in Boston where her passion was training and coaching and focuses on leadership, persuasion, sales training, relationship building, and character development. Robin is an accomplished stand-up comedian and is also the founder and producer of Boston Comedy Chicks, a group devoted to supporting Women in Comedy through development and providing opportunities. She is currently the founding partner of http:// mindsetcommunication.com, an international training and coaching firm.

Michelle Hege, M.S., APR, is the president and CEO of DH, an advertising, public relations, and research firm based in Spokane, Washington. She has 20 years of experience in designing research-based communications and marketing programs for organizations. She also works with executive teams in facilitating strategic planning and internal communications improvement processes.

Robin Hinkle, Ph.D., director of the Master of Science in Business Communication (MSBC) and assistant professor, School of Business, Spalding University, previously taught at the University of Louisville and worked for various organizations, including Humana and the US Army Research Institute. She holds a Ph.D. in leadership development from the University of Louisville.

Dakota C. Horn, MA, is an Ed.D student at Illinois State University specializing in communication education and instructional design. Dakota received his BA and MA degrees from Western Illinois University in communication. His work experience includes training and marketing development at State Farm Insurance offices as well as curriculum design and communication planning for k-12 school districts.

Dr. Renee Kaufmann, Ph.D., specializes in Instructional Communication and Instructional Technology. She is assistant professor of Communication at the University of Kentucky. Renee has a graduate certificate in distance learning from the University of Kentucky and, prior to her role as an assistant professor, served as an e-learning specialist for UK.

Helen Lie, Ed.D. is a lecturer in the Oral Communication Program and the Program in Writing and Rhetoric at Stanford University, where she teaches, delivers workshops, and provides consultations to students, researchers, and staff on general presentation skills, preparing academic presentations, effective communication, and visual design.

DeeDee Smartt Lynch, B.S. in Organizational Communication, University of Texas at Austin, is a global interaction strategist and consultant specializing in team coaching and development. Certified in the United Kingdom and now a leading Belbin Team Roles expert in the U.S., she has provided team training and services to small businesses, corporations, and the U.S. government and military.

Michael J. Lynch, M.Sc., C.Eng., MIET, has more than 30 years of experience of Project Management in the international civil nuclear engineering and construction arena (managed projects up to $3.5 billion). He saw first-hand the power of Belbin Team Roles in his project teams and delivered superior results because of it.

Lauren Mackenzie, Ph.D., is professor of Military Cross-Cultural Competence at the Marine Corps University Center for Advanced Operational Culture Learning in Quantico, VA. She conducts research relating to cross-cultural competence, oversees culture-related curriculum development, and outcomes assessment, and delivers intercultural communication presentations across the Professional Military Education spectrum.

Robin Smith Mathis, Ph.D., is an assistant professor of Organizational Leadership at Mercer University. She designs, delivers, and assesses training in the Penfield College's workforce training program. She earned her Ph.D. from Texas A&M University in Educational Human Resource Development with an emphasis in Communication.

Kristen A. McIntyre (Ph.D., North Dakota State University) is an associate professor in the Department of Applied Communication at the University of Arkansas at Little Rock. Her co-authored publications in communication education include *Communication Quarterly, Communication Teacher, The Communication Centers Movement in Higher Education,* and *Best Practices in Experiential and Service Learning in Communication*.

Lori B. Miraldi, MA, is a Ph.D. candidate in Workforce Education at The Pennsylvania State University and Director of the Engineering Ambassadors Program and Student Engagement Initiatives in the College of Engineering.

Peter N. Miraldi, Ph.D., earned his Ph.D. in Communication Studies from Kent State University and is a Teaching Professor in Communication Arts and Sciences at The Pennsylvania State University.

Kristine M. Nicolini, Ph.D., is an assistant professor in the Journalism department at the University of Wisconsin, Oshkosh. Her research examines cognitive, behavioral, and normative processes associated with navigating difficult conversations. Nicolini has over 15 years of professional experience in public relations, strategic marketing, and corporate communication.

Jessica Parker-Raley, Ph.D., is an associate professor at Texas State University and postdoctoral fellow at UT Health Science Center San Antonio. She conducts training programs focused on improving communication in healthcare settings. Topics include: interdisciplinary communication, patient handoffs, patient discharge, breaking bad news, and consenting patients/families.

DeAnne Priddis, Ph.D., is an assistant professor in the Department of Communication at Middle Tennessee State University, Murfreesboro, TN. Her research includes conflict in families and organizations. Priddis has over 15 years of corporate and non-profit professional experience primarily in human resources and training prior to her career in academics.

Brett W. Robertson, MA, is a doctoral student at The University of Texas at Austin. His research examines how individuals use social media in the workplace and in crisis contexts. He has published research related to organizational communication and technology use and has received several top paper awards.

Brent D. Ruben, Ph.D., is a distinguished professor and executive director of the Center for Organizational Leadership at Rutgers University. He is author of numerous publications including *Excellence in Higher Education, Communication and Human Behavior,* and *A Guide for Leaders in Higher Education: Core Concepts, Competencies, and Tools.*

Hannah R. Seagrave, MS, is an adjunct lecturer at Eastern Washington University and program coordinator at Pacific University. She has instructed undergraduate and graduate level research methods courses, contributed to publications within organizational communication as well as human communication and technology, and consulted with diagnostic teams for organizations throughout the Inland Northwest.

Robert J. Sidelinger, Ed.D., is an associate professor and communication internship director in the Department of Communication and Journalism at Oakland University. His main research focus is instructional communication. Much of his work centers on student-to-student connectedness and its impact on learning processes and educational outcomes.

Jeffrey L. Stafford, Ph.D., is a professor of organizational communication & leadership at Eastern Washington University. He teaches graduate seminars on organizational diagnosis, leadership, & organizational improvement. His Students conduct diagnostic projects for community organizations. He is also the founder of a consulting firm, Stafford & Associates, LLC, which specializes in applied research.

Susan L. Steen, Ph.D., is an assistant professor of Cross-Cultural Communication at the Air Force Culture and Language Center where she designs and develops curricula, conducts research, teaches, trains, and advises students. Her work involves military service members from enlisted through General Officer, in-residence and online, at the graduate and undergraduate levels.

Keri K. Stephens, Ph.D., is associate professor of Organizational Communication & Technology and an associate director for the Center for Health Communication in the Moody College of Communication at The University of Texas at Austin. Her research focuses on organizational communication technology use and she has trained over 100 different clients.

Dr. Michael G. Strawser, Ph.D., specializes in Instructional and Organizational Communication. He is an assistant professor of Communication at Bellarmine University and the director of graduate programs in the School of Communication. Additionally, he has worked with Leadership Louisville, Young Professionals of Louisville, and the Kentucky Department of Education as a communication trainer through his firm Legacy Communication Training and Consulting.

Greta R. Underhill, MS, is an educator with interests in organizational health and inclusion. She has instructed undergraduate level courses in basic communication and research methods, including the development of several online courses. In addition to her corporate human resource experience, she has consulted on communication audits for a range of organizations.

Don Waisanen, Ph.D., is an associate professor in the Baruch College, CUNY Marxe School of Public and International Affairs, where he teaches courses in communication and leadership. He is the founder and president of Communication Upward and received a Ph.D. in Communication from the University of Southern California's Annenberg School.

Lisa Waite, MA, brings three decades of experience teaching undergraduate communication courses and as a passionate practitioner. She provides executive coaching and consulting for teachers, trainers, and business professionals. Through a people-centric approach, Lisa leads organizations to build healthy cultures that support success, civility, accountability, and innovation to compete.

Jennifer H. Waldeck, Ph.D., has 100+ scholarly articles, books, and presentations regarding instructional, organizational, and business communication. She is an associate professor of Communication at Chapman University. She has extensive consulting experience in a variety of manufacturing, health, and public service sectors and has co-edited (with David Seibold) *Consulting that Matters: A Handbook for Scholars and Practitioners,* 2016.

Marian L. Ward, MA, teaches the introductory communication course at the University of Arkansas at Little Rock. Previously, Marian worked as a political consultant on campaigns from mayoral races to the U.S. presidential contests. Marian's most recent publication can be found in *Communication Law Review.*

Hope Zoeller, Ph.D., Founder and President of HOPE (Helping Other People Excel), LLC, consults with organizations on leadership development. She is also an adjunct professor at Spalding University in the MSBC program. She holds a Doctorate in Leadership Education from Spalding University. Zoeller recently published a book titled HOPE for Leaders Unabridged.

Introduction
Best practices for communication training

This volume is an outgrowth of the ongoing work of the National Communication Association's Training and Development Division but is certainly not limited to its membership or interests. To be sure, communication training remains a stalwart of the T & D universe. However, since most of the work has been internal NCA's T & D division some background to its development is appropriate.

Rationale

The National Communication Association's (NCA) Training and Development Division's leadership requested the development of a slate of "Best Practices for Communication Training and Development" both for the Division and also as resource of guidance for the NCA. Ideally these would be accessible both by members and nonmembers to establish NCA scholars as a substantive voice in the field of training and development.

This was appropriate and served the interests of Communication Consultants, Coaches, Teachers & Trainers (CCCTTs) but also the interests of the National Communication Association. Aside from being an educational resource, it is appropriate for four overarching reasons:

1 Give guidance and benchmarks which both practitioners and academics can use to establish threshold competencies.
2 Allow those who are proficient in those competencies to gain additional visibility by some form of recognition of the standards to which they already adhere.
3 Provide consumers of communication training and development, regardless of setting a guide for assessing quality.
4 Contribute to the fulfillment of the NCA fundamental values and visionary goals.

It also helps align the T & D division with NCA's broader strategic plan and organizational vision. This was consistent with a number of categories in NCA's Strategic Plan that are parallel with most organizational CCCTTs. These include "the cultivation of communication knowledge," "dissemination of communication knowledge," "supporting pedagogy," "facilitating professional development for communication scholars, educators, and practitioners," and "fostering and modeling civil discourse and open and ethical communication."

Background

The National Communication Association's (NCA) Training and Development Division charged a Blue Ribbon Task Force on Best Practices for Training and Development to provide a slate of areas to be considered as guidelines and building blocks for strengthening the quality of communication services and information delivered CCCTTs from academic or practitioner groups. Members of the panel included both practitioners and academics. Participants included: Dr. Dennis Becker, Principal & Senior Coaching Partner for The Speech Improvement Company; Dr. Timothy P. Mottet, professor and Dean of the College of Fine Arts and Communication at University of Texas-San Marcos; Dr. Robert C. Chandler, professor and Director of the Nicholson School of Communication at University of Central Florida; and Dr. J. D. Wallace, (chair) professor of communication at Abilene Christian University and former chair of NCA's Training and Development Division. The practices that emerged reflected a broad framework for CCCTTs of competence, accountability, and transparency. Supporting material for the multi-year long inquiry included, but were not limited to:

- Evaluation of 400+ occupations from the bureau of labor statistics, 40 % of which had training as their most significant source of education
- Examination of all 50 U. S. state governmental materials for standards regarding communication and speech certification
- Review of NCA's previous/current standards concerning speaking, listening, and media literacy
- An extensive literature review involving 949 peer reviewed articles, generating 9,533 (3,840 unique) topics
- A review of 66 online training course syllabi from human resources, business, psychology, education, and communication
- Survey of 148 practitioners concerning the efficacy academic's literature top fifty-two training and development related topics

These results were consolidated and presented at the NCA annual conference in New Orleans. A special panel was created at the conference to solicit feedback from NCA's training and development division membership. The membership re-tasked the task force into creating a language for practices that would do two things:

First, establish a common set of core principles around which CCCTTs could advance their related pursuits.

Second, ensure usability that would legitimize, distinguish, and reward those CCCTTs who recognized and adhered to those principles.

The results were presented and accepted at the Training and Development Division's annual business meeting. Subsequently, the division conducted a small-scale survey to solicit endorsements to test inherent value of the best practices. Initial endorsements came from a 80/20 per cent academic/practitioner mix including over 100 Universities representing a potential reach to more than 1 million undergraduate students. The resulting Best Practices involved seven best practices in 12 general areas of application. These were not considered to be all inclusive but rather as illustrative of the more common areas of application and scholarship emerging from the Task Forces Review.

The following details the seven best practices for communication training as well as affiliated expectations of this handbook. The practices as they stand reflect three strong umbrella themes of competency, accountability, and transparency.

Best practices for communication training competency, accountability, and transparency

Best practice 1 – Maintain transparency to clients and trainees

- Those involved in Training and Development acknowledge a framework of best practices that provides structure for their training and consulting.
- Trainers and consultants should have readily available standards to which their activities can be evaluated by participants. Language should include demonstrable benchmarks.
- Trainers and consultants must abide by a documented code of ethics that is easily obtainable by clients and assessment groups.

Best practice 2 – Use assessable methods

- Trainers and consultants must have identifiable deliverables that can be internally and externally assessed.
- Trainers should be able to demonstrate expertise in training transfer.

Best practice 3 – Demonstrate technology proficiency

- Trainers should have proficiency in technology needed for delivering and executing training content.
- Trainers should have proficiency in digital technology.

Best practice 4 – Demonstrate professional development

- Subject and performance competency should be acquired and maintained.
- Professional development should provide on leverage for the communication trainer.

Best practice 5 – Develop and maintain organizational expertise

- Communication trainers and consultants should be familiar with organizational catalysts for training such as leadership, management, planning, and culture.
- Communication trainers and consultants should be familiar with employee catalysts for training such as career development, human resources, innovativeness, selection, and appraisal.

Best Practice 6 – Demonstrate effective and appropriate instructional design

- Communication training should be built around implementable models of instructional design.
- Instructional design should accommodate different learning styles and their corresponding instructional methods.

Best Practice 7 – Demonstrate communication proficiency

- Communication trainers should demonstrate executable communication proficiencies including, but not necessarily limited to, presentations skills, interpersonal skills, organizational culture, and group techniques.

Maintain transparency to clients and trainees

- Those involved in Training and Development acknowledge a framework of best practices that provides structure for their training and consulting.
- Trainers and consultants should have readily available standards to which their activities can be evaluated by participants. Language should include demonstrable benchmarks.
- Trainers and consultants must abide by a documented code of ethics that is easily obtainable by clients and assessment groups.

Transparency is a two-way street that needs to be handled authentically by all parties in a communication training relationship. Consultants and trainers must understand expectations of clients and trainees. Conversely clients and trainees must understand expectations and limitations of those involved in communication training and development. Too often, both parties are involved (sometimes unknowingly) with bait and switch techniques. The first chapter, "Mobilizing a client for change" shows how trainers and consultants can obtain and build "Request for Proposals" that use clear frameworks to clarify expectations. The next chapter, "Communication training's higher calling", demonstrates how a civic frame can be used both to promote transparency and elevate the value of services. Finally, "The F-word changes a circular message" demonstrates even controversial frames have extended value when mutual interests are clearly expressed.

Chapter 1

Mobilizing a client for change

Best practices for proposing training

Jennifer H. Waldeck

Abstract

The ability to write a clear, persuasive, thorough, and marketable training proposal is the foundation for training that serves both client and trainer. This chapter details how to develop responses to formal Requests for Proposals (RFPs) common throughout government and industry. However, many proposals lack strategy or influence. Procedures, techniques, and considerations are provided to enhance professionalism for both novice and experienced trainers as well as to advance their submission response rate.

The proposal is the primary opportunity for a trainer to show an organization why he or she is best suited for the work, describe the training plan, provide a timeline and budget for the project, and to formalize a relationship with the client. It is critical for authentic and transparent training. Yet, trainers create proposals that often go unnoticed, unread, and/or unfunded. Many trainers are shortsighted in their thinking about what the proposal represents, and view it as little more than a formal means to obtain work. As a result, these important documents often lack strategy and influence. At its best, the proposal is a powerful tool for persuading clients to begin the progressive trajectory that great training makes possible—a path toward organizational development and improvement.

An effective training proposal defines the scope, objectives, rationale, and cost of a training intervention. It is well-organized, well-written, and, ultimately, highly persuasive. Further, the best proposals are highly client-centered. Each element must be written with careful attention to the unique nature of the client organization's culture, people, communication climate, structure, politics, and system (both internal and external). This chapter provides perspective on how to plan, write, and deliver proposals that will help the trainer win work, and that represent the first step toward influencing clients to make productive changes. This is essential to establishing fit with what the trainer offers and what the client desires.

A training proposal should address six primary topics (Waldeck, Plax, & Kearney, 2016):

- The trainer's credentials, experience, and technical ability to deliver the proposed services.
- The objectives of the proposed instruction.
- A detailed description of the training plan – the content, training methods, and assessments that the trainer is proposing based on an individualized client needs assessment (Jorgensen, 2016; Plax, Waldeck, & Kearney, 2016).

- A timeline for carrying out the training along with logistical details of project management for multi-phase training plans.
- The estimated costs and expenses associated with the project.
- The method(s) for evaluating the effectiveness of the proposed plan.

Example 1.1 features a flexible outline that can be adapted for most training proposals (Waldeck et al., 2016), into which these six topics can be situated. To produce a proposal that will have the greatest short- and long-term impact, trainers should spend an appropriate amount of time assessing the client's needs and collecting relevant data about the organization.

Title Page
Transmittal Letter
Table of Contents
Executive Summary

Introduction and Overview
Provide relevant history of the project
Overview needs assessment methods and summarize results
Establish a compelling need for action and improvement based on available evidence
Illustrate the trainer's (or training team's) credibility relative to the project (include professional bios and vitae or resumes as Appendix)

Training Objectives and Scope
Provide well-written observable, measurable, attainable, and specific training objectives for each phase (if multi-phased)
Summarize the target audiences for each phase of the training (specific groups and/or individuals from the organization who will be involved)

Training Plan
List and describe the content modules that correspond to each objective
Discuss the instructional strategies that will accomplish each content module
Explain any considerations such as employee time away from work, space, or physical resources the client should know about

Timeline
Provide a descriptive, visual timeline for the training intervention. When will each phase (if multi-phased) and module be facilitated? How much time will each phase and module require?
Explain how project management will be handled. How will the logistics of the project be managed? Who is accountable for project management in multi-phase, long-term training engagements?

Methods of Evaluation
Specify how the training will evaluated in terms of process, content, and delivery
Explain how evaluations will reveal whether training objectives were accomplished and will enable clients to realize a return on investement
Address formative and summative evaluation techniques

Budget and Costs
List, explain, and justify amounts requested for the training

Summary and Conclusion
Summarize the overall purpose of the project, close warmly, and ask for the business

Appendices
Bibliography

Example 1.1 Suggested Table of Contents for training proposals.

The proposal's backstory: Organizations and their training needs are rarely simple

Understanding an organization's training needs and how to best address them in a proposal requires a sophisticated understanding of organizing and organizational communication in general, and an ability to assess the specific organization relative to the expressed need – sometimes with little direct access. Organizations are complex structures; their needs rarely simple. For example, a client once requested a proposal for a four-hour customer service training session that would involve front line employees. Driving his perception of the need for this course were negative online customer reviews. To him, the solution was simple and straightforward. But when I began asking questions and observing the underlying informal organization, I realized that although what he was asking for was appropriate, even more critical was work with middle management. The front line experienced morale and motivation problems due to lackluster in-store management and oversight. If we implemented only front line customer service training, we would be patching a deep hole instead of filling it in. The question then becomes *how do trainers learn the nature and extent of the 'holes' that they are working with and expected to fix?* This backstory to the training proposal begins with how the trainer and client find one another.

The nature of the proposal is dependent, to an extent, on how the trainer came to bid on the job – in response to a Request for Proposal (RFP) or after a systematic needs assessment. An RFP is an invitation to qualified organizations or individuals to bid for specific work, typically without the benefit of a thorough needs analysis.[1] For instance, in 2016, working with a consulting group, I responded to a RFP from a U.S. Department of Defense (DOD) agency. The project involved developing training on communication in virtual team environments. Like many RFP-driven proposals, this proposal was very difficult to create. I had limited experience consulting with this particular agency. Although others on the team had worked with different units within DOD for many years, they had not worked with this particular project manager or target audience. Thus, we were constrained in our ability to understand the politics of the agency and the backstory of the RFP easily or accurately. We had to base our assessment of the client's needs strictly on the very general RFP. In addition to providing the qualifications that consultants had to meet (e.g., in terms of education, experience, and publication history), this document simply stated that the agency was requesting bids for a 10-hour curriculum on virtual teamwork and communication that could be delivered online or in an instructor-led environment.

From this example, you should see that trainers writing proposals in response to a published RFP have access to the limited, general information provided in the request. The inexperienced trainer will provide a generic response to a generic RFP. Conversely, the seasoned trainer knows that organizational culture, politics, structure, and personalities all interact to create the needs expressed in the RFP (Ross & Waldeck, 2016). An effective trainer networks with organizational insiders and does the kinds of informal research necessary to contextualize the often-vague contents of an RFP. This resource-intensive, behind-the-scenes work is essential for creating an influential proposal. My team ultimately won the contract to develop the virtual team communication course. However, we had generated many previous proposals for other agencies within the DOD that were unsuccessful because we had not yet built the connections, knowledge, and client-specific expertise necessary to understand the complexity of the needs expressed in the RFPs we had received. Thus, our proposals did not stand out. Over time, we sought a great deal of feedback on proposals submitted but unfunded and work completed, and built relationships that helped us develop the kind of understanding necessary to be successful.

When an RFP is issued, the client typically has a designated official who will respond to consultants' queries. However, the insight that contact offers is nothing like the type of information trainers can acquire through a needs assessment and by establishing an ongoing communication relationship with a prospective client. Thus, in contrast to the DOD bid, most of the work that I do is for clients with whom I have pre-existing relationships. Aware of my expertise, interests, background, and experience, these people approach me with a particular need. Even with well-established relationships, clients may require a written proposal and often question or resist aspects of my recommendations. My proposals must be persuasive, well-supported, well-written, and strategically aimed at the organization and its needs. I will ask the prospective client for the opportunity to speak with key stakeholders, and to do a formal needs assessment when appropriate (Jorgensen, 2016; Plax, Waldeck, & Kearney, 2016). These conversations and research methods allow me to create an effective, targeted proposal. In the next section, I discuss the strategies that underlie the process I follow for writing proposals for training and other consulting work.

Strategies for creating a successful proposal for training

Approach the proposal as persuasion

Proposals are, first and foremost, persuasive messages. They allow trainers to establish their credibility, convince clients of the urgency of organizational needs and problems, propose workable solutions, and persuade readers to accept recommendations. Influential proposals enable trainers to present themselves as a valuable asset to the organization who recognizes its needs – a partner that is able to make appropriate recommendations for addressing them. As with any persuasive message, readers of training proposals will fall into three groups – those who (1) already support the plan, (2) are neutral or undecided/uninformed about the issues addressed in the proposal, and (3) disagree with the need for training or with the recommended training solutions. As we will explore in this chapter, the persuasive proposal must be written for each of these audiences. After reading the proposal, previously agreeable readers should be even more motivated to accept the trainer's recommendations, neutral or undecided people should be more knowledgeable and invested in the issue, and disagreeable decision makers should feel respected, unthreatened, and more open to a reasonable amount of change. With this last group, the trainer must be cautious not ask for too much commitment at once to any issue or recommendation that the reader resists; rather, the training proposal should acknowledge potential objections to the plan, propose incremental change, and provide ample evidence of the plan's feasibility. Be very careful not to create resistance by offending readers with an approach that suggests that their organization is behind the times, uninformed, noncompetitive, or poorly managed (even if you believe that any of these conditions are true).

As with any persuasive message, the trainer should support the project in general and each recommendation in particular with clear, convincing reasoning. Link each training recommendation to one or more of the project objectives. Substantiate the proposal with needs assessment data, and wherever possible, with a theoretical or research-based rationale from the literature. My own training and consulting work is influential with organizational clients because it is grounded in credible, rigorous research and theoretical frameworks (Waldeck, 2016). But I write proposals in a style appropriate for the target audience – organizational decision makers who may not fully understand these research-based and theoretical approaches but seek positive change. Be sure to use relevant language to translate areas of your expertise that might be unfamiliar to the client. Effective trainers make their recommendations familiar and consumable to diverse readers in applied settings.

Persuasive proposals should conclude with specific action steps for the organization to take. In other words, ask for the work. Once you have created a sense of urgency surrounding the organization's needs and proposed a relevant and realistic solution, you must be clear about what the client needs to do in order start a formal working relationship with you. Leave the reader confident and comfortable that you will be able to credibly and reliably assist this organization in making needed improvements.

Communicate frequently with the client

Whether face-to-face or mediated (e.g., video calling or conferencing, e-mail) (Stephens & Waters, 2016), frequent, in-depth communication with clients results in the best proposals. This point is critical. Trainers should work closely and check in with the client as they specify objectives for the training, create the instructional design plan, and develop a budget. Working closely with the client at this stage ensures buy-in and a realistic proposal that is aligned with the client's needs, expectations, and available resources. To build the best possible relationship with contacts, practice active listening, rapport-building skills, verbal and nonverbal immediacy, and affinity seeking strategies (Beebe, 2016).

The more engaged the client is in the entire process, beginning with the formulation of the proposal, the more likely the client will be satisfied with the proposal the trainer generates, and ultimately, with the results of the training engagement. If the client is disengaged, or if the trainer does not communicate with the client during the formulation of the proposal, the trainer will have a difficult time getting buy-in and approval. Clients that are less involved in the early stages of the trainer's work tend to be more critical than engaged clients because they lack an appreciation of the process and product. Conversely, clients that give input into the proposal already feel a sense of ownership relative to the training and its potential benefits.

Some clients may want to be over-involved and attempt to control the direction of the work. For instance, a manager of a department within a large city government contacted me with a very specific training request. This client, concerned about costs and a sensitive political climate inside his organization, insisted on writing the description of the program, as well as the training objectives he wanted me to build my training plan around. I knew that the program I would propose should incorporate his input, but that I would need to carefully probe and assess his assertion that there were no other issues to address. The tactful trainer considers the client's concerns and addresses them in the proposal, but still makes recommendations based on an objective assessment of the organization's needs.

Whether clients are withdrawn or domineering, the best consultants leverage and manage their interactions with them, but do not rely solely on their input. Trainers should listen carefully, educate their clients about the training process, ask good questions, seek additional input from within the organization, and use the information they gather to write a strong proposal. Treat everything you observe and hear as valuable data. Working with experienced mentors in the fields of training and organizational consulting, I learned very early the importance of integrating clients into my work beginning with the proposal stage. Doing so gives them a feeling of ownership and investment in that work and gives me greater insight into the organization. As a result, the trainer has a heightened chance of successful engagements, additional contracts, and satisfying, long-term relationships.

Write strategically and well

Trainers must write their proposals strategically, with a great deal of attention to detail. First, this means that the document must be tailored to the specific client for which it is being written. Trainers must write their proposals with the knowledge that multiple people inside the organization will read them. I ask my primary contact on any engagement who will be receiving a copy of the proposal, and who the decision makers are. I obtain as much information as I can about those individuals in advance. Trainers should know what these readers' concerns or objections might be, their previous role in training and development initiatives on this and other issues within the organization, their attitudes toward external consultants, how much weight their opinion carries, and what support they might have to lend the project. After learning about the audience, the trainer is prepared to speak to each reader carefully in the proposal.

As the trainer gets to know the unique culture, needs, expectations, and challenges of an organization, he or she should incorporate this knowledge into the proposal through the language and approach used to frame it. The proposal needs to illustrate to the organizational stakeholders who read it that the trainer has unique, insider's insight into the issues the training will address. The goal is to customize the proposal to the organization's specific challenges, use the jargon and overall language that decision makers use and will understand, and leave readers thinking "this consultant really 'gets' us."

I have trained (among others) police officers, tool and die makers, and Fortune 500 corporate employees; management, front line workers, and executives. The nature of the target audience's work and position will inform many aspects of my plan, including the length of the program I recommend; the types of instructional strategies I plan to use; and whether the training should occur face-to-face, online, or in a blended format. There are no "cookie cutter" approaches to effective training that apply across learners or organization type, and the proposal must reflect the trainer's understanding of this critical point.

Next, the strategic proposal must be a perfect document, both in terms of content and presentation. The information included must be accurate; the grammar, punctuation, sentence, and paragraph structure polished and professional. Consider these recommendations (Waldeck et al., 2016):

- Apply a consistent format for lists and use italicized, boldfaced, and underlined text to emphasize important information. Create or use an existing style guide.
- Keep the proposal organized by using section headings and logical paragraphs. Business audiences tend to prefer deductively structured paragraphs. Ensure that paragraphs are coherent and flow with one another smoothly.
- Use internal previews, summaries, and signposts to keep the reader focused.
- Use high quality visuals and graphics such as tables, figures, graphs, and other images where appropriate to enhance the readability of the document (Boster, 2016).
- Present ideas in small, digestible units that will be easy for readers to comprehend and remember. Miller (1956) found that readers effectively process between just five and nine units of information at a time.
- Follow the instructions in the RFP if you are working from one. If you deviate from the prospective client's requirements at this stage in your relationship, you are demonstrating that you may not listen later, either.

- Be sure to allow sufficient time to write your proposal. In my experience, rushed proposals are rarely funded because I (or we, in the case of the team) have not taken the time to be detailed and accurate. Determining how long a proposal will take depends on many idiosyncratic factors including how fast you write, how many people are contributing, and how much information you need to compile to create an appropriate submission.
- Complete a thorough cycle of review and revisions. The proposal should be:
  - Concise
  - Written in the appropriate tone and using terminology the client will understand
  - Accurate, with proper attributions
  - Free of passive voice, spelling, punctuation, and grammatical errors.

On large, high stakes projects, I utilize professional copyeditors. In addition, the larger the project or organization, the more difficult the process will be to create an acceptable proposal, and working closely with your client will be very helpful. When I integrate a client into the process of developing the proposal, that contact will often pre-read and evaluate elements of the proposal, providing feedback that I can use for the copy I submit. For example, a number of years ago when working full time in the performance improvement consulting field, I was involved in complex, multi-year training initiative for one of the Big Three U.S. automakers. The proposal took six months to develop. Proactively, we scheduled regular conference calls with key members of the client organization to discuss needs and parameters for the program. As the agenda for the project became clear, these "champions" of the initiative reviewed the proposal and gave us helpful feedback based on their insight about other decision makers (some of whom would be less supportive) and aspects of the plan that would be difficult for anyone other than an insider to comment on. Over time, my team created a clear, relevant, and realistic training plan. The final proposal anticipated the concerns and suggestions of key decision makers. Ultimately, the project met the client's expectations and fulfilled the goals established at the beginning of the project. After five years, the contract was renewed and we moved on to help this organization achieve additional objectives.

The subtle facets of proposal strategy take time and effort to learn, often through trial and error. For example, my team responded to a number of RFPs from the Department of Defense, obtaining only small contracts for very short training programs (and having many proposals rejected) before being awarded the large virtual team communication project mentioned earlier in this chapter. Our proposals were written well, and submitted for training that we were highly qualified to facilitate. But, as any experienced consultant knows, a lot of work goes into figuring out how to get one's foot in the door. In our case, the principal consultant spent *years* learning the political landscape of this government agency, performing fairly small-scale training programs, getting to know decision makers, seeking feedback on failed proposals, and acquiring inside information about the agency's expectations. Only after this effort did we have an understanding of how to create a successful proposal to do larger projects that had more impact for both the trainers and the organization.

In sum, effective proposals require a trainer's time, effort, and sometimes, direct expense (e.g., payment to professional editors to proofread or improve your work). New or inexperienced trainers must understand that the costs of developing proposals for work they do not obtain are out of pocket. With experience, feedback, and mentoring, trainers become proficient at writing proposals and building relationships that will lead to profitable contracts and fulfilling, interesting work.

Be clear and thorough in explaining the client's needs

To write a comprehensive proposal, trainers need an understanding of the client's needs relative to the training topic (Jorgensen, 2016). Psychological reactance theory (Brehm, 1966) suggests that proposal evaluators, and ultimately, training participants, may not only be resistant to the trainer's recommendations, but to the very existence of the problem(s) or need(s) that the training is designed to resolve. Monroe (1935) developed a long-used, time-tested approach to persuasion that can be helpful to trainers in framing their proposals. Monroe's Motivated Sequence was rooted in the assumption people require enough of the right information to accept and even welcome change-oriented messages. Although this model is not necessarily a suggested format for consulting proposals, Monroe's emphasis on listener/reader needs in a persuasive situation is highly relevant for consulting proposals.

The most critical piece of information that clients require relates to their needs or problems surrounding the issue. Importantly, readers of training proposals may be unaware of the existence of such needs, or resistant to acknowledging them. The trainer must thoroughly establish that needs are clear and urgent, yet unfilled, before recommending solutions. The proposal should document the extent of the problem, as well as the source of the data that point to it. For instance, Ross and Waldeck (2016) worked with an organization that, on the surface, appeared to have some minor problems with transparency and communication openness. However, they conducted an organization-wide survey, interviews, and focus groups with employees from all units and ranks within the organization. This process revealed damaging dynamics related to how power was used by high-ranking officials. These perceived problems led to serious mistrust among lower-ranking employees. Because the problems identified in the needs analysis implicated some of the individuals who would be evaluating the proposal, the trainers anticipated resistance and objections.

Thus, when addressing problems and needs in a proposal, trainers must be aware that not all readers will understand or accept them – and must document them sensitively and thoroughly. Provide evidence of their existence and explain how that evidence was collected. Training objectives, and each recommendation the trainer makes in his or her plan, must be logically tied to documented needs. For instance, in a project for an organization now known as the National Association of Landscape Professionals (Waldeck, 2008), I worked with a team to evaluate skill competencies of green industry employees. Our analysis indicated competence gaps in several areas. Using statistical data taken from the skills tests as a rationale, we showed the extent of existing needs and made corresponding training recommendations. Whether the trainer learns about client needs through an RFP, background research on the client, formal needs assessments, or informal discussions, he or she must use these needs to persuade the client that the recommended interventions will be worth the effort and financial investment.

Pose realistic, relevant objectives for training

Once the trainer identifies the client's needs and defines them, he or she must translate those into desired results. Through conversations with the client, the trainer should identify:

- What specific outcomes should result from the intervention(s) at the organization and group levels.
- At the individual level, how organizational members should think, behave, or feel differently as a result of the training.

Writing useful training objectives takes a great deal of thought of and time. They must be observable, measurable, attainable in the agreed-upon timeframe and with the available resources, and specific (Beebe, Mottet, & Roach, 2013). Objectives that meet these criteria give the trainer direction on what kinds of training content and instructional activities will be effective, because they specify what should result from the training. For example, in a leadership training project, my client and I agreed that the client's existing courses were populated with outdated, unsubstantiated advice about leadership that was drawn from the popular press literature. My charge was to update and strengthen the curriculum with greater emphasis on recent peer-reviewed research and credible thought leaders. I reviewed literature published in the prior five years for research findings to include in the courses, and selected a formal theoretical framework (transformational leadership) for the curriculum. I then wrote specific learning objectives for each course – statements of what training participants should know and be able to do after completing the course. Having a theoretical framework and a set of training objectives guided me in organizing the content, eliminating that which was not consistent with the selected theory, and ensuring that what remained was credible. Taken together, the objectives ultimately enabled me to evaluate the success of the program.

Regardless of the focus of a trainer's engagement or the target audience, writing clear, realistic, and relevant objectives is critical. Objectives help the trainer illustrate for the client what is possible in terms of change, and then to create, implement, and evaluate training. A client, then, can easily see a valid, reliable set of results.

Provide an overview of your plan

Once the problem is defined and project objectives are specified, the trainer's task is to describe in clear, concrete detail, his or her recommendations for solving the problem and meeting the client's needs via training and instruction. In addition to describing the nature of the training, the proposal should be specific in indicating a timeline for implementation and delivery, methods for keeping the project on schedule, and who will be responsible for what aspects of the process. The proposal should also discuss issues of project management, specifying who will perform functions such as scheduling people and space or ordering supplies and other necessary items.

Typically, my recommendations are specific enough to give the client an understanding of what the training will entail, but not specific enough that it could be replicated. At the proposal stage, I avoid providing detailed content outlines or proprietary information. Remember, an internal consultant or trainer could decide he or she is capable of facilitating your content. I recommend providing a title for the program; an overall description that encompasses the program objectives; titles and objectives for each content module; an overview of the training methods you intend to use (based on the understanding you have of the target audience); and a general description of your assessment plan. Include a reference list for any specific material you cite in the proposal, and a representative bibliography of the kinds of sources you plan to consult for training content. As you determine the fine line between too much detail and too little, consider your specific readers. Your goals are to (a) provide a proposal that the client will read with interest, not annoyance because it is too long or filled with too many details; and (b) provide enough detail that will allow the client to make an informed decision or ask good questions and keep the relationship moving forward.

In describing your training and other deliverables, be sure that all recommendations are well-substantiated. The client must be able to see the link between the trainer's recommendations and the organization's need. The proposal must further demonstrate the efficacy of the solution. For instance, in work for the educational loan industry, Plax, Kearney, Allen, and Ross (2006) explored the problem of students defaulting on their loans. Based on clear evidence collected from their target population that existing educational materials (e.g., brochures, posters, and brief workshops) were inadequate, their proposal recommended a blended online and instructor-led training solution aimed at the problem of financial illiteracy that was scalable for undergraduates, graduate students, professional students, and recent college graduates.

Complex organizational problems and needs require complex solutions, and rarely can one individual provide all of the necessary skills and expertise. Some training programs require the skills and expertise of a training team. Thus, when making recommendations, trainers should be specific in describing each team member's roles and related background qualifications. This will establish the training team's credibility and aid the reader in determining that the recommendations are efficacious (since one individual cannot likely perform all aspects of a complex training plan and is not likely to have all of the skills and required knowledge to facilitate all aspects of a large engagement).

Indicate an assessment plan

A thorough, convincing proposal addresses exactly how the trainer plans to assess the effectiveness the recommended instruction. The goal of evaluation is to provide useful feedback to key stakeholders in the consultation's impact. Evaluative feedback provides clients with evidence that their investment in the project was worthwhile, often in the form of return on investment (ROI); such evidence allows clients to argue for additional resources, programs, or continuation of any of the initiatives begun. Evaluation offers trainers feedback on what worked and what did not, and speaks to whether or not the project's objectives were accomplished. Without a proper evaluation, trainers do not know how to improve their facilitation skills or the content and style of their programs, and clients can only speculate about the training's value. In the absence of a systematic evaluation plan, all stakeholders can do is base their conclusions on anecdotal evidence of questionable reliability and validity.

My approach in evaluating my training and other consulting work relies heavily on the scientific method and I typically use a mixed method approach. As a result, I obtain data that are as objective, reliable, valid, and impartial as possible and triangulate these with employees' narratives and my observations of organizational members' behavior and interactions relative to the training topic(s). Organizational decision makers appreciate and understand the results of quantitative measures when it comes to demonstrating bottom-line success of a consultation, but they also appreciate understanding their environments in terms of the stories and day-to-day experiences of other members, customers, and other stakeholders. Thus, I often also collect open-ended, qualitative data.

Every trainer needs to determine what types of evaluative methods to employ based on a careful analysis of key decision makers within the organization. For instance, by observing your client's listening style (Bodie & Worthington, 2010), you can determine what kinds of data and outcomes he or she will be most interested in. See Beebe (2016) for an explanation of how to understand listening styles and use this information in the training and consulting context.

Further, trainers should conduct both formative and summative evaluations (Waldeck, Kearney, & Plax, 2017). *Formative* evaluations assess participant reactions to the training before and during implementation. I rely on formative evaluations to determine trainees' level of readiness (e.g., with a pre-test), and to refine my training as I facilitate workshops. For instance, I ask participants to complete simple feedback forms at the conclusion of the first day (or hour, or module) of training. These forms typically include Likert-type and semantic differential scales for evaluating the content and trainee reactions to the facilitator. Simple skills tests or quizzes offer insight into training effectiveness after a content module. Other simple techniques used in academic settings, such as having trainees anonymously record one or two "muddiest" or confusing points from the training that the trainer will then address when the session resumes, are highly effective. These formative evaluation techniques not only provide the trainer with valuable feedback, but they heighten participant engagement in the training experience.

Trainers conduct *summative* evaluations at the conclusion of a program. Typically more formal than formative evaluations, they measure the outcomes of an intervention and are linked to program objectives. Trainers should investigate the availability of existing instruments that assess attainment of each objective, or create their own reliable, valid assessments. Common summative evaluation techniques include tests or demonstrations, anonymous surveys, exit interviews, and both short- and long-term outcome indicators. These measure impacts, benefits, or changes brought about by the training. Clients are often interested in the long-term impacts of training, but the value of the intervention isn't measurable immediately, or clients want to know if the immediate value lasts or grows. For example, I was involved in the development of an online learning program for corporate employees that included video clips of motivational keynote speeches delivered by business leaders. At the conclusion of each talk, participants were asked to complete a goal-setting exercise based on the speaker's content and overall program objectives. Follow-up emails at 4-week, 6-month, and 1-year intervals prompted them to complete summative assessments of their progress toward established goals.

Summary: Proposal development

Taken together, proposal development strategies should suggest several important takeaway points to trainers. First, training requires careful, strategic planning. Effective trainers think through every detail of planning, facilitating, and evaluating a program prior to submitting a proposal. Well-crafted proposals anticipate readers' concerns, questions, and objections. Second, high-quality proposals furnish credible, compelling evidence relevant to each recommendation. They convince the reader that the recommendation will work, and they minimize client objections or concerns about implementation by clarifying the trainer's expertise and ability to facilitate the interventions smoothly. Third, successful proposals list attainable objectives and how the trainer's recommendations will help the organization realize those objectives—and how client will know (i.e., through what evaluation methods). Finally, the proposal must be a technically flawless document. Any errors, gaps in reasoning, editorial mistakes, or missing information will result in the proposal being discarded in favor of one that has been more thoughtfully prepared. One of the most important details a client will need is the project's cost.

How much should I charge? Advice for estimating costs and determining your worth

First, do not underestimate the time that a training project will require. A careful proposal that serves both client and trainer offers an accurate estimate of resources required to carry out the project. For example, a one-day training workshop involves much more than the eight hours spent at the training site. Determining the time associated with any project becomes more difficult the larger and more complex the consultation is. For any engagement, Plax (2008) advises that trainers carefully consider:

- *Preparation time* (e.g., assessing the training audience; formally meeting with the client; conducting a needs analysis; writing objectives; research; designing content, pedagogical strategies, and evaluation measures).
- *Delivery time* (e.g., the actual facilitation of the training; setting up the physical space; arranging for participant comforts such as food and beverages, parking, and commuting expenses).
- *Debriefing time* (e.g., analyzing evaluation data; writing a report; briefing the client).

Costing out time for a proposal does not include the time spent finding the work, writing the proposal, talking informally with the client, or negotiating the terms. Trainers incur some indirect costs in proposing and acquiring work – but these tasks can be factored in to the rate they charge for the project. Estimating time using the categories of preparation, delivering, and debriefing can help trainers be accurate in computing just how many hours they will spend on a particular project.

In my experience, everything takes longer than anticipated and projects often grow in unexpected ways as clients ask for more and contingencies arise. For example, I created an online training course for a client that required learning a software program that was much more difficult to use than the client had initially suggested to me. Then, well into the project, the client asked me to assume responsibility for evaluating the course's 508(c) compliance, which ensured accessibility and usability by learners with disabilities. The problem grew complex when the client was unwilling to furnish an increase in the financial terms of the contract for this added time and work. Trainers cannot anticipate all of the complications that might lead to added time on a project, therefore they should always overestimate their time at the proposal stage.

What dollar amount should trainers associate with the time spent on their work? Plax (2008) recommends that academics new to training calculate an hourly rate based on their salary as a college professor. More experienced consultants can charge a great deal more. (If you are not a full-time faculty member at a college or university, you can use the average gross annual salary figure for that position in your geographic region and your discipline; or, you can research what in-house and contract trainers are paid in your area.) Before using that hourly fee to multiply by time spent to calculate a total project cost, consider that:

- Consulting work is contract work, which does not include benefits normally associated with permanent employment. If the trainer does not have health insurance or a retirement benefit from another employer, he or she will need to fund them from consulting fees.

- Training and consulting fees are taxable, yet the payment a trainer receives is pre-tax money. Contractors need to set aside a portion of what they earn to pay taxes owed.
- The trainer's fee must cover any expenses not specified elsewhere in the contract (e.g., meals, commuting).
- The fee is a one-time payment for services rendered, and because there is no guarantee of future work with this client, the trainer will spend more time and money to generate additional work.

All of these considerations suggest that trainers must be careful to account for the hidden costs associated with their work in order to generate a profit. So, using Plax's formula, for example: If your base salary at your academic institution is $85,000, that works out to $1,770.83 per week and $44.27 per hour based on a 40-hour work week. But when you subtract the expenses just discussed from $44.27, you are left with a very small number. Thus, Plax recommends adding additional time into your initial estimate; for instance, although each 8-hour day of training typically requires 40 hours of total (i.e., preparation, delivery, and debriefing) time, he advises adding another 20 hours to calculate an overall cost of the project that will cover expenses and yield a profit for the consultant. The fee for the 8-hour workshop has now gone from about $1770 (or $221/hour) to $2655 (or $332/hour). This sample calculation represents the cost of one trainer. The costs of all contractors must be included in the budget.

The Plax (2008) formula represents a framework for how to determine the expense categories for which trainers need to charge clients, time spent on these activities, and how to calculate a total cost for services. Costing out the budget for a training project is not a science. Many factors will influence what trainers can charge, including *history with the client* (trainers with a history of trust, reliability, and caring can charge more than those with a less solid history with any particular client); *the client's perception of the trainer and training's value* (when clients really need what a trainer has to offer, they will pay more than situations in which the trainer's recommendations are targeted at low organizational priorities); *the trainer's credentials and experience* (those with relevant work history, terminal degrees, research publications, books, or an affiliation with a prestigious university or firm can charge more than those trainers who do not) (Waldeck et al., 2016).

A final factor that distinguishes highly paid trainers from those who cannot charge as much is the *ability to communicate a sense of self-confidence*. "Projected self-confidence is worth money. Individuals who come across as experts, confident in what they know and what they can do, are also those the client is likely to hire and be willing to pay the most" (Plax, 2008, p. 246). The proposal should communicate the trainer's expertise and self-confidence in terms that the client will understand and appreciate. In this way, the proposal will maximize client confidence that the proposal is a good one, and that the trainer is the right person for helping the organization achieve its goals.

Conclusion

The ability to write a clear, persuasive, thorough, and marketable proposal is the foundation for training work that will serve your client well, and in turn, be personally and professionally fulfilling to you. Successful proposals demonstrate compelling, substantiated needs within the client organization; advance appropriate objectives; and make efficacious recommendations. A strong proposal asks for the business, is transparent, and gives the client confidence in you, the trainer, and your recommendations. Like any persuasive message, an influential proposal is both art and science. The science involves competent business writing skills (Waldeck et al., 2017) and logic. The art involves understanding your client and your own abilities in a meaningful way. Trainers who apply the strategies and insights offered in this chapter will, with time and experience, generate proposals that stand out to their readers and help them create authentic partnerships that will lead to organizational development and improvement.

Note

1 Consultants can find RFPs in a variety of databases relevant to their interests and expertise. For example, findrfp.com is a subscription-based service with a database dedicated to state and local government RFPs for consulting, leadership, and strategic planning; rfpdb.com provides RFPs and bid opportunities from the public and private sectors; fbo.gov provides access to federal government contracts up for bid; bidnet.com lists RFPs for contract opportunities in education, social services, health and medical, sports, recreation, and arts. Many institutions and organizations release RFPs on their own websites. Finding relevant RFPs is a research task and a networking task; once a consultant establishes him or herself in an area, organizations may ask for a bid.

References

Beebe, S. A. (2016). Communication skills for consulting excellence. In J. H. Waldeck & D. R. Seibold (eds.), *Consulting that matters: A handbook for scholars and practitioners* (pp. 127–146). New York, NY: Peter Lang.

Beebe, S. A., Mottet, T. P., & Roach, K. D. (2013). *Training and development: Communicating for success* (2nd ed.). Boston, MA: Pearson.

Bodie, G. D., & Worthington, D. L. (2010). Revisiting the listening styles profile (LSR-16): A confirmatory factor analytic approach to scale validation and reliability estimation. *International Journal of Listening, 24*, 69–88.

Boster, F. J. (2016). Providing research services for clients. In J. H. Waldeck & D. R. Seibold (eds.), *Consulting that matters: A handbook for scholars and practitioners* (pp. 259–276). New York, NY: Peter Lang.

Brehm, J. W. (1966). *A theory of psychological reactance.* New York, NY: Academic Press.

Jorgensen, P. F. (2016). Building an evidence-based practice: Conducting valuable needs assessments. In J. H. Waldeck & D. R. Seibold (eds.), *Consulting that matters: A handbook for scholars and practitioners* (pp. 49–62). New York, NY: Peter Lang.

Miller, G. A. (1956). The magical number seven, plus or minus two: Some limits on our capacity for processing information. *Psychological Review, 64*, 81–97.

Monroe, A. H. (1935). *Principles and types of speech.* Chicago, IL: Scott, Foresman.

Plax, T. G. (2008). Raising the question #2: How much are we worth? Estimating fees for services. *Communication Education, 55*, 242–246.

Plax, T. G., Kearney, P., Allen, T. H., & Ross, T. (2006). Using focus groups to design a nationwide debt management educational program. In L. R. Frey (ed.), *Facilitating group communication in context: Innovations and applications with natural groups* (vol. 2., pp. 89–107). Creskill, NJ: Hampton Press.

Plax, T. G., Waldeck, J. H., & Kearney, P. (2016). Collecting and using narratives that matter. In J. H. Waldeck & D. R. Seibold (eds.), *Consulting that matters: A handbook for scholars and practitioners* (pp. 87–108). New York, NY: Peter Lang.

Ross, S., & Waldeck, J. H. (2016). White shirts, blue shirts: A case study of leadership development consulting for law enforcement. In J. H. Waldeck & D. R. Seibold (eds.), *Consulting that matters: A handbook for scholars and practitioners* (pp. 319–330). New York, NY: Peter Lang.

Stephens, K. K., & Waters, E. D. (2016). How and why technology matters in consulting and coaching interventions. In J. H. Waldeck & D. R. Seibold (eds.), *Consulting that matters: A handbook for scholars and practitioners* (pp. 239–258). New York, NY: Peter Lang.

Waldeck, J. H. (2008). The development of an industry-specific online learning center: Consulting lessons learned. *Communication Education, 57,* 452–463.

Waldeck, J. H. (2016). How communication theory and research make consulting matter. In J. H. Waldeck & D. R. Seibold (eds.), *Consulting that matters: A handbook for scholars and practitioners* (pp. 3–10). New York, NY: Peter Lang.

Waldeck, J. H., Kearney, P., & Plax, T. G. (2017). *Strategic communication at work: Contemporary perspectives on business and professional communication* (2nd ed.). Dubuque, IA: Kendall Hunt.

Waldeck, J. H., Plax, T. G., & Kearney, P. (2016). Planning and proposing consulting work. In J. H. Waldeck & D. R. Seibold (eds.), *Consulting that matters: A handbook for scholars and practitioners* (pp. 109–126). New York, NY: Peter Lang.

Chapter 2

Communication training's higher calling

Using a civic frame to promote transparency and elevate the value of services

Don Waisanen

Abstract

Communication trainers can make a greater case for their work by positioning all of their training, at its highest level, within a *civic frame*. A civic frame
raises the stakes for training components such as listening or diversity and puts
the benefits of corporate social responsibility and similar efforts into practice in
training contexts. This chapter details why and how trainers can use this frame
to create transparency and elevate the value of their services.

As both a communication trainer and professor, I have worked with just about every type
of group and organization. I've found training extraordinarily valuable for helping people
in my local community and around the world do their work more effectively, testing new
ideas about communication, and bridging theory with practice. The greatest surprise in
carrying out this work over the years, however, has been my discovery of the robust connections between communication training and societal improvement. This chapter makes
a case for implementing this connection in an intentional and visible way within all communication training to create transparency with clients and elevate the value of our services.

For decades, communication "training, a specific type of consulting intervention,"
has been "aimed at developing organizational members' skills in target areas that can
enhance organizational outcomes" (Houser, 2016, p. 217). Given the pressures for immediate skill building or organizational advisement built into most contracts, communication trainers should continue to make these goals a priority. Yet a next step is
to underscore how communication training further connects with societal improvement. Focusing on societal improvement isn't simply a "nice add on" for existing
training programs, but rather a pragmatic, robust way to signal trainers' accountability
to higher standards, broader audiences, and—even in the most bottom-line focused
environments—make a greater case for the types of outcomes clients seek. Based on
a review of extant literatures, Stephan et al. (2016) argue that market-based organizations in particular should "*proactively initiate*" positive social change (PSC) through "a
multilevel, 'bottom-up' process where changes in patterns of thoughts, behaviors and social
relationships among individuals underlie changes in organizations, industries, communities, regions, or even nations" (pp. 1252–1253, italics in original). They argue, for
example, that sustainable production practices throughout supplier networks only come
into being "from aggregated changes in the behaviors of individual decision makers

working in these organizations" (p. 1253). A civic frame for training builds upon this research, providing a bottom-up way to put such ideas into practice.

Some reading this chapter may be looking for a larger conceptual framework for communication training or simply a primer on implementing some elements of this perspective. Others could benefit from a frame that raises the stakes for specific communication training components such as listening or diversity, while providing a concrete way for training to connect with increasing organizational emphases on corporate social responsibility (CSR), sustainability, and more. For trainers seeking to make more compelling pitches for funding training (e.g. to an organization, the HR department, etc.), a civic frame translates the benefits of CSR and similar ideas into practice in training contexts. Many investors now believe that addressing economic returns and social developments is critical to their success (Mair & Hehenberger, 2014).

All communication trainers should be "working from a solid theoretical framework and thoughtfully allowing empirical knowledge to guide our decisions during consulting," which "makes consultants credible, effective, and valuable to the organizations which seek their help" (Waldeck & Seibold, 2016, p. xi). There is "no theory-free consulting; we are all driven by explicit and/or implicit human and organizational theories" (Pettegrew, 2016, p. 308), and using frames strategically impacts leadership, management, and self-assessments (Sasnett & Ross, 2007). Trainers hence need to be more conscious about the frames that guide their training, conducting strategic "design work" to address organizational challenges (Jackson & Aakhus, 2014, p. 125). In fact, the communication training literature hints at the need for civic design in this work. Seibold (2016) notes that organizational communication consulting mutually enhances theory and practice "for the growth of knowledge... for the benefit of our discipline," and "*for the well-being of society and its institutions*" (p. 13, emphasis added). Some institutional trends have also been moving in this direction, such as "citizenship" becoming a commonly used term in many organizations (e.g. Organ, 2017), and a belief that organizations need to engage in activities that signal legitimacy to the broader public (Jacobs, van Witteloostuijn, & Christe-Zeyse, 2013, p. 777; see also see Stephan et al., 2016).

With these opportunities in mind, I define a civic frame as the structuring of communication training intentionally and visibly as a way to improve society through an accountability to the larger public. Some guiding questions driving this frame include: What would training objectives and outcomes look like starting from a societal viewpoint? What benefits does a training offer participants both inside and outside an organization? And, for any individual skills covered in a training, what if more participants acted in this way? For example, for a corporate diversity workshop focused on how to work well across differences, a human resources or full-time trainer might write a proposal speaking to the individual benefits of being able to work with vastly different communication styles, the organizational rewards of employee retention, *and* the societal return for easing relations, anticipating risks, and averting crises between people in a world where more cultures are coming into contact than ever before (see Lull, 2007).

What's critical to recognize is how the last point heightens the value of the individual and organizational objectives. With the civic frame, a larger case can be made for embedding and scaling trainings that focus on a staff's ability to work across differences. A civic frame works with all the individual and organizational outcomes trainers hope to effect (e.g. greater productivity, better teamwork, etc.), but elevates the value of these services by highlighting their connections with the public good. Debriefs, for instance, can raise the stakes for communication training by toggling between "I hope this new skill helps you with your lives and work" to "The world would be a much better place if more people used this skill in their interactions with others." In turn, communication training becomes more transparent by making interventions guided by a higher, global level of accountability. With the civic frame in mind, trainers can articulate that their content and processes have interlocking value for individuals, organizations, and societies.

A civic frame promoting transparency and other ethical standards is already implicit within communication training. For instance, at a corporate staff development workshop that teaches how to communicate well up, down, and across organizational silos, we're essentially modeling ways to be better citizens outside of an organization too. Or, in helping a nonprofit consider audiences it doesn't typically work with, we're attempting to build civic and communal bonds where there were none, helping people imagine and make actionable ways of working across divides. Such projects "facilitate collaborations among previously unconnected actors to build weak-tie (or *bridging*) social capital" (Stephan et al., 2016, p. 1263). A civic frame forwards "the strength of weak ties" and the access to critical information and development of new ideas that it affords (Granovetter, 1983, p. 201). In conducting teambuilding sessions or training in how to facilitate better meetings, we're also underscoring essential ways to build trust, manage conflicts, and bring diverse voices to the table writ large. These aren't just useful activities to help people in organizations do their work better, they're what our world needs.

In Table 2.1 I address integration and adoption issues for the three different audiences likely to read this chapter: those who have already adopted a civic frame and are searching for criteria and evidence to affirm this perspective (adoptive audience); those who are receptive to these ideas or who are already down this road but looking for ways to implement and further justify their work (receptive audience); and those who for whom these ideas may initially seem uninteresting or unimportant (skeptical audience). Following the issues identified in this table, the rest of this chapter will build a case for why and how a civic frame can benefit each of these audiences.

At a minimum, adopting a civic frame means explicitly drawing attention to and marketing the individual, organizational, and societal outcomes for training. In the teambuilding session mentioned above, a trainer might present tools for building trust among employees and highlight the global dimensions for using such a tool in a cross-cultural business meeting. A session on professional writing may seem like it's only relevant to improving staff members' abilities to communicate well via email, or to unclog an organization's voluminous pipeline of unnecessary online communication each work day. But a written component can also adopt a civic frame and a higher level of transparency about why trainers are doing what they're doing by being tied to, for example, the "curse of knowledge" (the idea that we all struggle to move outside of our own frames of reference in writing) that has led to more misunderstanding between all people than perhaps any other communication issue (Pinker, 2015). Before detailing how communication trainers of all kinds can further benefit from and employ a civic frame, the next section will provide a deeper background, context, and rationale for training guided by an accountability to the larger public.

Why use a civic frame for training?

In many ways, the challenges that individuals and groups face in organizations directly parallel the problems that we face as a society. The social and political problems of polarization, tribalism, and conflict run rampant throughout public life. In the U.S., Pew polls show that people are increasingly distrustful and isolated from one another

Table 2.1 Adoption and integration issues for applying a civic frame in communication training

Adoption and Integration Issues	Adoptive Audience	Receptive Audience	Skeptical Audience
Corporate Social Responsibility (CSR) in Training	Promotes visibility for CSR work	Provides a roadmap for CSR integration	Wake-up call to absence of CSR
Transparency and Accountability	Affirms an accountability to the broader public	Promotes a broader view of an organization's potential stakeholders; advances legitimacy and aligns internal and external expectations or perceptions about the organization; expanded sense of possibilities for influence	Advances a process of moving beyond shareholders to stakeholders; further activates the "strength of weak ties" (Granovetter, 1983, p. 201)
Citizenship	Recovers or establishes civic part of mission and rebuts "ivory tower"-type objections	Addresses needs for organizational citizenship and global leadership; raises the stakes for training by emphasizing broader applications	Provides a tangible way to practice increasing corporate emphasis on organizational citizenship; links with "employee helping behavior" (Mossholder et al., 2011, p. 33)
Benefits for Trainers	Fits calls in the literature to have a clear, developed frame for training; sense of purpose and efficacy	Positions choices about training fees, content decisions etc. credibly in terms of social capital; constructs case for more systemic (rather than one-shot) training opportunities	Builds trust that the trainer sees her or himself as open and accountable to a larger community and is not simply self-interested
Risks for Trainers	Civic and political apathy; potential perceptions that, like CSR, the civic/social aspects of training mask less altruistic motivations; perception that this is just an "add on" and not central to training	Civic and political apathy; potential perceptions that, like CSR, the civic/social aspects of training mask less altruistic motivations; perception that this is just an "add on" and not central to training	Organizational desires for short-term results may impede longer term positive civic/social developments; more research needed to see how a civic frame impacts many KPIs

Organizational Purpose and Meaning	Puts into motion one way that the organization is practicing what it preaches	Connects with the "purpose economy" (Hurst, 2014) and the way that practitioners increasingly think about their work; employee retention and loyalty; plays into the ethos of social entrepreneurship and sustainability	Contributes to employee satisfaction and brand enhancement
Training ROI for Clients	In addition to targeting traditional training outcomes, a civic frame makes training a form of public engagement infused with social purposes	Increased trust with internal and external stakeholders; more motivated employees; emphasizes teamwork and productive conflict management; aligns economic returns with social developments	Increased trust with internal and external stakeholders; more motivated employees; emphasizes teamwork and productive conflict management; aligns economic returns with social developments
Trainer's Identity	World-class trainer with deep and broad perspectives exemplified by a commitment to the public good	World-class trainer with deep and broad perspectives exemplified by a commitment to the public good	Niche trainer; missed opportunity to make a greater case for the value of communication training
Leadership	Fits with current trends in leadership research emphasizing distributed and connective models	Repositions training as less about developing extraordinary people than promoting tools and perspectives that can make a difference in the lives of everyone	Gets with the times; constructs an integrated view of organizational responsibilities for CSR, training, and collective commitments
Promotes Diversity, Inclusion, and Cultural Sensitivity	Provides a frame in which diversity, inclusion, and cultural sensitivity all fit; raises the stakes for these matters beyond minimalist employee compliance to a maximalist, motivating purpose for why the world and organization needs more training	Underscores the importance of both unique contributions and common causes in the work culture; provides a frame in which diversity, inclusion, and cultural sensitivity all fit; raises the stakes for these matters beyond minimalist employee compliance to a maximalist, motivating purpose for why the world and organization needs more training	Compliance with diversity initiatives; employee competence and performance with different individuals and teams; signals a relationship to the larger world and an awareness of how communication strategies should vary across cultural and microcultural contexts

(Pew Research, 2014). In the last two decades, especially, "our politics seems more un-accountable and dysfunctional than ever, and outright hostility toward anything public seems increasingly common" (Snyder-Hall, 2015, p. 1).

When the communication training and civic engagement literatures are positioned together, the possibility for training to address many of the most vexing societal prob-lems becomes clear. Scully and Diebel (2015) note that "in too many communities, the inherent democratic capacities of citizens, organizations, and networks to address com-plex public programs remain unrecognized and underutilized" (p. 1; see also Nabatchi & Gastil, 2012). Jarvis, Nold, and Barroquillo (2016) further find that civic education (at least in the United States) historically became "scientized, sanitized, and national-ized" in a way that emphasized knowing rather than doing or feeling a "civic pulse" (p. 15). A lot of ink has been spilled about what democratic communication should look like (e.g. Habermas, 2006), but communication training actually provides one route for putting these ideas into practice. By working with individuals and targeting social im-provements from the ground up, communication training constitutes an ethical, civic intervention for clients and trainees.

If community development "implies that the quality of interaction among the people living in a locality improves over time" (Flora, Flora, & Gasteyer, 2015, p. 364), then it's chiefly in improving the one-to-one interactions between people that trainers can most make their mark in promoting positive communities. According to theories such as the coordinated management of meaning, "organizations and their concerns are made through the ongoing and combined interactions of their people. Therefore, if you want to change anything about the organization, you begin with the relevant interactions of its people" (Sostrin, 2016, p. 154). The same goes for societal engagement, which can only start with the quality of discourse between people. With a civic frame, this kind of skill development also links to the variable of "employee helping behavior," or "in-terpersonal organizational citizenship behavior (OCB) that is affiliative, co-operative, and directed at other individuals" (Mossholder, Richardson, & Settoon, 2011, p. 33).

Since communication consulting and training involves "the application of organiza-tional communication principles and theories to real-world problems" (DeWine, 2016, p. xv), communication trainers need to take seriously how their work can influence both institutions and society. As research shows, training can effectively address many societal problems, such as the poor relationships between police officers and different publics (Ross & Waldeck, 2016). In this study, a civic focus offered a societal benefit *and* linked to bottom-line outcomes, with "clients report[ing] cost savings associated with the negative outcomes averted by practicing the principles and engaging in the behav-iors recommended by our programs" (p. 320; see also Aguinis & Kraiger, 2009, p. 468).

Although this may require a shift in mindset for some readers, a civic frame can be applied intentionally and visibly in any and all organizational trainings. As Pearce (2010) highlights, if civic engagement gets characterized as only about traditional city council meetings and public hearings, we miss opportunities to make it matter through more creative and unusual processes (p. 8). Mathews (2014) too expands the definition of civic engagement by suggesting that "practicing democratic practices creates its own space. There is no street address; the space appears whenever people take advantage of opportunities to go about familiar routines in a more democratic way" (p. 120).

As research repeatedly shows, "when time and energy are applied to building the communication skills of learners – and the communication-skills of leaders, this has an immediate impact [on] improving productivity, quality, morale, turnover among low-performers and retention among high-performers" (The skills, 2017). Yet, as two millennia of communication research highlights, communication training shouldn't be left behind the minute trainees walk out of their organizations: it's meant to foster transparent and ethical improvements in individuals, organizations, and public life as a whole.

In my experience, this larger civic framing stands out as distinctive and credible for communication training proposals to foundations and other funding entities, especially in persuading funders that communication training should be carried out through a long-term, sustained, and ecological commitment to improvements that can be tracked and assessed (i.e. the other best practices in this volume). A civic frame further fits emerging themes from meta-analyses of training research that look to the "different levels of analysis" we might use to frame our work (see Bell et al., 2017, p. 305). Overall, by using a civic frame and terms that attempt to improve individuals, organizations and, as its highest purpose, society, we build a higher calling into our work.

How to use a civic frame for training

Trainers can apply a civic frame in countless ways. My goal here is less to provide an exhaustive list of examples than to introduce some of the means by which trainers can use this frame. One example is David Kantor's ideas about "Dialogic Leadership," which invites individuals to expand their repertoire of communication skills by thinking through how much they practice using their voices, how well they listen to others, how much they engage in respectful opposition, and how much they are neutral rather than reactionary in different situations (Isaacs, n.d.). Listening alone is one of the top predictors for effective leadership (Romig, 2001), but it's also the starting point for working across differences in a complex society. Without good listening skills, the communication in organizations and societies devolves into monologues. Communication frameworks like dialogic leadership ask trainees to become more open, transparent communicators committed to getting unstuck from common, unproductive patterns in their personal lives and as citizens in society.

We can even use a civic perspective to raise the stakes for these skills more broadly by constructing training as a counterfactual with national or international leadership. As much as two participants in a training may perform better from a role-play practicing conscious neutrality, they stand to benefit from thinking about how an international negotiation between two world leaders might have gone differently had this technique been employed. To use a civic frame for training, trainers should continually link concepts and skills to this level of reference and outcomes.

Trainers should tell participants that they apply these learnings in their everyday lives, focusing their investment in improving conversations and the quality of public discourse. Patton (2016) argues that self-identity is one of the top communication training variables. If trainers see themselves as transparent, ethical, and civically-engaged professionals, then they will tend to act this way, and many participants will follow suit. One way that I try to model a spirit of transparency and openness in my small leadership communication trainings is by having everyone sit in a circle for most of our time together. In doing so, I take on the role of "facilitative leader," demonstrating to trainees what democratic communication can look like. I use established moderating techniques from dialogue initiatives such as the National Issues Forums (www.nifi.org) to highlight process practices that stand to improve communication both within and outside organizations.

To best adapt to different audiences, trainers need to be boundary spanners (see Waisanen, 2014). Communication training is about helping people connect with others, skillfully crossing boundaries and borders toward that end. From a civic perspective, "'fixers' don't work alone; they are enmeshed in any number of overlapping networks of people" (Mathews, 2014, p. xv). To conduct consulting well, Plax, Waldeck, and Kearney (2016) too relate how that they had to become "literate in a range of sectors and concerns that our advanced degrees in communication never would have prepared us for" (p. 100). Drawing from a range of research, Beebe (2016) identifies seven behaviors that communication trainers should exhibit, which can equally be seen as ways to span boundaries and model a civic frame: assume equality, be perceived as comfortable, keep conversational rules, practice dynamism, invite disclosure from others, encourage enjoyment, and establish rapport nonverbally (pp. 134–135). Additionally, however, using a civic perspective means reframing training from what clients and trainees too often perceive as only about individual "soft skills" to the "hard skills" that it takes to make societies work well.

Three themes tend to run through communication training best practices: relationships and transparency; a tailored rather than off-the-shelf, generic approach to training; and evaluation or assessment/measurement (Fahs & Brock, 2016). Each of these themes can be developed under a civic framing. Whether communicated on our websites, in contracts, or orally at the beginning of a training, to develop relationships and transparency trainers can tell participants that they're accountable to and willing to learn from everyone. Using a tailored approach highlights that trainers are responsive to the needs of trainees and committed to working with a diverse citizenry. Engaging in evaluation and assessment/measurement further shows that trainers see themselves as accountable to broader social data and evidence beyond their own intuitions or traditions. In each of these ways, there's more than meets the eye in communication training—we're aiming to be transparent, accountable, responsive, sensitive to diversity, and willing to go where the evidence leads in meeting others' needs.

For those who are primarily communication practitioners, using this framing can add greater depth, stakes, and accountability to a variety of services. For those who are primarily academics, using this framing can better communicate how this outside work connects with every university's public service mission. Those who cross these worlds can speak about civic purposes with both vocabularies. In this spirit, let me detail a few ideas for practitioners, academics, and both for putting a civic frame into practice.

For practitioners

If you run or are part of a business or a nonprofit, it's worth recognizing the alignment between a civic frame and hybrid public–private developments like social entrepreneurship, the ethos of corporate social responsibility, or sustainability programs that look beyond profit to concerns for people and the environment. Corporations, in particular, need to find new ways "to look at the relationship between business and society that does not treat corporate growth and social welfare as a zero-sum game," since "perceiving social responsibility as an opportunity rather than as damage control or a PR campaign requires dramatically different thinking—a mind-set… that will become increasingly important to competitive success" (Porter & Kramer, 2006, para. 4).

There's a reason so many companies have invested heavily in corporate social responsibility: it broadcasts a transparency to the larger public beyond shareholder needs, looking more realistically to the range of stakeholders and the broader environment at play. Additionally, the organizational change literature is clear that "what works well in one organization, culture, or country, may well produce failure in another organization, culture, or country" (Jacobs, van Witteloostuijn, & Christe-Zeyse,

2013, p. 775). A civic frame signals that communication strategies should vary across contexts, accounting for the diversity that now exists within just about every organization. At the same time, all kinds of individual and organizational benefits follow from recasting company goals along these lines, from employee satisfaction to brand enhancement. I'm arguing for exactly the same move to take place in communication training – social responsibility isn't simply a nice accessory to what we do, it's an opportunity to elevate the meaning and value of training itself. Ultimately, transporting this frame to the communication training space makes sense given the impacts of organizational social responsibility (e.g. Deng, Kang, & Low, 2013).

In working with for profits, I'm unabashed about the idea that a primary training goal is to improve communication skills and spread this work as far as possible. After all, the tools that make for better conversations at work are also effective outside of it. Almost every communication training and development exercise can be inflected in this way. Trainers don't have to be preachy here, they can get the civic calling into their work subtly through questions such as, "What do you think would happen if every corporate and nonprofit leader engaged in this listening practice?"

There may be no better role that a civic frame can play in business and other forms of training than in its links with the "purpose economy" (Hurst, 2014). Different than prior eras, Hurst finds that people are moving into an age in which meaning, relationships, personal growth, and "service to something greater than themselves" have become the most important motivators for careers (p. 4). We know from research that "motivated project teams are more likely to be engaged and willing to build project capabilities and opportunities" (Stephan et al., 2016, p. 1264). The establishment of private–public organizations like B-corporations and the growth of industries such as life coaching further testify to these desires (Hurst, 2014, pp. 72, 107). As much as people may need communication training for their individual and organizational goals, then, a civic frame opens up an opportunity for trainers to connect with the ways that corporate and nonprofit practitioners are increasingly thinking about their work.

For academics

Countering outdated views that communication training is somehow at odds with what academics do, it's now more clear than ever that communication consulting can enrich and share a reciprocal relationship with teaching and research (Waldeck & Seibold, 2016, p. ix). But a civic frame can make an additional, higher level case that academics (especially in the communication field) should be conducting communication training along the lines set forth in this chapter. Boyte (2004) notes that "academic culture at many of today's colleges and universities has produced a widespread sense of powerlessness in their faculties, disappointment in their students, and dismissiveness from the public at large" (p. 1). If you're at a university, applying a civic frame addresses what many perceive to be the lost civic missions of colleges across the nation. This isn't only an ethical commitment to public service, it's a way of improving full-time university work. In my experience, students love hearing about any time I help local nonprofit staff present their cause more effectively. It quickly rids the classroom environment of objections such as "this is just theory," "ivory tower," and other remarks that you're disconnected from what's happening "out there."

A civic frame would have us be more transparent and available to broader publics in training, testing our developing ideas about communication in the process. Since adding training to my work, even when conducting research I find myself thinking through trainees' feedback about how a tool for group communication may not be useful in every type of meeting. I've observed different models of leadership and management communication in organizations and rethought my theories of how good decisions can be made or what it might take to develop more positive work cultures. Communication training with a civic focus forces you get to become more interdisciplinary, applied, and engaged.

When academics frame their training, at its highest level, in terms of improving publicness, they participate in a form of civic engagement that some evidence suggests also results in more fulfilling careers. Interviewing 39 academics from all over the country, Snyder-Hall (2015) found that "all those interviewed felt positive and energized by their civic engagement, found that it helped them do their academic jobs better, and experienced increased levels of connection with others and meaningfulness in their work" (p. 3).

By communicating the societal value of training to clients and trainees, as well as fellow scholars and administrators, a civic frame provides a transparent, sense-making model for this work. As a civic act, trainers move beyond their silos and establish presence with diverse people. Writing to an audience of rhetoricians, Pezzullo implicitly makes a case for this frame in highlighting how:

> Some might consider it ironic that academics dedicated to studying public address and public culture need to reflect on why some of us conduct research in public spaces and/or with publics. Given that ancient rhetorical scholars commonly moved between their roles as teachers, advocates, consultants, poets, and more, it should be uncontroversial to affirm rhetorical analysis that draws on critical ethnographic practicalities and sensibilities.
>
> (Pezzullo, 2016, p. 178)

In shifting between the types of roles Pezzullo highlights, communication trainers who are academics bring value to both the public and their university settings. Keyton (2016) notes how her national expertise in gender communication, especially sexual harassment, was discovered mostly through presentations to non-academic organizations (p. 34). Plax (1991) further finds that "there are clear conceptual and operational parallels between what high quality university communication researchers do in a simulated setting and what high quality communication consultants do in the field" (p. 56). Adding a civic frame to communication training only amplifies these connections and makes us public actors who care for how communication gets practiced at every level of society.

Four key terms for civic training

I'd like to propose four key terms as benchmarks for civic-focused, globally-minded communication training. My hope is that trainers can use these ideas to build additional concepts and connections with societal engagement into their work. The first best practice in this handbook focuses on being *transparent*, and it's at the center of what this chapter means by using a civic frame. If we're concerned about communicating in open and honest ways, frequent communication with clients is a must. From putting together to actually implementing a training, we have to ask ourselves every step of the way how much we're opening or closing space for others (see Asen, 2009, p. 263). To be transparent, we have to approach clients and trainees as "open books," being ready to justify our choices (i.e. training content decisions, how we arrived at our fees, etc.), while always being open to the possibility that we could be misguided or wrong. How we listen to others also matters. Trainers should use verbal listening skills such as paraphrasing and asking questions (Bodie et al., 2015). As civic, public beings, we should unconditionally accept others (Rogers, 2012) and their rights to know about what we do and why we do it at every stage of the communication training process.

Civically informed communication training becomes more transparent when we highlight that communication should be *distributed*. Everyone's voice matters. "Adaptive leadership" remains attentive to how voices and power get distributed throughout organizations and societies (Heifitz, Grashow, & Linsky, 2009). Many concepts in the communication field have similar underpinnings. As communication trainers, we should take every opportunity to let others know how much we care about their voices being heard and advise putting organizational processes in place that can sustain open, democratic, and diverse dialogues. Those in managerial positions should especially "maintain nonverbal immediacy and frame prosocial-type messages to preserve their credibility in the workplace" (Teven, 2007, p. 155).

Trainers should also be *reflexive*, or practice continuous self-examination about what they're doing. Individual, organizational, and societal communication problems all beg the same three questions: "how was this made," "what are we making together," and "how can we make better social worlds," with answers always highlighting that "we have power – a limited power, to be sure, but power nonetheless – to make the worlds in which we want to live" (Pearce, 2010, pp. 30–31). The worlds made in organizations affect the worlds made outside of them, and vice versa. A civic frame would have us be reflexive about the worlds we and our participants are constantly in the process of creating, using a dynamic rather than static understanding of how communication works to both create and solve most human problems. Among many ways of reflexively thinking about the social worlds that we're creating in training spaces, using different lenses from the communication field – such as systems, interpretive, symbolic, and even critical communication theories – can help both trainers and trainees see their worlds anew (Keyton, 2016).

Finally, a civic framing geared toward acting in transparent, distributed, and reflexive ways implicates a *humanitarian* perspective. The sine non qua of communication training is clients' needs; indeed, "training that does not address a need or specific job function of a trainee is not effective training" (Beebe, Mottet, & Roach, 2013, p. xii). The greatest need for communication training may be bridging differences between people so that they can act in more human and humane ways with one another. In PSC projects, such "shared visions can be particularly powerful by instilling a sense of positive collective identity and purpose. The very nature of this work emphasizes making a positive difference to others, appealing to individuals' universal basic need for relatedness" (Stephan et al., 2016, p. 1264; Ryan & Deci, 2000). A civic frame for communication training can align individual, organizational, and societal needs along these lines. Compared with other approaches, a negotiation training that gets trainees to create rather than claim value with one another (Malhotra & Bazerman, 2008), for example, tends to create better individual results, establish a more positive organizational climate, and sets in motion a way of acting that's helpful for all citizens. This kind of humanitarian thought has a long history. The "categorical imperative" asks us to think about individuals' actions and consequences in terms of the question: What if everyone acted in this way (Kant, 2013/1785, p. 490)? Similarly, communication training can be a means by which trainees learn to think about and act in more humanitarian, global ways with one another.

In applying a civic frame to communication training, trainers should be careful to protect clients' confidential and proprietary information, committing to nonmalfeasance and beneficence, while applying reasonable standards of care (Keyton, 2016, pp. 41–43). Discussing training in civic terms can still be accomplished by hewing closely to clients or trainees' needs for private, safe spaces to practice their skills individually or collectively. Overall, a civic frame for communication training that is transparent, distributed, reflexive, and humanitarian promotes sensitivity to people and contexts.

Recovering and evolving higher training purposes

In many ways, establishing a civic frame for transparent and accountable communication training is a recovery project. Whether you're a full-time management consultant or working from a university platform, it's worth recognizing how many of the communication field's earliest figures moved seamlessly between the worlds of practice and reflection for civic purposes. A father of organizational communication research, Charles Redding, trained military officers in communication skills, and saw wearing many hats as integral to his work and community development (Waldeck, 2016, p. 4). Many of our forebears sought to improve society through their "disciplinary attachment not only to ideas but to the ground, to the messiness of practice, to the hesitations of the real world, and to the inconsistencies and brutalities of social, economic, political, cultural, and public life" (Zelizer, 2011, p. 15). Even ancient communication experts like Cicero and Quintilian put civic inflections over all their work. On different days, they'd teach communication skills to students, advise government leaders, and write reflections for public audiences informed by all these efforts.

By using a civic frame, trainers can contribute to the development of people everywhere, pulling society upward. Communication consultant and scholar Pearce (2007) says that "the pull upward consists of new ideas, institutions and practices that elevate and enhance human beings and society," as contrasted to the "downward pull of the old, familiar ways of being" (p. 9). When communication training focuses on individual skill building or organizational development alone, it misses an opportunity to make a greater case for the value of the work that communication trainers do. Without this larger civic context, one risks engaging in great person narratives that talk about extraordinary people and results (Mathews, 2014, p. xvi), rather than the tools and perspectives that can make a difference in the lives of everyone. A civic frame also forwards current trends in leadership research emphasizing distributed and connective models that put the exercise of leadership within more people's reach (see Gagnon, Vough, & Nickerson, 2012; Stephan et al., 2016).

As a practical matter, putting a civic frame over communication training can also help trainers see new opportunities for work. A civic frame focuses systemic ways to apply training. For instance, trainers could seek foundation funding to embed and scale communication training across organizations to make more of a societal impact. One public program that I have worked with, The New York Community Trust Leadership Fellowship, is a perfect example. To make training matter, the program has funded, sustained, tracked, and assessed impacts for cohorts of nonprofit participants who otherwise would not have had the opportunity to receive cutting-edge professional development (The New York Community Trust Leadership Fellows, 2017).

In this chapter I have sought to "get the ball rolling" by framing communication training more firmly as a matter of social responsibility, especially as a means to greater transparency with clients and trainees. While I've provided reasoning for doing so, what's now needed is more evidence, data, and examples that explore the connections between communication training and civic capacities. Macromanagement research itself has been

> largely dominated by theories that conceive of organizations as 'closed' and guarded, top-down controlled places of rational transactions and competition that are focused on shareholders but disconnected from local communities and most stakeholders .... Conversely, the organizational practices associated with deep-level PSC strategies characterize organizations that are 'open' to stakeholder influences, 'embedded' in communities, 'relational' in that they create social connections, [and] 'purposeful' as they are infused with meaning.
>
> (Stephan et al., 2016, p. 1268)

Along with work in PSC, and just as CSR research started with a few ideas that have burgeoned into its own subfield in recent decades, we need further empirical work to test the benchmarks in this chapter and explore the social responsibilities of communication training in different contexts.

There's one final benefit of applying a civic frame in training: It stands to improve the communication field as a whole. Whether you're a practitioner or academic, engaging with broader publics through communication training provides one avenue for making known all that our discipline has to offer. In my own experience, using the benchmarks in this chapter (e.g. the need for distributed communication) often has participants realizing how much they need to make communication skills and perspectives a priority in their lives. When joined with civic and societal purpose, we amplify those needs as a matter for global development. Toward that end, it's time to settle for nothing less than transparent communication training that can affect individuals, organizations, and societies.

References

Aguinis, H., & Kraiger, K. (2009). Benefits of training and development for individuals and teams, organizations, and society. *Annual Review of Psychology, 60*, 451–474.

Asen, R. (2009). Ideology, materiality, and counterpublicity: William E. Simon and the rise of a conservative counterintelligensia. *Quarterly Journal of Speech, 95*, 263–288.

Beebe, S. (2016). Communication skills for consulting excellence. In J. Waldeck & D. Seibold (eds.), *Consulting that matters* (pp. 127–146). New York, NY: Peter Lang.

Beebe, S. A., Mottet, T. P., & Roach, K. D. (2013). *Training & development: Communicating for success.* Upper Saddle River, NJ: Pearson Higher Education.

Bell, B. S., Tannenbaum, S. I., Ford, J. K., Noe, R. A., & Kraiger, K. (2017). 100 years of training and development research: What we know and where we should go. *Journal of Applied Psychology, 102*, 305–323.

Bodie, G. D., Vickery, A. J., Cannava, K., & Jones, S. M. (2015). The role of "active listening" in informal helping conversations: Impact on perceptions of listener helpfulness, sensitivity, and supportiveness and discloser emotional improvement. *Western Journal of Communication, 79*, 151–173.

Boyte, H. (2004). *Going public.* Dayton, OH: Kettering Foundation Press.

Deng, X., Kang, J. K., & Low, B. S. (2013). Corporate social responsibility and stakeholder value maximization: Evidence from mergers. *Journal of Financial Economics, 110*, 87–109.

DeWine, S. (2016). Foreword. In J. Waldeck & D. Seibold (eds.), *Consulting that matters* (pp. ix–xiii). New York, NY: Peter Lang.

Fahs, M. L., & Brock, S. (2016). The top twenty communication variables for actualizing and achieving NCA's training and development best practices. Paper presented for the Training and Development Division at the National Communication Association conference, Philadelphia, PA.

Flora, C. B., Flora, J. L., & Gasteyer, S. (2015). *Rural communities: Legacy + change.* Boulder, CO: Westview Press.

Gagnon, S., Vough, H. C., & Nickerson, R. (2012). Learning to lead, unscripted: Developing affiliative leadership through improvisational theatre. *Human Resource Development Review, 11,* 299–325.

Granovetter, M. (1983). The strength of weak ties: A network theory revisited. *Sociological Theory, 1,* 201–233.

Habermas, J. (2006). Political communication in media society: Does democracy still enjoy an epistemic dimension? The impact of normative theory on empirical research. *Communication Theory, 16,* 411–426.

Heifetz, R. A., Grashow, A., & Linsky, M. (2009). *The practice of adaptive leadership: Tools and tactics for changing your organization and the world.* Cambridge, MA: Harvard Business Press.

Houser, M. (2016). Facilitating training. In J. Waldeck & D. Seibold (eds.), *Consulting that matters* (pp. 217–238). New York, NY: Peter Lang.

Hurst, A. (2014). *The purpose economy.* Boise, ID: Elevate Publishing.

Isaacs, D. (n.d.). Dialogic leadership. *Systems Thinker.* https://thesystemsthinker.com/dialogic-leadership/

Jackson, S., & Aakhus, M. (2014). Becoming more reflective about the role of design in communication. *Journal of Applied Communication Research, 42*(2), 125–134.

Jacobs, G., van Witteloostuijn, A., & Christe-Zeyse, J. (2013). A theoretical framework of organizational change. *Journal of Organizational Change Management, 26,* 772–792.

Jarvis, S. E., Nold, S. T., & Barroquillo, K. (2016, March). Civic engagement: Sharing the responsibility. *Spectra, 53,* 14–19.

Kant, I. (2013/1785). Groundwork of the metaphysics of morals. In R. Shafer-Landau (ed.), *Ethical theory* (2nd ed., pp. 485–498). Malden, MA: Wiley-Blackwell.

Keyton, J. (2016). Many paths. In J. Waldeck & D. Seibold (eds.), *Consulting that matters* (pp. 31–45). New York, NY: Peter Lang.

Lull, J. (2007). *Culture-on-demand: Communication in a crisis world.* Malden, MA: Wiley-Blackwell.

Mair, J., & Hehenberger, L. (2014). Front-stage and backstage convening: The transition from opposition to mutualistic coexistence in organizational philanthropy. *Academy of Management Journal, 57,* 1174–1200.

Malhotra, D., & Bazerman, M. H. (2008). *Negotiation genius.* New York, NY: Bantam.

Mathews, D. (2014). *The ecology of democracy: Finding ways to have a stronger hand in shaping our future.* Dayton, OH: Kettering Foundation Press.

Mossholder, K. W., Richardson, H. A., & Settoon, R. P. (2011). Human resource systems and helping in organizations: A relational perspective. *Academy of Management Review, 36,* 33–52.

Nabatchi, T., & Gastil, J. (eds.). (2012). *Democracy in motion: Evaluating the practice and impact of deliberative civic engagement.* New York, NY: Oxford University Press.

Organ, D. W. (2017). Recent developments in research pertaining to Organizational Citizenship Behavior (OCB). *Annual Review of Organizational Psychology and Organizational Behavior, 5.*

Patton, G. (2016). The twenty key variables for actualizing and achieving training and development's best practices. Paper presented for the Training and Development Division at the National Communication Association conference, Philadelphia, PA.

Pearce, K. (2010). *Public engagement and civic maturity: A public dialogue consortium.* Redwood City, CA: Pearce Associates.

Pearce, W. B. (2007). *Making social worlds.* Malden, MA: Wiley-Blackwell.

Pettegrew, L. (2016). A delicate balance. In J. Waldeck & D. Seibold (eds.), *Consulting that matters* (pp. 305–317). New York, NY: Peter Lang.

Pew Research Center (2014, March 7). Millennials in adulthood: Detached from institutions, networked with friends. www.pewsocialtrends.org/2014/03/07/millennials-in-adulthood/

Pezzullo, P. (2016). Afterword: Decentralizing and regenerating the field. In S. L. McKinnon, R. Asen, K. R. Chávez & R. G. Howard (eds.), *text + FIELD* (pp. 177–188). University Park, PA: Penn State University Press.

Pinker, S. (2015). *The sense of style*. New York, NY: Penguin Books.

Plax, T. G. (1991). Understanding applied communication inquiry: Researcher as organizational consultant. *Journal of Applied Communication Research, 19*, 55–70.

Plax, T., Waldeck, J., & Kearney, P. (2016). Collecting and using narratives that matter. In J. Waldeck & D. Seibold (eds.), *Consulting that matters* (pp. 87–108). New York, NY: Peter Lang.

Porter, M. E., & Kramer, M. R. (2006). Strategy and society: The link between competitive advantage and corporate social responsibility. *Harvard Business Review*. https://hbr.org/2006/12/strategy-and-society-the-link-between-competitive-advantage-and-corporate-social-responsibility

Rogers, J. (2012). *Coaching skills: A handbook*. Berkshire, UK: McGraw-Hill Education.

Romig, D. A. (2001). *Side by side leadership: Achieving outstanding results together*. Marietta, GA: Bard Press.

Ross, S., & Waldeck, J. (2016). White shirts, blue shirts. In J. Waldeck & D. Seibold (eds.), *Consulting that matters* (pp. 319–330). New York, NY: Peter Lang.

Ryan, R. M., & Deci, E. L. (2000). Self-determination theory and the facilitation of intrinsic motivation, social development, and well-being. *American Psychologist, 55*, 68–78.

Sasnett, B., & Ross, T. (2007). Leadership frames and perceptions of effectiveness among health information management program directors. *Perspectives in Health Information Management, 4*, 1–15.

Scully, P. L., & Diebel, A. (2015). The essential and inherent democratic capacities of communities. *Community Development, 46*, 212–226.

Seibold, D. (2016). The communication scholar's unique perspective. In J. Waldeck & D. Seibold (eds.), *Consulting that matters* (pp. 11–30). New York, NY: Peter Lang.

Sostrin, J. (2016). A collaborative approach to examining and addressing organizational challenges. In J. Waldeck & D. Seibold (eds.), *Consulting that matters* (pp. 149–169). New York, NY: Peter Lang.

Stephan, U., Patterson, M., Kelly, C., & Mair, J. (2016). Organizations driving positive social change: A review and an integrative framework of change processes. *Journal of Management, 42*, 1250–1281.

Synder-Hall, C. (2015). *Civic aspirations: Why some higher education faculty are reconnecting their professional and public lives*. Dayton, OH: Kettering Foundation Press.

Teven, J. J. (2007). Effects of supervisor social influence, nonverbal immediacy, and biological sex on subordinates' perceptions of job satisfaction, liking, and supervisor credibility. *Communication Quarterly, 55*, 155–177.

The New York Community Trust Leadership Fellows (2017). https://trustfellows.org/the-fellowship/

The skill that has the highest ROI. (2017, March 7). *Learning and Development Professional*. www.ldphub.com/general-news/the-skill-that-has-the-highest-roi-233845.aspx

Waisanen, D. J. (2014). Toward robust public engagement: The value of *deliberative* discourse for *civil* communication. *Rhetoric & Public Affairs, 17*, 287–322.

Waldeck, J. (2016). How communication theory and research make consulting matter. In J. Waldeck & D. Seibold (eds.), *Consulting that matters* (pp. 3–10). New York, NY: Peter Lang.

Waldeck, J., & Seibold, D. (2016). Preface. In J. Waldeck & D. Seibold (eds.), *Consulting that matters* (pp. ix–xiii). New York, NY: Peter Lang.

Zelizer, B. (2011). Journalism in the service of communication. *Journal of Communication, 61*, 1–21.

Chapter 3

The F-word changes a circular message

Linking a profession's history to communication training's unique organizational role

Robin Smith Mathis

Abstract

This chapter provides key strategies to ensuring transparency in your training. Maintaining authenticity in a masculine management-driven organization can be difficult. Establishing influence and power and yet remaining true to your style and audience is possible. This chapter discusses the best practice of transparency in regard to trainee adaptation and communicative behaviors. Though I discuss a feminine/relational approach, this chapter highlights how different lenses and paradigms are best developed when they are intentional and thoughtfully integrated into training.

I am a relational communication consultant, coach, teacher, and trainer (CCCTT). According to Beebe, Mottet, and Roach (2004) communication is inescapable, irreversible, complicated, and emphasizes content and *relationships*. "Relationships involve more implicit cues about feelings, emotions, attitudes, or power involved between the communicants" (p. 12). The relationship can establish power in the training environment when the CCCTT/trainee relationship is based on "positive respect you have for the person asking you to do something" (p. 304). Furthermore, Mottet, Richmond, and McCroskey (2006) state, "instructional communication as a relational process. Both teachers [trainers] and students [trainees] mutually create and use verbal and nonverbal messages to develop a relationship with each other" (p. 24). So, once a CCCTT agrees to design and deliver a training program for the organization, you identify how you can meet the trainees' needs to be effective and beneficial to their organization and establish relational power. Various best practices can yield power, and this chapter will discuss the best practice of trainee adaptation and transparency and behaviors that communicate such.

If you were trained under a communication or human resource development lens then you have probably heard of some variation of a "relational CCCTT" before.

> Let's get back to what we bring back to the table as communication scholars and teachers .... But even in our discipline, we know a bit about how to engage trainees in learning. For example, we know that CCCTTs can engage students or trainees by making things understandable.
>
> (Dannels et al., 2014, p. 372)

I say this to you because I feel organizations focus on the macro, and I understand why. Obviously, performance and external communication are vital to the organization. However, an effective CCCTT has to focus on that dyadic relationship first, and this micro level consideration in the overarching organization. Miller (2012) presents emotions, empathy, intuition, and connectedness as feminist characteristics. Therefore, the practice of maintaining the relational or feminine lens in a masculine and management driven organization can be problematic (Dannels et al., 2014).

Thus, this chapter will discuss how to authentically present one's self in training, explain the best practices such as self-disclosure to communicate transparency, and illustrate adaptation. The practice of transparency and adaptation in training positions it within the organization as an influential component. Therefore, the CCCTT directly impacts the perception of communication training. Communication training has a unique ability to embrace the training field's history for enhanced communication effectiveness.

One lens for authenticity would be deconstructing communication training as gendered. However, my feminist lens approach in practicing authentic training also explains how relational communicative strategies position training within the organization. Regardless of lens or perspective it is appropriate when engaging in the best practices of any profession to intentionally engage the roots of the profession first.

Communication training roots are relational

Dannels et al. (2014) present a creative narrative that will be discussed throughout the chapter, and Act II is titled *This Above All: To Thine Own Self Be True*. This title reflects the core thought of my best practices and lens for training. The creative narrative is an interpretivist analysis strategy that allows a small group of people to present their thoughts through a united narrative. It is also a creative way to get advice and opinions from a collection of experts. A feminine lens is used to describe my practice of transparency. Narrative scholars know that people will fill in an incomplete story; so, it is necessary to be as open and honest as possible for learning to occur. Feminist studies have been labeled the other F-word without an understanding of what we mean by feminist or feminine studies (Miller, 2012). By feminine, I mean relational and under-represented in the traditionally masculine organizations (Miller, 2012; Mumby & Putnam, 1992; Putnam & Fairhurst, 2015). Health care, practicing law, and management are three areas I will explore later in this chapter to provide a few concrete examples. The notion of critically examining the training practices through a feminist lens has emerged in the twenty-first century (Brown, Cervero, & Johnson–Bailey, 2000; Howell, Carter, & Schied, 2002). Training practices contribute to organizational socialization, change, identity, and resistance.

A survey at the turn of the twenty-first century revealed that human resource managers feel that training and development is the most vital role. (Desimone, Werner, & Harris, 2002). I approach training from a "getting back to our roots" type of philosophy that works well. Years ago, I wrote about the history of training in the rationale for studying leadership and communication in the organizational training context (Mathis, 2010). After the Great Depression and World Wars, the USA desperately needed quality training to fill war and domestic work needs (Ruona, 2001). The civil rights movement, economic conditions (Herr, 2001), and women's liberation created a vision of hope and a better future. People wanted jobs that were personally satisfying and revealed elements of self-efficacy (Pope, 2000).

The 1960s and 1970s saw educational policy and legislature that would improve the development of all employees. The training field was shifting from the skills needed for the organization to skills needed for the organization's human resources. The 1980s and 1990s, the decade of *Wall Street* and titan movies, began a shift for CCCTTs and other human resource development professionals in neglecting our roots. This economic boom in our country and the portrayal of the masculine titan romanticized the individualistic approach of performance and "every man/woman for themselves."

Buzzanell (2000) discusses the dichotomy of the private and public spheres. I consider the two spheres to be *training* and *management*. A communicative feminist theory reveals the contradictions that exist within these spheres. Bullis and Stout in Buzzanell discuss how biologists are seen as the marginalized group within the tree harvesting industry. Given this example from Buzzanell, organizational training and development departments could be a marginalized group within traditionally patriarchal organizations. The creative narrative mentioned earlier appeared in *Communication Education*, and it illustrates patriarchal management influence on our training (Dannels et al., 2014).

> I hate to say this but I'm now imagining how my administrators and legislators might respond. We need to be preparing students [trainees] for the workplace, plain and simple.
>
> (p. 370)

> Administrators and legislators and accreditation agencies—not to mention students [trainees]—want results. And in this climate, results do not equal holistic, transformative learning. They equal jobs. We need to be preparing our communication students to get jobs. It is part of our responsibility and this discipline, in particular, has a unique contribution to make to healthy and productive workplaces. I, for one, don't think we should apologize for this contribution …. This is an age-old debate. I mean right before World War II, in a time period when scientific, practical, and military knowledge— content knowledge— was presumably valued, Abraham Flexner, the founding director of the Institute for Advanced Studies in Princeton wrote an essay "The Usefulness of Useless Knowledge." He argued that the most important discoveries have been made by those driven by the desire to satisfy curiosity, rather than the need or desire to be useful. Let's teach students [trainees] to be curious. Not simply to get jobs.
>
> (p. 371)

More than ever, with the discussion of Millennials in the workplace, we know that by stretching the minds and helping trainees think critically and problem-solve, we help them be productive within the organization. Then, on the other hand, those skills might not be directly transferable or easily measured. This is when such "best practices" can help you establish your credibility in the task driven world. The examination of the communication processes is missing from various methods developing our human resources (Ashcraft & Mumby, 2004; Dannels et al., 2014). Moreover, there is a need to explore the practices and processes from your authentic lens in order to position the field to claim their identity. Mine is a feminist approach, and it helps me to examine the creation and meaning of the messages and behaviors in the organizational training and development environment that position the field of HRD in a place of power. Furthermore, an interpretivist lens, social constructivist lens, and postmodern lens, to name a few, opens the minds of trainees to ultimately be critical thinkers approaching the task of communicating. This should be clear to communication trainees as it is incumbent on any CCCTT to be clear about perspectives, approaches, or techniques that heavily influence the nature, tenor, or philosophy of their training.

Fenwick (2005) encouraged HRD to explore the field from a critical perspective in order to stay true to their foundation. There is evidence that scholars are beginning to take her charge to heart. However, it is not possible that HRD will acquire the sovereign model of power (Ashcraft & Mumby, 2004); nor should we argue that they should rise to capitalism and bureaucracy. Establishing the importance of understanding and explaining what your role is within the organization clarifies transparency with the trainees. Hopefully, in the examples to come, I can exemplify how to take this critical lens and put it into practice for you.

Training is a central key to learning that occurs in organizations (Hanscome & Cervero, 2003). Training and development was created to enhance and help individuals. Training is not only central to the organization's development of human resources, but it has a powerful position when it comes to creating and establishing the organizational culture (Hanscome & Cervero, 2003). This can establish a tension when organizational performance goals and employee needs clash. It isn't difficult to see that the CCCTT can be pulled in two different directions. Research in organizational training and adult learning reveals resistance, contradictions, and ironies that implies CCCTTs are focusing on the masculine/task needs of the organization and not the relational roots (Brown et al., 2000, Hanscome & Cervero, 2003, Howell et al., 2002; Tisdell, 1993). I would not dare say that the task is not critical in training. After all, it is the core of behavioral change and enhancing necessary skills. However, I would say that transparently adapting to the trainees' needs was at our core in the field's beginning, and it is still a best practice today. Training has been identified as a critical component in the organization's success; therefore, it is imperative that we provide you the best practices discovered by communication and organizational studies scholars.

Relational is revived or reinvented

Communication Education journal has explored the need for understanding how communication functions in training and organizational contexts (Beebe, 2007; Horan & Afifi, 2014; Kearney, 2008; Lucier, 2008). Though many communication training scholars have written in *Communication Education* concerning the need as early as 2008, by 2012 a database search of *Communication Education* had 93 hits for immediacy, 0 for trainer or trainee immediacy, 20 for relevance, and 0 for training and relevance. Dannels et al. (2014) raised critical questions relevant to this chapter and remind us that there are many ways to measure learning. "Immediacy doesn't always work" (p. 398); however, we always explore immediacy in the instructional setting (Christensen & Menzel, 1998; Christophel, 1990) in the same context with similar power structures. Through the same creative-narrative discussed earlier, the authors raise awareness of how communication scholars were contributing to a "productive workplace" helping students [trainees] understand and establish credibility, and that communication is a communal process.

> I think we have lost focus on the big picture. We get so focused on the minutia that we lose what is important: do we, as teachers, really know much about learning? And it is not just teachers who have lost perspective: do doctors know much about healing? How much do lawyers know about justice?
>
> (Dannels et al., 2014, p. 371)

This excerpt from the journal *Communication Education* stimulates you to think about what you really know about the process, the training and learning process. As a CCCTT, do not fall victim to the practice of the act. Like the excerpt says, we assume that the lawyer understands the process, but s/he may only know the act of practicing law, objecting, persuading, or cross-examining. This act influences the justice process just like your act of "training" influences the trainee and the organization. However, how much do you really know about the trainee and their process of learning and what that means to the organization? I mentioned earlier that CCCTTs are trained to adapt to the learner; however, it is easy to get co-opted by the organization's focus and not align with a now marginalized practice of training. Now, a foundational argument for authentic and transparent training adaption. It really is possible to stay true to *thine own self.*

Relational is authentic trust and respect

Well, although some teachers [CCCTTs] worry about things like clarity, there are many, many other concerns facing today's teachers [CCCTTs]. The concerns are complicated. We know clarity is important, but so are multiple other concerns like establishing credibility, negotiating teacher–student relationships, managing authority, acknowledging difference, and providing feedback, for example.

(Dannels et al., 2014, p. 372)

Recently, I conducted sessions with two separate groups on communication strategies to help them with various organizational challenges. One of the most pressing concerns was bridging generational differences. Therefore, I will use examples from my training experiences with members of the State Public Health Department and county business leaders seeking communication skills to bridge generational gaps in the workplace by illustrating practices on building relationships, credibility, etc. This topic can easily turn into a venting and complaining session. However, using somewhat self-deprecating disclosure allowed all generations to recall that they were difficult to the generation before them, and established credibility and respect with the younger generations. Horan and Afifi (2014) encourages more exploration in the traditional classroom and organizational concepts within the training context. Transparently communicating relevance and applicability by practicing trainee adaptation (Mathis, 2010) establishes an important relationship with the trainee. This instructional concept made instrumental in the traditional classroom was also found to be important in workplace training. Your ability to clearly and authentically communicate the relevance and applicability by understanding the "big picture" process gives you credibility and value to the organization because you will earn their trust (Mathis, 2010).

Furthermore, research has been conducted on the role disclosure plays in learning. We utilize a number of best practices where the CCCTT "attempts to get a trainee to like him/her or encourages the trainee to talk by asking questions and reinforcing the trainees for talking" (Beebe, Mottet, & Roach, 2013, p. 242). Furthermore, the CCCTT's willingness to self-disclose appropriately also establishes transparency. "That sounds like an interesting challenge, but now we have to ask the looming question: How?" (Dannels et al., 2014, p. 372).

Putting authentic training into transparent practice

I use disclosure and videos to establish trust and respect. Brene Brown developed the acronym BRAVING to deconstruct trustworthiness.

The teacher [CCCTT] presents self as trustworthy and reliable by emphasizing his or her sense of responsibility, reliability, fairness, dedication, honesty, and sincerity. The teacher also maintains consistency among their stated beliefs and behaviors, fulfills any commitments made to the student, and avoids 'false fronts" by acting natural at all times.

(Bell & Daly, 1984 cited in Mottet,
Richmond, & McCroskey, 2006, p. 199)

Trust is critical for all CCCTTs, and I find it particularly difficult when I have limited time as an external CCCTT. The acronym stands for boundaries, reliability, accountability, vault, integrity, nonjudgment, and generosity. I use disclosure carefully as a CCCTT to establish that I am reliable and accountable. I communicate guidelines and boundaries for the training session. Disclosure is a tricky instructional communication practice. I am careful to self-disclose in a way that it doesn't communicate with my trainees that I will not open my "vault." In other words, I tell my trainees that they can trust me and share with the class; so, I must communicate in a way that they know their sharing is safe and protected. Communicating nonjudgmentally encourages trainees to engage in discussion.

There are levels of respect in the training context (Mottet, Richmond, & McCroskey, 2006). Organizational legitimate power based on title or rank does not require a relationship. On the other hand, when trainees perceive the CCCTT as an expert, a relationship has developed. The highest level of respect is when a trainee "complies with a tough or disliked request when it comes from a leader they respect … students [trainees] respect their teachers [CCCTT], see them as credible and, to some degree, role models." (p. 120). When I trained county business leaders on communication strategies to bridge generational gaps, I established trust and respect by acknowledging my generational differences, explaining the history of our generations, and making it clear how they will see communication in the workplace differently after this training/workshop. Stating your agenda, objectives, and perception checking with them is transparent communication that yields trust and respect for me as I train. Take a moment and think through the questions below.

1   How do you measure or assess your relationships with your trainees?
2   Do you know that your clients trust you? Why have they asked you to conduct the training?
3   How do you communicate trust and respect that is unique?

So, what I am asking you to do at this moment is to consider how you make abstract outcomes concrete to establish your worth to the trainees. If you have a method that works for you, keep using it. However, if you need a more explicit model, I will share the first one I used and have adapted appropriately given my training audience.

I first used the EDIT process in unpacking traditional classroom activities. Beebe, Mottet, and Roach (2012) first mentioned that this model for unpacking the learning experience could be used in the training context. This is not a new practice of unpacking, but I want to summarize and illustrate how it speaks to the CCCTT's transparency. The (E) represents the learning experience (discussion, case study, video, etc.). Then, during the (D) phase, we ask the trainees to describe or paraphrase what they heard or saw and felt. I tend to stick firmly to the EDIT process in the traditional classroom set-ting. In the training context, however, I have found that revising the (D) stage, making it more concise, or deleting has worked. On the other hand, it has been vital given the communication skill and the organization or department's history. So, you can adapt and emphasize components on this model based on your training audience. The (I) represents inference and the (T) refers to transference. Inference guides the trainees to articulate what they learned from the experience, or what has them questioning an old idea. I find this conversation key for adult learners in a training context. Articulating the learning for them helps with the internalization of knowledge. It also complements what I have mentioned previously about guiding the trainee to be a critical think-ing problem-solver, needed in our millennial booming workforce today. Finally, the trainee communicates how they plan to immediately transfer (transference) on the job what they just learned. This part of the model guides the discussion to enhance the learning. In the inference stage questions are asked to spark discussion about what the trainee learned in the training experience then and there. Then, the trainee is encour-aged to examine how the new knowledge can be transferred to work or personal lives. It is important to reflect on the construction of these discussion questions, and to what extent gender, class, and race play in their construction, and the invitation to contribute to the learning.

Years ago, I spoke with A fortune 500 company's director of compliance during my research. A Fortune 500 manufacturing company typically has a masculine or patriar-chal traditional culture. Publicly traded companies were feeling the pressure to ensure ethical compliance with the Sarbanes–Oxley in the aftermath of Enron. He told me that taking the time to adapt training to the trainees to meet organizational demands was worth it. He could see through assessments that by adapting the training to what they know and understand on a personal level helped them to reach a higher level of learning. Finally, we can apply the same small changes/practices to the implementation of de-signing training programs, delivering the training content, and/or assessing the training program. I mention "or" in the previous sentence because there have been times when I was limited on the design or assessment pieces. Nevertheless, I was able to implement the adaptation into my delivery style, and these small changes have made an impact. Because I am aware of the HRD professional or CCCTT's job only applying to one area of the training process, I will break up the training process into design, delivery, and assessment to examine the micro-level practices of all three areas.

Constructing objectives and selecting instructional methods is the core of authentic relational training. The organizational CCCTT or instructional designer design mod-ules around individual needs as well as those of the organization. Now, I have been in a training situation where the objectives and content were previously selected for me; however, I discussed with the key stakeholders to clarify the objectives. As authenti-cally transparent CCCTTs, we have to use our communication knowledge to "manage up" the management. What I mean by this is, if faced with ambiguous and abstract objectives, gain clarification to ensure that the trainees leave transferring the skill. It is within the training delivery and activities that I authentically address the objectives.

Also, the CCCTT might have the freedom to explore how individual needs are also met while designing training to meet organizational needs. So, when considering training from a feminine or relational perspective the following questions are impor-tant to ask in the designing process: 1) How will the training objectives meet gendered needs; 2) How will training objectives explore gender, race, and class experiences; and, 3) How do objectives address the gender, race, and class of the trainees? Recounting a legal training will help demonstrate an exemplar of how you might bring the feminine/relational lens into a traditionally masculine and task-oriented field.

How the "F-word" works within design, delivery, and assessment

Design

Attorneys expressed a problem with a particular task; however, the reality of what was impeding their achievement of their task was actually neglecting the relational aspect. The likelihood that they would admit that or agree, is slim. As a CCCTT, my job wasn't necessarily to convince them of the root, but rather to provide impactful design and delivery of effective training. What follows is a description of how feminine/relational issues were implemented into a training module designed for trial lawyers. The program objective is that attorneys will discuss the role that communication concepts have in the voir dire (jury selection) process, and understand how to implement components of immediacy, perceptions, and interviewing into the voir dire process. Lawyers see this phase of the trial as instrumental in the outcome; however, their communication competence hinders their success in this process. The study of the law is inherently masculine and the misconception that a charismatic speaker is a competent communicator is common in this field.

The program was broken down into specific course objectives. The key to transparent design is establishing observable, measurable, attainable, and specific objectives (Beebe, Mottet, & Roach, 2013; Noe, 2005). Furthermore, Caffarella (2002) provides worksheets to design program objectives on page 198 and on pages 199–202 provides brainstorming sheets for delivery and assessment as well. The clear objectives show alignment with task needs and frustrations. For illustration, we will explore just a few objectives.

- The attorney will be able to differentiate between credibility and trustworthiness.
- The attorney will be able to understand homophily and the role it plays in the *voir dire* (jury selection) process. (In other words, how does the potential juror connecting with the attorney and feeling the same rather than highlighting the differences impact the jury selection process?)
- The attorney will understand the difference in willingness to communicate and communication apprehension.

CCCTTs, trainees, and clients can look at objectives and ask: How do gendered, racial, and class identities define or experience immediacy, credibility, and trustworthiness? Also, how is asking attorneys to be aware of "homophily" engaging in essentialist praxis? Considering the description of the previous objectives and their perceptions of their communication, can CCCTTs help or expect attorneys to be able to understand the concept of adapting messages in establishing credibility, creating immediacy, and developing effective questions while listening actively to conduct/build a successful voir dire (jury selection).

Delivery

In addition to thinking through our objective construction, we need to examine why we select specific instructional methods. Delivery is considered in the design phase (Caffarella, 2002; Noe, 2005), but for the purpose of this best practice analysis, we are discussing the actual delivery; the delivery that connects us with the trainee (Beebe, Mottet, & Roach, 2013). Often we select methods due to time constraints and to demonstrate use of technology which only reinforces what the dominant structure expects. Hopefully, the methods that we use are not used because they best meet the needs and values of the organization over the employees' development. However, in this case, CCCTTs still have creativity in the delivery and planned content. For example, if the organization is relentless about delivering training virtually to save money, your methods in that lean channel can make all the difference for trainee learning. The training program I am using as a descriptive example used the movies *Runaway Jury* and *A Time to Kill* to illustrate objectives. Along with self-disclosure, adaptation of appropriate movie clips encourages the lawyers to disclose to one another to increase higher levels of learning. The designer of a training program should deconstruct these movies and examine how these movies reinforce power and communication as we know in the patriarchal notion of law practice.

Assessment

Again, like delivery, Caffarella (2002) discusses assessment in the design phase; however, I am focusing on the actual assessment process. Assessment "is a systematic process that ultimately recycles itself "(p. 257) and confirms the quality of the training (Beebe, Mottet, & Roach, 2013). Though assessment may be embedded in a pre-packaged training, you may always add your internal inventories and perception checks for assessment purposes. Affective learning is value for content, behaviors, and/or the CCCTT. I have found assessing affective learning is vital in training and development. Finally, patriarchal practices of assessing training are concerned with the most basic level of learning transfer and cognitive learning. I can absolutely see the need to be able to ensure that trainees can transfer. The literature is vast on this matter, and I would not want to be misunderstood that I was arguing otherwise. Nevertheless, training can be assessed in terms of affective learning and should not be ignored. In fact, high affect is needed for transfer. This lends us to understand how the training met the individual values and beliefs of the trainees. Affective learning is impacted by gender, race, and class where cognitive learning may not be.

The CCCTT can relate back to the design to see that on some level feminine, racial, or cultural needs are being addressed, discussed, and assessed in organizational training; hence, meeting the needs of the trainee makes them more effective and productive. For example, with attorneys, I disclose that I come from a home of attorneys. There are three in my family. I share specific stories building empathy for their communicative challenges, rather than evaluating and judging their communication. Though a family attorney may be skilled at presentational speaking or persuasion, more than likely, they suffer in establishing an empathic relationship with their clients. Using self-disclosure establishes affect for me and helps create affect for the content and behavior. Nevertheless, I evaluate at the end of sessions with open-ended questions. Micro level training practices provide resistance to less relational training practices which in turn empower the profession intended to service the individuals within organizations. A CCCTT who considers the relational approach to design, delivery, and affective learning will see cognitive learning and behavioral change.

Summary

This chapter provides an argument for positioning yourself (the CCCTT) in a unique and powerful position. You may not approach training from a feminist lens, but sometimes your lens can be just as shocking as the "F-word" of feminism if it does not follow traditional embedded models. Hopefully, this chapter has established a firm rationale for being an authentic trainer and the positive impact it has on the process. Training and development is still a key element of human resource development, yet I argue that when we are not transparent with our clients and trainees we are marginalized in organizations. Gender, race, and class play a huge role in the development of the individuals that we service and in the practice of HRD. At the very least, this chapter revealed exclusions that appear to be common to many communication CCCTTs. It also looked at the way training and development professionals can position themselves as powerful and more authentic through their own act of micro practices of resistance to established norms. This can be done through more intentional inclusion of feministic, relational, and affective elements from professional literature and the practice of design, delivery, and assessment.

Finally, all lenses and paradigms are best developed when they are intentional and thoughtfully integrated into training. In that regard, if you are interested in advancing the practitioner-scholar body of research on the embracing the feminist paradigm, more qualitative or postmodern work needs to be conducted that explores the practices of such social masculine pressures that exists in HRD (Dick & Hyde, 2006). More research will provide rich descriptions of how resistance to various paradigms of practice can take various forms (Collinson, 2005; Dick & Hyde, 2006; Thomas & Davies, 2005). Hopefully, this chapter addresses transparency, prompts discussion, and initiates exploration in some of those areas including:

- Be transparent in your authentic feminine (or paradigm) training.
- Paradoxically, transparent authentic relational/feminine training will likely establish trust and respect vital in traditionally masculine fields.
- Find new ways/strategies of using traditional "best practices."
- Priority of assessing affective learning.

Best wishes in your quest to make your training process your own authentic best.

References

Ashcraft, K. L., & Mumby, D. K. (2004). *Reworking gender: A feminist communicology of organizations*. Thousand Oaks, CA: Sage.

Beebe, S. A. (2007). Raising the question #6: What do communication trainers do? *Communication Education, 56*, 249–254.

Beebe, S. A., Mottet, T. P., & Roach, D. (2004). *Training and development: Communicating for success*. Boston, MA: Allyn & Bacon.

Beebe, S. A., Mottet, T. P., & Roach, D. (2013). *Training and development: Communicating for success*. Boston, MA: Allyn & Bacon.

Bell, R. A., & Daly, J. A. (1984). The affinity-seeking function of communication. *Communication Monographs, 51*, 91–115.

Brown, A. H., Cervero, R. M., & Johnson-Bailey, J. (2000). Making the invisible visible: Race, gender, and teaching in adult education. *Adult Education Quarterly, 50*(4), 273–288.

Buzzanell, P. M. (2000). *Rethinking organizational & managerial communication from feminist perspectives*. Thousand Oaks, CA: Sage.

Caffarella, R. S. (2002). *Planning programs for adult learners: A practical guide for educators, trainers, and staff developers* (2nd ed.). San Francisco, CA: Jossey-Bass.

Christensen, L. J., & Menzel, K. E. (1998). The linear relationship between student reports of teacher immediacy behaviors and perceptions of state motivation and of cognitive, affective, and behavioral learning. *Communication Education, 47*, 82–90.

Christophel, D. M. (1990). The relationship among teacher immediacy behaviors, student motivation and learning. *Communication Education, 39*, 322–340.

Collinson, D. (2005). Discussion of Thomas and Davies: Refuting Romanticism: The value of feminist perspectives for understanding resistance. *Organization, 12*(5), 741–747.

Dannels, D. P., Darling, A., Fassett, D. L., Kerssen-Griep, J., Lane, D., Mottet, T. P., Nainby, K., & Sellnow, D. (2014). Inception: Beginning a new conversation about communication pedagogy and scholarship. *Communication Education, 63*(4), 366–382. DOI: 10.1080/03634523.2014.934849

Desimone, R. L., Werner, J. M., & Harris, D. M. (2002). *Human resource development* (3rd ed.). Mason, OH: Thomson South-Western.

Dick, P., & Hyde, R. (2006). Consent as resistance, resistance as consent: Re-reading part-time professionals' acceptance of their marginal positions. *Gender, Work, and Organizations, 13*(6), 543–564.

Fenwick, T. (2005). Conceptions of critical HRD: Dilemmas for theory and practice. *Human Resource Development International, 8*(2), 225–238.

Hanscome, L., & Cervero, R. M. (2003). The impact of gendered power relations in HRD. *Human Resource Development International, 6*(4), 509–525.

Herr, E. L. (2001). Career development and its practice: A historical perspective. *The Career Development Quarterly, 49*, 196–211.

Horan, S. M., & Afifi, T. D. (2014). Advancing instructional communication: Integrating a biosocial approach. *Communication Education, 63*(4). DOI: 10.1080/03634523.2014.934851

Howell, S. L., Carter, V. K., & Schied, F. M. (2002). Gender and women's experience at work: A critical and feminist perspective on human resource development. *Adult Education Quarterly, 52*(2), 112–127.

Kearney, P. (2008). Special issue: Instructional communication in organizational contexts: Innovations in training and consulting. *Communication Education, 57*(2). DOI:10.1080/036345 20802324116

Koopans, H., Doornbos, A. J., & Van Eekelen, I. M. (2006). Learning in interactive work situations: It takes two to tango why not invite both partners to dance? *Human Resource Development Quarterly, 17*(2), 135–158.

Lucier, K. H. (2008). A consultative training program: Collateral effect of needs assessment. *Communication Education, 57*(4). DOI: 10.1080/03634520802094305

Mathis, R. S. (2010). Participants' perspectives of training experiences: An exploratory qualitative study. Unpublished doctoral dissertation, Texas A&M, College Station, TX. Pro Quest Dissertations (UMI No. 3416249).

Miller, K. I. (2012). *Organizational communication* (6th ed.). Boston, MA: Cengage.

Mottet, T. P., Richmond, V. P., & McCroskey, J. C. (2006). (eds.), *Handbook of instructional communication: Rhetorical and relational perspectives* (pp. 271–278). Boston, MA: Pearson.

Mumby, D., & Putnam, L. L. (1992). The politics of emotion: A feminist reading of bounded rationality. *Academy of Management Review, 17*(3), 465–486.

Noe, R. A. (2005). *Employee training and development* (3rd ed.). Boston, MA: McGraw Hill.

Pope, M. (2000). A brief history of career counseling in the United States. *The Career Development Quarterly, 48*, 194–211.

Putnam, L. L., & Fairhurst, G. T. (2015). Revisiting "organizations as discursive constructions: 10 years later. *Communication Theory, 25*, 375–392.

Ruona, W. E. A. (2001). The foundational impact of the training within industry project on the human resource development profession. *Advances in Developing Human Resources, 3*(2), 119–126.

Thomas, R., & Davies, A. (2005). What have the feminist done for us? Feminist theory and organizational resistance. *Organization, 12*(5), 711–741.

Tisdell, E. J. (1993). Interlocking systems of power, privilege, and oppression in adult higher education classes. *Adult Education Quarterly, 43*(4), 203–226.

Best practice 2

Use assessable methods

- Trainers and consultants must have identifiable deliverables that can be internally and externally assessed.
- Trainers should be able to demonstrate expertise in training transfer.

Of course not everything is conveniently assessed, and too often clients are attracted to consultants and trainers who over-promise and then fail to demonstrate value. The illusive return on investment of training is often improperly assessed by both parties. Certainly better work satisfaction should arguably make better employees, but it also may make employees more complacent. Without assessment it is difficult to tell. Once again, assessment is often obfuscated around returns that are so intangible that benefits, if any, could never really be attributed to the training given. Such things as undefined future gains, risk reduction, and training satisfaction can look like there are benefits when in fact the impact, or lack thereof, can never really be connected to the communication training at hand.

Assessment includes both diagnostics and also making sense of the findings. "Help, communication is broken and we need training!" identifies several diagnostic techniques as well as helps and hinders to such activities. "Greater alignment, greater success" gives step by step protocols that can be used for assessment as well a number of levels of appropriate implementation. "Observational assessment at the core of your communication training program" provides a real-world technique that converts observations into data that demonstrate level of return for a wide range of training programs.

Chapter 4

Help, communication is broken and we need training!

How diagnosing the organizational needs leads to better interventions, outcomes, and profit

Jeffrey L. Stafford, Michelle Hege, Amber Barnes, Greta R. Underhill, and Hannah R. Seagrave

Abstract

This chapter discusses the role of diagnosis in improving organizational communication, interventions, outcomes, and profit through an interdisciplinary approach, including the field of communication, organization development, business, and consultancy After laying a foundation for understanding diagnosis, several significant processes, methods, and models are presented in addition to lessons learned in the field. Focused benefits are highlighted for internal and external consultants, faculty, and trainers as well as ways to use diagnosis as a profit strategy.

In this chapter we provide an overview of diagnosis. When a leader or someone in an organization reaches out for help with communication, diagnosis helps professionals provide an effective type of "help." Unfortunately, it's not uncommon for people to self-diagnose, "communication is broken," and then self-medicate, "we need communication training." The problem is that communication has lots of moving parts. It involves people, processes, structures, culture, resources, etc. It's not as simple as, say, a broken arm. In that case it would make sense to say, "my arm is broken and I need a cast." Communication challenges are more like heart pain. It would be unwise for someone to say "my chest hurts and I need heart surgery."

Our premise is that effective diagnosis saves leaders from wasting time, money, and energy on solutions, such as training, that may not result in improved communication. We've brought together frameworks from the field of communication, organization development, business, and consultancy to provide an interdisciplinary approach to diagnosis. Effective diagnosis is not just gathering data, but rather what happens before, during, and after data collection. Thus, this chapter includes a process for diagnosis as well as ways to understand and interpret data.

Diagnosis is complex and, like communication, it has a lot of elements. Training solutions are often sought by clients and this kind of purchase model puts the onus primarily on the client. However, assessment of organizational needs and the implementation of the training solution may be contracted by a consultant, expected of a human resources department, or deemed a necessity by the trainer to determine kind and fit of their particular training specialties. Unfortunately, training is not the only intervention, but organizational assessment is necessary to determine if it is a desired option. This chapter provides an overview of some of the basic logistics of organizational diagnosis, making it strongly aligned with this handbook's Best Practice 2 – Use Assessable Methods.

This chapter will:

- Provide a foundation for understanding diagnosis.
- Highlight different processes, methods, and models for diagnosis.
- Offer guiding principles via lessons learned in the field.
- Summarize benefits and ways to use diagnosis as a profit strategy.

What follows are lessons from the field, from seasoned professionals who have been deeply involved in communication assessment, consulting, and training. We know that no single method of assessment is appropriate for all situations and so present the following that have proved to be mainstays for ourselves and other communication consultants and trainers.

This chapter is also directed to those of you who are seeking to bolster your capabilities in this Best Practice. As trainers and teachers this chapter will help you strengthen your communication training/teaching skills.

Foundations of diagnosis

The concept of diagnosis isn't new. It's been used since the pre-modern era in the medical field (Berger, 1999) and is now used across many different disciplines and practices. In the organizational setting, its commonly associated with organization development (OD), which is a specific field that deals with planned change in organizations (Jamieson & Worley, 2008), but it's also used in a variety of ways across other business functions.

Definition of diagnosis

We define diagnosis as a process in which we "gather, organize, and interpret information" (Levinson, 1994) to understand how an organization is functioning in order to achieve a specific goal or outcome (Cummings & Worley, 2009). It's a process that can be applied either broadly to an organization as a whole, or narrowly to a specific area of focus such as communication. Diagnosis can be part of a larger project, or a project in and of itself.

Diagnostics professionals

Understanding how communication is functioning within an organization doesn't require a specific degree or certification; however, it's a best practice to consider the experience and education of those involved. As we mentioned earlier, diagnosis involves gathering, organizing, and interpreting information, meaning that the individual or team responsible for diagnosis will have a significant impact on outcomes (Levinson, 1994). Although it's not uncommon in the field to see a functional manager engaging in various types of diagnosis, we recommend partnering with a skilled professional to lead the project or at minimum to serve on the diagnostics team. We aren't partial to the professional being internal or external; both options have pros and cons (Anderson, 2016).

External professionals generally refer to the organizational leaders or person or group being served as a "client", whereas internal professionals sometimes use "internal customer", or simply the department or team name. Throughout this chapter, we'll use "client" to represent anyone who engages a professional in diagnosis.

Processes for diagnosis

In the case of diagnosis, the process is just as important as outcomes. Schein (1999) asserts, "everything you do is an intervention" and "every interaction [has] consequences" (p. 17). For this reason, it's critical to choose and adhere to a process that acknowledges what happens before, during, and after diagnosis. In this section we share three processes: two from specific fields (communications and OD) and a general consulting process.

The ICA Communication Audit

This process "provides an organization with advance information that may prevent major breakdowns that limit overall effectiveness" (Goldhaber & Krivonos, 1977, p. 41). It's unique from other diagnostic processes in three ways:

1   It was designed specifically to diagnose communication based on perceived "problems" with other approaches that were focused on the organization as a whole.
2   The process is standardized, which gives professionals the ability to compare data across different organizations while also establishing baselines and benchmarks.
3   The ICA Communication Audit is an all-inclusive process. It incorporates not just a framework, but also a defined method for data collection as well as defined deliverables.

Two common critiques of this process include: It's too scholarly and rigid for the average professional and it's too atheoretical for scholars (Tracy, 2017). In our experience, these are irrelevant for the professional who is both trained in the process and has no interest in publishing research. One of our favorite aspects of this process is the list of deliverables for clients, which includes profiles, maps, and summaries to illustrate a complete picture of how communication works, where it breaks down, and possible causes (Goldhaber & Krivonos, 1977).

A general consulting process

A well-known process in the consulting world comes from Peter Block, author of *Flawless Consulting: A Guide to Getting Your Expertise Used*. He suggests four steps: contracting, discovery and data collection, feedback and a decision to act, and engagement and implementation (Block, 2011).

We appreciate Block's approach because it's relevant for internal and external professionals and is broadly and narrowly applicable across disciplines and fields. One critique is it takes an investment of time, energy, and possibly money to master Block's process in its entirety (including all the sub-steps and skills). Professionals can, however, use the four steps as a simple roadmap for diagnostic projects.

An OD consulting process

The third process is one that's common among OD practitioners. It includes elements with sub-tasks and skills like previous models. The names of the steps change slightly depending the source, but we've attempted to provide a basic summary of the elements below:

- Entering and contracting (starting the project and making agreements);
- Diagnosing (figuring out what's happening/not happening);
- Analyzing (making sense of the data);
- Designing interventions (choosing strategies and solutions to influence change);
- Evaluating (assessing interventions for effectiveness and sustainability);
- Exiting (wrapping up the project).

In our experience, the language involved with the process can come across as technical or clinical to clients. But like other approaches, it provides a roadmap for engaging in diagnostic projects. Professionals can share this process, and others, with clients or reserve it for use in an internal process.

To summarize, there is no one best approach, or even a preferred approach, among diagnostics professionals. Interview one hundred different professionals about diagnostic processes and you'll get one hundred different ideas. For the purposes of self-reflection, project assessment, and continual improvement, we recommend choosing a process and sticking with it. Ultimately, we agree with Joel Brockner (2017), author of *The Process Matters*, "the problem is that all too often our obsession with results blinds us to the reality that how we get there, the process, also makes a big difference" (p. 2).

In this section we introduced three processes that can be used for diagnostics projects. Each process painted a picture of what to do before, during, and after diagnosis.

Diagnostic methods

There are literally hundreds of different quantitative, qualitative, and interpretive (Ragin & Amoroso, 2011) approaches to gathering data, also known as diagnostic methods. In this section, we highlight some commonly used methods as well as methods that we've found to be particularly useful. For each one we provide an overview and a summary of advantages and disadvantages.

Interviews, focus groups, and Town Hall Meetings

We consider the interview the most basic methodology for gathering information. It's used primarily to gather data from a selected group of participants who are chosen for strategic reasons. Interview guides are used for continuity as well as process improvement. Downs and Adrian (2004) recommend scheduling two rounds of interviews to maximize their "organic nature," refine interview guides if need be, and see whether trends hold over time (pp. 77–78).

Focus groups (Krueger & Casey, 2015; Morgan, Krueger, & King, 1998) are also excellent ways to gather qualitative data from a select group of individuals. Focus groups consist of "6–15 people led by a moderator" (Downs & Adrian, 2004, p. 210),[1] who engage in an intensive exploration of open questions designed to facilitate discussion. Many various sources can be used to develop focus group details and logistics (Morgan, 1997).

Town Hall Meetings are useful for gathering information from a lot of people all at once. It's really a group interview using a variation of Nominal Group Process (Delbecq & Van de Ven, 1971; Pyzdek, 2001) to gather and collapse the data.[2] For an overview of advantages and disadvantages see Table 4.1.

Table 4.1 Interviews, focus groups, and Town Hall Meetings

Advantages	Disadvantages
• Rich qualitative information • Opportunity for process improvement between interviews or focus groups	• Time intensive (from scheduling to processing the data) • Confidentiality between participants (focus groups and Town Halls)

Surveys and standardized instruments

The diagnostics team may choose to utilize a survey to collect data. According to Babbie (2016), "surveys include the use of a questionnaire – an instrument specifically designed to elicit information that will be useful for analysis" (p. 248). Professionals can design a survey or they can use a standardized instrument such as the Downs-Hazen Communication Satisfaction Questionnaire[3] (Downs & Adrian, 2004; Zwijze-Koning & De Jong, 2007). Some standardized instruments beneficial for organizational diagnosis measure leadership, organizational commitment, supervisor communication, etc. (Rubin, Palmgreen, & Sypher, 2009). Additional sources can be found in the Buros mental measurements yearbook (Carlson, Kurt, & Jonson, 2017). Though there are many to choose from, the ComSat is a standardized instrument developed specifically to be used in communication audits. For an overview of advantages and disadvantages see Table 4.2.

Table 4.2 Surveys and standardized instruments

Advantages	Disadvantages
• Can be cost effective • Minimizes time and geographic constraints • Maximizes the number of people who can participate	• Survey design can be tedious • Language and socioeconomic status can serve as barriers for participants

Network analysis

A network analysis is an approach that results in mapping out communication patterns and networks within the organization (Downs & Adrian, 2004, pp. 187–209). There are several ways to do this; size and complexity of the organization will determine the size and complexity of the analysis. The simplest form is to ask people several possible questions or combinations of questions, such as:

• Who do you need to talk to the most or who do you talk to the most? (Note: these questions give slightly different sets of information.)
• How satisfied are you with these communications? (This leads to a distinct set of questions.)

From these questions, professionals build a visual representation of communication channels within an organization. Ultimately, we want a picture that is far more organic than an organizational chart and utilizes lines, arrows, double arrows, and dotted lines to show the patterns. There are software packages that facilitate the development of the network diagram, however, it can be done by simply laying out notecards on a large table and then tracing and drawing arrows and lines. The better diagrams have lines and arrows with a legend that demonstrates a variety of weights and types that help with the visual representation. Our biggest take away, whether you use a high or low-tech solution, is to stay consistent across projects. This will help with ongoing quality improvement efforts. For an overview of advantages and disadvantages see Table 4.3.

Table 4.3 Network analysis

Advantages	Disadvantages
• Provides information about patterns of communication, strengths, and levels of satisfaction	• Can be difficult for organizations with more than 40 people

Critical incidents

The critical incident is a very simple, yet elegant way to track messages throughout the organization and to determine patterns or themes of communication behavior (Downs & Adrian, 2004, pp. 158–172). The critical incident questionnaire consists of two, open-ended questions which are analyzed using a thematic sorting approach. The two questions must mirror each other, for example:

• Please describe a positive communication incident in your organization that has occurred in the last 6 months.
• Please describe a negative communication incident in your organization that has occurred in the last 6 months.

After sorting the two questions (positive and negative), the diagnostics team looks for patterns and themes in the reports. Interestingly, people tend to report on similar incidents. For instance, out of 100 people, perhaps 40 would respond and 15 of them would describe the same incident. For an overview of advantages and disadvantages see Table 4.4.

Table 4.4 Critical incidents

Advantages	Disadvantages
• Relatively easy to administer and process the data	• Information may be vague or one sided

Diagnostic models

The purpose of this section is to introduce ways or models to organize, understand, and interpret information post data collection. Using a model can help you gain clarity quickly by creating visual representations of insights from data collection. Professionals often modify existing models or create new ones in order make sense of information for themselves and the client.

The Burke-Litwin model

This model is highlighted regularly in OD books and articles. It's based on the premise that we need to understand the tactical and strategic aspects of an organization as well as the levers for change (Burke & Litwin, 1992). Though it was designed for organizational diagnosis, we've used it to understand communication systems, experiences, and problems.

The model has 12 areas that Burke and Litwin (1992) determined to be most important based on previous models, including: external environment, leadership, mission and strategy, organizational culture, management practices, structure, systems, work unit climate, motivation, task and individual skills, individual needs and values, and individual/organizational performance.

In the context of communication we recommend exploring the function, strengths, weaknesses, and impact of each area. For example:

- What did we learn about how leadership impacts communication?
- What did we learn about how leadership communicates?
- What are the strengths and weaknesses of leadership communications?

Force field analysis

Although it's not typically referred to as a model, we consider this a useful approach for interpreting information. It's especially helpful when interpreting qualitative data from interviews and group meetings. The model is derived from Kurt Lewin's model of change – unfreezing, changing, and refreezing (Cummings & Worley, 2009). It helps us understand elements of communication that maintain or enable status quo, as well as those that help or hurt communication systems, activities, and experiences. Waclawski and Rogelberg (2002) assert that it's a practical model because "the outcome typically suggests actions for improvement, such as barriers to [communication] that need to be removed and enabling forces that need to be maintained and strengthened" (p. 110).

The Johari Window

This model is traditionally used as part of personal or leadership development, specifically when giving feedback. The premise of the model is that each person has four quadrants that represent what we consciously and unconsciously communicate to others. Imagine a square split into four sections: the upper right quadrant represents our open self (what's known to us and others); the upper left quadrant represents our concealed self (what's known to us and unknown to others); the lower right quadrant represents our blind self (what's known to others but unknown to us); and the lower left quadrant represents our unknown self (what's unknown to us and others) (Schein, 1999).

In our experience, this model can be leveraged for understanding and interpreting information about teams, departments, and companies in communication. For example, what does a team know about itself, but doesn't share with others? What does a leadership team not know about themselves, but everyone else knows? These types of insights foster self and others awareness, particularly around communication. It helps them reflect on the alignment of their words, actions, and non-verbal strategies.

The SWOT

An acronym for strengths, weaknesses, opportunities, and threats. Although this model is commonly used to gather data, it can also serve to organize data collected via other methods. We use this to make sense of qualitative and quantitative data. Because the SWOT is used in a variety of fields for various reasons, we recommend documenting how you're defining each aspect of SWOT as well as the criteria used to sort the data.

For example, if a scale of 1–5 is used on a survey, perhaps classify 4s and 5s as strengths (things to continue), 1s and 2s as weaknesses (things to change or improve), 3s as opportunities (opportunities for attention), and threats anything where there are major gaps in perception between various demographics. This is a sample of how professionals can modify existing models and use personal lenses to interpret data. It is not supported by research and isn't considered valid in many regards, but if it fosters understanding and inspires positive change, it has utility for the client.

Interpreting data

Data are meaningless to clients unless they tell a story. As professionals, it's our job to help clients understand what's going on and what that means. To be clear, this isn't about proposing solutions, but rather pinpointing root causes. If we do a good job of interpreting information then it's much easier to identify effective solutions. Pulling from OD, we present three classes of issues to consider when interpreting information: human process issues, techno-structural issues, and human resource issues.

Human process issues

Common challenges with communication often stem from interpersonal issues, meaning the way information is shared between people, groups, departments, and stakeholders. Challenges involving people and the processes they use are referred to as human process issues (Cummings & Worley, 2009). People exchange all kinds of information including, but not limited to:

Decisions	Feedback	Updates
Problems	Wants/needs	Successes
Goals	Ideas	Failures
Expectations	Solutions	

As a diagnostic professional, it's your job to illuminate root causes and help clients see what's helping, hindering, or hurting communication. In our experience, clients can make some immediate and easy changes in this area. In other cases it helps clients identify skills, knowledge, awareness, or tools that are missing or being used ineffectively.

Techno-structural issues

Techno-structural issues stem from an organization's "technology (for example, task methods and job design) and structure (for example, division of labor and hierarchy)" (Cummings & Worley, 2009, p. 158). Questions to ask include:

- How is the design or structure of the organization affecting communication?
- How is the way in which people work affecting communication (independent, collaboration, cross-functional, etc.)?
- How are people's attitude and perception towards their work affecting communication?

Human resource issues

Another type of issue that affects communication is categorized as human resource issues. These issues pertain to talent management activities such as hiring, rewarding, developing, onboarding, and setting expectations (Cummings & Worley, 2009). Questions to ask include:

- How are hiring practices affecting communication?
- How is poor communication reinforced (for example, if the culture is one of competition, people might get rewarded for withholding information)?
- How are expectations set around communication?
- What type of training do people receive in order to communicate well?

Lessons from the field

In this next section we share lessons from our experience working with clients (collectively we have done hundreds of projects). There's support for each of these lessons in the literature and there are many tips and tricks out there, however, experience is ultimately the best teacher. We strongly recommend keeping field notes about successes, challenges, and lessons learned. This helps professionals with ongoing process improvement as well as professional development.

We've organized lessons into four categories: interpersonal, process, personal, and client. Interpersonal relates to relationships, process to execution, personal to the professional or team of professionals, and client to people receiving the benefits of diagnosis.

Interpersonal lessons

- **Executive and leadership support is essential** – Without commitment and active participation from top leadership it will be difficult, though not impossible, to affect change. Kouzes and Posner (1995) state that leaders must model the way for others.
- **Trust (or the lack there of) impacts everything** – John Gottman (2011), a relationship expert, says that trust is built in small moments over time. Trust influences how much people are willing to share (refer to the Johari Window). Be mindful and intentional about the things you do and say.
- **Confidentiality and anonymity are helpful** – We've found that employees are more open and willing to share with confidentiality and anonymity agreements in place. It helps to reduce fear and anxiety (when agreements are honored). Executive level leadership must agree to this condition.[4] If you have reason to believe that confidentiality and anonymity are at stake or if agreements aren't made ahead of time, be transparent with people.
- **Voice to others** – Remember that part of your job is to give voice to underrepresented groups (Ragin & Amoroso, 2011). Voice to others is perhaps the most

difficult of all to achieve. We must constantly remind ourselves during this process that some groups will feel more comfortable sharing information and the different approaches to gathering data might have advantages over others. It's also important to remember that we (the diagnostic team as well as leadership) might be blind to the concerns of groups of which we are not a part.

Process lessons

- **Diagnosis can be disruptive** – Gathering data takes employees and leaders away from goals and tasks temporarily. This can have an adverse impact on productivity and performance short-term. If successful, the diagnostic process will result in improved productivity and performance long-term, but leaders and employees should know about the short-term investment.
- **Form follows function** – Pick methodologies that are congruent with your purpose and that will lead you to insights that will be valuable to the organization. Hundreds of methodological approaches exist.
- **Diagnosis is an intervention** – Heisenberg's Uncertainty Principle[5] suggests that when dealing with humans and organizations asking a question like, "tell me about the leadership style of your boss," raises awareness of the boss's leadership and leadership in general just by asking the question. Employees will quite naturally be talking with colleagues as well. All of this tends to create an interaction effect that is an intervention in and of itself. It's also possible that this intervention can either be positive or negative in its impact on the organization. Our goal is to maximize the positive and minimize the negative, considering diagnosis as an influencer of change (Sagor, 2011).
- **Use mixed methods** – Also called triangulation of data, a combination of methods serves as a way to cross-check the data and to better understand how things are currently functioning.
- **Utility matters as much as validity** – A working definition of validity is: *Are we measuring what we think we are measuring?* Methods textbooks list multiple types of validity and ways to measure them depending upon the methodological approach being used. Utility is potentially a far more important concept. Do the diagnostics process and the outcomes have utility for the organization? Will they help us to design interventions and solve problems?

Personal lessons

- **Credibility (or the lack there of) impacts everything** – Credibility is linked to believability and believability is linked to trust (Blanchard, Olmstead, & Lawrence, 2013). If you don't have it now, figure out ways to develop and build credibility. One way is through integrity – aligning your actions, words, and values (Brown, 2015).
- **Know your limits** – Being a consultant can be seductive. We ride in on a white horse, tell them what to do, get paid big bucks, and leave before the challenging work of change gets done. We feel it is important to help the client and at the same time, know that there is only so much we can do.
- **Keep learning** – Based on both our experience and the experiences of many others, it is important to constantly improve one's own processes, skills, and abilities. A critical skill to master for diagnosis is asking the right questions. We would suggest that one of the most important questions to reflect on is, "what can be done 'better' next time?"

Client lessons

- **The cost of poor communication** – Lack of communication post data collection is a huge risk as well. Depending on the organization's history with diagnostics, including employee surveys, employees may be cynical or apathetic which may influence the quality of the data. When clients make decisions during diagnosis, especially post-data collection, without explaining the 'why' and 'how' it can leave employees thinking they haven't been heard.
- **Ownership** – It's not uncommon for a client to pass problems onto professionals, expecting us to own or fully solve the problem without their involvement (Schein, 1999). We recommend a collaborative role, but be mindful of taking ownership for problems and solutions for which you have little or no control.
- **Ask for old data** – To avoid duplication of efforts, find out what the client has already done in terms of data collection and diagnosis. It can hurt our credibility if we're asking questions that were asked six months ago. Additionally, old data can be useful at various points of the diagnostic process.

Benefits of diagnosis

The goal of diagnosis is to accurately diagnose so that organizations can improve and the lives of stakeholders also improve. An additional benefit of diagnosis is that it's an intervention itself. The sheer act of gathering input, or letting employees know diagnosis is happening, creates a new level of awareness.[6] Many organizations begin to see changes long before formal interventions are recommended and executed.

For internal consultants

Internal consultants can help their organization grow and provide empirical support to organizational leadership and stakeholders about what they (the internal consultant) already know or suspect. The diagnostic process facilitates their ability to focus training and other interventions on the root causes of problems, thus increasing the probability of success.

For external consultants

External consultants can also sell the diagnostic process to clients. For external consultants, we recommend treating diagnosis and training (or other interventions) as two separate contracts.[7]

For faculty and academic tenure

Academics are driven by a different type of personal and professional ROI. Professionally, they are working towards creating knowledge, etc. Personally, faculty are driven by the systemic requirements related to tenure and promotion. Research of this type is often not publishable in the traditional sense. This may discourage some faculty, especially junior faculty, from embarking on diagnostics due to their focus on getting tenure and eventually promotion to full professor.

Certainly, one can take some of the work from organizational diagnosis and use it as scholarship, but institutions are slow to see this as equivalent to a refereed article.

Diagnostic projects are often not appropriate as articles because they almost always contain proprietary information. Numerous projects can be turned into books and articles, but that is not possible until a meta-analysis can be done (Clampitt, 2013).

We would also note that diagnosis easily qualifies as service when done for a nonprofit, or teaching when it involves a class in service learning for a nonprofit. Diagnostic projects are a great learning tool for graduate students and a wonderful way to contribute pro bono to the community.

Tenure ultimately depends upon policies at the institution. We would suggest looking at the work of Ernest Boyer (1990) in *Scholarship Reconsidered*. Boyer made the argument that we needed to enlarge and broaden the perspective of the American professoriate. And in doing so, identifies four levels of scholarship. This work by Boyer provides the basis for an argument allowing the faculty member to make a case that even though many diagnosis projects do not result in unique studies that can be published in journals, they are worthy of consideration as they are sound academic studies. Faculty members should examine Boyer's work and policies that are unique to their institution to make diagnosis work count towards their reviews.

For training

When training interventions are supported by diagnostic data highlighting gaps in skills, knowledge, or ability, the rationale for training is much clearer for participants. Training is also appropriate to support changes in attitude, mindset, and behavior if changes are first modeled by senior leaders and reinforced over time. Diagnostic data also serve as a form of pre and post training assessment and measurement. This not only fosters accountability for employees to apply the learning post training, but also serves as a gauge for training effectiveness (Bell, Tannenbaum, Ford, Noe, & Kraiger, 2017). An example from one of our projects demonstrates this.

A local computer company of about 60 employees that delivered services nationally and internationally requested some interpersonal communication training. We convinced the owner that we should undergo a diagnostic process. It was discovered that the real issue was that employees were leaving after going through some excellent IT training and certifications. The company was not profitable because they were, in effect, training their competitors' workforces.

It was discovered that there were three key issues. They were:

- A benefits package that was good for the eight employees that had been with the organization for twenty plus years, but not good for employees who were concerned about pre-natal care, orthodontics and other programs that one would expect from talented younger employees. SOLUTION: Redesigned the benefits package to a menu driven system that gave choice to employees.
- They had a problem in that their internal systems were not as cutting edge as the systems and software they installed for their customers. SOLUTION: They took materials out of their own inventory and had their own technicians install and maintain them.
- They did need training on listening, which primarily consisted of awareness and attitude adjustments to get the "bosses" to slow down, focus, and really listen. SOLUTION: Training of all in listening and worked with leadership (most of whom were from technical backgrounds) to raise "awareness" of the need for focus and listening.

Questions for reflection

Diagnosis has many different parts. Engaging in reflection throughout and post-diagnosis helps professionals strengthen their skills and effectiveness. Below are some of our favorite questions:

- What were the strengths and weaknesses of our process?
- How helpful was the information we uncovered using diagnostic methods?
- Did the information we shared make sense to the client?
- Did the information we shared foster understanding of root causes?
- What changes happened as a result of engaging in diagnosis?
- What would we do differently next time?
- What successes and wins will we celebrate?

Summary

In this chapter we shared a foundation for diagnosis, including a brief history and working definition. We highlighted three processes to guide professionals before, during, and after diagnosis. Effective diagnosis includes gathering, understanding, and interpreting information in order to help clients identify and choose effective solutions improving communication. For gathering information we shared several methods as well as advantages and disadvantages for each option. To organize and understand data, we shared four diagnostic models. We offered three different ways to interpret the data. These include human process, techno-structural, and human resource issues. In support of diagnostic effectiveness, we shared lessons from the field as well as questions for reflection. At this point our suggestion is that you explore and experiment with diagnostic approaches to see what works for you. And that you build on your successes and learn from each project. And remember to have fun while building on your craft.

Notes

1 Many sources suggest different numbers, our experience is 8 to 12 is a better number. The guiding principle is: enough participants for a synergistic group discussion and not so many that focus and control are lost.
2 The largest group we have done is around 500 participants, but larger can be done if you have enough facilitators to assist.
3 The ComSat offers an accessible questionnaire (60 questions), while also providing insights into multiple dimensions of communication satisfaction. Responses received from the Downs-Hazen Communication Satisfaction Questionnaire (Downs & Adrian, 2004; Zwijze-Koning & De Jong, 2007) has been factor-analyzed into "eight main dimensions of communication satisfaction" (Downs & Adrian, 2004, pp. 140–141).
4 One time, even though Stafford had commitment from the executive level leadership, that leadership demanded to know who had made some critical remarks. Upon reaching impasse, and being threatened with nonpayment, the team stood up, gathered all materials and results, and walked out of the conference room. They were not paid. Stafford paid the team members providing an example of the "right thing to do" and has served him well when conducting many more projects in terms of credibility and expectations.
5 *Heisenberg's Uncertainty Principle*: The principle states that one cannot measure with certainty the position and motion of a particle because the act of measurement impacts the position and motion (Jha, 2013). In other words, at the subatomic level, even a laser measuring the

distance between two walls is having an impact on the molecules and particles. With humans, the impact is far greater.

6 Heisenberg's Uncertainty Process at work.

7 In some cases, the diagnostic process is worth more in profit to the consultant. It also helps them to better deliver solutions.

References

Anderson, D. L. (2016). *Organization development: The process of leading organization change* (3rd ed.). Thousand Oaks, CA: SAGE.

Babbie, E. (2016). *The practice of social research* (14th ed.). Boston, MA: Cengage Learning.

Bell, B. S., Tannenbaum, S. I., Ford, J. K., Noe, R. A., & Kraiger, K. (2017). 100 Years of training and development research: What we know and where we should go. *The Journal of Applied Psychology, 102*(3), 305–323. doi: 10.1037/apl0000142

Berger, D. (1999). A brief history of medical diagnosis and the birth of the clinical laboratory: Part 1 – Ancient times through the 19th century. *Medical Laboratory Observer, 31*(7). Retrieved from https://www.ncbi.nlm.nih.gov/pubmed/10539661

Blanchard, K., Olmstead, C., & Lawrence, M. C. (2013). *TrustWorks! Four keys to building lasting relationships* (1st ed.). New York, NY: William Morrow.

Block, P. (2011). *Flawless consulting: A guide to getting your expertise used* (3rd ed.). San Francisco, CA: Pfeiffer.

Boyer, E. (1990). *Scholarship reconsidered: Priorities of the professoriate.* Princeton, NJ: Carnegie Foundation for the Advancement of Teaching.

Brockner, J. (2017). *The process matters: Engaging and equipping people for success.* Princeton, NJ: Princeton University Press.

Brown, B. (2015). *Rising strong.* New York, NY: Spiegel & Grau.

Burke, W. W., & Litwin, G. H. (1992). A casual model of organizational performance and change. *Journal of Management, 18*(3), 523–545. Retrieved from https://ezproxy.library.ewu.edu/login?url=https://search-proquest-com.ezproxy.library.ewu.edu/docview/215258879?accountid=7305

Carlson, J. F., Kurt, F., & Jonson, J. L. (eds.). (2017). *The twentieth mental measurements yearbook.*, NE: Buros Institute of Mental Measurements.

Clampitt, P. (2013). *Communicating for managerial effectiveness: Problems, strategies, solutions* (5th ed.). Thousand Oaks, CA: SAGE.

Cummings, T. G., & Worley, C. G. (2009). *Organization development and change* (9th ed.). Mason, OH: South-Western Cengage Learning.

Delbecq, A. L., & Van de Ven, A. H. (1971). A group process model for problem identification and program planning. *The Journal of Applied Behavioral Science, 7*(4), 466–492. doi: 10.1177/002188637100700404

Downs, C., & Adrian, A. D. (2004). *Assessing organizational communication: Strategic communication audits* (Guilford communication series). New York, NY: Guilford Press.

Goldhaber, G. M., & Krivonos, P. D. (1977). The ICA communication audit: Process, status, and critique. *The Journal of Business Communication, 15*(1), 41. Retrieved from http://job.sagepub.com/content/15/1/41

Gottman, J. (2011, October 29). John Gottman on betrayal and trust. *Greater Good Magazine.* Retrieved from https://greatergood.berkeley.edu/article/item/john_gottman_on_trust_and_betrayal

Jamieson, D. W., & Worley, C. G. (2008). The practice of organization development. In T. G. Cummings (ed.), *Handbook of organization development* (pp. 99–122). Thousand Oaks, CA: SAGE.

Jha, A. (2013, November 10). What is Heisenberg's uncertainty principle? *The Guardian.* Retrieved from https://www.theguardian.com/science/2013/nov/10/what-is-heisenbergs-uncertainty-principle

Kouzes, J. M., & Posner, B. Z. (1995). *The leadership challenge: How to keep getting extraordinary things done in organizations* (2nd ed.). San Francisco, CA: Jossey-Bass.

Krueger, R., & Casey, M. A. (2015). *Focus groups: A practical guide for applied research* (5th ed.). Thousand Oaks, CA: SAGE.

Levinson, H. (1994). The practitioner as diagnostic instrument. In A. Howard (ed.), *Diagnosis for organizational change. Methods and models* (pp. 27–52). New York, NY: Guilford.

Morgan, D. (1997). *Focus groups as qualitative research* (2nd ed.; Qualitative research methods, vol. 16). Thousand Oaks, CA: SAGE.

Morgan, D., Krueger, R. A., & King, J. A. (1998). *Focus group kit.* Thousand Oaks, CA: SAGE.

Pyzdek, T. (2001). *The six sigma handbook: A complete guide for greenbelts, blackbelts, and managers at all levels.* New York, NY: McGraw-Hill.

Ragin, C., & Amoroso, L. M. (2011). *Constructing social research: The unity and diversity of method* (2nd ed.; Sociology for a new century). Los Angeles, CA: SAGE.

Rubin, R., Palmgreen, P., & Sypher, H. E. (2009). *Communication research measures: A sourcebook* (Guilford communication series). New York, NY: Routledge.

Sagor, R. (2011). *The action research guidebook: A four-stage process for educators and school teams* (2nd ed.). Thousand Oaks, CA: Corwin.

Schein, E. H. (1999). *Process consultation revisited: Building the helping relationship.* Reading, MA: Addison-Wesley Publishing Company, Inc.

Tracy, C. J. (2017). Practical application in organizational communication: A historical snapshot and challenge for the future. *Management Communication Quarterly, 31*(1), 139–145. doi: 10.1177/0893318916675736

Waclawski, J., & Rogelberg, S. G. (2002). Interviews and focus groups: Quintessential organization development techniques. In J. Waclawski & A. H. Church (eds.), *Organization development: A data-driven approach to organization change* (pp. 103–126). San Francisco, CA: Jossey-Bass.

Zwijze-Koning, K., & De Jong, M. (2007). Evaluating the communication satisfaction questionnaire as a communication audit tool. *Management Communication Quarterly, 20*(3), 261–282. doi: 10.1177/0893318906295680

Chapter 5

Greater alignment, greater success

Communication needs assessments and training program assessments

Piyawan Charoensap-Kelly

Abstract

This chapter illustrates why assessment is widely valued and considered a Best Practice by the training and development community. It presents an overview of the knowledge and skills communication consultants, coaches, teachers, and trainers (CCCTTs) should possess to conduct effective needs assessment and evaluation. The chapter seeks to familiarize novice CCCTTs with the language and basic how-to's of assessments as well as provide veteran CCCTTs with new ways to refine their assessment approaches.

How do you ascertain if your training will meet your clients' needs or address problems they are trying to solve? How do you ensure you have effectively delivered to clients what you promised? The work of communication consultants, coaches, teachers, and trainers (CCCTTs) does not simply start on the first day of the training and end when the training is completed. Most practitioners and scholars agree training and development initiatives should begin with an effective assessment of individual and organizational needs (Altschuld & Watkins, 2014; Arthur, Bennett, Edens, & Bell, 2003; Beebe, Mottet, & Roach, 2013; DeWine, 2001; Fyke & Buzzanell, 2014; Sleezer, Russ-Eft, & Gupta, 2014). A post-training assessment also should be conducted to measure the quality of the training program (Altschuld & Watkins, 2014; Beebe et al., 2013; DeWine, 2001; Fyke & Buzzanell, 2014).

This chapter focuses on Best Practice 2 – Use Assessable Methods. It aims to illustrate why assessment is widely valued and considered a Best Practice by communication specialists and the broader T&D community (Beebe et al., 2013; Gilbert, 1978; Harless, 1970; Kaufman & Guerra-López, 2013; Phillips & Phillips, 2016; Rossett, 1987; Sleezer et al., 2014; Stufflebeam, McCormick, Brinkerhoff, & Nelson, 1985). The chapter provides an overview of the knowledge and skills CCCTTs should possess in order to effectively adopt this best practice. Assessments at the front-end and back-end of the training process will be discussed because both types are crucial and go hand in hand (Beebe et al., 2013; DeWine, 2001). For clarity, front-end assessment and back-end assessment will be referred to as needs assessment and training evaluation, respectively.

The first part of the chapter describes the what, why, and how of a needs assessment. Five basic steps of conducting a needs assessment and a real-life needs assessment case study are provided. The second part explains what a training evaluation is, why it is important, and how to evaluate a training program using the influential Kirkpatrick evaluation model. Sample evaluation questionnaires are provided as a useful guide for developing one's own training program evaluation. The chapter concludes with practical points readers might find useful for developing pre- and post-assessments for their training and development programs.

Needs assessments

> If you don't know where you are going, every road will get you nowhere.
>
> Henry Kissinger

What is a needs assessment?

A need is a measurable gap between what currently is and what should or could be (Altschuld & Watkins, 2014; Sleezer et al., 2014; Watkins, West, & Visser, 2012); for example, a gap between employees' current and desired sales negotiation or customer relations skills. A needs assessment identifies what the gap or problem is, what causes it, and what should be done to reduce it (Sleezer et al., 2014). When training is determined to be the best intervention, assessment data enable CCCTTs to create effective training objectives, develop relevant content, select workable delivery methods, and use appropriate evaluation measures (Arthur et al., 2003; Beebe et al., 2013; Lawson, 2015). A needs assessment also helps CCCTTs avoid jumping to a wrong solution, including providing training when other interventions are needed. For example, a low performance level among a company's accountants may be caused by an outdated accounting software. Providing a communication training program to all accountants would not solve the issue but upgrading the software would.

In addition, the process of collecting data, asking for input from various internal and external stakeholders and letting them be part of the solutions, can also increase their buy-in for the recommendations that will follow (Sleezer et al., 2014; Watkins et al., 2012). Moreover, a needs assessment ensures that the benefits of conducting the training or adopting a proposed intervention will be greater than the problems caused by the performance deficiency (Kaufman, 1998). Since organizations invest billions of dollars in training every year (Grossman & Salas, 2011), it is critical to ensure all training and development budget is spent on actual needs. To summarize, a needs assessment ensures that interventions are relevant and address the needs, helps stakeholders make better decisions about what course of action should be taken to better current performance issues, and supports organizations' objectives.

Needs assessment models and approaches

In the needs assessment literature, several models and frameworks are provided (Lepicki & Boggs, 2014), each with its own jargon and steps (Sleezer et al., 2014). According to leading assessment scholars Altschuld and Watkins (2014), two seminal and influential models are the three-phase needs assessment approach (Witkin & Altschuld, 1995; Altschuld, 2010) and the Organizational Element Model (OEM; Kaufman, 1992, 2000; Kaufman & Guerra-Lopez, 2013). The three-phase needs assessment approach includes:

- *Phase 1 pre-assessment*: Investigate the situation and determine the scope and plan for the assessment by reviewing existing information, discussing with key stakeholders, and collecting some preliminary information as needed;
- *Phase 2 assessment*: If Phase 1 did not provide enough information, conduct in-depth research, using methodologically sound methods, to thoroughly explore the needs and their root causes, and prioritize solution strategies; and

- *Phase 3 post-assessment*: Communicate findings to the stakeholders, implement the action plans, and evaluate the recommended solutions as well as the needs assessment process itself (Altschuld & Watkins, 2014; Watkins et al., 2012).

For detailed information about the three-phase approach, read Altschuld (2010).

The OEM proposes that assessors identify and align needs (i.e., gaps between current and desired results) across five levels:

- *Mega*: The societal level such as the quality of life or safety;
- *Macro*: The organizational level such as profit, brand recognition;
- *Micro*: The individual/team level such as production quota met, operation completed, employees well-trained;
- *Processes*: Methods, interventions, or activities such as operation line, training, communication practices; and
- *Inputs*: Resources such as funding, equipment, policies that the organization uses to achieve its desired results.

By filling the gaps across and aligning these five levels, the organization can add value to both internal stakeholders (e.g., employees, senior management) and external stakeholders (e.g., client and society), thus maximizing performance and ensuring continuous growth. For further study, Kaufman and Guerra-Lopez's (2013) book provides specific steps for conducting a need assessment for each of the five levels and how to link them together.

In addition to these two models, Human Performance Technology (HPT) is another comprehensive model focused on improving performance at the societal, organizational, process, and individual performer level. HPT uses a wide range of tools and interventions (both training and non-training) for improving human performance and business results. For a thorough discussion of HPT see Chapter 15 within this handbook by Burk and Birk. Within the communication field, Goldhaber and a team of scholars from the International Communication Association (ICA) developed the ICA Communication Audit as a multi-instrument method for auditing communication behaviors in organizations (Goldhaber, 1976, 2002; Goldhaber, Porter, & Yates, 1977). The ICA Communication Audit uses five diagnostic tools including a 122-item questionnaire, interviews, diaries, critical communication incidents, and network analyses (Clampitt, 2009; Goldhaber et al., 1977). These tools can be administered independently or in any combination depending on the needs of the organization (Goldhaber, 2002; Goldhaber et al., 1977). The ICA Communication Audit survey instrument has become the go-to tool for academics and practitioners (Goldhaber, 2002). Despite some criticism, it is considered one of the "most comprehensive attempts to measure all aspects of an organization's communication system" (Clampitt, 2009, p. 59).

Given the multiplicity of needs assessment models, how do CCCTTs decide which model to use? First, consider the nature of the problem or whether the needs you are addressing are strategic, tactical, or operational.

- *Strategic needs* (equivalent to Kaufman's Mega level) focus on the long-term organizational goals typically concerning the relationship between the organization and the clients and society in which they serve. For example, a city government is developing a downtown revitalization project and needs to know what changes are of greatest interest to the populace and how to best communicate new services to them.

- *Tactical needs* (Kaufman's Macro level) involve short-range plans including policies and procedures put in place to support strategic decisions and guide operational decisions. The focus is on the organization itself. For example, customer complaints in a hotel company have dramatically increased and the number of customers has dropped by 40 per cent in the last six months. You are charged with investigating and fixing the problem.
- *Operational needs* (Kaufman's Micro level) involve implementing projects or programs and carrying out tasks to produce results. This type of need typically concerns individuals or teams' performance. For example, employees in the production department have exhibited low morale and often miss work. Their manager is requesting a training program to help the employees improve interpersonal relationships and increase their morale.

Strategic and tactical needs are typically more complex than operational needs and therefore require more comprehensive assessment models such as the three-phase approach and OEM. These types of needs usually involve a variety of interventions beyond training. When the need is operational, the assessment has a narrower scope and is often executed on a smaller scale. However, strategic, tactical, and operational needs do not function independently and successful assessments align all three of them. Efforts to fulfill the organization's strategic plans and serve the clients should not ignore the needs of individual employees. Likewise, efforts to improve individual and team performance should be aligned with organizational objectives, missions, and visions. Oftentimes, projects may specifically involve assessing training needs for a group of employees and does not call for a large-scale strategic assessment.

Second, resources such as time, money, and skills also influence what needs assessment approaches to use. Large-scale needs assessments are time-consuming and costly. Most organizations are more concerned about implementing solutions than about investing time and money assessing needs (Sleezer et al., 2014). For such cases, an abbreviated form of needs assessment is commonly used (Lawson, 2015). Third, effective CCCTTs realize that there is no one-size-fit-all approach. Lepicki and Boggs (2014) recommended that "rigid adherence to one needs assessment model almost always will not work" (p. 73) and customizing from multiple models following the context of your project is key to a successful assessment.

No matter what models or frameworks you use, a needs assessment follows five basic steps that CCCTTs should be familiar with. The next section describes the five steps for conducting a needs assessment with a specific focus on developing a communication training program. •

How to conduct a basic needs assessment

Step 1: Identify the problem or need

At the first meeting with your client or senior management, listen carefully about the problem or condition they are facing. It may be an increase in employee grievances, a low production rate, a decrease in sales, or a development of a new onboarding program, to name a few. Next, study the organization's visions, missions, values, and goals so you have a complete understanding of its business needs (i.e., strategic planning) and align your program objectives accordingly. This preliminary investigation will help you understand the gap between the current condition and desired condition. Importantly, you will gain a basic idea about the scope of the project, whether training is the right solution, and what you can and cannot deliver. As guided by the handbook's Best Practice 1 – Maintain Transparency to Clients and Trainees, you want to be transparent with your client about your capability. You may need to get help from other colleagues or consultants with relevant expertise or you may agree to delivering a certain part of the project that you are specialized in. This will help you set a practical goal for your project that will meet the client's needs and that you can effectively deliver.

Step 2: Design your research methodology

Your goal at this stage is to gain an in-depth understanding about the problem or need and what causes it so you can offer the best recommendations. You need to determine what to ask, who to ask, and how to ask. Table 5.1 shows a summary of analyses you might perform (i.e., types of questions to ask), the people involved in each analysis, some sample questions, and methods to use.

What to ask. Your questions or types of analyses can be divided into three categories. *Organizational analysis* reveals what an organization needs or is lacking in order to accomplish its missions and goals. *Task analysis* identifies a set of skills trainees need to perform their job more effectively. *Individual analysis* reveals who needs the training, what they already know on the subject, what they yet need to learn, when would be the best time to train them, and what their learning styles are. An individual analysis helps CCCTTs create an audience-centered training program (Beebe et al., 2013). Grouping your questions in this way helps you align the organization's strategic, tactical, and operational needs as mentioned earlier. Although you will be asking different questions to different groups of people, you can use similar techniques to collect data.

Who to ask. Who to ask depends on the nature of the problem, the goal of your assessment, and the types of questions you are asking. Sources of information can be senior management; potential trainees; potential trainees' managers, direct reports, and coworkers; human resource personnel; and external stakeholders (e.g., vendors, customers, and community members). Gathering data about the client's competitors such as sales results and market share from trade publications can identify your client's position in relation to its competitors and pinpoint areas for improvement (Lawson, 2015). Additionally, subject matter experts (SMEs: people who have a rich knowledge and skills on how to perform a task) are great sources of information, especially when conducting a task analysis. Research has shown that consulting SMEs during a needs assessment can maximize the benefits of training (Aguinis & Kraiger, 2009).

How to ask. Several methods are available for collecting data to identify the gap in performance or learning. The most frequently used methods include *questionnaires, interviews, observations,* and *organizational records,* each having its strengths and weaknesses.

Questionnaires. A questionnaire is a series of questions or statements that examine the knowledge, beliefs, attitudes, and (self-report) behaviors of respondents. Surveys are a cost and time efficient approach to collect data from a large number of people. Questionnaires assure greater anonymity for the respondents, increasing likelihood of open feedback. Additionally, both quantitative data (e.g., standardized questions) and qualitative data (e.g., open-ended questions) can be gathered simultaneously (Frey, Botan, & Kreps, 1999; Ruel, Wagner, & Gillespie, 2016).

Table 5.1 Data collection guide: What to ask, who to ask, and how to ask

Type of Analysis	Sources of Information	What to Look For	Sample Questions*	Data Collection Methods
Organizational Analysis	Senior management	Business goals; current business concerns; organization's strengths, weaknesses, opportunities, and threats (SWOTs)	• What are your organization's mission and vision? • What are the strengths and weaknesses of your company? • What organizational issues require an immediate attention?	Survey/questionnaires Individual interview Focus group interview Document review Observation
	Clients; patients; community members	Attitudes, expectations, or satisfaction, etc. about the organization's products or services.	• Based on your experience with [product], would you recommend this product to a friend? • Based on your experience with [product], how likely are you to buy [product] again?	
	Competitors	How your client is doing compared with its competitors	• Using data from competitors' annual reports or trade publications, find out how they do in terms of market share, brand loyalty, stock prices, etc.	
Task Analysis	Manager; human resource personnel; subject matter experts (SMEs)	A better or preferred way to do a task to get the best results	• HR personnel: What tasks is the person in this role expected to fulfill? • Manager: What is the standard or most effective way to perform this task? • SME: What steps are involved in performing the skill? What do you do first, second, and so on?	
Individual Analysis	Potential trainees; managers; coworkers; direct reports	Potential trainees' levels of skills and knowledge; what they already know; what they need to know; their learning styles; work schedule; best time to train	• Trainee: How satisfied are you with your current level of performance? What additional skills do you think can help you do your job better? • Manager: What are the important issues or problems your employees currently face? • Coworkers/direct reports: What would you like your supervisor/coworkers to do differently?	

Note: The SME sample question is borrowed from Beebe et al. (2013).

A disadvantage of questionnaires is the lack of in-depth data. For example, you might discover from a questionnaire that employees are dissatisfied with their management's practices but cannot identify what specific practices cause the dissatisfaction. Moreover, people often do not return their questionnaires and a limited number of responses you have may not represent your survey population. In such cases, it is hard to make a meaningful interpretation of the problem or situation you are investigating. Finally, it can be difficult to design a questionnaire that is both valid and reliable. There are several ways to ensure the most usable survey responses. At the very least, develop questions that are clear, specific, simple, and concise. Avoid double-barreled questions (i.e., asking about multiple issues in one question) and avoid biased questions that lead respondents to answer questions in a specific way (Frey, Botan, & Kreps, 1999; Ruel, Wagner, & Gillespie, 2016).

Interviews. Assessors can conduct individual or one-on-one interviews or focus group interviews consisting of multiple participants. Unlike a questionnaire with fixed questions, interviewers can rephrase their questions or ask follow-up questions during an interview to clarify points or probe for more information. Additionally, interviewees can talk in their own words without being limited to a pre-determined set of answers (Lindlof & Taylor, 2010). Therefore, assessors can gain a richer and wider understanding about participants' perspectives (Kvale & Brinkmann, 2009). The primary disadvantage of interviews is that they are time-consuming in administration and data analysis. It can also be difficult to identify consistent themes especially when the interviewer conducts multiple individual interviews or focus group interviews and varies his or her questions considerably. Furthermore, an interviewer must have good interpersonal and listening skills, particularly when facilitating a focus group interview.

Before conducting an interview, CCCTTs should develop an interview guide, a set of open-ended questions and possible follow-up questions that will help them stay on track during the course of each interview. The interviewer should begin the interview by building rapport with the interviewee, explaining the purpose of the interview, allowing them to ask questions about the process, and ensuring confidentiality. The interviewer then proceeds to ask questions of concern and take notes as she/he proceeds. It is helpful to record the interview but only with permission from interviewees or gatekeepers. The major drawback of audio- or video-recording is that the interviewee may feel uncomfortable giving you honest responses. Toward the end of the interview, signal the interview is over and allow respondents to add further comments or ask questions. Interview notes should be filled out immediately after the interview so the interviewer does not forget the details (Beebe et al., 2013; DeWine, 2001).

Observations. Another way to gather data is to watch behaviors, interactions, or note physical environments in their natural setting. There are two types of observations. A *structured observation* is when you monitor and record specific behaviors that are determined before the observation. For example, you could monitor the number of times sales associates in a retail store smile at their customers. An *unstructured observation* is when you watch everything that is happening without predetermined notions of which behaviors to observe. For example, you could observe the same retail store and record all behaviors you consider prominent or important. Through observation you can identify if there is any gap in employees' knowledge, skills, or behaviors that can be addressed by a training program or an intervention (Gillham, 2008; Sleezer et al., 2014).

The primary advantage of observation is that it gives the observer a first-hand account and more realistic data of "whether what people say they do is the same as what they actually do" (Mulhall, 2003, p. 307). Another advantage is that observational data can illuminate existing but unrecognized communication patterns within an organization. They can yield insights that "stimulate discussion and potential change among organization members" (Meyer, 2002, p. 476). Observation also can be less disruptive to the employee's work compared with an interview approach. However, observations can take a considerable amount of time and talent on the part of the observer. It can be costly and impractical for using with large groups. Results also can be tainted by observer bias or the "Hawthorne effect," where people alter or improve their behavior when they know they are being observed (Schwartzman, 1993).

Organizational records. Organizational records can be useful sources of information to determine a performance deficiency or a gap that you want to fill. Organizational records refer to any written or printed material from an organization including, for example, customer complaints, accident and safety reports, job descriptions, organizational charts, personnel records, performance appraisal results, sales and cost records, attendance records, handbooks, samples of work, and company memos. If customer complaints have been dramatically increasing, it would be wise to review customer calls, grievance reports, or return policies before conducting customer service training. If a university department seeks to update its undergraduate curriculum, it would be important to review the existing curriculum, student course evaluations, and the department's mission and vision statements as part of the gap analysis. Organizational records are factual and objective sources of information that can reveal a lot about areas of concern. The drawbacks are that the records may be out of date and no longer relevant. Also, CCCTTs may not always have permission to access certain documents they deem necessary.

In sum, each of the methods discussed above has its strengths and weaknesses. What methods to use depends on the scope of the project, time, cost, manpower, and skills of the assessor among other factors. Whenever possible, assessors should combine both quantitative and qualitative methods to allow for triangulation of results and the most fruitful findings. Example 5.1 provides a real-life illustration of how multiple data collection methods can be used to understand the needs and their causes and offer more effective intervention.

Example 5.1 A Needs Assessment Case Study

A client, a mid-size telecommunications company, asked me for assistance with organizational restructuring. The initial request was straightforward: "we need a new organization chart." After the first meeting with my contact, the human resources director, I learned more things that were troubling her. Employees had low morale and poor interpersonal relationships with each other, new engineers made a lot of mistakes, and there was high turnover in the information technology (IT) engineering department. Clearly, a new organization chart alone would not address her concerns. I started the project with a needs assessment to understand the causes of the problems for developing proper interventions. I conducted a company-wide survey, individual interviews with the CEO, senior management, and SMEs in the IT department, and observed the day-to-day interactions among employees. Results showed that 1) job manuals and career advancement plans were not in place for IT engineers, 2) an onboarding program had not been implemented in the past few years, 3) the silo mentality prevailed across the board, and 4) employees had poor communication and interpersonal relationships.

With these findings, I proposed a training program for all employees that would pro-mote open, positive communication and improve their relationships. For four months after that, I worked closely with the human resource director, IT department head, and senior management to produce 1) a job manual and career advancement program for the IT department (to reduce mistakes and turnover rate); 2) an onboarding program for new employees; and 3) a new organization chart. At the end of the project, I delivered another training program to introduce the new organization chart and explain how all departments function together to achieve the same goal for the company and produce the final outcomes for its external stakeholders. The needs assessment data unearthed the stumbling blocks to this company's performance efficiency leading to more effective solutions.

Step 3: Collect data

After identifying sources of information, selecting data collection methods, and cre-ating instruments (e.g., questionnaires, interview guides), it is important to pilot test instruments to ensure their validity and reliability. *Validity* refers to the extent to which you are accurately measuring what you intend to measure (Patten, 2012). For example, are you asking the right people? Will your questions help you uncover the cause of the problem or are you wasting time with irrelevant questions? *Reliability* refers to the degree to which an instrument produces consistent results (Patten, 2012). For example, if you use a scale composed of 10 items that aim to measure customer satisfaction, all items on the scale must deal with customer satisfaction for the scale to be consistent within itself and considered reliable. If two researchers observe a group of employees at work and interpret what they see, they should consistently yield a similar interpretation for it to be reliable. For more information about validity and reliability, see Creswell (2014) or Patten (2012). Based on the pilot test results, revise the instruments as nec-essary (e.g., rephrase certain questions to improve clarity or avoid misunderstandings). When validity and reliability are achieved, coordinate data collection procedures with the client. For example, obtain documents to be reviewed, schedule interviews, and prepare to launch the survey via the organization's email listserv or Intranet. There are no hard and fast rules about what to do first, second, and so forth when you employ multiple data collection methods. However, when time and resources permit, start with reviewing organizational records to form an idea about the problems or needs and familiarize yourself with the language used in the organization. With that knowledge, you can develop more effective and appropriate interview questions. Next, conduct individual interviews followed by focus group interviews. Based on the results from the interviews, you can then create a questionnaire for a larger group of employees.

Step 4: Analyze data

After gathering needed information, the next step is to analyze data in a meaningful way. Remain neutral as much as possible when analyzing the data. For quantitative data (such as close-ended questionnaires or structured observation), look at the data in terms of frequency, averages, and percentages. For qualitative data (such as interviews, open-ended questionnaires, or unstructured observation), classify the data into categories and identify major themes. More importantly, the data should concretely inform you about the problem, what causes it, and what will be the best solutions. If CCCTTs cannot answer these questions with confidence at this point, they should repeat Steps 2 and 3.

Based on the findings, prioritize the needs and develop a list of recommended interventions considering the size, urgency, and relative importance of needs as well as the cost of interventions. Calculate expected **return on investment** (i.e., the benefit of an investment relative to the cost of the investment). The two most common measures for calculating return on investment are the *benefit-cost ratio* (i.e., program benefits divided by program cost) and the *ROI formula* (i.e., net program benefits divided by cost multiplied by one hundred). Phillips and Phillips's (2016) *Handbook of Training Evaluation and Measurement Methods* can serve as a great guidebook for calculating ROIs. When training is appropriate, define the specific objectives the training program will meet to fill the gap you identified. Setting effective training objectives allows for more effective evaluation of a training program.

When analyzing data, note any factors that may impact training results. Research has identified a host of variables that can inhibit the transfer of learning to the job environment including, for example, trainee cognitive ability, self-efficacy, perceived utility of training, career planning, willingness to learn, training method, supervisor support, peer support, opportunity to apply new knowledge and skills, and follow-up (Baldwin & Ford, 1988; Burke & Hutchins, 2007; Chiaburu & Marinova, 2005; Charoensap-Kelly, Broussard, Caldwell, & Lindsly, 2016; Grossman & Salas, 2011; Noe & Schmitt, 1986). For example, trainees might express disappointment with how they were not able to apply knowledge and skills from previous training to their jobs. They might report that such inability stems from the lack of positive reinforcement from supervisors or the organizational culture that impedes innovation. This is invaluable to know before the training so that CCCTTs can be proactive about the situation (to be described later in the chapter). Include this information in your report to the decision makers under the potential barriers section (to be explained next) so proper measures can be taken. Training transfer variables will be discussed further in the training evaluation section.

Step 5: Present the results

The last step of a basic needs assessment is to report findings and recommendations. Make your written report clear, clean, and crisp (DeWine, 2001). Facilitate clients' decision-making process with sufficient and critical information and avoid overwhelming them with too much information. This will increase the likelihood for a proposal approval. The written report should include an executive summary, project background and objectives, the data collection process (the methods used and people involved), summary of findings, recommendations, expected benefits, potential barriers, and an implementation guide. For the oral presentation, keep it concise. Facilitate understanding with slides and highlight important information using simple charts and graphs. Be prepared to answer questions and concerns related to training implementation. The oral presentation is an opportunity to hear feedback from key players, discuss the next action, and get buy-in (Lawson, 2015).

Once CCCTTs have completed the five basic steps of a needs assessment as described above, the next step is to develop an intervention or a training program that will meet both individual and organizational needs. Instructional design best practices can be found elsewhere in this handbook. In the next section, I discuss training evaluation and how it links to needs assessment.

Training evaluation

> If you don't have a good understanding of what impact you have had in the past, you can't expect to be able to predict with any certainty how successful you will be in the future.
>
> Sue DeWine

What is a training evaluation?

Training evaluation is the process of measuring the effectiveness of a training program to make sure that the program has met its objectives. When evaluating a training program, CCCTTs can use the same data collection methods (e.g., questionnaires, interviews, observation, organizational records) previously mentioned for needs assessment. However, the two types of assessments seek to answer different questions. Whereas a needs assessment identifies gaps in performance or learning, a training evaluation determines if the intervention has successfully filled those gaps and answered individual and organizational needs. Results from an evaluation can improve existing programs, justify new programs, or gain additional support. Evaluation data also inform CCCTTs on how to keep improving their own skills to remain competitive in the field.

There are two common types of evaluation. *Formative evaluation* gathers feedback that can be used to guide improvements while a training program is forming or occurring. For example, CCCTTs pilot-test a training activity with a small group of trainees or gain feedback from trainees at the end of each day of a week-long training program to see if any modifications are needed. *Summative evaluation* measures the level of success or proficiency that has been obtained after the training has been completed. For example, CCCTTs gather data about trainees' amount of learning, degree of behavior change, and return on investment. Summative evaluation determines whether the training program has attained its objectives, what adjustments can be made to increase the quality of the training, and if it is worthy of continued investment.

Kirkpatrick's training evaluation model

Among many training evaluation models, Kirkpatrick's (1959) four-level model has been the most enduring and widely used (Arthur et al., 2003; McLean & Moss, 2003; Rajeev, Madan, & Jayarajan, 2009; Smidt, Balandin, Sigafoos, & Reed, 2009). It is included on the certification exam of the Association for Talent Development. With the limited space, I will focus on this model and explain how it can be used. Kirkpatrick (1959) proposed four criteria for evaluating the effectiveness of a training program: reaction, learning, behavior, and results (Kirkpatrick, 1959; Kirkpatrick & Kirkpatrick, 2006).

Level 1: The *reaction* level measures trainees' favorable responses to the training. Although researchers and practitioners argue that the extent to which trainees are satisfied with the training does not necessarily translate to learning and behavioral change, this criterion has been the most widely used compared with other criteria (Arthur et al., 2003; Fyke & Buzzanell, 2014). Students' liking for the course or subject area can motivate them to achieve higher levels of cognitive learning and self-directed learning (Mottet & Richmond, 1998). Therefore, the reaction criterion should not be totally ignored. You can measure trainees' attitudes toward the trainer, training content, training delivery, and training environment using questionnaires or interviews. For sample questions examining trainees' reactions to a training program see Example 5.2, Section 1.

Example 5.2 A sample evaluation questionnaire using Kirkpatrick's reaction and learning criteria.

Participant's Training Evaluation Survey

Instructions: Thank you for participating in the _____ training program. Please take a few minutes to answer the following questions about your training experience and what you have learned from the training today. Your answers will be confidential and will be used only for improving the program. Your feedback is highly appreciated.

Section 1: Satisfaction with the Training: Please rate your level of agreement with the following statements.

	Strongly Disagree	Disagree	Neutral	Agree	Strongly Agree
The training content was relevant to my job.	O	O	O	O	O
The activities helped me to understand course concepts better.	O	O	O	O	O
The presenters were knowledgeable.	O	O	O	O	O
The presenters were engaging.	O	O	O	O	O
All information was presented clearly.	O	O	O	O	O
I enjoyed the class atmosphere.	O	O	O	O	O
I can apply what I learned to solve conflicts in the future.	O	O	O	O	O
The training met my expectations.	O	O	O	O	O
I will recommend this training program to others.	O	O	O	O	O

Comments:

1. What did you like the most about the training?

2. What do you think should be improved in the future?

3. What other comments or suggestions would you like to share?

Section 2: Comprehension: Please select the **best** answer for the following questions.

1. Which of the following statements is *true* about how to deal with emotions in conflict negotiation?
    a. Be totally rational and neglect any and all emotions.
    b. Stop having emotions in negotiation.
    c. Deal directly with emotions.
    d. Recognize emotions you and the other are experiencing.

2. Please identify five basic ways of handling conflict as covered in this training.

    _____

    _____

    _____

    _____

    _____

3. Which of the following statements is *false?*
    a. There is no single best way to respond to conflicts.
    b. Which conflict style to use depends on the situation, the other person, and your goals.
    c. For a win–win solution, consider the needs of yourself and those of others.
    d. Paraphrasing is irrelevant during a conflict negotiation.

Directions: Re-write the each of the following statements so that it becomes a confirming message, conducive to creating a supportive climate. For example:

Disconfirming Message: That idea will never work.
More Confirming Message: That idea is very creative. I'm afraid we do not have enough time to execute it though.

4. Shut up and listen to me!

5. How did you get into this management position? You don't know what you are doing.

6. Everyone gets a promotion sooner or later. Don't be too excited about it.

Level 2: The *learning* level measures the degree to which trainees acquire the intended knowledge, skills, attitude, confidence, and commitment based on their participation in the training. You can examine trainees' learning using multiple-choice, matching, fill-in-the-blanks, or essay questions. See Example 5.2, Section 2 for sample questions measuring trainees' learning.

Level 3: The *behavioral* level assesses the extent to which trainees apply what they learned from training in their job. In other words, this is a measure of **training transfer**, the extent to which the acquired knowledge, skills, or attitudes are generalized to the job setting and maintained over time (Baldwin & Ford, 1988). You can measure behavioral change by using surveys, interviews, or observations. A self-report questionnaire is certainly not the most reliable measure of behavioral improvement but can provide the organization with preliminary data about the applicability and transferability of the training when time and resources do not permit other more concrete approaches. See Example 5.3, Section 1 for sample questions measuring trainees' behavior change after a training program. It is important to note that this type of follow-up questionnaire should be administered a period of time after the participant has completed the program and had time to apply the new skills and knowledge. The questions in Section 1 should be consistent with your training objectives and reflect the exact skills you teach in your training as identified by your needs assessment.

Example 5.3. A Sample Evaluation Questionnaire Using Kirkpatrick's Behavioral Change Criteria.

Participant's Post-Training Follow-Up Survey

Instructions: Three months ago you completed the _____ training program. The purposes of this follow-up survey are to understand your experiences of applying the new skills and knowledge from the training; to see if any additional support is needed; and to improve the future program. Your answers will be confidential and are highly valued.

Section 1: Practical Application: Please rate your level of agreement with the following statements.

	Strongly Disagree	Disagree	Neutral	Agree	Strongly Agree	N/A
In the past three months...						
1. I have become more flexible in adopting a conflict style that fits the situation and the person I am dealing with.	O	O	O	O	O	O
2. I have actively considered the needs of myself *and* those of others when seeking solutions.	O	O	O	O	O	O

3. I have practiced paraphrasing skills with others to make sure I fully understand their thoughts or feelings.   ◯   ◯   ◯   ◯   ◯   ◯

4. I have been using more supportive messages.   ◯   ◯   ◯   ◯   ◯   ◯

5. I have become more cautious to avoiding defense-provoking messages.   ◯   ◯   ◯   ◯   ◯   ◯

6. I have less conflict with my supervisors.   ◯   ◯   ◯   ◯   ◯   ◯

7. I have less conflict with my coworkers.   ◯   ◯   ◯   ◯   ◯   ◯

8. I have received fewer complaints from my clients.   ◯   ◯   ◯   ◯   ◯   ◯

Section 2: Knowledge and Skills Transfer Climate: Please rate your level of agreement with the following statements.

	Strongly Disagree	Disagree	Neutral	Agree	Strongly Agree	N/A
In the past three months...						
9. I have been determined to apply my new knowledge in every possible occasion.	◯	◯	◯	◯	◯	◯
10. I have felt capable to apply my new knowledge in my job.	◯	◯	◯	◯	◯	◯
11. I have had opportunities to apply what I learned into my job.	◯	◯	◯	◯	◯	◯
12. I have been able to practice my new skills with my coworkers.	◯	◯	◯	◯	◯	◯
13. My immediate supervisor has encouraged me to apply the course material in my job.	◯	◯	◯	◯	◯	◯
14. I have received positive feedback from my supervisor when I successfully apply my new skills.	◯	◯	◯	◯	◯	◯
15. I have received positive feedback from my colleagues when I successfully apply my new skills.	◯	◯	◯	◯	◯	◯
16. I have been able to effectively apply what I learned from the training thanks to my previous experience.	◯	◯	◯	◯	◯	◯

17. Please provide a specific example of how the course has helped you achieve positive results in your job.

18. Would you like any further assistance or support that would enable you to apply what you learned more effectively? Please specify.

19. What other comments or suggestions would you like to share?

A more valid and reliable approach is the *360-degree survey* method administered before and some time after the training. The 360-degree survey method gathers data about the behavior or performance level of trainees from the trainees themselves as well as their colleagues, supervisors, direct reports, and, where relevant, external stakeholders (e.g., vendors or clients). The multisource feedback (hence the name, 360 degrees) can provide a more accurate picture of the employee behavior.

Another method to explore how well trainees are using what they learned in their job activities is through interviews. For example, Bowles, Mackintosh, and Torn (2001) evaluated a communication skills training program for nurses using a pre- and post-training survey and a focus group interview six months after the training completion. The survey identified the exact area of behavior change; trainees were more willing to communicate with troubled patients. Focusing on changes to trainees' practice, the group interview further revealed that trainees' interaction with patients shifted from being negative and problem oriented (i.e., "nurses must solve all problems for patients") to being positive and solution focused (i.e., empowering and working with patients to find solutions). This shift increased trainees' confidence to interact with patients as well as reduced their feelings of inadequacy and emotional stress. The most accurate measure to examine post-training behavioral change is probably observation. For example, in a sales presentation skills training program, CCCTTs can have trainees video-record their presentations before and after the training and observe trainees' skill improvement. After a customer service training, CCCTTs may also observe how well trainees apply knowledge and skills from the training to their real-life job settings.

As mentioned previously, multiple variables can promote or inhibit training transfer. A good needs assessment can give CCCTTs some inkling about what those variables might be for the organization they are working with so they can be proactive about it. For example, CCCTTs can encourage training transfer by making training content highly relevant to the trainees' job. An effective task analysis will help with this. Communicating, at the very beginning of the program, the value of training and how it can make a difference in trainees' job can motivate trainees to learn and apply new knowledge and skills. Furthermore, training methods that promote the application of knowledge should be considered. Recent studies have identified *behavior modeling* (i.e., showing trainees a desired behavior and guiding them to practice it) (Taylor, Russ–Eft, & Chan, 2005); *error management* (i.e., encouraging trainees to make errors and learn from them) (Keith & Frese, 2008); and *realistic training environment* (i.e., conducting training and practice in environments that mirror the workplace) (Grossman & Salas, 2011) as training designs that enhance training transfer. Because a number of factors can impact the training transfer and the factors can vary from organization to organization (Aguinis & Kraiger, 2009), CCCTTs should find ways to account for these variables when evaluating a training program. That way, CCCTTs can determine whether the trainees' change in behavior (or lack thereof) comes from the training itself or other external causes. Example 5.3, Section 2 provides sample questions you can include in your post-training follow-up survey to account for those causes. The sample questions measure factors (individual, organizational, and previous experience) that may promote or impede training transfer. By accounting for these non-training related factors, CCCTTs will be able to examine more accurately the impact of the training program on participants' behavioral change.

Level 4: The *results* level gauges improvements in tangible individual or organizational outcomes as a result of the training and subsequent reinforcement. Tangible outcomes can be, for instance, increased productivity, reduced cost, improved workplace climate, and high ROI. Results criteria are regarded as the most difficult to evaluate, particularly for soft skills training like communication programs (Charoensap-Kelly et al., 2016; Redford, 2007). However, they are regarded as the most credible measures (Rajeev, Madan, & Jayarajan, 2009) and can be carried out with careful planning. Redford (2007), for instance, suggested one can calculate the ROI of soft skills training when the cost-benefit assessment is done before training starts, when the training solution is aligned with core business needs, when an ongoing skills audit is conducted, and when clear training objectives and key performance indicators are identified. Platt (2008) and his colleagues' successful ROI calculation for their assertiveness training services to a client serves as a stellar case study. Prior to the training, Platt (2008) and his team conducted a thorough training needs analysis and refined assertiveness into observable and precise skills (e.g., active listening, objective setting, praising, and reprimanding). They then identified traceable outcomes in line with departmental and organizational goals (e.g., increased productivity, decreased absenteeism, and lower error rates). Further, the consultants kept track of identified outcomes and used a control group that did not receive training to compare against the trained group of employees. Finally, they presented to the client a financial analysis two years after the training was conducted. Besides demonstrating how tangible outcomes can be measured for communication training programs, Redford's suggestions and Platt's (2008) case study also reemphasize the importance of needs assessment and the notion that needs assessment and training evaluation work in tandem.

In summary, the Kirkpatrick's model suggests that you examine whether the trainees liked the training, learned the material, can apply the new knowledge and skills, and if all of these outcomes make a tangible, measurable impact on the organization. Data on all four levels can help you take your training to the next level and demonstrate concretely how effective the program was in filling the gap you identified in your needs assessment. This information helps organizations make informed decisions as to whether they should continue investing in your program.

Now, should CCCTTs always evaluate their training programs using all four criteria? It depends on two major factors. First, your evaluation criteria must correspond to your training objectives and contents developed from the needs assessment. Some training programs may stress on some training outcomes (and corresponding evaluation criteria) more than others. For example, you are a training manager at a hospital and discovered from a needs assessment that employees need training on a patient tracking software the hospital just purchased to follow a new HIPPA regulation. Your training goals would be more on trainees' comprehension (learning level) and ability to use the new software (behavior level). In this case, asking trainees what they feel about the training content (reaction level) would not be relevant; they have to go through the training nonetheless to fulfill legal requirements.

Second, the scope of the project, time, and resources also influence what evaluation criteria to use. If you are an external consultant hired to provide a one-time two-hour training session on improving workplace climate, your assignment is rather narrow in scope and the training time too limited to shoot for reducing the turnover rate by 20 per cent in a month. Instead, you may aim to teach trainees on Gibb's (1961) categories of defense-provoking versus supportive behaviors and encourage them to keep a journal for four weeks of how they use three of six supportive messages and avoid the corresponding three defense-provoking messages with their coworkers. At the end of the two-hour training, you have the trainees complete an evaluation form measuring their satisfaction (level 1) and comprehension (level 2). After four weeks, you collect and analyze trainees' journals to measure their behavior change (level 3). For this one-shot training, you may measure only the first three evaluation criteria (reaction, learning, and behavior change). You may then proceed to present your findings at those three levels to the company decision-makers and propose a long-term training program where you aim to help the company reduce their turnover rates and improve the overall workplace climate. Once that long-term training proposal is accepted, you can include the results criterion in your new evaluation. To illustrate further, McLean and Moss's (2003) case study involving a comprehensive evaluation of a national leadership development program suggested that applying all four levels of the Kirkpatrick's model may be more appropriate for larger and relatively expensive programs than smaller or less expensive training programs. The takeaway is to evaluate your training using the criteria most appropriate for your program objectives, scope, and time and resources availability. Where possible, use all four criteria.

Conclusion

Needs assessment and training evaluation are crucial processes that ensure the quality of communication training and development efforts. They both involve a systematic ap-proach for collecting data that will guide decisions and actions. While needs assessments set the direction and goals for training and development initiatives, training evaluations determine whether you have accomplished those goals. Developing and implementing an intervention without a needs assessment is like embarking on a journey without know-ing where you are going. Finishing a training and development program without eval-uating its effectiveness is comparable to arriving at a destination and disregarding how you got there or if you are still in good shape. A good understanding and skillful use of these pre- and post-program assessments will help CCCTTs develop high-quality train-ing programs that meet clients' needs and expectations. Adhering to this Best Practice together with the others presented elsewhere in this book will help increase consultants', coaches', teachers', and trainers' competency, accountability, and transparency.

References

Aguinis, H., & Kraiger, K. (2009). Benefits of training and development for individuals and teams, organizations, and society. *Annual Review of Psychology, 60*, 451–474. DOI: 10.1146/annurev.psych.60.110707.163505

Altschuld, J. W. (ed.). (2010). *The needs assessment kit.* Thousand Oaks, CA: Sage.

Altschuld, J. W., & Watkins, R. (2014). A primer on needs assessment: More than 40 years of research and practice. In J. W. Altschuld & R. Watkins (eds.), *Needs assessment: Trends and a view toward the future* (New directions for evaluation, no. 144; pp. 5–18). San Francisco, CA: Wiley (Jossey-Bass).

Arthur, W., Jr., Bennett, W., Edens, P. S., & Bell, S. T. (2003). Effectiveness of training in organizations: A Meta-analysis of design and evaluation features. *Journal of Applied Psychology, 88*, 234–245. DOI: 10.1037/0021–9010.88.2.234

Baldwin, T., & Ford, J. K. (1988, March). Transfer of training: A review and directions for future research. *Personnel Psychology, 41*(1), 63–105. DOI: 10.1111/j.1744–6570.1988.tb00632.x

Beebe, S. (2007). Raising the question #6: What do communication trainers do? *Communication Education, 56*, 249–254.

Beebe, S. A., Mottet, T. P., & Roach, K. D. (2013). *Training and development: Communicating for success* (2nd ed.). Boston, MA: Pearson.

Bowles, N., Mackintosh, C., & Torn, A. (2001). Nurses' communication skills: An evaluation of the impact of solution-focused communication training. *Journal of Advanced Nursing, 36*, 347–354. DOI: 10.1046/j.1365–2648.2001.01979.x

Burke, L. A., & Hutchins, H. M. (2007, September). Training transfer: An integrative literature review. *Human Resource Development Review, 6*, 263–296. DOI: 10.1177/1534484307303035

Chiaburu, D. S., & Marinova, S. V. (2005). What predicts skill transfer? An exploratory study of goal orientation, training self-efficacy and organizational supports. *International Journal of Training & Development, 9*, 110–123. DOI: 10.1111/j.1468–2419.2005.00225.x

Charoensap-Kelly, P., Broussard, L., Caldwell, M., & Lindsly, M. (2016, June). Evaluation of a soft skills training program. *Business & Professional Communication Quarterly, 79*(2), 154–179. DOI: 10.1177/2329490615602090

Clampitt, P. G. (2009). The questionnaire approach. In O. Hargie & D. Tourish (eds.), *Auditing organizational communication: A handbook of research, theory, and practice.* Retrieved June 15, 2017 from https://www.routledgehandbooks.com/doi/10.4324/9780203883990.ch3

Creswell, J. W. (2014). Research design: Qualitative, quantitative, and mixed methods approaches. Thousand Oaks, CA: SAGE Publications, Inc.

DeWine, S. (2001). *The consultant's craft: Improving organizational communication* (2nd ed.). Boston, MA: Bedford/St. Martin's.

Frey, L., Botan, C., & Kreps, G. (1999). *Investigating communication: An introduction to research methods* (2nd ed.). Boston, MA: Allyn & Bacon.

Fyke, J. P., & Buzzanell, P. M. (2014). Meeting the communication challenges of training. In V. D. Miller & M. E. Gordon (eds.), *Meeting the challenges of human resource management: A communication perspective* (pp. 97–108). New York, NY: Taylor & Francis (Routledge).

Gibb, J. R. (1961). Defensive communication. *Journal of Communication, 11*, 141–148.

Gilbert, T. F. (1978). *Human competence: Engineering worthy performance.* New York, NY: McGraw-Hill.

Gillham, B. (2008). *Observation technique: Structured to unstructured.* London & New York, NY: Continuum International Publishing Group.

Goldhaber, G. M. (1976). The ICA communication audit: Rationale and development. Paper prepared for the special edition of "Communication, Journal of the Communication Association of the Pacific" compiled for the C.A.P. Convention, Kobe, Japan. Retrieved June 27, 2016 from http://files.eric.ed.gov/fulltext/ED127637.pdf

Goldhaber, G. M., Porter, D. T., & Yates, M. (1977). ICA communication audit survey instrument: 1977 organizational norms. Paper presented at the Annual Meeting of the International Communication Association (27th, Berlin, Germany, June 1977). Retrieved June 27, 2017 from http://files.eric.ed.gov/fulltext/ED140375.pdf

Goldhaber, G. M. (2002, February). Communication audits in the age of the Internet. *Management Communication Quarterly*, *15*, 451–457. DOI: 10.1177/0893318902153007

Grossman, R., & Salas, E. (2011). The transfer of training: What really matters. *International Journal of Training & Development*, *15*, 103–120. DOI: 10.1111/j.1468–2419.2011.00373.x

Harless, J. (1970). *An ounce of analysis (is worth a pound of objectives)*. Newman, GA: Harless Performance Guild.

Ivatury, R. R., Guilford, K., Malhotra, A. K., Therese, D., Aboutanos, M., & Martin, N. (2008). Patient safety in trauma: Maximal impact management errors at a Level 1 trauma center. *Journal of Trauma and Acute Care Surgery*, *64*(2), 265–272.

Kaufman, R. (1992). *Strategic planning plus*. Thousand Oaks, CA: Sage Publishing.

Kaufman, R. (1998). *Strategic thinking: A guide to identifying and solving problems* (rev. ed). Washington, D.C. & Arlington, VA: The International Society for Performance Improvement and the American Society for Training and Development.

Kaufman, R. (2000). Mega planning: Practical tools for organizational success. Thousand Oaks, CA: Sage.

Kaufman, R., & Guerra-López, I. (2013). *Needs assessment for organizational success*. [Books24x7 version.] Available from http://common.books24x7.com.lynx.lib.usm.edu/toc.aspx?bookid=104320

Keith, N., & Frese, M. (2008). Effectiveness of error management training: A meta-analysis. *Journal of Applied Psychology*, *93*(1), 59–69. DOI: 10.1037/0021–9010.93.1.59

Kirkpatrick, D. L. (1959). Techniques for evaluating programs. *Journal of the American Society of Training Directors (ASTD)*, *13*(11), 3–9.

Kirkpatrick, D. L., & Kirkpatrick, J. D. (2006). *Evaluating training programs* (3rd ed.). San Francisco, CA: Berrett-Koehler Publishers.

Kvale, S., & Brinkmann, S. (2009). *InterViews: Learning the craft of qualitative research interviewing* (2nd ed.). Thousand Oaks, CA: Sage.

Lawson, K. (2015). *The trainer's handbook*. Retrieved June 27, 2017 from http://ebookcentral.proquest.com

Lepicki, T., & Boggs, A. (2014). Needs assessments to determine training requirements. In J. W. Altschuld & R. Watkins (eds.), *Needs assessment: Trends and a view toward the future* (New directions for evaluation, no. 144; pp. 61–74). San Francisco, CA: Wiley (Jossey-Bass).

Lindlof, T. R., & Taylor, B. C. (2010). *Qualitative communication research methods* (3rd ed.). Thousand Oaks, CA: Sage.

McLean, S., & Moss, G. (2003). They're happy, but did they make a difference? Applying Kirkpatrick's framework to the evaluation of a national leadership program. *The Canadian Journal of Program Evaluation*, *18*(1), 1–23.

Meyer, J. C. (2002, February). Organizational communication assessment: Fuzzy methods and the accessibility of symbols. *Management Communication Quarterly*, *15*, 472–479. DOI: 10.1177/0893318902153010

Mottet, T., & Richmond, V. P. (1998). Newer is not necessarily better: A reexamination of affective learning measurement. *Communication Research Reports*, *15*, 370–378.

Mulhall, A. (2003). In the field: Notes on observation in qualitative research. *Journal of Advanced Nursing*, *41*, 306–313. DOI: 10.1046/j.1365–2648.2003.02514.x

Noe, R. A., & Schmitt, N. (1986). The influence of trainee attitudes on training effectiveness: Test of a model. *Personnel Psychology*, *39*, 497–523. DOI: 10.1111/j.1744–6570.1986.tb00950.x

Patten, M. L. (2012). Understanding research methods: An overview of the essentials (8th ed.). Glendale, CA: Pyrczak.

Phillips, J. J., & Phillips, P. P. (2016). *Handbook of training evaluation and measurement methods* (4th ed.). New York, NY: Routledge.

Platt, G. (2008, August). The hard facts about soft skills measurement. *Training Journal*, 53–56.

Rajeev, P., Madan, M. S., & Jayarajan, K. (2009). Revisiting Kirkpatrick's model – an evaluation of an academic training course. *Current Science, 96*, 272–276.

Redford, K. (2007, July). The measure of all things soft. *Training & Coaching Today*, 10–11.

Rossett, A. (1987). *Training needs assessment.* Englewood Cliffs, NJ: Educational Technology Publications.

Ruel, E., Wagner, W. E., & Gillespie, B. J. (2016). *The practice of survey research: Theory and applications.* Thousand Oaks, CA: Sage Publications.

Schwartzman, H. B. (1993). *Ethnography in organizations* (vol. 27). Newbury Park, CA: Sage.

Sleezer, C. M., Russ-Eft, D. F., & Gupta, K. (2014). *A practical guide to needs assessment* (3rd ed.). San Francisco, CA: Wiley & Sons, Inc.

Smidt, A., Balandin, S., Sigafoos, J., & Reed, V.A. (2009). The Kirkpatrick model: A useful tool for evaluating training outcomes. *Journal of Intellectual & Development Disability, 34*, 266–274. DOI: 10.1080/13668250903093125

Stufflebeam, D. L., McCormick, C. H., Brinkerhoff, R. O., & Nelson, C. O. (1985). Conducting educational needs assessments. Boston, MA: Kluwer-Nijhof.

Taylor, P. J., Russ-Eft, D. F., & Chan, D. W. L. (2005). A meta-analytic review of behavior modeling training. *Journal of Applied Psychology, 90*, 692–709. DOI: 10.1037/0021–9010.90.4.692

Watkins, R., West, M. M., & Visser, Y. (2012). *Guide to assessing needs.* Retrieved June 27, 2017 from http://ebookcentral.proquest.com

Witkin, B. R., & Altschuld, J. W. (1995). *Planning and conducting needs assessments: A practical guide.* Thousand Oaks, CA: Sage.

Chapter 6

Observational assessment at the core of your communication training program

Authentic design and use of observational survey instruments

Jessica Parker-Raley and Amber N. Finn

Abstract

You identified a communication problem and determined training is the solution, but how do you design a training program that will resolve the issue? We share a pragmatic approach to developing and using an observational assessment technique to improve communication. We introduce a communication problem, explain how an assessment was created to facilitate a communication training program for that problem, and explain how assessments can be used before, during, and after communication training program implementation.

Assessment, defined as "a wide variety of methods or tools that educators use to evaluate, measure, and document readiness, learning, progress, skill acquisition, or educational needs" (Hidden Curriculum, 2014), plays a central role in the teaching and learning process, and it is arguably one of the most important Best Practices for training professionals. When done well, assessment can benefit the trainer, the trainees, as well as the organization. For example, it can be used to help ensure training is the right solution to an organizational problem and identify the specific needs of the trainees (Silberman & Biech, 2015), improve training programs, maximize transfer of learning, and demonstrate the value of the training to the organization (Kirkpatrick & Kirkpatrick, 2016). Assessment most frequently occurs prior to the training, which is often referred to as a *needs analysis* or *needs assessment*, and following the training, also known as *training evaluation*. Beebe, Mottet, and Roach (2013) describe assessment as the "bookends" of training, explaining that "the needs assessment identifies what trainees *need to learn*, and the final assessment identifies *whether trainees learned* what they were supposed to learn" (p. 257). Assessment can also be utilized throughout the training. For example, it can be employed to measure trainees' perceptions of the training along the way, check knowledge and skill acquisition of trainees at the end of one module prior to moving on to another module, and to provide feedback to trainees following structured simulations. Kirkpatrick and Kirkpatrick (2016) recommend that assessment begin prior to training and continue long after training ends.

Assessment should play a central role in the design and execution of any *communication training program*. One way of ensuring assessment stays front and center in your communication training program is to create an assessment instrument and employ it in various stages throughout your training. In this chapter, we will share a pragmatic approach for developing instruments that are particularly useful in observational assessment. While the chapter has both content analysis and survey elements, for reasons of familiarity and applicability, the more familiar survey research terms will be used (Treadwell, 2017). First, we describe two important steps that need to be taken prior to creating an observational instrument to ensure your training and the assessment focus on a specific problem associated with a desired organizational outcome. Then, we review the five-step process for creating an observational instrument that can be utilized to accomplish key training tasks prior to, during, and following training. In order to provide context and enhance understanding, we use a real-world example from a healthcare setting throughout the chapter.

Prior to creating an observational instrument

Determining the organizational outcome and communication problem

Prior to creating an observational survey instrument, or designing any part of a training program for that matter, it is imperative that you understand both the expected *organizational outcome* as well as the exact *problem* the training will address. Let's begin by discussing the expected organizational outcome or result of the training. According to Kirkpatrick and Kirkpatrick's (2016) New World Kirkpatrick Model, evaluation works best if you (the trainer) work with organizational stakeholders to identify desired results (e.g., increased sales, employee retention, employee satisfaction, etc.) up front, prior to, the training. This helps ensure the training leads to the expected organizational outcome(s) and can help the trainer demonstrate the value of the training to the organization. In the healthcare industry, for example, an expected outcome or result of training might be decreased medical errors. Following the model, it would be important to work with the healthcare organization to ensure that all stakeholders are in agreement that this is the targeted outcome.

In addition to identifying the organizational outcome(s), you must also determine the exact problem associated with the desired outcome(s). In other words, what is currently impeding performance? This may be something the organization determines and shares with you, something you need to research and identify, or some combination of the two. Even if the organization indicates what they perceive the problem to be, it is advisable to do some of your own research as well.

In the event you need to determine or verify the problem, one way of doing so is to immerse yourself in the internal workings of the organization without interrupting work flow. The *participant as observer* method can be employed, allowing you to take part in ongoing activities and become a central "player" in the action as you record observations (Spradley, 2016). You can conduct informal interviews as you follow employees throughout their workday asking questions about potential barriers impeding progress. Listen to frustrations and concerns ensuring you are interacting with all hierarchical levels embedded in the organizational framework. Additionally, you can hold focus groups with employees to allow for richer descriptions of problems impacting individual work performance or organizational progress. During the focus groups, ask questions about the frustrations expressed by employees and potential barriers you noted during observations.

After you have identified what you perceive to be the most pressing barrier or problem associated with the organizational outcome(s), go to the literature and study what researchers know about this issue. Make sure to conduct an interdisciplinary literature review to ensure important findings from all fields are considered. Use your findings from the observations, focus groups, and literature review to define the problem clearly. It is crucial that you, and other key players within the organization, know exactly what the problem is, why it is relevant, and how it is related to the desired organizational outcome(s).

In the healthcare industry, a common problem associated with medical errors involves poor communication skills, such as miscommunication between interdisciplinary team members in emergent settings (i.e., trauma teams). In fact, over the last decade, multiple studies have demonstrated that communication breakdowns between team members in emergent settings leads to medical errors and even patient deaths (Bower et al., 2003; Brennan et al., 1991; Courtenay et al., 2013; Davis et al., 1992; Grumbach & Bodenheimer, 2004; Ivatury et al., 2008; Kohn et al., 2000; Pucher et al., 2014; Risser et al., 1999; Stahl et al., 2009). Consequently, organizations like the Accreditation Council for Graduate Medical Education and The Joint Commission released mandates directing hospital administrators and clinicians to focus on *non-technical skills* such as team communication in an attempt to reduce miscommunication in critical care environments. To date though, the national organizations have not created the instructional materials program directors and hospital administrators need to effectively teach team communication skills in emergent settings.

One of the underlying reasons or contributing factors to this problem has to do with the lack of specificity of non-technical skills. That is, the specific verbal and nonverbal communication behaviors needed to improve miscommunication between team members have not been identified. This is oftentimes accomplished through the creation and use of a survey instrument, but to date, there are few, if any, measurement tools available to evaluate the non-technical skills needed in emergent settings. There are plenty of valid tools available to assess the technical skills of healthcare providers when caring for patients in critical care contexts, but the same tools have not emerged for non-technical skills, such as communication. Although other high-risk industries such as aviation, nuclear energy, and motorcar racing have adopted surveys to assess non-technical skills with proven benefits, evaluating communication skills in emergency care settings has been difficult to achieve due to high patient volume and turnover, especially in busy Level 1 trauma centers (Rehim et al., 2017). Nevertheless, non-technical skill assessments for high risk fields of medicine exist, such as cardiopulmonary resuscitation and general surgery. The Trauma Nontechnical Skills Scale (T-NOTECHS) developed by Steinemann and colleagues (2012) and the Team Emergency Assessment Measure (TEAM) (Cooper & Cant, 2014) developed by Cooper and colleagues (2016) are tools designed to measure teamwork during high risk situations, but these tools generally lack the necessary scope to describe, model, and measure how trauma teams communicate effectively when caring for acutely injured patients (Rehim et al., 2017). This measurement gap exists due to a paucity of research focused on how trauma teams communicate effectively during trauma resuscitations. It is difficult to measure communication effectiveness when clinicians, students, and scholars have yet to describe or model what effective team communication looks or sounds like during trauma resuscitations.

Real-world example: Ineffective communication in emergent settings

In order to better understand this underlying problem associated with the desired organizational outcome (i.e., reduced medical errors) and to identify the specific team communication skills trauma teams need when caring for patients in the trauma bay, the first author became a participant as observer at a Level I Trauma Center in central Texas. She watched trauma teams treating critically injured patients on a regular basis during evenings, week-ends, and dayshifts. During downtime, she also read trauma protocols, studied trauma team diagrams, and reviewed job performance expectations to better understand the trauma setting and work environment. Additionally, she conducted interdisciplinary focus groups with trauma team members and asked the "pit boss" (supervisor of the trauma bay) and other trauma team members informal interview questions right after they finished caring for a pa-tient. Aside from taking on the role of participant as observer to watch trauma teams in live settings, she also watched trauma teams caring for patients on pre-recorded video to ensure she observed teams taking care of all types of patients with various injury severity scores.

Following the observations, focus groups, and multiple reviews of protocols/literature, she decided to hold additional focus groups and informal interviews to further narrow down the specific communication problems and skills. During these focus groups, trauma team members including surgeons, residents, nurses, medical students, respira-tory care, and medical technicians provided feedback about her insights. Feedback from team members allowed her to ask more informal interview questions and clarify her knowledge and understanding of the central communication problems or breakdowns that occur between team members when caring for injured patients. Additionally, she demonstrated the relevance of this problem by locating research highlighting com-munication and other non-technical skills as the root causes of most medical errors in trauma settings (Davis et al., 1992; Pucher et al., 2014).

Creating an observational survey instrument

Although there are many ways of going about designing, facilitating, and evaluating a training program to address this and other communication problems in the healthcare setting, as well as in other contexts, in this chapter, we argue that the creation of a sur-vey instrument could prove to be invaluable before, during, and following training. A well designed survey instrument can help ensure assessment plays a central role in your training program. Below we outline a five-step process to create a survey instrument and then we provide suggestions for using the tool in all phases of a training program.

Step one: Identify core communication competencies

The first step in creating a survey instrument is to ask yourself what specific *communica-tion skills* trainees need to master in order to overcome the identified problem. Doing so will help you identify the core communication competencies or skill sets that trainees should use to maximize their work goals and avoid being hindered by the communication problem you identified. This task may require focus groups, interviews, and reviews of literature, concentrating on specific trainee behaviors that could mitigate communication barriers or proposed solutions to the communication problem you identified.

Step one in action

To identify the core communication competencies for team members in a trauma bay, the first author used focus groups and informal interviews to identify the particular non-technical skills trauma teams should use when caring for patients. Specifically, she asked what barriers they encountered when trying to communicate with other team members. Team members recalled specific problems they encountered that could be remedied by better "teamwork". She compiled her notes from these focus groups and identified barriers to teamwork in the trauma bay including: organization, attitude, space, noise, response, and leadership. Next, she went to the literature and conducted more observations to determine what particular communication skills or competencies could be used to overcome the identified barriers. Ultimately, she identified six core team communication competencies (i.e., Team Flow, Team Relationships, Team Space Negotiation, Team Noise Management, Team Listening, Team Emergent Leadership) that can be used to minimize communication barriers that occur in emergent settings (Parker-Raley et al., 2012).

Step two: Identify and define communication behaviors

Once you are certain about the communication competencies you will include in your new measurement tool, the next step is to identify the particular verbal and nonverbal behaviors that adequately describe each competency. To do this, ask yourself, what did the communication competencies you identified in step one look or sound like during your observations or reviews of literature? What particular verbal or nonverbal examples did employees use when describing behaviors during focus group discussions about the communication problem? What direct quotes or behaviors did you capture? Go back to your notes to pick out specific verbal or nonverbal behaviors that allowed team members to overcome communication barriers or circumvent the communication problem. Make a master list of different communicative behaviors trainees enacted to define each of the communication competencies you want to include in your assessment instrument. Additionally, categorize the list of communication behaviors with the communication competency it aligns best with. Once all behaviors are assigned to a specific competency, you have identified verbal/nonverbal behaviors that can be used to measure each competency.

Step two in action

To complete step two, the first author created a master list including all verbal and nonverbal behaviors she observed or read about that described what the identified team communication competencies (i.e., Team Flow, Team Relationships, Team Space Negotiation, Team Noise Management, Team Listening, Team Emergent Leadership) looked or sounded like in the trauma setting. Once the list was finished, she grouped the communication behaviors with the corresponding team communication competency. For example, she grouped the behaviors: assertive, responsive, task talk, social talk, competent, caring, and trustworthy under the Team Relationships competency because they all explained the team's ability to manage interpersonal relationships while caring for patients. More specifically, team members did not use hurtful or hostile messages. Instead, they offered their assistance verbally or nonverbally by asking "how can I help," or volunteering to execute an essential task. Teammates provided positive feedback, encouragement, or support. They said "well done," "nice job," "thank you," or "great work." She also grouped the behaviors: interruption, talking over one another, and asking irrelevant questions under the Team Relationship competency because those actions communicated a lack of respect and detracted from the management of interpersonal relationships among team members. For a complete list of the verbal and nonverbal behaviors associated with each team communication competency, see the Trauma Team Communication Assessment (TTCA-24) in Example 6.1 for quick reference or the TTCA-24 Codebook in Example 6.2 for a more detailed view. In the codebook, the communication competencies are in bold and the behaviors are in italics.

Step three: Create the survey instrument

Example 6.1 Trauma Team Communication Assessment (TTCA-24)

Instructions: Using the following scale, indicate how well the team performed.
(1 = poor, 2 = fair, 3 = good, 4 = excellent)
Team Flow (The team's efforts to be...)

_____ 1. emotionally controlled
_____ 2. collaborative/organized/structured
_____ 3. focused and alert
_____ 4. *global perception*

Team Relationships (Team member's demonstrating...)
_____ 5. assertive/responsive behaviors
_____ 6. appropriate task/social talk behaviors
_____ 7. competent/caring/trustworthy behaviors
_____ 8. *global perception*

Team Space Negotiation (The team's efforts to...)
_____ 9. yield to each other when necessary
_____ 10. remain at bedside only when necessary
_____ 11. get-in/get-out
_____ 12. *global perception*

Team Noise Management (The team's efforts to...)
_____ 13. manage environmental noise
_____ 14. manage team member noise
_____ 15. *global perception*

Team Listening (The team's efforts to...)
_____ 16. pay attention to each other
_____ 17. understand each other
_____ 18. respond to each other
_____ 19. *global perception*

Team Emergent Leadership (The team's efforts to...)
_____ 20. instruct each other
_____ 21. delegate roles and duties
_____ 22. compensate for others
_____ 23. ask insightful questions to close gap
_____ 24. *global perception*

Instructions: For each category, add the items and insert the totals below.

1. Team Flow = _____
2. Team Relationships = _____
3. Team Space Negotiation = _____
4. Team Noise Management = _____
5. Team Listening = _____
6. Team Emergent Leadership = _____
7. Team TTCA Total = _____

Scoring:
Scale Range = 24–96, Midpoint = 60
> 60 = Effective Team Communication, < 60 = Ineffective Team Communication

After you have identified and defined the communication competencies and corresponding behaviors you want to include in your new measurement tool, it is time to create the survey instrument. You will need to decide if you want to create an *atomistic assessment* or an *analytic assessment*. Beebe et al. (2013) explain that the atomistic assessment, described as "the identification of small, observable behaviors," should be used when you are interested in determining *if* the behaviors were performed, whereas the analytic assessment, defined as "assessing how *well* each individual behavior was performed," should be used when you are interested in determining the level or quality of performance (Lavrakas, 2008, p. 269). If you simply want to know if the behaviors were performed, you can create a checklist of the behaviors. An observer (or coder) can then use the checklist to indicate which of the behaviors were performed. If you are interested in assessing how well the behaviors were performed though, you will need to select a scale that indicates quality of performance (Beebe et al., 2013). For example, you could use a 5-point scale such as 1 = very poor, 2 = poor, 3 = fair, 4 = good, and 5 = very good. Scales typically range from 4 to 7 points. If an analytic assessment is used, an observer (or coder) would use the tool to indicate level of performance for each behavior. It is also a good idea to insert a *global score* option for each of the identified competencies. This way the observer (or coder) could provide specific scores for the communication behaviors and then one global score for the communication competency. If you are using an analytic assessment, you will also need to determine the range of the total assessment score and the midpoint. Midpoint scores could be true mid-points, midpoints from other assessments, or midpoints from the current assessment. For example, using a 5-point scale, the first kind of midpoint would have 3 as a middle number. In the second case, if all the numbers from the previous assessment using a 5-point scale ranged from 3 to 5, the midpoint would be 4. The third kind of midpoint might take average or median scores from the current assessment and see who is above or below. Of course, there are other standards from which midpoints can be determined as well. Regardless of which midpoint you decide to utilize, you can use the midpoint to indicate that scores higher than the midpoint signify effective communication and scores lower than the midpoint denotes ineffective communication.

Step three in action

For step three, the first author decided to use an analytic assessment. The complete measure can be seen in Example 6.1. Within each team communication competency (i.e., Team Flow, Team Relationships, Team Space Negotiation, Team Noise Management, Team Listening, Team Emergent Leadership) the corresponding communication behaviors are measured individually and the competency is measured globally. She elected to use a 4-point scale, with answer options ranging from poor to excellent. Ultimately, 6 competencies, with 18 corresponding communication behaviors and 6 global perceptions, are examined. The total score can range from 24 to 96 with a true midpoint of 60. Scores above 60 indicate effective team communication and below 60 signify ineffective team communication. This was a useful delineation as it is determined across a range of items if the teams were performing poor or fair vs good or excellent.

Step four: Develop a codebook for observers

Example 6.2 TTCA-24 codebook

TTCA-24 Codebook Introduction

The trauma team communication assessment (TTCA-24) is an instrument designed to assess the communication effectiveness of interdisciplinary teams during trauma resuscitations. The instrument was developed to ensure that trauma team members receive proper instruction and develop competency in effective team communication. Communication competencies were developed for trauma teams. These competencies are assessed using a 4-point scale. Team competencies include team flow, team relationships, team space negotiation, team noise management, team listening, and team emergent leadership. Within each competency communication behaviors are measured resulting in one global score for each competency. Six competencies are examined that include 18 communication behaviors and 6 global perceptions. The total score can range from 24 to 96 with a midpoint of 60. Scores above 60 indicate effective team communication. The instrument was developed by two communication researchers based on current communication literature that was adapted to this specific context. Additionally, contextual information was obtained from focus group participants, in-depth interviews, and observations of mock and live trauma activations.

Instructions for TTCA-24 coders

Before using the TTCA-24 coders must read the codebook, key terms, and coder notes to become familiar with the six competencies and 18 communication behaviors included in the instrument. Once these materials are reviewed coders can assess the communication effectiveness of trauma teams using the TTCA-24 either by viewing a live or recorded trauma activation.

Key terms

- **TTCA-24** = Trauma Team Communication Assessment (24 stands for # of items)
- **Competencies** = 6 team communication competencies included in the TTCA-24. Each competency is an umbrella term or construct that represents the communication behaviors included under it.
- **Global perception** = Overall assessment of a team competency.
- **Communication behaviors** = Verbal/nonverbal messages or actions under each competency.
- **Descriptor** = Excellent, Good, Fair, Poor
- **TTCA-24 ratings**
  - 4 indicates Excellent – Team members exceeded expectations
  - 3 indicates Good – Team members met expectations
  - 2 indicates Fair – Team members somewhat met expectations
  - 1 indicates Poor – Team members did not meet expectations

- **Team TTCA Total** = Sum of all 24 items
- **Effective team communication score** = 60 or higher
- **Verbal communication** = Written/spoken language that creates meaning for someone.
- **Nonverbal communication** = Communication other than written or spoken language that creates meaning for someone such as a person's use of posture, movement, gestures, eye contact, space, or vocal tone.

Coder notes

- Do not restrict coding to examples given in codebook. Other instances or examples may occur that are not specified in codebook descriptions.
- Competencies are in no particular order.
- The TTCA-24 can be completed during or after viewing a live or videotaped trauma activation. Take notes on the TTCA-24 while watching/observing activations.

How to use the TTCA-24

1   Review codebook and key terms to make sure communication behaviors and competencies are understood.
2   Assign a trauma activation number to the assessment form.
3   When rating each communication behavior under each competency establish a valence. Ask yourself is the communication behavior negative (i.e. poor or fair) or positive (i.e. good or excellent).
4   After deciding on a valence indicate the rating that best reflects the performed communication behavior.
5   To rate the global perception of each competency make an overall assessment of that particular competency. Ask yourself overall how did the team perform the competency; don't focus on one team member.
6   After assigning a rating for all communication behaviors and global assessments add your scores. You should have one team communication effectiveness score. Write the score in the blank at the bottom of the assessment and indicate if the score reflects effective or ineffective team communication.

Inter-rater agreement

- To properly assess team member communication effectiveness during pediatric trauma resuscitations coders must be completely separated when using the TTCA-24.
- Coders must come together and check inter-rater agreement after every five TTCA-24 assessments have been independently completed.
- Inter-rater agreement is calculated by obtaining the number of agreements (Na) divided by the number of agreements (Na) and disagreements (Nd), all multiplied by 100 as follows: $[Na \div (Na + Nd)] \times 100$.
- Coders must obtain a minimum of 80% agreement during each inter-rater agreement check.
- If coders fail to reach the appropriate percentage of agreement they should go back and reread the codebook, key terms, and coder notes in order to clarify disagreements.

Assessment Items

Team Flow

Team's ability to manage emotional, relational, and organizational climate. Able to remain emotionally controlled, foster a collaborative approach, and retain an organized structure. Used verbal and nonverbal behaviors to control flow of info given during the resuscitation. Eye contact, posture, gestures, facial expressions, and body position used to indicate when team members should make requests, provide patient descriptions, or listen to others. For example, a verbal regulatory cue would include phrases such as hold up, back up, or wait a minute while a nonverbal regulatory cue would include holding up a hand to control flow of conversation or tapping a watch to indicate the urgency of a task.

Team Emotional Control

Team members used verbal and nonverbal messages that were normal in tone, volume, and rate for the trauma bay. They were calm and controlled but maintained a proper sense of urgency and seriousness for the ED. Their nonverbal messages were not overly exaggerated, extreme, abrupt, clipped, or too relaxed. Team members did not appear to be behaving in a lackadaisical, nervous, uneasy, apprehensive, or fearful manner, nor were they acting aggravated, annoyed, or upset.

Collaboration, Organization, Structure

Team members were responsive and cooperative with each other. They maintained fluidity and cohesiveness. Performed roles with ease. Little hesitation when they decided who was to perform a certain task. The team acted together instead of in individual silos. When team members needed a particular person to complete a task, they used the person's name or formal role and stated the task to be completed.

Focused and Alert

Team members were prepared, attentive, and equipped ready to react. They were decisive and purposeful about current duties/next steps. Teammates accepted input and directives. They were receptive to concerns, requests, or feedback and did not display defensiveness, aggravation, or reluctance when asked to complete a task.

Team Relationships

Team's ability to manage interpersonal relationships while participating in the activation. Team members did not use hurtful or hostile messages. Instead they offered their assistance verbally or nonverbally by asking "how can I help", or volunteering to execute an essential task.

Teammates might have provided positive feedback, encouragement, or support. They may have even said well done, nice job, thank you, or great work. Teammates did not interrupt each other by requesting items, asking question or listing patient info while their teammate was communicating important info to the team.

Assertive/Responsive Behaviors

Team members were confident, firm, but also approachable. They were quick to respond or react using both verbal messages (yes Greg I got the syringe) and behaviors (walking to the station to retrieve syringe). They did not use aggressive, antagonistic, destructive or evaluative (you) language. They refrained from eye rolling, mocking, harsh vocal tones, or ridiculing their teammates.

Appropriate Task/ Social Talk
Team members stayed on task by talking about patient needs, injuries, and calling out procedures that are both needed and completed. Teammates avoided talking over each other. They refrained from personal communication until after patient was stabilized.

Competent, Caring, Trustworthy Behaviors
Team members were perceived by their teammates as credible/knowledgeable, helpful/considerate, and dependable/reliable.

Team Space Negotiation

Team's ability to function in their appropriate spots and share the limited space around the bedside by negotiating when they should move in and do their job and when they should yield to their teammates to avoid unnecessary hovering or crowding. Key personnel stood at the bedside and continuously moved to work on patient. All non-key personnel stood at least two steps back from the bedside to allow the team to work efficiently.

Team Members Yielded to Each Other When Necessary
Team members stepped back from the bed to give their colleagues sufficient space to assist the patient.

Team Members Remained at Bedside Only When Necessary
Team members did not crowd their colleagues, violate personal space needs, or gesture for teammates to stand back when trying to assist the patient.

Team Members Got-in/Got-out
Team members assumed their positions by the patient in order to complete their task and then stepped aside without lingering. They were ready for direction and did not have to be told twice.

Noise Management

Attempts to manage the presence of messages or sounds that may interfere with communication between team members.

Team Management of Environmental Noise
Team members attempted to manage noise made from machines used to assist the patient (i.e. beeping, ringing, suctioning, etc.) so that it did not interfere with the team's ability to communicate with one another.

Team Management of Team Noise
Team members refrained from side conversations or discussions both around the bedside of the patient and in the background that could interfere with team communication during the resuscitation. All communication between members was task oriented.

Team Management of Interpersonal Noise
Team members attempted to manage any patient noise (i.e. screaming, crying, thrashing, seizing, etc.) and family member communication (i.e. soothing the patient, asking questions, making requests, etc.) so that it did not interfere with the team's ability to communicate with one another. For example, team members may provide the patient with a video or blanket to try and quiet their crying or remove an emotive parent if necessary.

Team Listening

Refers to the amount and quality of listening that takes place among team members. Listening takes place when directions, suggestions or comments are made.

Team Members Pay Attention to Each Other
Team members exhibited attentiveness when listening to another teammate. They used direct eye contact, walked closer to teammates, or gave head nods or back-channeling cues.

Team Members Understand Each Other
Team members asked questions and paraphrased responses to ensure message sent equaled message received.

Team Members Respond to Each Other
Teammates used verbal messages or nonverbal behaviors to reply to each other. For example, they said something like, "Ok Ernie I'm getting the blanket", or "Roger that" which demonstrated that they heard their teammate. They may have also responded nonverbally by giving a thumbs up or cupping their ear with their hand to indicate they did not hear they wanted the teammate to repeat message.

Team Emergent Leadership

Although trauma activation protocols have designated leaders, other members of the team stepped up to lead patient care. They emerged as leaders and adapted to the needs of their team. They filled in where necessary in regards to knowledge, experience, or clinical opinions. They taught and cued their teammates to provide effective patient care.

Team Members Instructed Each Other
Team members demonstrated how to carry out duties or asked teammates to try a new skill or procedure and commented on their performance. They may have even verbally walked a teammate through a procedure cuing them each step of the way.

Team Members Delegated Roles and Duties
Team members named tasks to be completed and assigned teammates by name to those specific tasks. They may have even given a preview before the patient arrived about a plan of action. They indicated the overall goal or plan of action in addition to listing action items.

Team Members Compensated for Others
Team members respectfully stepped in and helped each other with difficult tasks or knowledge gaps. They may have even verbally cued a teammate while completing

another task or procedure. Teammates stepped up when needed to meet the team needs and avoided complications or struggles in patient care.

Team Members Asked Insightful Questions to Close the Gap
Team info or asked recorder to repeat info. Team members sought necessary detail about patients' and teammates' decisions to provide the best care possible.

Once the survey instrument (Example 6.1) is complete, you will need to create a *codebook* (i.e., an instructor manual) for coders or observers (Example 6.2). It should contain six sections: (1) codebook introduction, (2) instructions for coders, (3) key terms, (4) coder notes, (5) how to use the tool, and (6) competency definitions. Each one of these sections will ensure coders (i.e., observers) can train themselves to use your new assessment properly by ensuring they are evaluating the specific verbal and nonverbal communicative acts that you want them to. It is important to make sure your definitions contain several specific examples of what the communication competencies and verbal/nonverbal behaviors look and sound like. You may even want to include examples indicating what the competency or corresponding behaviors are not intending to measure. This level of specificity will help to ensure coders are able to differentiate between each communication competency and train each other to achieve *inter-rater agreement*. This is the degree of agreement among coders when using the same instrument to measure an identical theory/concept (Cook & Beckman, 2006; DeVon et al., 2007; Haidet et al., 2009). Lastly, ensure that the purpose or intention of the instrument is clearly described in the codebook introduction.

Step four in action

As you can see in Example 6.2, the TTCA-24 codebook contains six sections: (1) TTCA-24 codebook introduction, (2) instructions for TTCA-24 coders, (3) key terms, (4) coder notes, (5) how to use the TTCA-24, (6) competency definitions. The codebook was written to ensure that clinicians, researchers, communication studies experts, and students could all use the tool to measure team communication effectiveness in emergent settings. All six sections were written to ensure all team communication competencies and corresponding behaviors were clear and distinguishable. The key terms and inter-rater agreement sections were included to remind users that it is important to achieve inter-rater agreement among two or more coders when assigning communication scores to trauma teams. If coders encounter problems obtaining similar team communication scores, they can always go back to the codebook to review definitions, examples, or key terms before returning back to the field.

Step five: Pilot-test the survey instrument

Once your survey instrument and codebook are complete, it is time to pilot-test your new assessment. To do this, you will need to use the survey instrument to assess the communication behaviors as they occur naturally in the field or context you are studying. For example, if you developed a survey instrument to measure communication effectiveness during clinical trial recruitment and consent (Morgan et al., in press), you would take that instrument to a clinical trial recruitment conversation to assess the clinical research professional's use of verbal and nonverbal communication behaviors during the conversation. This pilot-test phase is a chance for you to take your new survey instrument on a "test drive" to see if the tool is adequately assessing the communication behaviors you want it to. Chances are you will notice that you have a hard time determining which communication behaviors fall under the communication competencies included on the assessment. If this happens, you will know that you need to refine your survey instrument to ensure the specified competencies are mutually exclusive by changing wording or adding more detail in the codebook. You may also find that the communication behaviors you included on the survey instrument never occurred during your pilot-test so you found it impossible to assess them. This is a red flag that perhaps you should spend more time in your field of interest to determine if you should remove a particular competency from your instrument. After you make the necessary changes to your survey instrument, it is a good idea to ask someone else from your field to try out the edited survey instrument and get their feedback using it in the field when communication behaviors are naturally exhibited. These would be subject matter experts (SMEs) who would be highly familiar with what you are intending to observe. It is also important to go back and read your codebook to ensure the changes you made to the survey instrument are also made throughout the codebook to ensure consistency between documents.

Step five in action

Before finalizing the TTCA-24, the first author and two of her colleagues pilot-tested the measure during live and video recorded trauma activations. Following the individual pilot-tests, it was decided that the TTCA-24 should be edited slightly to increase the specificity of the Space Negotiation competency. Specifically, the second communication behavior under the Space Negotiation competency was changed from "*the team's ability to not hover over each other*" to "*the team's efforts to remain at beside only when performing a necessary task*" (DeMoor et al., 2017; Parker-Raley et al., 2013a, 2013b). The second edit made to the original TTCA-24 was to substitute the word "*effort*" for "*ability*" throughout the assessment. Rather than assessing the team's "*ability*", it was decided the goal was to assess the "*effort*" made to communicate effectively. Lastly, the TTCA-24 was edited to make all communication behaviors more descriptive and take out any words such as "not" or "avoid" that indicated how team members should refrain from acting. More descriptive communication behaviors were easier to assess. For example, under the Team Relationships competency, "*The teams' ability to avoid defensiveness*" was changed to the "*team's efforts to remain open to messages from each other.*" Following the TTCA-24 edits, the first author edited the TTCA-24 codebook by incorporating more examples and descriptive language for each communication behavior listed under the six team competencies.

Using the observational survey instrument

Now that we have reviewed how to create an observational survey instrument, let's look at some of the different ways it can be utilized prior to, during, and following your training.

Prior to training

Numerous crucial training tasks occur prior to delivering the training, in the design phase (Beebe et al., 2013). If an observational survey instrument has not yet been created, the previous five steps may be the first steps you want to take to begin preparing your training program. Once the instrument is available though, it can be used in the design phase to effectively assess participants' needs, conduct a pre-test, and to explain and market your training program.

Needs assessment. As previously mentioned, the needs assessment occurs prior to training, and the purpose of it is to determine trainee and organizational needs (Beebe, 2007; Beebe et al., 2013; Silberman & Biech, 2015). One of the primary goals is to identify what specifically those attending the training need to learn in order for the organization to succeed (Silberman & Biech, 2015). Trainers frequently conduct needs assessments by (1) distributing questionnaires to trainees, (2) visiting one-on-one with trainees, (3) conducting focus groups, and (4) observing trainees at work (Beebe, 2007; Beebe et al., 2013), with perhaps the easiest and most efficient way being to distribute a needs assessment questionnaire electronically to potential participants prior to training.

Without a lot of additional work on the part of the trainer, the observational survey instrument can be easily converted into a *self-assessment questionnaire* and distributed to participants. This could be as simple as changing the instructions to ensure the participants know they are rating their own behavior. For example, using the TTCA-24, you could change the instructions to read "Using the following scale, indicate how well your team performed during your last interaction," or "Using the following scale, indicate how well your team performs generally." In addition to changing the instructions, you may also want to change the scale, depending on your unique needs. For example, participants could indicate the extent to which they agree they currently perform the behaviors identified on the assessment tool, with options ranging from (1) strongly disagree to (5) strongly agree. Additional ways to modify the assessment tool would be to have participants (1) indicate how confident they felt performing the behaviors (i.e., 1 – extremely unconfident to 5 – extremely confident); (2) rank order the behaviors according to how much they felt like they needed to work on them; or simply (3) place a check next to the behaviors they wanted to improve (Beebe et al., 2013). Regardless of the scale you decide to use, the purpose is to have participants assess their own behaviors so you can learn more about their training needs. Also, additional questions can be added to the self-assessment questionnaire so that you are gathering all the information you need about participants prior to training. For example, Silberman and Biech (2015) suggest that you should gather information about participants' needs, the nature of their work situations, their knowledge, skills, and attitudes, and the conditions that will affect participant involvement in the training program. These should be linked to competencies and behaviors determined in steps one and two of design.

Pre-test. Pre-tests are frequently given to participants prior to training to assess their current knowledge and skill. The results of the pre-test can be used to determine learning objectives, training methods, and content, and the scores on the pre-test can be compared with post-test scores to see how much learning actually occurred as a result of the training. The survey instrument can be easily utilized for pre-testing purposes. For example, the trainer could observe the employee(s) on the job performing the current skill (e.g., watching the team interact during a trauma activation) and use the survey instrument to evaluate current skill level. In the event a live observation is not possible, with written consent, the employee(s) could be video-taped while on the job. The trainer could then watch the video of the employee(s) and, while watching, use the survey instrument to evaluate performance. If, however, it is not possible to observe (or video) employees on the job, authentic simulation exercises can be used instead. For example, the trainer could organize a mock trauma activation and observe participants during the exercise. Irrespective of how employees are observed (i.e., on the job, via video, during a mock exercise), the point is to use the survey instrument to evaluate employees' performance and use the information obtained to make key design decisions about the training program (e.g., training objectives, training methods, etc.) and, later, assess the effectiveness of the actual training (post-test).

Explain and market. Trainers oftentimes need to explain and market their training programs to potential clients, key organizational decision-makers, prospective trainees, etc., and the survey instrument and codebook can provide the language needed to ac-complish these goals. Highlight the *communication competencies* (i.e., key communication skill sets from your assessment tool) you will focus on in training and use your rationale for the survey instrument to explain what need or problem your training will specifi-cally address as well as the desired organizational outcome it will help accomplish There may even be times when it would be appropriate and helpful to make available the sur-vey instrument and codebook. Organizational members commonly have financial and measurement concerns and it would be beneficial to explain how the survey instrument will be utilized for pre- and post-testing purposes. This level of detail and organization can speak volumes for your training program.

During training

The observational survey instrument can also be employed during your training pro-gram. In this Handbook and also in Beebe and colleagues (2013) the 5-step process of *tell, show, invite, encourage,* and *correct* is recommended to teach skills, such as communi-cation skills. The survey instrument can be utilized during each of the five steps.

Tell. The purpose of the tell step is to describe how to perform the communication skill you are focusing on in the training (e.g., assertive communication, listening, group problem-solving, team communication, etc.). In this step, you would want to explain the appropriate and effective communication behaviors associated with that skill. That is, you would need to describe the core communication competencies. The benefit of creating a survey instrument first is that you have already taken the time to identify the core communication competencies that would need to be taught during training. Taking our example of team communication during trauma activations, you would want to explain in detail each of the communication competencies from the survey instrument (e.g., team noise management, team listening, etc.). The subcategories and the codebook can be used to provide further detail and examples. In other words, the content for your training is already in your survey tool and codebook, and thus, you can rely heavily on those sources to prepare the content for your training. The most com-mon way for describing the skill in this step is a brief lecture, but other methods such as having participants read the material (i.e., read the assessment tool and codebook) could also be utilized (Beebe et al., 2013).

Show. The aim of the show step is to demonstrate how to perform the skill. Thus, in this step, you would want to show an example of someone performing the skill well (e.g., effective team communication during a trauma activation). This could be accomplished by personally demonstrating the skill or showing a video of others performing the skill. One way you could incorporate the survey instrument into the show step is to provide each participant a copy of the survey tool. Then, have participants watch the video (or live demonstration) and assess the actor(s) communication behaviors using the survey tool. Afterwards, facilitate a brief discussion about what participants observed. The goal is to make sure that all the participants were able to see, and that they understand, each of the communication competencies.

Invite. The goal of the invite step is to have participants practice the skill (e.g., effective team communication during a trauma activation). To accomplish this, you would need to design a training activity that would give participants (team members) an opportunity to practice communicating appropriately and effectively during a trauma activation. Following our example, if you are working with more than one team at a time, one option would be to have one team complete the activity while the other team observed. The observing team could use the survey tool to evaluate the performing team's communication skills during the activity.

Encourage and correct. The last two steps involve providing feedback following the performance. The goal is to describe what the trainees did well (encourage) and what they need to continue working on (correct). Feedback can be provided any number of ways – via the trainer, via peers, or even self-assessment. Regardless of who provides the feedback (i.e., trainer, peers, self), the survey tool should be utilized in the process. If in the invite step you had one team observing, then in this step, you could have the team share and discuss their completed assessments with the performing team. This way, the feedback is structured and focuses on the specific communication competencies associated with the skill. Encourage the feedback provider(s) to first share what the performing team did well and then explain what they could do better next time.

Following the training

The survey tool can also be used to accomplish several training tasks at the conclusion of training. For example, it can be employed for post-testing, demonstrating training value, and train the trainer workshops.

Post-test. Like the pre-test, the purpose of the post-test is to determine participants' current knowledge and skill, but this time, it is after they have attended the training program. The goal is to determine what *new* knowledge and skills participants have as a result of attending the training. If the assessment tool was utilized for the pre-test, it is advisable to use it again as the post-test. You can observe participants in a mock exercise at the end of the training program or once they are back on the job, and the observations can take place live in-person or via video. If possible, assess behavior using the post-test on multiple occasions. Irrespective, the goal is to use the survey tool to evaluate current behavior. It is important to note here too that the results (comparing pre- and post-test scores) should be used to make necessary changes and improvements to the training program and as a way to explain the overall benefits of the training program to important organizational decision makers.

Demonstrating training value. In order to show the value of your training, it is important to compare the changes in pre- and post-test scores with changes in the desired organizational outcome. For example, if the desired organizational outcome is decreased medical errors in the trauma bay, it would be helpful to know the number of medical errors prior to the training as well as after the training. Then, the change in pre- and post-test scores could be compared with the change in number of medical errors in the trauma bay. According to Kirkpatrick and Kirkpatrick (2016):

> Success factors and instances of success should be analyzed to determine if there is a way to propagate them across the initiative. Barriers to success and areas where training graduates are not performing to standards should be identified, analyzed for root causes, and resolved. Instead of sweeping performance problems or outcome shortfalls under the rug, embrace them as opportunities to reconnect with managers, participants, and stakeholders to talk about what is going on and how to get the program reengaged.
>
> (p. 30)

Additionally, it should be noted that while assessments can be used for improvement, they can also be employed to determine if current standards are being met, as a safety check of behaviors, or as a comparison with other performance groups or models. For example, you may have training that does not increase performance of the current team; however, that team might outperform other teams. The current team may have hit a ceiling or the training may not be necessary as they know the material already.

Train the trainer. Finally, it is not uncommon for multiple people to be responsible for facilitating the same (or similar) training to different employees within the same organization or to people in other organizations altogether. Thus, train the trainer programs are quite common and popular. The observational survey tool and codebook provide a great way to design these types of training programs as well.

Conclusion

Assessment is an important and necessary component of training (Kirkpatrick & Kirkpatrick, 2016; Silberman & Biech, 2015), and it should play a key role in all communication training programs (Beebe et al., 2013). In this chapter, we argued that a well-designed observational survey instrument provides a way to keep assessment at the forefront of your training program and provides a useful tool for addressing an identified problem and showing how the communication behaviors taught during training are associated with a desired organizational outcome. We outlined a 5-step process for creating an observational survey instrument and then explained how it could be easily incorporated into designing, facilitating, and evaluating a communication training program. It should be noted that although we applied this process in a healthcare setting, it could be utilized in any context. Finally, whether you take the approach discussed in this chapter or another approach altogether, we strongly urge you to make assessment a key ingredient, rather than an after-thought, in all your training programs.

References

Anderson, P. O., Jensen, M. K., Lippert, A., Østergaard, D., & Klausen, T. W. (2010). Development of a formative assessment tool for measurement of performance in multi-professional resuscitation teams. *Resuscitation, 81*, 703–711.

Beebe, S. A., Mottet, T. P., & Roach, K. D. (2013). *Training and development: Communicating for success* (2nd ed.). Boston, MA: Pearson.

Bower P., Campbell, S., Bojke, C., & Sibbald, B. (2003). Team structure, team climate and the quality of care in primary care: an observational study. *Quality Safe Health Care, 12*, 273–279.

Brennan, T., Leape, L., Laird, N., Hebert, L., Localio, A., Lawthers, A., Newhouse, J., Weiler, P., & Hiatt, H. (1991). Incidence of adverse events and negligence in hospitalized patients. Results of the Harvard Medical Practice Study I. *New England Journal of Medicine, 324*, 370–376.

Briggs, A., Raja, A. S., Joyce, M. F., Yule, S. J., Jiang, W., Lipsitz, S. R., & Havens, J. M. (2015). The role of nontechnical skills in simulated trauma resuscitation. *Journal of Surgical Education, 72*, 732–739.

Cook, D. A., & Beckman, T. J. (2006). Current concepts in validity and reliability for psychometric instruments: Theory and application. *The American Journal of Medicine, 119*(2), 166.e7–16.

Cooper, S., & Cant, R. (2014). Measuring non-technical skills of medical emergency teams: An update on the validity and reliability of the Team Emergency Assessment Measure (TEAM). *Resuscitation, 85*, 31–33.

Cooper, S., Cant, R., Connell, C., Sims, L., Porter, J. E., Symmons, M., Nestel, D., & Liaw, S.Y. (2016). Measuring teamwork performance: Validity testing of the Team Emergency Assessment Measure (TEAM) with clinical resuscitation teams. *Resuscitation, 101*, 97–101.

Courtenay, M., Nancarrow, S., & Dawson, D. (2013). Interprofessional teamwork in the trauma setting: A scoping review. *Human Resource Health, 11*, 57.

Davis J. W., Hoyt, D. B., McArdle, M. S., Mackersie, R.C., Eastman, A. B., Virgilio, R. W., Cooper, G., Hammill, F., & Lynch, F. P. (1992). An analysis of errors causing morbidity and mortality in a trauma system: A guide for quality improvement. *Journal of Trauma, 32*, 660–666.

DeMoor, S., Rehim, S., Myers, J., & Parker-Raley, J. A. (in press). Evaluating trauma team performance in a level I trauma center: Validation of the trauma team communication assessment (TTCA-24). *Journal of Trauma.*

DeVon, H. A., Block, M. E., Moyle-Wright, P., Ernst, D. M., Hayden, S. J., Lazzara, D. J., Savoy, S. M., & Kostas-Polston, E. (2007). A psychometric toolbox for testing validity and reliability. *Journal of Nursing Scholarship, 39*, 155–164. doi:10.1111/j.1547–5069.2007.00161.x

Grumbach, K., & Bodenheimer, T. (2004). Can healthcare teams improve primary care practice? *JAMA, 291*, 1246–1251.

Haidet, K. K., Tate, J., Divirgilio-Thomas, D., Kolanowski, A., & Happ, M. B. (2009). Methods to improve reliability of video-recorded behavioral data. *Research Nursing Health, 32*, 465–474. doi:10.1002/nur.20334

Hidden Curriculum (2014). In S. Abbott (ed.), *The glossary of education reform*. Retrieved from http://edglossary.org/hidden-curriculum

Ivatury, R. R., Guilford, K., Malhotra, A. K., Duane, T., Aboutanous, M., & Martin, N. (2009). Patient safety in trauma: Maximal impact management errors at a level 1 trauma center. *Journal of Trauma, 64*, 265–272.

Kirkpatrick, J. D., & Kirkpatrick, W. K., (2016). *Kirkpatrick's four levels of training evaluation.* Alexandria, VA: ATD Press.

Kohn, L. T., Corrigan, J. M., & Donaldson, M. S., & Institute of Medicine (US) Committee of Health Care in America (eds.). (2000). *To err is human: Building a safer health system.* Washington, DC: National Academy Press.

Lavrakas, P. J. (2008). *Encyclopedia of survey research methods.* Thousand Oaks, CA: Sage Publications Ltd. doi: 10.4135/9781412963947

Morgan, S. E., Finn, A., Raley, J. A., Occa, A., MacFarlane, S., Peng, W., & Potter, J. (in press). Assessing communication practice during clinical trial recruitment and consent: A measurement tool. In M. Prostran (ed.), *Clinical trials in vulnerable populations.* InTech.

Parker-Raley, J., Cerroni, A., Mottet, T. P., Lawson, K. A., Duzinski, S. V., Mercado, M., & Yanez, K. (2013a). Investigating pediatric trauma team communication effectiveness phase two: Achieving inter-rater reliability for the Assessment of Pediatric Resuscitation Communication Team Assessment. *Journal of Communication in Healthcare, 6,* 145–157.

Parker-Raley, J., Mottet, T. P., Lawson, K. A., Duzinski, S. V., Cerroni, A., & Mercado, M. (2012). Investigating pediatric trauma team communication effectiveness phase one: The development of the assessment of pediatric resuscitation communication. *Journal of Communication in Healthcare, 5,* 102–115.

Parker-Raley, J., Yanez, K., Cerroni, A., Mottet, T. P., Duzinski, S. V., & Lawson, K. A. (2013b). Assessing trauma leader communication in an ED setting. *Journal of Communication in Healthcare, 6,* 197–207.

Pucher, P. H., Aggarwal, R., Batrick, N., Jenkins, M., & Darzi, A. (2014). Nontechnical skills performance and care processes in the management of the acute trauma patient. *Surgery, 155,* 902–909.

Risser, D. T., Rice, M. M., Salisbury, M. L., Simon, R., Jay, G. D., & Berns, S. D. (1999). The potential for improved teamwork to reduce medical errors in the emergency department. *Annals of Emergency Medicine, 34,* 73–83.

Rehim, S.A., DeMoor, S., Olmstead, R., Dent, D. L., & Parker-Raley, J. A. (2017). Tools for assessment of communication skills of hospital action teams: A systematic review. *Journal of Surgical Education, 72,* 341–351.

Silberman, M., & Biech, E. (2015). *Active training.* San Francisco, CA: Pfeiffer-John Wiley & Sons.

Spradley J. S. (2016). *Participant observation.* Long Groves, IL: Waveland Press.

Stahl, K., Palileo, A., Schulman, C. I., Wilson, K., Augestein, J., Kiffin, C., & McKenney, M. (2009). Enhancing patient safety in the trauma/surgical intensive care unit. *Journal of Trauma, 67,* 430–435.

Steinemann, S., Berg, B., DiTullio, A., Skinner, A., Terada, K., Anzelon, K., & Ho, H. C. (2012). Assessing teamwork in the trauma bay: Introduction of a modified "NOTECHS" scale for trauma. *American Journal of Surgeons, 203,* 69–75.

The Joint Commission (2015). Sentinel event data – root causes by event type as of November 13, 2015. Available from www.jointcommision.org/sentinel_event.aspx

Treadwell, D. (2017). *Introducing communication research: Paths of inquiry* (3rd ed.). Thousand Oaks, CA: Sage Publications.

Demonstrate technology proficiency

- Proficiencies in technology needed for delivering and executing training content
- Digital technology

Clearly technology does not always include digital elements. Communication trainers can use items such as flip charts, room arrangements, index cards, etc., to produce amazing results. So at the outset trainers need to be proficient in the technologies necessary for the communication training. That being said, this chapter focuses primarily on digital elements that are common in communication training and consultation.

"Online training tools in an interconnected world" recommends the integration of online tools with more traditional training and provides guidance for multi-modal training. "Mobile devices in training" tackles the very real issue of trainees bringing their technology to the training environments. "Best practices in slide design" uses research to propose a reconceptualization of traditional slide design that should increase retention in a range of situations. "Training in a flash" takes communication training online using adult learning theory to help in the creation and execution of communication webinars.

Chapter 7

Online training tools in an interconnected world

Michael G. Strawser, Renee Kaufmann, and Marjorie M. Buckner

Abstract

The third communication training Best Practice, demonstrate technology proficiency, should be a focus for twenty-first century communication consultants, coaches, teachers, and trainers (CCCTT). The demonstration of a technology proficiency includes knowing what online tools are available, and their proper use for training development and delivery. This chapter discusses the rise of unique training modalities, especially e-learning, and previews tools available for CCCTTs. This chapter also provides a best practices framework for trainers who engage in online and blended training.

In the corporate world, employees need to develop skills to collaborate and work across spatial constraints (O'Brien, 2009). The corporate communication trainer, as Hemingway (2008) delicately defines, becomes a vehicle, "to deliver training to the right person, in the right place and at the right time" (para. 1). Thus, trainers should be proficient with technology but should also be capable designers of training initiatives that give employees hands-on practice, accountability, and breathing room (Li, 2016). As you navigate best practices in communication training, it is important to remember that technology is important in training initiatives. The Training and Development Division of the National Communication Association, after years of research, developed several training and development best practices. The third communication training Best Practice, demonstrate technology proficiency, is a necessary twenty-first century pillar. Proficiencies in technology are necessary for delivering and executing training content and digital technology is a principal trainer competency in an interconnected world.

The modern corporate training context is ripe for opportunity. One specific challenge for the online training industry is to bridge the gap "between the traditional concept of instructional design, where a tutorial was designed with clear measurable objectives and testing to check that those objectives were met, and the lack of any design model in some forms of user-generated content" (O'Brien, 2009, p. 58). These are weighty issues for the twenty-first century communication trainer. To answer these challenges, this chapter serves as an overview of the background and rise of unique training modalities, especially e-learning, and offers a preview of what is available for training initiatives. This chapter will also provide you with a best practices framework along with additional resources for trainers who engage in online and blended training.

The evolution of corporate training: F2F (face-to-face) to online/hybrid

Communication training initiatives have rapidly become dependent on flexible instruction and flexible trainers. According to Smart, Witt, and Scott (2012), traditional teaching has too often been based on a "passive lecture model, dependent on an expert teacher who funnels knowledge into the somewhat retentive minds of students while more current learning theory suggests a different role for teachers, that of facilitators" (p. 392). This facilitation shift is driven by an enhanced toolbox for instructional modalities as well as an increased opportunity for students and trainees to take control of their own learning. One particular avenue that spurred flexible training is the development of unique training modalities, such as online and hybrid offerings.

The twenty-first century training environment necessitates a widespread technology proficiency for both communication trainers and trainees. As such, it is important that communication scholars highlight a data-driven and standardized conceptual framework for training and professional development for online contexts (Hewett & Powers, 2007). Technology promises easier access to information through a wide variety of media and ultimately encourages greater levels of accessibility and interactivity (Worley, 2010). The new information avenues available to trainers and trainees dictate twenty-first century training competencies. For the purposes of this chapter, technology refers to the hardware and software used to supplement training sessions that are hosted both F2F (face-to-face) and online. Further, the technologies discussed will help foster multi-modal training, which we define as training that uses multiple modes, modalities, and platforms. F2F, hybrid, and online would all be considered modalities.

One industry report compiled by *Training Magazine* (2015) revealed pertinent information about the training landscape, especially online and hybrid components. First, we know that training in the United States continues to be a popular source of corporate expenditure, as highlighted by US training costs that surpassed $70 billion in 2015. Additionally, the cost of training expenditures (e.g., travel, facilities, and equipment) doubled from $13 billion in 2014 to more than $28 billion in 2015. For the context of this chapter, maybe the most appropriate factor in terms of resources will revolve around learning management systems, online learning tools and systems, and mobile learning. Further, training delivery has increased in terms of hours delivered in blended learning environments and has continued to remain popular in online formats. Even training using mobile devices continues to be prominent in training initiatives. Technology use in training is higher than in previous years and learning management systems, rapid e-learning tools as well as application simulation tools, continue to represent oft-used learning technologies for professional development and skill training.

Technology allows you to move away from a course-centered model for training to that of a user-centered model (O'Brien, 2009) but, without sound instructional design, these principles are null and void. According to Armstrong and Sadler-Smith (2008)

> What emerges from the voice of the training industry is that timing (on-demand and chunked); mode of delivery (face-to-face blended with more flexible methods); and an instrumental focus (on job-related knowledge and skills) are becoming crucial components in the provision of training and that its delivery is increasingly being assigned to external providers.
>
> (p. 572)

What does this mean? External providers, communication scholars and practitioners, and especially communication trainers must continue to focus on this flexible training phenomenon.

Demonstrate technology proficiency: Best practice overview

The twenty-first century training audience must overcome unique challenges. For instance, the modern learner is often distracted, impatient, and overwhelmed. Consider the following information from Deloitte (2014). The average employee may be online 27 times through-out the workday, compared with only five in the early days of the Internet. Additionally, most learners won't watch videos longer than 4 minutes and online designers have only between 5 and 10 seconds to grab someone's attention before they leave a site for something else (Deloitte, 2014). Deloitte (2014) would argue that even our "work" is often interrupted as frequently as every 5 minutes, usually by work applications and collaboration tools. The constant distraction, impatience, and overwhelmed sense of existence has led us to a place where trainers recognize that 1 per cent of a typical work week is all an employee has to truly focus on training and development (Deloitte, 2014). Therefore, engaging, flexible, and tech-savvy training initiatives become even more important. You can no longer rely on technology as a vehicle for training without demonstrating a legitimate proficiency that addresses the challenges of the modern employee and the modern learner.

On the other hand, while it is true that the modern employee is distracted, over-whelmed, and impatient, the professional emphasis on technology has brought positive developments to the workplace and, as a result, to training and development platforms. Employees are untethered, on-demand, collaborative, and empowered (Deloitte, 2014). This creates an exciting opportunity for trainers. Because of the flexibility of the modern worker, trainers can now incorporate technology that may help alleviate information overload, if used effectively. For instance, training initiatives can now be distributed in flexible platforms. This means that employees no longer need to devote a F2F morning (afternoon, or entire day/week) to training. Additionally, tools available to companies like blogs, forums, podcasts, or e-portfolios, allow for flexibility and consistent feedback for learners who desire these elements (O'Brien, 2009; see Table 7.1 for an overview of the tools available for multi-modal training). Furthermore, Screen & Audio Capture Software such as narrated PowerPoint and others, allow trainers to repurpose their F2F content. This content can be efficiently modified for digital delivery to current and subsequent audiences. This results in a corporate training best practice where digital technologies are used for information exchange and to facilitate learning (Hemingway, 2008).

Demonstrating a digital technology proficiency is a best practice because trainers who are proficient with technology can address rapid evolutions in the modern workplace by effectively and efficiently providing unique training options. Corporations have the luxury of using technology to harness the power of informal learning, which experts say can contribute to 70–90 per cent of learning in organizations (O'Brien, 2009). Fur-ther, and an added benefit, Hemingway (2008) says that the

> Challenge faced by corporate training professionals is to parlay informal learning events into skill acquisition, and e-learning as a platform is well suited for this challenge because of its flexibility and portability. Applying information-exchange technologies and other informal channels to facilitate performance development will be an exciting and evolving trend for e-learning in the coming years.
>
> (para. 6)

Table 7.1 Examples of tools for multi-modal training

Tool	Description/Integration	Strengths	Weaknesses
Learning Management System	Offering trainings via a learning management system (LMS) allows for trainers to monitor trainees' progress, house all information in one place, and even embed assessments to ensure material is learned. There are a variety of LMS platforms to choose. Using an LMS to house videos, files, and assessments for trainings is key to organizing a multiple modality training.	– Trainees' progress and engagement can be monitored. – Messaging capabilities. – Universal format. – Depending on the LMS, additional feature options for communication and integration of outside tools.	– Time consuming for upfront design. – Not all LMS platforms are easy to navigate. – Most require subscription for services.
Websites/Blogs/ Forums	A website is another option for housing information for training sessions. Websites provide trainers with the opportunity to link information, post videos, and lead discussions with trainees.	– Space for discussions.Ability to post information for all trainees. Generally low cost (even free).Easy to maintain once established.	– Time consuming for upfront design. – Not always easy to implement for the designer/manager. – Difficult to monitor progress or engagement.
Web Conferencing	Options for synchronous trainings include web conferencing. This service allows for file and screen sharing. Trainers can use this service to meet with trainees (e.g., for office hours or meetings) and to host real-time training sessions.	– Fosters immediacy. – Allows for people to see one another. – Inclusion of nonverbal cues. – Real-time experience. – Inclusion of people who may not have originally participated.	– Bandwidth issues. – Trainees need hardware (e.g., microphone, web cam) to participate. – Can be costly. – Some are limited in amount of people who can participate.
Screen & Audio Capture	There are several programs that allow for voice over and embeds of screen content. Trainers may also embed assessment questions for transfer checks. These recorded sessions allow trainees to go back to the content discussed in the training session and review information.	– Great for dissemination of information beyond text on the slide.Trainees can review content anytime.Once contentis made the sessions are persistent.	– Requires additional time. – If content changes, edits must be made. – Can entail cost for initial software.

As a vehicle for informal learning, technology proficiency for the modern trainer is a necessary reality.

Technology proficiency is even more pressing in light of the "checkered past" that has, at times, occurred between technology and trainers. O'Brien (2009) believes that

> The novelty of education being delivered over a computer was often sufficient initially to motivate learners and entice corporate training budgets. Sometimes poorly created content was passed off as learning, simply because it was the latest thing. However, learners quickly became disillusioned with early page-turners until sound pedagogical and usability design models were brought to bear. Similarly, it will be important for e-learning providers and learners alike to be aware that simply posting and accessing files on the latest technology platform does not necessarily constitute a valuable learning experience.
>
> (p. 59)

This reinforces the need for design-based training, no matter the modality. Further, this exemplifies how you should remain cognizant of the new and effective ways content is shared.

You can, and should, engage in training development that reinforces sound instructional design principles and utilizes multiple modalities. While blended learning (i.e., a mix of F2F and online content) has become a popular avenue for training, especially soft-skill training, e-learning still remains a substantial and robust training solution. E-learning, a $100 billion industry, is otherwise known as "the instructional content or learning experiences delivered or enabled by internet technology to enhance an individual's knowledge and performance" (Monika, 2013, p. 75). Practically, e-learning training technology can incorporate m-Learning (mobile learning), 3-D virtual learning, instant messaging, and social networking but are often delivered in isolation (O'Brien, 2009).

Traditional training methods, with their expensive outputs and loss of workdays, no longer suit the needs of the modern organization. Monika (2013) believes that e-learning allows the learner to control and make decisions on their own which affords a flexible schedule. Further, e-learning "meets current demands to rapidly create learning resources to address business events, competitive developments, product trainings or other business needs and it helps minimize the time and resource contribution from the student" (Monika, 2013, p. 75). Technology-rich modalities have continued to become more popular training platforms, which results in a content-rich and learner-centric endeavor.

Furthermore, traditional training has suffered from a large number of inherent deficiencies that are beyond the single trainer or even some training teams. Trainers know that some training components would be beneficial but do not have the time or expertise to execute them in their current resource allocations. Being open to both free and for-pay outsourcing may be a viable solution. Digital and web-based content have allowed for a wide array of plug-ins that provide stop-gap solutions for some of these diminished components. These could include prepackaged content, instant audience polling, assessment modules, boiler plate training modules such as ice breakers, mobile applications for additional penetration, and others.

Ultimately, all of this means that trainers must embrace this changing landscape. The viability of technology as a training reinforcement, or foundation, presents an exciting trajectory for communication trainers. As corporations latch on to e-learning as a viable training option for various educational contexts, online training will continue to form the core of numerous business plans (Joo, Lim, & Kim, 2012). Moreover, digital technologies provide unique tools that can add value to traditional training initiatives including content accessibility, management of learners and courses, and even enhanced delivery channels (Joo et al., 2012). Technology driven trainings are easily distributed and provide flexibility for organizational budgets and presents opportunities for blended learning initiatives to supplement basic knowledge, classroom concepts, and instructor-led training (Hemingway, 2008). The necessity for trainers to demonstrate a technology proficiency is assuredly a best practice and a non-negotiable for the twenty-first century trainer.

Rationale: Necessity of multiple modalities

Despite the inordinate benefits, training and development should not, solely, focus on technology-driven initiatives. Although training and development that incorporates online instruction is effective, corporate training should go beyond knowledge, or information transfer, by inviting collaboration with peers and the trainer and, resultantly, co-engagement in the learning process. Technology adds interactive elements that can move beyond solely face-to-face instruction. With that said, the most effective trainers tend to incorporate purposeful modalities (Hester, Hutchins, & Burke-Smalley, 2016) that reinforce the content and create a user-centered instructional experience.

To foster learning, social interaction is crucial and online training should follow a model similar to that of online courses (Rodriguez & Armellini, 2013). This model should incorporate learner–content interaction, learner–learner interaction, and learner–teacher interaction (Rodriguez & Armellini, 2013). Technology has the potential to

> provide the type of management training where learning is distributed at the time of need, embedded in a work context, and delivered in rapid bite-sized pieces, which aim to meet participants' needs in terms of depth of information coverage, timeliness of delivery, and job readiness.
>
> (Armstrong & Sadler-Smith, 2008, p. 571)

In terms of collaboration and community, online interactions have the potential to enhance training effectiveness in multiple ways (Rodriguez & Armellini, 2013).

Training modalities must focus on delivery and content. The end goal, no matter the modality, should be to support the diverse needs of learners in organizations. To reach a variety of learners, trainers may incorporate several approaches:

1   Instructor-led: Traditional, F2F training.
2   Virtual instructor-led: Virtual training with synchronous or asynchronous interactions with an instructor.

3   E-learning or web-based: Online training that may, or may not, utilize an active instructor or trainer presence.
4   Gamified: Training that presents content and delivery in game-like form.
5   Blended: A mix of online and F2F training content.
6   Mentored: One-on-one training and coaching.
7   Microlearning or mobile learning: Training programs developed specifically for a mobile device.

Regardless of the approach, you should design an experience that engages the modern learner through a means that is most effective and efficient.

The effective use of a particular modality should be a central concern for trainers and content developers. With that said, a modality that incorporates technology, and a trainer that exemplifies a technology proficiency, could ultimately achieve a greater effectiveness because of the flexibility and design options involved. While the study and use of multiple modalities is not new, and in effect has been examined since at least the 1970s (Reinwein, 2012), the twenty-first century capabilities of multi-modal training are unmatched. As such, consideration of scalability of content to multi-modal environments is becoming a requisite proficiency for all communication trainers.

Blended modalities allow corporations to increase learning opportunities while reaching the emerging workforce. In our modern training context, learners want small pieces of content loosely joined together more so than something monolithic, which leads to, naturally, an increase in user-generated content like social networking and wikis (O'Brien, 2009). This bears a great deal of responsibility. Trainers who utilize technology are no longer responsible for just placing a document on a learning management system, instead, brain science techniques, personalized micro-learning, and gamification are expected in the training environment. If used correctly, companies who incorporate multiple modalities can expect significant time and cost savings compared with traditional models (Joo et al., 2012). A renewed, or continued, emphasis on technology proficiency in training initiatives can lead to innovative learning systems built on a foundation of cognitive science and workplace learning behavior (Hemingway, 2008).

Training in multiple modalities

The use of technology to facilitate trainings (i.e., whether the trainings are F2F or hosted online) can be difficult to navigate at first. In F2F trainings, the trainer(s) have the ability to read trainee nonverbals. This affordance can be replicated in an online setting, but nonverbals do not always translate in mediated settings (Walther & Tidwell, 1995). This means the trainer needs to incorporate additional time for misconception or miscommunication checks to provide additional clarity if needed. Using technology in training settings also allows the trainer to model appropriate use of digital technology and provides trainees an opportunity to experience the technology prior to implementing it in their work processes.

There are several strategies for using multiple modalities. First, you need to consider how the inclusion of technology enhances the session's outcomes (e.g., helps to visualize or reach an audience not geographically close). Additionally, trainers should evaluate the strengths and weaknesses for the potential technology (see Table 7.1) and how those technologies could be incorporated into different contexts (e.g., F2F, hybrid, online; see Table 7.2 later in the chapter). Further, Bonk (2002) notes that most trainees report not completing online based trainings because of one of the following

Table 7.2 Example integrations and use of digital tools

Tool	Integration: F2F/Hybrid	Integration: Online Specific
Learning Management System	Facilitates discussions, assess knowledge, and can store files to share with trainees. Trainees can view sessions and ask questions of the group. Can "flip" training environments so content is off loaded and skill development is central.	Needs to be seen as the sole platform for trainees to gain information and learn content. Provides asynchronous training configurations. Often minus many of the synchronous interaction characteristics of F2F/ hybrid configurations.
Websites/Blogs/ Forums	Provides a place for comments and questions. This is useful during a F2F training because it allows for real-time questioning and engagement of materials without disrupting the flow of the training presentation. Allows for the opportunity to go back to information at anytime and anyplace. Great place to store needed files for trainees to access.	You often may not be able to identify users who are non-participants. Often minus the accountability in other configurations.
Web Conferencing	Facilitate "help" desk hours when trainees are not in close proximity. Can bring in additional sources (i.e., people; experts) for informational sessions to have "live" conversations with trainees or Subject Matter Experts not readily available.	Often limited in amount of trainees that can be accommodated depending on the purpose. Makes individual coaching or training time and cost effective. Enhances availability while reducing travel times. Can be used to build a community of learners.
Screen & Audio Capture	Offloads word critical training content into "perfect package" to be plugged in when needed. Training modules can be used across multiple training topics. Allows for review and remediation of material by trainees at later times.	Introduces audio and video cues typically absent in many online training environments. Often minus the accountability in other configurations.

reasons: (1) amount of time, (2) not incentivized, (3) not designed or implemented well, or (4) too costly for the trainee. To address these concerns, trainers need to strategically plan sessions around learning outcomes and be aware of how the addition of technology may contribute to not completing a training session. Waldeck (2008) encourages pilot testing and assessing training sessions to ensure flow and understanding of content. When designed and implemented well, trainees can reduce the actual training time as a result of the streamlined nature and control most online trainings provide (Bell & Kozlowski, 2007). In addition, providing incentives to trainees for completing training may help with completion of training sessions (Bonk, 2002).

Second, trainers need to be aware of their audiences' access to the chosen technology. When planning, trainers need to be aware of whether the technology (i.e., software or hardware) in use is free (i.e., supplied by organization) or if the trainees would need to purchase additional technology (e.g., webcams, subscriptions, apps) to participate, and furthermore, trainers need to consider if their potential audience has access to the Internet (Bell & Kozlowski, 2007). More specifically, trainees may already have access to a webcam via their mobile device and can access the training sessions, but they may not have access to the platform or app, which requires them to pay then download or subscribe. Assuming that all will have access and understanding of the technology echoes Bonk's (2002) caution regarding trainees' successful completion of training sessions.

Third, while multiple-modality training (or training that incorporates options beyond solely F2F) "offers cost-savings and other practical benefits, it also offers the potential to revolutionize training effectiveness by making training better targeted and more learner centered and personalized" (Bell & Kozlowski, 2007, p. 41). Trainings that are multi-modal can be perceived as lonely or isolating if lacking F2F components (Oomen-Early & Murphy, 2009). In order to avoid these negative perceptions and provide a learner centered, personalized approach, trainers need to incorporate a support plan for trainees. This can be accomplished by providing information or links for technology help, offering virtual office hours, along with providing "knowledge bases, FAQs or self-help documents" when technology help or virtual office hours are not available (Oomen-Early & Murphy, 2009, p. 235).

By considering how the technology ensures successful completion, checking trainees' access and capabilities to use the training delivery platforms, and implementing a trainee support plan, trainers can maximize the effectiveness of technology-based or technology-enhanced trainings. Understanding barriers to trainee completion and devising plans for navigating or overcoming these barriers prior to implementing the training can circumvent problems others have encountered. Investigating trainee access and capability for participating in the training may lead to proactive solutions that ensure training success. Further, determining access and capability prior to training development and implementation may allow for other choices regarding instructional strategies, technology platforms, or facilitation techniques such that trainees are empowered to complete the training via familiarity with technology and training delivery methods. Moreover, forecasting potential questions or problems trainees may encounter and developing support materials for trainees to access at their convenience may further ensure trainees' successful and satisfactory experience during the training that leads to completion. Ultimately, without trainee completion, the training is ineffective. Hence, taking these steps to maximize completion is critical for companies and individuals to reap the benefits of employee training.

Fundamentals of digital training application

The sheer magnitude of US training costs, and the emphasis corporations place on training initiatives, reinforce the importance of trainers for the modern workforce. While a technology proficiency is, assuredly, a best practice for communication trainers, it is important to also think strategically about how trainers can demonstrate a technology proficiency when developing training programs. This section summarizes two overarching relevant application points for trainers who desire a more tech-driven training regimen.

First, you should be proficient with technology but a technology proficiency does not negate the importance of instructional design. Trainers should continue to build training programs that have clear outcomes, interactive activities, hands-on application, etc. Trainers should consider how technology can reinforce the session's outcomes.

Second, develop programs that are user-centered, not trainer-centered. Trainers who use multiple modalities, such as online and blended platforms, can reach trainees in new and innovative ways. Technology-driven trainings can encourage trainee flexibility and may further create a rich user-centered learning experience. Trainers should know the audience, know the needs of the organization, and develop programs that are targeted and personalized. A user-centered emphasis also outlines specific outcomes (i.e., learning goals) for the trainee. For example, the trainer should articulate what skills or content the trainee will learn and how the new information will benefit him or her.

These two principles are foundational for trainers. Effective instructional design and user-centered training should be of primary concern for trainers. To deliver training in multiple modalities, trainers should familiarize themselves with tools available and additional resources available for consultation.

Tools available for training in multiple modalities

To accomplish the two principles mentioned directly above, there are several tools available for delivering and developing a training session. These tools (i.e., software and hardware) range in cost, the level of technological expertise needed to facilitate or participate in the training, and use of integration (see Table 7.2). Hybrid integration has all of the characteristics of F2F plus some additional characteristics. Online integration has all of the characteristics of hybrid integration plus some addition features.

These tools can enhance the learning experience but trainers would be well-served to approach tech-enhanced training with purposeful intentionality. A trainer proficient in technology will design pedagogically sound courses that use instructional strategies that incorporate technology with a clear outcome and create a learner-centered environment that ensures successful training completion for trainees.

Conclusion

The inclusion of technology into training sessions affords trainers and trainees a variety of benefits and opportunities to experience the content in innovative ways. By incorporating training programs that use multiple modalities, trainers have the ability to reach a wider audience, create trainings that are cost and time effective, and customize content. When sessions are streamlined and compensate the trainee, Bonk (2002) explains the trainee is more likely to complete the training. Ultimately, most trainers, especially communication trainers, would probably agree that every context is not suited to an emphasis on technology. As proficient trainers, we must strive to continue to ensure human touch while recognizing that technology can serve as a nice supplement to traditional F2F initiatives.

To this end, this chapter has detailed how the use of digital training proficiencies have migrated from nicety to necessity. Additionally, it detailed helps and barriers provided by those technologies as well as providing a number of digital tool options for the communication trainer. Lastly, it provided an overview of strengths and weakness of the tools as they stand currently. Although any number of exemplars could be provided to "Demonstrate Technology Proficiency", these have the potential for increasing the reach, efficiency, and flexibility for solo and team communication providers alike.

References

Armstrong, S. J., & Sadler-Smith, E. (2008). Learning on demand, at your own pace, in rapid bite-sized chunks: The future shape of management development? *Academy of Management Learning & Education, 7*, 571–586.

Bell, B. S., & Kozlowski, S. W. (2007). Advances in technology-based training [electronic version]. In S. Werner (ed.), *Managing human resources in North America* (pp. 27–43). Abingdon, UK: Routledge.

Bonk, C. J. (2002). *Online training in an online world*. Bloomington, IN: CourseShare.com.

Deloitte (2014, November 26). Meet the modern learner [infographic]. Retrieved from https://www.bersin.com/Practice/Detail.aspx?id=18071

Hemingway, M. (2008, September). Going "digital native": Putting e-learning to practice with an emerging workforce. *Online Education*. Retrieved from www.utility-automation.com

Hester, A. J., Hutchins, H. M., & Burke-Smalley, L. A. (2016). Web 2.0 and transfer: Trainers' use of technology to support employees' learning transfer on the job. *Performance Improvement Quarterly, 29*(3), 231–255.

Hewett, B. L., & Powers, C. E. (2007). Guest editors' introduction: Online teaching and learning: Preparation, development, and organizational communication. *Technical Communication Quarterly, 16*(1), 1–11. doi:10.1207/s15427625tcq1601_1

Joo, Y. J., Lim, K. Y., & Kim, S. M. (2012). A model for predicting learning flow and achievement in corporate e-learning. *Educational Technology & Society, 15*, 313–325.

Li, M. (2016). The 3 things that make technical training worthwhile. *Harvard Business Review*. Retrieved from https://hbr.org/2016/03/the-3-things-that-make-technical-training-worthwhile

Monika, C. (2013). Analysis of perceptions of conventional and e-learning education in corporate training. *Journal of Competitiveness, 5*, 73–97.

O'Brien, M. (2009, August). The e-learning industry: Facing the challenges of Web 2.0. *Forum: New Media, New Relations, 6*, 57–61.

Oomen-Early, J., & Murphy, L. (2009). Self-actualization and e-learning: A qualitative inves-
tigation of university faculty's perceived needs for effective online instruction. *International Journal on E-Learning, 8*(2), 223–240.

Reinwein, J. (2012). Does the modality effect exist and if so, which modality effect? *Journal of Psycholinguistic Research, 41*(1), 1–32. doi:10.1007/s10936-011-9180-4

Rodriguez, B. C. P., & Armellini, A. (2013). Interaction and effectiveness of corporate e-learning programmes. *Human Resource Development International, 16,* 480–489.

Smart, K. L., Witt, C., & Scott, J. P. (2012). Toward learner-centered teaching: An inductive approach. *Business Communication Quarterly, 75*(4), 392–403. doi:10.1177/1080569912459752

Training Magazine (2015). *2015 Training industry report.* Retrieved from https://trainingmag.com/trgmag-article/2o15-training-industry-report

Waldeck, J. H. (2008). The development of an industry-specific online learning center: Consulting lessons learned. *Communication Education, 57,* 452–463.

Walther, J. B., & Tidwell, L. C. (1995). Nonverbal cues in computer-mediated communication, and the effect of chronemics on relational communication. *Journal of Organizational Computing and Electronic Commerce, 5*(4), 355–378.

Worley, R. B. (2010). Business communication and new media. *Business Communication Quarterly, 73*(4), 432–434. doi:10.1177/1080569910385327

Chapter 8

Mobile devices in training

What are our trainees doing and what can trainers do?

Keri K. Stephens and Brett W. Robertson

Abstract

This chapter connects training and development practices with scholarly research that helps CCCTTs develop their technology proficiency; a best practice integral to improving instructional design and communication proficiency. Our chapter addresses both the problems created when people are constantly connected, and the impact those practices have on focus and attention during training. We share best practices, consistent with the multicommunicating and learning motivation literature, that will help trainers accommodate the needs of their connected learners.

Mobile devices have pervaded the contemporary workplace. As trainers and teachers, we often wish we could pull the plug on wifi and, voilà, a captive audience. But that is not reality. It is nearly impossible for trainees to disconnect from the outside world and give their full attention to learning – and as trainers, we need to be proficient with our own technologies.

This technology-infused training environment is due in part to expectations that people are reachable and available at all times. These norms of connectedness (Bayer, Campbell, & Ling, 2016; Licoppe, 2004; Ling, 2012) not only permeate work, but are integral to most people's lives. This reality means that as trainers we must understand the different ways our trainees use mobile technology and how that interacts with learning motivation. Only then can we begin to change our own practices to help our trainees be effective in a technology-omnipresent environment.

This chapter bridges the gap for CCCTTs who want to develop their technology proficiency by linking technology use, learning motivation, and classroom strategies. Technology proficiency is one of the seven best practices identified by Training and Development Division of the National Communication Association, and by developing these strategies, trainers can also improve other best practices like instructional design and communication proficiency. Table 8.1 highlights the practical strategies developed in this chapter that are built from scholarly research. We have shared this table here because is concretizes the chapter's key take aways.

We begin this chapter by explaining the practice of multicommunicating – carrying on more than one conversation simultaneously, typically using technology (Reinsch, Turner, & Tinsley, 2008). Whether trainees are sending and receiving emails and text messages on their mobile phones or searching the Internet on their laptops during a training session, trainers first need to understand why this is happening and what it means for learning motivation.

Table 8.1 Trainers' strategies to accomplish technology proficiency using learning motivations

Learning Motivation	Description	Training Context	Trainers' Strategies
Intrinsic (IMES)	People's participation in an activity with the goal of experiencing stimulating sensations.	Intrinsic motivators and trainers often rely on sensory pleasure, fun, excitement, and activities to encourage participation.	• Go laptop-less. • Create a culture of mindfulness. • Require physical movement during the training. • Use technology interactivity on mobile devices, including integrative quizzes and polls.
Extrinsic	Other people or stimuli, external to the individual, provide a motivational push.	Rewards—tangible and intangible—are examples of extrinsic motivators and trainers often can use these to encourage and reward desirable behaviors.	• Create windows of availability where trainees let others know when they will be available.
Amotivation	A lack of motivation. This is a feeling that external forces fully control individuals' behaviors.	Amotivated trainees may view training as unnecessary and feel that they do not need to be actively involved or achieve the learning outcomes.	• Have trainees "clear the desk, clear the mind," pack up materials and mobiles, and allow for reflection.

Learning motivations adapted from Deci, Vallerand, Pelletier, and Ryan (1991).

Here we elaborate on habits and connectedness norms (Bayer et al., 2016; Licoppe, 2004; Ling, 2012), and individuals' desires to be available to other people (Stephens, 2012).

Next, we explain learning motivation theories that are relevant for andragogy and adult learning environments. We elaborate on self-determination theory (Deci & Ryan, 1985) to understand motivation in an adult learning context and then we link that theory to multicommunicating (Stephens & Pantoja, 2016). Finally, in the section titled "What's a trainer to do?" we provide practical strategies to accommodate and combat the reality that trainees are often only partially present in the training classroom.

Multicommunicating and multitasking are reality, but why?

Multicommunicating (MC) is related to multitasking, but research suggests that MC can be more difficult to accomplish successfully because it specifically involves engaging with multiple people almost simultaneously (Reinsch et al., 2008). Multitasking, in comparison, is doing two activities simultaneously (or nearly simultaneously). Both of these practices can and do happen in training environments; they can be used with trainees who are on- or off-task, and they are increasingly more common with the use of technology.

People who multicommunicate often are considered inattentive or rude (Cameron & Webster, 2011; Stephens & Davis, 2009). There are many examples in both academic and popular press literature suggesting that when it is a person's turn to speak in a group, if that person is multicommunciating, he or she will miss the cue and act temporarily confused while gathering his or her thoughts. Some people even make errors in their written or verbal communication (Cameron & Webster, 2011; Turner & Reinsch, 2010), including mixing up the messages and sending them to the wrong people (Turner & Reinsch, 2010). When these work activities occur during a training session, they compete with the training content, resulting in less learning. This definition also can include multicommunicating with others for reasons of diversionary entertainment. In a classroom context, Cheong, Shuter, and Suwinyattichaiporn (2016) explain that students often juggle attention between classroom lecture and digital media.

So why can't we keep people from multicommunicating and multitasking in our training sessions? Why do you multicommunicate? Next, we will cover four primary reasons that are intertwined with each other: technology pervasiveness, habits, norms of connectedness, and a desire or need to be available to others.

Technology pervasiveness

Using information and communication technologies (ICTs) at work is important largely due to the range of technologies available (Stephens & Waters, 2016). In a given workday, people bounce from using email, to the Internet, to the phone (D'Urso & Pierce, 2009; Stephens, Waters, & Sinclair, 2014), and many people also use social media tools while at work (Smith & Brenner, 2012). While organizations provide many of these ICTs for their workers, the pervasive use of mobile devices – for personal and work use – further expands technology options (Stephens, in press). Quite simply, people have more access to ICTs and that affords them many options for retrieving and sharing information with others. Think about the ICTs that you have at your fingertips.

Mobile habits and norms of connectedness

One of the byproducts of having mobile devices with us all the time is that we develop a conscious and/or unconscious reliance on that communication tool. Habits are often unconscious because they are an automatic response that is provoked by an environmental stimulus or by remembering a goal (LaRose & Eastin, 2004).

Soror and colleagues (2015) explain that habits develop from routine, daily activities (e.g., brushing teeth, tying shoes, driving to work), but they also arise when people use a mobile device; receiving a text message is a routine occurrence that triggers an automatic response.

There are two reasons people might develop mobile habits: ease of customizing and social pressure, or norms of connectedness. Throughout the past decade, mobile phones have become highly personalizable, something that can enhance people's over-attachment to these devices (Takao, Takahashi, & Kitamura, 2009). This is an active process, where by adapting mobile devices, people make them so useful, they become dependent on the functionality (Oulasvirta, Rattenbury, Ma, & Raita, 2012). The other reason for habit development rests outside of the device itself; by providing a way people can connect easily, the mobile affordance of availability can create external pressure that practically forces people to respond and be reachable (Bayer et al., 2016). Are there things you have done to control your mobile habits, or is this no problem for you?

Desire or need to be available to others

Stephens (2012) found that *being available* to others was a key reason why people wanted to multicommunicate in the workplace. She claims that this desire to be available "highlights the importance people place on using communication technologies to be reachable by others even when engaged in another activity like an organizational meeting" (Stephens, 2012, p. 206). Behaviors related to being available to others all the time include responding to text messages as soon as possible and checking emails frequently (Stafford & Hillyer, 2012); behaviors that also increase the likelihood of engaging in multicommunicating. Campbell and Russo (2003) explain how an individual's personal communication network (PCN) can actually shape the speed at which people respond; they share norms and those norms can create expectations (Stephens, in press). If an individual's PCN expects members to be available all the time, he or she is more likely to provide a fast-response to others. As we wrap up this section, think about your need to be available to others. Are there people in your own life who expect—or demand—your constant availability?

Training and learning motivations vary

Mandating training

Typically trainers are concerned with achieving learning objectives, and the learner's motivation can impact those outcomes. When attendance in a training session is forced – managers mandate it – versus voluntary, researchers suggest that this negatively influences trainees' motivation to learn (Guerrero & Sire, 2001; Hicks & Klimoski, 1987). But there is also evidence that the topics and messages of the training can mediate trainee motivation (Mathieu & Martineau, 1997). Required training courses can be perceived as a commitment toward skill and performance excellence by management, and in that case, employees can be motivated to learn, even if the training is mandatory. However, when organizations provide training that is perceived by employees as manipulative, their motivation to learn is lessened (Mathieu & Martineau, 1997). How many trainees in your sessions are forced to attend?

Self-determination theory

In addition to the organizational and managerial influences on training motivation, individuals vary in what they want from the training. We define training motivation as people's intentional behavior to engage in actions that allow them to achieve their desired outcomes in a training session (Deci et al., 1991; Vallerand et al., 1992). This definition is derived from self-determination theory (SDT), and it explains that people vary in how they are best motivated in training sessions.

SDT explains three types of motivation: internal, external, and amotivation (Deci et al., 1991). There are three more nuanced types of intrinsic motivation (Vallerand et al., 1992), but the one more directly related to how trainees use technology to communicate in a training session is intrinsic motivation to experience stimulation (IMES). IMES is defined as people's participation in an activity with the goal of experiencing stimulating sensations like sensory pleasures and fun (Vallerand et al., 1992). This is something many trainers incorporate into their in-person and online training.

Some individuals are extrinsically motivated, meaning that other people or stimuli, external to the individual, provide a motivational push. Rewards, tangible and intangible, are examples of extrinsic motivators and trainers can often use these to encourage and reward desirable behaviors (Vallerand et al., 1992). People who solely rely on extrinsic motivation often seek the approval of others as a way to gain a sense of self-worth.

Amotivation is an additional type of motivation and is explained as a lack of motivation. This is a feeling that external forces fully control individuals' behaviors (Vallerand et al., 1992). In a training environment, amotivated trainees may view training as unnecessary and feel that they do not need to be actively involved or achieve the learning outcomes.

SDT often is applied in classrooms where it is used to explain students' needs for autonomy, competence, and belongingness (Kerssen-Griep, Trees, & Hess, 2008; Kerssen-Griep & Witt, 2012). This theory argues that individuals have choices when regulating their own behavior (Deci & Ryan, 1985; Deci et al., 1991). When people act in a self-determined manner, their actions are intrinsically motivated, and there are many benefits for people acting this way. These trainees engage in proactive learning behaviors for the pleasure and satisfaction they receive from accomplishing the task (Vallerand et al., 1992). Research on this topic has found that people with higher levels of intrinsic motivation enjoy learning and show more positive emotions than those who feel their learning is regulated by external forces (Ryan & Connell, 1989). All of these forms of motivation can affect your training efforts. Which of these three types is most helpful when you are helping people learn?

Specific learning motivations are linked to multicommunicating behaviors

A growing body of research is focusing on how mobile devices are used in classrooms and how they impact learning (e.g., Finn & Ledbetter, 2013; Lancaster & Goodboy, 2015; Stephens & Pantoja, 2016). Stephens and Pantoja's (2016) work on learning motivations and multicommunicating provides a link to explain how different types of motivation can influence learners in training environments. Although their work was rooted in classroom settings, these same ideas can be applied to trainers and trainees. Using the three types of motivation in self-determination theory—amotivation, extrinsic, and intrinsic—their study directly links multicommunicating behaviors and motivation.

While reading the descriptions in the following section, see where you think you fall into these types of motivation. The answer to that question alone will give you the insight into your own understanding around technology and how you learn in different environments. Understanding where you fall can help you recognize your learners' motivations and help you adjust your training and coaching strategies.

Amotivation

Specifically, learners who feel forced to learn or believe they have little to no control over their learning environment, experience a sense of amotivation (Vallerand et al., 1992). Stephens and Pantoja suggest that as the level of amotivation increases, learners use their mobile devices more often for distraction purposes and to keep themselves entertained during class.

Researchers examining mobile device use in contexts other than a training environment have often found that when it is used for entertainment purposes, negative outcomes, like excessive Internet use, result. Using a uses and gratifications approach,

Wei (2008) notes that mobile devices are used for both instrumental (e.g., staying informed on news reports) and ritualistic (e.g., passing time) reasons. People using mobiles for instrumental reasons are more productive, whereas ritualistic motives are linked to playing video games on the mobile device. Younger users are most likely to be ritualistically using their mobile devices.

Extrinsic

People with an extrinsic motivation to learn want to be available others; a desire consistent with past research. This finding implies that people who like to multitask anyway, who are also extrinsically motivated, multicommunicate in class with a goal of being available to other people. Being available is not unlike a habit because it is likened to "breathing," which makes some people feel "alive"; that is, available for information exchange at all times (Reinsch et al., 2008, p. 398).

Intrinsic

People with an intrinsic motivation to experience stimulation (IMES) are more likely to multicommunicate for reasons of understanding course material, influencing others, and giving and receiving social support. This finding explains that those who are intrinsically motivated will actually engage in productive multicommunicating practices with others, and this can enhance learning beyond the classroom (Jones, 2008).

What's a trainer to do?

Trainers face an often-unpleasant reality that there are many things beyond their control in a training environment. In this chapter we have explained how ICTs – mobile devices, in particular – combine with learning motivations to create challenges for trainers. Though there is no magic solution to fix all these problems, there are examples from literature and our own training experiences that provide guidance as we experiment and learn to address pervasive technology, and many of them are related to the same concepts we shared for why people are multicommunicate in training sessions: habit, norms of connectedness, and desire to be available. We begin this discussion by sharing the challenge of having to work around pre-set schedules of trainees who have a mobile in their pocket at all times, then we translate these three reasons why people multicommunicate into practical advice for trainers.

> At 8:30am, the designated start time, 14 of our 15 trainees were in the room, so we kicked off our session on time. We began by asking if anyone had scheduled meetings where they needed to leave the training for the next two days. Three people raised their hands and said they had teleconferences at 11:30am, a 12:30pm, and 2:30pm. We were now up to 3 attendees who had prior commitments.
> By the way, we had spoken with management and they had assured us that we would have their undivided attention for the two days. This is often the case: management commits their employees' time, but things come up at the last minute.
> Still waiting on our last person to arrive, we spent 5 minutes arranging our schedule for the day so that we accommodated everyone but Sam, who had an

11:30am call. Sam agreed to contact his customer and re-schedule the call during lunch or afternoon break.

He was successful. Larry, our late arriver walked in and one of the trainers met him at the door, walked outside, and got his private agreement on the negotiated schedule:

> *Break from 10–10:30, lunch from 12:15–1:15, and afternoon break from 2:30–3pm. We would end promptly by 5pm, per the original schedule.*

Next, we discussed why we negotiated this schedule and why the breaks are a full 30 minutes. Our philosophy as trainers is to work with our clients' schedules, but then hold them accountable for being prompt when returning from breaks and being fully present during each focused-training session. This approach is based on the concept of reciprocity (Cialdini, 1984); we accommodate the trainees, and in turn, they feel a sense of obligation to meet our requests. We also explained what being focused meant, and that we were committed to promptly ending prior to each break, so people felt comfortable putting mobile devices out of their regular reach. Finally, we got everyone's verbal commitment to the schedule and the ground rules.

Every time we gave a two-day training session to this high-tech company, we spent the first 15 minutes creating a mutually agreed upon schedule that included designated times that our trainees would be available and reachable by others. And some of our trainees went into their email programs, created an out-of-office message, and listed the exact times they would be available for the two days. We found this approach essential for achieving our learning objectives.

Habitual mobile device use

Addressing mobile phone habits can be challenging in a training environment because many people are unaware that they have habits. Whereas we can share the latest research on mobile habits with our college students and try to affect their classroom behaviors, that pedantic approach does not work as well with adult learners in a training environment. The tactics we just shared focusing on negotiation and reciprocity, are one option, but there are other methods.

Laptop-less. Companies have tried going laptop-less for quite a while (Chudoba, Watson-Manheim, Lee, & Crowston, 2005; Marquez, 2008), and some groups ban mobile devices completely from meetings and trainings. In fact, news media and popular press recently have shared stories about executives mandating that mobile devices be stripped from meeting spaces (e.g., Hedges, 2014). But the problem with taking devices from people is that many of them will become very anxious (Cheever, Rosen, Carrier, & Chavez, 2014).

Other organizational employees find workarounds that "obey" the policy, but still distract them from their training/meeting goals. For example, Stephens (in press) shares a story of two managers in their late 60s who were in a session that banned their mobile devices. During her observations, she found that they complied with this request, but when it was getting close to lunch, she saw one gentleman lean into the aisle and pass a folded note to his peer. This happened when the manager's back was turned, but they acted like junior-high school students by sneaking around to pass notes and accomplish what they needed. She later learned that they were trying to coordinate their lunch plans, and yes, they did pass notes to do that.

Reflect on your own mobile device habits. Have you experienced a compelling need to quickly glance at your incoming text messages? What about check social media when you find your mind wandering? Next, we share some recovery and advanced-planning techniques that can get trainees refocused.

Physical movement makes mobile use inconvenient

One of the best strategies to help trainees get back on task when their noses are stuck in their phones is getting them up on their feet. We share two tangible examples next.

> We [1]rarely conduct training where participants sit for extended periods of time. When people are practicing a simple skill and everyone in the room is going to participate, we do not call on people to come up to the front one at a time. Instead we make this announcement: "Everyone up and line up around the room to take your turn practicing."
>
> This gets all the trainees out of their seats, and we find that they pay closer attention to their peers and provide stronger feedback when they are standing.

> *Every time we have used this approach it gets trainees engaged.*

A second strategy is to put people into groups and have them move from the comfort of their normal seats. Here, flip-chart paper is a real friend. When a group has to work together to create a written plan, they interact and often stand around a piece of flip-chart paper. Working in groups to create objects, play meaningful games, and exchange information, also can be a productive recovery strategy. There is social pressure that keeps many people off of their mobile devices when they are interacting directly with others (Stephens, in press; Stephens & Davis, 2009).

Interactivity and training salience to address engagement

Trainers also should examine the frequency of their interaction-based activities as part of the design of their training. In a National Communication Association Training and Development Panel presented in 2012, Marie-Claire Bouchal, Michael Fahs, Seth Frei, Jeff Martin, Greg Patton, and Keri Stephens presented 100 different ways to infuse interactivity into training. The document they created describes techniques ranging from traditional training classroom exercises, like sentence completers and trainee demonstrations, to using technology to engage learners.

Create windows of availability for trainees

In the high-tech training example in this chapter, one of the subtle practices that we used was creating breaks that matched our trainees' needs. A good way to accomplish this is to talk with the trainees as they arrive and understand their existing commitments. In our example, we needed to make longer breaks and we shifted lunch to accommodate one of their pre-existing commitments. Then, and most importantly, we shared the times they would all be available with the entire group and we kept our commitments.

Trainees who are knowledge workers – meaning their work is more cerebral and their work is more autonomous (Drucker, 1969) – typically create their own schedules and they use their mobile phones differently than hourly and shift-based workers (Stephens, in press). One of the luxuries of training hourly workers is that if their managers approve their training, they likely have limited other commitments during that time. Another advantage is they are accustomed to worked for a fixed time and having a scheduled break.

Knowledge workers are different, and while that is not new, having constant access to mobile devices has heightened these differences when conducting training courses. Trainers need to create windows of availability (Stephens, in press) and give these workers time to let people know their schedules. Breaks function differently in the daily lives of these workers – they are irregular and often under their personal control – so we need to realize this and change our communication around how to use these breaks when knowledge workers attend training.

In our extended example, we lengthened breaks to 30 minutes, but there are many other ways to handle breaks. Some groups respond well when given 5 to 10-minute breaks at least once an hour. This is especially the case when the training material is less interactive or if trainees need to be responsive to people outside the training room. Some breaks can be combined with a group activity. Giving groups 45 minutes to take a break and accomplish a goal gives them flexibility; however, be sure and specify how much time they get for the break or you will have frustrated team members who think the break is 10 minutes and others will not return for half an hour.

Morning breaks can be on a different schedule than afternoon breaks. Finally, trainers are typically quite good a reading an audience. Give trainees a 5 minute bio break when they need it. But don't forget about yourself. Most trainers know there are particular times of the day when their attention wanes.

Helping trainees be present

The final strategy we share is a concrete example of how to get trainees to focus on the task at hand; it is called Clear the Desk, Clear the Mind. We return to our extended example of the high-tech company.

> At the end of the second day of training, our trainees are always exhausted. We push people pretty hard in this course and they work through some emotional baggage as they try to understand the value of changing their habitual speaking patterns. For example, one young man began every sentence with the word *and*; it was his filler and he was completely unaware that he did this in every conversation. We warn our participants they will be frustrated at the end of day one and after all this struggle, they will not leave "fixed," but instead they will leave the training with in-depth knowledge and a plan for how to create new speaking habits that will help them make a positive impact on others.
>
> So how do we accomplish this and make sure their individual plans are crystalized in their minds, despite being physically and emotionally exhausted? We clear the desk. An hour before our training ends, we instruct our trainees to pack up all

their materials, including mobile devices, and move them off their desks next to the back door of the class. The tone of the class changes and there is an immediate human connection established in the room. Some people would call this a mindfulness setting. We pass out blank notecards and pens, but that is all they have to work with for the final hour. For some exercises, they write their own notecards, but for other exercises, they have a trusted peer capture information and give it to them. It is as if removing all the clutter from the desk, sets the stage for them to reflect on their learning and be committed to the plan they develop.

Trainers need to think about how they use technology

So far, the strategies we have shared concerning how to handle mobile device use during training have focused on addressing this in a traditional training room, and hopefully you have self-reflected on your own technology behaviors. Next we share strategies that look at training as a process: trainers and trainees can use technology before, during, and after their training sessions. Before we dive into tactics, it is important to return to adult learning theory and consider how using technology to teach and learn functions.

Andragogy. How do adult learning environments influence trainees' desires to engage in training while battling multicommunication behaviors, especially when individual-learning behaviors also are changing the way trainers have to train? We turn to the literature on technology and andragogy for an explanation. Knowles (1970) defines andragogy as "the science and art of educating adults" (p. 43). Andragogy is studied often within an adult higher-education context (Halx, 2010) as a way to explain how adult learners in college classrooms process information differently than their younger counterparts. These same ideas can be applied in a training context. Technology also plays a role in determining how adult learners can engage with course material and training information. Because mobile devices, knowledge management software, and the Internet have influenced educational practice, there have been substantial changes to the how teaching and learning happen.

Heutagogical learning. Andragogy moved trainers into the realm of considering adult learners, as opposed to young learners, but many of these adults now must engage in constant learning to thrive at work. According to Blaschke (2012), a heutagogical approach to teaching and learning stresses that learners are autonomous and self-determined. It emphasizes developing learner capacity and capability, with the overall goal of producing learners who are well prepared for the challenges in workplaces while dealing with multiple communication complexities. Previously, heutagogy has been used to explain learning during the growth in emerging technologies used for distance education (Anderson, 2010; Wheeler, 2011), although its relevance to training is also apparent because trainees, in a self-determined fashion, seek autonomy in understanding content. Traditional distance learning requires the learner to be autonomous.

Strategies. Because heutagogy has generally been used to understand adult learners – working adults with extensive life experience and more maturity than campus-based students (Peters, 2004; Richardson, Morgan, & Woodley, 1999) – it serves as an appropriate framework to understand trainers and trainees. We need to show our trainees the value of our training content so they will be more motivated to engage. Learners need to know how to reflect upon what they have learned, so educators must focus on teaching learners how to teach themselves (Kamenetz, 2010; Peters, 2004). Reflection and self-directed action plans are just as important today as ever; we cannot afford to run out of time at the end of the day and skip this crucial step in helping our trainees achieve their desired outcomes.

When we think in terms of heutagogy, this invites us to consider whether we can use technology effectively to prime our learners and then again to reinforce learning. There are many technology tools – online systems, webconferences, social media – available to help us interact, and actually teach our trainees important concepts before we enter a physical classroom. There are also times that we can use technology during our class to enhance participation and learning (Stephens, Murphy, & Kee, 2011). Finally, there can be some added benefits of using technology to engage learners; they can like the trainer more and that can translate into added learning (Stephen & Mottet, 2008).

Comfort in using technology. It is worth a reminder that if trainers use technology in training we need to know how to use it, and we must learn methods for dealing with changes in technology habits. For trainers to be capable of integrating technology successfully, they must remain current with available technology options and programs, as well as knowing the needs of their trainees. (Taylor, 2006). Some technology works well and some people use technology in training very well. But it is not magic. The fundamentals of instructional design and instructor-led training/online training always should be considered before using the latest tool. Technology is here to stay and we must learn to deal with the influx of potential changes. For example, combining high-quality video conferencing with robots-on-wheels may make is possible for us to bring virtual guests into our training room without them leaving the comfort of their desk. We may be expected to enter production studios, learn gamification strategies, and create online learning modules that supplement instructor-led training. As consultants, trainers, and teachers we need to constantly reassess our skills and knowledge to understand how to use technology creatively in our own work.

Conclusion

The ideas shared in this chapter invite you to think about the next two training sessions you will lead. (Do not think back to the last few where you have been frustrated that mobile phones are a distraction.) Consider your audience and how they like or need breaks. Think about how you will set the stage for gaining commitment to presence during the training, while simultaneously providing opportunities for them to get urgent work done. How will you re-set the group if your trainees are on their phones during training or if they constantly step out to take calls? Finally, how can you re-design your training course to take advantage of heutagogical learning, possibly involving some form of technology? Through self-reflection and by considering the needs of the trainees and their motivations, communication coaches, consultants, trainers, and teachers can develop their technology proficiency and stay agile as training evolves.

Note

1 All references to the high-tech training scenarios are the experiences of the first author and her training partner Rebecca Esposito of Esposito Consulting.

References

Anderson, T. (2010). Theories for learning with emerging technologies. In G. Veletsianos (ed.), *Emerging technologies in distance education* (pp. 23–40). Edmonton, Canada: Athabasca University Press.

Bayer, J. B., Campbell, S. W., & Ling, R. (2016). Connection cues: Activating the norms and habits of social connectedness. *Communication Theory, 26*(2), 128–149. http://dx.doi.org/10.1111/comt.12090

Blaschke, L. M. (2012). Heutagogy and lifelong learning: A review of heutagogical practice and self-determined learning. *The International Review of Research in Open and Distributed Learning, 13*(1), 56–71. http://dx.doi.org/10.19173/irrodl.v13i1.1076

Campbell, S. W., & Russo, T. C. (2003). The social construction of mobile telephony: An application of the social influence model to perceptions and uses of mobile phones within personal communication networks. *Communication Monographs, 70*(4), 317–334. http://dx.doi.org/10.1080/0363775032000179124

Cameron, A. F., & Webster, J. (2011). Relational outcomes of multicommunicating: Integrating incivility and social exchange perspectives. *Organization Science, 22*(3), 754–771. http://dx.doi.org/10.1287/orsc.1100.0540

Cheever, N. A., Rosen, L. D., Carrier, L. M., & Chavez, A. (2014). Out of sight is not out of mind: The impact of restricting wireless mobile device use on anxiety levels among low, moderate and high users. *Computers in Human Behavior, 37*, 290–297. http://dx.doi.org/10.1016/j.chb.2014.05.002

Cheong, P. H., Shuter, R., & Suwinyattichaiporn, T. (2016). Managing student digital distractions and hyperconnectivity: Communication strategies and challenges for professorial authority. *Communication Education, 65*(3), 272–289. http://dx.doi.org/10.1080/03634523.2016.1159317

Chudoba, K. M., Watson-Manheim, M. B., Lee, C. S., & Crowston, K. (2005, August). Meet me in cyberspace: Meetings in the distributed work environment. Paper presented at the Academy of Management Conference, Honolulu, HI.

Cialdini, R. B. (1984). *Influence: The psychology of persuasion.* New York, NY: William Morrow and Company.

Deci, E. L., & Ryan, R. M. (1985). *Intrinsic motivation and self-determination in human behavior.* New York, NY: Plenum.

Deci, E. L., Vallerand, R. J., Pelletier, L.G., & Ryan, R. M. (1991). Motivation and education: The self-determination perspective. *Educational Psychologist, 26*, 325–347. http://dx.doi.org/10.1207/s15326985ep2603&4_6

Drucker, P. F. (1969). *The age of discontinuity: Guidelines to our changing society.* London: William Heinemann Ltd.

D'Urso, S. C., & Pierce, K. M. (2009). Connected to the organization: A survey of communication technologies in the modern organizational landscape. *Communication Research Reports, 26*(1), 75–81. http://dx.doi.org/10.1080/08824090802637098

Finn, A. N., & Ledbetter, A. M. (2013). Teacher technology policies and online communication apprehension as predictors of learner empowerment. *Communication Education, 62*, 301–317. http://dx.doi.org/10.1080/03634523.2013.794386

Guerrero, S., & Sire, B. (2001). Motivation to train from the workers' perspective: Example of French companies. *International Journal of Human Resource Management, 12*(6), 988–1004. http://dx.doi.org/10.1080/713769684

Halx, M. D. (2010). Re-conceptualizing college and university teaching through the lens of adult education: Regarding undergraduates as adults. *Teaching in Higher Education, 15*(5), 519–530. http://dx.doi.org/10.1080/13562517.2010.491909

Hedges, K. (2014, June 5). How to get people off their phones in meetings without being a jerk. Retrieved from www.forbes.com/sites/work-in-progress/2014/06/05/how-to-get-people-off-their-phones-in-meetings-without-being-a-jerk/

Hicks, W. D., & Klimoski, R. J. (1987). Entry into training programs and its effects on training outcomes: A field experiment. *Academy of Management Journal, 30*(3), 542–552. http://dx.doi.org/10.2307/256013

Jones, A. C. (2008). The effects of out-of-class support on student satisfaction and motivation to learn. *Communication Education, 57*, 373–388. http://dx.doi.org/10.1080/03634520801968830

Kamenetz, A. (2010). *Edupunks, edupreneurs, and the coming transformation of higher education.* Chelsea, VT: Chelsea Green Publishing Company.

Kerssen-Griep, J., Trees, A. R., & Hess, J. A. (2008). Attentive facework during instructional feedback: Key to perceiving mentorship and an optimal learning environment. *Communication Education, 57*, 312–332. http://dx.doi.org/10.1080/03634520802027347

Kerssen-Griep, J., & Witt, P. L. (2012). Instructional feedback II: How do instructor immediacy cues and facework tactics interact to predict student motivation and fairness perceptions? *Communication Studies, 63*, 498–517. http://dx.doi.org/10.1080/10510974.2011.632660

Knowles, M. S. (1970). *The modern practice of adult education* (Vol. 41). New York, NY: Association Press.

Lancaster, A. L., & Goodboy, A. K. (2015). An experimental examination of students' attitudes toward classroom cell phone policies. *Communication Research Reports, 32*, 107–111. http://dx.doi.org/10.1080/08824096.2014.989977

LaRose, R., & Eastin, M. S. (2004). A social cognitive theory of Internet uses and gratifications: Toward a new model of media attendance. *Journal of Broadcasting & Electronic Media, 48*(3), 358–377. http://dx.doi.org/10.1207/s15506878jobem4803_2

Licoppe, C. (2004). Connected presence: The emergence of a new repertoire for managing social relationships in a changing communication technospace. *Environment and Planning D: Society and Space, 22*(1), 135–156. http://dx.doi.org/10.1068/d323t

Ling, R. (2012). *Taken for grantedness: The embedding of mobile communication into society.* Cambridge, MA: MIT Press.

Marquez, L. (2008, March 31). *Why Silicon Valley employees are going to meetings "laptop-less".* Retrieved March 31, 2008 from http://abcnews.go.com/Technology/story ?id=4560823Going topless to office meetings

Mathieu, J. E., & Martineau, J. W. (1997). Individual and situational influences on training motivation. In J. K. Ford (Ed.), *Improving training effectiveness in work organizations* (pp. 193–222). New York: Lawrence Erlbaum Associates, Inc.

Oulasvirta, A., Rattenbury, T., Ma, L., & Raita, E. (2012). Habits make smartphone use more pervasive. *Personal and Ubiquitous Computing, 16*(1), 105–114. http://dx.doi.org/10.1007/s00779-011-0412-2

Peters, O. (2004). *Distance education in transition – New trends and challenges* (4th ed., vol. 5). Oldenburg, Germany: Bibliotheks- und Informationssystem der Universität Oldenburg.

Reinsch, N. L., Turner, J. W., & Tinsley, C. H. (2008). Multicommunicating: A practice whose time has come? *Academy of Management Review, 33*(2), 391–403. http://dx.doi.org/10.5465/AMR.2008.31193450

Richardson, J. T. E., Morgan, A., & Woodley, A. (1999). Approaches to studying distance education. *Higher Education, 37*, 23–55. http://dx.doi.org/10.1023/A:1003445000716

Ryan, R. M., & Connell, J. P. (1989). Perceived locus of causality and internalization: Examining reasons for acting in two domains. *Journal of Personality and Social Psychology, 57*(5), 749–761. http://dx.doi.org/10.1037/0022-3514.57.5.749

Smith, A., & Brenner, J. (2012). Twitter use 2012. Retrieved from: http://www.pewinternet.org/files/old-media/Files/Reports/2012/PIP_Twitter_Use_2012.pdf

Soror, A. A., Hammer, B. I., Steelman, Z. R., Davis, F. D., & Limayem, M. M. (2015). Good habits gone bad: Explaining negative consequences associated with the use of mobile phones from a dual-systems perspective. *Information Systems Journal, 25*(4), 403–427. http://dx.doi.org/10.1111/isj.12065

Stafford, L., & Hillyer, J. D. (2012). Information and communication technologies in personal relationships. *Review of Communication*, *12*(4), 290–312. http://dx.doi.org/10.1080/15358593. 2012.685951

Stephens, K. K. (in press). *Negotiating control: Organizations & mobile communication*. Oxford University Press.

Stephens, K. K. (2012). Multiple conversations during organizational meetings: Development of the multicommunicating scale. *Management Communication Quarterly*, *26*, 195–223. http://dx.doi.org/10.1177/0893318911431802

Stephens, K. K., & Davis, J. D. (2009). The social influences on electronic multitasking in organizational meetings. *Management Communication Quarterly*, *23*, 63–83. http://dx.doi.org/10.1177/0893318909335417

Stephens, K. K., & Mottet, T. M. (2008). Interactivity in a web conferencing training context: Effects on trainers and trainees. *Communication Education*, *57*, 88–104. http://dx.doi.org/10.1080/03634520701573284

Stephens, K. K., Murphy, M., & Kee, K. (2011). Leveraging multicommunication in the classroom: Implications for participation and engagement. In S. P. Ferris (ed.), *Teaching and learning with the net generation: Concepts and tools for reaching digital learners* (pp. 269–288). Hershey, PA: IGI Global. http://dx.doi.org/10.4018/978-1-61350-347-8.ch015

Stephens, K. K., & Pantoja, G. E. (2016). Mobile devices in the classroom: Learning motivations predict specific types of multicommunicating behaviors. *Communication Education*, *65*(4), 463–479. http://dx.doi.org/10.1080/03634523.2016.1164876

Stephens, K. K., & Waters, E. D. (2016). How and why technology matters in consulting interventions. In J. H. Waldeck & D. R. Seibold (eds.), *Consulting that matters: A reader for scholars and practitioners* (pp. 239–258). New York, NY: Peter Lang Publishing.

Stephens, K. K., Waters, E. D., & Sinclair, C. (2014). Media management: The integration of HR, technology, and people. In M. E. Gordon & V. D. Miller (eds.), *Meeting the challenge of human resource management: A communication perspective* (pp. 215–226). New York, NY: Routledge.

Takao, M., Takahashi, S., & Kitamura, M. (2009). Addictive personality and problematic mobile phone use. *CyberPsychology & Behavior*, *12*(5), 501–507. http://dx.doi.org/10.1089/cpb. 2009.0022

Taylor, M. L. (2006). Generation NeXt comes to college: 2006 updates and emerging issues. *A Collection of Papers on Self-Study and Institutional Improvement*, *2*(2), 48–55.

Turner, J. W., & Reinsch, N. L. (2007). The business communicator as presence allocator: Multicommunicating, equivocality, and status at work. *Journal of Business Communication*, *44*, 36–58. http://dx.doi.org/10.1177/0021943606295779

Turner, J. W., & Reinsch, N. L. (2010). Successful and unsuccessful multicommunication episodes: Engaging in dialogue or juggling messages? *Information System Frontiers*, *12*, 277–285. doi: 10.1007/s10796-009-9185-y

Vallerand, R. J., Pelletier, L. G., Blais, M. R., Briere, N. M., Senecal, C., & Vallieres, E. F. (1992). The academic motivation scale: A measure of intrinsic, extrinsic, and amotivation in education. *Educational and Psychological Measurement*, *52*, 1003–1017. http://dx.doi.org/10.1177/0013164492052004025

Wei, R. (2008). Motivations for using the mobile phone for mass communications and entertainment. *Telematics and Informatics*, *25*(1), 36–46. http://dx.doi.org/10.1016/j.tele.2006.03.001

Wheeler, S. (2011, July 8). Learning with e's: Digital age learning. [Blog post.] Retrieved from http://steve-wheeler.blogspot.com/2011/07/digital-age-learning.html

Chapter 9

Best practices in slide design

Lori B. Miraldi and Peter N. Miraldi

Abstract

Communication consultants, coaches, teachers, and trainers need to demonstrate their technology proficiency with well-designed presentation slides that effectively communicate information to a variety of audiences. However, the common practice of slide design is not based on theories and research of how audiences process and learn information. Therefore, in this chapter, we introduce the Assertion-Evidence slide design style which can help presenters increase their audience's comprehension and retention of important content.

As educators and trainers, we often encounter technological challenges in delivering content to our audience. One of the main culprits in teaching and training is bad slide design. Undoubtedly, you have sat through seminars that tend to confuse and confound more than they inform or inspire. Even though you can sense, intuitively, that slide presentations could be better, you may not know how to improve them. Therefore, we chose to address Best Practice 3 – Demonstrating Technology Proficiency by explaining the learning process and how you can design presentation slides to complement the way in which we learn. Understanding these fundamentals and how to apply them proficiently can enhance your teaching and training. In addition, these insights can be applied to various programs and platforms. Demonstrating proficiency in slide design can have a positive impact on the other best practices introduced in this handbook as well.

Training itself is a technology that seeks to teach an audience methods for achieving goals. Rogers (2003) noted that technologies often include both hardware and software components. The hardware component is a physical device whereas the software component is the information or instructions for using the tool. Typically, trainers and educators design and present digital slides to help them organize and illustrate their lessons (Simons, 2004). Therefore, we need to develop and demonstrate proficiency with the slide design technologies we use to deliver our content.

Slideware programs, such as the ubiquitous PowerPoint, are used to create and give countless presentations each day (Thielsch & Perabo, 2012). These presentations occur in a variety of educational and organizational settings, including the delivery and implementation of training content. You may use slide presentations to disseminate information to clients and stakeholders both orally and with printouts. Unfortunately, the common practice of formatting presentation slides is not based on the sound principles of cognitive psychology and multimedia learning. These common-practice slides lead to missed opportunities for learning. The use of new, research-based slide design formats is needed to maximize audience comprehension and retention of information. Improving your audience's comprehension and retention of information can lead to more effective training programs, saving time and money. Research from multimedia learning and cognitive psychology has informed the creation of a new slide design format called the Assertion-Evidence design. This new format is firmly rooted in research and has been tested for effectiveness. Both you and your clients can benefit from these best practices in slide design style.

A cognitive theory of multimedia learning

Researchers in cognitive and educational psychology have contributed a number of important concepts that inform how you can create effective presentation slides. Richard Mayer (2005, 2009), a leader in the field of multimedia learning, integrated a number of relevant theories into his cognitive theory of multimedia learning. Drawing on theories of cognitive processing, Mayer claimed that people actively process information during the learning process by paying attention, organizing information, and integrating information with knowledge in their long-term memory. We process visual and verbal information separately (i.e., dual-channel processing) and there are limits to the amount of information we can process (i.e., processing limits). Understanding these processes can provide you with insights on how to better design your presentation slides so you can train your audience more effectively.

Dual-channel processing

At the heart of Mayer's theory is the multimedia principle, "People learn more deeply from words and pictures than from words alone" (Mayer, 2005, p. 31). Essentially, there are two ways in which you process information: visually and verbally (Mayer, 2005, 2009; Mayer & Moreno, 2002; Paivio, 1986). You can process images and sounds that are not language-based independently from language that is spoken or written. This dual-channel processing approach assumes that one system can be functioning at a time or both systems may be functioning at the same time.

Visual and verbal information are complementary. The learner can process both types of information simultaneously via the dual-channel processing systems of the working memory. This process allows the learner to draw connections between the two and enhance learning. A study by Mayer and Anderson (1991) supported the application of this technique. During the study, they created four conditions based on the type of training that was provided: a visual with words, a purely verbal explanation, a purely visual presentation, and no training. Following the training, the group who saw the visual with the words demonstrated superior problem solving in comparison with the other three groups.

Processing limits

However, there is a limit to what you can process in each channel at one time, and too much information can overload your processing ability (Mayer, 2005, 2009). Understanding the relationship between working memory and long-term memory is essential for effective training. When you process new information, you use your working memory which is extremely limited and short-term. It is estimated that your working memory can handle two to four elements and may retain information for less than a minute. By contrast, your long-term memory holds all the knowledge you have gained through adaptation to your environment. Sweller (2005) defined learning as a change in your long-term memory. The challenge for you, as a trainer, is to overcome the limitations of your audience's working memory in order to change their long-term memory.

One way to do this is by maximizing effortful learning, or germane cognitive load, that results in changes to long-term memory (Mayer, 2009; Sweller, 2005). Training that provides learners with a variety of evidence to help them process and understand a new concept results in germane cognitive load.

An additional technique is to manage the information, or intrinsic cognitive load, so it does not overwhelm your audience. Slides that are filled with vast amounts of data and information may be doing a disservice to your audience by overloading them, causing them to withdraw from your presentation. The modality principle has been shown to reduce intrinsic cognitive load (Mayer, 2009; Mayer & Moreno, 1998, 2002; Moreno & Mayer, 1999). The modality principle states that learning is improved with the use of images and spoken words rather than with the use of images and printed words. Baddeley (1999, 2003) proposed that written language enters through the visual processing channel. The modality principle holds that presenting verbal information in spoken rather than written form will avoid overloading the visual channel (Mayer, 2009). The learner can process more information by taking full advantage of both processing systems simultaneously without overload.

Another technique is to eliminate extraneous information from your instructional design. For example, using more words than necessary increases the extraneous cognitive load on your audience and can be especially overwhelming when the germane and intrinsic cognitive loads are demanding as well. Rather, a picture may be more appropriate and effective than a detailed description.

There are five multimedia principles that you can apply to reduce extraneous cognitive load: coherence, signaling, redundancy, spatial contiguity, and temporal contiguity. The coherence principle calls for the removal of irrelevant words, pictures, sounds, and music. In addition, unnecessary words and symbols should also be excluded from presentations. More concise, focused information will lead to better learning because working memory is limited. This principle is particularly important for learners who do not have much knowledge on the subject.

Second, the signaling principle states that learning is improved when cues highlighting the organization of key pieces of information are included (Mayer, 2009). This signaling helps the learner to identify and pay attention to the key points in your lesson. It also helps your audience draw connections between the key points by highlighting the relationships between ideas. Focusing your audience members on the most important elements of the presentation and highlighting the structure of the information reduces the demand on their working memory.

Third, the redundancy principle states that removing redundant text from your presentation will increase your audience's learning (Mayer, 2009; Mayer & Moreno, 2002). You learn more from visuals and spoken text than you do from visuals, spoken text, and written text. The spoken and written texts overload the verbal processing system and reduce learning. Eliminating the redundant verbal information reduces the extraneous load and allows the learner to integrate the visual and verbal information being received. It is helpful to note that labels used to highlight and describe parts of a graphic can be used effectively (Mayer & Johnson, 2008). However, in order to avoid extraneous load, these labels should be kept to a few words.

Fourth, when written text is used on the screen, tests of the spatial contiguity principle have supported that you should place text near the graphic it is describing (Mayer, 2009; Mayer & Anderson, 1992; Mayer & Moreno, 2002; Moreno & Mayer, 1999). When you locate labels far from the graphic being described, your audience members have to use more cognitive processing to search the screen and make connections between the two elements. Placing graphics and descriptors close together reduces their extraneous cognitive load. This is particularly helpful when the information is complex, the visual cannot be understood without words, or when the audience does not have a lot of knowledge of the subject.

While the previous principle focused on the spatial proximity of information, the fifth principle, temporal contiguity, focuses on the proximity of information in time. Experiments on the temporal contiguity principle have supported that learning is enhanced when verbal and visual information are presented simultaneously (Mayer, 2009; Mayer & Anderson, 1992; Mayer & Moreno, 2002; Mayer, Moreno, Boire, & Vagge, 1999; Mayer & Sims, 1994). It is easier for audience members to hold both pieces of information in their working memory when they are received at the same time. Having verbal and visual information accessible in the working memory can lead to better mental connections and improved learning.

Slide design

Common practices

Unfortunately, the format used for most presentation slides is not based on cognitive theory of multimedia learning. Although there are a variety of slideware programs, PowerPoint is the mostly widely used one (Thielsch & Perabo, 2012). Robert Gaskins (2012), co-founder of PowerPoint, explained some of his motivation for creating the program. He pointed out that it was originally created as an alternative tool for creating transparencies and 35 mm slides and expedited the creation of presentation aids. Gaskins had a background in computers and business but not in multimedia learning or cognitive psychology. Therefore, the default template that guides the slides' format was not based in the principles of educational psychology outlined above. This is evidenced by the common complaints about the use of PowerPoint (Cooper, 2009; Doumont, 2005; Tufte, 2003; Vik, 2004): too many words, busy backgrounds, distracting animations and sounds, overly complicated graphics, and a lack of organization.

Based on the PowerPoint default template, the common practice for formatting slides is to use a phrase headline (i.e., an incomplete sentence title) followed by a bulleted list (Garner, Alley, Gaudelli, & Zappe, 2009). In a survey of more than 2,000 slides created by professionals, Garner et al. found that more than 80 per cent of the slides used a phrase headline. More than 60 per cent of those slides had a bulleted list. This bulleted list may be helpful to you, as the speaker; however, the bulleted list poses significant hurdles for your audience (Doumont, 2005; Garner & Alley, 2011). It may be difficult for your audience to infer the hierarchy and organization of your information. Also, it may be difficult for your audience to pick out the most important points.

In addition, the use of phrase headlines and bulleted lists runs counter to many of multimedia principles described by Mayer (2009). The common phrase-headline, bulleted-list structure leads to too many words on the screen and extraneous information, violating the principle of coherence (Garner & Alley, 2011). As discussed earlier, the coherence principle calls for the elimination of extraneous information, animations, and sounds (Garner et al., 2009; Mayer, 2009). Typically, presenters rely on a text-filled screen while verbally sharing the same information, often reading directly from the screen (Garner & Alley, 2011). This practice is a violation of the redundancy principle, which highlights the importance of avoiding identical written and spoken information (Garner et al., 2009; Mayer, 2009).

Although a bulleted list gives the illusion of organization, it violates the signaling principle (Garner et al., 2009; Mayer, 2009). It does not provide the recommended cues that highlight the importance and organization of the key ideas in a presentation. Also, the phrase headline followed by the bulleted list results in a slide that has a lot of written text and little room for relevant graphics (Garner & Alley, 2011). When graphics are used, they typically repeat something that is already presented in the text or they are merely decorative. This practice runs counter to the multimedia principle which calls for relevant visuals to be coupled with a spoken explanation (Garner et al., 2009; Mayer, 2009).

Based on the common practices of PowerPoint and other slide presentation software outlined above, there is a need for an improved slide-design style. You and your audience could benefit from slides that apply our understanding of information processing and its limitations. As educators and trainers ourselves, we have adopted the Assertion-Evidence slide design style in our teaching and training with positive results and reception.

The Assertion-Evidence structure

The Assertion-Evidence (A-E) slide structure is an alternative format to the common phrase-headline, bulleted-list structure and is based on the cognitive theory of multimedia learning. A-E structure was developed to improve professional presentations in science and engineering. However, it has become popular in a variety of professional fields due to its clear structure that overcomes the defaults of PowerPoint (Alley & Neeley, 2005; Garner & Alley, 2011). The A-E structure has three important assumptions (Alley, 2003). First, you should use slides appropriate for the presentation. When your slide is not contributing to the comprehension or retention of the specific information you are presenting, you should use a blank slide instead. Second, your slides should not have as much information as your handout. These should be two different documents. Third, slides are for your audience, not for you as the speaker. In other words, your slides should not serve as your speaker's notes.

The A-E structure is based on a slide design that was first used at Lawrence Livermore National Lab in the 1980s (Alley, 2003). Michael Alley and his colleagues have since refined the structure to maximize audience comprehension and retention of information (Alley & Neeley, 2005). The first key element of the A-E structure is a left-justified sentence headline that clearly communicates the main point of that scene of the presentation (see Figure 9.1). This strategy has been supported in independent slide-design recommendations by Atkinson (2005) and Doumont (2005). The sentence headline should be an assertion emphasizing the key idea of the relevant part of a talk. Using this assertion has a number of advantages to a phrase headline (Alley, Schreiber, Diesel, Ramsdell, &

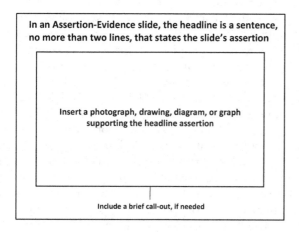

In an Assertion-Evidence slide, the headline is a sentence, no more than two lines, that states the slide's assertion

Insert a photograph, drawing, diagram, or graph supporting the headline assertion

Include a brief call-out, if needed

Figure 9.1 An Assertion-Evidence slide layout.

Borrego, 2007; Alley, Schreiber, Ramsdell, & Muffo, 2006). A full sentence assertion effectively orients your audience to the purpose of your slide. The typographical prominence of the assertion helps to emphasize the most important piece of information on the slide. The left justification allows the viewers eye to take a natural z-pattern that has been encouraged in multimedia research (e.g., Cooke, 2005). Lastly, it helps you to focus the audience on your key ideas, arguments, and assumptions (Alley et al., 2006, 2007).

Initially, it may seem that creating a sentence headline runs counter to the redundancy principle described earlier. However, this sentence summarizes the slide and re-inforces an average of ten spoken sentences (Alley, 2003). The use of this full-sentence assertion results in an average of 20 words displayed per minute, compared with an average of 35 to 40 words displayed per minute on a common practice slide. Therefore, the use of the full-sentence assertion applies the signaling, coherence, and redundancy principles because it focuses and highlights the relationships among key ideas and focuses the information being presented (Garner & Alley, 2013).

Alley et al. (2006) tested the effectiveness of the sentence headline in multiple sections of an introductory, university course. They found that, on average, students who viewed slides with sentence headlines performed 10 per cent better than those who viewed slides with the traditional phrase headline (p <.001). In a second study, they tested the effectiveness of the sentence headline again but added an active learning element (Alley et al., 2007). Similar to the previous study, this study found an average increase in test performance of seven percentage points (p <.001).

After establishing a clear and focused assertion headline, the second key element of the A-E structure is purposeful visual evidence that supports the assertion (Alley, 2003). The visual evidence in the body of the slide can include images, graphs, drawings, diagrams, film clips, small tables, and charts (see Figure 9.1). The type of visual evidence should be heavily dependent on the assertion and should be explanatory and functional rather than decorative (Alley, 2003; Markel, 2009). Using this relevant explanatory visual evidence to support a sentence assertion creates a slide that follows the multimedia technique (Mayer, 2009). Garner and Alley (2011) pointed out that the visual and verbal information should not just reiterate the same information and definitely should not conflict with one another. The visual and verbal information should be complementary, adhering to the modality and redundancy principles that claim multimedia messages should utilize both channels of processing and should avoid redundant text on the slide (Mayer, 2009).

Alley (2003) articulated a number of formatting guidelines for A–E slide design that follow the coherence principle of multimedia learning that calls for the elimination of extraneous details and distractions. These guidelines were refined through the use of critique sessions of more than 400 presentations (Alley & Neeley, 2005). Alley (2003) recommends that the assertion headline is left justified in the top left corner of the slide, does not exceed two lines, and uses a 28-point, bolded, sans-serif font. You should create your slides with simple, high contrast backgrounds (e.g., black or white). Do not use decorative backgrounds because they contain extraneous images that can distract and diminish learning. You can use animations to heighten the signaling principle by drawing the audience's attention to particular parts of the visual evidence. However, it is important to limit animation to the *appear* animation and avoid potentially distracting animation, like *fly in* and *checkerboard* transitions. The more elaborate animations are extraneous and do not adhere to the coherence principle. Overall, your slides should contain only the information and elements necessary to support your verbal explanation. These formatting guidelines follow Doumont's (2005) recommendation to maintain a high signal-to-noise ratio. In other words, you should filter all extraneous details (i.e., noise) out of your slides so that the main message (i.e., signal) reaches your audience without distraction.

Mayer (2009) stated that "understanding occurs when learners are able to build meaningful connections between pictorial and verbal representations" (p. 7). You can facilitate these connections with your oral explanations to explain the assertions and evidence on the screen. You should act as the tour guide, leading your audience through the evidence on the screen and filling in relevant details and explanations. Markel (2009) pointed out that although oral presentations can be done well without slides, using slides without an oral presentation is much less promising. Using eye tracking devices, Bucher and Niemann (2012) found that referring actions, such as spoken cues (e.g., "as seen on the left") and use of a laser pointer, focused an audience's attention on the presentation slide.

A–E structured slides have been shown to have positive effects on the trainer, the presentation, and the audience (Alley, 2003). However, A–E slides take longer to prepare than common practice slides. As a speaker, you must spend time crafting focused assertions and developing helpful, audience-centered visual evidence to support those headlines. However, you will tend to be more familiar with your material because of this additional investment of time. As a result, you can focus more on your audience during the presentation, creating a more engaging delivery. In addition, crafting the assertions forces you to filter out extraneous details and clearly articulate the key ideas of your talk. This tends to result in a more focused and clear presentation (Alley, 2003).

Finally, the A–E slides have been shown to increase audience comprehension and retention of information. Garner and Alley (2013) exposed different groups to either common practice slides or A–E slides, both using the same recorded oral script. Their results support the application of multimedia learning principles through A–E style slides. Learning outcomes were significantly higher in the group that viewed A–E slides than in the group that viewed the common practice slides. The A–E group demonstrated better comprehension of the information, reported fewer misconceptions, showed comparable recall of facts, and reported the use of less mental effort to understand the information than the common practice group. In addition, subjects in the A–E slide condition demonstrated better retention of the information a week-and-a-half after the experiment. A study by Kustritz (2014) further supported that A-E slides increase the audience's retention of information. This study tested an audience a month after a lecture and found that the common practice group had a significant decline in retention of information while the A-E group retained the knowledge they had gained. This suggests that information communicated with the help of A-E slides is successfully reaching long-term memory and learning is taking place. However, if you are relying on the common use of PowerPoint slides in your teaching and training, you may be missing an opportunity to deliver enduring content.

Adoption of alternative slide styles

Our design and use of slides are responsible for some of the potential shortcomings in our presentations. Doumont (2005) stated that PowerPoint is a tool; it is not the product. Several researchers and consultants have advocated for a better informed use of PowerPoint, applying multimedia learning principles to slide design (Alley & Neeley, 2005; Atkinson, 2005; Doumont, 2005; Duarte, 2008; Jennings, 2009; Markel, 2009; Reynolds, 2008). However, it may be challenging for many of us to convert from the practice of using a phrase headline with a bulleted list. Doumont (2005) suggested that business culture is a significant barrier to adopting alternative slide designs. He highlighted the pressures that young professionals face when entering the workforce. These young professionals want to fit in and, therefore, conform to their organization's norms, one of which is often ineffective presentation slides. Time limitations also make it difficult to adopt an informed, yet time consuming use of PowerPoint. In addition, company templates often hamper efforts to improve slide design (Doumont, 2005; Neeley, Alley, Nicometo, & Srajek, 2009). The prospect of adoption can be more promising when an influential person in the organization is supportive of the change (Neeley et al., 2009).

Limitations and future directions

Although there is evidence that the use of a sentence headline supported by visual evidence is more effective than the common practice slide design, most of this research has been conducted with undergraduate students in a traditional educational setting. Furthermore, much of the research has been within the fields of science and engineering. More research is needed to understand the applicability of this slide design style in a variety of other knowledge domains and among a wider range of audiences. Although the A-E slide design style is being used in professional settings, research of its effectiveness with a variety of professional populations is necessary.

In addition, the challenge of changing the status quo needs further consideration. The common practice of a phrase headline and bulleted list is so widely used that audiences and managers expect it (Garner et al., 2009). Even Robert Gaskins, the co-founder of PowerPoint, did not expect children to be using his program in grade schools (Gomes, 2007). In order for alternative slide design styles to be adopted by trainers and employees, barriers in the organizational climate need to be explored and understood better.

In the meantime, you can be an agent of change in your organization by adopting this best practice of slide design and demonstrating your proficiency with the technology. We encourage you to incorporate the Assertion-Evidence principles in your next slide presentation so you can improve your audience's comprehension and retention of your training content. Also, encourage others to adopt the Assertion-Evidence, slide-design style so we can all benefit from more effective presentations.

Summary

Best practices in slide design

- Incorporate more relevant visual and nonverbal information, rather than redundant written information, to support your spoken words.
- Provide a variety of evidence to help learners process and understand new concepts.
- Present verbal information in spoken rather than written form.
- Eliminate extraneous information from presentations (e.g., irrelevant words, pictures).
- Highlight the organization and connections of key pieces of information with visual and verbal cues such as highlighting sections of the slide or stating, "as seen on the left."
- Use labels sparingly and sparsely in proximity to relevant graphics to highlight illustrations.
- Present verbal and relevant visual information simultaneously.
- Use handouts to provide details rather than cluttering slides used for the presentation.
- Write your speaker's notes in a separate document rather than in the presentation slides.
- Use a left-justified, full-sentence headline to clearly state the assertion for each slide.
- Assertions should be 28-point, bolded, sans-serif font and should not exceed two lines.
- Focus on only one assertion per minute of your talk which can include several slides/images.
- Slides should be created with simple, high contrast backgrounds (e.g., black and white).
- Avoid using decorative backgrounds, elaborate animations, or clashing color schemes.
- Use purposeful, explanatory visual evidence that supports the relevant assertion.
- Visual evidence may include images, graphs, drawings, diagrams, film clips, tables, etc.
- Limit animation to the *appear* animation and avoid distracting movements and patterns.
- Visual and verbal information should be complementary and cohesive.
- Explain, verbally, how the visual evidence supports the assertion.
- Only use slides if they directly contribute to the comprehension or retention of the information; a bad slide is worse than no slide at all.

References

Alley, M. (2003). *The craft of scientific presentations* (2nd ed., vol. 41). New York, NY: Springer. http://doi.org/10.1023/B:PHOT.0000027556.80339.c7

Alley, M., & Neeley, K. A. (2005). Rethinking the design of presentation slides: A case for sentence headlines and visual evidence. *Technical Communication, 52*(4), 417–426.

Alley, M., Schreiber, M., Diesel, E., Ramsdell, K., & Borrego, M. (2007). Increased student learning and attendance in resources geology through the combination of sentence-headline slides and active learning measures. *Journal of Geoscience Education, 55*(1), 85–91.

Alley, M., Schreiber, M., Ramsdell, K., & Muffo, J. (2006). How the design of headlines in presentation slides affects audience retention. *Technical Communication, 53*(2), 10. Retrieved from http://www.ingentaconnect.com/content/stc/tc/2006/00000053/00000002/art00007

Atkinson, C. (2005). Beyond bullet points: Using Microsoft PowerPoint to create presentations that inform, motivate, and inspire. Redmond, WA: Microsoft Press.

Baddeley, A. (1999). *Essentials of human memory.* Hove, UK: Psychology Press.

Baddeley, A. (2003). Working memory: Looking back and looking forward. *Nature Reviews Neuroscience, 4*(10), 829–839. http://doi.org/10.1038/nrn1201

Bucher, H.-J., & Niemann, P. (2012). Visualizing science: The reception of PowerPoint presentations. *Visual Communication, 11*(3), 283–306. http://doi.org/10.1177/1470357212446409

Cooke, L. (2005). Eye tracking: How it works and how it relates to usability. *Technical Communication, 52*(4), 456–463. Retrieved from http://www.ingentaconnect.com/content/stc/tc/2005/00000052/00000004/art00006

Cooper, E. (2009). Overloading on slides: Cognitive load theory and Microsoft's slide program PowerPoint. *AACE Journal, 17*, 127–135. Retrieved from http://www.editlib.org/p/28143

Doumont, J.-L. (2005). The cognitive style of PowerPoint: Slides are not all evil. *Technical Communication, 52*(1), 64–70.

Duarte, N. (2008). *Slide:ology*. Sebastopol, CA: O'Reilly Media.

Garner, J. K., & Alley, M. (2011). PowerPoint in the psychology classroom: Lessons from multimedia learning research. *Psychology Learning and Teaching, 10*(2), 95–106. http://doi.org/10.2304/plat.2011.10.2.95

Garner, J. K., Alley, M., Gaudelli, A. F., & Zappe, S. E. (2009). Common use of PowerPoint versus the assertion-evidence structure: A cognitive psychology perspective. *Technical Communication, 56*(4), 331–345.

Garner, J. K., & Alley, M. P. (2013). How the design of presentation slides affects audience comprehension: A case for the assertion–evidence approach. *International Journal Engineering Education, 29*(6), 1564–1579.

Gaskins, R. (2012). *Sweating bullets: Notes about inventing PowerPoint*. http://doi.org/10.1007/s13398-014-0173-7.2

Gomes, L. (2007, June 20). PowerPoint turns 20, as its creators ponder a dark side to success. *The Wall Street Journal*. Retrieved from http://www.wsj.com/articles/SB118228116940840904

Jennings, A. (2009). Creating marketing slides for engineering presentations. *Technical Communication, 56*(1), 14–27.

Kustritz, M. V. R. (2014). Effect of differing PowerPoint slide design on multiple-choice test scores for assessment of knowledge and retention in a theriogenology course. *Journal of Veterinary Medical Education, 41*(3), 311–318. http://doi.org/10.3138/jvme.0114-004R

Markel, M. (2009). Exploiting verbal-visual synergy in presentation slides. *Technical Communication, 56*(2), 122–131. Retrieved from http://search.ebscohost.com/login.aspx?direct=true&db=ufh&AN=40102031&site=ehost-live

Mayer, R. E. (2005). Cognitive theory of multimedia learning. In R. E. Mayer (ed.), *The Cambridge handbook of multimedia learning* (pp. 31–48). New York, NY: Cambridge University Press.

Mayer, R. E. (2009). *Multimedia learning* (2nd ed.). New York, NY: Cambridge University Press.

Mayer, R. E., & Anderson, R. B. (1991). Animations need narrations: An experimental test of a dual-coding hypothesis. *Journal of Educational Psychology, 83*(4), 484–490. http://doi.org/10.1037/0022-0663.83.4.484

Mayer, R. E., & Anderson, R. B. (1992). The instructive animation: Helping students build connections between words and pictures in multimedia learning. *Journal of Educational Psychology, 84*(4), 444–452. http://doi.org/10.1037/0022-0663.84.4.444

Mayer, R. E., & Johnson, C. I. (2008). Revising the redundancy principle in multimedia learning. *Journal of Educational Psychology, 100*(2), 380–386. http://doi.org/10.1037/0022-0663.100.2.380

Mayer, R. E., & Moreno, R. (1998). A split-attention effect in multimedia learning: Evidence for dual processing systems in working memory. *Journal of Educational Psychology, 90*(2), 312–320. http://doi.org/10.1037//0022-0663.90.2.312

Mayer, R. E., & Moreno, R. (2002). Aids to computer-based multimedia learning. *Learning and Instruction, 12*(1), 107–119. http://doi.org/10.1016/S0959-4752(01)00018-4

Mayer, R. E., Moreno, R., Boire, M., & Vagge, S. (1999). Maximizing constructivist learning from multimedia communications by minimizing cognitive load. *Journal of Educational Psychology, 91*(4), 638–643. http://doi.org/10.1037/0022-0663.91.4.638

Mayer, R. E., & Sims, V. K. (1994). For whom is a picture worth a thousand words? Extensions of a dual coding theory of multimedia learning. *Journal of Educational Psychology, 86*(3), 389–401. http://doi.org/10.1037/0022-0663.86.3.389

Moreno, R., & Mayer, R. E. (1999). Cognitive principles of multimedia learning: The role of modality and contiguity. *Journal of Educational Psychology, 91*(2), 358–368. http://doi.org/10.1037/0022-0663.91.2.358

Neeley, K. A., Alley, M., Nicometo, C. G., & Srajek, L. C. (2009). Challenging the common practice of PowerPoint at an institution: Lessons from instructors. *Technical Communication, 56*(4), 346–360.

Paivio, A. (1986). *Mental representations: A dual coding approach.* New York, NY: Oxford University Press.

Reynolds, G. (2008). *Presentation zen.* Berkeley, CA: New Riders.

Rogers, E. M. (2003). *Diffusion of innovations* (5th ed.). New York, NY: Free Press.

Simons, T. (2004). Does PowerPoint make you stupid? *Presentations, 18*(3), 24–31.

Sweller, J. (2005). Implications of cognitive load theory for multimedia learning. In R. E. Mayer (ed.), *The Cambridge handbook of multimedia learning* (pp. 19–30). New York, NY: Cambridge University Press.

Thielsch, M. T., & Perabo, I. (2012). Use and evaluation of presentation software. *Technical Communication, 59*(2), 112–123. Retrieved from http://www.scopus.com/inward/record.url?eid= 2-s2.0-84865482234&partnerID=40&md5=9626854a9f9350306f72826c73cb97b9

Tufte, E. R. (2003). *The cognitive style of PowerPoint.* Cheshire, CT: Graphics Press LLC. http://doi.org/10.1027/1016-9040.2.3.258

Vik, G. N. (2004). Breaking bad habits: Teaching effective PowerPoint use to working graduate students. *Business Communication Quarterly, 67*, 225–228.

Chapter 10

Training in a flash

Considerations of learning outcomes and storytelling in building webinar training

Donna M. Elkins, Robin Hinkle, and Hope Zoeller

Abstract

Technology allows organizations with shrinking professional development budgets to provide less expensive and more time-conscious training to employees. Creating webinars is a practical delivery method to meet these training needs if trainers have developed technical proficiency. Through a case study approach using a delivered webinar, this chapter provides trainers with a foundation in adult learning theory to create effective learning outcomes and in storytelling to build effective delivery method in the webinar modality.

Due to shrinking training budgets, many organizations are looking for inexpensive and time-conscious ways to provide training to employees. The Association for Talent Development: State of the Industry Report website (2017) states that organizations spent an average of $1,252 per employee in 2015 on direct learning expenditures such as the design, administration, delivery costs, and salaries of staff associated with learning programs. Typically, professionals interested in expanding their skills or learning a new topic would self-select in-person training or online options depending on their preferences. Recent decreases in the amount of corporate funds available for professional development and travel have created fewer options and professionals may be forced to learn using delivery formats that are not their first choice (Buxton & DeMuth, 2012; Czeropski, 2012). One option that has become easier and more cost effective with technological advances is to create short "webinars" or online seminars to provide training on a variety of topics. Webinars may also save time and provide greater scheduling flexibility (Ho, 2016). This chapter explores incorporating one of the National Communication Association (NCA) Training and Development Division best practices, the best practice of demonstrating technology proficiency, to address these communication training challenges in the specific context of creating and delivering webinars.

Learning challenges in webinar training

Delivery methods for webinar training, even those with a goal of providing practical communication skill training, vary widely from slides to streaming video to interactive chatting (Lande, 2011). Though there has been a proliferation of webinars, trainers often struggle to present effectively through this delivery method. Communication trainers must make difficult decisions about how to distinguish and communicate key concepts of complicated communication skills in a limited timeframe (sometimes with no visual presence), appeal to a diverse audience of adult learners, and assess how viewers apply what they have learned, while also meeting the expectations and goals of the organization for which they are providing the training.

The term "webinar" is credited to Eric R. Kolb, who in 1998 derived the new term from two words, "web," a common reference to the Internet, and "seminar" or interactive meeting (Lande, 2011, p. 6). David Godfrey (2009) of the American Bar Association has written about webinars as "short attention-span theater" that require short, engaging bursts of a single story much like a prime-time television sitcom (p. 30). Most webinars are short-term, usually a length of 60 to 90 minutes. In the past individuals used a telephone to listen and a computer to watch slides or other visuals (Lande, 2011). Technology improvements have created more and more options for live-streaming through computer speakers and producing live interaction between the webinar trainer and the audience. However, many webinars are recorded and watched by participants after the live event has taken place.

Despite popularity and proliferation of webinars as a training tool, Lande (2011) found a lack of serious research and scholarly consideration of the best practices for training in this venue. That finding was confirmed by the authors of this chapter in a more recent search. Not only is research lacking, but experienced webinar trainers and professionals often publish contradictory or only surface-level information about their practices.

Studies comparing computer and Web-based instruction with live classroom instruction on college campuses have generally concluded that there is little difference in the learning or satisfaction of students. In a study of pharmacy students, Buxton (2014) found no difference in scores on identical final examinations comparing campus-based and remote students. Others have argued that the individualized and analytical opportunities in online instruction actually increase students' attainment of learning outcomes over the traditional face-to-face classroom (Gupta & Anson, 2014). Studies examining the factors of satisfaction and ability to apply what was learned in the professional training environment in-person versus online have shown similar results (Buxton & DeMuth, 2012; Czeropski, 2012). The individual student's level of interest in computers also influences the amount of interaction and activity with which they engage the learning process online (Sansone et al., 2011).

The following sections of this chapter are designed to assist trainers in developing habits and principles of technology proficiency for webinar creation. The chapter reviews considerations when establishing learning outcomes for adult learners, storytelling as a training method, and presents a case study that demonstrates successful integration of many of these principles in a web-based training environment.

Learning outcomes and adult learners

Cyril O. Houle began research in the 1950s to explore the differences between teaching adult learners and children. His results, which have been expanded upon over the pursuant years, pointed to three motivations that led adults to continue their education (as reported in Knowles, Holton, & Swanson, 2012). First, goal-oriented learners use education to reach clear objectives they have for themselves. Second, activity-oriented learners take part because they enjoy the process of learning no matter the content or purpose. Third are those who are learning-oriented and seek knowledge for the sake of knowing, apart from any practical use or application of the content of the learning (Knowles, Holton, & Swanson, 2012). Adults are more engaged by what Malcolm Knowles has termed the "androgogical model" than by typical pedagogical models. This model includes six factors that improve learning for adults: (1) Adults need to know why they are learning something before they begin; (2) adults have a sense of being responsible and in control of their own lives so they do not react well to educators who treat them like children; (3) adults come into learning situations with a volume of experiences; (4) adults have a readiness to learn based on need to perform in real-life situations; (5) adults have a life-centered (sometimes called a problem-centered or task-centered) approach to learning; (6) finally, adults have external motivators (promotions, higher salaries, job requirements) and internal motivators (quality of life, self-esteem, increased life and job satisfaction) (Brockett, 2016; Daly & Vangelisti, 2003; Knowles, Holton, & Swanson, 2012).

Unlike typical school teaching experiences, trainers who are working with adults in the workplace are called upon to see the process of teaching differently. Though the trainer may be working with a captive audience due to required attendance by the organization, if the training session is to be beneficial, the trainer must prepare learners to participate and develop their own expectations or outcomes for the training event (Kirwan, 2013; Knowles, Holton, & Swanson, 2012). The training may take place synchronously, but in attempts to meet employee schedules, the training is often asynchronous with little to no interaction between participants themselves or between trainer and participants (Buxton, 2014; Czeropski, 2012). In a short-term webinar format this means that the trainer may have limited ability to evaluate the needs of the learners who will view the webinar. Since the webinar may well be viewed by a wide-ranging audience across time and locations, the learning outcomes established for the training should be clearly outlined for anyone who may take part.

Establishing the learning outcomes for a webinar training will guide the creation of the content, create a learning climate for those taking part, and provide a way for individual learners, the trainer, and the organizational partners to evaluate the effectiveness of the webinar. Webinars give little opportunity to practice or build on the content that is transmitted, therefore having clearly defined and well-written learning outcomes is crucial for the participants' learning and the practice of learning to continue after the webinar is completed.

Benjamin Bloom and his colleagues are recognized for developing a taxonomy of learning which distinguished cognitive (knowledge acquisition and increased understanding), affective (changes in feelings and values), and behavioral (changes in behavior and skill acquisition) domains of learning (Bloom, Engelhart, Furst, Hill, & Krathwohl, 1956). Learning outcomes are generally written to impact affective, cognitive, and/or behavioral learning, with well-established acknowledgement that there are positive relationships between cognitive and affective learning (Knowles, Holton, & Swanson, 2012). Behavioral learning is also associated positively with affective and cognitive learning as well as with the behaviors of the instructor (Lane, 2015; Weber, Martin, & Myers, 2011). Typically, "training focuses more on the behavioral learning domain, whereas education typically emphasizes the cognitive learning domain" (Beebe, 2007, p. 250). Training often emphasizes doing and achieving a certain level of skill attainment, many times focused on performing a specific task in a specific step-by-step fashion for a specific job. However, training has grown to encompass more affective and cognitive outcomes over time. This is especially true in the field of communication where training often focuses on the affective and cognitive learning domains, with a goal of inspiring behavioral outcomes in the trainee (Lane, 2015; Beebe, 2007).

A trainer creating a webinar must make clear decisions about what specific outcomes he or she is hoping to achieve because the decisions about whether the training is intended to change cognitive, affective, and/or behavioral outcomes will drive the instructional model (Brockett, 2016). This does not alleviate the need for the trainer to understand adult learning theory and view his or her role less as a lecturer but more as a facilitator. Effective trainers should follow this advice: It is better to get a message out of people than to put one in them. Adult learners bring their own experiences to the training session; they also want to focus on real problems that are in their literal or metaphorical 'in basket' or on their 'to do' list.

(Beebe, 2007, pp. 250–251)

In webinars where trainers may or may not have direct interaction with their trainees, clearly established learning outcomes can motivate the individual learners by connecting to their job-related goals. Carol Sansone and colleagues found

students [are] more active in how they used the online lesson, particularly when the initial framing of the lesson made explicit connections for how the skills could be used in real life. When provided information that enhanced goals-defined motivation, therefore, students with higher individual interest were even more likely to regulate the experience.... These results suggest that individual interest may increase the importance of the situational experience while working toward the goals, rather than making the experience less important.

(2011, p. 208)

Adult learners attending training are motivated by individual goals, but are also motivated, engaged, and pushed to use prior knowledge by a training experience that proves to be "interesting" (Daly & Vangelisti, 2003, p. 876).

Storytelling as a training method

Organizations are brimming with stories and the use of them in training settings is not new. Stories play a critical role in efficiently communicating many important organizational concepts. Ideas, values, and lessons are all made more believable and memorable through effective storytelling. Leaders have long conveyed their vision for the future of the organization, cautioned against the dangers of the status quo, and inspired their employees to change through stories. Statistics can seem powerful to the teller, but the listener often forgets them immediately. People remember a good story. Listeners take another person's story and unconsciously relate it to their own experience. This personalization is what makes the story memorable (Morgan & Dennehy, 1997). The story often centers on a particular problem and the meaning behind the problem can be explored or presented to the audience through questions (Kirwan, 2013). The amount of information corporations attempt to instill into their leaders to increase their effectiveness can be overwhelming and prohibitively expensive, in terms of resources for development and the time it takes for the leader to attend the training. Vivid stories that entertain, evoke emotion, create empathy, and inspire can take time to develop and to tell, but this time does not compare with the amount of time it would take another person to relive the scenario. The goal is for the listener to take away the lesson from the story without actually experiencing the situation. To this end, stories provide an abbreviated way of learning (Tyler, 2007).

Storytelling is a subjective social process using a natural medium that creates a shared purpose. The National Storytelling Network ("What is storytelling?," n.d.) defines storytelling as an interaction between words and actions to tell a story that allows the listener to summon their imagination, past experiences, and beliefs. The completed story forms in the mind of the listener, who, therefore, becomes the co-creator of the story. While storytelling is steeped in oral tradition within cultural groups, stories can be told across a variety of modern technological platforms, including web-based (Chen, Dong, Ball-Rokeach, Parks, & Huang, 2012) and digital media (Alexander, 2011). Developing content for use in multiple locations and in different contexts improves the return on investment in the training. Allowing employees to access training at their choosing, either because they have the time to devote to it or because they require the information just-in-time, increases the likelihood the lessons will be retained and applied. With the latest technology, organizations are able to capitalize on the expediency of storytelling as a management tool to expand beyond their physical boundaries and trainers have the mandate to select and adapt stories normally used in the classroom (Ho, 2016).

Although a number of studies exist that support storytelling as instrumental in disseminating information (Boje, 2006), promoting cultural norms (Breuer, 1998; Wilkins 1984), and supporting business goals within organizations (Wacker & Silverman, 2003), there is little guidance for trainers to incorporate storytelling into their virtual training efforts. Bower (2011) cautions against the assumption that successful face-to-face approaches simply transfer to the online environment. Most trainers find delivery via web-conferencing in general to be an "intense and demanding experience" as their attempts to replicate the learning atmosphere of their face-to-face classrooms fail (Cornelius, 2014). The addition of storytelling compounds the difficulty of training online. The lack of visual feedback from the audience prevents the trainer from gauging the effect of the story in real time and determining the need for spontaneous alterations. In the absence of immediate and interactive feedback, Mezirow's (1991) requirements for a rational discourse provide a framework for effective storytelling. He discusses the seven conditions a learner must experience: information that is accurate and complete, freedom from coercion and self-deception, the ability to weigh evidence and evaluate arguments, the ability to reflect, openness to differing perspectives, opportunity to participate, and acceptance of a rational, informed, and objective consensus as a legitimate validity test.

In Mezirow's list there are a few items beyond the trainer's control. It is difficult to know if the audience is open to differing opinions or willing to accept a rational conclusion. For developing a story for online delivery, there is the challenge of giving the learner an opportunity to participate. Although many virtual training sessions are delivered synchronously, the ability to record the session and view it at a more convenient time is a major advantage of the delivery method. This precludes the learner from commenting or asking questions. If the story is concrete, with real people and events, and set in a recognizable place and time, then the learner's imaginative ability to live the story along with the teller plays the role of participation. In fact, this may connect the learner to the organization's philosophy and culture in a more profound and personal way. However, this places the added burden on the trainer as the storyteller to have the linguistic and presentational prowess to evoke the imagination of the learner to the extent the learner can live the story vicariously. Morgan and Dennehy (1997) provide guidance for trainers to determine if their stories possess elements that will make them resonate in the organizational context and persist in the learner's memory. This guidance is summarized for quick reference in Table 10.1.

Table 10.1 Checklist for characteristics of a good story

Concrete	Is the story about real people, events, and actions?
	Is it during a time that the learner can identify with?
	Does it connect to the organization's mission, philosophy, or culture?
Common Knowledge	Do most people in the organization know about the story?
	Does the story provide guidance about the organization's mission, philosophy, or culture?
Believable	Can the learner accept that the story is true of the organization?
Social Contract	Does the story describe how things are done or not done in the organization?
	Can the learner become socialized to the organization's norms without having to make costly mistakes?

Chip and Dan Heath (2007) in their book *Made to Stick* argue stories are one of the key factors to making messages memorable because stories aid in visualization. For athletes, doing nothing more than imagining a performance through mental practice produces about two thirds of the benefits of actual physical practice. Heath and Heath (2007) argue that good stories are simulations that provide a context which information delivered in a non-narrative form cannot do. They coined the term "Velcro theory of memory" (p. 214) to explain why stories make information stick. Based on their research, they argue that the most impactful stories follow one of three plots – the Challenge Plot (overcoming a challenge to succeed); the Connection Plot (bridging a gap to form a relationship); or the Creativity Plot (using innovation to solve a problem or make a breakthrough).

Webinar case study – What are you serving as a leader?

To assist trainers in developing skills and principles that will lead them to technology proficiency in the creation of webinars, the remainder of the chapter provides a case example of developing and delivering a webinar. The case follows the webinar through creation, presentation delivery, audience reaction, and follow-up. The webinar used in this case was a one-hour training created and delivered by Hope Zoeller, founder and president of HOPE (Helping Other People Excel), LLC, a firm that specializes in leadership development. It is titled "What are you serving as a leader?" and has been delivered to various organizations.[1] The case study presented here describes the webinar as delivered specifically to 191 leaders in the senior care industry.

One of the largest challenges of the webinar format in its synchronous or asynchronous form is that the audience may be multi-tasking in a myriad of ways while listening to the webinar: carrying on conversations, working on projects, checking email, surfing the web, or doing a variety of other personal or work tasks. In many cases, the learning environment for the distance learner will be much different than it would be if the adult learner traveled to attend a live educational event. These distractions may not be as conducive to learning as those associated with classroom-type instruction (Buxton & DeMuth, 2012). Linda Lande (2011, p. 7) reports two surveys published in *Training* magazine that question the efficacy of training in the webinar format. In a short article published in *Training* in February 2010, survey results showed that 66 per cent of participants found webinar training to be effective, but that was 12 per cent lower than those who had the same training in a traditional face-to-face setting. The researchers in these articles point to three key areas that might create the difference for successful webinars: pre-work, participation, and post-work (Lande, 2011).

Pre-work for webinar development

Pre-work involves designing a webinar that has clear learning outcomes that highlight the benefits to the audience and the goals of the organization. Even choosing a title that draws participants in is a part of the pre-work.

The topic for this webinar case was chosen by the organization hosting the training from a list of courses provided by and developed by HOPE. Training outcomes are often focused on changing behaviors (Beebe, 2007). In a short amount of time, it can be difficult if not impossible to impact behavior in a substantial way without building cognitive and affective outcomes first, even though the ultimate goal is often to inspire behavioral outcomes in the trainee (Lane, 2015; Beebe, 2007). The trainer who is creating a short webinar must make clear decisions about what specific behavioral outcome is desired and build a short instructional path to get there. The learning outcomes in this case included three cognitive learning outcomes that build to one behavioral outcome:

- Define what it means to be a servant leader (cognitive).
- Define the differences between a self-serving leader and a servant leader (cognitive).
- Identify the seven traits of a true servant leader (cognitive).
- Assess your own effectiveness as a servant leader (behavioral).

The pre-work involved several conference calls with the hosting organization, so that Zoeller could better understand the leadership challenges and needs of the participants and customize the content accordingly. The hosting organization, one which provides hiring software to those in the senior care industry, offered this webinar to their clients, so responsibility for recruiting participants and handling all scheduling logistics fell on the organization rather than the trainer.

In an effort to prepare and engage the participants of the webinar before it began, a pre-course handout was created and sent in advance to the senior care leaders registered to attend the webinar. The content included a self-assessment of the seven traits of a servant leader to be presented during the webinar. The senior care leaders were asked to self-identify their perception of personal success regarding each trait. To extend and encourage actual practical follow-up from the webinar, the trainer challenged the senior care leaders to share this self-assessment after the webinar with their teams to confirm whether their self-perception was in alignment with that of their teams.

Also included on the handout were questions for the senior care leaders to explore beyond the webinar to help them put the traits discussed in the webinar into action in their everyday leadership practices and reach the behavioral outcome established for the training (Zoeller, 2016). The questions included:

- Do you want the input of others, or do you just want them to agree and validate your opinions and ideas?
- Do you truly listen to what other people are saying with their work and actions, as well as what they're not saying? Do you listen to understand, or do you just listen to respond? Are you perceived as having listened?

- Do you communicate effectively through your words and behavior? Are your words and actions aligned? Do you "walk the talk"?
- Do you take time for regular personal reflection as a way to grow? Do you seek feedback from others to ensure others' perceptions are in alignment with your own?
- Do you seek challenges for personal and professional growth? Are you continually seeking to learn and develop yourself and others?
- Do you advocate for others even when it means you may not get what you want?
- Are you willing to put your own personal agenda aside for the betterment of others?

In addition, questions for the senior care leaders to discuss with their teams before or after the webinar were included to provide additional assistance in reaching the behavioral outcome, such as (Zoeller, 2016):

- What obstacles are in the way of performing your job to the best of your ability?
- How would you assess the feedback you're getting about how you are performing?
- What needs do you have that are not being met?
- If you could change just one thing about your job, what would it be?
- What aspects of your job performance do you believe you need to improve upon?
- What frustrates you most about your job?
- What ideas do you have to help improve your department? The organization?
- How would you assess your job satisfaction?
- How would you assess my performance as a leader?
- How specifically could I improve as a leader?
- What would you do differently if you were in my role?
- How can I better support you?
- How could the organization better support you?

Table 10.2 synthesizes adult learning principles from the model provided by Brockett (2016) and Knowles, Holton, and Swanson (2012) and the way these principles were applied in this webinar.

Even with pre-work, it is challenging to ensure those individuals who sign up for a webinar will actually attend and complete the entire webinar, especially at the scheduled synchronous time. Of the 399 senior care providers who pre-registered for this webinar, 208 did not attend or log in to the live webinar. However, of the 191 who were documented as live attendees, some attended as a group rather than as an individual which was evidenced by responses to questions during the event where attendees indicated they had more than one person listening to the webinar with them. Therefore, it is always challenging for a trainer to gauge with certainty the number of individuals in the webinar audience and the extent of their participation.

Fostering participation during webinar delivery

After reviewing results from multiple webinar studies, Lande (2011) concluded, "Moving face-to-face presentations directly to the webinar venue without considering the audience's perspectives and making the adjustments necessary to engage and hold their attention are destined to fail" (p. 7). Others have cautioned about taking face-to-face training online as well (Bower, 2011; Cornelius, 2014). Common complaints about webinars from participants and trainers include the lightness of material, lack of

Table 10.2 Applying adult learning theory in webinar pre-work, participation, and post-work

Factors in Adult Learning Model	Application in this Webinar
Identify why learning is important before you begin	• Trainer interacted with hosting organization leaders to plan realistic outcomes • Trainer established clear cognitive learning outcomes that lead to one behavioral change outcome
Make attendees responsible and in control of their own choices about how to incorporate what they learn	• Trainer supplied pre-webinar handout of questions for self-assessment to assist attendees with ideas and options for reaching a personal behavioral change outcome • Trainer supplied pre-webinar handout with questions attendees could choose to use with their teams after the conclusion of the webinar to reach behavioral change outcome • Follow-up question required attendees to choose a characteristic they want to continue building (reinforcing behavioral change outcome)
Lean on the attendees' own volume of experiences	• During storytelling, trainer encouraged attendees to consider similar situations they had experienced • Trainer included time for attendees to voice questions and experiences of their own at close of webinar (could be done at points throughout the webinar)
Connect the learning content to the performance needs in real-life situations	• Trainer customized terminology for this specific work industry • Trainer related leadership stories told during the webinar to specific workplace needs in this industry • Trainer supplied a handout of questions that could be applied by attendees individually or with their work teams that included specific job-focused questions
Present a problem-centered or task-centered approach	• Stories told about each characteristic of a servant leader were workplace experience stories that addressed a problem encountered and in some cases solved • Trainer encouraged attendees to consider problems or tasks they were trying to accomplish with their teams specifically through questions in webinar and handout
Link to external motivators (promotions, higher salaries, job requirements) and internal motivators (quality of life, self-esteem, increased life and job satisfaction)	• Host organization and the industry itself required training hours for certification of leaders in these positions • Trainer's handout questions and questions during the webinar required attendees to consider ways to increase their team motivation and satisfaction • Topic related to personal life goals as well as workplace accomplishments

student-to-student interaction, and the difficulty in teaching hands-on skills or leading complicated activities using this modality (Lande, 2011). Trainers should not try to act as both moderator and trainer because of the frustration the audience can quickly develop if technology goes awry. Having a moderator who can monitor incoming messages, handle any technology questions, and provide support so the trainer can stay on task is important.

Engaging the audience is another challenge and one that trainers new to this modality may struggle to carry out effectively. As the webinar progresses the moderator and trainer can generally see people leaving the event.

> Limiting your topic is critically important …. One way to approach it is to think of a Webinar as a prime-time television sitcom—a short, single story presented in 6 to 10 minute segments. Plan to communicate your message in short segments and include "commercial breaks" in the form of polls and quizzes to break the program up.
>
> (Godfrey, 2009, p. 30)

Questions that require the audience to do something like click a button rather than always write a chat response are crucial to keeping everyone involved (Lande, 2011).

In the "What are you serving as a leader" webinar, responses from the audience were limited to questions or comments posted via chat at the end of the webinar and may have limited engagement from attendees.

Gathering complete and accurate data from a host organization or webinar vendor is also a challenge. In this case, the organization tracked attendance during the webinar, but most likely due to technical problems was only able to report details on the attendance of 127 of the 191 live attendees. This report shows six attendees left the webinar before 15 minutes. Another five left before 20 minutes. Following that, the next seven left between 41–45 minutes. Five more left between 46–49 minutes. Another 12 left near the end between 50 and 54 minutes. The remaining attendees (83 or 65 per cent of those tracked) stayed in the webinar for the full training (55–57 minutes). Therefore, 75 per cent of those tracked remained for the bulk of the training (at least 50 minutes). Completion rate in webinars is a problem. As mentioned earlier, distractions for those engaged in webinar training are many. Often attendees are still in their typical workspace which means they are facing work or other online distractions. Therefore, it is not unusual for attendees to leave early or to be away from the training even if technically it appears they are present. Looking at the positive evaluations for this training provided in Table 10.3, it can be surmised the applicable value of the content and the topic engagement were factors in maintaining the majority of attendees for the full training.

Pace is also a challenge for webinar trainers, requiring that they not spend too much time on one slide or visual. Limiting the amount of text on slides is as important in webinar presentations as in typical in-person presentations. Voice and vocal delivery that include passion and emphasis as well as tone and word choice that keeps the audience interested are also important as the trainer does not have physical presence, body language, and facial expressions to play this role (Lande, 2011).

The delivery methods for Zoeller's "What are you serving as a leader?" included slides throughout, trainer storytelling, and interactive chatting at the end of the webinar to address specific content-related questions. A moderator introduced the topic and trainer at the beginning of the webinar and facilitated the question and answer session at the conclusion. Because the trainer had no visual presence with the audience, the slides were designed to be engaging and thought-provoking for the adult learner. Minimal words were used on each slide and included a picture relating to the content. The trainer also created the acronym SERVANT to communicate the traits of a servant leader and provide a mnemonic device for attendees to remember (Zoeller, 2016).

To engage the audience through storytelling, the trainer shared a story about various leaders that she had coached or worked for who demonstrated each one of the traits. She also included examples of leaders who did not demonstrate these traits and shared how it limited their ability to successfully lead themselves and their teams. This storytelling provided a continuous single story presented in short segments to hold interest throughout the training (Godfrey, 2009) and was used to impact the memory of attendees, as well as impart complex ideas in a concrete way during the short time frame (Heath & Heath, 2007; Tyler, 2007).

As previously discussed, stories play a vital role, even more so in leadership development, in communicating important learning points and helping participants more easily remember them. Also, stories allow for learners to live vicariously through another person's experiences and challenges of leading. One leader's hindsight can become another leader's foresight. Relying on Mezirow's (1991) requirements for a rational discourse (as described earlier) to provide a framework for effective storytelling in this case, the information in this story line was accurate and complete, free from coercion, and allowed attendees to weigh evidence and evaluate arguments. Listeners could participate by reflecting on their own leadership experiences and move toward a rational, informed, and objective consensus as to how a servant leader behaves as opposed to other types of leaders through this use of story.

When writing learning outcomes for the webinar, it is important to consider the specific needs of the audience as much as possible, especially if designing the training for a specific organization or industry (Daly & Vangelisti, 2003; Sansone et al., 2011). As discussed earlier, beginning with the behavioral outcome that is most desired, the trainer can establish cognitive and affective outcomes that build to that ending point. For the "What are you serving as a leader?" webinar, the trainer also customized the content to include language appropriate for the specific audience. For example, in the senior care industry customers are referred to as "residents." The trainer also included in the examples of the seven traits of a servant leader specific challenges of being a senior care provider such as a higher than average turnover rate for certain positions in their facilities. The trainer stressed the importance of living these servant leader traits, so employees would be motivated and encouraged to stay with the organization and most importantly be committed to providing quality care to their residents.

Post-work: evaluation and follow up

Evaluations of a webinar or any training can provide two important functions. One is to encourage participants to continue their thoughts about and implementation of what they have learned through self-assessment. The second is that the trainer can use the information to inform and improve on this particular webinar or others for future delivery.

For an evaluation after the webinar to draw the best return rate, the questions should be selected carefully. Ambiguity in evaluation questions leads to misinterpretation. Asking questions that are too complex or require too much thought in answering leads to cognitive overload and can discourage participants from responding (Lande, 2011). Only asking questions that can be helpful for improvement, either to prompt the attendee to complete next steps or to help the trainer prepare for the future, is also important (Hart, 2004). Following up with evaluations, copies of materials, contact information, and maybe a summary of the webinar is post-work that provides another opportunity to reinforce the relationships and reiterate the important facts from the training (Lande, 2011).

A follow-up survey was sent online to many of those who attended the "What are you serving as a leader?" webinar. Questions on the survey included (Zoeller, 2016):

- As a senior care leader, which of the seven traits could you be better at serving?
- How would you rate the content of the webinar?
- How would you rate the appropriateness of this content for senior care?
- Would you like additional information on senior care hiring and best practices?

By asking attendees to respond with a trait needing improvement on the follow-up evaluation, it is ensured that those responding at least consider how the information could be applied to their own work, thus engaging cognitive and behavioral learning. Table 10.3 provides results for the questions about the content and appropriateness of the webinar for those who attended.

The content of the webinar received a "better than average" or "excellent" rating from more than 90 per cent of the respondents as did the appropriateness of this training for senior care. Of the 104 who responded to the follow-up evaluation, 25 (24 per cent) requested further information on senior care hiring and best practices to continue their learning. However, a limitation of this evaluation is that there is no way to measure if the audience practiced any of the seven traits of a servant leader presented in the webinar and as a result experienced improved performance with their teams. The evaluation respondents also do not represent the majority of people who originally signed up (only 191 or 48 per cent of the 399 who signed up actually attended for any length of time and only 106 or 55 per cent of those who attended for any length of time completed

Table 10.3 Responses on follow-up evaluation

Evaluation Question	Excellent	Better than Average	Average	Total Respondents
How would you rate the content of the webinar?	49 46%	53 50%	4 4%	106
How do you rate the appropriateness of this content for senior care?	63 61%	33 32%	8 7%	104

Note: The information from this table is taken directly from the raw evaluation responses provided to the trainer after the webinar was complete. The total number of attendees at the webinar was 191 which means the follow-up evaluation had a completion rate of 55 per cent.

the evaluation). The evaluation was completed by some attendees who did not stay for at least 50 minutes (as only 95 attendees participated for at least that amount of time). Many attendees who have negative experiences may leave the webinar very early and not respond to the follow-up evaluation. The percentage of attendees and the numbers of those who completed the webinar highlight the challenges trainers face in this delivery modality. However, for this particular webinar, most of those who responded to the evaluation did report an excellent or better than average experience indicating that their affective response to the topic content was positive. The results also indicate that a significant number of those completing the evaluation (93 per cent) found the training's information appropriate for their work needs. As such, the webinar was considered substantial in its Return on Investment and value to the host organizations' goals. This type of feedback along with the percentage of those attending and completing the webinar are crucial pieces of information for trainers to continue improving content and delivery strategies for future training.

Conclusion

Presenting content in an online webinar includes a wide array of challenges and requires that trainers demonstrate the best practice of technology proficiency. Trainers are often faced with an asynchronous audience so participation is limited. The audience may be distracted by many other things in their working environment. Speaking about a substantial topic in a way that leads to behavioral outcomes in such a short timeframe is difficult. Technology provides another layer of separation and obstacle between the trainer and attendee that may limit the interaction and the desired learning. Simply taking a face-to-face training session into the webinar delivery format is likely to fail.

To be successful in this delivery mode, trainers need to engage in pre-work with their prospective audience or the organization for which they are training. A large component of this pre-work is writing specific learning outcomes relevant to adult learners (Daly & Vangelisti, 2003) that are clearly communicated and set the stage for the "short-term theater" (Godfrey, 2009) that will engage and hold the interest of the attendees. To successfully train adults, the trainer needs to be aware of adult learning theory and be sure that attendees' experience, real-life task needs, and motivations are considered throughout the content presentation. Perhaps the most effective way to engage the audience is through storytelling that will garner and hold attendees' attention while they are faced with many possible distractions. As this case demonstrates, however, storytelling as a training method resulted in about 75 per cent of attendees staying for the bulk of the training (at least 50 minutes). Finally, the trainer must partner with the organization holding the training to follow-up with an evaluation of the webinar that again prompts attendees to apply what was learned.

It is impossible in one chapter to give a thorough perspective of all elements required for presenting an effective webinar. Vendor selection, with vendor variance in media richness and technical limitations, is an important consideration not addressed here. The role of the host organization, the organization's openness and expectations for the trainer and for the attendees, are also important considerations.

More rigorous study about conducting training using the webinar modality is needed. Trainers themselves are best situated to collect data and evaluate best practices for training using webinar technology. Though it is possible to look to the research conducted in traditional classroom settings which compares face-to-face and online learning as one source of information, the need is great to further understand best practices when training adults in the online world. Adult learning theory and the difference between training and classroom instruction highlights the different expectations of these two venues (Beebe, 2007). As training budgets continue to decrease and technology proficiency continues to increase, the call for webinars as a training delivery system will only increase as well. This chapter explored the NCA Training and Development Division best practice of demonstrating technology proficiency to address communication training challenges in the specific context of creating webinars. Trainers using webinars effectively have a robust opportunity to expand understanding of this growing modality through continued collecting and sharing of data and experience with other scholars and trainers.

Note

1 *"What are you serving as a leader?"* is certified for one recertification credit hour toward PHR and SPHR recertification through the Human Resource Certification Institute (HRCI) and approved by the National Continuing Education Review Service (NCERS) of the National Association of Long Term Care Administrator Boards (NAB) for 1.00 clock hours.

References

Alexander, B. (2011). *The new digital storytelling: Creating narratives with new media.* Santa Barbara, CA: Praeger.
Association for Talent Development (2017). *State of the industry.* Retrieved from https://www.td.org/research-reports/2017-state-of-the-industry
Beebe, S. A. (2007). Raising the question #6: What do communication trainers do? *Communication Education, 56*(2), 249–254. doi: 10.1080/03634520601145266
Bloom, B. S., Englehart, M. D., Furst, E. J., Hill, W. H., & Krathwohl, D. R. (eds.). (1956). *Taxonomy of educational objectives: The classification of educational goals, Handbook 1: The cognitive domain.* New York, NY: McKay.
Boje, D. M. (2006). *Storytelling organizations.* Thousand Oaks, CA: Sage.
Bower, M. (2011). Synchronous collaboration competencies in web-conferencing environments: Their impact on the learning process. *Distance Education, 32*(1), 63–83.
Breuer, N. L. (1998). The power of storytelling. *Global Workforce, 77*(12), 36–41.
Brockett, R. G. (2016). A dozen things you need to know about adult learning. In *Teaching adults: A practical guide for new teachers* (pp. 31–42). San Francisco, CA: Jossey-Bass.
Buxton, E. (2014). Pharmacists' perception of synchronous versus asynchronous distance learning for continuing education programs. *American Journal of Pharmaceutical Education, 78*(1), 1–7.
Buxton, E., & De Muth, J. (2012). Adult learners' perceptions of a professional development program comparing live distance learning versus live local learning. *The Journal of Continuing Higher Education, 60*, 12–19. doi: 10.1080/07377363.2012.649125
Chen, N. N., Dong, F., Ball-Rokeach, S. J., Parks, M., & Huang, J. (2012). Building a new media platform for local storytelling and civic engagement in ethnically diverse neighborhoods. *New Media Society, 14*, 931–950. doi:10.1177/1461444811435640
Cornelius, S. (2014). Facilitating in a demanding environment: Experiences of teaching in virtual classrooms using web conferencing. *British Journal of Educational Technology, 45*(2), 260–271. doi:10.1111/bjet.12016

Czeropski, S. (2012). Use of asynchronous discussions for corporate training: A case study. *Performance Improvement, 51*(9), 14–21. doi: 10.1002/pfi.21304

Daly, J. A., & Vangelisti, A. L. (2003). Skillfully instructing learners: How communicators effectively convey messages. In J. Greene & B. Burleson (eds.), *Handbook of communication and social interaction skills* (pp. 871–908). Mahwah, NJ: Lawrence Erlbaum.

Godfrey, D. (2009). Short attention-span theater: Training tips for webinar presenters. *Bifocal, 31*(2), 30–31. Retrieved from: http://www.americanbar.org/content/dam/aba/publications/bifocal/dec_09_bifj.authcheckdam.pdf

Gupta, S., & Anson, R. (2014). Do I matter? The impact of individual differences on a technology-mediated end user training process. *Journal of Organizational and End User Computing, 26*(2), 60–79. doi: 10.4018/joeuc.2014040104

Hart, G. (2004). Practical and effective metrics. *Intercom, 51*(2), 6–8.

Heath, C., & Heath, D. (2007). *Made to stick: Why some ideas survive while others die.* New York, NY: Random House.

Ho, M. (2016). Investment in learning increases for the fourth straight year. (Cover story). *Talent Development Magazine, 70*(11), 30–35.

Kirwan, C. (2013). *Making sense of organizational learning: Putting theory into practice.* New York, NY: Routledge.

Knowles, M. S., Holton, E. F., & Swanson, R. A. (2012). *The adult learner: The definitive classic in adult education and human resource development* (7th ed.). New York, NY: Routledge.

Lande, L. M. (2011). *Webinar best practices: From invitation to evaluation* (Master's Thesis). University of Wisconsin-Stout, Menomonie, WI. Retrieved from http://www.uwstout.edu/static/lib/thesis/2011/2011landel.pdf

Lane, D. R. (2015). The instructional communication affective learning paradox. *Communication Education, 64*(4), 510–515. doi:10.1080/03634523.2015.1066020

Mezirow, J. (1991). *Transformative dimensions of adult learning.* San Francisco, CA: Jossey-Bass.

Morgan, S., & Dennehy, R. F. (1997). The power of organizational storytelling: A management development perspective. *Journal of Management Development, 16*(7), 494–501. doi:10.1108/02621719710169585

National Storytelling Network (n.d.). What is storytelling? Retrieved July 24, 2017, from http://www.storynet.org/what-is-storytelling.html

Sansone, C., Fraughton, T., Zachary, J. L., Butner, J., & Heiner, C. (2011). Self-regulation of motivation when learning online: the importance of who, why and how. *Educational Technology Research and Development, 59,* 199–212. doi: 10.1007/s11423-011-9193-6

Tyler, J. A. (2007). Incorporating storytelling into practice: How HRD practitioners foster strategic storytelling. *Human Resource Development Quarterly, 18*(4), 559–587.

Wacker, M. B., & Silverman, L. L. (2003). *Stories trainers tell: 55 ready-to-use stories to make training stick.* San Francisco, CA: Jossey-Bass/Pfeiffer.

Weber, K., Martin, M. M., & Myers, S. A. (2011). The development and testing of the instructional beliefs model. *Communication Education, 60*(1), 51–74. doi: 10.1080/03634523.2012.759243

Wilkins, A. L. (1984). The creation of company cultures: The role of stories and human resource systems. *Human Resource Management, 23*(1), 41–60.

Zoeller, H. (2016). Webinar: What are you serving as a leader? Retrieved from https://attendee.gotowebinar.com/register/3548191470175459586

Best practice 4

Demonstrate professional development

- Subject and performance competency acquisition and maintenance
- Leveraging professional development

Professionalism is the essence of professional and personal relationships that allow clients and trainees to trust the products and services that are being delivered in communication training and consulting. There are three elements that characterize professionalism development. it must be acquired, maintained, and demonstrated. Without any one of these elements, the professionalism is either impoverished, degrades over time, or both.

"Career and professional development as levels of engagement in the communication training and development field" proposes one view of professionalism that engages clients, trainees, and the broader society that allows for a beneficial product outcome that tries to benefit all stakeholders. "The communication trainer as bricoleur" expresses universal elements of professionalism that need to be attended to meet expectations to maintain standards in the training and consulting community. "Deliberate practice activities of communication professionals …" uses interviews from the field to reveal 16 specific practices that align themselves with five specific areas needed for professionalism. "Professional development" is a view of elements and expectations from a seasoned trainer that sets both benchmarks for and expectations of elements that should be present in communication training and consulting.

Chapter 11

Career and professional development as levels of engagement in the communication training and development field[1]

Ross Brinkert

Abstract

This chapter addresses Best Practice 4 – Demonstrate Professional Development by offering a stage model allowing self-assessment and assessment of others. Becoming a Communication Training and Development practitioner and demonstrating ongoing professional development involves being active in a community of practice in that area, learning the language of the field, contributing to field-related conversation, and possibly becoming a leader in that conversation in addition to more formally demonstrating relevant competencies.

What is professional development and why do we need to demonstrate it?

As you read this section, you are invited to consider … What makes you or anyone competent as a Communication Training and Development professional? What is involved in maintaining competency? How might clearly establishing and maintaining competency be important to you, your clients, the field, and society?

While we may generally think of professional development as an established professional's periodic efforts to take time out to participate in a training seminar and related assessment to keep on track with curated content changes in their field, there are reasons to think about professional development more expansively. First, professional development can happen anywhere along the continuum from first encountering a field to rising to and maintaining standing in its most senior ranks. Second, professional development can happen in a discrete manner, but it also happens as someone goes about their daily activities in a field. Third, it may be concentrated in contained units of knowledge apart from more contemporaneous undertakings, but it is, arguably, most ideally encountered as practically-situated and momentarily-evolving knowledge.

The ongoing demonstration and assessment of professional competency are important for the individual practitioner, for those the practitioner engages as prospective and actual clients, for academics studying and theorizing about the field, and for the field itself. The maintenance of competency in a changing environment requires professional development activity. It is insufficient for someone to simply "learn it once" in a field and assume they are competent or will remain competent. Consequently, there needs to be one or more guiding frameworks within the field so that self-assessment and assessment by others is not only possible and encouraged but widely expected. For an individual professional to commit to the field and develop, he or she must be supported with a reasonably clear map for doing so. Prospective clients need clarity and confidence in approaching the field and making hiring and contracting decisions. The field itself needs definition, direction, and sustainable professional development processes to attract internal and external stakeholders and justify their commitments over time.

The many needs for clarity around competency and professional development for Communication Training and Development professionals along with the fluid and complex quality of these topics justify the creation of a comprehensive approach to career development. The remainder of the chapter is dedicated to proposing, elaborating, and determining next steps for a model intended to support growth in this area.

The logic of blending career development and professional development

As you read this section, you are invited to consider … What are your current opinions about career development and professional development? What shaped your current opinions? How have you acted upon them?

The comprehensive approach to professional development advanced in this chapter is derived, in part, from incorporating elements from what we typically expect in terms of both career development and professional development. The following definitions are meant to reflect general understandings of these two concepts. The proposed model that follows pushes career development by, for example, making it less of an individual process. The proposed model pushes professional development by, for instance, making it more embedded in regular professional practice.

Career development – Career development is the process by which individuals may progress in a professional field. This process can be clarified by indicating stages that are generally applicable. Career development tends to be conceived as a multi-year, even multi-decade undertaking that applies to those considering entry and extends to those who are at the profession's senior most stage. Career development is often associated with mentoring. Career development is primarily about meeting the needs of individuals who want to advance.

Professional development – Professional development is the process by which individuals stay up to date in a professional field. Professional development tends to be conceived as a once yearly or once bi-yearly undertaking that is mainly aimed at keeping established professionals informed and knowledgeable about industry changes. Professional development attempts to meet the needs of clients, prospective clients, and the field itself as well as well as the needs of professionals themselves.

Functions of a robust model addressing career and professional development in communication training and development

As you read this section, you are invited to consider … What matters most to you in a model addressing career and professional development in this field? Who are other stakeholders of such a model? What is likely to matter most to each stakeholder group?

Prior to offering a model, it is worthwhile identifying what is expected of such a model. Here is a proposed list of functions of an appropriate and effective model:

•   Promote a communication approach to competency, career development, and professional development.

- Provide guidance to any level of professional, from entry-level prospect on up.
- Provide guidance to those seeking to mentor professionals at any level.
- Provide guidance to those seeking to hire professionals.
- Account for competency and professional development sometimes involving discrete knowledge units and traditional methods of assessment.
- Account for competency and professional development largely involving ongoing engagement in the field.
- Build the overall field while also building the careers of individual professionals and empowering prospective clients.
- Maintain relevance in a rapidly changing field and larger world.

A social constructionist approach to developing the model

As you read this section, you are invited to consider … What is an example from your life when communication with one or more other people made a longstanding impact on how you think about your identity and relationships? What is a time you recall having to learn the unique language of a community before being able to act as an impactful speaker or writer in that community? Why is it easy or difficult for you to think about the individual and community as co-composed through communication?

Social construction is an academic perspective that assumes language and context are central to our sense of reality, our production of knowledge, and our experience of other fundamental human concepts such as identity (Gergen, 2015). Although scholars and practitioners in various fields subscribe to the social constructionist paradigm, it can be viewed as inherently communication based since even concepts commonly understood as solitary (e.g., personal identity) are explained in social construction in communicative terms. For instance, someone's sense of self is understood in largely linguistic terms (even in terms of internal self-talk) and the meaning of those words is shaped by the relationships in which that person has been and is engaged.

The social constructionist perspective is most pertinent to a proposal for a Communication Training and Development career model in that initial exposure and intensifying levels of integration within the field of Communication Training and Development, including identification as a Communication Training and Development professional, are thoroughly communicative processes. In general terms, it can be understood as hearing the language of the field, participating in conversations in the field, and playing a leading role in conversations in the field. Terms such as 'hearing' and 'conversation' are used broadly here to refer, respectively, to more receptive and more interactive communication events, regardless of the dominant medium.

The Communication Career and Professional Development Model

As you read this section, you are invited to consider … What does it mean for you to develop from your existing strengths? How does Communication Training and Development fit into your current professional narrative (i.e., story) and how do you want your narrative to advance? What has been your experience of learning in "real life" situations and what is the potential value for you in using this kind of learning in the near future?

The model offered here is intended to be relevant throughout an individual's professional life and to position professional development as broader in scope and importance than is typical. With social construction as the paradigmatic core, the Communication Career and Professional Development Model also incorporates appreciative inquiry, career construction, narrative theory, networking theory, and the theory of situated learning. These approaches and theories are used to both conceptualize and operationalize the model. Appreciative inquiry (Cooperrider, 1986; Cooperrider & Whitney, 2005) is a philosophy and approach to human change that builds from existing strengths, the crafting of key questions, and the importance of conversation for creating positive future states. Career construction (Hartung & Taber, 2013) is a theory and system of career counseling. Narrative theory (Kellett & Dalton, 2001; Vannini, 2015) addresses the nature and function of stories for making sense of human experience. Network theory (Granovetter, 1973; Scott, 2017) explains interactions among interconnected individuals. The theory of situated learning emphasizes learning within the social situation in which it applies (Lave & Wenger, 1991). Appreciative narrative work in the conflict management field (Brinkert, 2006; Jones & Brinkert, 2008), including work in broad support of positive narrative expansion (Brinkert, 2016) have also been an influence here. These approaches and theories are combined in the Communication Career and Professional Development Model. It should also be noted that the model is shaped by my 12 years of experience mentoring students in a Corporate Communication program (sometimes including a strong learning and development focus) as well as other work I have performed over the years, including coaching international MBA students specifically in the career arena, coaching executives on development related goals, and co-leading the National Communication Association Training and Development Division Mentoring Program.

The model has been designed to not only highlight needs and pathways for professional development but also to provide a map for an individual's career in the Communication Training and Development field, offer theoretical and practical guidance for a related approach to mentoring, and point the way for a mid-to-long term effort to strengthen the quality of participation of those in the field and increase the number of people involved.

Specific stages in the Communication Career and Professional Development Model

As you read this section, you are invited to consider … What stage best captures your present professional positioning in the field? What is the highest stage to which you aspire?

The model conceives of a fully developing individual within the field moving from experiencing basic curiosity toward the field to determining initial strengths and interests to solidifying strengths and interests within one or more sub-areas to increasing their fluency, relationships, and networks within one or more sub-areas to developing an expert voice and amassing expert accomplishments within one or more sub-areas. While the model is intended as a good general guide, its relevance will be limited for various individual cases. Some people may entirely bypass one or more stages. The time needed to progress from one stage to another may be quite different for different individuals and different stage transitions. Progression to the top stage will not be a desirable goal for all individuals. Nonetheless, the model may be particularly useful for identifying and nurturing well-rounded professionals in the field, especially at the higher stages. The model is depicted in Table 11.1. Each model stage and its corresponding professional descriptor is depicted in Table 11.2. The model stages are explained immediately below.

Table 11.1 The Communication Career and Professional Development Model

Stage 1: Casual exposure experiences
Stage 2: Focused exposure experiences – level one
Stage 3: Focused exposure experiences – level two
Stage 4: Initial community integration
Stage 5: Intermediate community integration
Stage 6: Advanced community integration
Stage 7: Expert community integration

Table 11.2 Model stages and general professional descriptors

Stage	General Professional Descriptor
1 2 3	Not applicable – individuals at these stages have not yet committed to the field and demonstrated basic competencies
4	Entry level professional
5	Intermediate level professional
6	Advanced level professional
7	Expert level professional

Stage 1: Casual exposure experiences. This stage is characterized by basic awareness of and curiosity about the Communication Training and Development field. Little effort is required on the part of the individual. The individual has some basic knowledge of the field and has a sense of its possible personal resonance. Maybe the individual has had incidental contact with someone studying or working in the field. Maybe he or she has seen someone depicted in the media and is intrigued. Maybe he or she has simply read a description and wants to learn more. An example of someone in stage one is a student who hears a professor speak about their training and development work and the student thinks this may possibly suit their own interests. Another example is a professional in an allied field who is a recipient of training and development services and, similarly, is intrigued at the idea of what it takes to offer such services.

Stage 2: Focused exposure experiences – level one. This stage involves the individual determining initial strengths and interests relevant to this professional field. Some concerted effort is required on the part of the individual. The individual learns more about the field and more about himself or herself, typically guided by easily accessible teachers or mentors. Reflective activities involving the mentor and combining additional information about the field and exploration of personal talents and qualities are often primary here. One example here is an interested person who takes part in a training development event as a participant but who does so while making a special effort to consider the perspective and role of the leader of the event. This individual and this event leader may have made a pre-arrangement to meet after the event to have a substantial conversation to discuss the leader's role and the participant's comfort and interest in taking on such a role in the future, albeit with considerable preparation.

Stage 3: Focused exposure experiences – level two. This stage involves the individual further clarifying strengths and interests within the field, likely within a sub-area. A moderate effort is needed on the part of the individual. The individual's growing awareness of her or his passions, talents, and interests relative to the field leads to more specialized development. The individual often takes a more planned approach here, likely meeting with at least one or more individuals in the field beyond the academic- and/or practice-based mentor. The individual may also participate in field-based events such as programs hosted by professional associations or an internship with the purpose of learning the relative basics of the field. The individual is very much discovering the field and his or her position in it. An example of someone in this stage is a person who, with the help of an initial contact in the field, attends a few professional association events as a guest and makes arrangements to hold informational interviews with a few different people in the field to figure out whether he or she wants to commit to joining the field and, if so, identifying a likely specialty area.

Stage 4: Initial community integration. This stage involves the individual increasing his or her fluency as well as the number and quality of his or her relationships and networks, likely within a sub-area. The individual should, ideally, be demonstrating ongoing participation. The individual enters the conversation as a full-fledged community member within the field. The person is certainly carrying out some field-related work. This could involve the individual more purposely taking on a particular internship or even taking on an entry-level paid position because he or she is relatively clear about how this will help him or her progress. It could also involve the individual joining and becoming active in a professional association. A person at this stage almost certainly requires considerable supervision to handle client work and would likely function as an assistant or junior team member. One example of someone in this stage is a student who joins a professional association, gets involved as a member of a committee, and begins working on field-related projects in an internship for a consulting company. Another example is a professional from an allied field who joins a training and development professional association, regularly attends meetings and participates in an association subcommittee, and begins to segue into doing training and development work by first working under the guidance of a more established training and development professional on a client project.

Stage 5: Intermediate community integration. This stage involves the individual developing a unique voice within the field. The individual makes one or more substantial contributions. The person begins to contribute accomplishments that situate her or him as a full-status peer within the field. The span and depth of field-related work is increasing. This may mean the individual has made one or more notable contributions at an internship or, more likely, a paid position. It may also mean the individual has made notable contributions in the activities of a professional association. The individual is not only committed to the field but has shown he or she is a competent contributing member. The person has at least a basic understanding of the overall field. An individual at this stage can likely work with a high degree of independence on client projects but likely still requires oversight from a more senior colleague. One example of a training and development professional at this stage is a newly graduating student who has completed an industry internship, has been active in a professional association for a couple of years, and is able to present an insightful 20-minute professional development segment on an emerging topic for professional association peers based on his or her knowledge and experience.

Stage 6: Advanced community integration. This stage involves the individual developing as a leading voice in the field. The person does so by earning recognition as an emerging leader based on ongoing peer standing and the provision of one or more excellent contributions. The individual goes beyond making a competent contribution to making a high quality leading contribution, especially as judged by those who are established leaders in the field. The person not only has a solid understanding of the overall field but is fully capable in all general field-related competencies. An individual at this stage is a senior professional in the field. An example of someone at this stage is a person who originally shifted into training and development from an allied field and now has a years-long track record of providing training and development services within that allied field. He or she speaks from knowledge and experience to other training and development professionals about how to offer industry services within a specialized professional culture.

Stage 7: Expert community integration. This stage involves the individual interacting as an established leader in the field. The person does so by exhibiting excellence across projects and relationships. The individual stands out as an established leader based on a body of excellent study, work, and professional-to-professional interaction. The individual is routinely acting as a leader in the field. The person has a sophisticated understanding of the overall field and maintains capability in all general field-related competencies. An individual at this stage stands out even among other senior professionals in the field. One example is an individual who has an advanced degree in a training and development related area and has a 10-year plus history of doing high quality and innovative client work as well as a 10-year plus record of regularly publishing, training, coaching, mentoring, and leading others in his or her professional association.

Core processes of the model

As you read this section, you are invited to consider … What is your mix of core processes (listening, contributing, and leading) in your current professional stage? Regardless of your current professional stage, what is an example of you enacting each of the core processes in the future? (Even purely hypothetical examples are fine for this second question.)

The following three core processes are present throughout the model. These processes involve individual agency and occur in relationship to other people, including other proximate individuals in the field, the field as a whole, and society in general. All are necessary for dedicated professionals at any stage of development in the field but the core process ratio will generally shift depending on the individual's developmental stage. A depiction of core processes in relation to model stages is presented in Figure 11.1. A description of the core processes follows immediately below.

Core process #1: Listening. Listening is an interactive process. For instance, a person can ask questions inwardly or outwardly as he or she listens. A listener certainly has some level of self-awareness about processing information. Nonetheless, relative to speaking, listening is more receptive. It makes sense that someone new to the field is engaging in a considerable amount of listening (with listening defined broadly here), as he or she is learning from more experienced individuals and sources of field-related information. Notably, listening remains important, even for an advanced practitioner or expert in the field, as other individuals and other individuals' ideas deserve recognition, relationships are initiated and maintained, and because listening plays an important role in all forms of learning as well as the maintenance of an adequate degree of professional development.

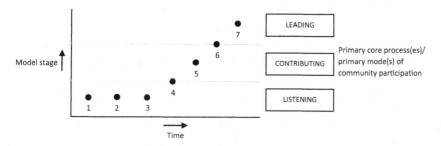

Figure 11.1 Core processes in relation to time and model stages.

Core process #2: Contributing. Contributing can be understood as providing value to a relationship when that value is not better characterized as leading. For example, value can consist of a piece of useful new information expressed in one conversational turn or a substantial amount of basic work to support others in the field. The relationship can be to one individual, two or more individuals, and even the overall field or society. Substantial contributing tends to happen after an individual has at least an initial understanding of the field and has made some sort of commitment to the field. For individuals who rise to the higher stages of involvement in the field, contributing remains important in addition to leading because of the more peer-to-peer nature of contributing versus leading.

Core process #3: Leading. Leading involves using influence and/or power in the service of establishing a meaningful direction for others. It is probably the case with leadership that less people can lead than contribute in a certain situation and, accordingly, there is elevated status associated with leading. This is not to suggest that there must be many contributors and few leaders. Contributing actions may very well fill much of an individual's time, even as he or she acts as a clear leader in some circumstances. Arguably, the most credible and revered leaders continue to find ways to modestly contribute to the growth of others, even as they also more boldly chart a path for others.

Applying the model to guide an individual's development

As you read this section, you are invited to consider … Given your current stage positioning, which of the accompanying listed questions seems most pertinent for your own development? What is an additional question (not listed) that is important for you to consider at this time?

One application of the model is for individuals to self-assess their stage placement and use the model and its related tools to progress. The following questions are designed for individual self-reflection to generally determine career stage position and advance professional development accordingly.

Stage 1: Casual exposure experiences.

- What about this field is capturing my attention?
- What is the resonance for me?
- Am I interested in making a modest commitment to learning more about it and my place in it?

Stage 2: Focused exposure experiences – level one.

- How can I come to know the basics of this field?
- What are the characteristics of those making contributions or leading in this field?
- How have I already demonstrated one or more important characteristics?

Stage 3: Focused exposure experiences – level two.

- Given my richer understanding of the field, what sub-area(s) do I most want to learn more about?
- What are some specific field-related interaction opportunities that I want to experience?
- What more do I need to learn about this field before considering strongly committing?

Stage 4: Initial community integration.

- How am I committed to regularly participating in one or more semi-formal or formal networks (e.g., communities, associations, organizations) in my field?
- How am I committed to one or more sub-areas in my field?
- How might I contribute now that I have basic fluency in the language of my field?

Stage 5: Intermediate community integration.

- What is a contribution that might establish me as a full peer among other professionals in my field?
- How am I active in professional relationships with individuals at various levels in my field?
- What might be my unique place in my field?

Stage 6: Advanced community integration.

- How do I contribute as a leading voice in my field from a content standpoint?
- How do I build significant professional relationships with individuals at various levels in my field?
- How do I contribute to developing the careers of others (including those less senior) in my field?

Stage 7: Expert community integration.

- How do I regularly contribute as a leading voice in my field from a content standpoint?
- How do I sustain significant professional relationships with individuals at various levels in my field?
- How do I make significant ongoing contributions to developing the careers of others (especially those less senior) in my field?

Applying the model to structure mentoring relationships

As you read this section, you are invited to consider ... What stage of professional might you mentor, even in a limited way, at present time? It is normal for early stage professionals to seek mentors; how might later stage professionals be encouraged to act not just as mentors but as mentees as well?

A second application of the model is for informal or formal mentoring relationships. Below are stage-specific questions for mentors. Notably, there is an assumption that individuals can benefit from mentoring at any career stage.

Stage 1: Casual exposure experiences.

- To what degree am I providing useful information for those who may be prospective contributors to this field?
- How might I best make myself available as a mentoring resource?

Stage 2: Focused exposure experiences – level one.

- How might I best provide a more nuanced overview of my field?
- How can I best support possible new entrants in identifying current strengths relevant to my field?

Stage 3: Focused exposure experiences – level two.

- To whom might I introduce the possible new entrant to assist him or her in clarifying specialty areas?
- What additional types of support might I provide to the possible new entrant to help them make a decision about whether to commit to this field?

Stage 4: Initial community integration.

- To what degree is the possible new entrant clear about what it means to make a commitment decision in this field?
- How can I best support the new entrant now that he or she has made a basic commitment?

Stage 5: Intermediate community integration.

- To what degree have I made the mentee aware of basic contribution options suiting his or her unique profile?
- How might I support the mentee in making an initial contribution that is sustainable?

Stage 6: Advanced community integration.

- To what degree have I supported the mentee in identifying one or more exemplary leadership opportunities related to his or her profile?
- How have I fostered the identification of ways for the mentee to support others?

Stage 7: Expert community integration.

- To what degree have I supported the mentee in identifying related, successive exemplary leadership opportunities?
- How have I fostered the mentee's ongoing appreciation and support of others?

Applying the model to advance professional development across the overall field

As you read this section, you are invited to consider … Given your current stage of professional development, how might you most effectively act as steward of the overall field? What should the field-as-a-whole prioritize in terms of stewardship of professional development?
   A third application of the model is to foster reflection at the field-level for whether career and professional development is sufficiently supported at each of the various stages. These questions are offered for those wanting to act as stewards of the overall field by striving to further improve career advancement and professional development opportunities.

Stage 1: Casual exposure experiences.

- How can we best produce and share accurate yet easy-to-grasp depictions of the field for those who have not encountered it before?
- What information platforms and avenues for interaction exist for those with an initial curiosity in the field?

Stage 2: Focused exposure experiences – level one.

- What easy-to-access experiences should we be promoting to those trying to determine whether this is a field in which they might want to work?
- How might a prospective entrant to the field be best supported in exploring their strengths and interests in the context of the field?

Stage 3: Focused exposure experiences – level two.

- What are some richer experiences we can make available to individuals who are seriously considering committing to work in the field?
- How can established professionals in the field best support the decision process of individuals thinking about committing to the field?

Stage 4: Initial community integration.

- What does it mean for an individual to commit to the field?
- How can we most effectively welcome and integrate newly committed individuals in the field?

Stage 5: Intermediate community integration.

- How are individuals supported in their ability to make contributions, especially notable initial contributions to the field?
- How might individuals be able to maintain status as competent contributing members or be supported in achieving a higher status?

Stage 6: Advanced community integration.

- How are individuals supported in their ability to make leading contributions to the field?
- How might individuals be able to maintain status as advanced members of the community or be supported in achieving expert status?

Stage 7: Expert community integration.

- How are individuals supported in their ability to become longstanding leaders in the field?
- How might individuals sustain expert status while also supporting the growth of others?

Model-supported professional development metrics

As you read this section, you are invited to consider … Where do you currently stand in terms of the four metrics? How, specifically, are you committed to advancing in one or more of the metric areas in the coming year? Are additional metrics needed and, if so, what are they?

An additional application of the model is in identifying more concrete measures of career stage achievement and related professional development expectations. These metrics can be used inside the field to more formally determine the career and professional development status of individual professionals. Entry level professionals (i.e., Stage 4 status) would at least, to some degree, demonstrate Metric #1: Evidence of general participation in the field and Metric #2: Evidence of the development of the professional self. Intermediate level professionals (i.e., Stage 5 status), advanced level professionals (i.e., Stage 6 status), and expert level professionals (i.e., Stage 7 status) would also be expected to variously demonstrate Metric #3: Evidence of work to develop the field for the benefit of diverse others and Metric #4: Evidence of field-related work for clients. It is important to point out that some activities would satisfy two or more metrics, as would be the case with a trainer who carried out a *pro bono* training or an academic who published an article for those inside and outside the field. Both examples could fulfill Metric #3 and Metric #4. The four metrics are presented in Table 11.3. Descriptions of the four metrics follow immediately below.

Metric #1: Evidence of general participation in the field. To enter the field is to commit to participate in the field. Interaction in the field is fundamental to not only becoming but remaining an active member. This is particularly the case in a field and broader

Table 11.3 Four metrics

Metric No.	Description
1	Evidence of general participation in the field
2	Evidence of development of the professional self (demonstration and advancement of general and specialized competencies)
3	Evidence of work to develop the field for the benefit of diverse others (advancing the interests of fellow professionals in the field, prospective entrants to the field, the overall field, and society in general as supported by the field)
4	Evidence of field-related work for clients (effectively serving clients' interests and legitimate immediate self-interests)

environment marked by considerable change. To maintain awareness of the changing field, it is important to be involved in the field on an ongoing basis. Therefore, the demonstration of adequate professional development includes evidence of an individual's involvement in routine field-related activities.

Metric #2: Evidence of development of the professional self (demonstration and advancement of general and specialized competencies). While membership in the field may consist of simple participation in field-related activities, the performance of work for clients and the representation of the field in academic and other writing presupposes that a member is competent. Therefore, it is in the best interests of the overall field to ensure that individual members (offering professional services or representing the field in other ways) are appropriately knowledgeable, skilled, and motivated. While many will work in one or more sub-areas of the field and should demonstrate competency in such areas, a general understanding of the overall field and evidence of generally applicable skills will also be useful to in contextualizing specializations as well as to maintaining and growing the visibility and integrity of the overall field.

Metric #3: Evidence of work to develop the field for the benefit of diverse others (advancing the interests of fellow professionals in the field, prospective entrants to the field, the overall field, and society in general as supported by the field). Because advancement of the individual member and advancement of the field are thoroughly interconnected, individuals benefiting from community identification have an obligation to show how they are contributing to or leading the field itself, essentially putting the field's interests above self-interests for at least part of what is accomplished professionally.

Metric #4: Evidence of field-related work for clients (effectively serving clients' interests and legitimate immediate self-interests). Serving the training and development needs of clients and publishing related academic and applied writing are the primary outputs of the field. They can be highly impactful. They are the primary deliverables for which professionals are financially compensated. Training and development professionals should strive to achieve and maintain a certain level of professional activity in these areas. And professionals should be willing to offer at least a certain level of transparency and accountability for their professional activities, not only for clients and prospective clients but also for fellow professionals, including senior leaders, in the field.

How the model and metrics can be of value to prospective clients

As you read this section, you are invited to consider … Which of your current metric-related accomplishments matter most to those you serve and/or strive to serve? What additional metric-related accomplishments would be most valued by these individuals or organizations?

Just as assessment of training interventions has become increasingly important for training clients (Beebe, Mottet, & Roach, 2013), so too does initial assessment of prospective training contractors seem of growing importance. The four metrics represent a relatively compact yet comprehensive way of summarizing a given professional's standing in the field and indicating their suitability for client work. A given professional could use these metrics to compose a personal introduction that provided transparency to prospective clients while also establishing or enhancing professional credibility. The metrics could informally be used in this way immediately. The field may, in time, decide to formalize the presentation of these or similar metrics by professionals to prospective clients.

Limitations and next steps

As you read this section, you are invited to consider … What points about the model or, more broadly, professional development in the Communication Training and Development field do you feel need further consideration? How might you contribute to addressing these issues?

The model proposed here is relatively bold in its scope. Consequently, its presentation in this chapter is necessarily limited, especially as various implications remain only partially explored or wholly unexplored. More research, dialogue, and debate are needed to clarify metrics by stage and general professional descriptor, particularly if the metrics will be strongly enforced to facilitate or block practice opportunities. The Communication Training and Development field must try to learn from the Executive Coaching field, which found itself promoting an ethical code that was an obstacle to ethical practice (Diochon & Nizet, 2015). Details of initial competency assessment and periodic assessment of professional development are yet to be determined. This process should occur with a degree of modesty given the complexity of the field and the pace of change both in the field and general environment. Additionally, the field needs to reconcile the need for general standards in a time of considerable specialization. As a related matter, there is almost certainly a paradox in individuals largely rising to the top of the field as experts and then having considerable power and influence over the general field – and a field, as noted by Beebe, Mottet, and Roach (2013), often needing generalists. Further, efforts must be made to apply the model to individuals taking temporary leave from the field or working on the periphery of the field and possibly identifying heavily with one or more allied fields. Also, the formation of the individual's own professional story formation in relation to developmental stage and the ever-evolving stories of the field itself merits exploration.

Conclusion

This chapter began by clarifying the importance of professional development for the Communication Training and Development field. The case was then made that an expansive approach was needed, in part to address the needs of multiple stakeholders and individuals in different developmental stages. The Communication Career and Professional Development Model was then introduced. This model positions meaningful interaction in the professional field as the central feature of career development and professional development. The model's stages provide a relatively precise way to support individual professionals, mentors, and stewards of the field as they seek growth. While the model facilitates developmental growth, it also offers a clear conception of competency metrics that will be of particular value to prospective clients of Communication Training and Development services and products. The application of the Communication Career and Professional Development Model has substantial implications for growing the field, providing transparency, and ensuring quality. Given the stakes involved, more work should be done to elaborate and examine its tools before mandating its use.

As you reflect on the overall chapter ... How do the views expressed in this chapter enhance your existing perspective(s) on career and professional development? How do the views expressed in this chapter possibly prompt you to think in transformative new ways? How, if at all, does this chapter make you likely to act differently when it comes to your own career and professional development and/or your involvement with others in the Communication Training and Development field?

Note

1 This book chapter was developed out of a paper the author prepared for the 8th Annual Mentoring Conference "New Perspectives in Mentoring: A Quest for Leadership Excellence and Innovation" at the Mentoring Institute at the University of New Mexico. The paper, titled "Constructing Storied Careers in Strategic Communication: A Mentoring Model," was presented on October 21, 2015, appeared in the official conference proceedings, but has not been published.

References

Beebe, S. A., Mottet, K., & Roach, D. (2013). *Training and development: Communicating for success.* Upper Saddle River, NJ: Pearson.

Brinkert, R. (2006). Conflict coaching: Advancing the conflict resolution field by developing an individual disputant process. *Conflict Resolution Quarterly, 23,* 517–528.

Brinkert, R. (2016). Gratitude communication as conflict management: Advancing a strategy and tactic for positive narrative expansion. In P. M. Kellett & T. G. Matyok (eds.), *Transforming conflict through communication: Personal to working relationships* (pp. 313–332). Lanham, MD: Lexington.

Cooperrider, D. L. (1986). *Appreciative inquiry: Toward a methodology for understanding and enhancing organizational innovation.* PhD. Case Western Reserve University, Cleveland, OH.

Cooperrider, D., & Whitney, D. D. (2005). *Appreciative inquiry: A positive revolution in change.* Oakland, CA: Berrett-Koehler Publishers.

Diochon, P. F., & Nizet, J. (2015). Ethical codes and executive coaches: One size does not fit all. *The Journal of Applied Behavioral Science, 51,* 277–301.

Gergen, K. (2015). *An invitation to social construction* (3rd ed.). Thousand Oaks, CA: Sage.

Granovetter, M. S. (1973). The strength of weak ties. *American Journal of Sociology, 78,* 1360–1380.

Hartung, P. J., & Taber, B. J. (2013). Career construction: Heeding the call of the heart. In B. J. Dik, Z. S. Byrne, & M. F. Steger (eds.), *Purpose and meaning in the workplace* (pp. 17–36). Washington, DC: American Psychological Association.

Jones, T. S., & Brinkert, R. (2008). *Conflict coaching: Conflict management strategies and skills for the individual*. Thousand Oaks, CA: Sage.

Kellett, P. M., & Dalton, D. G. (2001). *Managing conflict in a negotiated world: A narrative approach to achieving dialogue and change*. Thousand Oaks, CA: Sage.

Lave, J., & Wenger, E. (1991). *Situated learning: Legitimate peripheral participation*. Cambridge: Cambridge University Press.

Scott, J. (2017). *Social network analysis* (4th ed.). Los Angeles, CA: Sage.

Vannini, A. (2015). Stories and storytelling. In S. W. Littlejohn & K. A. Foss (eds.), *Encyclopedia of communication theory* (vol. 2, pp. 934–936). Thousand Oaks, CA: Sage.

Chapter 12

The communication trainer as bricoleur

Craig Engstrom, Michael Forst, and Lacey Corey Brown

Abstract

Developing and maintaining organizational expertise (Best Practice 5) is partly driven by competency (Best Practice 4). Using a case study, we present an interpretivist orientation to continuing education, professional development, and stakeholder engagement labeled BRIC: be humble, read broadly, involve all stakeholders, and collaborate with others. BRIC operationalizes the best practice of *demonstrating* professional development as a precursor to maintaining organizational expertise. Practitioners using BRIC will be more creative, more flexible, and stronger process consultants.

Excellent trainers, developers, and consultants focus on the growth of others; however, training and development professionals (TDPs), especially communication consultants, coaches, teachers, and trainers (CCCTTs), recognize the need to prepare for projects and improve themselves through ongoing training, development, and consultation with other experts and resources. Recognizing the need for continuing education and client engagement, the National Communication Association's Training and Development Division included the following two best practices as part of its seven best practices that emerged from a multi-year study ("Best Practices...," n.d.): Best Practice 4 (BP4) – Demonstrate Professional Development and Best Practice 5 (BP5) – Develop and Maintain Organizational Expertise.

We understand these two best practices to be intertwined and reinforcing. BP4 recommends that TDPs should (1) engage in subject and performance competency acquisition and maintenance and (2) leverage professional development of internal and external stakeholders. BP5 recommends that TDPs (1) recognize organizational catalysts for training (e.g., leadership, management, planning, and culture) and (2) recognize employee catalysts for training (e.g., career development, human resources, innovativeness, selection, and appraisal). These two best practices suggest TDPs should have extensive knowledge before entering into a contract with a client but should not forget they have a lot to learn from their clients. In short, these best practices require CCCTTs to be humble. Humility can be learned and demonstrated in practice. As you read this chapter, think about how we demonstrate humility to our client by involving all stakeholders, by recognizing our knowledge gaps and reading more material to improve our trainings, and by collaborating with others. Also, reflect on how you might have approached things differently than we did. By engaging and reflecting with our examples and heeding advice in our recommendations, you will grow and develop, brick by brick, a stronger foundation for training and consulting success.

In this chapter, we share our experiences through a case study of a 1.5-year long communication training and consulting relationship with a university's food service operation (100+ employees). Despite various challenges, such as having very limited training time (a total of 1.5 hours for each training session), significant gaps between trainings (as much as 9 months), trainees with significant variations in age (18–65+) and formal education (GED to MA), and strict union rules (limiting our interaction with employees onsite and data reporting to our client), the consulting relationship we developed with our client, University Dining Services (UDS), ensured successful training sessions. Our success is reflected in questionnaire data (Engstrom, Forst, & Brown, 2017) and by trainees who twice voted our training programs "most favorable" out of all other trainings.

Through this experience, we realized the value of purposeful application of BP5 (participation with stakeholders to develop and maintain organizational expertise during consultancy), which *demonstrated* our own preparation and continuing education while in the field (BP4). We present our experience as a case study that operationalizes BPs 4 and 5 into a set of four practices, which form the acronym *BRIC*: be humble, read broadly, involve all stakeholders, and collaborate with others. Although these four practices are comprehensive, we recognize they are not absolute. Nevertheless, these practices form the story of our consulting success, which we attribute to our *training-as-bricolage* or *trainer-as-bricoleur* approach. Thus, we use the acronym strategically to capture the set of practices that made this project successful. BRIC forms the prefix for the words *bricoleur* and *bricolage*, which are obviously not everyday terms. We explain these terms in detail later; however, for now, note that bricolage refers to a creative outcome (like a jazz performance or unique training session) and a bricoleur is a broadly trained, creative individual who is a master-craftsperson. A trainer-as-bricoleur, in other words, is a trainer who can adapt to changing circumstance and creatively respond to unanticipated trainee needs. We believe the four practices explained in this chapter will usefully guide other TDPs' application of best practice guidelines and assist them in engaging training, development, and consulting as bricoleurs.

Our chapter explains bricolage, describes how it suits communication training and development best practices, and explicates how CCCTTs can use BRIC to adequately improvise when faced with unique, dynamic, and challenging training and consulting situations. To prevent our presentation from leading us into academes and abstraction, we first provide a brief overview of the actual training and consulting situation we encountered with UDS. Second, we explain BRIC by drawing on publications in process consulting, organizational development, and entrepreneurship studies. In this section, we illustrate BRIC in practice; specifically, how we resolved problems we faced as trainers–consultants committed to *developing and maintaining organizational expertise* during our 1.5-year consultancy. We conclude by summarizing the communication trainer as bricoleur and by providing propositions that may be useful for future study of this BRIC approach.

Case overview: Resolving conflict in UDS through BRIC approach

In October 2015, University Dining Services (UDS) sent a request for proposal (RFP) to units across campus to assist with a new training program for its unionized civil service employees. They sought expert advice from various academic and operational units, who would offer sessions during their training series. UDS provided the trainings in response to external and internal pressures to increase efficiencies, lower operating costs, increase student satisfaction of dining and residential living, and meet new state training guidelines for food service handlers.

In accordance with BP5, we scheduled a meeting with the UDS administrator who authored the call. By meeting prior to writing and submitting an RFP response, we sought to better understand UDS's needs and the catalysts for training, and to determine if we could offer anything substantive to the project. The initial meeting indicated management felt workplace stress was significant among line-service staff and this, along with employee diversity (e.g., age, race, class, and educational background), was generating unproductive workplace conflict. Following this meeting, we reviewed publications on food service environments and workplace stress (BP4). We determined stress and negative conflict drive employee burnout, conflict, and sabotage in hospitality sectors (Boles & Babin, 1996; Kao, Cheng, & Huang, 2014). By reviewing research, we demonstrate continuing education (BP4) and obtained a better picture of possible catalysts for employee training (BP5).

Drawing on our backgrounds in organizational communication and conflict training, additional research, knowledge of the diversity of the trainees, and limitations imposed by training workshop constraints (we could only have maximum 1 hour and 30 minutes for any single training), we developed a proposal we felt best served UDS's interests. Our plan embraced a *participatory approach to consulting* – a type of approach that may also be referred to as humble consulting because it de-centers the trainer as expert (Schein, 2016) – and extended the relationship beyond a single instance of training, as had been initially called for, to multiple instances of consultation and training over a 1.5-year period.

UDS administrators approved of our ideas and suggestions. Their objective was to provide "any training that would engage, entertain, and improve communication skills of line staff with diverse educations." After months of additional research and brief informational interviews with shift supervisors, we ultimately determined workplace conflict was a topic likely to appeal to and benefit trainees. Conflict is a relatable topic and interpersonal communication tactics of humor, metaphor reframing, and negotiation jujitsu, from our prior experience teaching interpersonal conflict using Hocker and Wilmot (2014), are easy for trainees with any level of education or experience to grasp and employ.

Our plan presented modest objectives, illustrated in Table 12.1, which demonstrate our commitment to professional development through the first two aspects of BRIC. First, we demonstrated a willingness to *be humble* by acknowledging the need to learn about hospitality and food service industries to better situate our communication expertise. Second, we *read broadly* to ensure we addressed our lack of expertise and developed objectives specific to our client, rather than providing generic remedies.

Objective 1 was an overarching objective for the entire training and consulting activity. Objective 2 was the primary objective for the first training session, which we conducted prior to any substantive engagement with trainees because we had limited access to them outside of trainings (concern for union rules prohibited us from contacting them). Objectives 3 and 4 were the primary focus of the second training session. The third and final training's curriculum was designed to accomplish objective 5; however, just before this training we significantly deviated from our initial curriculum plan, which we had sketched more than 1.25 years earlier. Initially, the curriculum was to lean heavily on lecture-style delivery and short engagement exercises. Based on our observations from the first two training sessions and ongoing consultations with supervisors and senior staff, we improvised by changing our roles from trainers to facilitators and allotted substantial time for open forum discussion. This allowed participants to

Table 12.1 Training objectives developed from review of literature

Objectives	Relevant Literature (Select)
Objective 1. Provide broad communication tactics that are known to mitigate conflict in situ, are easy to teach and use in almost any circumstance (i.e. they can be ready-at-hand), and fit the short training timeframe and diverse audience of trainees.	Beverland, Kates, Lindgreen, & Chung, 2010; Grandey et al., 2007; Han, Bonn, & Cho, 2016; Hocker & Wilmot, 2014.
Objective 2. Explain positive and negative humor with specific examples of positive communication strategies to use in the workplace.	Bateson, 1969; Van den Broeck, Vander, De Lange, & De Witte, 2012; Lynch, 2009; Sclavi, 2008; Tews, Michel, & Stafford, 2013.
Objective 3. Teach participants to be more observant of their uses of metaphor to describe conflict.	Buzzanell & Burrell, 1997; Hocker & Wilmot, 2014; Lakoff & Johnson, 1980; McCorkle & Mills, 1992; Yang, Cheng, & Chuang, 2015.
Objective 4. Provide examples of positive metaphors that shift participants' cognitive frames of conflict from predictably negative to positive.	
Objective 5. Explain principled negotiation and how humor and metaphor framing can tactically be used as negotiation jujitsu.	De Dreu, van Dierendonck, & Dijkstra, 2004; Fisher & Ury, 1991; Menkel-Meadow, 2006; Taylor, Mesmer-Magnus, & Burns, 2008.

engage in open dialogue with each other and for us to solicit useful information we could provide to senior staff, which they could use to improve the workplace. The new training curriculum for the third session generated useful information and deliverables for all parties (in order of importance): line staff, managers, and researchers.

Overall, the training and consulting relationship consisted of (1) three trainings for line staff on *simple and actionable* communication tactics for mitigating conflict; (2) three consulting meetings with managers to discuss training and research outcomes and to provide guidance for developing conflict mediation protocols that would satisfy the union representatives, employees, and managers; and (3) useful research data for scholarly publication on training. Through participatory design, embracing BRIC, and improvisation, our training and consulting was successful despite time and access constraints. Our embrace of BRIC allowed us to continue modifying our approach from the initial proposal to final deliverables. We entered the relationship without significant expertise about food service; however, we took steps to show our investment in leaderships' and employees' catalysts for training and demonstrated willingness to adapt based on their feedback. In the next section, we explain BRIC/improvisation so that our case provides value to other CCCTTs through operationalization of best practices.

What is BRIC?

The concept of the *bricoleur*, first introduced by anthropologist Claude Lévi-Strauss, is popular in organizational development, entrepreneurship, and education. A bricoleur is often defined *as someone who makes do with whatever is at hand* and is ascribed with traits such as artfulness, craft, resourcefulness, flexibility, and inventiveness (Stinchfield,

Nelson, & Wood, 2013). Researchers in entrepreneurship and organization studies argue bricoleurs are largely creative due to their knowledge and skills, which allow them to improvise. Weick (1993), for example, likens the jazz improviser to Lévi-Strauss's (1966) concept of *bricolage*, the art of making usage of whatever is at hand. The bricoleur, like the jazz musician, examines the raw materials available and entices some order, creating unique combinations through the process of working with the resources they find.

The metaphor of bricolage entered the field of communication most notably through the work of organizational communication theorist Eric Eisenberg (1984, 1990). However, despite articles in other disciplines discussing the teacher as bricoleur (Hanley, 2011), the entrepreneur as bricoleur (Baker & Nelsen, 2005), and the leader as bricoleur (Koyama, 2014), there is little mention of *the communication trainer as bricoleur*. This is surprising; like trainers, bricoleurs are process oriented and disciplined. Bricoleurs bring together a set of techniques (bricolage) that must be used at the opportune moment to solve problems and respond to trainees' needs.

In popular press literature and talent development industries, the academic concept of *bricolage* is most closely associated with *improvisation* (a current training trend; see Kulhan, 2017). Improvisation is similarly defined as making do with what is at hand: "Improvisation is not so much a creation of something out of nothing as much as it is the creation of something out of everything—everything one has been taught, everything one experiences, everything one knows" (Kulhan, 2017, p. 9). TDPs who can *make do with what is there* are likelier to succeed in consulting contexts marked by uncertainty and ambiguity (Allen, Jimmieson, Bordia, & Irmer, 2007).

To lessen the impact of uncertainty and change, organizational consultants and trainers draw on the iterative, process-oriented form of consulting defined by Edgar Schein. He defines process consultation as "the creation of a relationship with the client that permits the client to perceive, understand, and act on the process of events that occur in the client's internal and external environment in order to improve the situation as defined by the client" (1999, p. 20). While there are more sets of techniques TDPs can bring together to do process consulting as bricoleurs, we propose four that represent an effective orientation to BPs 4 and 5: be humble, read broadly, involve all stakeholders, and collaborate with others. This BRIC approach requires continuing education (BP4) and working with organizational stakeholders (BP5). Each element of BRIC is described next and summarized in Table 12.2.

Be humble

According to Schein (1999), there are five core principles of process consultation: (1) "always try to be helpful" (p. 6); (2) "always stay in touch with the current reality" (p. 6); (3) "access your ignorance" (p. 11); (4) "everything you do is an intervention" (p. 17); (5) "it is the client who owns the problem and the solution" (p. 20). Following these principles in the field requires a high level of self-awareness, useful conceptual models and guidelines, and extensive training and experience. It requires being open to the possibility that the answers already reside with the client and TDPs must intervene (inherently causing disruption) to help identify the answers.

Recently, Schein published two useful books that organize the five principles into accessible concepts, which he calls humble inquiry (2013) and humble consulting (2016). Humility is an important starting point for trainers and practitioners who want to be

Table 12.2 BRIC summarized

BP		Practice	Supporting Literature	Application
Best Practice 4 – Demonstrate Professional Development	Best Practice 5 – Develop and Maintain Organizational Expertise	**B**e Humble	Beal, 2017; Cameron & Caza, 2004; Langer, 1997; Owens & Hekman, 2012; Schein, 1999, 2013, 2016.	Do less telling, and ask more. Listen and acknowledge others' perspective. Get action through good communication; good communication requires a trusting relationship; and a trusting relationship requires here-and-now humility. Start the consultancy by recognizing you know less than the client does about their problems. Your tool kit of solutions may need additions.
		Read Broadly	Boles & Babin, 1996; Cunningham & Stanovic, 2001; Kao, Cheng, & Huang, 2014; Kulhan, 2017; Millán et al., 2014; Ritchie et al., 2013; Schein, 1999; Shane, 2000, 2008; Shiu, 2014	Do not simply explore one aspect of the stakeholder's need. Read beyond their field to examine how similar problems have been solved outside of this particular context. Keep literature broad to satisfy a diverse audience. You might find pieces of the puzzle in the most unexpected places. Create training and consulting objectives supported by literatures (e.g., Table 12.1).
		Involve All Stakeholders	de Blois et al., 2016; Frick, 1983; Herremans et al., 2016; Ozanne et al., 2017; Purvis et al., 2015; Scheba & Mustalahti, 2015; Schein, 1999; Striley, 2016; Thory, 2016.	Involve all stakeholders, even those with the least amount of authority. Ask the stakeholder community how they feel about and understand the larger needs of their work environment. This is an opportunity to learn more deeply about the nuance details of the client's needs. Involving all stakeholders in finding a solution will ensure buy in from the entire community.
		Collaborate with Others	Hocker & Wilmot, 2014; Heath & Isbell, 2015, Lowitt, 2013; O'Grady & Orton, 2016; Orton & O'Grady, 2016; Schein, 1999; Weick, 1993.	The client owns the solution. Ensure all voices can be heard. Sharing various perspectives of all stakeholders will uncover aspects of the client's needs that might have previous gone unnoticed. Remain flexible as collaboration might shift your previous understanding of the client's needs.

Note: As illustrated, there is overlap between BP4 and BP5 relevant to BRIC practices. Supporting literature is scholarly publications.

open to learning (BP4) and understand catalysts for change (BP5). He defined humble inquiry as "the fine art of drawing someone out, of asking questions to which you do not already know the answer, of building a relationship based on curiosity and interest in the other person" (2013, p. 2). To summarize, as a humble inquirer, you should do less telling and more listening. It is a form of inquiry that requires speaking with and building reliable communication across different hierarchical boundaries. It is a form of inquiry based on here-and-now humility, which requires depending on someone else, usually a lower-level employee, who can facilitate upward change. As a trainer, you could ask, for example: How will I facilitate a relationship of curiosity and interest with my trainees?

Humility is founded upon sincerely admitting mistakes and limitations, as well as celebrating successes and competencies. Though given different names in academic and popular press publications, like coaching habit, humble leadership (Beal, 2017), and mindful learning (Langer, 1997), empirical research supports the usefulness of humility in training and development work. As a core organizational virtue, humility produces exceptional performance, amplifies altruistic and prosocial behavior, improves relationships, enhances team effectiveness, and intensifies ethos (Cameron & Caza, 2004; Owens & Hekman, 2012, 2016). Humble consulting requires a mutual understanding that the consultant brings certain skills and knowledge to the relationship but is not an expert in all matters. Both parties must understand the relationship will evolve over time. Each party must remain committed to open communication and to the idea that solutions do not reside in one party but are context specific and mutually achieved.

At the outset of our consulting relationship, we expressed concern to UDS administrators about time constraints and limitations on contact with the trainees, acknowledging these might negatively impact the success of the training. Despite these barriers, we started with basic questions, many of which exposed our ignorance: *Why are you doing these trainings? What kind of communication principles do you think we should teach? What are some of the communication challenges you think employees have? What challenges do they say they have? Can we speak with others? What do trade magazines in food service say are major challenges to workplace productivity? How have you been managing these challenges? Why do you think you need outside help?*

By asking these types of questions, we demonstrated we were interested in *their* problems, we were willing to reveal *our* limitations, and we were interested in *helping*, not preaching. (How can you incorporate similar questions into your training and consulting relationships?) According to research, conflict is pervasive in food service; however, instead of making assumptions, we needed to know if UDS reflected industry norms or was an outlier. Throughout the entire consultation, we did not *tell* UDS what they needed to do, rather we *asked* what they needed. Of course, this stance decentered us from the position of *expert* and made us vulnerable. However, as Schein (2013) notes – and we experienced to be true – when TDPs express genuine interest in listening to understand, the communicative process (and relationships it establishes) overshadows the real or perceived information deficit.

Of course, humble inquiry requires ongoing commitment to genuine interest, not simple posturing during an intake meeting. Therefore, we continued to ask questions throughout the 1.5-year consultation and treated all employees, from line level employees to higher-level administrators, as experts. During our second training session, for example, we provided our trainees with a conflict scenario, which presented the fictional story of a conflict between a line-level dining hall employee and his supervisor. While the scenario generated meaningful discussion among most, the story did not resonate with a few of the line-level employees who found it unrealistic. To build a relationship based in genuine curiosity and interest (Schein, 2013), we asked the employees to share their critiques and explain how the scenario could be changed to more fully reflect the workplace conflicts they had experienced. Humbly inquiring about the trainees' critiques of the activity accomplished three things: (1) it valued their expert knowledge; (2) it acknowledged that the client already "owns the problem and the solution" (Schein, 1999, p. 20); and (3) it allowed us to improvise and alter the scenario used during our third training session to better reflect conflict among UDS employees. How could you have improvised during your own training experiences? How has improvising led to solutions?

We remained focused on learning from each stakeholder; an asking orientation is essential to BP5. Even in trainings, where we did a lot of telling, we focused on reporting back what we learned from trainees through conversations and polls. Asking allowed us to develop a rapport with UDS administrators and to build a trusting relationship with all stakeholders. Our positive relationship with UDS administrators resulted in trust. This trust led them to grant our request for them to leave our final training to enable open dialogue with line-level employees about their feelings toward managers. The line-level employees trusted us enough to share their thoughts in our brief meeting. Everyone's willingness to be vulnerable ultimately allowed us to understand catalysts for change in UDS.

Read broadly

As noted above, we entered the initial meeting with some knowledge of the types of conflict inherent to the food service industry (Boles & Babin, 1996; Kao, Cheng, & Huang, 2014). In the first meeting, we obtained information that *improved our knowledge* of what we did not know. We then set out to *read broadly*. While we are not opposed to reading deeply, we ascribe greater value to reading broadly to learn from training and development situations involving many different stakeholders. Good improvisation is achieved through *making something out of everything*, thus our broad reading included food service operations, conflict in the food service industry, and conflict training. We identified useful training activities from the *Harvard Program on Negotiation* and specific conflict and communication training simulations from food services industry groups. This literature allowed us to build our credibility with UDS administrators because our training objectives were supported by existing literature (see Table 12.1).

Even so-called experts cannot become complacent in terms of their own preparation because each training situation always presents unique circumstances. Research exploring success in business, leadership, and client relations shows a strong correlation between reading volume and cognitive mindfulness (Cunningham & Stanovich, 2001). Mindfulness is a key factor in improvisation (Kulhan, 2017) and improvisation is necessary for professional success in creative fields, such as training and development (Shiu, 2014).

What is more, there are many indicators that autodidacts are better at business, better at adapting, better at leading, and better at communicating (Cunningham & Stanovich, 2001; Ritchie et al., 2013). In studies of entrepreneurship, researchers have found human capital obtained through education, whether self-education or formal education, is one of the strongest drivers of entrepreneurship performance (Millán, Congregado Román, van Praag, & van Stel, 2014). There are other positive links between education and entrepreneurial success. For instance, the more formal education entrepreneurs have, the greater probability their businesses will survive past five years, obtain higher profits, and discover more opportunities (Millán et al., 2014; Shane, 2000, 2008). In these articles, emphasis is placed on the activity of reading for cognitive awareness, not necessarily on technical expertise. Reading broadly, therefore, should not be limited to technical information. Rather, it should include all forms of information gathering. As Shane (2000) notes, identifying creative ways to resolve problems or discover new opportunities requires *prior knowledge*, knowledge that comes from both experience and ongoing education.

The three of us entered the consulting challenge with different, but complementary experiences; however, we also set out to read broadly about a variety of topics related to conflict, food service, and training and development. While the deliverables we provided UDS were supported by our specific research efforts related to the project, reading broadly proved most useful when answering impromptu questions during trainings (demonstrating competence) and helping resolve random problems as they arose (demonstrating value).

One random problem that was creatively resolved came to be called "the paper towel game." In a random conversation with UDS administrators, they said they were perplexed by the fact that line employees were stockpiling rolls of paper towels at their workstations. We determined line employees were stockpiling; turned out, they preferred paper towels to microfiber towels because they were faster to clean with (wipe and toss versus wipe and rinse). Management had failed to effectively communicate the important financial implication of this change to line-level employees or to train them how to effectively use the microfiber towels to reduce rinsing. We suggested to management that they physically show employees how to use the new microfiber towels and encourage them to use them more than paper towels. We also suggested, since one of us was reading broadly on the topic of gameful learning at the time, they educate employees on the benefits of microfiber towels through gamification. This approach would arguably accelerate employee adoption and increase use-efficiency of microfiber towels. Gamification could be achieved, we suggested, by rewarding points daily to each shift that used the least paper towels during a shift. At the end of a specified period (we recommended a month), the shift with the most points would get a reward. This unique suggestion, one that they really thought was clever but did not ultimately use, was an opportunity to demonstrate competence and value to the client. A key question CCCTTs committed to BP4 ask is *How can our interests and continuing education creatively help solve our clients' problems?*

Involve all stakeholders

It is important to enter the consulting and training relationship with an understanding that the whole is smarter than the sum of its parts. That is, all stakeholders should, whenever possible and within reason, be included in discussions and decisions. *Involve all stakeholders* puts into service findings from articles showing the positive outcomes of participatory research and audience adaptation (Frick, 1983; Thory, 2016), stakeholder engagement (Herremans, Nazari, & Mahmoudian, 2016), and iterative processes in creative projects (de Blois, Lizarralde, & De Coninck, 2016). While a client may want to limit interaction with internal and external stakeholders, it is important you negotiate access to these parties (when applicable to context). This is not only to understand catalysts for change (BP5), but also to subject matter experts who can be leveraged (BP4) to identify problems and solutions that reside with clients (Schein, 1999). In our case, we began by negotiating access to line staff.

While we were allowed some interaction with union representatives, concern about union regulations limited our ability to interact with line staff outside of the three training sessions. To address this limitation, we incorporated small group discussions into our training program. Trainers moved among the discussion groups, participating in conversations when appropriate, and made notes about the topics of discussion, specific ideas, and potential solutions expressed by trainees. Notes derived from small group discussions broadened our understanding of line staff's catalysts for change (BP5) and participation in small group discussions allowed trainers to demonstrate competency (BP4) by sharing insights gleaned from *reading broadly* in preparation for the training. *Involving all stakeholders* in one-on-one discussion strengthened our consulting relationship because all stakeholders were engaged in the training, improving our likelihood of successful intervention (Striley, 2016).

Research supports the positive impact of stakeholder engagement in the consulting relationship. Direct benefits include increased creativity (Baker & Nelson, 2005; Barrett, 1998; Kulhan, 2017; Shane, 2000) – the primary antecedent to bricolage and improvisation – and improved audience adaptation and solution implementation (Ozanne et al., 2017; Purvis, Zagenczyk, & McCray, 2015; Scheba & Mustalahti, 2015). Moreover, when consultants involve others it increases expectancy of positive outcomes, which increase self-fulfilling predictions about program success. When people see their ideas implemented into a solution, they are more motivated to make the solutions work (Purvis et al., 2015).

Involving others also reduces problems that arise when a consultant excludes certain stakeholders, which can lead to failed intervention attempts (Striley, 2016). This is a primary reason BP5 suggests a non-comprehensive list of possible catalysts ("Best practices…," n.d.). CCCTTs who do not consider all catalysts will likely lose the buy-in necessary for a successful intervention. For this reason, we focused on building rapport up and down the hierarchy, including with union representatives who helped us find creative ways to protect line staff as we collected information that would be useful to managers. Union reps are catalyst for change as well, so including them ensured we identified all possible sources of miscommunication and conflict. How will you create a training environment to facilitate all stakeholders' voices in your next training?

Collaborate with others

The final practice comprising a BRIC orientation is collaboration, which builds upon the premise of involving everyone. It is one thing to involve others in data collection, discussion, and feedback, it is another to involve others in analysis and invention of strategy. Collaboration is often defined in communication as working together with others in a manner that retains a high concern for self and other, with engagement ultimately producing something greater than could have been achieved individually (Hocker & Wilmot, 2014). In business literatures, effective stakeholder engagement and creativity are often described as requiring a "collaborative mindset," which is why organizations increasingly want to recruit people who are adept at building relationships with a range of stakeholders (Lowitt, 2013).

As Schein (1999) notes, "we make sense of ambiguous situations by sharing perceptions and thoughts" (p. 102). We must share, however, with expectation of joint sensemaking and mutual expectation that each party engages in a sincere effort to "figure out and define the situation so that we know how to operate in it" (p. 102). This important point requires reflective pause. Schein articulates two important starting points many consultants may not begin with: (1) stakeholders are engaged in the process of resolving problems already and (2) trainers engage with the client with a vested interest from the beginning. There is no need for cajoling, persuading, or making demands. There simply needs to be an interest in *helping*, in *working with others*, in *listening to understand* with a collaborative goal of inventing solutions.

A collaborative approach to identifying solutions guided our third training session with UDS. During this training we built upon discussions that *involved all stakeholders* and asked trainees to help develop strategies to lessen workplace conflict, specifically responding to the following question: *What changes can be made to resolve unproductive workplace conflict through collaboration?* Line staff, managers, and administrators collaborated with trainers to *imagine and invent solutions* to previous or ongoing conflicts. For instance, line staff expressed frustration with the unidirectional, top-down nature of communication in the workplace. Together, line staff and administrators decided sessions moderated by third party representatives, such as our trainings, helped to address this frustration. Collaboration among stakeholders resulted in a proposed solution that directly addressed the situation and was agreeable to all parties.

Of course, collaboration is not easy. Weick (1993), for example, showed sensemaking becomes rather fragile if there is a loss of trust or a lack of coherent processes. As TDPs, we may enter some organizations or situations that are in disarray and we may need to be more assertive than collaborative (Orton & O'Grady, 2016). However, even in these extreme cases (e.g., O'Grady & Orton, 2016), we should set up the process for collaboration to occur and teach others the value of collaboration, which is fundamentally about "communicat[ing] in such a way as to facilitate mutual understanding" (Schein, 1999, p. 103). Through collaboration, we create and demonstrate processes that make organizational stakeholders more resilient and able to adapt to changing contexts. That is to say, we generate bricolage. Consultants adhering to BP5, in embracing collaboration, model behaviors that may rub off on others in the organization. As Weick, Schein, and others have shown us, collaboration is a catalyst to change.

We were fortunate to enter a situation that was generally well managed. Despite some common workplace gripes, data from our surveys and ethnographic interviews showed UDS was well managed and a positive workplace (Engstrom et al., 2017). Had we entered the organization with the assumption they hired us to resolve a problem, this would have been a significant error on our part and against training best practices. Instead, we embraced best practices through a BRIC model. We recognized UDS administrators had already embraced a worldview that sees collaboration as key to their success. Our goal was not to teach them collaboration, but to validate their approach. We used their worldview to our advantage, suggesting a creative training–consulting relationship that would lead to productive outcomes for all parties.

Summarizing BRIC

As the above sections highlight, our BRIC approach presents a novel way to understand *communication trainers as bricoleurs*, an orientation that embodies the objectives of BP4 and BP5. Though novel, BRIC is empirically grounded in existing research, including Schein's process philosophy, which has guided TDPs for 50 years. To summarize, *be humble* draws upon Edgar Schein's (2013, 2016) concepts and strategies of humble inquiry and humble consulting. *Read broadly* points to existing publications on the direct relationship among reading, other forms of continuing education, and success. *Involve all stakeholders* focuses findings from articles showing the positive outcomes of participatory research and audience adaptation (Frick, 1983; Thory, 2016), stakeholder engagement (Herremans, Nazari, & Mahmoudian, 2016), and iterative processes in creative projects (de Blois, Lizarralde, & De Coninck, 2016). Finally, *collaborate with others* comes from studies in the communication discipline on the usefulness of collaboration for project and relational success (e.g., Heath & Isbell, 2015; O'Grady & Orton, 2016).

Chapter summary and key takeaways

In this chapter, we demonstrated BRIC in practice and showed how this framework can be instructive when approaching training-as-bricolage. Specifically, our BRIC approach allowed us to resolve two specific problems we faced as trainers–consultants: (1) lack of knowledge of client's needs and (2) issues between employees and management during trainings. Approaching the training with a desire to *be humble*, we acknowledged areas we needed to *read broadly* in order to expand our knowledge about conflict in the food service industry. In addition, we *involved all stakeholders* during the first training to better understand employee needs and asked them, again through humble inquiry and involvement, to help us generate solutions through *collaborative* communication efforts.

The overall training relationship proved effective because of our willingness to draw on different communication theories, training models, and stakeholder feedback. We continued to learn and adapt throughout the process, even throwing away some of our initial plans. In short, we were effective because we engaged in *bricolage*. Approaching training as bricolage, we created "something out of everything" (Kulhan, 2017, p. 9), which resulted in a stronger training program. More importantly, we were guided by antecedents to bricolage, which align with the NCA's Training and Development Division's best practices of ongoing professional development (BP4) and working with others as catalysts of change (BP5). In practice, this meant continuing education and doing after-training-reviews (ATRs); these proved critically important during and after training sessions and project completion.

Our case and the BRIC approach have implications for both practitioners and academics. For practitioner readers, we foremost hope you will add bricolage and bricoleur to your vocabulary and share stories of application of BRIC in training and development activities. Our first key takeaway argues humility is related to personality, but it is also a communicative performance. For those wanting an introduction to humility, consider reading Schein's books; however, humility is also achieved by reaching out to peers. Second, we cannot over-emphasize the need to read broadly. We all risk getting comfortable with what we know works in the field. But we must ensure we are bringing new and useful insights to our clients. For this reason, BP4 emphasizes *subject and performance competency acquisition and maintenance*. Third, BP5 requires developing and maintaining organizational expertise. As we learned in our case, however, employees are often the catalyst for change (BP5) and should not be overlooked during the consulting and training process. As our case highlighted, they are often the source and force of consulting and training success.

For academic readers, we have explained that BRIC operationalize best practices, which can be summarized with four propositions. We hope you will study or test these propositions in future studies, since a study of BRIC can validate best practices 4 and 5:

Proposition 1: Consulting relationships and training outcomes will be positively improved when CCCTTs demonstrate humility in communication.
Proposition 2: Consulting and training success improves with continuing education because it provides more resources for improvisational communication *in situ*.
Proposition 3: Communication with all stakeholders within training, development, and consulting situations will positively influence training and consulting outcomes.
Proposition 4: Collaboration as communication style is influenced by and influences humility, improvisation, and involvement; collaboration leads to unique training and consulting outcomes.

To build upon and study these propositions, we recommend beginning with a review of literature listed in Table 12.2. Those wanting a crash introduction to training as bricolage, specifically, should begin their study with this handbook and Schein's *Humble Inquiry* and *Humble Consulting*.

While not every training and consulting situation lends itself to this participatory orientation, a BRIC approach can be achieved when BP4 and BP5 are embraced by CCCTTs. These intertwined best practices reminded us to approach the field with some humility and to draw on others' expertise as we recognized that they are ultimately the catalysts for change. The BRIC approach, which simply proves an easy-to-remember acronym, enabled us to deliver training and consulting expertise that met the client's goals; however, and perhaps most importantly, we found creative solutions to problems encountered throughout the project.

Thus, the four sets of practices explained in this chapter should usefully guide others' application of best practice guidelines, which, as demonstrated in Table 12.2, are overlapping and reinforcing. These best practices should guide you to engage training, development, and consulting as a bricoleur (BRIC approach). The communication trainer, by adhering to all best practices, but especially BPs 4 and 5 ("Best Practices...," n.d.), is, in practice, a trainer-as-bricoleur.

References

Allen, J., Jimmieson, N. L., Bordia, P., & Irmer, B. E. (2007). Uncertainty during organizational change: Managing perceptions through communication. *Journal of Change Management*, 7(2), 187–210. doi:10.1080/14697010701563379

Baker, T., & Nelson, R. E. (2005). Creating something from nothing: Resource construction through entrepreneurial bricolage. *Administrative Science Quarterly*, 50(3), 329–366.

Barrett, F. J. (1998). Creativity and improvisation in jazz and organizations: Implications for organizational learning. *Organization Science*, 9(5), 605–622.

Bateson, G. (1969). The position of humor in human communication. In J. Levine (ed.), *Motivation in humor* (pp. 159–178). New Brunswick, NJ: Aldine Transaction.

Beal, B. (2017). Leaders' courage in showing humility. *Human Resource Management International Digest*, 25(2), 28–40.

Best practices background. (n.d.). *NCA Training and Development Division*. Retrieved from http://ncatraininganddevelopment.com/training-best-practices/best-practices-background

Beverland, M., Kates, S., Lindgreen, A., & Chung, E. (2010). Exploring consumer conflict management in service encounters. *Journal of the Academy of Marketing Science, 38*(5), 617–633. doi:10.1007/s11747-009-0162-0

Boles, J. S., & Babin, B. J. (1996). On the front lines: Stress, conflict, and the customer service provider. *Journal of Business Research, 37*, 41–50.

Buzzanell, P. M., & Burrell, N. A. (1997). Family and workplace conflict: Examining metaphorical conflict schemas and expressions across context and sex. *Human Communication Research, 24*, 109–146.

Cameron, K. S., & Caza, A. (2004). Contributions to the discipline of positive organizational scholarship. *American Behavioral Scientist, 47*, 731–739.

Cunningham, A. E., & Stanovich, K. E. (2001). What reading does for the mind. *Journal of Direct Instruction, 1*(2), 137–149.

de Blois, M., Lizarralde, G., & De Coninck, P. (2016). Iterative project processes within temporary multi-organizations in construction: The self-, eco-, re-organizing projects. *Project Management Journal, 47*(1), 27–44. doi:10.1002/pmj.21560

De Dreu, C., D. van Dierendonck, & Dijkstra, M. (2004). Conflict at work and individual well-being. *International Journal of Conflict Management, 15*, 6–26.

Eisenberg, E. M. (1984). Ambiguity as strategy in organizational communication. *Communication Monographs, 51*(3), 227–242.

Eisenberg, E. M. (1990). Jamming: Transcendence through organizing. *Communication Research, 17*(2), 139–164. doi:10.1177/009365090017002001

Engstrom, C., Forst, M., & Brown, L. (2017, November). In search of civil service: An à la carte approach to training university dining staff in conflict reduction tactics. National Communication Conference (Training & Development Division), Dallas, Texas.

Fisher, R., & Ury, W. (1991). *Getting to yes: Negotiating agreement without giving in.* New York, NY: Penguin.

Fricke, W. (1983). Participatory research and the enhancement of workers' innovative qualifications. *Journal of Occupational Behavior, 4*, 73–87.

Grandey, A. A., Kern, J. H., & Frone, M. R. (2007). Verbal abuse from outsiders versus insiders: Comparing frequency, impact on emotional exhaustion, and the role of emotional labor. *Journal of Occupational Health Psychology, 12*, 63–79.

Han, S. J., Bonn, M. A., & Cho, M. (2016). The relationship between customer incivility, restaurant frontline service employee burnout and turnover intention. *International Journal of Hospitality Management, 52*, 97–106. doi:10.1016/j.ijhm.2015.10.002

Hanley, L. (2011). Mashing up the institution: Teacher as bricoleur. *Radical Teacher, 90*, 9–14.

Heath, R. G., & Isbell, M. (2015). Broadening organizational communication curricula: Collaboration as key to 21st-century organizing. *Management Communication Quarterly, 29*, 309–314. doi:10.1177/0893318915571351

Herremans, I., Nazari, J., & Mahmoudian, F. (2016). Stakeholder relationships, engagement, and sustainability reporting. *Journal of Business Ethics, 138*(3), 417–435. doi:10.1007/s10551-015-2634-0

Hocker, J. L., & Wilmot, W. W. (2014). *Interpersonal conflict* (9th ed.). Boston, MA: McGraw Hill.

Kao, F.-H., Cheng, B.-S., Kuo, C.-C., & Huang, M.-P. (2014). Stressors, withdrawal, and sabotage in frontline employees: The moderating effects of caring and service climates. *Journal of Occupational & Organizational Psychology, 87*, 755–780. doi:10.1111/joop.12073

Koyama, J. (2014). Principals as bricoleurs: Making sense and making do in an era of accountability. *Educational Administration Quarterly, 50*(2), 279–304.

Kulhan, B. (2017). *Getting to "yes and": The art of business improv.* Stanford, CA: Stanford Business Books.

Lakoff, G., & Johnson, M. (1980). *Metaphors we live by.* Chicago, IL: University of Chicago Press.

Langer, E. (1997). *The power of mindful learning.* Reading, MA: Addison-Wesley

Lévi-Strauss, C. (1966). *The savage mind* (trans. G. Weidenfeld & N. Nicolson). Chicago, IL: University of Chicago Press.

Lowitt, E. (2013). *The collaboration economy: How meet business, social, and environmental needs and gain competitive advantage.* San Francisco, CA: Jossey-Bass.

Lynch, O. H. (2009). Kitchen antics: The importance of humor and maintaining professionalism at work. *Journal of Applied Communication Research, 37,* 444–464.

McCorkle, S., & Mills, J. L. (1992). Rowboat in a hurricane: Metaphors of interpersonal conflict management. *Communication Reports, 5*(2), 57–66.

Menkel-Meadow, C. (2006). Why hasn't the world gotten to yes? An appreciation and some reflections. *Negotiation Journal, 22,* 485–503.

Millán, J. M., Congregado, E., Román, C., van Praag, M., & van Stel, A. (2014). The value of an educated population for an individual's entrepreneurship success. *Journal of Business Venturing, 29,* 612–632. doi:10.1016/j.jbusvent.2013.09.003

O'Grady, K. A., & Orton, J. D. (2016). Resilience processes during cosmology episodes: Lessons learned from the Haiti earthquake. *Journal of Psychology & Theology, 44*(2), 109–123.

Orton, J. D., & O'Grady, K. A. (2016). Cosmology episodes: A reconceptualization. *Journal of Management, Spirituality & Religion, 13*(3), 226–245. doi:10.1080/14766086.2016.1159975

Owens, B. P., & Hekman, D. R. (2012). Modeling how to grow: An inductive examination of humble leader behaviors, contingencies, and outcomes. *Academy of Management Journal, 55*(4), 787–818. doi:10.5465/amj.2010.0441

Owens, B. P., & Hekman, D. R. (2016). How does leader humility influence team performance? Exploring the mechanisms of contagion and collective promotion focus. *Academy of Management Journal, 59*(3), 1088–1111. doi:10.5465/amj.2013.0660

Ozanne, J. L., Davis, B., Murray, J. B., Grier, S., Benmecheddal, A., Downey, H.,... Veer, E. (2017). Assessing the societal impact of research: The relational engagement approach. *Journal of Public Policy & Marketing, 36*(1), 1–14.

Purvis, R. L., Zagenczyk, T. J., & McCray, G. E. (2015). What's in it for me? Using expectancy theory and climate to explain stakeholder participation, its direction and intensity. *International Journal of Project Management, 33,* 3–14. doi:10.1016/j.ijproman.2014.03.003

Ritchie, S. J., Luciano, M., Hansell, N. K., Wright, M. J., & Bates, T. C. (2013). The relationship of reading ability to creativity: Positive, not negative associations. *Learning & Individual Differences, 26,* 171–176.

Scheba, A., & Mustalahti, I. (2015). Rethinking 'expert' knowledge in community forest management in Tanzania. *Forest Policy and Economics, 60,* 7–18. doi:10.1016/j.forpol.2014.12.007

Schein, E. H. (1999). *Process consultation revisited.* Reading, MA: Addison-Wesley Publishing Company.

Schein, E. H. (2013). *Humble inquiry: The gentle art of asking instead of telling.* San Francisco, CA: Berrett-Koehler Publishers, Inc.

Schein, E. H. (2016). *Humble consulting: How to provide real help faster.* Oakland, CA: Berrett-Koehler Publishers.

Sclavi, M. (2008). The role of play and humor in creative conflict management. *Negotiation Journal, 24*(2), 157–180. doi:10.1111/j.1571–9979.2008.00175.x

Shane, S. A. (2000). Prior knowledge and the discovery of entrepreneurial opportunities. *Organization Science, 11*(4), 448–469.

Shane, S. A. (2008). *The illusions of entrepreneurship: The costly myths that entrepreneurs, investors, and policy makers live by.* New Haven, CT: Yale University Press.

Shiu, E. C. C. (2014). *Creativity research: An inter-disciplinary and multi-disciplinary research handbook.* Hoboken, NJ: Routledge.

Stinchfield, B. T., Nelson, R. E., & Wood, M. S. (2013). Learning from Levi-Strauss' legacy: Art, craft, engineering, bricolage, and brokerage in entrepreneurship. *Entrepreneurship: Theory & Practice, 37*(4), 889–921. doi:10.1111/j.1540–6520.2012.00523.x

Striley, K. (2016). Corruption, addiction, and scandal: Lessons learned from a failed attempt to engage a community's youth. In C. Engstrom & J. Frye (eds.), *Qualitative communication consulting: Stories and lessons from the field*. Dubuque, IA: Kendall Hunt.

Taylor, K. A., Mesmer-Magnus, J., & Burns, T. M. (2008). Teaching the art of negotiation: Improving students' negotiating confidence and perceptions of effectiveness. *Journal of Education for Business, 83*(3), 135–140.

Tews, M. J., Michel, J. W., & Stafford, K. (2013). Does fun pay? The impact of workplace fun on employee turnover and performance. *Cornell Hospitality Quarterly, 54,* 370–382.

Thory, K. (2016). Developing meaningfulness at work through emotional intelligence training. *International Journal of Training and Development, 20*(1), 58–77.

Van den Broeck, A., Vander Elst, T., Dikkers, J., De Lange, A., & De Witte, H. (2012). This is funny: On the beneficial role of self-enhancing and affiliative humour in job design. *Psicothema, 24*(1), 87–93.

Weick, K. E. (1993). The collapse of sensemaking in organizations: The Mann Gulch disaster. *Administrative Science Quarterly, 38*(4), 628–653.

Yang, M.-Y., Cheng, F.-C., & Chuang, A. (2015). The role of affects in conflict frames and conflict management. *International Journal of Conflict Management (Emerald), 26,* 427–449.

Chapter 13

Deliberate practice activities of communication professionals and implications for training and consulting

Helen Lie

Abstract

This chapter presents an interview-questionnaire study that explored expertise development activities of 22 professional speakers utilizing the deliberate practice framework. Sixteen deliberate practice activities used to enhance presentation excellence in professional speaking were identified and grouped into five themes: access to resources and community; audience connection; self-development and learning; experience and rehearsal; and self-monitoring and feedback. Implications for CCCTTs in terms of professional development and instructional design for presentation skills training are discussed.

The ability to speak and communicate ideas clearly and convincingly is a highly valued skill among employers and college students (Hart Research Associates, 2015; Hooker & Simonds, 2015). This is likely why the market for presentation skills training is booming, and why nearly 80 per cent of surveyed colleges and universities are including an oral communication course in their general education requirements (see Morreale, Myers, Backlund, & Simonds, 2016). How can communication consultants, coaches, teachers, and trainers (CCCTTs) working in this context effectively guide their clients, trainees, and students in the art of oral communication and help them develop speaking expertise?

In its *Best Practices for Communication Training and Consulting* (Best Practices Background, n.d.), the National Communication Association's (NCA's) Training and Development Division outlines a comprehensive framework of skills that are necessary to be an effective CCCTT. In the realm of presentation skills training, demonstrating effective and appropriate instructional design competence is particularly important. The subjective, interactive and context-dependent nature of communication performance (Morreale, Backlund, Hay, & Moore, 2011) makes it possible for any earnest listener to offer valid critique and advice. Without detracting from layperson perspectives, CCCTTs are behooved to deliver more value and expertise to their clients. One way they can do this is by developing training goals and methods that address the specific learning needs of the client or trainee (NCA's Training ..., n.d.), and by grounding their advice and instructional methods not just on practical experience, which is invaluable, but also on research. CCCTTs who use research-based training methods and techniques are able to facilitate with a clear rationale and conceptual framework. Explaining the empirical grounding for training plans, goals, and activities enhances credibility with clients and trainees, which helps them become more receptive to learning.

This chapter describes an exploratory study on the expertise development activities of professional speakers and discusses the implications of this research to the work of CCCTTs. Professional speakers are individuals who get paid to speak; their livelihoods depend on their maintaining excellence in the art of public speaking. CCCTTs may find empirically-based strategies for designing effective presentation skills training and inspiration to continue their own professional development from the disciplines of these speaking experts.

The interpretive framework for the study was a theory of expertise development called deliberate practice (Ericsson, Krampe, & Tesch-Römer, 1993). Past studies have identified deliberate practice activities in work settings including teaching (Dunn & Shriner, 1999), insurance sales (Sonnentag & Kleine, 2000), and organizational consulting (Van de Wiel, Szegedi, & Weggeman, 2004). In a similar vein, the aim of the present study was to investigate what constitutes deliberate practice in the domain of professional speaking.

What is deliberate practice?

Deliberate practice refers to individualized and structured training, typically designed by a teacher or coach, that facilitates improvement in performance (Ericsson & Charness, 1994). Whereas routine practice may involve practicing what one already knows to do well, deliberate practice involves identifying weaknesses or areas of improvement and practicing until those areas are strengthened. Ericsson generally asserts that over a 10-year period, individuals who engage in more deliberate practice will outperform their peers who possess comparable years of experience (Ericsson, Roring, & Nandagopal, 2007; Ericsson & Charness, 1994). Once expert performance levels are attained, continued improvements in performance can be accomplished through ongoing deliberate practice.

A deliberate practice activity has several characteristics: 1) the task is well-defined; 2) the level of difficulty must be appropriate for the learner; 3) the task is designed specifically to improve performance; 4) the learner receives feedback regarding the results of their performance; and 5) the learner has opportunities to repeat and correct any errors (Ericsson & Charness, 1994; Ericsson et al., 2007). Examples of deliberate practice activities found in professional domains include reflection on what is and is not working in teaching (Dunn & Shriner, 1999); reading academic articles and self-directed studying in the fields of medical study (Moulaert, Verwijnen, Rikers, & Scherpbier, 2004) and organizational consulting (Van de Wiel et al., 2004); asking for feedback and engaging in mental simulation in insurance sales (Sonnentag & Kleine, 2000).

Description and methods of the study

In the study of professional speakers, deliberate practice was defined as any activity that: a) had a goal of performance or competence improvement; b) was maintained with some frequency for at least one year; and c) was considered relevant to performance or competence improvement. These definitional criteria were similar to those of previous deliberate practice studies in professional contexts (Sonnentag & Kleine, 2000; Van de Wiel et al., 2004).

The study involved 22 highly experienced and elite members of the National Speakers Association, a leading professional association for developing and professional speakers that provides training, resources, and support to its roughly 3400 members. All 22 participants had earned the NSA's Certified Speaking Professional (CSP) designation, which represents the top 10 per cent of the professional speaking community. Ten of the speakers had also earned an honorary award within the NSA known as the Council of Peers Award for Excellence (CPAE) – considered to be the organization's Speaker Hall of Fame. Participants had an average of 28.45 years of professional speaking experience (range was 8–50 years). The average age of the participants was 58.1 years. The participants included 14 men and 8 women. Twenty (91 per cent) of the participants were white/Caucasian, one (4.5 per cent) Asian, and one (4.5 per cent) Hispanic. All the participants resided in the United States; seven in the Western region, six in the South, three in the Midwest, and six in the Northeast region. Participants were initially identified via a combination of referral, snowball, and random selection methods, and their participation was completely voluntary and uncompensated.

Each speaker participated in a 30–60-minute semi-structured phone interview. A standard guide of questions was used, with flexibility for additional probes or clarification questions. To establish content validity, the interview guide was developed in consultation with two members of the NSA – a CSP and the Chair of Research at the NSA Foundation. The interview guide was also piloted with four other NSA members. All but one interview was voice-recorded and transcribed (one interview was documented via notetaking).

16 activities and 5 deliberate practice themes

To analyze the interview data, a general analysis mode called bricolage was used to identify recurring themes and potential deliberate practice activities. Bricolage is a common approach to interview analysis, in which the researcher uses whatever tools, approaches, and concepts are available to generate meaning (Kvale & Brinkmann, 2009). In this case, the researcher reviewed the transcripts noting any unit or idea expressed by a speaker that represented a behavior, activity, or sentiment that was considered an element in his or her growth, training, or practice. To consolidate the units, similar ideas were clustered together, and general activities were identified. Activities were determined based on their being mentioned at least three times by speakers across the 22 interviews. The researcher then looked for any correspondence between the 16 activities and the components of deliberate practice that are described in the literature. Specifically, deliberate practice involves goal setting, feedback, monitoring, and repetition (Ericsson et al., 1993). Some of these components became labels for themes. Other themes emerged by finding a logical relationship between the various units. The researcher reviewed the interview notes and transcripts to see if there was any evidence that had been missed, or any data that might deviate from the generated units or themes.

To confirm initial interpretations of the interview data, a follow-up questionnaire was developed and administered that measured frequency of engagement, effort required, and perceived relevance of each activity to expertise development. The questions were similar to those found in deliberate practice studies that used structured interviews or questionnaires (Dunn & Shriner, 1999; Sonnentag & Kleine, 2000). A total of 18 speakers participated in the survey, yielding a response rate of 82 per cent. The 16 activities were grouped into five deliberate practice themes. The themes and activities are described below.

Theme #1: Access to resources and community

The first theme was participating in a community of like-minded professionals, such as the National Speakers Association. All but one speaker attributed NSA membership as a major source of skill development and maintenance. Participation in NSA activities could involve attending national conferences and workshops, local chapter meetings, conference calls and tele-seminars. At each of these events, effective speaking techniques are both discussed and modeled. Two additional activities placed in this theme were attending other speaking group meetings and observing other speakers.

Joining a community of peers and professionals provided speakers with *access* to resources; e.g., mentors, models, coaches, and skills training that they may otherwise not have had if working in isolation. This finding supports Ericsson et al.'s (1993) assertion that in order to engage in deliberate practice, individuals need to overcome what he called a resource constraint—the need for access to training materials, equipment, or quality coaches and teachers. Speaker 8 commented:

> I could just walk up to any speaker there and pretty much ask any question I wanted. So the ability to have the access to people that are at all levels of success or failure ... was something that really helped me with my career.

Participating in a community of speaking professionals appears to supply speakers with the synergy that not only motivates them to get better but provides guidance and resources to help support their development. Speaker 11 said:

> The business can be lonely if you're just on your own all the time feeding yourself your own stuff. You don't even know what you don't know. And by going to the meetings, I found that I knew – I got to learn what I didn't know.

Social interaction behaviors such as consulting peers and professionals have also been identified as important contributors to skill development in previous studies of teachers, insurance agents, and organizational consultants (Dunn & Shriner, 1999; Sonnentag & Kleine, 2000; Van de Wiel et al. 2004). Whether new to the field, or seeking fresh motivation and insight, CCCTTs who participate in a community of practitioners position themselves to find support, share resources with peers, and thereby accelerate their growth.

Theme #2: Audience connection

The second theme that emerged was audience connection. Professional speakers emphasized the importance of keeping the audience at the forefront of their minds to have meaningful and genuine interaction. Three activities that were placed in this theme were focusing on the audience, "committing to give 100%" to a speech performance and being "authentic."

Focusing on the audience involved getting to know the audience, tailoring the presentation to the audience's need, and working with the client to understand expectations and desired outcomes. Referred to in the professional speaking industry as customization (Speakers 3, 9, 11), the practice of making slight adjustments in a speech for a particular audience was considered key to speaking effectiveness. Speaker 18 said: "Regardless of who your audience is and how many times you've presented something, you always need to be on top of your game." Focusing on the audience could also involve building positive rapport with the audience before the speech event. Speaker 10 said, "I learned to stand at the door, whether it was 2000 people or 20, and greet people, call them by name, ask them questions." Speaker 12 expressed a similar practice: "I go early so I can scope out the audience and get a feel for what they're like."

Focusing on the audience was typically mentioned in contrast to focusing on one's own ego, or being in an "arrogant, auto–pilot state of mind" (Speaker 15). Speaker 3 talked about the importance of making a good impression with the client, or event organizer: "exhibiting as much patience as needed and certainly not coming across as a prima donna." Focusing less on themselves and more on the audience may have required struggle and experience. Speaker 6 said:

> For me, the most difficult thing is getting my ego out of it... I mess myself up if I start thinking about, 'Okay, I really hope they like me. What can I do that will make them like me?' ... If I remember that it's about them and about the ideas, then I'm fine.

Speaker 18 described his current audience-centered mindset as something that developed over time: "I don't want to be a superstar. I don't want to be obtuse. I don't want to be anything except clear... I think 10 years ago, it would have been much more about being on stage."

Being focused on how to best connect with the audience rather than on oneself was considered to be the ideal state of mind. This mindset was also described as "making a commitment to give 100%" to a speech performance, "not holding anything back" on the platform, and being "fully present." Speaker 8 would say to himself, "This is going to be the best one yet... let everything else go," or "Stop thinking about delivery." Speaker 10 put it this way:

> [I]f you are focused on the message, your mission, and the meaning of what you're bringing, it enhances presence. If you're focused on money, marketing, and media, it stands in the way of presence. There's nothing worse than a hungry salesman.

Closely related to audience focus was the notion of "authenticity," which meant seeking to be the same person on the stage as off the stage. "Really walking my talk," was how Speaker 22 put it. Speaker 10 described it as "being comfortable in one's own skin." If a speaker was not being himself or herself, the inherent falseness in the speaking situation would be a turn-off for the audience. Thus, "authenticity" was also related to credibility. A speaker should not address topics on which they have no expertise or give advice that he or she did not live by. Speaker 22 said this message was emphasized at an NSA convention: "Speak from your heart, your truth, your passion, and tell your story."

As expert speakers suggested, achieving audience connection through activities such as customization and being yourself is easier said than done. For beginning speakers, developing a sense of one's own style and message can take time. But emphasizing audience connection as a primary objective at all times will stand CCCTTs – and their clients and trainees – in good stead.

Theme #3: Self-development and learning

The third theme was self-development and learning. Professional speakers engaged in activities that would stimulate their minds, foster creativity, and inspire new speaking material. Speakers sought out new ideas to apply to their speaking practice and improve their performance.

One speaker, a business expert, read newspapers and periodicals, like *Forbes Magazine* and the business section of *The New York Times*, diligently looking for new ideas that could be applied to a speech for a client. Another speaker, an expert in a specific niche market, spent 2 hours a day, or 10–12 hours per week researching relevant reports and national statistics related to his topic. Other reading materials included biographies, inspirational books, and self-help books.

Writing was another way speakers developed content expertise. One speaker maintained an extensive online presence, including four professional websites and two fan pages, produced an e-zine, and used blogging and tweeting to generate and test material:

> Blogs are open for comment so it creates dialogue. Blogs also get reposted and almost every platform ... will tell you how many times it's been reposted. Twitter's even better because... in 140 characters, I can really play with words and I know if it struck a chord by how many times it gets re-tweeted.

Another speaker sent out a weekly tip to clients and considered how to integrate the tip as a "bit" or "chunk" in a presentation. Publishing a book was often a means to increase name recognition and be invited to speaking engagements: "[Publishing] gives you a platform that you didn't have before."

Some speakers hired a speech coach, who would meet one-on-one to review video footage and suggest ways the speaker could improve his or her delivery and technique. Speaker 2 had been a full-time professional speaker for six years when he hired a speech coach, and described the coach's feedback on his video as follows:

> Well, some of it was kind of philosophical. For instance, in the first few minutes I had done a bunch of humor, and then I got serious. I remember [the coach] said, 'You know, people are wondering what happened to the funny guy. If you're too funny at the beginning, you set up the expectation that you're going to be funny throughout.' Then some of it was real specific, like, 'Notice how you didn't pause long enough there.'... So I would say [the coach] was good at both the philosophical as well as the pragmatic—the mechanics, if you will.

Speaker 2 went on to explain that when working with a coach, easily a dozen things could be identified for improvement. However, only one or two changes can realistically be made at a time. Examples of goals speakers worked on with a coach included using specific and concise language, developing a speaking style that was more in line with the speaker's off-stage personality, storytelling, writing, and speaking with more authority, directness, and conviction. CCCTTs working with advanced speakers, or speakers who are at later stages of their presentation preparation, might consider any of these target areas for designing a session.

Not all speakers commissioned a speech coach. One concern was that ineffective coaching can cause speakers to become too focused on mechanics or cause them to become artificial. Speaker 10 said, "I've chosen not to get training because I've seen that training can squelch great speakers. They all begin to be cookie cutters, you know?" This caveat is a helpful warning for CCCTTs to be careful not to impose their own communication style when coaching their clients, and to avoid prolonged emphasis on specific nonverbal behaviors.

In addition to hiring speaking coaches, some speakers hired a vocal coach, a business coach, or an executive coach. A vocal coach might work on accent reduction, or general voice quality and breathing. A business coach would help develop marketing and employee management strategies to build the speaker's business. An executive coach might identify a speaker's personality strengths and weaknesses and offer practical advice on self-care and how to handle professional issues. The finding that accomplished professional speakers enlisted the help of a coach is an important insight for CCCTTs, because it highlights the value of coaching even for advanced learners.

Theme #4: Experience and rehearsal

The fourth theme was experience and rehearsal. Speakers emphasized the importance of seeking any opportunity to get in front of people; whether it be practicing at a Lion's Club meeting, attending a Toastmaster's meeting or a peer speaking group, or serving in a leadership position. A few speakers engaged in regular rehearsals on their own or with a coach. Speaker 3 reported spending 2–3 hours per week rehearsing new chunks of material. Speaker 1 regularly read his manuscript out loud, then committed the speech to memory. After that, he recited his entire speech quietly on a plane, or out loud while on a walk. In this manner, an hour-long speech would be rehearsed in 35–40 minutes. These rehearsal methods may be adapted by CCCTTs for their clients or for their own personal preparation.

Gaining speaking experience and having repeated opportunities to practice speeches were valuable for several reasons. First, getting experience was a way to build confidence. Speakers 11 and 7 both overcame stuttering gradually each time they spoke before larger and larger audiences and received positive feedback. Before going professional, another speaker was advised to go out and give 100 speeches, whether paid or unpaid, to test her ability and desire for the profession. After three years of tracking her performance, she came to the conclusion with encouragement from a peer that she could succeed as a professional speaker.

Second, by gaining experience, speakers had opportunities to give different versions of the same speech and thereby refine their delivery. With each successive version, they could pay attention to the effects of making small changes in the nuances of delivery, such as placement of pauses, or changes in vocalics. A keynote speaker described this process: "[Y]ou repeat the same scenario, and you're honing it. And you're developing how to say it and how to change the way you say it ... As we hone those keynotes, as we give them over and over, they become perfected."

Third, by gaining experience, speakers learned how to handle various situations, such as speaking in front of thousands, dealing with hecklers, dealing with difficult questions, and in one case, dealing with an audience member who had a heart attack during a presentation! Being willing to be open to new and uncomfortable situations was important to skill development. Speaker 21 explained: "[I give] myself permission to be uncomfortable so I can grow and that's not easy." This last point, that growth can involve discomfort is important for all CCCTTs to remember. This is not to say CCCTTs should take on gigs that are outside their area of expertise. Rather, CCCTTs should welcome opportunities to move outside of their comfort zones in order to expand and strengthen their skills.

Theme #5: Self-monitoring and feedback

The fifth theme was self-monitoring and feedback. Activities grouped into this theme were reflection (thinking about what worked and what did not work after a speech), watching oneself on video, and seeking feedback. Speaker 18, commenting on the importance of video review, said, "I was surprised at how much I was touching my clothing, pulled on my jacket." For audience feedback, speakers took note of nonverbal feedback during a presentation, obtained written evaluations, spoke with audience members directly after a presentation, or debriefed with the client after a presentation. Speakers would also ask friends, colleagues, and family members for feedback. Speakers often had to encourage their sources to be honest and constructive because they found people were typically reluctant to give anything but positive feedback.

Speakers also handled types of feedback differently. Audience evaluations were generally treated with caution. Speakers tended to give less weight to a single negative evaluation, and give more weight to a point of criticism when received by more than a few audience members. Speaker 18 said, "There's always that one person who is extremely dissatisfied and you have to make sure not to let that one person get under your skin – which is really easy to do." Notwithstanding, some speakers had learned to persist to find a constructive point to grow from even mean-spirited comments: "there's always a kernel of truth in every criticism." Some speakers also advised that audience feedback forms provided relative indicators of listeners' immediate reactions, rather than concrete data on the impact of a speech, or specific feedback that helped the speaker identify areas of improvement. Speakers 1, 2, and 8 cautioned that numeric ratings, such as "I give this speaker a 6 out of 10" are less helpful. "It just gives you a relative sense of how you did and there's no absolute benchmark" (Speaker 2).

Several speakers described client feedback as more valuable than audience feedback. The explanation was that the client, being the person who hired the speaker, was in the best position to inform the speaker whether they had fulfilled the job expectations. Speakers also took note of referrals, repeat business, and audience interest in purchasing the speaker's products. Speaker 20 said referrals, or lack thereof after a presentation, was the "ultimate form of feedback." Speaker 10 said, in contrast to audience feedback, which is vague and may be based on a subjective and fleeting sentiment, referrals are actual and concrete: "I'm going to trust that reality."

Another valuable source of feedback was peers, mentors, or coaches in the speaking community. Speakers might invite their peers or mentors to sit in on a live speech or send their peers or coach a video of their performance and request a critique. Speaker 2 explained:

> The best feedback comes from those who know enough about the profession who are proven in their own abilities that they can tell you not just the what but the why and the how. Here's what you did or didn't do. Here's why you should or shouldn't do it, and here's how to do it better. That's really key.

When considering the different modes and sources of feedback that were described here, an important note for CCCTTs is that not all feedback is equally valuable. When designing audience evaluation forms, for instance, CCCTTs may find that a few simple, open-ended questions, such as, "What was the most impactful moment in this presentation and why?" or "What would you suggest the speaker improve?" may yield more specific and helpful comments than a form that asks for numerical ratings. When facilitating peer feedback during a group session, CCCTTs may improve the quality of feedback by giving participants general guidelines regarding the desired tone of feedback, appropriate length of feedback, and how to balance constructive comments with affirming statements.

Frequency, relevance, and effort ratings of deliberate practice activities

To test the validity of the interview findings, a questionnaire was developed that featured the 16 activities that had been distilled from the interview data, generally maintaining the terminology used by the professional speakers in the interview. The speakers were asked to rate each activity according to frequency of engagement, effort required, and relevance to skill development.[1] The questionnaire data indicated on average, professional speakers considered all 16 activities relevant to developing expertise in speaking and engaged in most but not always all of the activities with some degree of regularity with the goal of skill improvement. Table 13.1 presents the 16 deliberate practice activities, delineated by theme, with mean ratings and affiliated standard deviations for frequency, relevance, and effort. Statistical tests supported that the questionnaire's three subscales were highly reliable using Cronbach's alpha [frequency (.85), relevance (.86), effort (.85)]. Responses of N/A and instances when a respondent left an item blank were treated as missing data and the mean response for an item was inserted. This involved a small percentage (4 per cent) of the total data. Activities that received the highest and lowest mean scores in each category are noted in the next few sections.[2]

Frequency

Deliberate practice activities that received the highest frequency scores in the three subscales included: "commit to give 100%" ($M = 6.83$, $SD = .38$), be "authentic" ($M = 6.67$, $SD = .59$), focus on the audience ($M = 6.22$, $SD = 1.26$), reflection ($M = 6.17$, $SD = 1.47$), and observe other performers ($M = 4.06$, $SD = 1.06$). The first four items were rated using a 7-point scale and the fifth was rated using a 5-point scale (see Table 13.1). Deliberate practice activities that received low frequency scores included: meet with a coach ($M = 1.78$, $SD = .88$), meet with a mentor ($M = 2.06$, $SD = .87$), and attend other speaking group meetings outside of the NSA ($M = 2.28$, $SD = .90$). For these items, a rating of 1 indicated a frequency response of "never"; a rating of 2 indicated a frequency of 1–2 times a year.

Relevance

Participants indicated how relevant each of the 16 activities was to their skill development, improvement, and maintenance. Response choices ranged from 1 to 5, with 1 meaning irrelevant, and 5 meaning extremely relevant. Deliberate practice activities that received the highest ratings for relevance to skill development were: "commit to give 100%" ($M = 4.94$, $SD = .24$), focus on the audience ($M = 4.83$, $SD = .51$), and be

Table 13.1 Mean ratings and standard deviations for frequency, relevance, and effort of deliberate practice activities in professional speaking (N = 18)

Theme	Activity	Frequency[1]	Relevance[2]	Effort[3]
Access to Resources and Community	Participate in NSA activities	2.94, 1.21 (Scale 2)	4.12, 1.17	3.06, .85
	Attend other speaking group meetings	2.28, .90 (Scale 2)	3.5, 1.37	2.62, .96
	Observe other performers	4.06, 1.06 (Scale 2)	4.17, 1.10	2.76, .90
Audience Connection	Focus on audience	6.22, 1.26 (Scale 3)	4.83, .51	3.83, 1.34
	Commit to give 100%	6.83, .38 (Scale 3)	4.94, .24	3.39, 1.20
	Be authentic	6.67, .59 (Scale 3)	4.67, .59	3.44, 1.15
Self-development and Learning	Read to stay current	4.00, 1.14 (Scale 1)	4.50, .79	3.06, 1.06
	Write	3.94, 1.11 (Scale 1)	4.39, .78	3.41, 1.00
	Meet with a coach	1.78, .88 (Scale 2)	3.07, 1.53	3.11, .60
	Meet with a mentor	2.06, .87 (Scale 2)	3.37, 1.50	2.77, 1.01
Experience and Rehearsal	Seek as many speaking opportunities as possible	3.50, 1.30 (Scale 1)	4.17, 1.30	3.76, 1.09
	Pay attention to details and nuances	5.67, 1.50 (Scale 3)	4.61, .70	2.94, 1.16
	Rehearse portions of my speech out loud	3.67, 2.22 (Scale 3)	4.31, 1.69	3.31, 1.03
Self-monitoring and Feedback	Reflection	6.17, 1.47 (Scale 3)	4.56, 1.04	3.00, .97
	Video critique	2.94, 1.06 (Scale 2)	3.83, 1.34	2.88, .70
	Seek feedback	3.78, 1.35 (Scale 2)	4.06, 1.16	2.82, .95

[1] The instrument featured three sub-scales to measure frequency of engagement for each activity. The scale ratings were as follows: Frequency Scale #1: 1 = Never; 2 = Once in a while; 3 = Monthly; 4 = Weekly; 5 = Daily; Frequency Scale #2: 1 = Never; 2 = 1–2 times/yr; 3 = 3–6 times/yr; 4 = 7–12 times/yr; 5 = more than 12 times/yr; Frequency Scale #3: 1 = Never; 2 = Seldom; 3 = Occasionally; 4 = Somewhat often; 5 = Often; 6 = Very often; 7 = Always.
[2] 1 = Irrelevant; 3 = Moderate Moderately relevant; 5 = Extremely relevant.
[3] 1 = No effort; 2 = Minimal effort; 3 = Moderate effort; 4 = Very effortful; 5 = Extremely effortful.

"authentic" (M = 4.67, SD =.59). Deliberate practice activities that received the lowest relevance ratings still received moderate relevance scores: meet with a coach (M = 3.07, SD = 1.53), meet with a mentor (M = 3.37, SD = 1.50), and attend other speaking group meetings (M = 3.5, SD = 1.37). Thus, all of the 16 activities on average received moderately strong to strong relevance ratings. Table 13.2 lists the 16 activities in order of relevance rating, from highest to lowest with rank number 9 reflecting a tie.

Effort

Participants ranked each of the 16 activities for degree of effort required to engage in that activity. The response choices for all 16 items ranged from 1 to 5, with 1 meaning no effort, 2 corresponding to minimal effort, 3 corresponding to moderate effort, 4 corresponding to very effortful, and 5 meaning extremely effortful. Practice activities that received the highest ratings for effort were: focus on the audience (M = 3.83, SD = 1.34), seek as many speaking opportunities as possible (M = 3.76, SD = 1.09), and be "authentic" (M = 3.44, SD = 1.15). Activities that received the lowest ratings for effort

Table 13.2 Ranked list and description of 16 deliberate practice (DP) activities in professional speaking in order of highest to lowest relevance ratings

Rank by Relevance	DP Activity	Description
1	Commitment to give 100%	Being fully present, an emotional commitment to focus all on connecting with the audience
2	Focus on the audience	Tailor the presentation to the audience's need, work with the client to make sure desired outcomes are understood
3	Be authentic	Be the same person on stage as off-stage, speak only on areas of personal expertise
4	Pay attention to details and nuances	Experiment with changes in stress, pause, intonation and observe effects on the audience to refine delivery
5	Reflection	Think about what worked and didn't work after a speech performance
6	Read to stay current	Read biographies, periodicals, self-help books, research relating to area of content expertise
7	Write	Maintain a blog, tweet, publish to develop content and increase name recognition
8	Rehearse portions of my speech out loud	Regular rehearsals to practice new material or commit portions of a talk to memory
9	Observe other performers	Learn from other speakers of what works and doesn't work, get inspiration from watching artistic performers
	AND	
	Seek as many speaking opportunities as possible	Be proactive to gain speaking experience to develop confidence, move out of comfort zone
10	Participate in NSA activities	Attend conferences, workshops, local chapter meetings, and tele-seminars
11	Seek feedback	Consult colleagues, audience members/client, friends and family for constructive comments
12	Video critique	Watch a recording of themselves with or without a coach to identify areas of improvement and assess performance
13	Attend other speaking group meetings	Toastmasters, small groups of colleagues where speakers can learn from others and practice with peer feedback
14	Meet with a mentor	Get advice from people who give honest feedback on how to develop speaking skills and the business
15	Meet with a coach	A speech coach can help identify areas of improvement for delivery and technique

were: attend other speaking group meetings (M = 2.62, SD =.96), observe other performers (M = 2.76, SD =.90), and meet with a mentor (M = 2.77, SD = 1.01). All of the 16 practice activities on average received low-moderate to moderately strong effort ratings.

The survey data reveal specifics about how much time and effort speakers put into the 16 deliberate practice activities on average in order to develop their speaking craft. What may be of particular interest to CCCTTs is that professional speakers engaged in some form of writing and reading on an almost-weekly basis, and considered these activities even more relevant to cultivating speaking excellence than meeting with a coach or mentor. CCCTTs might consider how much time they are currently setting aside for self-study, and establish a regular schedule if they are not already doing so. CCCTTs should also take note of three activities that appear to stand out for ranking in the top 5 for frequency, relevance, and effort: "commit to give 100%", focus on the audience, and be "authentic." Three additional activities that received high frequency ratings were: pay attention to details, reflection, and observe other performers. CCCTTs might ask themselves, to what extent am I currently engaging in these activities? What may be hindering me? How might I incorporate these activities as part of my professional practice in order to strengthen my expertise?

Limitations

The research design of the study had limitations, including a small convenience sample size of 22 participants. Although 22 was well within the acceptable range of qualitative interview studies (Kvale & Brinkmann, 2009), the number was not sufficiently large to warrant strong conclusions about a population without additional research. Another limitation of the study was the lack of validity measures for the interview data and questionnaire. During the interviews, it is possible that participants were unable to recall or effectively speak about their practice behaviors accurately and completely. Moreover, items on the follow-up questionnaire may have been ambiguous or interpreted in different ways by participants, thus affecting the validity of the responses. However, on balance, recalled experiences may be more self-defining than actual experiences.

Implications for training and consulting

Assuming the above caveats, below are some implications for CCCTTs to consider when developing instructional materials, methods, and techniques for face-to-face training and consulting activities. These recommendations were developed primarily with oral communication teaching and training contexts in mind, but there are broader applications here for all CCCTTs in relation to ongoing professional development and demonstrating instructional design competence.

1   *Emphasize an audience-centered mindset.* Focusing on the audience received high frequency and relevance ratings and included practices such as focusing on the needs of the audience, and customizing a speech so that the language, style, and content would appeal to and be inclusive of the specific audience. Often referred to as audience analysis in speech pedagogy, the audience-centered principle is important for CCCTTs on two levels:

   a   When designing instructional methods and their training plan, CCCTTs should think carefully about their clients. Who are they? What are their concerns regarding speaking in public? What kinds of speaking do they do? What are their goals? CCCTTs who make an effort to align their training goals, methods, and assessments with the needs and interests of their clients will have greater success. People notice and respond positively when CCCTTs take the time to understand their specific needs, and tailor their training program accordingly. Client customization does not necessarily mean re-inventing the wheel for each new audience, but may simply involve swapping out more relevant examples, or developing a couple of new slides in your training slide deck in order to address the salient needs of the particular group.

b   The audience-centered mindset is also an important principle to teach trainees. CCCTTs may develop protocols or activities that help clients pose questions and find answers about their audience so they can frame and convey their message more effectively. CCCTTs can also emphasize that audience–centeredness should be maintained not just during the planning stages but also during the delivery phase of a presentation. Once clients are clear about their purpose and message, and are comfortable with the flow of their presentation, CCCTTs might coach them to focus on connecting with the audience. Professional speakers described maintaining audience focus as difficult and requiring great effort, because the natural tendency is to worry about one's own ego, or be preoccupied with one's delivery. Maintaining audience-focus during the delivery phase may be an advanced speaking skill for CCCTTs to work on with clients gradually over time.

2   *Introduce the concepts of commitment and authenticity.* Two deliberate practice activities that received high relevance and frequency ratings were being "authentic" and "committing to give 100%" to a speech performance. These activities were conceptualized as being in opposition to tendencies to "hold back," try to be someone they are not, or focus on technical details. Beginning speakers may have an image in their mind of "the charismatic speaker" and feel that they need to conform to that image to be effective, which inhibits their own style and authenticity. CCCTTs can explain that having models of good speakers is helpful to a point. Professional speakers on average observed other performers approximately 7–12 times per year and considered these observations – which may have included both good and bad models – highly relevant to developing speaking excellence (see Table 13.1). As learners gain speaking proficiency, imitating techniques of model speakers is one way they can expand their presentation lexicon. But ultimately, speakers must be true to themselves. What works for one speaker may fall flat for another.

"Commitment to give 100%" to a speech performance was described by speakers as an attitude of wanting to give their best to the audience and not worrying about delivery or their own egos. It is likely an advanced speaking skill. But CCCTTs can introduce this concept to novices and develop short speaking activities to practice commitment. Improvisation exercises may be helpful in this regard; games that require listening to others, discourage premeditating what you will say, and promote spontaneous and creative expression can help trainees experience the state of being fully present.

3   *Provide video critique and opportunities for reflection.* Seeing themselves on video in order to monitor and reflect on their performance was a deliberate practice activity for several professional speakers in this study. Without video reflection, a speaker may not be able to assess their performance completely or identify areas for improvement. Videotaping trainees, watching the video with clients, and offering feedback with the video are ways CCCTTs can help clients become aware of effective and ineffective behaviors, and reflect on how they can improve. This combination of reflection with CCCTT feedback also motivates the client to engage in ongoing targeted practice.

Recognizing the value of video critique, how should CCCTTs give feedback to their clients? Speakers in this study described optimal feedback as constructive in tone and having three components: 1) what can be improved; 2) why it needs to be improved; and 3) how it can be improved. Feedback from an untrained or less experienced listener typically focuses on the first component of feedback—naming what did not work. But CCCTTs who address all three components in a supportive tone bring greater value to their clients.

4   *Highlight the role of reading, studying and writing to develop material.* Professional speakers emphasized the importance of staying current in their area of expertise through ongoing study, reading, and writing. This principle relates to invention, the first canon of rhetoric, which includes the process of identifying relevant, interesting, and credible sources of information to find compelling material. The study findings underscored the importance of *continual* invention—not using the same old material past its timeliness and relevance. CCCTTs should encourage their clients to find ways to cultivate the mind with fresh ideas, keep up to date on developments in their field, and foster creativity. These activities are also relevant for CCCTTs' own professional development and instructional design process. CCCTTs who regularly devote time to read key publications in their area of expertise and research client-related interests to develop appropriate training material are likely to perform at higher levels.

5   *Encourage out-loud rehearsal and focused attention to the details.* CCCTTs understand and emphasize the importance of rehearsing a speech out loud. What sometimes receives less coverage, however, is the actual rehearsal process; for instance, the steps to move a speaker from reliance on a script to a conversational, extemporaneous style. Although there is no single "right" way to rehearse a speech, providing clients and trainees with general guidelines for effective, out loud rehearsal can demystify the preparation process and help trainees recognize that speaking effectively in front of an audience takes time and effort. To help clients improve their delivery, CCCTTs can identify specific target goals and design focused exercises for their clients. Examples of target goals mentioned by professional speakers included refining transitions, incorporating pauses, using appropriate inflection (e.g., managing up-talk), and tightening sections to be more concise. Patiently addressing one issue at a time is generally more effective than potentially overwhelming the trainee with too many goals at once.

Summary

Recognizing the ongoing interest in presentation skills training, and the importance of CCCTTs' ability to demonstrate both insight and instructional design competence in this area, this chapter presented findings from a study that identified deliberate practice activities of professional speakers and the implications for training and consulting. Deliberate practice activities generally have the following characteristics: the task is well-defined, the level of difficulty must be appropriate for the learner, the task is designed specifically to improve performance, the learner receives feedback regarding the results of their performance, and the learner has opportunities to repeat and correct any errors (Ericsson & Charness, 1994; Ericsson et al., 2007). Consistent with these characteristics, the research revealed 16 activities that could be arranged into five deliberate practice themes in professional speaking: 1) access to resources and community; 2) audience connection; 3) self-development and learning; 4) experience and rehearsal; and 5) self-monitoring and feedback. These five themes may be considered key components for effective presentation skills training programs.

CCCTTs will find these deliberate practice themes and activities instructive and insightful as they apply the NCA's Training and Development Division's Best Practices for Communication Training and Consulting. In particular, the empirically-based themes and activities can be adapted by CCCTTs to demonstrate instructional design competence. Insofar as deliberate practice is optimally designed at an appropriate level of difficulty for the learner, CCCTTs should be aware that some of the activities will be more suitable than others or require adaptation depending on the client's level of oral communication proficiency and the training situation. Audience connection, the second deliberate practice theme in professional speaking, is thus fundamental to effective instructional design. CCCTTs must take time to understand each client's needs and goals. This understanding will lead to insight on how to select and adapt an appropriate activity for the client. Moreover, considering deliberate practice is a well-defined task specifically designed for improvement, CCCTTs should clearly communicate to clients what the target objective is when setting up an activity, and how the activity will help them improve. This transparency helps clients buy into the training because it conveys the CCCTT's expertise and attention to their specific concerns.

Beyond the implications to instructional design in presentation skills training, the five deliberate practice themes in professional speaking have resonance for CCCTTs considering their own professional development. In view of the first theme (access to resources and community), aspiring and developing CCCTTs would likely benefit from actively participating in their professional association and organizing meetings with colleagues to exchange ideas, resources, and feedback. Being part of a community of practitioners is key because it is in such an environment that learners get exposed to knowledge they need for growth and motivation. A closing note is that every professional speaker in the study conveyed a passion for continual learning and a respect for their audience. These values, among others, fueled their commitment to excellence. In order to achieve and maintain high professional standards such as those outlined in the NCA TD&D's Best Practices, CCCTTs would be wise to guard against complacency, seek out a support system, be open to feedback, and reflect regularly on what is important to them.

Notes

1 There was a total of 65 items on the questionnaire, which also included questions on motivation, life satisfaction, and demographic information.
2 An activity was deemed high ranking if its mean score exceeded 6 (Frequency Scale #3) or 4 (Frequency Scale #2), or if its mean score was among the top three in its category. Lowest ranking activities for frequency occurred on average 1–2 times per year or less (Scale #2). Lowest ranking activities for relevance and effort received the bottom three mean scores in their respective categories.

References

Best practices background. (n.d.). Retrieved from http://ncatraininganddevelopment.com/training-best-practices/best-practices-background
Dunn, T. G., & Shriner, C. (1999). Deliberate practice in teaching: What teachers do for self-improvement. *Teaching and Teacher Education, 15*, 631–651.

Ericsson, K. A., & Charness, N. (1994). Expert performance: Its structure and acquisition. *American Psychologist, 49*(8), 725–747.

Ericsson, K. A., Krampe, R., & Tesch-Römer, C. (1993). The role of deliberate practice in the acquisition of expert performance. *Psychological Review, 100,* 363–406.

Ericsson, K. A., Roring, R. W., & Nandagopal, K. (2007). Giftedness and evidence for reproducibly superior performance: An account based on the expert performance framework. *High Ability Studies, 18*(1), 3–56.

Hart Research Associates (2015). *Falling short? College learning and career success.* Retrieved from https://www.aacu.org/leap/public-opinion-research/2015-survey-results

Hooker, J. F., & Simonds, C. J. (2015). From the outside looking in: Employers' views of the basic course. *Basic Communication Course Annual, 27*(1), 12.

Kvale, S., & Brinkmann, S. (2009). *Interviews* (2nd ed.). Thousand Oaks, CA: Sage Publications.

Morreale, S., Backlund, P., Hay, E., & Moore, M. (2011). Assessment of oral communication: A major review of the historical development and trends in the movement from 1975 to 2009. *Communication Education, 60*(2), 255–278.

Morreale, S. P., Myers, S. A., Backlund, P. M., & Simonds, C. J. (2016). Study IX of the basic communication course at two-and four-year US Colleges and Universities: A re-examination of our discipline's "front porch". *Communication Education, 65*(3), 338–355.

Moulaert, V., Verwijnen, M. G. M., Rikers, R., & Scherpbier, A. J. J. A. (2004). The effects of deliberate practice in undergraduate medical education. *Medical Education, 38,* 1044–1052.

NCA's Training and Development Division's Best Practices for Communication Training and Consulting (n.d.). Retrieved from http://ncatraininganddevelopment.com/training-best-practices/best-practices-for-communication-training-and-consulting/

Sonnentag, S., & Kleine, B. M. (2000). Deliberate practice at work: A study with insurance agents. *Journal of Occupational and Organizational Psychology, 73,* 87–102.

Van de Wiel, M. W. J., Szegedi, K. H. P., & Weggeman, M. C. D. P. (2004). Deliberate attempts at developing expertise. In H. P. A. Boshuizen, R. Bromme, & H. Gruber (eds.), *Professional learning: Gaps and transitions on the way from novice to expert* (pp. 181–206). Dordrecht: Kluwer Academic Publishers.

Chapter 14

Professional development

Lisa Waite

Abstract

This content explores four topics that frame a facilitator's professional development proficiency in organizational training contexts and their relationship to
best practices. Findings suggest that these topics warrant special consideration
for novice and experienced CCCTTs. The topics are not meant to exclude
other skills central to a development process. Instead they represent themes and
facilitator strategies identified throughout contemporary literature as essential,
thus relevant to establish as best practices.

If you have mastered the previous best practices, congratulations! The inclusion of *professional development* is intended to leverage your proficiency. Like the broad base of a
pyramid, it supports everything else placed upon it and underpins all of the best practices described in this handbook. There is much more to professional development than
technique. For communication coaches, consultants, trainers, teachers, and other like-
minded experts who are serious about ongoing personal success, these best practices
illustrate how to accomplish goals with the express intent to positively influence those
around you and develop a deeper way of engaging others with powerful results.

Let's begin with communication competence as the cornerstone skill to professional
development. In this context, communication competence is one's ability to select the
best communication behavior that is both appropriate and effective for a given situation to
establish understanding. Beebe, Mottet, and Roach (2013) further emphasize that understanding is ultimately created via listener perception (p.15). Communication competence
is not solely represented by presentation skills. Because everyone experiences learning
differently, perhaps the best skill to significantly improve effective communication is
to be empathetic and try to understand how others perceive the world. Seeing through
another's 'lens' allows you to adjust your own communication to create shared meaning
and helps participants to perform new skills.

Presentation skills, interpersonal IQ, understanding organizational culture, and
group techniques are critical components that contribute to professional development.
This list is by no means exclusive, but think of these four attributes as best practice
'non-negotiables.' They are included here because they are very prominent among
many gold standard theories, applications, and techniques rooted in adult learning research. They are also synthesized in a four-step model that demonstrates how people

learn best (Meier, 2000, p. 53). New information on learning styles, and more recently, even discoveries in neuroscience support their relevance and are grounded in a modern context now called *Accelerated Learning* (Kinard & Parker, 2007). They are also named in *The Accelerated Learning Handbook* (Meier, 2000), which describes the best training practices of the past five decades. Finally, be sure to consider blended learning, which is recognized in the training and development community as a particularly effective technique for traditional and online training. This book and best practice promotes understanding and skills for readers, learners, and researchers in organizational, classroom, and other development settings.

Working to sharpen communication competence is a mixed bag of necessary facilitator skills that will make or break a professional development experience. I've attended sessions where the facilitator was a tremendous content expert, but ineffective communication skills derailed his performance and left participants uninspired. It was a difficult eight hours for everyone. The intent of this book is to further your understanding of the value in these combined best practices and successfully adapt them to serve your specific professional development interests to evaluate, formulate, and replicate.

Readers likely come to the Professional Development best practice with some insight of basic platform skills. In this spirit, I offer more tactical suggestions that are derived from nearly three decades of training and development experience (and learning from my own mistakes), while others are empirically supported. These are the *"gee I wish I would have known..."* tools. Some are original, others come from great mentors and content experts. They are intended to take your development to a higher level whether you are a business practitioner, educator, or a student who is studying communication and training.

Presentation skills

Presentation skills are informed by public speaking skills, but in the training context these are distinct. In other words, public speaking is more monologue where training is dialogue. So let's begin with Waite's Words of Wisdom; *"1 point impact."* This is often called a 'take-a-way' and represents a facilitator's ability to determine his/her primary learning point. For example, in facilitating a module on team building, my 1 point impact is *collaboration leads to innovation*. Consider rings on a dart board (Figure 14.1). The outer circles represent content, hearty discussion, and a possible activity but *"collaboration leads to innovation"* is the 1 point impact at the bull's-eye. Too often facilitators assume that participants can identify key points. What happens when you assume? You get the idea. Lessons become buried in content or otherwise overlooked. The facilitator needs to present this key thought with absolute clarity before, during and in summarizing principle lessons.

Energy!

I'll offer a big takeaway right here: The energy and attitude you bring will frame your mindset for success and create the energy to get your audience engaged. Training specialists need to become effective in all aspects of their craft. This includes refining your message and delivering it with passion and conviction. This approach takes you from average to insightful and inspirational. Thus, polishing your technique is critical to supporting a strong performance. O'Hair, Stewart, and Rubinstein (2015) identify eye

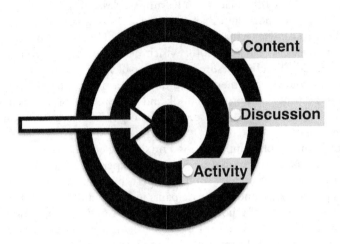

Figure 14.1 Collaboration leads to innovation.

contact, awareness of nonverbal signals, voice quality, and first impression management as principal skills. Beyond these, I wish to focus on energy. Some call it charisma or passion and, either way, you need to have it. The energy I speak of is actually two-fold: emotional energy and physical energy.

I often explain *emotional energy* this way: Audiences give more credibility and trust to presenters who display levels of high energy and enthusiasm for learning over those who do not. Bowman (2009) reinforces that "The human brain learns best when information is presented to it both emotionally and rationally" (p. 27). Enthusiasm is a quality that is difficult to fake. For instance, some academics who aspire to step into training and development (I call them *prac-ademics*) have difficulty transitioning from the classroom to the training room, where the 'bow tie and elbow patch' style fails to engage professionals who don't want to be 'lectured' to. A first-hand lesson about enthusiasm occurred when I played a YouTube video about leadership as part of my slide show. Evidentially the video was updated to include a Viagra® commercial cautioning users to seek immediate medical treatment for 'symptoms' lasting more than four hours. In addition to turning a delightful shade of red, I maintained enthusiasm and simply said, "Well, isn't that special!" The audience laughed, and the unexpected content was not a big deal. I attribute the ability to recover from this to my experience with enthusiasm and maintaining composure. I cannot stress this presentation quality enough!

Physical energy represents the literal demands of facilitating a long development session. Being in good physical shape is important. Standing for long periods, packing and unpacking materials, hours of engaged discussion is demanding. I find myself pleasantly exhausted for a day or two following a development session, but there is solid evidence to support the ability to engage on your feet. Antion (1999) elaborates on this significance via a University of Minnesota study that found, "When you stand up, you instantly command authority, attention, and interest" (p. 117). I particularly assign more credibility to facilitators who can handle the physical demands of a two or three-day development session. Good physical energy (and comfortable shoes!) helps maintain endurance in these marathon events.

Videotaping may provide a good metric for animation and vigor. Find an experienced mentor to review your film with candor and, in return, be open to feedback. I did this when I was new to training, and I was mortified at the soft voice projection and limited eye contact. It was a bit uncomfortable to watch but became the catalyst I needed to make improvements. Of course, even today I seek continued ways to develop my talents at every level, including video review.

Organized learning modules

Clarity begins with distinct learning modules. These are designed so that one lesson gives integrity to the next. Random lessons are less likely to 'stick' and they make it exceptionally difficult for participants to make sense of erratic content. Organize your learning modules and practice the transitions to connect lessons in a practical manner. Be sure to dedicate space in each module to assess learning, and to use an engagement opportunity or a Q&A session. If I am short on time, I'll simply ask participants, "*How is this beginning to make sense?*" One application that supports this is called a Learner-Led Summary (Bowman, 2009), "that gives you—the trainer—an opportunity to evaluate what learners know, and to further calculate misconceptions that would have been overlooked" (p. 213). We are reminded of the long time advice, "*Prior proper preparation prevents poor performance by the person putting on the presentation.*" There are many variations of this expression, which is believed to have originated in the military during World War II (Van Sickle, 1961, p. 553). The point is – you are the content expert. Know your material thoroughly only using slideshows as a visual reinforcement. Hint: If you are reading, you are not training! Learning modules are easy to build by adhering to a simple rule of thumb; have about three main points for every 10 minutes of speaking (Gallo, 2014, p. 191). Don't forget to engage participants with meaningful activities and hearty discussion. These enrich motivation, goals, and new skills.

The big four

The first lesson originates from Bob Kulhan (2017) and is a key to thriving in fast-paced and often unpredictable training events. The remaining skills come from my participation at a training event hosted by Barry-Wehmiller University where facilitators-in-training (BWU calls them 'Professors') are taught three cardinal rules for a successful training event (Vandermolen, 2013). I expand upon each of these via ways I hit a home run and other ways I fell short:

1   *Perform at the top of your intelligence.* This is Kulhan's (2017) take on "one's ability to draw upon all of their skills, talents and experiences to make fast choices about actions to take. This positions you to succeed when tasks take place in times of uncertainty or even chaos." Don't confuse this ability to shift gears quickly with flying by the seat of your pants. Kulhan emphasizes that performing at the top of your intelligence as a competent facilitator involves the ability to invoke well-developed muscle memory to master your task. For example, this tenet is present in a skilled surgeon who encounters a life and death decision during surgery and alters his approach by utilizing all of his skills, talents and experiences to make an immediate decision about which action to take. In short, when stripped down to its basic building blocks, this is about re-acting, adapting and communicating. You see what's happening around you. You quickly consider how to respond and support others. This improvisation skill helps you to manage the unexpected and arrive at the best solution at the moment (Kulhan, 2017, p. 9).

2   *Create the environment.* Through my experience this consists of a comfortable learning space (room set up, seating, lighting, temperature, food and beverage needs, emotional security, and privacy policies). Learning materials, office supplies, technology, and location logistics need to be arranged. Rules for mobile phones and other technology interruption should be addressed to limit distractions. Expect the unexpected. Training professionals who plan thoroughly can encounter hiccups, and they've happened to the best of us despite our genuine efforts to prevent them. For instance—the projector bulb burns out, your slide show won't open, the YouTube video you planned to show is no longer accessible. It happens. Been there, done that. A successful training event has a lot of moving parts and can easily break down. Competence in managing these unexpected issues in a flawless manner separates great presenters from average ones. I offer a few considerations to avoid these bleeps and blunders. This starts by becoming your own devil's advocate. Consider possible roadblocks and how to avoid them or at best manage them should they occur. For example, technology is a common failure. What is your 'plan B' if your computer fails? How will you progress? This is all part and parcel of communication competence. *The Consultant's Big Book of Organization Development Tools* (Silberman, 2003) offers tremendous training and development materials such as preparation checklists, needs assessments, post-training surveys, and a review of communication competencies that I find most helpful, especially for the new practitioner.

3   *Impart insight.* This begins with a clearly expressed rationale supporting the topic and a well-developed learning plan. Activities and discussion are purposeful where the facilitator is the host and primary content expert, but all participants bring a wealth of experiences and perceptions to the development event. Anticipate situations that may present challenges based upon diverse opinions, ideologies, and behaviors. Bowman (2009) offers additional methods that suggest this is best accomplished via a thorough needs assessment and exploring the culture (p. 262). Finally, seek opportunities to move discussion along when it stalls. This includes reflective listening, especially in managing controversies that envelop a diverse workplace. A thoughtful facilitator offers respectful feedback and provides a safe 'space' for these exchanges.

4   *Inspire change.* In a communication skills development session for example, the ultimate goal is behavior change. Consider how to foster this and offer a post-training plan for sustainability. Know the purposes, processes, and methods of your topic and facilitation strategies. Accomplish this by reviewing content and have a progression plan. The latter can be most difficult. As dynamic as a training session might be, learning can't be rushed. People arrive at understanding via different paths. This is where proficiency with a learning cycle can assist to manage these lesson outcomes with an individual focus. There are a number of traditional 'learning cycles' for review, probably as many as there are training and development books. Here is one that is both simple and effective. Linda Adams, President and CEO of Gordon Training International (2016), expands upon a model for acquiring new skills conceptualized by former GTI employee, Noel Burch in the 1980s. This builds upon best practice #6, *Effective Instructional Design*, but at its foundation *directly impacts* professional development when trainers and participants realize that learning is a gradual (and sometimes uncomfortable) process. Here is a brief overview of the Gordon Training model:

The four stages for learning any new skill (Gordon, 2001)

Stage 1 — Unconsciously unskilled. This is generally born of inexperience and is most often seen in participants who are less familiar with a topic versus participants who have more foundational knowledge. Making assumptions or one's tendency to oversimplify a subject are common examples of being unconsciously unskilled. An insightful facilitator understands how to illustrate the value in new knowledge for all participants. For instance, I am interested in earning my pilot's license. In a recent conversation with a pilot friend, I suggested that the invention of autopilot makes it easy for most anyone to fly an airplane, or at least learn the skill more readily. My friend chuckled politely at my naiveté and explained a variety of flight dynamics that inexperienced aviation enthusiasts don't consider.

Key point: In a training scenario, participants should anticipate learning new skills and be offered insight where learning gaps exist.

Stage 2 — Consciously unskilled. This is born of understanding. We begin to 'get it' and see that a topic is more complex than we initially thought. My pilot friend continued to engage me in the previous conversation and said, "Actually Lisa, autopilot is great, but other variables of lift, thrust, drag and pull impact the aircraft's performance and thus a pilot's decision to use autopilot or manual operation."

Key point: In a training scenario, participants are not yet using the new skills, but they can anticipate further understanding of these.

Stage 3 — Consciously skilled. This is born of expanded understanding and the ability to *practice* the skill. Taking flight lessons and actually commanding the plane allows me to perform the skill at a novice level. I still require supervision and value opportunity to be coached, counseled, and mentored in the process.

Key point: In a training scenario, the facilitator supports my learning beyond the single training session via constructive feedback as participants become more comfortable with new skills.

Stage 4 — Unconsciously skilled. This is born of enlightenment. It is a full paradigm shift where my anxiety and new pilot skills are refined through much practice. I can reflect on my journey, and I am in a position to pass the knowledge onto the next generation of student pilots.

Key point: In a training scenario, the facilitator becomes confident that participants have mastered a lesson or skill. This is similar to 'muscle memory' where an individual masters something via repetition and with little thought.

Interpersonal IQ

I think of training participants as guests in my home. I greet them by name and provide them with an experience that has been planned with their specific needs in mind. The entire event is organized and executed with attention to detail. Despite a facilitator's sincere efforts to establish a welcoming environment, some participants arrive with emotional baggage that makes their negative energy easily identifiable. I refer to them as 'psychic vampires' who suck positive energy right out of the room. Where most attendees arrive with a hearty attitude for learning, some attend *because the boss said so*.

To manage the latter participant and other interpersonal issues, the facilitator needs to assess his/her relational management skills. We find validation from Kouzes and Posner (2012) who agree that, "competent trainers know how to paraphrase, summarize, express feelings, disclose personal information, admit mistakes, respond non-defensively, ask for clarification, solicit different views, and so on." The ability to facilitate in this manner creates better training and better learning. Integrating these emotionally intelligent components into the training approach will boost a mutually rewarding outcome for both the facilitator and participant.

Plan, prepare, and organize. In the case of difficult topics such as conflict resolution, workplace bullying, or failed leadership, the skilled facilitator prepares to deal "constructively with problems that emerge from behavioral diversity" (VanderMolen, 2013, p. 2). This includes finding ways to establish trust, deter conflict, clarify perceptions, and encourage motivation by understanding others. Additionally, this helps to deal with difficult people and sensitive emotions as well as methods to discuss problems and possible solutions. This *other-orientation* carves a path for an empathic climate. In doing so, you are in a more proficient position to 'gift' them your full attention, withhold judgment, and listen, reflectively. This shifts accountability allowing a participant to feel valued and visible to you.

Group techniques

When I was a new facilitator, I didn't fully understand the difference between contract and open enrollment training that impact group dynamics. Contract training involves participants from the same organization. They likely know each other and thus their familiarity more readily opens the door to discussion. Open enrollment training includes participants from a variety of organizations, often representing different industries and, thus, varied organizational cultures. In a recent open enrollment session, participants represented aviation, education, snack food, health care, and manufacturing. Talk about a diverse group! Both circumstances pose a benefit and a challenge in managing discussions. The more over-assertive vocal folks may leave introverts feeling left out. To balance small group and tabletop discussions, I impose this one rule: No one speaks twice until everyone has a *chance* to speak once. This creates an inclusive rather than exclusive environment. Beebe et al. (2013, p. 127) offers a technique adhering to eight ground rules for competent group interactions:

1   Do not interrupt others.
2   Remain respectful of others' opinions.
3   Describe rather than evaluate what it is about others' opinions that you find problematic.
4   Self-disclose how others' comments and opinions make you feel.
5   Realize that you can understand another's point of view without necessarily agreeing with it.
6   Monitor verbal and nonverbal behavior such as evaluative language, crossed arms, eye rolling, sighs, etc.

7   Use a 'yes, and' response to indicate active listening and build upon another's idea. This is also a great strategy to establish common ground.

8   Practice mindfulness. This self-check allows creativity and awareness of how you are fitting into a situation and how you affect people.

Organizational culture

Professional development is further demonstrated in understanding organizational culture. This matrix of shared assumptions, values, and beliefs will shape your content and most certainly impact your facilitation approach (West & Turner, 2013). Knowing your target audience establishes a rapport and the ability for strong interactions. Watkins (2013) emphasizes jointly held beliefs that emerge in shared narratives and rituals to reinforce the behavior. Understanding culture connects lessons to 'reality' in ways that provide a basis for alignment of purpose and shared action. Content and organizational culture varies with each group of training audiences. Through all of the ways that we embrace diversity, culture awareness allows us to manage diverse perspectives that are informed by distinctive circumstances. This offers the opportunity to understand the nuances (I call it *learning DNA*) that make us unique and capture ideas and greatness from each training participant. Therefore, the best trainers prioritize the ability to demonstrate understanding and they are well aware of how their facilitation skills impact participant needs with every initiative.

Summary

Academics and training industry specialists recognize that professional development is driven more by action than theory. I once heard that professional development is a contact sport necessary to build trust, gain buy-in, and meet individual learning needs. I fully agree and echo the words of a famous talk show host, "When you know better, you do better." The ability to demonstrate these critical skills enables facilitators to maximize their training efforts. Understanding these best practices and seeking ongoing opportunities to refine them will leverage participant learning and contribute to organizational success.

It is my fondest hope that these tips and tools generate excitement and confidence as you refine presentation skills, interpersonal IQ, understanding organizational culture, and group techniques. In three decades of bringing professional development to various audiences, I've learned that my role as a competent facilitator becomes the heartbeat for the best outcomes. Leading the charge requires a laser focus, vision, commitment, time, and most of all courage. Sharpening your proficiency with these techniques will help execute strategy, foster creativity, and enhance motivation, innovation, and adaptability.

All seven of the best practices introduced in this handbook are connected by a common thread: They reflect a growing industry that is ever-changing yet built upon the conviction that the training and development process is a continuous cycle of learning and reflecting. Whether you are a seasoned training specialist, an academic looking to enter the training and development profession, or other industry practitioner wanting to sharpen your skills, this book helps to produce powerful results. The world's greatest psychologists agree that we have a deep human desire to connect with others and to be understood. In this context, it involves training ourselves to explore possibilities and respond to challenges. It begins and ends with communication proficiency (It begins and ends with communication proficiency) that is strengthened through professional development.

References

Adams, L. (2016, November 12). The four stages for learning any new skill. Gordon Training International. Retrieved from http://www.gordontraining.com/free-workplace-articles/learning-a-new-skill-is-easier-said-than-done/

Antion, T. (1999). *Wake'em up: How to use professional techniques to create alarmingly good presentations.* Andover Hills, MI: Anchor Publishing.

Beebe, S., Mottet, T., & Roach, D. (2013). *Training and development: Enhancing communication and leadership skills.* Boston, MA: Pearson.

Bowman, S. (2009). *Training from the back of the room; 65 ways to step aside and let them learn.* San Francisco, CA: Pfeiffer Publishers.

Gallo, C. (2014). *Talk like Ted: The 9 public-speaking secrets of the world's top minds.* New York, NY: St. Martin Press.

Gordon, T. (2001). *Leader effectiveness training book.* New York, NY: Berkley Publishing.

Kinard, K., & Parker, M. (2007). *The Accelerated Learning Cycle: Are you ready to learn? Am I ready to lead?* Retrieved from http://www.sdaccelerate.com/wp-content/uploads/2013/04/breakout2_4.pdf

Kouzes, J., & Posner B. (2007). *The leadership challenge: How to make extraordinary things happen in organizations.* San Francisco, CA: Wiley and Sons.

Kouzes, J., & Posner, B. (2012). *The leadership challenge.* Retrieved from http://www.leadershipchallenge.com/about-section-our-approach.aspx

Kulhan, B. (2017). *Getting to "yes and."* Stanford, CA: Stanford University Press.

Meier, D. (2000). *The accelerated learning handbook.* New York, NY: McGraw-Hill.

O'Hair, D., Stewart, R., & Rubinstein, H. (2015). *A speaker's guidebook: Text and reference.* New York, NY: Bedford/St. Martin's.

Silberman, M. (2003). *The consultant's big book of organization development tools.* New York, NY: McGraw-Hill.

VanderMolen, D. (2013). Evaluating effectiveness. In *Communication skills professor training course. Selected facilitator lessons.* St. Louis, MO: Barry-Wehmiller University Press.

Van Sickle, N. (1961). *Modern airmanship.* Princeton, NJ: D. Van Nostrand Company Inc.

Watkins, M. D. (2013, May 15). What is organizational culture? And why should we care? *Harvard Business Review, 3.* Retrieved from https://hbr.org/2013/05/what-is-organizational-culture

West, R., & Turner, L. H. (2013). *Communication theory: Analysis and application.* New York, NY: McGraw-Hill.

Best practice 5

Develop and maintain organizational expertise

- Organizational catalysts for training such as leadership, management, planning, and culture
- Employee catalysts for training such as career development, human resources, innovativeness, selection, and appraisal

Understanding the organizational context is beneficial for all training and indispensable for consulting. Aligning leadership, organizational goals, and idiosyncratic cultures are accelerants for any individual or systemic developmental activities. These factors are often improved and diminished by the quality of the employees that are chosen, reside, and depart from the organization.

"From training to performance improvement" details the Human Performance Technology (HPT) framework to provide a path of how to analyze organizations' gaps and provide a road forward. Additionally, it shifts consulting practices from purely communication training solutions to justified performance improvement. "The role of communication theory in leadership training and development" provides an integration of leadership development and communication training that considers aspects of training and development that can be controlled and predicted. Furthermore, organizational factors that extend beyond the control of individuals responsible for a training initiative are integrated into a more comprehensive development solution.

Chapter 15

From training to performance improvement

Using a holistic approach to demonstrate organizational expertise and achieve results

John E. Burk and Thomas A. Birk

Abstract

Developing and maintaining organizational expertise as a communication consultant, coach, teacher, and trainer (CCCTT) necessitates knowing and facilitating a holistic discovery and intervention process that leads to improved individual, group/team, and organizational results. A best practice is the Human Performance Technology (HPT) framework, which is an evidence-based approach to conducting needs assessments, determining proper inventions (training and non-training), and informing change management practices to improve human and organizational performance by evaluating results.

Using a holistic approach to demonstrate organizational expertise and achieve results

Organizations are operating at ever faster rates while navigating increasingly complex environments to achieve business objectives. Organizations have a perpetual need to change to keep pace with marketplace demands. Change requires improving human and organizational performance to achieve desired results. Organizations often seek expertise to make changes and improve results, which is where you as a communication consultant, coach, teacher, and trainer (CCCTT) will find opportunities to utilize your expertise. A way to demonstrate your organizational expertise is by using Human Performance Technology (HPT) to diagnose and solve business problems. This chapter provides a primer in the HPT framework as a holistic approach and best practice for training and development consulting; it is not prescriptive but descriptive of the factors and processes to use when working with organizations to improve their performance. Using the HPT framework allows you to understand how and why organizations perform the way they do and to develop interventions that make changes to achieve desired business results. When using the framework, you become an *architect of performance* (Addison & Tosti, 2012) in partnership with your clients and provide a breadth and depth of expertise well beyond training. In other words, the focus is not on training but performance improvement to enable learning and change within organizations. Your value as a consultant increases significantly when using the HPT framework to establish your expertise with clients and collaborate with them to address human and organizational performance improvement opportunities.

Organizational expertise as a best practice

In the role of a CCCTT, demonstrating organizational expertise starts with establishing credibility, both in *content knowledge* and in *process* capability to diagnose and solve organizations' problems. Content knowledge in Communication is the reason why you as a CCCTT might be hired by an organization (e.g., an organization wants an expert to deliver leadership training sessions). Understanding and offering a robust process that leads to improving individual, group/team, or organizational results is a holistic consulting approach that adds more value than content expertise alone. Expert and process consulting are not mutually exclusive but are mutually beneficial to you and your clients and a best practice when used in tandem (Keyton, 2016). The best practices recognized by the National Communication Association in this handbook also enable you to demonstrate content and process expertise when applying them to solve corporate challenges.

CCCTT's expertise includes the ability to gain and share organizational insight in partnership with clients (Seibold, 2016). Facilitating robust diagnostic and discovery processes to understand "what is really going on" before recommending any solutions is essential organizational expertise to share with clients by conducting needs assessments to determine root causes of perceived human and organizational problems. A needs assessment is an evidence-based practice of gathering facts about the current conditions within an organization to document actual performance and determine catalysts for change (Jorgensen, 2016). Your role is to facilitate the process and document the evidence so that decisions can be made to improve performance.

Using a holistic approach: The Human Performance Technology framework

One such best practice model for conducting needs assessments, determining proper inventions to improve performance, and informing the change management process is the HPT framework (see Figure 15.1). "Human Performance Technology is the study and ethical practice of improving productivity in organizations by designing and developing effective interventions that are results-oriented, comprehensive, and systemic" (Pershing, 2006, p. 6). Farrington (2012) synthesizes the many definitions and attributes of HPT into the following:

> HPT is the systemic application of a system approach to improving the performance of individuals, teams, and organizations. The means for doing this must be grounded in observation and supported by evidence. The results must be measured to ensure that the desired results were obtained.
>
> (p. 29)

HPT draws from a 50-year body of work from disciplines such as training, instructional systems design, educational technology, industrial and organizational psychology, organizational development, and human resource development among others. In the literature, HPT is also called Human Performance Improvement (HPI) or Performance Improvement (PI). It is championed by the International Society for Performance Improvement (ISPI) and codified in a Certified Performance Technologist (CPT) program. The multidisciplinary approach of HPT adds to your capabilities by broadening skills and knowledge used in business and industry to solve complex problems.

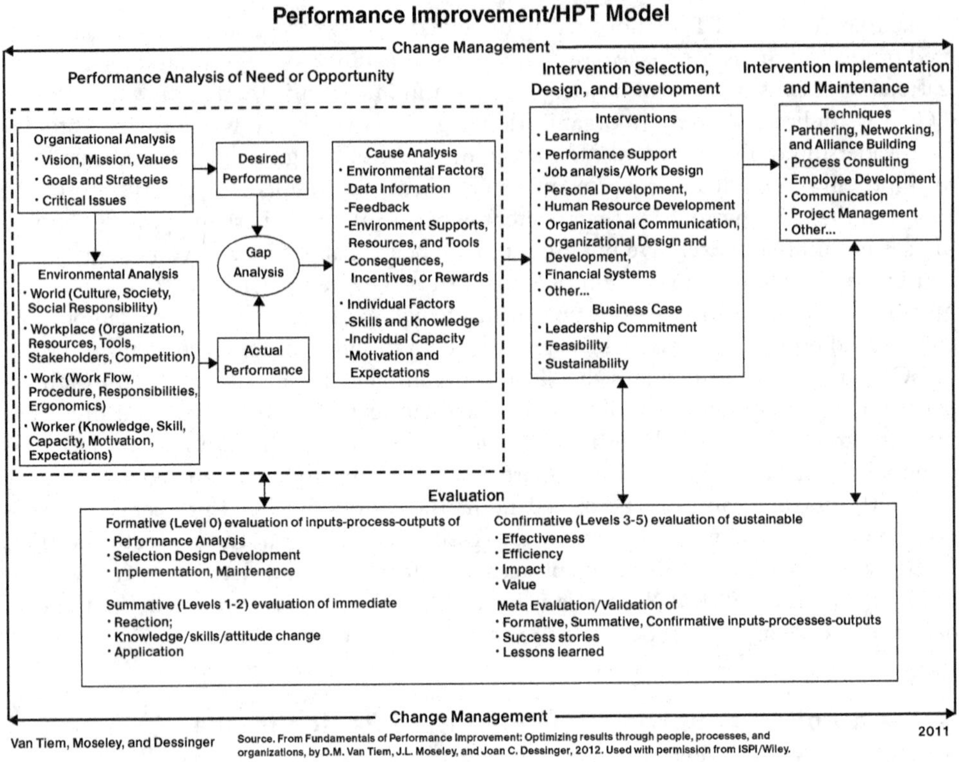

Performance Improvement/HPT Model

Figure 15.1 Performance Improvement/HPT model.

Why is the HPT framework relevant and useful to you? It begins with the end in mind (Covey, 2013): *What are the desired results and outcomes that organizations want to achieve?* At its root, HPT is results-oriented; value is created and positive impacts are achieved when desired results are measurably attained (Pershing, 2006). The comprehensive, systemic, and systematic principles of HPT enable you to add value by achieving results in partnership with clients (Addison & Haig, 2006). It also helps you understand the business perspectives of organizations so that any change recommendations are in language clients will understand (Silber & Kearny, 2006). Each component of the framework helps you analyze appropriate interventions to implement and evaluate for their effectiveness in improving individual, group/team, and organizational performance.

To illustrate how this approach works in a consultation, a case study from our consulting practice is provided throughout the chapter; the case will highlight the organizational expertise CCCTTs can demonstrate when practicing performance improvement. We will describe each stage of the consulting process using the HPT framework and the case study to illustrate each part. Questions that you should consider are provided to empower your learning and practice of the framework. The consultation stages we describe are:

Stage 1: Entry and background
Stage 2: Contracting
Stage 3: Organizational research and analysis

Stage 4: Performance analysis
Stage 5: Cause analysis
Stage 6: Intervention selection, design, and development
Stage 7: Implementation and change management
Stage 8: Evaluation and exit

These stages allow you to organize and articulate the work throughout client engagements to demonstrate your organizational expertise and meet expectations to achieve desired results.

Stage 1: Entry and background

A consultancy begins with establishing a relationship with potential clients and understanding the business problems they are trying to solve. There are a myriad of ways to connect with potential clients (e.g., direct marketing, conferences, associations, referrals, etc.). Once the connection is established, seeking to understand the marketplace conditions and challenges the organizations face is the first step in establishing a relationship with your client and building trust. Asking relevant questions establishes your credibility and engenders a dialogue about the content and process expertise that clients' need to solve their business problems. It may take several conversations to understand the work and hone the specific issues that need to be addressed. At this stage, you must assess your "goodness of fit" with the organizations and the required work and determine if you will proceed to the next stage of contracting.

BOX 15.1 Case study: Onboarding/Integration Performance Improvement

Note: Each stage of the consulting process is presented accompanied by focus questions that enable your learning and practice and our notes that highlight additional information.

Stage 1 – Entry and background

Entry and background	A high-tech global company was seeking expertise and best practices in onboarding and integrating new employees into the organization. We were referred to the company through our professional network and met with members of the executive leadership team and the Human Resources Director to understand their business challenges and the results they wanted to achieve. After several conversations, we understood the work required and were comfortable that our organizational expertise was a good fit. We also understood onboarding/integration as a process organizations use for new employee orientation and assimilation into the workplace. Fundamentally, onboarding/integration is a communication process wherein new employees are socialized to learn the organization's culture and how to be successful in their roles.
Focus questions	*What background research should you do on prospective organizations to learn more about them?* *What are intangible factors that contribute to "goodness of fit" with clients assuming you have the content and process expertise they need?*

> Our notes   The work came to us through our network of Human
> Resources professionals under the rubric of Organizational
> Effectiveness. CCCTT work often comes through
> Organizational Development or Human Resource
> Development designations. Participation in industry
> associations such as the National Communication
> Association, the Society of Human Resource Management,
> the Association for Talent Development, and others helps
> develop and maintain organizational expertise and access
> potential clientele. The best practices in this Handbook
> also empower you to demonstrate organizational expertise
> throughout CCCTT consultancies. Use them!

Stage 2: Contracting

Organizational expertise is also demonstrated through a *clear contract* that establishes project scope, membership, roles and responsibilities, milestones, and deliverables. Stating clearly what the CCCTT consultancy will and will *not* accomplish also adds to credibility and setting realistic expectations for all involved in the contracting process. This essential work upfront is insightful for both you and the client as you establish a working relationship and begin the process of understanding what the organization needs to succeed. The initial engagements with clients establish your content and process expertise that will be used throughout the project to achieve desired organizational results.

BOX 15.2 Stage 2 – Contracting

Contracting   The project began in the contracting phase with the scope
of work discussed with a key business leader and Human
Resources (HR) Director. Boundary conditions were established
to keep the engagement focused on a limited number of topics
and to meet an aggressive schedule for the first deliverable:
an organizational assessment and recommendations for
performance improvement. The project team was established
that included the key business leader in the role of project
sponsor, an executive administrative assistant, a recent new
hire who was working to improve the intern program, and
us. Project milestones, deliverables, and deadlines were
documented in addition to a clear charter for the project team
at which point the work commenced.

Focus   *Why are establishing boundary conditions important for you and the client?*
questions   *What should you consider when establishing the project team and why is*
a team charter important?

Our notes   The project core team was formed after some initial discovery
of the way the business operated. Each core team member was
working on "pieces of the puzzle" and functioned at different
levels in the organization (front-line to executive) that proved
invaluable in diagnosing performance gaps; we were able to be
holistic in our analysis of the organizational system.

Stage 3: Organizational research and analysis

The challenge when consulting is to learn what organizations do and how they operate very quickly to include understanding their marketplace competition. This is where having industry expertise is very helpful (e.g., healthcare, transportation, high-tech, nonprofit, education, etc.). However, the organizational expertise needed in any industry is research skills that can be applied to learn the organizational system and use the appropriate content knowledge with the HPT process to solve business problems. Your ability to employ reliable and valid research methods demonstrates your expertise to discover what is really going on inside and outside organizations. The first step is to align the consulting work to the business objectives that organizations want to achieve.

BOX 15.3 Stage 3 – Organizational Research and Analysis

Organizational research & analysis	The primary research methods used were documentation analysis, surveys, and one-on-one interviews with front-line managers and individual contributors. An appreciative inquiry approach was used in the interviews to learn what was working well in addition to identifying gaps; this approach focused on positive attributes in the organizational system and recognized best practices that could be replicated. Best practices from outside the organization were also investigated and used as benchmarks to evaluate the current onboarding/integration program.
Organizational summary	The high-tech enterprise was a $2B business with a goal of becoming a $10B business within five years. It was hiring 20 per cent more employees annually to meet demand for its products. One of the business objectives was to implement an effective onboarding/integration program that enabled new employees' rapid productivity and contributed to retention through a positive experience. There was clear alignment between the business objectives and the program.
Focus questions	*What is the benefit of using an appreciative inquiry vs. a strictly needs based approach? How would you go about discovering positive attributes in the organizational system?* *What other research methods might you use in this situation? What would be your research design?*
Our notes	The appreciative inquiry approach helped us find best practices and acknowledge them in our reports to the executive team, which added the value of recognizing employees who were role-modeling desired behavior. While multiple one-on-one interviews were time-consuming, it provided an invaluable qualitative assessment of what was and was not working in the organizational system. Online surveys served to validate our findings and check ourselves for bias (i.e., were the interview findings the norm vs. discovering outlier behavior). We felt we gathered enough data to describe human and organizational behavior accurately.

Stage 4: Performance analysis of need or opportunity

The performance analysis begins by viewing organizations as systems of interrelated and interdependent parts (Brethower, 2006). The systems view helps keep a holistic perspective that informs the analysis of the discrete parts of organizations. As you engage different parts, begin by putting the parts together to form a broader understanding of how organizations operate and the opportunities they have to improve performance. The performance analysis includes the fundamentals of needs assessments that promote employees' inputs and buy-in for change and permits you to translate organizational information into organizational knowledge to empower change (Jorgensen, 2016). Fundamentally, a systems perspective is understanding that any changes made in one part will impact other parts and the degree to which more systemic changes are made will influence the longevity and return on investment of the changes.

The performance analysis determines the gaps in actual vs. desired work performance through several inputs. The performance analysis includes both an organizational and environmental analysis. The organizational analysis contains an assessment of organizations' vision, mission, values, goals, and strategies to understand what organizations espouse to achieve. This analysis frames the desired state for individuals, teams, and organizations as a whole contrasted against actual performance where gaps may exist. The concomitant environmental analysis looks at four different levels that inform desired vs. actual performance: the workers, the work, the workplace, and the world (Van Tiem, Moseley & Dessinger, 2012). This helps diagnose where performance gaps exist by being discrete in the performance analysis and discovering the many variables influencing performance. The details of environmental analysis help you ask the right questions at the right level to pinpoint the performance gaps and continue the process within the HPT framework.

BOX 15.4 Stage 4 – Performance Analysis

The Workplace	The competition for talent in this high-tech market was fierce. The immediate productivity and retention of newly hired talent was a priority for the Chief Executive Officer (CEO) who codified it as one of five strategic objectives the business would achieve. The workplace provided the necessary resources for employees to be productive once on board.
The Work	The onboarding/integration process started with recruiters during the hiring process ensuring the most qualified candidates were matriculated into the organization. Once candidates accepted their offers, the managers then triggered the HR system to document future start dates and first-day-office activities. On the first day, all new hires completed a standard orientation set by the corporate office that included an overview of the organization, completing benefits elections on forms, and getting issued laptops with proper system access. After these onboarding activities, the recommended practice was for hiring managers to meet their new employees and complete a checklist of tasks to ensure the new hires had everything they needed to begin working (i.e., desk, I.T. peripherals, lab space, etc.). Managers used the checklists to complete the minimum requirements for onboarding and integration that included initial employee training requirements, team introductions, buddy assignments (i.e., peers assigned to help new hires navigate successfully), additional work systems access, etc.

The amount of time required to complete the work was dependent upon each manager and highly variable: it was subject to the investment managers made doing it.

The Workers   Managers were responsible for the onboarding and integration of their new employees. Some did receive support from administrative assistants who provided documentation to help complete the checklists for the managers. The managers knew they were responsible for the process as a standard business practice and had the basic skills, knowledge, and capacity to perform the tasks. Their motivation was to add productive employees who would contribute to the business's growth. The disincentive was the time required to complete the work given managers' demanding schedules.

Gap Analysis   Desired performance (What should be)
Managers deliver a consistent onboarding/integration experience across the organization that enables new employees to be productive individually and within their teams within 90-days and new employees are retained for one-year or longer. Managers use organizational support systems to deliver the program and results are measured quarterly and annually.

Managers and employees   Actual performance (What is)
The new hires' onboarding and integration experiences varied widely. In some cases, they had a positive experience where managers and teams made them feel included and helped them learn the tools, business practices, and production methods quickly. In many cases, employees were welcomed by managers on the first day after Human Resources and Information Technology onboarding activities but were left to self-navigate their work environments thereafter; they spent limited time with their managers and team integration was left to chance. Managers indicated they had little time to provide a robust experience and those Managers who were hiring many employees felt overwhelmed by the tasks. Not all managers received support from the administrative assistants during the process. There was almost no accountability for the managers' performance and survey data were not being used to provide feedback to managers or summarize results for the CEO. A simple checklist was the only performance tool managers used to execute their tasks.

Organizational structure   Structurally, the organization had several subdivisions and locations. The corporate office housed half of the 1200 employees with the remainder divided amongst several offices in the U.S. and Canada. There were onboarding/integration program "champions" within subdivisions who provided limited support to managers for events (e.g., orientation training, team socials, etc.). Subdivisions spanned different office locations so site-managers at each office played an active role in the onboarding/integration experience. Best practices were happening at office locations where site managers provided highly structured first week experiences. Feedback from new employees in these locations was generally positive as they could see and feel the attention paid to them. The first week experience included welcome sessions with site managers, pre-scheduled one-on-one meetings with hiring managers, team members, and other stakeholders important to their work. Orientation workshops were provided by subject matter experts in technology development and instruction was delivered in business processes, tools, and operations.

(Continued)

	Managers hiring new employees at these locations had organizational support systems to deliver a robust onboarding/integration experience whereas other locations and the corporate office did not.
Organizational data	A corporate survey taken of new employees after their first two weeks, 90-days, and one-year found that less than half of all new employees were assigned a "buddy" – a peer assigned to help a new employee navigate work tasks, business practices, policies, team dynamics, and organizational culture. "Buddy" assignments were perceived as a best practice and used a measure of program performance; if managers were not performing this basic task, then they were not following the checklist or providing the minimum support for new employees. Lack of "buddy" assignments was symptomatic of the program's health.
Organizational support	Managers who received support from administrative assistants were more prepared to perform their tasks. An executive administrative assistant at the corporate office had been given system access to see when new hires were starting and had created a database to prompt her to send reminders to other administrative assistants of hiring managers to prepare and customize the onboarding/integration checklists for their managers. The best practice occurred when administrative assistants had a week's notice to help their managers but that practice was limited to the corporate office site.
Focus questions	*What communication complexities are inherent in the organization's subdivision and site structure that might create other gaps in human and organizational performance? What challenges and opportunities do you see for improving communication and program performance across the organization?*
Our notes	Our challenge was filtering the data we gathered into information that described what was really going on in the organizational system (i.e., summing the site and subdivision specifics into an organizational whole). Presenting the information clearly to the client was an essential task and demonstration of organizational expertise. "The consultant's primary task is to present a fresh picture of what has been discovered. This is 70 percent of the contribution you have to make. Trust it" (Block, 2011, p. 217).

The four levels of environmental analysis

The workers: what are their skills, knowledge, motivations, expectations, and capacity to do the work in the given situation?

The work: what are the workflows, procedures, responsibilities, and ergonomics that influence the situation?

The workplace: what are the organizational resources, tools, stakeholders, and competition that influence the situation?

The world: what are the cultural, societal, and social responsibility factors that influence the situation?

(Van Tiem et al., 2012, p. 46)

The four levels allow you to analyze the situation holistically and discretely and account for many variables that may contribute to the gap between actual and desired performance and ascertain what may be a training need or not.

Stage 5: Cause analysis

Once the performance analysis is completed and the gaps are clear, then the causes of the gaps need to be investigated. There are generally two categories of causes: environmental factors (e.g., lack of information and feedback, resources and tools, consequences, incentives, or rewards) and individual factors (e.g., lack of skills and knowledge, individual capacity, motivation and expectations) (Van Tiem et al., 2012, p. 46). This is also the point at which organizational culture becomes very important. The causes may have long histories that may not be overcome easily (or at all). For example, if workers are not getting sufficient performance feedback and there is only one annual performance review tool that is insufficient but has been used for the last 30 years, then the organization's willingness to change will be important in intervention selection. The challenge is to determine true root causes.

The cause analysis allows you and the client to sort out "why" the performance gaps exist. While appropriately identifying a skills/knowledge gap can be challenging,

---

BOX 15.5 Stage 5 – Cause Analysis

Environmental factors	The organization did not have sufficient support systems in place to ensure consistent program delivery and did not have a specific method for evaluating managers' performance or compliance. There were no consequences, incentives, or rewards for managers to deliver a positive onboarding/integration experience for new employees and they had been given no feedback on their performance. They did have access to the minimum information and data required to perform the tasks but not a consistent standard to follow.
Individual factors	Managers had the basic skills and knowledge to deliver the program in the form of checklists and they understood that onboarding and integrating their new employees was part of their job. There were intrinsic motivations demonstrated by some managers who wanted to perform these tasks well. There were no extrinsic motivations and minimum expectations that managers should develop and execute a robust onboarding/integration program.
Focus questions	*What are other environmental factors that may contribute to performance gaps in this case?* *What are other individual factors that may contribute to performance gaps in this case?*
Our notes	We discovered organizational culture norms in the cause analysis in that managers were expected to perform the onboard/integration tasks for their new employees; whether managers should perform the task was never questioned as it was a job expectation. Likewise, there were no special rewards or recognition for performing the task since it was inherent in managers' responsibilites. Accountablilty and program evaluation were needed to measure managers' performance formatively and summatively.

it is a prerequisite for selecting training as the proper invention in the next step. Is it one worker or a whole team, department, or division that lacks skills or knowledge to perform their work? How does the client know? The same is true when analyzing the cause of work and workplace performance gaps. What are the indicators of a lack of information and feedback, resources, tool, incentives, etc.? This is when qualitative and quantitative research methods are used to assess causes via interviews, surveys, focus groups, content analyses of documents, etc., that contribute to whole system discovery and help construct a picture of "what is really going on" (Block, 2011).

Stage 6: Intervention selection, design, and development

There may been one or many interventions that are selected, designed, and developed to close the gaps between actual and desired human and organizational performance. The HPT framework (see Figure 15.1) highlights several possibilities: performance support (instructional and non-instructional), job analysis/work design, personal development, human resource development, organizational communication, organizational design and development, and financial systems (Van Tiem et al., 2012). Most organizational circumstances will warrant more than one intervention to ensure recommended changes are implemented effectively and have longevity. Organizational expertise as a best practice is demonstrated as both content and process expertise. You may have the content expertise to design and develop the appropriate interventions but you can also partner with experts within organizations, or bring in additional experts, to design and develop interventions too. The value added is identifying and collaborating with a team of experts to develop interventions that will improve performance and achieve desired results.

BOX 15.6   Stage 6 – Intervention Selection, Design, and Development

---

	Best practices were selected from inside and outside the organization and placed within a redesigned program that was developed with a program team from within the business. The initial core team added two members from subdivisions that had elements of best practices already established. We shared the best practices with the program team and developed initial products and processes that the team members iterated to form final recommendations that the CEO and his executive team endorsed to proceed. We also communicated the implementation plan that the CEO also endorsed.
Intervention categories	Learning
	Managers and administrative assistants required training to understand new program elements, processes, and requirements to ensure consistent application across the organization.
	Performance support
	An onboarding/integration workbook was developed as a customizable job aid for managers and administrative assistants to use with new hires that provided all corporate resources in one place. The design criterion was ease of use by managers, administrative assistants, and new employees.

The workbook included a first two-week schedule for new employees to adopt the best practice of a highly structured entry experience. Each subdivision appointed program "champions" that met regularly to share lessons learned and iterate best practices as needed (*not* a one-size-fits-all solution). Managers had support from the "champions" for any unique site or subdivision requirements. All administrative assistants would provide the same level of support to managers across the organization. A program team would oversee implementation and gather feedback to continuously improve the process and provide support to managers corporately.

Job analysis/work design

The front-end of the process was redesigned so that all administrative assistants received new hires' future start dates in a weekly report that enabled them to pre-populate and customize the onboarding/integration workbook for their hiring managers. Once completed, the administrative assistants could cut and paste portions of the workbook into a welcome email to the new hires that provided them essential information about their first day; the workbooks were also sent to hiring managers for their preparation and further completion. The workbook was redesigned from a simple checklist to a robust set of active hyperlinks that identified requirements for both new employees and managers to complete over 30, 60, and 90-days culminating in career development conversations at six months from hire. Key performance indicators were included so employees and managers could measure their progress together. The workbook was designed for managers and employees to have purposeful conversations about the onboarding/integration process and enable a positive and successful integration experience – and focus managers' and employees' time on relationship development as opposed to completing a checklist of tasks.

Personal development

The program was endorsed by the organization's executive team and approved by the CEO; the executive team was now accountable for the program within their subdivisions and for oversight of the managers delivering the program. Quarterly online surveys were designed and implemented to provide feedback on managers' performance that was shared with the executive team and imparted to managers for further action. The program team also shared survey results with subdivision "champions" to provide further feedback and modulate support to managers as needed. Managers' performance was effectively supervised through consistent feedback that contributed to their personal development.

Organizational communication

Each subdivision "champion" was chartered to develop a "101" presentation about their organization that was compiled and shared during new employees' first week experience. The content was also stored on an intranet site for anyone to use to promote cross-group knowledge sharing and collaboration.

(Continued)

Focus Questions	*Do the interventions address the "whole system?" Were any "parts" left out and what risk does that pose to successful implementation? Do the interventions address managers' motivations and incentives sufficiently? What do you recommend?*
Our notes	We did not select, design, and develop the interventions ourselves. We did it in partnership with the program team who pilot-tested early versions and helped us iterate to improve final versions. This supports our consulting approach that the solutions to problems reside within the organizational system and not solely from consultants-as-experts; it is the people within the organization who have to buy-in and take action to solve their own problems (Block, 2011).

Stage 7: Implementation and change management

The next step in the HPT framework is to implement the interventions. You play two important roles as a CCCTT at this stage: 1) technical expert when delivering interventions and 2) coalition builder to help create internal commitments and partnerships to deliver and sustain the interventions as part of the change management process (Block, 2011). Organizational communication is exceptionally important to keep employees and the organization informed and aligned to the goals and expected outcomes of the

BOX 15.7 Stage 7 – Implementation and Change Management

Change process	Change management started with presenting the organizational analysis, current state assessment, and best practice recommendations to the CEO and executive team who deliberated the need for performance improvement of the onboarding/integration process. Once the CEO and executive team decided to proceed, change was underway; they had endorsed the recommended changes and would support its implementation. The next step in the change process was selecting, design, and developing the interventions and getting feedback from the program team on their utility and probability for adoption given the organizational culture. The team encountered resistance from some subject-matter-experts who pilot-tested early versions of the interventions. The resistance centered on "why" the change was needed, which the program team articulated and captured for future organizational communication. Recommended improvements from the pilot tests were incorporated and solidified the changes that would be instituted throughout the organization. A progress report to the CEO and executive team confirmed the changes to be made and included the communication process the program team would use to initiate the changes organization-wide.

Organizational communication & training	Organizational communication and training were significant parts of the change management process. Process and product documentation was developed and stored on an intranet site for use by the program team, hiring managers, and administrative assistants, and served as the content for the organizational communication. The executive team was provided pre-packaged organizational communication (developed by the program team) that they shared within their subdivisions and through the "champions" who were closest to the hiring managers. The executive administrative assistant sent the same communication to all administrative assistants that included an invitation to training. The program team executive leader/sponsor sent the same communication to all managers so they received it directly with an invite to training. Training was scheduled as one-hour luncheon "brown bag" sessions with a primary focus on answering questions and were led by program team members and/or subdivision "champions." Attendance was mandatory for administrative assistants and voluntary for managers. Change management continued in the evaluation phase.
Focus questions	*Were there other training opportunities to maximize the impact of the change? What would you recommend?* *What elements of the organization's culture should be considered during implementation and change management?*
Our notes	Change management is often not planned by organizations as they tend to underestimate the work required to change employee and organizational behavior. The HPT framework has change management surrounding it because there is change being introduced at each step. It this case, we worked with the program team to ensure the recommended changes were implemented across the organization with results measured quarterly and annually, which follows the axiom: "that which gets measured gets done."

interventions. It is also important to ensure that HPT-based decisions align with the organization's strategic direction (Watkins, 2006). Interventions facilitate organizations' transition from current state to desired state, which is the essence of the change management process (Conner, 1992).

Change management

Utilizing the HPT framework is about using a disciplined, evidence-based approach to make organizational changes that achieve desired results – the crux of the framework is change management. The process defines the changes needed to improve human and organizational performance that includes utilizing best practices in change management, which is its own domain of knowledge that is well documented (see Bridges, 2003; Kotter, 1996). You should be aware that your work *introduces* change into organizational environments but whether the changes "stick" is a true measure of effectiveness.

Organizational change is also dependent on effective organizational communication. Developing messages that help promote and instill changes through formal and informal networks, open forums, team meetings, social media, etc., is expertise that you can provide. There is a need for information, incentive, and recognition strategies to promote adoption of the changes (Malopinsky & Osman, 2006). Developing the plans to execute such strategies is another point in the change management process that can be co-developed between you and your clients if part of the scope of work.

Stage 8: Evaluation and exit

Evaluation is required throughout the HPT process to assess progress, make midcourse corrections, and measure outcomes, both short and long-term. Dessinger and Moseley (2006) developed a full-scope evaluation model that describes the types of evaluation used in HPT:

> Formative evaluation focuses on the HPT process of performance, gap, and cause analysis; intervention selection, design, development, and implementation and change; and process outputs and outcomes.
>
> Summative evaluation focuses on the immediate intervention outcomes, such as reaction, accomplishment and immediate impact.
>
> Confirmative evaluation focuses on the long-term intervention outcomes of efficiency, effectiveness, impact, and value.
>
> Meta evaluation focuses on attributes of the evaluation process itself, such as validity, reliability, and accountability.
>
> (p. 319)

BOX 15.8 Stage 8 – Evaluation and Exit

Evaluation   Formative feedback was used throughout the project through both formal and informal means. Informally, the program team assessed progress at each stage by asking: "How are we doing as a team (intragroup performance)? Are we getting the inputs we need? Are we achieving what we said we would do?" Answers to these questions promoted quick course corrections as needed and helped us and program team members hold each other accountable. Formal formative feedback came from pilot-tests of the interventions by subject-matter-experts that helped improve the final products before implementing them. Additionally, an online survey was developed to measure managers' performance that provided initial summative feedback of the current state but was used subsequently as a formative feedback tool for managers to improve their performance; results were captured and shared quarterly. The survey became part of change management as results were also shared with the CEO and executive team and were measured against the business' strategic objectives to assess achievement. Evaluation was integral to change management and the HPT consulting process to measure results.

Exit	Once implementation began, the program team assessed what needed to happen to sustain the changes long-term. The program team decided to formalize its charter to oversee execution and evaluation of the onboarding/integration program; they also added subject-matter-experts and a focus on continuous improvement of the program. At this point, our scope-of-work was completed and we received a summative evaluation from the program's executive leader/sponsor. The program team had identified another opportunity to improve technical training for new hires that required an additional scope-of-work and we were asked to stay onboard to assist. Given the technical depth of expertise required, we declined but found the right resource with whom the business contracted to develop and manage the technical training program; a win/win for all parties.
Focus questions	*What confirmative feedback methods could be designed to measure return on investment of the program's improvements?* *How can you translate your scholarly evaluation expertise into organizational expertise in a CCCTT consultancy?*
Our notes	Sustaining the organizational changes meant keeping the program team intact to continue process improvement and measure results. Part of our success was enabling the program team to continue their work without need of further consulting; the organizational support systems were in place to sustain the changes. Ultimately, the key performance indicators were:

1   The onboarding/integration program infused best practices and the process was implemented easily by managers and administrative assistants across the organization.
2   The program focused on improving the frequency and quality of communication between managers and new employees to contribute to individual, team, and organiational success.
3   Formative and summative feedback tools were in place to measure results against the CEO's strategic objectives.

Evaluation requires using qualitative and quantitative research methods to gather and interpret data to measure results. Interviews, focus groups, surveys, questionnaires, direct observation, content analyses of documents and organizational communication, and other methods are used to gather and analyze data that become useful information to learn the impact of the changes made in organizational systems. The full scope of evaluation may not be needed or wanted but the appropriate level should be done to confirm results. Evaluation is expertise that you should include in the scope of work and make the case that it is required to complete the process.

Chapter summary

This chapter highlights for you the necessary and sufficient conditions when organizational expertise is developed, maintained, and demonstrated as a best practice in your role as a CCCTT. A broad and deep understanding of the HPT framework helps you use a holistic approach to analyze organizations' gaps and determine proper inventions that improve human and organizational performance by evaluating results. Utilizing the HPT framework also moves consulting practices from a focus on training to performance improvement, which is more comprehensive and inclusive of the work that organizations need to solve their business problems. Your role becomes one of *performance architect* as an agent of organizational change to enable businesses to overcome barriers and achieve desired results. Demonstrating both communication content and performance improvement process expertise adds value when solving business problems; the HPT framework provides a holistic method to engage organizations' challenges from beginning to end as a best practice. The rapid pace of change required for organizations to remain competitive in their marketplaces demands comprehensive solutions to complex problems. You can address such demands by demonstrating organizational expertise that delivers improved human and organizational performance by using the Human Performance Technology framework to achieve desired results.

References

Addison, R. M., & Haig, C. (2006). The performance architect's essential guide to the performance technology landscape. In J. Pershing (ed.), *Handbook of human performance technology: Principles, practices, and potential* (3rd ed., pp. 35–54). San Francisco, CA: Pfeiffer.

Addison, R. M., & Tosti, D. T. (2012). Two views of ISPI and the future of performance improvement. *Performance Improvement Quarterly, 25*(1), 23–26.

Block, P. (2011). *Flawless consulting: A guide to getting your expertise used* (3rd ed.). San Francisco, CA: Jossey-Bass.

Brethower, D. M. (2006). Systemic issues. In J. Pershing (ed.), *Handbook of human performance technology: Principles, practices, and potential* (3rd ed., pp. 111–137). San Francisco, CA: Pfeiffer.

Bridges, W. (2003). *Managing transitions: Making the most of change* (2nd ed.). Cambridge, MA: Da Capo Press.

Conner, D. R. (1992). *Managing at the speed of change: How resilient managers succeed and prosper where others fail.* New York, NY: Villard.

Covey, S. R. (2013). *The seven habits of highly effective people: Powerful lessons in personal change.* New York, NY: Simon & Schuster.

Dessinger, J. C., & Moseley, J. L. (2006). The full scoop on full-scope evaluation. In J. Pershing (ed.), *Handbook of human performance technology: Principles, practices, and potential* (3rd ed., pp. 312–333). San Francisco, CA: Pfeiffer.

Farrington, J. (2012). A rose by this or any other name. *Performance Improvement Quarterly, 25*(1), 27–34.

Jorgensen, P. (2016). Building an evidence based practice: Conducting valuable needs assessments. In J. H. Waldeck & D. R. Seibold (eds.), *Consulting that matters: A handbook for scholars & practitioners* (pp. 63–86). New York, NY: Peter Lang.

Keyton, J. (2016). Many paths: The role of the consultant's paradigms, values, and ethics. In J. H. Waldeck & D. R. Seibold (eds.), *Consulting that matters: A handbook for scholars & practitioners* (pp. 31–45). New York, NY: Peter Lang.

Kotter, J. P. (1996). *Leading change.* Boston, MA: Harvard Business School Press.

Malopinsky, L. V., & Osman, G. (2006). Dimensions of organizational change. In J. Pershing (ed.), *Handbook of human performance technology: Principles, practices, and potential* (3rd ed., pp. 262–286). San Francisco, MA: Pfeiffer.

Pershing, J. (2006). Human performance technology fundamentals. In J. Pershing (ed.), *Handbook of human performance technology: Principles, practices, and potential* (3rd ed., pp. 5–34). San Francisco, CA: Pfeiffer.

Seibold, D. R. (2016). The communication scholar's unique perspective on organizational consulting: Personal reflections and a design approach. In J. H. Waldeck & D. R. Seibold (eds.), *Consulting that matters: A handbook for scholars & practitioners* (pp. 11–30). New York, NY: Peter Lang.

Silber, K. H., & Kearny, L. (2006). Business perspectives for performance technologists. In J. Pershing (ed.), *Handbook of human performance technology: Principles, practices, and potential* (3rd ed., pp. 55–92). San Francisco, CA: Pfeiffer.

Van Tiem, D., Moseley, J. L., & Dessinger, J. C. (2012). *Fundamentals of performance improvement: Optimizing results through people, process, and organizations* (3rd ed.). San Francisco, CA: Pfeiffer.

Watkins, R. (2006). Aligning human performance technology decisions with an organization's strategic direction. In J. Pershing (ed.), *Handbook of human performance technology: Principles, practices, and potential* (3rd ed., pp. 191–207). San Francisco, CA: Pfeiffer.

Chapter 16

The role of communication theory in leadership training and development

Ralph A. Gigliotti and Brent D. Ruben

Abstract

Demonstrating communication proficiency is an important best practice for any CCCTT, regardless of one's context. This chapter highlights a number of core concepts and insights regarding communication theory that may be of use for training and development. Providing examples from the context of a university-wide Center for Organizational Leadership, this chapter examines various ways of understanding the nature of communication as it relates to the design and delivery of training and development initiatives.

Consistent with other approaches found in this *Handbook of Communication Training*, the practice of communication training calls for a deeper understanding of the nature of communication theory and the ways that this theory is manifested in formal and informal training interventions. As noted throughout this volume, communication training and development can be approached in any number of ways. The format depends on the needs, goals, and expectations of those seeking the training, the preferred methods of the individual(s) or organization(s) conducting the training, and, not unimportantly, the conceptualization of *communication* and *training* that guide the effort. Particularly for readers who are new to the area of communication training, coaching, teaching, or consulting, it is important to first identify what one means when they refer to these concepts of *communication* and *training*. In our view, considerations relative to one's understanding of these issues lie at the heart of training and development design and implementation efforts, and for this reason, our chapter will focus on these issues. We will illustrate the way these concepts play out by referring to our work in training and development in the Center for Organizational Leadership (OL) – a university-wide center at Rutgers University that designs and delivers programs and consultation in the areas of organizational advancement and academic and administrative leadership. The themes presented have relevance and applicability in any organizational context and for any individual communication consultant, coach, teacher, or trainer.

For the wide array of communication consultants, coaches, teachers, and trainers (CCCTT) both within and outside of higher education, this chapter highlights a number of core concepts and insights regarding communication theory that may be of use for training and development. The chapter begins with an overview of the existing programs and services offered by OL to clarify our specific organizational context. The second section of the chapter will examine various approaches to understanding the nature of communication as it relates to the design and delivery of training and development initiatives. Specifically, we will compare a traditional information-transmission view of communication – one that is frequently common in training and development interventions – with the interactional view and systems view (Ruben & Gigliotti, 2016). The chapter concludes with a discussion of the design and implementation implications that flow from the view of communication, training, and development that we have presented. It is our hope that the concepts and implications offered in this chapter can advance organizational best practices in training and development in a way that leads to more nuanced leadership education programs – programs that will ultimately address the challenges and opportunities facing leaders in this particular moment. Furthermore, by interrogating this important topic in the pages ahead, readers with an interest in communication training and development may more carefully consider their understanding of communication theory and the ways in which this way of thinking shapes their approach to applied practice.

Addressing gaps in training and development

It is important to begin by noting that unlike the widely-recognized value of leadership training and development in the military and business (Association for Talent Development, 2015; Conger & Fulmer, 2003), there has been a scarcity of formal leadership education programs for individuals in higher education with academic and administrative leadership responsibilities (Flaherty, 2016; Gigliotti, 2017; Ruben et al., 2017). To a greater extent than in previous years, an increasing number of colleges and universities are focusing more attention on leadership development in recognition of the growing need for specialized organizational and leadership knowledge and skill (Gmelch & Buller, 2015; Gmelch, Hopkins, & Damico, 2011; Ruben et al., 2017). As with other training and development efforts, we recognize the important role of communication in both training and implementation, and we utilize an approach to training and development that aligns with Best Practice 5 – Develop and Maintain Organizational Expertise.

Taking this perspective a bit further, there are a number of different ways to define and operationalize communication, ranging from the view of the communication as a tool or technique, on the one hand, or the fundamental process through which leadership takes place, on the other. While we see value in the technique-oriented approach, we have chosen to emphasize a process view of leadership (Ruben, 2005; Ruben et al., 2017; Ruben & Gigliotti, 2016), As we will discuss, we see communication as critical to leadership in higher education, and we have become convinced of the importance of a nuanced view of leadership, communication, and training in thinking about the conceptualization, design, and delivery of leadership development programming. As asserted by the Association for Talent Development Competency Model (2017), the skills and knowledge required for professional leadership training are expansive and evolving, and this is especially the case within institutions of higher education that are undergoing significant change and transformation. It is our belief that this rapidly shifting environment calls for a more conceptually expansive view of both communication and training, as described in the pages ahead.

Organizations and sectors that once failed to recognize the value of communication and leadership training are increasingly investing in the development of these skills. The convergence of interests in this area, coupled with the growing number of individuals involved in formal and informal communication training and development, all point to the relevance of a volume on this topic.

The Organizational Leadership (OL) approach

Our institution has found it useful to have a centralized unit that focuses on organizational development and leadership initiatives, and our approach to this topic will help to set the stage for exploring some of the more general training and development insights discussed later in the chapter. Both our approach to organizational development and leadership, along with the underlying principles discussed ahead, may be instructive for any CCCTT, regardless of one's context. In our case, OL provides programs and consultation in the areas of organizational advancement and academic and administrative leadership development designed to help administrators, faculty, staff, and graduate and medical students throughout Rutgers University develop and enhance their personal leadership and organizational knowledge and competencies.[1] Now reporting to the Office of the Senior Vice President of Academic Affairs, OL also remains affiliated with the School of Communication and Information. OL coordinates a portfolio of collaborative leadership programs within the domain of academic and administrative leadership development, and OL faculty and staff provide programming in the areas of leadership and communication for the Rutgers PhD in Higher Education program and Robert Wood Johnson Medical School. Related to the theme of organizational advancement, OL offers programs and services in the areas of strategic planning, organizational assessment, outcomes measurement, workplace culture and climate, and organizational communication and change.

The leadership programs offered by OL are designed for a wide array of campus audiences, including deans and current and newly appointed department chairs, mid-career faculty and staff, doctoral students, and medical students. The curriculum for these various leadership programs consists of a number of modules that are grounded in relevant communication, leadership, and organizational theory, and we use these modules as a way of disseminating core leadership and communication principles to our various audiences. One way to organize these offerings that we have found useful is across three topical areas: Core Leadership Modules (e.g., What is Leadership, Leadership-Communication Connections, Formal and Informal Leadership), Higher Education Modules (e.g., Higher Education Landscape, College and University Missions, Higher Education's Multiple Stakeholders), and Leadership and Communication Strategy and Tools (e.g., Personal Assessment and Leadership Development, Communication Strategy and Implementation, Strategic Planning, Understanding and Leading Change).

This curriculum focuses on domains of knowledge and skill that are cross-cutting – core organizational and leadership concepts and competencies, on the one hand, and also the unique issues associated with the campus, national, and international landscape of higher education, medical education, or the particular disciplines or technical areas for which the programming is being designed. These modules draw upon diverse leadership and communication theories, philosophies, and models – selected and created for their particular relevance to higher education and academic medicine and health (Gigliotti & Ruben, 2017; Ruben et al., 2017). Collectively, the modules are intended to focus on the most salient topics of higher education leadership and are designed to meet the current and future needs of academic and administrative leaders. Each module contains supplemental readings and a series of case studies and experiential exercises that can be customized based on the goals of the specific unit, department, or leadership team. The central goals underlying all of our leadership programs are three-fold: 1) To promote organizational advancement through the development, study, and adoption of best practices; 2) to develop increased internal capacity for leadership among our existing academic and administrative leaders; and 3) to prepare leaders to address higher education's current challenges, and to help to shape its future.

At a conceptual level, the following five precepts guide our approach to training and development (Gigliotti & Ruben, 2017), and we offer them here as guiding design principles, all of which would likely apply equally to internal organizational programs as well as CCCTTs that would be recommending leadership and training interventions. Each of these views of communication adds something important to the way one understands, internalizes, adopts, and implements training and development initiatives, and CCCTTs wishing to bolster their own skill set may find it useful to evaluate their own level of capability and competence in relation to these five underlying precepts.

Blend knowledge and skill. Leadership issues often arise due to the existence of a gap between theory and practice, or what Pfeffer and Sutton (2000) refer to as the "knowing-doing gap." Many of our leadership programs offer a blend of theory and practice, allowing for greater understanding of the core concepts and the opportunity to put these concepts and strategies into practice through experiential exercises and activities. Our sense is that specific skills and best practice information are vital for individuals as they move into specific leadership roles. At the same time, theories and competencies related to higher education, organizational leadership, and communication, more generally, provide a foundation designed to equip leaders to adapt to new roles, changing environments, and emerging challenges which they will encounter over the course of their professional careers.

Integrate vertical and horizontal competencies. Our approach to training and development highlights the various competencies required for effective leadership – some of which are position-specific, and many others that are cross-cutting and generic in nature (Ruben, 2012; Ruben & Gigliotti, in press). As depicted in Figure 16.1, these competencies are depicted as both "vertical" and "horizontal," both of which are significant to the work of leadership in higher education. It is our view, one supported by a growing body of theory and research, that a judicious blend of these two types of competencies is essential to the development of outstanding leaders – leaders who are able to integrate an understanding based on intensive knowledge of their discipline, role, institution, and industry, combined with well-developed analytic, communication, organizational, and personal competencies.[2] Figure 16.1 illustrates the ways in which these competencies come together in effective leadership practice (Agnew, 2014; Ruben, 2012; Ruben & Gigliotti, in press; Ruben et al., 2017).

Recognize the importance of informal as well as formal leadership. Typically, the primary focus of leadership development training is on preparing individuals in formal, titled positions of authority. While undeniably an appropriate emphasis, we also recognize that within higher education, as well as other sectors, much significant influence is initiated by informal leaders and is often manifested through informal channels. It is also worth noting that the competencies that are utilized in effective informal influence are also extremely useful in formal leadership roles. Given this, we believe that informal leadership practices and concepts are an important focus for training and development, acknowledging the important role informal leaders can play and the competencies that are most beneficial for effectiveness in both formal and informal leadership.

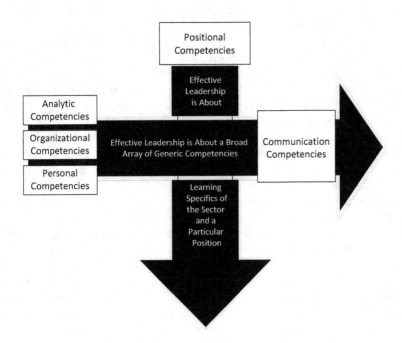

Figure 16.1 Vertical and horizontal leadership competencies (Ruben, 2012; Ruben, et al., 2017).

Build bridges between work roles and cultures. In the case of higher education, the focus of this principle is on the relationship between faculty and staff. Although faculty and staff often operate in their individual silos, we have found leadership development to be an important bridge for connecting these two groups (Gmelch & Buller, 2015; Ruben et al., 2017). The challenges facing higher education demand collaborative solutions from both faculty and staff. Furthermore, the roles of faculty and staff are intimately intertwined in relation to leadership knowledge and skill. Regardless of the sector or setting, through formal and informal opportunities for leadership development, employees in various work roles benefit from a deeper understanding of and appreciation for other cultures, roles, responsibilities, and priorities, and how to work effectively across the work-role divides.

Fostering collaborative sponsorship. Few programmatic themes are mentioned more often than leadership in discussions of the present and future needs of organizations. This is particularly true in higher education. Not surprisingly then, programming efforts may spring up in a great many locations and levels within a college or university. This growing popularity validates the importance of the theme, and yet it also leads to potential confusion, waste, and duplication of resources in program development efforts. The popularity of such efforts is a problem in some respects, but it can also be an opportunity for collaborative engagement and sponsorship across multiple units and levels of the institution. Although programs may be tailored to the specific needs of a given audience, there are also common elements that can be approached in a collaborative way. This shared approach to leadership programming helps to provide the training venues where individuals from throughout an organization can interact with and learn from one another, allows sponsoring units to conserve scarce resource, and models one of the core concepts of leadership development – interdisciplinary and interdepartmental collaboration.

Approaches to leadership communication

So, while there are a range of options available, we believe that the starting point for the design of any leadership training or development initiative is a clearly articulated view of what exactly constitutes leadership. This issue is framed succinctly by the question: "How do we define leadership, other than that we know it when we see it?" (Andrews, 2016). Of course, there are many answers to this question (Grint, 2010; Hackman & Johnson, 2013; Northouse, 2015; Ruben, 2012), and CCCTTs have a particular responsibility for providing a coherent and thoughtful answer.

We view leadership as a process of social influence that is constituted through communication. It may be planned or unplanned, formal or informal, and used for good or evil (Gigliotti, Ruben, & Goldthwaite, 2017; Ruben & Gigliotti, 2016; Ruben et al., 2017). As noted at the outset of this chapter, it is therefore our view that communication and leadership are inseparable; and we believe communication is essential to any leadership development program. This view is supported by a growing number of communication scholars (Barge & Fairhurst, 2008; Fairhurst, 2007; Fairhurst & Connaughton, 2014a, 2014b; Fairhurst & Sarr, 1996; Witherspoon, 1997), who see communication as central to our understanding of leadership.

It is also through communication that leadership behavior is displayed, and as we shall discuss in the following section, attention to communication helps to explain the nature of the relationship between leaders and followers, which is vital to understanding leadership processes and the strategies necessary to achieve desired leadership outcomes. Furthermore, it is through communication that both formal and informal leader-follower relationships are created, shaped, and maintained. Without followership, there can be no leadership; and leadership effectiveness is the result of both the leader's actions and the needs, desires, and interpretations of the followers – an insight that has relevance in all organizations and all sectors.

With these connections in mind, in the following section we will compare a traditional information-transmission view of communication – one that is frequently common in training and development interventions – with the relationship view and systems view (Ruben & Gigliotti, 2016; Ruben et al., 2017). Each of these views of communication adds something important to the way one understands, internalizes, and implements training and development initiatives.

Classical linear model

Our view of the nature of communication and its relevance to leadership theory and practice is reflective of the evolution of understanding of the phenomenon in how we think about and understand the phenomenon of communication. In classical writings on the subject, leadership is described in terms of the intentional creation and transmission of messages with particular influence outcomes in mind. In this way of thinking, a leader begins with a goal, and then he or she creates and transmits messages designed to achieve the desired goal among those he or she wishes to influence. A simple example would be the case of a leader who announces a change to a work procedure in an email or memo, expecting employees to understand, accept, and embrace the change.

Essentially, such a view reflects a one-way, cause-and-effect-oriented characterization of the communication and influence process, which assumes that the message initiator – the leader – is able to have a strong effect on the outcome of the communication and influence process. But all too often, the reality is that seldom does message sent equal message received (Ruben & Stewart, 2016). Neither communication nor social influence operate in such a predictable manner.

As much as the "transmission," "exchange," or "sharing of information" is a familiar and customary way of describing and thinking about communication, this portrayal oversimplifies and actually obscures some critical dimensions of the process. The model can sometimes be helpful in thinking about how leader-follower influence works; however, in many more instances, it is not—as in the many situations where a leader's intended messages seem to be ignored, distorted, and not acted upon appropriately. It is worth noting here that this same set of issues applies with regard to the dynamics of communication training, where it is all-too-often that the transmission of concepts and skills is not a mechanistic, highly predictable, nor trainer-controlled process. Within the context of training and development, for example, one might consider the ways in which information is shared with program participants. The dissemination of information in a didactic session of a formal training program is common, yet nonetheless limited. Providing program participants with printed curriculum materials, for example, is a useful strategy for sharing relevant knowledge and insights. However, those of us involved in the design of training and development programs hope for our participants to understand the content *and* use the content as noted earlier. The classical linear model focuses mainly on the distribution of information or content, and not so much on the ways in which program participants might integrate and use the information gathered in a program, seminar, or workshop. Finally, we understand that this classical linear model is widely used among CCCTTs in leadership and communication training programs, and we would encourage individuals to consider more complex models of communication for application in their particular circumstances, such as the interactional or systems models discussed ahead.

Interactional model

An interactional perspective attempts to capture more of the complexity and two-way influence between a leader and follower – or a trainer and learners. The interactional perspective recognizes that communication is not a one-way process, but rather is best understood as multidirectional, with no distinguishable beginning or end (Ruben, 2003). This way of thinking about communication does not imply that influence is controlled by the leader and his or her messages, but rather that it results from interactions between leaders *and* followers.

This more contemporary understanding of communication recognizes that only some of the influence that occurs in communication situations is the result of direct, purposeful, and intentional leader-controlled words and actions. Instead, it suggests that a multiplicity of factors is at play in even the most basic situation, and the result is that the communication process associated with influence is far more complex and unpredictable than suggested by the classic one-way model. Indeed, many of the messages that make a difference in communication and influence situations are unplanned and unpredicted, nonverbal as well as very verbal—and the product of ongoing dynamics, rather than a single message-sending/message-receiving event. These key points are not well-captured by the classical linear model. Unlike the limited one-way linear model, the interactional model expands the focus to a more complex two-way interchange between sender(s) and receiver(s). This model explains why the leadership behaviors of an individual may not be received or reacted to as intended, and why outcomes can be very unpredictable.

Despite the more expansive focus of the interactional perspective, the focus is primarily on the intentional exchange of messages and this approach may still be seen as viewing communication and influence in terms of the exchange, sharing, or transmission of information. Even with the added interactional focus of this model, the complexity of communication is not fully explored. In our work in the area of training and development, for example, we are cognizant that followers – or in this case, training and development participants and learners – shape the outcome of any intervention. Learners' interpretation of the provided curriculum, along with the connections made both during and following the sessions, are as important – if not more important – than the original content designed by the program facilitators. Additionally, as is often the case, much of the learning in our programs occurs not solely from the content that we share, but rather from the insights shared by others participating in the session – a view that is consistent with this interactional model of communication.

Systems model

A systems view of communication addresses many limitations of these first two models and more adequately captures the complexity of leadership communication and social influence. As you review this model, you may want to also reflect upon the ways in which communication is manifested across the systems where you currently conduct training and development. This view of communication focuses directly on the way people create, convey, select, and interpret the messages that inform and shape their lived experiences – viewing communication as a basic life process rather than an exchange of information or meaning between people (Ruben & Stewart, 2016). This perspective recognizes that some of these messages are intentionally created, whereas others are produced accidentally. Some messages are constructed to achieve specific influence goals or intentions, whereas others may be unconsciously created by their initiator with no specific purpose in mind. Many messages are created in the moment in face-to-face settings, whereas others occur at remote times and places and are conveyed via print or electronic media (Ruben & Stewart, 2016). The model also allows for consideration of all messages that can be influential for communication outcomes but that have inanimate sources, such as a rained-out campaign event or a regional natural disaster – either of which could cause postponement of planned leadership events.

This view of communication takes into account the fact that throughout any message-sending/message-receiving process, followers and leaders bring their own unique "maps" and "personal luggage" to every interaction (Ruben, 2016). Each has his or her own unique needs, values, attitudes, goals, aspirations, styles, education, cultures, physical and emotional abilities and disabilities, life history, and present life circumstances that influence one's interpretation of messages that are part of the communication process. These "belongings," or what some may refer to as "mental models," travel with an individual and influence every aspect of the way messages are created (or not), made sense of (or not), and reacted to (or not) (Ruben, 2016). As Thayer (1968) describes the process, "needs, values, expectations, attitudes, and goals are brought to every communication encounter. These predispositions, susceptibilities, and take-into-account-abilities influence the outcome of the interaction and are equivalent to our individual make-meaningful-abilities" (p. 36). Often, the communication "luggage" of one individual does not align all that well with the expectations, attributes, outlooks, and orientations of others with whom they are engaging. Generally speaking, the greater the extent of mismatch, the less the likelihood that message-sent will equal message-received (Ruben, 2016; Ruben & Stewart, 2016). For example, the use of phrases such as "work-life balance," "mission alignment," and "the pursuit of excellence," will be interpreted differently based on individual experiences and expectations, and it is important for leaders to recognize these diverse perspectives and interpretations.

This perspective on communication addresses the limitations of the linear and meaning-transmission or information exchange views of communication and reminds us that single messages and single message-sending events seldom yield momentous message-reception outcomes. In this view, communication and social influence are parts of an ongoing process through which messages wash over individuals – somewhat analogous to waves repeatedly washing upon the shore. Over time these messages shape the sensibilities and responses of receivers, much as waves shape a shoreline (Ruben, 2016). The exceptions to this subtle process are those rare, life-changing messages that can have a tsunami-like impact on message reception, such as the doctor sharing a serious diagnosis with a patient or a boss sharing a termination letter with an employee. Within the context of leadership communication training and development, we can assume that no one workshop, multi-day program, or book can be expected to have a transformative effect on a person's leadership capability (Ruben et al, 2017). As Gmelch and Buller (2015) suggest, "if we assume that it takes ten to twenty years for a highly intelligent person to become an expert in an academic discipline, why do we assume that we can train academic leaders in a three-day workshop"? (p. 8). It is certainly the case that individual programs and leadership resources can introduce learners to new concepts, skills, and strategies, but leadership development is better understood to be an ongoing process that evolves over time and with practice.

Perhaps most importantly, this view of the influence process suggests that leaders and followers engage together in creating the situation through which interaction and the potential for influence takes place. Each brings his or her own intentions, perspectives, needs, understandings, and goals, and each takes away one's own interpretations and understandings. The idea that leaders and followers co-create and co-control the outcomes – outcomes that are often attributed solely to the behaviors of leaders – is a particularly significant contribution of this model. It also helps to explain why it is also often the case that a leader cannot be held solely responsible for leader-follower outcomes, because in fact, the leader does not have control over many important components of the communication and influence process. Having reviewed these three primary ways in which to understand the nature of leadership communication, you may also consider the advantages and liabilities of each lens in better understanding your work in communication training and development.

Implications for communication training and development

A communication-oriented way of thinking about leadership focuses on the role of communication in social influence – influence that may be immediate and highly visible, but also influence that occurs over time among members of a group, organization, or community. This perspective has important implications for understanding and practicing leadership, and it also has equally important implications for a nuanced understanding of training and development theory and practice (Gigliotti et al., 2017; Ruben & Gigliotti, 2016; Ruben et al., 2017).

Building upon our overview of the OL leadership development model and the three conceptual approaches to leadership communication, this final section will highlight what we see as some of the most critical implications for the study and practice of communication training and development, all of which are essential for a variety of practitioners which include communication consultants, coaches, teachers, and trainers.

- *Recognize the centrality and complexity of communication.* As important as communication is to training and development, the traditional and frequently utilized approach can be a barrier in training and development efforts because it offers an oversimplified view of the way in which trainers and program leaders can achieve their goals. As leadership scholars note that traditional views of leadership often overstate and romanticize the impact of leaders (Meindl & Ehrlich, 1987; Northouse, 2015), so too, traditional views of communication can potentially overstate and romanticize the impact of trainers. A more nuanced and comprehensive systems view of communication reminds us that whether our focus is on leadership communication, or on training and development, these processes are complex and multi-directional, and outcomes are not so easily controlled despite our best efforts at planning and implementation. Acknowledging this more comprehensive approach, training and development initiatives allow and compel us to bring richer conceptualizations and greater realism to our work in training and development.
- *Recognize that training and development occur by default as well as by design.* Training and development interventions are part of a continual process whereby individuals learn through their long-term socialization in an organization (e.g., through culture, a set of experiences, and ongoing role modeling) (Ruben et al., 2017). While we hope our intended messages are particularly influential, it is important to understand the extent to which we compete for impact with other current messages, as well as the history of messages that have gone before – and will go after – ours. In fact, from this perspective, some may take issue with the word "training," in part due to the ways in which this word reinforces a traditional information-transmission view of communication and the extensive influence that model affords to a trainer and his or her messages.

When we engage in planned and purposeful leadership and training endeavors, these efforts take place in – and are inevitably influenced by – a rich and complex environment of informal and unstructured leadership and training dynamics. Training influence – like leadership influence – is ongoing and takes place every day in an organization.

The central issue here is that training and development programs do not occur in a vacuum. The culture of a unit, department, or organization provides a pervasive laboratory for leadership learning, such that training and development are ongoing for individuals as they work within their organizational setting (Ruben et al., 2017).

- *Recognize the importance of assessing the strengths and weaknesses of the organizational culture and context.* Organizational cultures provide a powerful source of influence as it relates to defining and socializing leadership behavior. To the extent that the culture and the customary behaviors of leaders are exemplary of positive ideals of organizational and leadership effectiveness, the task of leadership development programs is primarily to reinforce those values and behaviors. Where organizational practices and leadership communication behaviors and practices are less than fully exemplary of ideal practices, or where organizational or leadership change are motivational goals in leadership development efforts, the challenges are substantially more complex. In these instances, leadership preparation initiatives must strive to address, overcome, or circumvent the undesirable consequences of the natural socialization processes that occur each day throughout an organization, and which create impediments to meaningful organizational advancement and change – breaking out of or creating an alternative to the dominant culture (Ruben et al., 2017).

- *Recognize the specific needs of the audience.* Regardless of the organizational and sector-specific context, a careful analysis of the audience is critical. Individuals responsible for training and development should assess and take account of the expectations and background knowledge of program participants, and also the traditions, culture, and values of the organization, as well as, past experiences with training and development in general, and leadership, in particular. Furthermore, within this domain, CCCTTs should more deeply consider their personal identity and the ways in which this sense of self is manifested in one's training and development efforts.

- *Recognize the multi-dimensional nature of communication and training.* Communication training and development should focus not only on what to say and how to say it, but also on the nonverbal, material, interactional, and symbolic aspects of human communication. For example, it is critical for leaders to understand and endeavor to influence not only the nature of communication in spoken and written channels, but also potential influences that take place through nonverbal and material modalities, such as through space, gestures, facial expressions, eye contact, and the use of silence. Furthermore, a more comprehensive understanding of communication allows one to more fully consider the communicative acts of observation, listening, and information synthesis – all of which are critical to training and development – as well as leadership – practice.

- *Recognize the critical need to bridge the knowing-doing/theory-practice gap.* To do this, experiential activities of both a short- and long-term nature are essential. For example, we have found that immersive and interactive activities such as exercises, simulations, case studies, and role playing are critical to supporting the integration of knowledge and skills.

For example, through the use of an interactive scenario-based simulation for leadership development, participants have an opportunity to think through problem definition and problem solving in real-time and to apply communicative problem-solving strategies iteratively with an opportunity to see consequences of those strategies. As noted in Ruben et al. (2011), "Simulation-games are particularly appropriate for subjects like leadership in which what needs to be taught and learned is dynamic and often unpredictable, as much an art as a science, and where enhancements in strategic thinking, creative thought, personal reflection, and efficacy are desired outcomes" (p. 1120). The same could be said for teaching communication strategy in real-time in a way that is both dynamic and experiential.

In addition to using traditional didactic sessions, case studies, and simulations, Fellows in the Rutgers Leadership Academy have opportunities to take advantage of the university as a living and learning laboratory when it comes to leadership training and development through site visits, examination of actual campus-based leadership challenges and problem-solving cases, and an extensive experience-based capstone project which requires them to take the lead in designing and implementing a new organizational initiative or improvement project over the course of six months – with opportunities for reflecting upon the leadership dynamics at various stages.[3] In addition to learning about the political dynamics of higher education leadership, for instance, Fellows in the PreDoctoral Leadership Development Institute learn directly from policy makers and influential figures in a forum in Washington, DC. Similarly, Fellows in the Leadership in Academic Healthcare program can pursue a formal distinction on their diploma by participating in two field experiences under the mentorship of senior leaders in academic medicine and through the completion a field-based project (Gigliotti & Ruben, 2017). These ideas exemplify the advice provided by Morris and Laipple (2015) in their empirical study on academic leadership development: "Reading, consultation, and interactive training in human behavior principles may go a long way in increasing the confidence and performance of university leaders. We would stress however that mere exposure to information is insufficient" (p. 9). This value of experience-based learning certainly extends beyond the sector of higher education, and we are witnessing the development and use of myriad experiential techniques, strategies, and activities across the corporate and public sector, such as simulations, case studies, and on the job training. Given the importance of experience-based learning, readers interested in strengthening their skills in this area may seek a number of means to pursue additional knowledge and practice in this area.

Conclusion

To conclude this chapter, we want to restate our view that like leadership training and development, the study and practice of communication training and development can benefit from a careful exploration into the dynamics of communication and social influence. From this perspective, a more intentional examination of what we mean by communication and social influence can help to shape the intended outcomes of leadership programming, and we believe it is especially important for CCCTTs to develop a deep and clear understanding of the nature of communication theory and the ways that this theory is manifested in formal and informal training interventions. This leads us to consider those aspects of training and development that can be controlled and predicted, and also to take account of those aspects of training and development that extend beyond the control of the individual responsible for the training initiative. Put another way, just as followers are critical to defining leaders and leadership outcomes, learners define teachers and program participants define training and development outcomes – and this relationship raises a number of very fundamental and enduring issues for all of us engaged in the important work of preparing leaders across sectors for the realities and nuances of contemporary organizational life.

Notes

1 The Center was created in 1993 to serve as a national leader in the areas of organizational effectiveness and self-assessment, leadership development, and communication improvement. As such, OL serves as a resource not only for Rutgers University, but to the higher education community more generally. For more information regarding the history and current work of OL, see http://ol.rutgers.edu/. A list of publications and resources created by OL for broader audiences can be found at http://ol.rutgers.edu/research-development/

2 For a more extensive discussion of concepts and research findings underscoring the importance of leadership competencies, including those competencies associated with emotional intelligence, the following sources may be useful: (Agnew, 2014; Dwyer, 2017; Goleman, 1995, 1998; Ruben, 2012; Salovey & Mayer, 1990; Smith, 2007; Wisniewski, 1999).

3 A complete list of projects completed by the inaugural cohort of RLA Fellows can be found at http://ol.rutgers.edu/leadership-programs/rla-fellows-capstone-projects/

References

Agnew, B. (2014). Critical incidents in the tenure of higher education presidents and the competencies which define their leadership. (Unpublished doctoral dissertation). Rutgers University, New Brunswick, NJ.

Andrews, M. (2016, May 30). Teaching leadership. *Inside Higher Education.* Retrieved June 25, 2017 from https://www.insidehighered.com/blogs/stratedgy/teaching-leadership?utm_source=Inside+Higher+Ed&utm_campaign=df5eb913b9-DNU20160531&utm_medium=email&utm_term=0_1fcbc04421-df5eb913b9-198447317

Association for Talent Development (2015). 2015 State of the industry. Retrieved June 24, 2017 from https://www.td.org/Publications/Research-Reports/2015/2015-State-of-the-Industry

Association for Talent Development (2017). Competency model. Retrieved June 24, 2017 from https://www.td.org/Certification/Competency-Model

Barge, J. K., & Fairhurst, G. (2008). Living leadership: A systemic constructionist approach. *The Leadership Quarterly, 4*(3), 227–251.

Conger, J. A., & Fulmer, R. M. (2003, December). Developing your leadership pipeline. *Harvard Business Review.* Retrieved June 24, 2017 from https://hbr.org/2003/12/developing-your-leadership-pipeline

Dwyer, M. (2017). Presidential selection and evaluation in higher education: Information, communication, and gender. (Unpublished doctoral dissertation). Rutgers University, New Brunswick, NJ.

Fairhurst, G. T. (2007). *Discursive leadership: In conversation with leadership psychology.* Thousand Oaks, CA: Sage.

Fairhurst, G. T., & Connaughton, S. L. (2014a). Leadership: A communicative perspective. *Leadership, 10*(7), 7–35.

Fairhurst, G. T., & Connaughton, S. L. (2014b). Leadership communication. In L. L. Putnam & D. K. Mumby (eds.), *The SAGE handbook of organizational communication: Advances in theory, research, and method* (pp. 401–423). Thousand Oaks, CA: Sage.

Fairhurst, G. T., & Sarr, R. (1996). *The art of framing: Managing the language of leadership.* San Francisco, CA: Jossey-Bass.

Flaherty, C. (2016, December 1). Forgotten chairs. *Inside Higher Education.* Retrieved June 25, 2017 from https://www.insidehighered.com/news/2016/12/01/new-study-suggests-training-department-chairs-woefully-inadequate-most-institutions?utm_source=Inside+Higher+Ed&utm_campaign=d0c8f0df63-DNU20161201&utm_medium=email&utm_term=0_1fcbc04421-d0c8f0df63-197335273&mc_cid=d0c8f0df63&mc_eid=ee2ce7463a

Gigliotti, R. A. (2017). Academic leadership education within the Association of American Universities. *Journal of Applied Research in Higher Education, 9*(2), 196–210.

Gigliotti, R. A., & Ruben, B. D. (2017). Preparing higher education leaders: A conceptual, strategic, and operational approach. *Journal of Leadership Education, 16*(1), 96–114.

Gigliotti, R. A., Ruben, B. D., & Goldthwaite, C. (2017). *Leadership: Communication and social influence in personal and professional settings.* Dubuque, IA: Kendall Hunt.

Gmelch, W. H., & Buller, J. L. (2015). *Building academic leadership capacity: A guide to best practices.* San Francisco, CA: Jossey-Bass.

Gmelch, W. H., Hopkins, D., & Damico, S. B. (2011). *Seasons of a dean's life: Understanding the role and building leadership capacity.* Sterling, VA: Stylus Publishing.

Goleman, D. P. (1995). *Emotional intelligence: Why it can matter more than IQ for character, health and lifelong Achievement.* New York, NY: Bantam Books.

Goleman, D. (1998). *Working with emotional intelligence.* New York, NY: Bantam Books.

Grint, K. (2010). *Leadership: A very short introduction.* Oxford: Oxford University Press.

Hackman, J. R., & Johnson, C. E. (2013). *Leadership: A communication perspective.* Long Grove, IL: Waveland Press.

Meindl, J. R., & Ehrlich, S. B. (1987). The romance of leadership and the evaluation of organizational performance. *The Academy of Management Journal, 30*(1), 91–109.

Morris, T. L., & Laipple, J. S. (2015). How prepared are academic administrators? Leadership and job satisfaction within US research universities. *Journal of Higher Education Policy and Management, 37*(2), 241–251.

Northouse, P. G. (2015). *Leadership: Theory and practice* (7th ed.). Thousand Oaks, CA: Sage.

Pfeffer, J., & Sutton, R. I. (2000). *The knowing doing gap: How smart companies turn knowledge into action.* Boston, MA: Harvard University Business School Press.

Ruben, B. D. (2003). General system theory: An approach to human communication. In R. W. Budd & B. D. Ruben (eds.), *Interdisciplinary approaches to human communication* (2nd ed., pp. 95–118). New Brunswick, NJ: Transaction Publishers.

Ruben, B. D. (2005). Linking communication scholarship and professional practice in colleges and universities. *Journal of Applied Communication Research, 33*(4), 294–304.

Ruben, B. D. (2012). *What leaders need to know and do: A leadership competencies scorecard* (2nd ed.). Washington, D.C.: National Association of College and University Business Officers.

Ruben, B. D. (2016). Communication theory and health communication practice: The more things change, the more they stay the same. *Health Communication, 31*(1), 1–11.

Ruben, B. D., De Lisi, R., & Gigliotti, R. A. (2017). *A guide for leaders in higher education: Core concepts, competencies, and tools.* Sterling, VA: Stylus Publishing.

Ruben, B. D., & Gigliotti, R. A. (2016). Leadership as social influence: An expanded view of leadership communication theory and practice. *Journal of Leadership and Organizational Studies, 23*(4), 467–479.

Ruben, B. D., & Gigliotti, R. A. (2017). Are higher education institutions and their leadership needs unique? Vertical and horizontal perspectives. *Higher Education Review, 49(3), 27–52.*

Ruben, B. D., Immordino, K. M., Tromp, S., & Agnew, B. (2011). Using interactive, scenario-based simulations for leadership development. In P. Felicia (ed.), *Handbook of research on improving learning and motivation through educational games: Multidisciplinary approaches* (pp. 1111–1147). Hershey, PA: IGI Global Publishers.

Ruben, B. D., & Stewart, L. P. (2016). *Communication and human behavior* (6th ed.). Dubuque, IA: Kendall Hunt.

Salovey, P., & Mayer, J. D. (1990). Emotional intelligence. *Imagination, Cognition, and Personality, 9,* 185–211.

Smith, Z. (2007). Creating and testing the higher education leadership competencies (HELC) model: A study of athletics directors, senior student affairs officers, and chief academic officers. (Unpublished doctoral dissertation). University of Nevada, Reno, NV.

Thayer, L. (1968). *Communication and communication systems.* Homewood, IL: Richard D. Irwin.

Wisniewski, M. A. (1999). Leadership competencies in continuing higher education: Implications for leadership education. *Continuing Higher Education, 47(1),* 14–23.

Witherspoon, P. D. (1997). *Communicating leadership: An organizational perspective.* Boston, MA: Allyn & Bacon.

Demonstrate effective and appropriate instructional design

- Implementable models of instructional design
- Different learning styles and their corresponding instructional methods

If professional development is the essence of competent communication training, instructional design is the brick and mortar of which it is made. It is a mixture of psychology, communication, and educational elements in a way to enhance desired outcomes. Some communication trainers do not choose to be instructional designers. Rather they leave those duties to others or purchase predesigned programs to deliver. Some instructional designers do not choose to be communication trainers but rather create the programs to be delivered by others. As long as delivery and design are attended to, communication training can create powerful touchstone points that can enhance the productivity for individuals and organizations.

This section starts with a detailed explanation of one of communication trainings most used models both within this text and elsewhere. In the first chapter Steven Beebe presents a detailed explanation of the Needs–Centered Training Model as well as best practice strategies for implementation. Additional elements of instructional design are amplified through the remaining chapters in areas such as debriefing, adult learning design, growth mindsets, team roles, and experiential learning.

Chapter 17

Best practices of training instructional design

The Needs-Centered Training Model

Steven A. Beebe

Abstract

This chapter will provide an overview of the Needs-Centered Training Model infused with describing best-practice strategies for implementing the model in communication training. The model is based on adult learning theory that suggests effective training addresses trainee needs. The primary objective is to provide training specialists a comprehensive overview of training instructional design best practices and identify specific strategies for teaching trainees specific skills in order to perform a job or task more effectively.

Instructional design is the process of identifying, describing, and developing a sequence of procedures and methods to implement a focused learning program to achieve desired learning outcomes. Best practice six is: demonstrate effective and appropriate instructional design. In the training context, instructional design processes describe the procedures that emphasize the development of skills that should be performed to achieve a specific goal (Beebe, 2007). The Needs-Centered Training Model (Figure 17.1), as developed by Beebe, Mottet, and Roach (2013), provides an overview of the sequenced, best practices of training instructional design. Based on the principles of adult learning theory (Knowles, Holton, & Swanson, 2015; Merriam, 2008), the Needs-Centered Training Model places identifying and assessing the needs of the trainee, as well as the needs of the organization, at the center of the training instructional design process. Focusing on trainee needs drives each step of the instructional design elements of planning and presenting a training presentation.

Using the Needs-Centered Training Model as a framework, this chapter identifies nine instructional design training best practices that are supported by research, based on time-tested experience, and embraced by those who provide communication training and development programs (Beebe, 2007; Beebe, Mottet, & Roach, 2013; Beebe & Frei, 2017). The ultimate best practice, according to the Needs-Centered Training Model, is to be ever vigilant in focusing on the needs of the individual trainees and the over-arching needs of the organization.

What is distinctive about the Needs-Centered Training Model is the consideration of the trainee needs throughout the entire instructional design process. It is also developed as an instructional design model for communication *training*. Training, according to Beebe, Mottet, and Roach (2013) is the "Process of developing skills in order to perform a specific job or task more effectively" (p. 5). In contrast to education, which emphasizes cognitive learning, training focuses on developing skills.

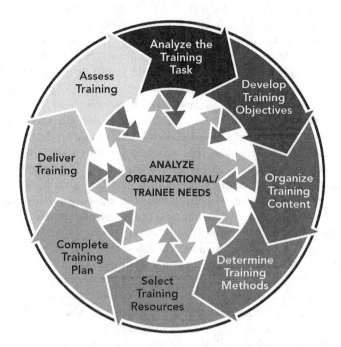

Figure 17.1 The Needs-Centered Training Model. © Beebe, Mottet, & Roach, 2013.

One classic instructional design model attributed to Florida State University's Center for Educational Technology, known by its acronym ADDIE, includes five steps: (1) Analyze, (2) Design, (3) Develop, (4) Implement, and (5) Evaluate (Andrews & Goodson, 1980). The first step, analyze, includes an assessment of learner needs. The Needs-Centered Training Model, developed specifically for the training context, emphasizes linking each instructional design step to meeting the needs of the learner not only at the beginning of the instructional design process but *throughout the training design process*. ASSURE is another instructional design model that is an acronym for six steps: (1) Analyze learning characteristics, (2) State objectives, (3) Select, modify, or design materials, (4) Utilize materials, (5) Require learner response, and (6) Evaluation (Aziz, 1999; Smaldino, Lowther, & Russell, 2008). Again, although analyze learning characteristics is the first step of the process, analyzing and adapting to learner needs is not emphasized in later stages of the instructional design process. The Needs-Centered Training Model makes analyzing organizational and trainee needs the central focus of the instructional design process from start to finish.

Analyze organizational and trainee needs

Instructional design begins with identifying the organizational and trainee needs. A *need* is simply that which is lacking, or that which is desired or required but not present. To assess the communication needs of an organization or trainee is to identify the requisite communication skills and behaviors that are lacking in order for the organization or the individual to effectively and appropriately perform a specific communication task. The Needs-Centered Training Model suggests that *all* effective instructional design begins with identifying organizational/trainee needs; each subsequent step in the design process should consider how the needs of the trainees are being met.

Conducting an effective needs assessment, by using a variety of tools and assessment methods, is vital to ensure that the planned training addresses the specific needs of those being trained. In fact, the answer to virtually any question about strategies, methods, or procedures for designing and implementing a training program is, "It depends on the trainee's needs." Such practical questions as: "How long should a training program be?" "What should the key content include?" and "What are the best methods of presenting training?" can each be answered by: *It depends on the needs of the trainees.*

The first step in assessing needs is to identify which learning domain should be addressed – cognitive, affective, or behavioral (Bloom, 1956). The cognitive domain of learning focuses on knowledge and information. The affective domain focuses on augmenting, diminishing, or changing attitudes, feelings, and emotions. The behavioral (also sometimes called the psychomotor) domain emphasizes developing skills, behaviors, or performance. Clarifying the difference between these three domains of learning can help the trainer ensure that the trainer is emphasizing the behavioral domain – the domain of training. Educational processes typically focus on the cognitive domain; schools, colleges, and universities emphasize learning principles, theory, facts, concepts, and ideas. Programs designed to motivate others focus on the affective domain of learning. Motivational speakers, who seek to encourage and inspire, also typically emphasize the affective domain of learning. *Communication training emphasizes developing communication skills* (such as listening, speaking, collaborating, relating) that can enhance individual and organizational effectiveness. Therefore, assessing the training needs of trainees typically emphasizes identifying the behavioral or skill deficiency of the trainees.

Best practices for assessing organizational or individual training needs include using a variety of techniques and strategies.

Conduct a survey: A survey or questionnaire is a series of written questions administered either on paper or online to assess the knowledge, attitudes, or skills of trainees related to the training topic. Survey methods include using a Likert scale, which assesses the degree to which a respondent strongly agrees, agrees, is undecided, disagrees, or strongly disagrees with a statement. A checklist, another method of gathering survey data, presents a list of skills or knowledge and asks respondents to identify the relative need they have to learn the skill or knowledge. Providing a list of skills or information to rank order or asking questions seeking "yes" or "no" responses are other survey formats. Asking open-ended questions seeking responses to such questions as, "What skills or information to you need to learn to improve your job?" can also elicit useful survey data.

Conduct personal interviews: Interviewing trainees one-on-one prior to a training session can glean in-depth information to help customize a training session. Interview question formats could include the same kinds of methods that were described for surveys. Greater emphasis is placed on open-ended questions and asking follow-up probing questions to gather more detailed information than gathering information using written survey responses. Although conducting personal interviews is a more time-consuming and less efficient method of assessing needs, it nonetheless may provide detailed information that will help a trainer develop a customized training program.

Conduct a focus group: A focus group is a group interview in which the interviewer seeks qualitative responses to assess needs and gather information to help customize a training session. One person typically serves as moderator or facilitator and asks open-ended question while other analysts listen and record the response looking for larger themes and generalizations. Focus group sessions are often video or audio recorded so that group member comments may be reviewed for further analysis and categorization.

Use observation methods: One of the most useful but often most time-consuming method of assessing organizational or training needs is to observe trainees on the job. Observing a meeting, for example, can result in learning about not only meeting and interaction skills, but can provide clues about organizational culture and norms. Observing sales personnel interacting with customers may provide important information that could be used to identify trainee communication needs.

Conduct a SWOT analysis: A SWOT analysis examines the strengths, weaknesses, opportunities and threats of an organization that provide a comprehensive environmental scan (Truelove, 2006). Strengths (such as a well-trained workforce) and weaknesses (lack of resources) are internal factors. Opportunities (e.g., increased population that results in a new market) and threats (higher taxes) are those forces external to the organization. A SWOT analysis provides a general scan of the organizational environment rather than analyzing specific communication skill deficiencies.

Whatever needs assessment method is used, the goal of assessment is to identify the specific skills that are needed to guide the trainer or curriculum developer in writing appropriate training objectives and content. Assessing and analyzing needs is not something only done once at the outset of the design and implementation of a training program. Needs assessment is an ongoing process, which is why analyzing trainee and organizational needs appears in the center of the model and touches all other aspects of training instructional design. Identifying trainee needs may necessitate revising other elements of the training including which training objectives should be developed and achieved.

Analyze the training task

To analyze the training task is to prepare a detailed, step-by-step outline providing a taxonomy of the specific skill steps that a trainee should perform to achieve the training goal. A task analysis is prepared in tandem with identifying a trainee's needs. Viewing the Needs-Centered Training Model as a clock, after noting the middle of the model is focusing on the needs of the trainee, begin at the top of the clock (the 12 o'clock position) and work around clock-wise to identify the instructional design steps of preparing and delivering a training presentation. Having a comprehensive understanding of the steps needed to perform a skill or set of skills may be helpful in designing a needs assessment instrument. Assessing individual needs reveals which of the skill steps included in the task analysis that a trainee can and cannot perform.

Preparing a task analysis involves three steps. First, become knowledgeable about the skill or behaviors you will be teaching. Identify and read books, articles, and research that provide a comprehensive summary of the behaviors required to perform the specific communication skill correctly. If, for example, you are teaching how to prepare for and facilitate a meeting, it is important to identify *all* steps, skills, and behaviors needed to plan and implement a successful meeting. A good source of information about the skills needed to perform a task may be found in books, especially communication textbooks that focus on skill development tasks. Textbooks are typically research-based and often include a detailed description of the behaviors that should be performed to achieve the communication task.

Second, with a clear understanding of the skills that are needed, identify the sequence of the behaviors that are needed to perform the skills. The order of the training content is based on the order of the specific tasks to be performed to achieve the desired skill. One strategy to identify the sequence of the skill steps is to first identify the larger, macro-level skills—those skills that would become the Roman numerals in an outline of the skills. After conducting research, brainstorm the skill steps and then organize the skill steps in the sequence in which they should be performed. Each skill step should begin with a verb—an action word that specifies the behavior that should be performed.

The third step in preparing a task analysis is to then go back to the list of macro skills and provide additional details, noting how each step and sub-step is performed. Begin each line of the task analysis with a verb such as perform, enact, develop, gather, or assess. Verbs that focus on cognitive processes such as, to know, understand, or explain suggest a more cognitive, educational task, rather than a training or behavioral task.

The two key obstacles to preparing an effective task analysis are: (1) the curriculum developer does not yet know how to perform the skill; additional research, observation, and reflection is needed, or (2) what is being analyzed is not a skill. It is not possible, for example, to conduct a task analysis on something that is not a task (skill). Intercultural communication is an important area of investigation, but unless one is analyzing a specific skill (such as how to create a third culture) it is difficult if not impossible to identify tasks (using appropriate verbs) when there are no actions to perform. A task analysis can only be performed on tasks, skills, or behaviors as opposed to theories, concepts, or ideas.

Develop training objectives

Objectives are precise statements that describe in specific, measurable, attainable, and observable terms, the desired training outcome. An alternative framework for training objective criteria uses the acronym SMART which stands for specific, measurable, achievable, responsible, and time-related (Doran, 1981).

To identify the objectives of a training session involves conducting a gap analysis— the comparison of what is required to perform the task (as detailed in the task analysis) with the specific skills that the trainee needs to perform the skill (as revealed in the needs assessment). The difference – the gap – between what is needed and what can already be performed helps identify the objectives that provide focus and direction for the training.

If, for example, the task analysis identifies six steps to successfully paraphrase a message, yet the needs assessment identified that the trainees could not perform these six steps, then the instructional designer has clear direction as to what the objective of the training should be. Based on a gap analysis, here is sample communication training objective: At the end of the training session, trainees should be able to describe and accurately perform the six-step process of paraphrasing a message with at least 90 per cent accuracy.

Without a task analysis that specifies the tasks needed to perform the skill (such as identifying the six-step process) and a needs assessment (to identify the deficiency) it will be difficult to identify an appropriate training objective that is observable, measurable, specific, or attainable.

Objectives should be observable. What would you see if the objective were achieved? In the example above, one could observe someone accurately performing each of the six steps. Using a verb such as *perform, role-play,* or *demonstrate* suggests that the objective, when enacted accurately, could be observed. As previously noted, verbs such as to *know,* to *understand,* or to *appreciate* are not observable behaviors, but rather, cognitive (educational) processes that would require additional more observable verbs (such as describe, explain, or compare and contrast) to be confirmed by observation.

Objectives should be measurable. A measurable objective is one that can be accurately assessed. If you cannot measure the level of effectiveness of the objective it is not a well-worded objective. Being able to paraphrase with 90 per cent accuracy is a measurable criterion.

Objectives should be specific. The key to making an objective specific is to ensure that the verb selected is specific rather than vague. To apply, assess, collect, practice, prepare, or provide are more specific verbs than to understand, know, or appreciate. A second way to make an objective specific is to identify the precise number of behaviors that should be performed. Identifying the number of steps (such as six steps of paraphrasing) involved makes the objective specific rather than general.

Objectives should be attainable. To be attainable means that the objective should be realistic. The performance of the objective should be accomplished within the time frame and limitations of the training and the background and competencies of the trainee.

Organize training content

The training content includes the core information and behaviors (principles, definitions, skills) presented in the training session to achieve the well-articulated training objectives identified. A successfully prepared task analysis explicates the essential content for the training session.

Once the essential training content is identified (through the gap analysis by specifying the difference between what is required to perform the skill and what is already known) the next task is to organize the training content. The sequence of presenting training content could be organized in one of at least three ways: chronological (in steps), by complexity (from easy to more complex), or topically (natural divisions).

Most training sessions are organized based on the logical, chronological sequence of the order in which the skill steps should be performed. For example, before teaching someone how to paraphrase accurately listening skills should be taught first.

The complexity strategy of organizing training content involves first teaching more elementary or less complex skills before teaching more complex skills. For example, informative speaking is typically taught before teaching someone to present a persuasive speech. Teaching someone to persuade involves more decisions, steps, and considerations than does teaching how to present an informative presentation. Or, the skill steps in preparing a meeting agenda are presented before the more complex skill of learning how to facilitate meeting interaction is presented.

A third way of organizing training content is to use a problem-solution organizational approach. Adult learning theory (Knowles, 2015) suggests that adult learners prefer to learn strategies that will solve problems. First, identify the problem that trainees will face, including skills needed to identify a problem, and then teach the strategies for developing a solution. Better yet, invite the trainees to identify the problems that they encounter and then offer skills and strategies to manage the specific problems or deficiencies. Andragogical, adult learning strategies (Knowles, Holton, & Swanson, 2015) focus on addressing the specific problems and concerns of the trainee that have been identified when assessing trainee needs.

Determine training methods

Methods are the strategies used by the trainer to present information and skills to a trainee. Trainers should consider the skill levels of the adults they are teaching to determine which methods are most appropriate for a specific training audience. Methods range from more passive learner strategies, such as listening to a lecture, reading, observing material on-line, to more interactive learner techniques such a role playing, case study analysis, group discussion, or simulations presented electronically or in real time.

The training methods for teaching a skill to adults follow these five over-arching instructional steps:

Tell (use lecture, reading, Internet presentations)
Show (demonstrate precisely how to perform the desired skill)
Invite (ask trainees to practice performing the new skill they have observed)
Encourage (provide positive reinforcement when the skill is performed correctly)
Correct (provide developmental feedback, when appropriate, to indicate that the trainee
    is not performing the skill effectively or appropriately).

These five lesson elements should be used to teach each learning objective. Trainees are first told (Tell) how to perform a specific skill followed by a demonstration (Show) as to how to perform the skills. Then the trainees are given an opportunity to practice performing the skill (Invite), followed by feedback that both provides positive reinforcement (Encourage) and notes errors or deficiencies (Correct). Appropriate training methods are selected to implement this recurring sequence of skill-development steps throughout a training session. As a trainer, consider which of these steps is the most natural for you to perform? Which of the steps are less familiar and may need additional attention? Effective training emphasizes each of these five steps in sequence.

The following check list provides a quick self-assessment to determine a person's familiarity with and applications of various instructional methods that could be used in training.

Use of Instructional Methods: A Self-Assessment

Evaluate each method below by numbering it:

I now use this method in my teaching
I am familiar with this method and can use it.
I am not familiar with this method but it sounds interesting and I would like to learn to use it.
I don't understand how this method can be used in training adult learners.

PRESENTATIONAL METHODS

_____Lecture
_____Illustrated lecture (using chalk/white board)
_____Read a chapter or article during a training session
_____Dramatic reading
_____Demonstration
_____Poetry reading
_____YouTube excerpt
_____Podcast
_____Audio recording
_____Video
_____Presentation by a group (panel, symposium, forum)
_____Out of class reading assignment
_____PowerPoint
_____PowerPoint with embedded media
_____Prezi

DISCUSSION METHODS

_____Group discussion
_____Question and answer
_____Circle response (sitting in a circle, each person responds to the same question)
_____Brainstorming
_____Buzz group (breaking into smaller groups for discussion)
_____Participative lecture
_____Video talk-back (structured conversation following a video)
_____Panel discussion
_____Forum (that includes audience participation)
_____Symposium (a series of related speeches)/forum

PARTICIPATION METHODS

_____Role play
_____Case study
_____Field trip
_____Interpretive art (painting, sculpture, etc.)
_____Creative writing
_____Interview
_____Book or video report
_____Demonstration
_____Think–pair–share (think and write, pair with another, share responses)
_____Interactive worksheets

(Continued)

_____Game
_____Instant assessment (ask for a show of hands or agreement ranging from 1–10 using fingers to respond)
_____Internet search on smart phone or other technological device

Results of the self-assessment can identify which training method (those coded 3 or 4) should be discussed in greater detail.

Communication training often incorporates experiential learning activities to help trainees master the specific communication skills being taught. The EDIT technique (Meyers & Meyers, 1976) is often used as a procedure for "unpacking" or processing experiential activities. EDIT is an acronym that stands for Experience, Describe, Infer, and Transfer. This simple and intuitive sequence helps learners identify how the skills practiced in a given activity can be transferred to the job setting. Here's a description of the four steps:

Experience: The trainees participate in a given activity, review a case study, participate in a role-playing scenario, or other experiential method.

Describe: Trainees are asked to describe what occurred during the activity using clear language rather than evaluative language. Questions to prompt trainees to describe the learning experience include:

What did you see, hear, feel, touch, and smell?
Describe the experience step-by-step of what occurred as though I was not there.
Rather than just describe what happened, show us what happened.

Infer: Ask trainees what they learned from participating in the activity. Have them make inferential predictions about what would happen if they used the skills at work or home. Ask:

What have you learned from this activity?
What do you know now that you did not know before participating in this activity?
What would happen if you used this strategy or specific skills where you work?

Transfer: The final phase of the EDIT technique is to clinch the application of the skill or strategy to the trainee's workplace or home. Specific questions to facilitate transfer include:

How do you plan to use this skill on the job?
How has this experienced helped you understand what is happening in your life or on the job?
What would you say to others in describing how this experience will enhance your job performance?

Select training resources

Training resources include all of the material, handouts, training participant manuals, videos, PowerPoint images, computer hardware and software that the trainer uses to implement the methods selected.

Trainers typically use a wide array of presentation aids to illustrate ideas or demonstrate skills or processes. The functions of presentation aids such as PowerPoint and Prezi are to: promote interest, clarify, demonstrate, enhance retention, or enhance training transfer. Research suggests that using PowerPoint does enhance learning somewhat (Yuviler-Gavish, Yechiam, & Kallai, 2011; Apperson, Laws, & Scepansky, 2008). Note that *somewhat* is a qualifier. Research has found that offering the trainee slide after slide of text or bulleted lists of terms and concepts may not be the best learning method (Shapiro, Kressen-Griep, Gayle, & Allen, 2006). What does seem to enhance learning is more liberal use of visual images (photos, drawings, illustrations) rather than cramming slides with tedious and lengthy text.

The two most violated principles of using visual presentation aids are (1) the information shown is too small to be seen clearly or (2) there is too much information being shown to the trainees (for example, there are more than seven lines of text on a single PowerPoint slide). General guidelines for using presentation aids include:

Simplicity: Use fewer words and usually no more than seven lines of text on a single slide.
Communicate with trainees, not to your presentation aids.
Be ready to present without presentation aids when there is a technology glitch.
Practice using your presentation aids.

Complete training plans

The next step in instructional design before presenting the training is to prepare a comprehensive written training lesson plan, which is also sometimes called a facilitator guide. Although training plan formats vary from very structured to more narrative, informal plans, all training plans typically include the following five elements:

Objectives: A specific, measurable, attainable, and observable statement of what the training should accomplish.

Training content: A clear, cogent summary of the information that the trainer presents either during lecture/discussion, video, computer-based instruction or essential information that is presented in the participant's guide.

Time: An estimate of the time frame for each portion of the training including the estimated time for lectures, activities, experiential activities, and assessment.

Method: A concise description of the training methods (e.g. lecture/discussion, group activity, role play) that will be used to achieve the training objective.

Materials: A description of all handouts, PowerPoint/Prezi, participant guide information, hardware/software that is needed to deliver the training.

Training formats vary in the amount of structure and detail included when incorporating these five lesson plan elements. The three typical training plan formats include:

Descriptive format: Information is presented as a narrative summary that first presents the training objective that is then linked to the training content, methods, and describes materials needed to implement the lesson. Time estimates are also included for each training block or module. Paragraphs and subheadings are used to organize individual modules or activities within each module.

Outline format: The lesson plan is structured following typical outline pattern. Major elements or individual modules of the training sessions are identified with Roman numerals, while sub areas and other elements of the lesson are organized around the major headings. The length of time of each module is noted along with attendant materials needed. Margin icons may be used to identify a change in methods or the use of video or other instructional materials.

Multicolumn format: This format organizes the five elements in the most structured of all formats. The learning objective for a given module is presented at the top of the page. Four columns support the learning objective. The first column, also the narrowest column, presents the time frame for each instructional element of the lesson (lecture/discussion or activity). A new time is noted for each change in method during the lesson. The second column, labeled "content," includes a description of the lecture/discussion or video information that is presented – "Tell" step of each training lesson. The only information that appears in column two is information related to the training content. The third column labeled "methods," includes a description of the strategies or methods (such as noting group activity, role play, video or any other method) used to process the training content described in column two. The final column is for "materials" and includes a description of all items needed to implement the training (including handouts, PowerPoint/Prezi slides, hardware/software). Page numbers in the participant's guide are also referenced.

Deliver training

Training may be delivered in person, online, via written materials, or through a combination of training techniques (often called a hybrid method such as when using both online and classroom delivery methods). Again, noting that the center of the model refers to trainee needs, effective training delivery adapts to the needs and learning style preferences of the trainees.

What are your best delivery skills as a trainer? What do you do well when you train others and what delivery strategies may need polishing? Consider taking a personal inventory of your training delivery skills honestly describing the delivery skills at which you excel and those that may need attention. Prescriptions for effective in-person instructional delivery include using direct eye contact, appropriate and natural vocal variation, natural gestures for emphasis, and meaningful movement. Appropriate and effective delivery enhances trainer credibility and also enhances the learning climate that results in improved learning (Beebe & Beebe, 2018; Faylor, Beebe, Houser, & Mottet, 2008).

Among the research-supported strategies to use during training are those that enhance trainer–trainee immediacy. To be immediate is to create a sense of physical and psychological closeness between trainer and trainee that engenders feelings of pleasure and trainer–trainee engagement (Witt, Wheeless, & Allen, 2006). Nonverbal immediacy behaviors (Pogue & Ahyun, 2006; Faylor, Beebe, Houser, & Mottet, 2008) include unspoken delivery elements that increase positive feelings and responses such as:

Looking directly at trainees in a natural way.
Leaning forward.

Standing closer to trainees.
Coming from behind a lectern or table.
Using appropriate gestures for natural emphasis.

Verbal immediacy behaviors are those statements and use of words that engender positive feelings and emotions that result in feelings of inclusion and psychological closeness.
Verbal immediacy behaviors include:

Using the names of the trainees.
Saying "us" and "our" rather than "me" or "my" or "you" in an effort to be inclusive.
Providing positive, reinforcing feedback.
Using personal examples or personal experiences.
Asking trainees about their feelings when given requests or assignments.

Because nonverbal messages play a major role in how trainees interpret messages and are
especially important in communicating feelings and emotions, the trainer's delivery is
vitally important in creating a dynamic and energetic training climate. Effective delivery enhances trainee attention, helps maintain interest, and facilitates increased learning
(Beebe & Beebe, 2018). Diminished eye contact, flat and uninspiring vocal inflection,
frequent vocal fillers (such as "um," or "you know," or "ok?"), distracting gestures or
mannerisms, and non-meaningful pacing or walking around during a training session
are nonverbal delivery behaviors to be avoided.

Assess the training

The final element in the Needs–Centered Training Model, training assessment, is the
systematic process of determining whether the training program met the needs of the
individual trainees as well as the needs of the organization. Using similar methods of
assessing trainee needs (surveys, interviews, focus groups, observations), training assessment methods are designed to determine if the trainees are able to implement the
training. Training assessment typically focuses on whether or not the trainees valued
the training (affective response), remembered what was presented (cognitive response),
and can now perform the desired skills (behavioral response) that enhances their job
performance.

Kirkpatrick's (1994) four levels of assessment provide a useful overview of the key
elements of assessing a training program.

Level one: Did they like it? The first level of training assessment is to determine whether
the trainees had a positive affective response to the training. Assessing training affective response is often measured through post-training surveys and Likert scale items.
Although improving liking or affect is typically not the ultimate goal of training, determining whether trainees liked or valued the training provides clues as to the overall
worth of the training from the trainee's perspective. A trainee's positive affective response
to the training is often a predictor that cognitive and behavioral learning will occur.

Level two: Did they learn it? The second level of the Kirkpatrick assessment model
focuses on the degree to which the trainees learned the information, principles, and
knowledge presented during the training. Level two considers the cognitive domain
of learning. Cognitive tests using multiple choice, short answer, definitional responses,
and essay responses are typical measures of cognitive learning.

Benjamin Bloom's (Bloom, 1956) taxonomy of cognitive learning provides an overview of the key cognitive learning outcomes:

Knowledge (to restate what was learned exactly as presented);
Comprehension (to summarize or paraphrase what was learned in a student's own words);
Application (to relate what was learned or to apply what was learned to a specific situation);
Analysis (to identify and break down elements in a process or system into its component parts);
Synthesis (to reconstruct elements of the system in new and creative ways);
Evaluation (to accurately and appropriately assess positive and negative aspects of what was observed or experienced).

Level three: Can they perform it? The third level of Kirkpatrick's assessment model assesses whether the specific skills or behaviors that were presented in the training program and be performed. The psychomotor domain of learning is emphasized. Questions such as, "Can the trainees now listen more accurately? Or, can trainees develop a more accurate and comprehensive meeting agenda?" are assessed by observing whether the skills can, in fact, be executed effectively and appropriately.

Level four: Can they use it? Ultimately communication training seeks to achieve positive outcomes on the job. Trainees may be able to perform a skill in a training session, but can they use the skill on the job? The fourth level of the Kirkpatrick model focuses on whether the behaviors taught that can now be performed and result in an overall positive effect for the individual and/or organization. Assuming that the trainee has a positive reaction to the material (level one), can understand or comprehend the information presented (level two), can perform the behavior (level three), is there an overall positive result to the individual or organization (level four)? The key assessment question of level four is, "Are whatever the desired outcomes (increased sales, reduced complaints, greater efficiency) actually occurring with greater frequency and accuracy now that the training has been presented?"

Besides documenting that affective, cognitive, and behavioral learning has occurred, an additional and important assessment goal is to document that the training has resulted in overall positive benefits, including financial benefits, for the organization. The Return on Investment (ROI) is calculated by identifying all of the costs of implementing a training program (such as the cost of developing and presenting the training as well as the lost productivity due to workers being trained) and comparing those costs with the overall financial benefits that result from the training. Improved sales, lower error rate, increased efficiency in meetings, fewer customer complaints can be quantified and specific cost savings can be identified to determine the overall training ROI.

Summary

Instructional design is the process of identifying, describing, and developing a sequence of procedures and methods to implement a focused learning program to achieve desired learning outcomes. Training is the process of developing skills to perform a specific job or task more effectively (Beebe, Mottet, & Roach, 2013; Beebe, 2007).

The Needs-Centered Training Model is based on the principle that effective training, as reflected in the instructional design process, addresses the specific needs of the trainee. This chapter provided an overview of the Needs-Centered Training Model infused with describing several best-practice strategies for implementing training. The model is based on adult learning theory (Knowles et al., 2015) that suggests effective training, first and foremost, addresses trainee needs. The primary objective of the chapter is to provide training specialists a comprehensive overview of training instructional design best practices and identify specific strategies for teaching trainee's specific skills in order to perform a job or task more effectively (Beebe, Mottet, & Roach, 2013).

The nine steps in the Needs-Centered Training Model include:

Analyze organizational and trainee needs: Identifying the trainee deficiencies and organizational needs should drive each step of the communication training process. Training exists to address the needs of individual trainees as well as those of the organization.

Analyze the training task: A task analysis is a detailed, step-by-step description of the precise behaviors that the trainee should before in order to perform the desired skill. Presented in outline form, the task analysis provides the essential information that informs the training content as well as identifies the skills that should be assessed.

Develop training objectives: Objectives are observable, measurable, specific, and attainable desired outcomes of the training. Objectives are developed by identifying the gap between the skills that are required (as detailed in a task analysis) and the needs of the trainee.

Organize training content: Best practices for organizing training content include a five-step sequence for teaching any skill: Tell, Show, Invite, Encourage, and Correct. In addition, training content may be organized chronologically, from simple to complex, or using a problem-solution structure.

Determine training methods: Training methods are the means by which training is presented. Lecture, discussion, video, activities, role play, case study are among the typical types of methods used to present training content. Increasingly more training is presented using computer-based instructional methods, online via the Internet, or using a comprehensive learning management system.

Select training resources: Training resources consist of all materials needed to implement the training. Resources include handouts, a participant's guide (a booklet that includes all training handouts and summarizes key content), as well as technological resources including hardware and software such as PowerPoint and Prezi.

Complete training plans: After key decisions are made about the instructional design and the resources needed, a training or lesson plan presents a detailed summary of how the lesson will be organized and presented. The five elements common to most training plans include: The training objective, time estimates, training content, a description of the training methods, and a comprehensive description of the training materials and resources.

Deliver training: Effective training delivery for live, in-person training sessions includes using effective and appropriate eye contact, vocal variation, and incorporating natural gestures and movement. The use of nonverbal and verbal immediacy behaviors that increase the physical and psychological closeness between trainer and trainee improves cognitive, affective, and behavioral learning.

Assess the training: Training assessment is the systematic process of determining whether the training program met the needs of the individual trainees as well as the needs of the organization. Key questions to address in assessing training include: Did they like it? Did they learn it? Can they, do it? Can they use it? Documenting the value of an investment in training is a critical element in the training and development process. Effective and appropriate training should be validated based not only on whether trainees can perform the desired skills, but also result in overall quantifiable benefits for the organization.

References

Andrews, D. H., & Goodson, L. A. (1980). A comparative analysis of models of instructional design. *Journal of Instructional Development, 3*(4), 2–16.

Aziz, H. (1999). Assure learning through the use of the ASSURE model. Office of Informational Technology at Valencia Community College. Retrieved August 2, 2017 from https://learn.vccs.edu/bbcswebdav/institution/SO/MODEL/Learning%20Unit%202/Assure%20Learning%20Through%20the%20Use%20of%20the%20ASSURE%20Model.pdf

Apperson, J. M., Laws, E. L., & Scepansky, J. A. (2008). An assessment of student preferences for PowerPoint presentation structure in undergraduate courses. *Computers & Education, 50*, 148–152.

Beebe, S. A. (2007). What do communication trainers do? *Communication Education, 56*, 249–254.

Beebe, S. A., & Beebe S. J. (2018). *Public speaking: An audience-centered approach* Boston, MA: Pearson.

Beebe, S. A., & Frei, S. S. (2017). Teaching communication to working adults. In P. L. Witt (ed.), *Handbooks of communication science*. Vol. 16. *Communication and learning.* Los Angeles, CA: De Gruyter.

Beebe, S. A., Mottet, T. P., & Roach, K. D. (2013). *Training and development: Communicating for success* (2nd ed.). Boston, MA: Pearson.

Bloom, B. (1956). *Taxonomy of educational objectives: Handbook I: Cognitive domain.* New York, NY: McKay.

Doran, G. T. (1981). There's a S.M.A.R.T. way to write management's goals and objectives. *Management Review, 20*(11), 35–36.

Faylor, N. R., Beebe, S. A., Houser, M. L., & Mottet, T. P. (2008). Perceived differences in instructional communication behaviors between effective and ineffective corporate trainers. *Human Communication, 11*, 145–156.

Kirkpatrick, D. L. (1994). *Evaluating training programs: The four levels.* San Francisco, CA: Berrett-Koehler.

Knowles, M. S., Holton, E. F., & Swanson, R. A. (2015). *The adult learner: The definitive classic in adult education and human resource development.* London: Routledge.

Merriam, S. B. (2008). Adult learning theory for the twenty-first century. *New Directions for Adult and Continuing Education*, 93–98.

Meyers, G. E., & Meyers, M. T. (1976). *Instructor's manual to accompany the dynamics of human communication.* New York, NY: McGraw-Hill.

Pogue, L. L., & Ahyun, K. (2006). The effective of teacher nonverbal immediacy and credibility on student motivation and affective learning. *Communication Education, 55*, 331–344.

Shapiro, E. J., Kerssen-Griep, J., Gayle, B. M., & Allen, M. (2006). How powerful is PowerPoint? Analyzing the educational effects of desktop presentational programs in the classroom. In B. M. Gayle, R. W. Preiss, N. Burrell, & M. Allen (eds.), *Classroom communication and instructional processes: Advances through meta-analysis* (pp. 61–75). Mahwah, NJ: Lawrence Erlbaum Associates.

Smaldino, S. E., Lowther, D. H., & Russell, J. D. (2008). *Instructional technology and media for learning.* Upper Saddle River, NJ: Pearson Education.

Truelove, S. (2006). *Training in practice*. London: Chartered Institute of Personnel and Development.

Witt, P. L., Wheeless, L. R., & Allen, M (2006). The relationship between teacher immediacy and student learning: A meta-analysis. In B. M. Gayle, R. W. Preiss, N. Burrell, & M. Allen (eds.), *Classroom communication and instructional processes: Advances through meta-analysis* (pp. 149–168). Mahwah, NJ: Lawrence Erlbaum Associates.

Yuviler-Gavish, N., Yechiam, E., & Kallai, A. (2011). Learning in multimodal training: Visual guidance can be both appealing and disadvantageous in special tasks. *International Journal of Human-Computer Studies*, *69*, 113–122.

Chapter 18

Debriefing

Enhancing skill acquisition and transfer of learning during training

Marjorie M. Buckner and Amber N. Finn

Abstract

A key best practice for CCCTTs is effective instructional design, which should include a robust debrief that guides trainees to reflect on learned skills and connect them to past experiences and future applications. In this chapter, readers will be introduced to debriefing, discover the rationale for debriefing, and learn best practices to facilitate a successful debrief. Subsequently, CCCTTs should be able to design more effective trainings that promote skill acquisition and transfer of learning.

An essential best practice for communication consultants, coaches, teachers, and trainers (CCCTTs) is intentional and meaningful instructional design. Instructional design, defined as "the systematic process of translating principles of learning and instruction into plans or specification for instructional materials or activities" (Elkilany, 2015, p. 147), is vital because, when done well, it can help foster long-lasting and deep learning, and of utmost importance in the training context, help ensure transfer of learning from the training classroom to the job. Instructional design informs not only what should be included in training, but also when certain things (i.e., activities, etc.) should occur in training. As noted by Silberman and Biech (2015), when you do things in training is paramount to the success of the training.

One of the most prevalent and influential instructional design models is Beebe, Mottet, and Roach's (2013) Needs-Centered Training Model, which was presented in detail in the preceding chapter. Following Beebe et al.'s (2013) model, one of the keys to successful and effective training is organizing the training content. For example, they suggest that training content should be organized chronologically (i.e., step by step) and by complexity (i.e., from easiest to most complex). Additionally, they propose a five-step training sequence (tell, show, invite, encourage, correct) that details one way communication trainers may organize training content. A trainer employing the sequence would explain to participants how to perform a communication skill (Step One), show them how to effectively and appropriately perform the communication skill (Step Two), and then invite trainees to participate in an activity or simulation to practice the communication skill (Step Three). Following the activity, the trainer would provide feedback to the participants – helpful information (Step Four) and/or criticism (Step Five) to improve performance of the communication skill. Although this is a well formulated and easily implementable plan for sequencing training, we will expand on one particular area, which we call debriefing.

It could be argued that the five-step sequence already includes debriefing (i.e., the final two feedback steps – encouraging and correcting); however, given the importance of debriefing, we suggest that this topic needs a more robust discussion and might even be considered for elevation to a sixth step in the process because of its importance.

In this chapter, we will define debriefing and discuss best practices for developing and facilitating a debrief. We will provide a rationale for including debriefing in your training plan and explain the value gained by concluding trainings with a robust debrief phase. Engaging in a thoughtful and research-based instructional design process is paramount to a successful training. Adding a comprehensive debrief to your skills training design will bolster your design and increase your training success.

The importance of debriefing

Debriefing, defined as "a process in which people who have had an experience are led through a purposive discussion of that experience" (Lederman, 1992, p. 146), is utilized in a variety of industries, such as the military, psychology, healthcare, business, corporate training, outdoor adventures, and education. Although debriefing always involves a discussion of a common experience, the goals and methodologies vary across industries and contexts (Lederman, 1992). For example, Lederman (1992) identifies three distinct ways debriefing has been utilized. First, it originated in the military, and it has been employed there for the purpose of bringing participants together after missions or exercises to discuss what occurred and to make strategic changes and improvements for future operations. Second, it has been used in psychology after deception studies to explain the purpose, nature, and importance of the deception to the study. Finally, debriefing has been employed in educational settings, such as in college classrooms and corporate training contexts, to help facilitate learning following an experiential activity (e.g., game, simulation, experience).

Lederman (1992) explains that despite these differences, all debriefing sessions involve a set of seven common elements: (1) the debriefer – the person who helps the participants process the experience; (2) the participants – the people who have participated in the experience; (3) the experience – the situation, simulation, exercise, or activity the participants have been through; (4) impact – the effect of the experience; (5) recollection – a recall of what happened during the experience; (6) report – a oral or written account of what happened during the experience; and (7) time – the interval given to process the experience. Further, the debriefing process is based upon two underlying assumptions: (1) The participants were impacted in some meaningful way by the experience, and (2) a discussion of the experience is necessary to "provide insight into that experience and its impact" (Lederman, 1992, p. 146).

Given the nature of this chapter, in the remainder of the time we will focus on debriefing for educational and training purposes. As we mentioned previously, debriefing in this sense follows some sort of simulation or experiential activity. Thus, it is assumed that the trainer has created and facilitated an activity, exercise, or simulation designed to provide the participants an opportunity to practice a communication skill set. Following the five-step training sequence reviewed previously, it is assumed then that a relevant activity was designed and facilitated in the invite step. Additionally, following Lederman's (1992) debrief assumptions outlined above, it is assumed that the experience was meaningful and a discussion of the experience is needed. Let's discuss these two assumptions in more detail before looking at best practices for debriefing.

First, when is an experience meaningful? We would argue that an experience is mean-ingful when it meets the needs of the trainees (Beebe et al., 2013). Aligning with Beebe et al.'s (2013) Needs-Centered Training Model, it is assumed that the trainer has con-ducted a thorough needs assessment to determine the specific needs of the participants and the organization (Silberman & Biech, 2015) and has designed an activity that provides the trainees with a relevant and practical opportunity to practice the specific communi-cation skill. For example, if the focus of training was handling customer complaints, the exercise should provide trainees an opportunity to practice handling relevant customer complaints, using the communication channel(s) common to that specific organization, and enacting the expected verbal and nonverbal communication behaviors according to current best practices identified in the literature, industry, and within the organization.

Next, when does an activity need to be debriefed? Drawing upon the work of edu-cational psychologists such as John Dewey (1916, 1929) and David Kolb (1983), those studying debriefing advocate that all experiential activities (e.g., games, simulations, exercises, etc.) need to be debriefed in order to maximize learning. In fact, the debrief is considered the most important component of the learning process (Lederman, 1984; 1992; McGaghie, Issenberg, Petrusa, & Scalese, 2010; Reed, Andrews, & Ravert, 2013; Ryoo & Ha, 2015) and a central and required, not ancillary, part of experience-based learning (Lederman, 1984). Similarly, based upon their review of current simulation based learning literature, Ryoo and Ha (2015) conclude that, "debriefing should not be an optional process but a required process of simulation based learning" (p. 544).

The goal of debriefing is for participants to reflect on, discuss, and process what they learned from the activity; making important and necessary connections to what they knew prior to the experience and determining how they can best use the information they learned in the future (Lederman, 1984, 1992). Nicholson (2012) suggests, "Without the debriefing time, the effectiveness of the activity may be greatly diminished" (p. 118). Similarly, Beebe et al. (2013) suggest, "If the experiential activity is not unpacked, many trainees will ques-tion the point of the activity and fail to make the appropriate learning connections" (p. 135). Nicholson (2012) goes on to explain that debriefing can surmount faults in the learning experience such that knowledge and skills are gained in spite of the learning experience producing unanticipated outcomes or otherwise not going well. Thus, the debrief helps par-ticipants make connections between what they learned from the activity and their previous and future experiences. This is of utmost important in the training context, where it is ex-pected that the information and skills learned during training will be transferred back to the workplace to improve organizational efficiency and effectiveness (Baldwin & Ford, 1988). However, as McKechnie (2016) so aptly stated, "recognizing its importance and implement-ing debrief in the most educationally effective way are very different things" (p. 184).

Debriefing best practices

Effective debriefing does not just magically happen; it takes a lot of preparation and skill on the part of the trainer. Without preparation, a trainer may poorly facilitate the session and demonstrate inappropriate or ineffective communication skills such as not asking relevant or thought-provoking questions, interjecting personal ideas or preju-dice, or allowing voices to be silenced during the debrief (Kessler, Cheng, & Mullan, 2014). These pitfalls of poor preparation, and thereby facilitation, may hinder "opti-mal learning" (Sawyer & Deering, 2013, p. 391). Although a wide variety of methods and suggestions have been proposed across diverse disciplines for how to effectively facilitate a debrief session, in this section, we summarize prior work and propose three best practices – (1) planning the debrief, (2) strategically structuring the debrief, and (3) engaging in effective communication skills to facilitate the debrief well.

Planning the debrief

The first best practice for debriefing involves planning the debrief session. Kessler et al. (2014) suggest that trainers must determine who, what, when, where, why, and how the debriefing will occur. Though Kessler et al. (2014) originally constructed this list for emergency room medical debriefs, these basic questions provide a comprehensive checklist that decisions trainers should make in order to facilitate a successful communication skills training debrief. Thus, we posit that establishing who, what, when, where, and why are essential to planning the debrief. (How will be addressed as part of the second best practice.)

Who describes the participants involved in the debrief. Though this may appear to be a simple question for a trainer who has been contracted to provide a singular training for a predetermined set of participants, determining who will participate in the debrief may vary in different situations. For example, if a trainer employed by a hotel chain is facilitating a training on mediating employee conflicts for department managers at a single hotel, then the trainer may also consider if the head of operations for the hotel should be included in the debrief. While including the head of operations might impress upon the trainees the gravity of the skills taught, the inclusion of the head of operations may jeopardize the learning environment by inducing anxiety for trainees or de-motivating employees to implement the skills as they may interpret the head of operations' presence as another managerial mandate rather than helpful and relevant skills necessary for effectively doing their job. Thus, depending on the goal(s) of the training, the trainer may need to include other organizational members in the debrief session.

After deciding who will be included in the debrief, the trainer must decide what will be debriefed. In the educational context, what needs to be debriefed is the activity, simulation, or game that provided trainees an opportunity to practice the communication skill(s). We argue that this always needs to happen in order to help ensure trainees learned from the experience and that they will utilize the knowledge and skills learned on the job. Thus, the trainer will need to plan a debrief session for all experiential activities, simulations, or games utilized in the training.

When involves establishing the time frame in which the debrief will occur. Though debriefings may be held directly following an activity or scheduled for a later date and time (Lederman, 1992), Kessler et al. (2014) suggests that participants are better able to recall actions and feelings and may be more likely to engage in discussion when the debrief occurs soon after the experience. Thus, we recommend that the debrief occurs immediately after the feedback steps (i.e., encourage and correct) in Beebe et al.'s (2013) sequence. In addition to determining when the debrief will occur, when also involves determining the length of the debrief. Although debrief durations can range from 10 minutes to more than an hour (Kessler et al., 2014), a meta-analysis of performance debrief research revealed an average debrief time of 18 minutes (Tannenbaum & Cerasoli, 2013). In order to decide on the length of the debrief, trainers should consider the total time allotted for the training. Likely, a 30-minute training will warrant less debrief time than a two-hour training. Additionally, the goals of the debrief, personal preferences, feasibility, and other factors may influence how much time is spent debriefing. While debrief durations may vary, a trainer will benefit from determining a specific allotment of time for the debrief and planning accordingly.

Deciding where the debrief will occur is an important consideration for establishing a learning environment that allows for all participants to engage in the debrief. Ambrose et al. (2010) suggest that a learning environment is comprised of four characteristics – intellectual (cognitive simulation and rigor), physical, social (interactions, involvement, and cooperation), and emotional. They posit that trainers' decisions on where the debrief is held should reflect concern for all four characteristics, though the physical space may take precedence in the decision. Generally, the location should be easily accessible for the trainees and convenient in relation to the activity space, particularly if the debrief will directly follow the activity. Attending to the social and emotional aspects of the environment, and recognizing feasibility and constraints, may be best illustrated in the following example. A trainer may be hired by an organization to teach employees about dissent and whistleblowing. The trainer may desire to conduct the debrief at a location not affiliated with the organization, but the organization may insist on using their own facilities. In addition to choosing a location, trainers must also consider the setup of the facility. Organizing chairs into small circles of five participants may encourage conversation and increase the opportunity for participants to thoroughly reflect on their personal perceptions and feelings about the experiential activity and receive peer feedback. However, creating this setup may not be possible and lecture–hall seating may be the only option available. All space arrangements present opportunities and constraints. A good trainer will recognize the opportunities and constraints afforded in the space chosen for the debrief, and when possible, a good trainer will seek to determine a location for the training that maximizes the learning outcomes of the debrief.

Finally, planning involves determining the why of the debrief. Beebe et al.'s (2013) Needs-Centered Training Model prompts trainers to "develop training learning objectives" prior to "organizing training content" (p. 19). Recalling these objectives should inform the specific outcomes determined for the debrief. That is, deciding why the debrief occurs requires syncing the purpose of the training with the purpose of the debrief. Why are you doing the debrief? What should trainees get out of the debrief? Kessler et al. (2014) recognize that a debrief may lead to changes in policy or procedure, behaviors, or assessments. However, in a communication skills training, the debrief outcome will likely echo the learning objectives for the training. For example, a training for managers about giving corrective feedback may have a learning objective of trainees articulating feedback in a series of praise a behavior, describe a behavior, recommend a correction, and praise a second behavior. The purpose of the debrief may be to accentuate how this practice can be implemented or to highlight the benefits of using this format. To underscore implementation, the debrief may prompt trainees to consider how they will remember to use this feedback format and how the trainees will hold themselves or each other accountable for using this format. Alternatively, to fulfill the purpose of highlighting the benefits of the format, the debrief may prompt trainees to reflect on how they felt when providing and receiving feedback in this format and list benefits they perceive to be associated with using this format. Deciding on the why of the debrief shapes and frames the prompts and questions included in the debrief to maximize trainee learning and ensure a productive outcome for the debrief.

Strategically structuring the debrief

Our second best practice – strategically structuring the debrief – addresses Kessler et al.'s (2014) how of debriefing. Establishing how the debrief will occur requires selecting a particular structure and developing prompts and questions. This is so important to debriefing that we consider this step to constitute a separate stage of debrief facilitation.

Over the years and across industries, those studying debriefing have described it as a systematic and structured communication process and subsequently have presented a variety of different models for effective debriefing. For example, Lederman (1992), summarizing several prior models, describes debriefing as a three-step process. The first step, systematic reflection and analysis, involves helping the participants reflect on what happened during the experience. The second phase, intensification and personalization, comprises having participants reflect on how they felt and what they learned from the experience. Finally, step three, generalization and application, helps participants move from their own experience to "broader applications and implications of the experience" (p. 152).

Similarly, Rudolph, Simon, Raemer, and Eppich (2008) present a three-step process that includes the reactions phase, the analysis phase, and the summary phase. The reactions phase involves having participants express their emotions associated with the experience and provides the instructor an opportunity to share facts related to the experience in order to prevent any confusion. The analysis phase includes a discussion regarding lessons learned, identification of gaps between desired and actual performance, feedback on performance gaps, and participants perspectives on what happened. Finally, the summary phase encompasses devising "lessons learned from the debriefing into memorable rules-of-thumb or concepts that trainees can take with them to improve practice" (p. 1013). In this last phase, participants have the opportunity to reflect on and share such things as what they might repeat in the future or what they might do differently in a real situation.

Likewise, Beebe et al. (2013) describe the four-step EDIT process for unpacking or debriefing an activity. It involves having participants engage (E) in an activity, describe (D) what happened during the activity, infer (I) what they learned during the experiential activity, and transfer (T) or share how they will use the new knowledge and skills on the job. Summarizing several models of debriefing, Nicholson (2012) concludes, "the key underlying concepts are having the learner describe what happened, asking them to analyze their performance, and encouraging them to talk about how this experience could be applied in the real world" (p. 119). And, as trainers gain experience, it is not unusual for trainers to use multiple debrief processes to best incorporate the facilitator's preference, learners' needs, and the debrief context (Krogh, Bearman, & Nestel, 2016). Though a novice communication skills trainer may benefit from a more explicit debrief plan, experience and continued practice with facilitation may help trainers develop strategic flexibility in debrief execution. However, as Nicholson (2012) posits, the most critical aspects of debriefing include description, reflection, and application. Thus, we suggest that regardless of which debrief model you utilize, the key is to recognize that the debrief is a structured process that involves the trainer (1) helping the participants reflect on and process the activity or experience; (2) ensuring the participants make the important and necessary connections to their prior knowledge and experiences; and (3) assisting participants to devise a plan for how they will use the newly acquired information and skills in the future. Planning and asking questions within these three areas should help ensure the effectiveness of the debrief.

Effective communication skills

The third, and final, best practice involves using effective communication skills to facilitate the debrief session. Surprisingly, to date, little empirical research has been done on effective communication skills in debriefing. Nonetheless, trainers report the importance of facilitating a supportive communication environment for learning to transpire and trainees to feel comfortable (Krogh et al., 2016). Similarly, scholars recommend that trainers use a variety of strategies in order to create this type of environment, including being honest, enforcing guidelines for civility, establishing an agenda for the debrief, and "sharing responsibility" (Krogh et al., 2016, para. 59). Effective communication skills, however, extend beyond information-centered behaviors (e.g., providing an agenda or guidelines) to specific ways in which we interact with others. Lederman (1984), for example, suggests that debrief facilitators need what she calls experience guidance skills. These include: (1) tolerance for ambiguity, (2) ability to observe and interpret behavior, (3) ability to form questions and listen to answers about behaviors, (4) ability to select appropriate directiveness and nondirectiveness, (5) a sense of timing, and (6) sound judgment calls. Additionally, grounded in instructional communication scholarship, Beebe et al. (2013) recommend that trainers engage in immediacy and affinity seeking behaviors, as well as "good eye contact, appropriate vocal volume and variation, professional posture, and illustrative gestures" (p. 232). Though all of these practices may help trainers facilitate a successful debrief, we put forth a synthesized and extended list of effective communication skills trainers should use to facilitate a debrief.

First, we suggest that trainers employ communication skills that foster a respectful, learning-centered communication environment. Although we acknowledge that a learning environment is co-constructed (Sidelinger & Booth-Butterfield, 2010) such that both trainers and participants influence how the environment is perceived, the trainer has a responsibility to demonstrate and encourage civility. In fact, an instructor's behaviors may have more influence on a learner's perceptions of the classroom environment than peers (Catt, Miller, & Schallenkamp, 2007; Gokcora, 1989; Kaufmann, Sellnow, & Frisby, 2016). Exhibiting and enforcing civility during a debrief may include (1) establishing guidelines for the debrief, (2) modeling and advocating descriptive language, and (3) employing verbal and nonverbal immediacy behaviors. First, we recommend that you establish guidelines with trainees prior to beginning the debrief. These could include such things as not interrupting another person and avoid blaming others. The goal is to ensure everyone knows what is expected of them and others during the debrief. Second, we recommend the use of descriptive language. Descriptive language may be used when discussing a particular event or behavior. In this instance, describe what happened and what the behavior was rather than articulating negative value to the person or people involved. Third, we recommend the use of verbal and nonverbal immediacy behaviors to create a perception of closeness between participants (Beebe et al., 2013; Mehrabian, 1971). Verbal immediacy behaviors include using participants' names (particularly when responding to a comment they have made or praising), using "we/our" language instead of "I/my" language, and asking trainees for their ideas or feelings (Beebe et al., 2013; Gorham, 1988). Nonverbal immediacy behaviors include decreasing space between you and the trainees, maintaining a positive facial expression, and making eye contact with participants (Beebe et al., 2013). The use of nonverbal immediacy behaviors in particular are associated with effective trainers (Faylor, Beebe, Houser, & Mottet, 2008). Avoiding non-immediacy or distancing nonverbal behaviors such as crossing your arms or putting your hands in your pocket, looking away or over-the-top of trainees' heads, and having "negative, sarcastic, or fake" facial expressions can negatively influence the debrief session (Beebe et al., 2013, p. 235). Additionally, trainers should manage the communication environment to discourage uncivil or distracting behaviors during the debrief. Fostering a respectful, learning-centered communication can increase what trainees learn during debriefing and how much they like the debrief process.

Second, trainers should ask open-ended (as opposed to closed-ended) questions. Open-ended questions invite the respondent to provide more information than will be elicited with closed-ended questions (Stewart & Cash, 2011). For example, "Tell me about your experience participating in this activity" is more open than "What emotion did you experience during the activity?" The first question prompts trainees to reflect on what happened and describe thoughts, feelings, and behaviors. The second question prompts trainees to provide a one-word answer reflective of the precise emotion experienced. Hence, the quality of answers provided by trainees, including depth and quantity, may increase if trainers use open-ended questions.

When asking open-ended questions, trainers should be mindful about waiting patiently for trainees to respond. Open-ended questions likely require additional thought before answering. Calmly and tolerantly waiting for someone to speak is important. One strategy is to count silently to ten before re-phrasing the question. Other strategies include prompting trainees to first write and share their answer with someone else before reporting back to the group (think–pair–share), asking a particular trainee to respond, or simply reassuring and encouraging participants to respond. To encourage participation, trainers can probe participant answers, particularly when the participant provides limited information, and praise respondents for their responses. Additionally, when trainers respond to participant responses, which should occur frequently, open-ended questions provide trainers with more information to more easily connect responses back to training objectives and highlight key conclusions or ideas related to the skill. Further, open-ended questions may be considered less threatening to participants (e.g., there is not one right answer to the question) and provide participants with greater agency in that they are empowered to decide "the amount and kind of information to give" (Stewart & Cash, 2011, p. 55). Yet, due to the open-ended nature of the answers, trainees' answers are less predictable. The trainer must be prepared to think on his or her feet in order to respond thoughtfully to trainees and connect their answers to the debrief outcomes and training objectives. The better the trainer knows the training content and the trainer spends contemplating the questions and possible answers, the more likely the trainer will adapt skillfully to participant responses. Asking open-ended questions incites rich reflection and discussion that increase learning, though it is important for a debrief facilitator to wait patiently for trainee answers, encourage participation, and adapt to trainee responses.

Third, the trainer should follow the debrief plan and structure constructed during preparation, but, at the same time, remain somewhat flexible. The objective of creating a plan and developing a debrief structure that strategically addresses training objectives, learner needs, and the purpose of the debrief is for the trainer to ensure that the debrief is meaningful and beneficial to trainees and for the trainer to feel prepared and confident about facilitating a successful debrief session. Departing from the plan at the last minute may invite common pitfalls such as inviting tangential conversations from the trainer or participants, asking poorly constructed or irrelevant questions, and ultimately devalue the debrief. However, trainers may encounter unexpected events or circumstances. For example, the time frame for the debrief may need to be adjusted because the activity took more or less time than anticipated or one of the questions in the debrief sparked more or less discussion than expected. As a result, the trainer may need to modify the debrief structure and add to or omit some of the questions or prompts planned. Additionally, as mentioned previously, another unexpected event might include participants responding to questions in surprising ways. Sometimes trainees may bring up connections to the experiential activity or simulation that the trainer is unaware of prior to the debrief. Spending time unpacking this connection to make sense of the activity and apply the communication skill to the trainees' jobs increases relevance for the trainees, which in turn enhances the learning experience (Beebe et al., 2013).

Fourth, the trainer should encourage multiple voices, thereby creating an inclusive environment and enabling a robust discussion. Encouraging multiple voices means inviting multiple perspectives by allowing more than one person to respond to questions. This may also mean that when one participant is the first to respond to more than one question in a row, the trainer may need to explicitly request that others offer answers and more attentively regulate when trainees respond. While asking participants to raise their hands to respond may seem elementary, this is a great way to manage who speaks. A more indirect strategy would be for the trainer to move to different places in the room. Decreasing distance between trainers and students is a display of nonverbal immediacy, which is a nonverbal behavior that increases perceived closeness (Mehrabian, 1971). Doing so may incite those closest to the trainer to offer responses and participate in the debrief. Perhaps most important to encouraging multiple voices is attending to the amount of time you are talking in the training. While you should include your own observations, feelings, and ideas, take care not to speak too soon or often (Beebe et al., 2013; Kessler et al., 2014). Dominating the conversation or going off on one's own tangents shifts the focus of the debrief away from trainee reflexivity, knowledge transfer, and skill retention to the trainer's knowledge and skill set. Instead, use your facilitation skills to spark dynamic conversation, involving as many trainees as possible for the time allotted. The combination of input from trainees and the trainer will create a rich learning environment where trainees can connect what they have learned to their own experiences and possible future applications and trainers can direct trainees' comments towards those connections or provide feedback to correct misunderstandings.

Lastly, the trainer should strive to connect trainees' responses during the debrief to trainees' experiences, training objectives, and the debrief purpose. When framing replies to participants' comments, draw on their own experiences to contextualize the communication skill. This helps trainees see the relevance and value of the communication skill in their own lives (Beebe et al., 2013). Additionally, leading them to reach these conclusions rather than simply telling trainees the value of the communication skill, for instance, helps the information resonate more deeply with the participants. It is important that debrief facilitators also connect trainees' responses to the training objectives and the debrief purpose. Sometimes, the trainer only needs to repeat the trainee's message in a way that demonstrates how the trainee's insight aligns with the training objective or brings to light the desire outcome of the debrief. For example, a participant in a customer service seminar on listening might say that listening is really important in the workplace in order to serve customers effectively. A trainer's response might re-state and elaborate on the participant's comments, explaining that, as discussed in the training, listening is a skill involving a six step process (hearing, understanding, remembering, interpreting, evaluating, and responding; Brownell, 2002; Floyd, 2011) and when used the same way as in the simulation, can help customer service representatives fulfill customers' needs with fewer mistakes. This response echoes what the participant has said, but also reiterates the training objective of using the six step listening process when listening to customer needs. Connecting trainees' responses to their own experiences increases relevance and understanding, while connecting trainees' responses to the training objective and purpose of the debrief accentuates the value of the training, reinforces why the trainees attended, and reiterates what they should get out of the training.

Conclusion

In this chapter, we explicate debriefing in training. Then, we propose that the debriefing phase be amplified and also provide the means by which it may be done. Debriefing consists of a purposeful, facilitated discussion that allows learners to reflect on their learning experiences and make sense of the skills taught during training (Fanning & Gaba, 2007; Fey & Jenkins, 2015; Raemer et al., 2011). Tannenbaum and Cerasoli (2013) estimate that effective debriefs "can improve individual and team performance by approximately 20% to 25%" (p. 231). Hence, planning a debrief when designing a training is an important component of effective instructional design. In order to ensure an effective debrief, we proposed three best practices necessary for facilitating a successful debrief session.

Facilitating a successful debrief session includes: planning the debrief, strategically structuring the debrief, and communicating effectively (see Table 18.1). Planning the debrief involves making decisions about who, what, when, where, and why the debrief

Table 18.1 Debrief best practices

Best Practices	Description
1. Plan the debrief	Decide on: • *who* will be included and who will facilitate the debrief • *what* needs to be debriefed • *when* the debrief will occur and for how long • *where* the debrief will occur • *why* the debrief will occur and what outcomes will be produced
2. Strategically structure the debrief	Choose a debrief structure that involves: • reflecting on what happened • connecting the exercise to prior knowledge and experience • developing a plan for implementation and execution in trainees' jobs
3. Communicate effectively	Demonstrate the following behaviors: • Foster a respectful, learning-centered communication environment • Ask open-ended (rather than closed-ended) questions • Follow your debrief plan, but be flexible • Encourage multiple voices • Connect responses to trainees' experiences, training objectives, and the debrief purpose

will occur. Structuring the debrief requires selecting a particular structure and developing prompts and questions that best fit the purpose of the debrief, training objectives, facilitator preferences, and learners' needs. Though there are several structures to choose from, any structure used should prompt trainees to reflect on the experiential activity, connect the exercise to prior knowledge and experience, develop a plan for implementing and executing the communication skill in their job. Communicating effectively during the debrief is essential to facilitating a successful debrief session. Fostering a respectful, learning-centered communication environment; asking open-ended questions; following your debrief plan and adapting as needed; encouraging multiple voices; and connecting trainees' responses to trainees' experiences, training objectives, and the debrief purpose are important verbal and nonverbal messages and behaviors that trainers need to demonstrate when facilitating a debrief session. All three best practices complement each other such that trainers are able to effectively guide participants through a valuable debrief.

Developing and implementing a robust debrief into Beebe et al.'s (2013) five-phase sequence may greatly improve the knowledge and skill trainees retain after participating in training. Debriefing allows trainees to reflect on what happened in the training exercise, connect the communication skill to their own experiences, understand how the skill works and the skill's value to the trainees, and apply the skill to their own lives. Thus, when trainers facilitate debriefing as the final phase of the sequence, trainees are able to receive instruction on a skill, watch the skill, perform the skill, receive positive and constructive feedback on the skill, and reflect on the skill. Overall, we argue that including debriefing in your instructional design will help ensure knowledge and performance gaps are minimized and the communication skill is transferred back to the workplace.

References

Ambrose, S. A., Bridges, M. W., DiPietro, M., Lovett, M. C., Norman, M. K., & Mayer, R. E. (2010). *How learning works: 7 Research-based principles for smart teaching.* San Francisco, CA: Jossey-Bass.

Baldwin, T., & Ford, J. K. (1988). Transfer of training: A review and directions for future research. *Personnel Psychology, 41*, 63–105.

Beebe, S. A., Mottet, T. P., & Roach, K. D. (2013). *Training and development: Communicating for success* (2nd ed.). Boston, MA: Pearson.

Brownell, J. (2002). *Listening attitudes, principles, and skills* (2nd ed.). Boston, MA: Allyn & Bacon.

Catt, S., Miller, D., & Schallenkamp, K. (2007). You are the key: Communicate for learning effectiveness. *Education, 127*, 369–377.

Dewey, J. (1916). *Democracy and education: An introduction to the philosophy of education.* New York, NY: MacMillan.

Dewey, J. (1929). *Experience and education.* New York, NY: MacMillan.

Elkilany, E. A. (2015). The impact of applying instructional design principles on students' attitudes towards the learning content. *Journal of Arab & Muslim Media Research, 8*, 147–169. doi:10.1386/jammr8.2.147_1

Fanning, R. M., & Gaba, D. M. (2007). The role of debriefing in simulation-based learning. *Simulation in Healthcare, 2*, 115–125.

Faylor, N. R., Beebe, S. A., Houser, M. L., & Mottet, T. P. (2008). Perceived differences in instructional communication behaviors between effective and ineffective corporate trainers. *Human Communication, 11*, 145–156.

Fey, M. K., & Jenkins, L. S. (2015). Debriefing practices in nursing education programs: Results from a national study. *Nursing Education Perspectives, 36*, 361–366. doi:10.5480/14–1520

Floyd, K. (2011). *Communication matters.* New York, NY: McGraw-Hill.

Gokcora, D. (1989, November). A descriptive study of communication and teaching strategies used by two types of international teaching assistants at the University of Minnesota, and their cultural perceptions of teaching and teachers. Paper presented at the meeting of the National Conference on Training and Employment of Teaching Assistants, Seattle, WA.

Gorham, J. (1988). The relationship between verbal teacher immediacy behaviors and student learning. *Communication Education, 37,* 40–53.

Kaufmann, R., Sellnow, D. D., & Frisby, B. N. (2016). The development and validation of the online learning climate scale (OLCS). *Communication Education, 65,* 307–321. doi:10.1080/03634523.2015.1101778

Kessler, D. O., Cheng, A., & Mullan, P. (2014). Debriefing in the emergency department after clinical events: A practical guide. *Annals of Emergency Medicine,* 1–9. doi:10.1016/j.annemergmed.2014.10.019

Kolb, D. (1983). *Experiential learning: Experience as the source learning and development.* Upper Saddle River, NJ: Prentice Hall.

Krogh, K., Bearman, M., & Nestel, D. (2016). "Thinking on your feet" – a qualitative study of debriefing practice. *Advances in Simulation, 1.* doi:10.1186/s41077-016-0011-4

Lederman, L. C. (1984). Debriefing: A critical reexamination of the postexperience analytic process with implications for its effective use. *Simulation & Games, 15,* 415–431.

Lederman, L. C. (1992). Debriefing: Toward a systematic assessment of theory and practice. *Simulation & Gaming, 23,* 145–160.

McGaghie, W. C., Issenberg, S. B., Petrusa, E. R., & Scalese, R. J. (2010). A critical review of simulation based medical education research. *Medical Education, 44,* 50–63. doi:10.1111/j.13652923.2009.03547.x

McKechnie, A. (2016). The importance and practice of debrief in medical simulation. *British Journal of Hospital Medicine, 77,* 184–186.

Mehrabian, A. (1971). *Silent messages.* Belmont, CA: Wadsworth.

Nicholson, S. (2012). Completing the experience: Debriefing in experiential education games. In *Proceedings of the 3rd International Conference on Society and Information Technologies* (pp. 117–121). Winter Garden, FL: International Institute of Informatics and Systematics.

Raemer, D., Anderson, M., Cheng, A., Fanning, R., Nadkarni, V., & Savoldelli, G. (2011). Research regarding debriefing as part of the learning process. *Simulation in Healthcare: The Journal of the Society for Simulation in Healthcare, 6,* S52–S57. doi:10.1097/SIH.0b013e31822724d0

Reed, S. J., Andrews, C. M., & Ravert, P. (2013). Debriefing simulations: Comparison of debriefing with video and debriefing alone. *Clinical Simulation in Nursing, 9,* 585–591.

Rudolph, J. W., Simon, R., Raemer, D. B., & Eppich, W. J. (2008). Debriefing as formative assessment: Closing performance gaps in medical education. *Academic Emergency Medicine, 15,* 1010–1016. doi:10.1111/j.1553–2712.2008.00248.x

Ryoo, E. N., & Ha, E. (2015). The importance of debriefing in simulation-based learning. *CIN: Computers, Informatics, & Nursing, 33,* 538–545.

Sawyer, T. L., & Deering, S. (2013). Adaptation of the US Army's after-action review for simulation debriefing in healthcare. *Simulation in Healthcare, 8,* 388–397. doi:10.1097/SIH.

Sidelinger, R. J., & Booth-Butterfield, M. (2010). Co-constructing student involvement: An examination of teacher confirmation and student-to-student connectedness in the college classroom. *Communication Education, 59,* 165–184. doi:10.1080/03634520903390867

Silberman, M., & Biech, E. (2015). *Active training.* San Francisco, CA: Pfeiffer-John Wiley & Sons.

Stewart, C. J., & Cash, Jr., W. B. (2011). *Interviewing: Principles and practices* (13th ed.). New York, NY: McGraw-Hill.

Tannenbaum, S. I., & Cesaroli, C. P. (2013). Do team and individual debriefs enhance performance? A meta-analysis. *Human Factors, 55,* 231–245. doi:10.1177/0018720812448394.

Chapter 19

Instructional design training as instruction

Delivering instruction for the adult learner

Robert J. Sidelinger

Abstract

This chapter explores the theories and applications of adult learning, as well as performance based instruction and learning within organizations. Trainers will be able to identify the major principles of adult learning, and transfer best practices from instructional communication scholarship to the workplace training environment. This chapter allows communication consultants, coaches, teachers, and trainers to integrate effective and appropriate instructional design while creating and delivering impactful training materials.

Following the National Communication Association's Training and Development Division identification of the seven best communication practices for training and workshop facilitation, this chapter provides you with the essential academic knowledge and proven instructional communication research insights for best practice in *delivering* effective and appropriate instructional design. Chory and McCroskey (1999) suggested that the classroom is similar to the organizational setting. Thus, the organizational system may operate similarly to the classroom system. With this in mind, trainers can identify the major principles of adult learning, and transfer best practices from instructional communication to the workplace training environment. Andragogy is the art and science of adult learning (Knowles, 1984). It centers on two main themes: The importance of the adult's existing knowledge and experience, and the emphasis of a learner-centered (rather than an instructor-centered) instructional approach. In support, Rachal (2002) stated, "The [adult] learner is perceived to be a mature, motivated, voluntary, and equal participant in a learning relationship with a facilitator whose role is to aid the learner in the achievement of his or her primarily self-determined learning objectives" (p. 219). Rhetorical and Relational Goals Theory (RRGT) offers the necessary skills on the path to becoming an effective communication coach, consultant, teacher, or trainer.

Through RRGT, you have the opportunity deliver instructional designs that unlock adult learners' potential to maximize their performance and career success. Rhetorical goals focus on the mastery of content and relational goals achieve positive relationships, while effective instructional design creates learning experiences that are efficient, effective, and appealing (Merrill, Drake, Lacy, Pratt, & the ID_2 Research Group, 1996). Nussbaum (1992) stated effective instructional communication behaviors "are related directly to either positive student outcomes or positive evaluations of teaching" (p. 167), and successful instructors enact a combination of effective instructional behaviors simultaneously to fulfill both rhetorical and relational goals (Myers, Goodboy, & Members of Comm 600, 2014). Likewise, the ability to implement RRGT within training sessions is paramount to the success of adult learners. To follow best practice, according to RRGT, you must be cognizant of balancing rhetorical and relational goals with appropriate instructional communication strategies. This chapter provides a number of actionable suggestions that can help increase effectiveness of material, verbal communication, nonverbal communication, and mechanics for face-to-face training situations to ensure your participants achieve their goals and desired learning outcomes.

What is instructional communication?

Instructional communication is the study of how communication relates to learning within any environment – including training in organizations (Myers, 2010). The foundation of instructional communication is interdisciplinary and it integrates theory and research from three interrelated disciplines: educational psychology, pedagogy/andragogy, and communication studies (Mottet & Beebe, 2006). Educational psychology focuses on learners and how they approach the learning process. Pedagogy/andragogy considers instructors and how they motivate, engage, and effectively delivery material to learners. Communication studies emphasizes communication as an inherent component to the teaching–learning process; it stimulates meaning through the effective use of verbal and nonverbal messages. Instructional communication provides relevant knowledge and skills for being an effective communication coach, teacher trainer, and consultant. Throughout the chapter when terms such as "classroom" or "student" are used, they are meant to also include individuals in nonacademic settings – for example, corporate workshops, in which "teaching" is called "training" and "students" are called "participants".

What is andragogy?

Knowles (1984) stated the aim of adult instruction should be self-actualization. Trainers assist adult learners to reach their full potential, and andragogy is the instructional practice used to achieve this outcome. Knowles, Holton, and Swanson (2015) included six characteristics of adult learners that influenced their approach to learning: (1) the need to know, (2) self-direction, (3) abundance of prior life and work experience, (4) learn when they are ready and when they have the need to learn, (5) life-centered in their orientation to learning, and (6) internally motivated. Andragogy offers the opportunity for the integration of knowledge learned from others with personal experience and reflection.

What is Rhetorical and Relational Goals Theory?

Learning is co-created between adult learners and the trainer. Therefore, trainers should assist adult learners to become self-directed learners (Darkenwald & Merriam, 1982; Davenport & Davenport, 1985). As you develop and implement instructional designs, you can employ RRGT of instruction. Mottet, Frymier, and Beebe (2006) said instructors and learners have relational goals to be liked and affirmed, and rhetorical goals to achieve a task and master content. Both goals are valued. Learning is more likely to occur when rhetorical and relational goals are met and learners' needs are fulfilled (Frymier, 2007; Mottet et al., 2006).

You have an arsenal of instructional communication behaviors that serve to achieve RRGT (McCroskey, Richmond, & Bennett, 2006) and make instructional designs more efficient, effective, and appealing. Instructor humor, relevance, and clarity satisfy rhetorical goals whereas instructor nonverbal immediacy, confirmation, and rapport satisfy relational goals. The inherent learning aims and outcomes associated with these instructional communication behaviors are consistent with RRGT (Mottet et al., 2006). In addition, the learning environment can be viewed as a community setting, characterized by supportiveness, empathy, participation, and trust among peers (Sidelinger & Booth-Butterfield, 2010). It is essential to facilitate a connected learning environment in which participants are integral to the learning community and take part in the responsibility for learning interactions.

Rhetorical goals of instruction

Kendrick and Darling (1990) stated interactive instructor–learner(s) communication is crucial to the effective learning experience. They explained, "communication enables teachers and students to engage in instructional tasks, facilitates social activity, and helps individuals to coordinate actions" (p. 15). In turn, rhetorical goals entail instruction that leads to the achievement of learning outcomes and course objectives. Rhetorical goals focus on how instructors create instructional messages that learners will understand, retain, and recall (Mottet & Beebe, 2006). Humor, clarity, and relevance are essential elements for creating messages that stimulate trainer-selected meanings in the participants' minds. When you maintain adult learners' interest through humor and present material in a clear, relevant manner, you follow best practice and deliver an instructional design that is conducive to learning.

Humor

According to Smith (2011) adult learners face many challenges. After working long hours already, one such challenge is remaining attentive and engaged during training modules or learning sessions. Humor alerts learners' attention and interest, and positively stimulates their mood (Hellman, 2007). Booth-Butterfield and Booth-Butterfield (1991) defined humor as, "intentional verbal and nonverbal messages that elicit laughter, chuckling, and other forms of spontaneous behavior taken to meant pleasure, delight, and/or surprise in the targeted receiver" (p. 206). Humor in the classroom includes jokes, riddles, puns, humorous comments, and funny stories (Bryant, Comisky, & Zillmann, 1979). Overall, appropriate, relevant humor benefits instructors and learners (Banas, Dunbar, Rodriguez, & Liu, 2011). Booth-Butterfield and Wanzer (2010) asserted instructor humor builds and maintains student attention and enhances instructor–student(s) relationships. Research also indicates that when learners perceive instructors as appropriately funny, they also positively evaluate the instructors (Bryant, Comisky, Crane, & Zillmann, 1980), report greater affective learning (Wanzer & Frymier, 1999), and enhanced learning comprehension (Gorham & Christophel, 1990).

Keeping humor relevant is essential to effective training. Individuals are more likely to learn and retain course material when humor is relevant to course content and generates affect for the instructor and course (Morrison, 2008). Like instructors, trainers can use humor as an affinity-seeking strategy (Booth-Butterfield & Booth-Butterfield, 1991), a class management technique (Banas, Dunbar, Rodriguez, & Liu, 2011), and a method to maintain control over course material while also enhancing learning (Hellman, 2007). When the situation allows, learners will appreciate humorous trainers.

You have a variety of relevant humor strategies at your disposal including funny media examples, humorous stories to illustrate concepts, and fun role-playing activities (Wanzer, Frymier, Wojtaszczyk, & Smith, 2006). Based on the above literature, to establish relevant humor, rhetorical goals include:

- Use humor to emphasize or explain important material. Humor alerts learners' attention and may help them retain and recall information.
- Incorporate humor *after* covering material, and then review the material again when the laughter subsides (Banas et al., 2011).
- Vary use of humor and select humorous strategies that are most comfortable and appropriate for you and the occasion – if you are not very good at telling jokes, then do not tell them. Instead, show a funny media clip.
- Limit humor to ensure it does not become a distraction. To be perceived as appropriately humorous, humor should be used no more than once every 15 minutes (Banas et al., 2011).
- Avoid humor that is disparaging or in poor taste (Wanzer, Frymier, & Irwin, 2010). Do not use vulgar language, make fun of specific groups of people – especially your participants, or humor irrelevant to training material.

Relevance

According to Knowles (1984), adult learners need to know the immediate relevance of what they are learning. If information is not relevant, adult learners may question why they need to know it and, in turn, may not be motivated to learn it (Fall, 2001). It is important for trainers to make the content relevant by connecting it to adult learners' past experiences, present life, and goals for the immediate future. When adult learners believe content is relevant to their professional life, they become open to learning.

Your efforts to make content relevant is empowering for adult learners. Research has demonstrated that content relevance is associated with intrinsic motivation, affective learning, effective learning behaviors, and learner empowerment (Frymier & Houser, 1998; Frymier, & Shulman, 1995). To ensure content relevance, rhetorical goals include:

- Establish content relevance by asking learners about their interests, and then connect those interests to instruction. Reinforce content relevance and show how content also connects to the future needs of your learners (Keller, 1983).
- Use information you learn about adult learners' interests (e.g., travel, hobbies) to create examples and analogies to illustrate concepts (Chesebro & Wanzer, 2006).
- Be current with the popular culture of your participants and use examples of popular culture in the workshop or training session (Frey & Tatum, 2016).
- Consider how material relates to adult learners' experiences and explain how the training session builds on adult learners' current skills (Chesebro & Wanzer, 2006).
- Create a more open and interactive relationship between you and the adult learners. With this in mind, Shulman and Luechauer (1993) suggested involving learners in designing the course interactively. If learners are active in the creation of the course or training session, content relevance will increase when the content complements their experiences and goals (Keller, 1987).

- Integrate problem-solving components relevant to adult learners' respective occupations. This verifies the relevance of course content and "assigns value to their ability to use prior experiences to solve problems" (Tainsh, 2016, p. 34).

These strategies encourage adult learners to "buy in" to content covered during training sessions. Knowles (1984) said it is essential that adult learners understand the relevance of course instruction.

Clarity

Course material and training objectives fall within the realm of your communicative responsibilities. In this way, instructor clarity emerges as necessary instructional behavior (Goldman, Cranmer, Sollitto, Labelle, & Lancaster, 2017). Instructor clarity focuses on the explicitness of instructional messages, and is central to teaching effectiveness (Rosenshine & Furst, 1971). Perceptions of instructor clarity are influenced by both oral and written communication in the classroom (Sidelinger & McCroskey, 1997). Clear instructors emphasize important material, offer numerous examples, and effectively respond to student questions. In addition, clarity includes understandable assessment questions, explicit course syllabi, and detailed outlines of projects or course objectives.

Instructor clarity aligns well with the andragogical assumptions that adult learners are self-directed, intrinsically motivated, and have a high degree of readiness. Previous research has shown links between instructor clarity and cognitive learning, perceived instructor effectiveness, and academic success (Hines, Cruickshank, & Kennedy, 1985; Smith & Land, 1980). Instructor clarity allows learners to better succeed in the educational environment and increases their affect for the instructor and course (Sidelinger & McCroskey, 1997). Clear instructors empower students (Finn & Schrodt, 2012) and further encourage motivated individuals to better understand course content (Chesbro & Wanzer, 2006). Prior research linked instructor clarity with learner perceived achievement (Goods & Grouws, 1977), and perceived teaching effectiveness (Powell & Harville, 1990). When instructors are clear, learners can stay on track and more effectively take notes (Titsworth, 2004).

Through clarity, you can enhance perceptions of participants' competence, while also fostering independent learning. Following best practices of instructor clarity, you should cover material at the appropriate pace to the topic and learners, give learners time to think and reflect, stay on topic, and offer relevant examples. Following synthesized research findings, to enhance clarity, rhetorical goals include:

- When possible and appropriate, have material prepared in advanced for learners to receive prior to or at the start of a training session, including reading material, outlines, and/or handouts. Keep in mind that participants may read ahead; therefore, it may be best to parse out material as the session moves forward.
- Avoid vague language and speak at the appropriate pace. Making sure all material is covered is less important than making sure material covered is understood.
- Make notetaking easy. Offer an initial overview, and clearly transition from one topic to the next. Summarize material at the end of a session.
- Answer all questions, offer feedback, and ensure any assignment or project expectations are understood (Titsworth & Mazer, 2010).
- Assess comprehension of training material. Frequently solicit feedback from the adult learners to determine if material covered is clear and easily understood.

Can they paraphrase or explain in their own words the content covered? Can they generate examples that illustrate concepts? Do not wait until the end; frequent assessment allows trainers to modify presentation of material and make immediate adjustments when necessary.

Ensuring instruction is clear allows adult learners to further value and understand the application and relevance of content covered.

Relational goals of instruction

Perceptions of instructor effectiveness and student learning are based on teaching methods employed in the classroom (Papo, 1999). Educators who incorporate an interactive teaching style encourage learner involvement and enhance affective learning (Sidelinger & Booth-Butterfield, 2010). In general, learners are more comfortable and learn more in training sessions or workshops with confirming, nonverbally immediate trainers who respond to questions and use an interactive teaching style. Nonverbal immediacy, confirmation behaviors, and rapport are essential elements of planning and delivering effective training sessions. No matter their origins, this points to certain relational expectations that participants have of your training style.

Nonverbal immediacy

Nonverbal immediacy behaviors help to reduce distance by reducing real and/or perceived distance (Mehrabian, 1971). These behaviors include smiling, eye contact, relaxed body posture, and vocal variety (Witt, Wheeless, & Allen, 2004). Andersen (1979) conceptualized immediacy as communication behaviors that predict teaching effectiveness.

Perceptions of instructors' nonverbal immediacy positively influence perceptions of the instructor and classroom (Titsworth, 2004). For example, Witt et al., (2004) stated when instructors are nonverbally immediate, learners have greater affect for the instructor and course, are more likely to engage in behaviors learned, and more likely to enroll in another course of the same type. When individuals perceive their instructors as nonverbally immediate, they also perceive them to be more caring, competent, and trustworthy (Teven & Hanson, 2004). Rocca (2004) found that students are more likely to attend classes when they perceive their instructors as nonverbally immediate. Nonverbal immediacy offers the possibility of establishing positive connections between you and adult learners. Nonverbal immediacy behaviors make training sessions more engaging. Research and practical experience suggest to enhance perceptions of nonverbal immediacy, relational goals include:

- Maintain eye contact to indicate engagement and attentive listening and smile at appropriate times to show warmth and approachability.
- Walk around the room, when space and time allows, to decrease spatial distance. Decreasing spatial distance creates a more informal, relaxed learning environment.
- Appear natural, appropriate, and spontaneous with nonverbal immediacy behaviors. Too much smiling or too much eye contact might seem contrived and insincere.
- Body movement should follow transitions within a presentation. For example, a trainer can simply take a few steps forward or to the side to indicate that the session is moving on to a new topic. Taking a few steps backward will let everyone know the session is nearing its end.

These nonverbal immediacy behaviors generate a positive, prosocial atmosphere for both trainers and adult learners. When this happens, you stimulate adult learners' attention and engagement.

Confirmation

Cissna and Sieburg (1981) stated confirming communication sets the emotional tone between individuals by creating a positive communication climate. In general, confirming communication allows others to feel endorsed, recognized, and acknowledged. Endorsement is displayed through acceptance and validation of another's feelings and thoughts. Recognition shows awareness of others' existence. Acknowledgement requires attentiveness to what another says, feels, or thinks. Confirming communication nurtures feelings of significance and offer opportunities to connect with others. Confirming communication is essential in learning environments and a best practice all trainers should employ. In support, Marzano (1992) said that individuals do not learn well if they do not have positive attitudes and perceptions in the classroom.

Ellis (2004) offered a pragmatic application for enhancing the learning experience with specific instructor confirmation behaviors. Three general behavioral patterns reflect instructor confirmation strategies: (a) instructors' responses to students' questions and comments, (b) demonstrated interest in students and their learning, and (c) interactive style of teaching (Ellis, 2004). Instructor confirmation is a strong predictor of student cognitive and affective learning, while also promoting student motivation. Instructor confirmation is one interpersonal communication behavior that encompasses ego support and referential skills (Schrodt et al., 2006), both of which are deemed essential for instructors (Frymier & Houser, 2000). Thus, learners are more comfortable communicating in the classroom when they perceive instructors as confirming (Schrodt et al., 2006).

The process of confirmation contributes to relational development between communicators (Watzlawick, Beavin, & Jackson, 1967). Likewise, andragogy creates an equitable classroom that allows all voices to be heard (Knowles, 1984). Confirming instructors, who endorse, acknowledge, and recognize students, offer a fair and just (Young, Horan, & Frisby, 2013) learner-centered instructional approach in the classroom that leads to a variety of effective learning outcomes such as affective learning and motivation (Goldman, Bolkan, & Goodboy, 2013). Instructor confirmation behaviors are in line with the aims of andragogy, which fosters an affirming, learner-centered environment. Instructor confirmation behaviors encourage instructor–student(s) relational communication (Ellis, 2004) and positively affect students' emotional experiences in the classroom (Goldman & Goodboy, 2014).

Confirmation behaviors should be used immediately to set the tone of your training session and then continue throughout the session(s). Taken together, research suggests to appear confirming, relational goals include:

- Learn everyone's names and begin to use their names immediately to demonstrate interest in them. Of the many objectives trainers have on the first meeting, it is essential to also set a positive tone for adult learners.
- Plan an icebreaker activity that will afford the opportunity to learn more about each participant. Icebreakers heighten the effectiveness of training sessions when targeted to the training or facilitation of material covered and the needs of the adult learners.

Icebreakers encourage interpersonal communication and when trainers get to know adult learners on a personal level, it will show them that they are valued.

- Ask good questions to encourage an interactive training session. Whenever possible ask open-ended questions that allow adult learners to go in many different directions. Closed-ended, such as yes–no questions do not give anyone room to discuss ideas. Closed-ended questions can be useful if there is an open-ended follow-up question (e.g., asking "why" after a "do you agree" type question).
- Do not answer your own questions. If the adult learners do not respond immediately, wait. They might need to think about the question or they may not understand the question. Whenever someone does respond, confirm that you understand them (Schrodt & Finn, 2011).
- Allow time for adult learners to ask questions and offer comments. Do not wait until the end of a training session. Encourage all questions to be asked, do not ignore or avoid questions.
- As questions are asked offer responses. If a question cannot be answered right away, follow up with an answer at the next meeting or with an email. This will confirm to everyone that all questions are important (Young, Horan, & Frisby, 2013).

In the end, a combination of confirming behaviors nurture feelings of significance and offer opportunities to connect with others.

Rapport

Learners report that rapport is an essential relational characteristic of an effective instructor (McLaughlin & Erickson, 1981). Rapport represents overall positive feelings between people comprised of trust and social bondedness (Catt, Miller, & Schallenkamp, 2007). In a training session or workshop, a trainer who establishes rapport with adult learners facilitates engagement and enhances perceptions of the trainer's commitment to adult learners. Further, building rapport can encourage social interactions by reducing anxiety (Coupland, 2003; Jorgenson, 1992). Instructor rapport serves to create a comfortable learning environment (Frisby & Martin, 2010).

You can develop rapport and establish connections with adult learners from the start of a training session. Following best practices, demonstrate respect, appear approachable, encourage open communication, and have a positive attitude are strategies that help create a sense of rapport between instructors and learners (Granitz, Koernig, & Harich, 2009). Practical experience and existing literature suggest a number of ways to establish and maintain rapport, relational goals include:

- Learn and use everyone's name, to enhance perceptions of rapport,
- Make interactions enjoyable (Frisby & Martin, 2010). Trainers should spend some time getting to know adult learners and allow time for adult learners to get to know them. Consider arriving to the training session early and staying after the session has ended to answer questions or for informal conversations.
- Use a combination of verbal (e.g., self-disclosure) and nonverbal behaviors (e.g., smiling). Appropriate self-disclosure is relevant to material covered and often used to clarify information or to enhance perceptions of credibility. Self-disclose about professional experiences, education, and at times even leisure activities or about

family and friends – all of which humanize you and make you appear more approachable (Myers, Brann, & Comm 600, 2009).

• Display the combination of behaviors implemented over time to create perceptions of rapport. Keep in mind that rapport is emergent, it happens over time and is made up of a combination of communicative behaviors (Buskist & Saville, 2001).

Overall, effective instructor-student (or trainer-participant) interactions are often a precursor to successful learning experiences (Kuh, Kinzie, Schuh, & Whitt, 2005).

Connected community of adult learners

Blackley and Sheffield (2015) suggested adult learners require deep learning. In part, deep learning includes critical thinking and collaborative learning with peers. You need to offer adult learners opportunities for reflection, feedback, and communication with fellow peers. A connected classroom climate reflects "student-to-student perceptions of a supportive and cooperative communication environment in the classroom" (Dwyer et al., 2004, p. 267). Most instructors and adult learners desire a constructive and positive classroom climate. The training session can be viewed as a community setting. Teaching and learning not only occurs between the instructor and learners but also among peers (Hirschy & Wilson, 2002).

What is a connected classroom climate?

Student-to-student connectedness represents the relational interactions that take place among learners in the classroom. Adult learners can express themselves freely and openly in nonjudgmental ways that allow strong bonds to exist in the connected classroom. These friendly, socially connected interactions include peers praising one another, sharing personal stories or experiences, and engaging in general small talk (Dwyer et al, 2004). Not only do learners enjoy a connected classroom climate, instructors report liking their students more in connected classrooms (Sidelinger, Bolen, Frisby, & McMullen, 2012a). The concept of the connected classroom climate implies the intent to establish and maintain a positive context that promotes learning and positive communication.

Facilitating a connected classroom climate optimizes the training session or workshop experience in many ways. First, a connected classroom climate enhances learning outcomes. It is positively associated with learners' affective learning (Ifert-Johnson, 2009), cognitive learning (Prisbell, Dwyer, Carlson, Bingham, & Cruz, 2009), and self-regulated learning (Sidelinger & Booth-Butterfield, 2010). Peers who connect with another in class are also more comfortable asking questions in class (Sidelinger & Booth-Butterfield, 2010) and getting extra help from their instructor and peers outside of class (Sidelinger, Bolen, McMullen, & Nyeste, 2015).

Second, a connected classroom climate positively affects communication. In connected classes, everyone participates more (Frisby & Martin, 2010), text less (Ifert-Johnson, 2013), and engages in civil behaviors (Myers, Goldman, Atkinson, Ball, Carton, Tindage, et al., 2016). It also provides individuals enrolled in presentation-based courses with a comfortable climate to present speeches (Sidelinger, Myers, & McMullen, 2011).

Third, a connected classroom climate is associated with effective instructional communication behaviors. Instructor confirmation behaviors (Sidelinger & Booth-Butterfied,

2010), rapport (Frisby & Martin, 2010), nonverbal immediacy (Ifert-Johnson, 2009), and humor (Sidelinger, Frisby, McMullen, & Heisler, 2012b) enhance students' perceptions of the connected classroom climate. When a connected classroom climate exists, instructors are also perceived as more flexible and approachable (Sidelinger et al., 2012a).

You can set goals and provide adult learners with opportunities to connect with one another early on. Use interactive and experiential learning – group discussions, problem-solving assignments, and role-playing activities – to engage adult learners in learning and help them to connect with their peers during the first few hours or days of a training session. Learners who are uncomfortable participating in a larger workshop or training session may speak up in a small group (Sollitto, Johnson, & Myers, 2013). Peer rapport (Frisby & Martin 2010) and appropriate, relevant self-disclosures with one another (Johnson & LaBelle, 2015) positively affect learners' perceptions of a connected classroom climate.

Once adult learners become familiar with one another, encourage participation. Not only will they connect with one another in small groups but also with the larger group. Research has shown instructors are more likely to ask questions early on, but as time progresses instructors may spend less effort attempting to stimulate involvement if earlier attempts fail (Howard & Henney, 1998). However, as the time progresses, learners are more likely to respond to instructor questions once student-to-student connectedness is established (Sidelinger & Booth-Butterfield, 2010). Be mindful that individuals may not be ready to participate at the start of a training session.

Be available to meet adult learners outside of training sessions and suggest they do the same with one another. A connected classroom climate strengthens involvement and communication outside of the training session or workshop. Learners are more likely to seek out instructors and peers outside of class when connections are established in class (Sidelinger et al., 2015).

Following best practices, trainers can employ a range of prosocial instructional communication behaviors to strengthen perceptions of a connected classroom climate. Confirming behaviors such as demonstrating interest, dynamic teaching style, and responding to student questions and comments serve to create a connected classroom climate (Sidelinger & Booth-Butterfield, 2010). Likewise, research has demonstrated that when instructors engage in appropriate, relevant humor (e.g., jokes related to the course material, role playing/activities) and are nonverbally immediate (Sidelinger et al., 2012b) perceptions of student-to-student connectedness are enhanced. Ifert-Johnson (2009) and Johnson and LaBelle (2015) suggested learners might mirror instructor behaviors in the classroom – not only with the instructor but also with one another. Trainers can build upon these ideas and develop peer connectedness in workshops and training sessions.

Conclusion

In this chapter I described how instructional communication, guided by andragogy and RRGT, offers you the opportunity to follow best practice and decide how course or training sessions can be successfully delivered. Rhetorical goals consider the effective dissemination of content and ensure information is delivered in a clear, memorable manner. Relational goals serve to develop positive relationships and foster affect for the trainer and training session or workshop (Mottet et al., 2006). Previous instructional

Table 19.1 Balancing rhetorical and relational goals

RRGT Strategies:	Humor	Relevance	Clarity	Nonverbal Immediacy	Confirmation	Rapport	Connectedness
Emphasize and explain important material	✓		✓				
Use appropriate and comfortable humor strategies	✓						✓
Limit use and avoid anything in poor taste	✓						
Generate examples that relate to participants' interests		✓	✓				
Be current with popular culture	✓	✓✓	✓				✓
Involve participants in development of training design		✓					✓
Integrate problem-solving activities		✓	✓✓				
Provide material when appropriate			✓				
Avoid vague language and speak at the appropriate pace			✓✓				
Allow time for and answer all questions			✓✓		✓		✓
Assess comprehension					✓✓	✓✓	✓✓
Maintain eye contact and smile				✓✓✓	✓✓	✓✓✓✓✓	
Create a comfortable environment	✓			✓✓	✓✓✓	✓✓✓	✓
Appear natural and spontaneous							
Learn everyone's name						✓✓✓	✓✓
Plan icebreaker activities							
Ask good questions		✓	✓				✓
Make interactions enjoyable	✓	✓				✓✓✓	✓✓✓
Use appropriate self-disclosure						✓✓✓	
Talk with participants before and after sessions			✓			✓	✓✓✓

communication research emphasizes the importance of *both* rhetorical and relational goals (Fassett & Warren, 2010) that work together to optimize learning outcomes (Mottet et al., 2006).

This chapter offered you best practice for balancing rhetorical goals (i.e. humor, relevance, and clarity) with relational goals (nonverbal immediacy, confirmation, and rapport) while developing a connected community of learners. A combination of rhetorical goals and relational goals (see Table 19.1) fulfills the needs and expectations of adult learners. Such learner-centered approaches offer trainers an array of possibilities for creating dynamic communication processes (Huba & Freed, 2000), engendering democratic learning spaces (Dallimore, Hertenstein, & Platt, 2008), and developing new ways of engaging adult learners. Indeed, similar to instructors, recognizing the trainer–learner relationship as interpersonal (Frymier, & Houser, 2000), and, for some, theorizing their method of training as friendship (Rawlins, 2000), it is likely learner-centered training will enhance participants' interest and overall learning. Essentially, these approaches demand that adult learners frequently interact with you and peers through continued dialogue and meaningful communication. These best practices are essential to the successful development of effective communication training.

References

Andersen, J. F. (1979). Teacher immediacy as a predictor of teaching effectiveness. In D. Nimmo (ed.), *Communication yearbook 3* (pp. 543–559). New Brunswick, NJ: Transaction Books.

Banas, J. A., Dunbar, N., Rodriguez, D., & Liu, S. (2011). A review of humor in educational settings: Four decades of research. *Communication Education, 60*, 115–144. doi:10.1080/03634 523.2010.496867

Blackley, S., & Sheffield, R. (2015). Digital andragogy: A richer blend of initial teacher education in the 21st century. *Issues in Educational Research, 25*, 397–414.

Booth-Butterfield, M., & Booth-Butterfield, S. (1991). Individual differences in the communication of humorous messages. *Southern Journal of Communication, 56*, 32–40.

Booth-Butterfield, M., & Wanzer, M. (2010). Humorous communication as goal-oriented communication. In D. Fassett & J. Warren (eds.), *SAGE handbook of communication and instruction* (pp. 221–240). Thousand Oaks, CA: SAGE Publications.

Bryant, J., Comisky, P. W., Crane, J. S., & Zillmann, D. (1980). Relationship between college teachers' use of humor in the classroom and students' evaluations of their teachers. *Journal of Educational Psychology, 72*, 511–519. doi:10.1037/0022–0663.72.4.511

Bryant, J., Comisky, P. W., & Zillmann, D. (1979). Teachers' humor in the college classroom. *Communication Education, 28*, 110–118.

Buskist, W., & Saville, B. K. (2001, March). Creating positive emotional contexts for enhancing teaching and learning. *Association for Psychological Science Observer.* Retrieved from http://www. psychologicalscience.org

Catt, S., Miller, D., & Schallenkamp, K. (2007). You are the key: Communicate for learning effectiveness. *Education, 127*, 369–377.

Chesebro, J. L., & Wanzer, M. B. (2006). Instructional message variables. In T. P. Mottet, V. P. Richmond, & J. C. McCroskey (eds.), *Handbook of instructional communication* (pp. 89–116). Boston, MA: Pearson.

Chory, R. M., & McCroskey, J. C. (1999). The relationship between teacher management communication style and affective learning. *Communication Quarterly, 47*, 1–11.

Cissna, K. N. L., & Sieburg, E. (1981). Patterns of interactional confirmation and disconfirmation. In C. Wilder-Mott & J. H. Weakland (eds.), *Rigor and imagination: Essays from the legacy of Gregory Bateson* (pp. 253–282). New York, NY: Praeger.

Coupland, J. (2003). Small talk: Social functions. *Research on Language and Social Interaction, 36,* 1–6. doi:10.1207/S15327973RLSI3601_1

Dallimore, E. J., Hertenstein, J. H., & Platt, M. B. (2008). Using discussion pedagogy to enhance oral and written communication skills. *College Teaching, 56,* 163–172.

Darkenwald, G. G., & Merriam, S. B. (1982). *Adult education: Foundations of practice.* New York, NY: Harper & Row.

Davenport, J., & Davenport, J. A. (1985). A chronology and analysis of the andragogy debate. *Adult Educational Quarterly, 35,* 152–159.

Dwyer, K. K., Bingham, S. G., Carlson, R. E., Prisbell, M. Cruz, A. M., & Fus, D. A. (2004). Communication and connectedness in the classroom: Development of the connected classroom climate inventory. *Communication Research Reports, 21,* 264–272.

Ellis, K. (2004). The impact of perceived teacher confirmation on receiver apprehension, motivation, and learning. *Communication Education, 53,* 1–20.

Fall, L. (2001). Three-weekend course format and adult student satisfaction. *Journalism and Mass Communication Educator, 55,* 39–48. doi:10.1177/107769580105500404

Fassett, D. L., & Warren, J. T. (2010). *The SAGE handbook of communication and instruction.* Thousand Oaks, CA: Sage.

Finn, A. N., & Schrodt, P. (2012). Students' perceived understanding mediates the effects of teacher clarity and nonverbal immediacy on learner empowerment. *Communication Education, 61,* 111–130. doi:10.1080/03634523.2012.656669

Frey, T. K., & Tatum, N. T. (2016). Hoverboards and "hovermoms:" Helicopter parents and their influence on millennial students' rapport with instructors. *Communication Education, 65,* 359–361. doi:10.1080/03634523.2016.1177841

Frisby, B. N., & Martin, M. M. (2010). Instructor–student and student-to-student rapport in the classroom. *Communication Education, 59,* 146–164. doi:10.1080/03634520903564362

Frymier, A. B. (2007, November). Teachers' and students' goals in the teaching–learning process. Paper presented at the annual conference of the National Communication Association, Chicago, IL.

Frymier, A. B., & Houser, M. L. (1998). Does making content relevant make a difference in learning? *Communication Research Reports, 15,* 121–129.

Frymier, A. B., & Houser, M. L. (2000). The teacher–student relationship as an interpersonal relationship. *Communication Education, 49,* 207–219. doi:10.1080/03634520009379209

Frymier, A. B., & Shulman, G. M. (1995). "What's in it for me?": Increasing content relevance to enhance students' motivation. *Communication Education, 44,* 40–50.

Goldman, Z. W., Bolkan, S., & Goodboy, A. K. (2014). Revisiting the relationship between teacher confirmation and learning outcomes: Examining cultural differences in Turkish, Chinese, and American classrooms. *Journal of Intercultural Communication Research, 43,* 45–63. doi:10.1080/17475759.2013.870087

Goldman, Z. W., Cranmer, G. A., Sollitto, M., Labelle, S., & Lancaster, A. L. (2017). What do college students want? A prioritization of instructional behaviors and characteristics. *Communication Education, 66,* 280–298. doi:10.1080/03634523.2016.1265135

Goldman, Z. W., & Goodboy, A. K. (2014). Making students feel better: Examining the relationships between teacher confirmation and college students' emotional outcomes. *Communication Education, 63,* 259–277. doi:10.1080/03634523.2014.920091

Goods, T. L., & Grouws, D. A. (1977). Teaching effects: A process-product study in fourth-grade mathematics classrooms. *Journal of Teacher Education, 28,* 49–54.

Gorham, J., & Christophel, D. M. (1990). The relationship of teachers' use of humor in the classroom to immediacy and student learning. *Communication Education, 39,* 46–62.

Granitz, N. A., Koernig, S. K., & Harich, K. R. (2009). Now it's personal: Antecedents and outcomes of rapport between business faculty and their students. *Journal of Marketing Education, 31,* 52–65. doi:10.1177/0273475308326408

Hellman, S. V. (2007). Humor in the classroom: Stu's seven simple steps to success. *College Teaching, 55*, 37–39.

Hines, C. V., Cruickshank, D. R., & Kennedy, J. J. (1985). Teacher clarity and its relationship to student achievement and satisfaction. *American Educational Research, 22*, 87–99. doi:10.2307/ 162989

Hirschy, A. S., & Wilson, M. E. (2002). The sociology of the classroom and its influence on student learning. *Peabody Journal of Education, 77*, 85–100.

Howard, J. R., & Henney, A. L. (1998). Student participation and instructor gender in the mixed-age college classroom. *Journal of Higher Education, 69*, 384–405.

Huba, M. E., & Freed, J. E. (2000). Learner-centered assessment on college campuses: Shifting the focus from teaching to learning. Boston, MA: Allyn & Bacon.

Ifert-Johnson, D. (2009). Connected classroom climate: A validity study. *Communication Research Reports, 26*, 146–157. doi:10.1080/08824090902861622

Ifert-Johnson, D. (2013). Student in-class texting behavior: Associations with instructor clarity and classroom relationships. *Communication Research Reports, 30*, 57–62. doi:10.1080/088240 96.2012.723645

Johnson, Z. D., & LaBelle, S. (2015). Examining the role of self-disclosure and connectedness in the process of instructional dissent: A test of the instructional beliefs model. *Communication Education, 64*, 154–170. doi:10.1080/03634523.2014.978800

Jorgenson, J. (1992). Communication, rapport, and the interview: A social perspective. *Communication Theory, 2*, 148–156. doi:10.1111/j.14682885.1992.tb00034.x

Keller, J. M. (1983). Motivational design of instruction. In C. M. Reogeluth (ed.), *Instructional design theories: An overview of their current status* (pp. 383–434). Hillsdale, NJ: Lawrence Erlbaum.

Keller, J. M. (1987). Strategies for stimulating the motivation to learn. *Performance and Instruction, 26*, 1–7.

Kendrick, W. L., & Darling, A. L. (1990). Problems of understanding in classrooms: Students' use of clarifying tactics. *Communication Education, 39*, 15–29. doi:10.1080/03634529009378784

Knowles, M. S. (1984). Andragogy in action: Applying modern principles of adult learning. San Francisco, CA: Jossey-Bass.

Knowles, M. S, Holton, E. F., & Swanson, R. A. (2015). *The adult learner* (8th ed.). New York, NY. Routledge.

Kuh, G. D., Kinzie, J., Schuh, J. H., & Whitt, E. J. (2005). *Student success in college: Creating conditions that matter.* San Francisco, CA: Jossey-Bass.

Marzano, R. (1992). *A different kind of classroom: Teaching with dimensions of learning.* Alexandria, VA: Association for Supervision and Curriculum Development.

McCroskey, J. C., Richmond, V. P., & Bennett, V. E. (2006). The relationships of student end-of-class motivation with teacher communication behaviors and instructional outcomes. *Communication Education, 55*, 403–414. doi:10.1080/03634520600702562

McLaughlin, M. L., & Erickson, K. V. (1981). A multidimensional scaling analysis of the "ideal interpersonal communication instructor." *Communication Education, 30*, 393–398. doi:10. 1080/03634528109378494

Mehrabian, A. (1971). *Silent messages.* Belmont, CA: Wadsworth.

Merrill, M. D., Drake, L., Lacy, M. J., Pratt, J., & the ID$_2$ Research Group (1996). Reclaiming instructional design. *Educational Technology, 36*, 5–7.

Morrison, M. K. (2008). Using humor to maximize learning: The links between positive emotions and education. Lanham, MD: Rowman & Littlefield.

Mottet, T. P., & Beebe, S. A. (2006). Foundations of instructional communication. In T. P. Mottet, V. P. Richmond, & J. C. McCroskey (eds.), *Handbook of instructional communication: Rhetorical and relational perspectives* (pp. 3–32). Boston, MA: Allyn & Bacon.

Mottet, T. P., Frymier, A. B., & Beebe, S. A. (2006). Theorizing about instructional communication. In T. P. Mottet, V. P. Richmond, & J. C. McCroskey (eds.), *Handbook of instructional communication: Rhetorical and relational perspectives* (pp. 255–282). Boston, MA: Allyn & Bacon.

Myers, S. A. (2010). Instructional communication: The emergence of a field. In D. L. Fassett & J. T. Warren (eds.), *The SAGE handbook of communication and instruction* (pp. 149–159). Thousand Oaks, CA: Sage.

Myers, S. A., Brann, M., & Comm 600 (2009). College students' perceptions of how instructors establish and enhance credibility through self-disclosure. *Qualitative Research Reports, 10,* 9–16. doi:10.1080/17459430902751808

Myers, S. A., Goldman, Z. W., Atkinson, J., Ball, H., Carton, T. S., Tindage, M. F., & Anderson, A. O. (2016). Student civility in the collage classroom: Exploring student use and effects of classroom citizenship behavior. *Communication Education, 65,* 64–82. doi:10.1080/03634523. 2015.1061197

Myers, S. A., Goodboy, A. K., & Members of Comm 600 (2014). College student learning, motivation, and satisfaction as a function of effective instructor communication behaviors. *Southern Communication Journal, 79,* 14–26. doi:10.1080/1041794X.2013.815266

Nussbaum, J. (1992). Effective teacher behaviors. *Communication Education, 41,* 167–180. doi:10. 1080/03634529209378878

Papo, W. D. (1999). Large class teaching: Is it a problem to students? *College Student Journal, 33,* 354–358.

Prisbell, M., Dwyer, K. K., Carlson, R. E., Bingham, S. G., & Cruz, A. M. (2009). Connected classroom climate in the basic course: Associations with learning. *Basic Communication Course Annual, 21,* 145–165.

Powell, R. G., & Harville, B. (1990). The effects of teacher immediacy and clarity on instructional outcomes: An intercultural assessment. *Communication Education, 39,* 368–379.

Rachal, J. R. (2002). Andragogy's detectives: A critique of the present and a proposal for the future. *Adult Education Quarterly, 52,* 210–227. doi:10.1177/0741713602052003004

Rawlins, W. K. (2000). Teaching as a mode of friendship. *Communication Theory, 10,* 5–26. doi:10.1111/j.1468–2885.2000.tb00176.x

Rocca, K. A. (2004). College student attendance: Impact of instructor immediacy and verbal aggression. *Communication Education, 53,* 185–195.

Rosenshine, B., & Furst, N. (1971). Research in teacher performance criteria. In B. Smith (ed.), *Research in teacher education: A symposium.* Englewood Cliffs, NJ: Prentice Hall.

Schrodt, P., & Finn, A. N. (2011). Students' perceived understanding: An alternative measure and its associations with perceived teacher confirmation, verbal aggressiveness, and credibility. *Communication Education, 60,* 231–254. doi:10.1080/03634523.2010.535007

Schrodt, P., Turman, P., & Soliz, J. (2006). Perceived understanding as a mediator of perceived teacher confirmation and students' rating of instruction. *Communication Education, 55,* 370–388. doi:10.1080/03634520600879196

Shulman, G., & Luechauer, D. (1993). The empowering educator: A CQI approach to classroom leadership. In D. Hubbard (ed.), *Continuous quality improvement: Making the transition to education* (pp. 424–453). Maryville, MO: Prescott Publishing.

Sidelinger, R. J., Bolen, D. M., Frisby, B. N., & McMullen, A. L. (2012a). Instructor compliance to student requests: An examination of student-to-student connectedness as power in the classroom. *Communication Education, 60,* 290–308. doi:10.1080/03634523.2012.666557

Sidelinger, R. J., Bolen, D. M., McMullen, A. L., & Nyeste, M. C. (2015). Academic and social integration in the basic communication course: Predictors of students' out-of-class communication and academic learning. *Communication Studies, 66,* 63–84.

Sidelinger, R. J., & Booth-Butterfield, M. (2010). Co-constructing student involvement: An examination of teacher confirmation and student-to-student connectedness in the college classroom. *Communication Education, 59,* 165–184. doi:10.1080/03634520903390867

Sidelinger, R. J., Frisby, B. N., McMullen, A. L., & Heisler, J. (2012b). Developing student-to-student connectedness: An examination of instructors' humor, nonverbal immediacy, and self-disclosure in public speaking courses. *Basic Communication Course Annual, 24,* 81–121.

Sidelinger, R. J., & McCroskey, J. C. (1997). Communication correlates of teacher clarity in the college classroom. *Communication Research Reports, 14*, 1–10.

Sidelinger, R. J., Myers, S. A., & McMullen, A. L. (2011). Students' communication predispositions: An examination of classroom connectedness in public speaking courses. *Basic Communication Course Annual, 23*, 248–278.

Smith, L. R., & Land, M. L. (1980). Student perceptions of teacher clarity. *Journal of Educational Psychology, 72*, 670–675.

Smith, R. L. (2011). Front-line facilitating: Negotiating adventurous learning within workplace programs. *Adult Learning, 22*, 18–22. doi:10.1177/104515951102200104

Sollitto, M., Johnson, Z. D., & Myers, S. A. (2013). Students' perceptions of college classroom connectedness, assimilation, and peer relationships. *Communication Education, 62*, 318–331. doi:10.1080/03634523.2013.788726

Tainsh, R. (2016). Thoughtfully designed online courses as effective adult learning tools. *Journal of Adult Education, 45*, 32–37.

Teven, J. J., & Hanson, T. L. (2004). The impact of teacher immediacy and perceived caring on teacher competence and trustworthiness. *Communication Quarterly, 52*, 39–53.

Titsworth, B. S. (2004). Students' notetaking: The effects of teacher immediacy and clarity. *Communication Education, 53*, 305–320.

Titsworth, B. S., & Mazer, J. P. (2010). Clarity in teaching: Conundrums, consequences, and opportunities. In D. L. Fassett & J. T. Warren (eds.), *The SAGE handbook of communication and instruction* (pp. 241–261). Thousand Oaks, CA: Sage.

Wanzer, M. B., & Frymier, A. B. (1999). The relationship between student perceptions of instructor humor and students' reports of learning. *Communication Education, 48*, 48–61.

Wanzer, M. B., Frymier, A. B., & Irwin, J. (2010). An explanation of the relationship between instructor humor and student learning: Instructional humor processing theory. *Communication Education, 59*, 1–18. doi:10.1080/03634520903367238

Wanzer, M. B., Frymier, A. B., Wojtaszczyk, A. M., & Smith, T. (2006). Appropriate and inappropriate uses of humor by teachers. *Communication Education, 55*, 178–196.

Watzlawick, P., Beavin, J., & Jackson, D. D. (1967). Pragmatics of human communication: A study of interactional patterns, pathologies, and paradoxes. New York, NY: Norton.

Witt, P. L., Wheeless, L. R., & Allen, M. (2004). A meta-analytical review of the relationship between teacher immediacy and student learning. *Communication Monographs, 71*, 184–207.

Young, L. E., Horan, S. M., & Frisby, B. N. (2013). Fair and square? An examination of classroom justice and relational teaching messages. *Communication Education, 62*, 333–351. doi:10.1080/03634523.2013.800216

Chapter 20

Training trainers growth mindset messaging

The role of Implicit Person Theory on training

Elissa A. Adame

Abstract

This chapter applies Implicit Person Theory (IPT) to the context of organizational training. IPT argues that individuals tend to ascribe to either growth or fixed mindset. Individuals with a fixed mindset believe abilities are fixed and constant; individuals with a growth mindset believe abilities are malleable and subject to development. This chapter demonstrates the central role that trainers have in shaping these mindsets. Four messaging methods to influence the trainees' receptiveness to the training are provided for consideration.

In my first job as a corporate trainer, I worked for an organization that hired an external training firm to design all the training programs. As a trainer in this organization, my primary role was to deliver the content that was developed by the external training firm. While the content was accurate, complete, and well structured, my fellow trainers and I became acutely aware that the instructional design of these training programs was not promoting the transfer of training to the job. Indeed, my colleagues and I were not alone in our concern for corporate training's effectiveness in making change in organizations. Despite the popularity of training research and implementation, corporate training tends to lack a track record of success in general (Kalev, Kelly, & Dobbin, 2006). This lack of success includes lackluster effects of training on financial performance (Tharenou, Saks, & Moore, 2007) and long-term soft skill acquisitions (Kalev et al., 2006).

As my colleagues and I spent more time implementing the training programs, we learned that we could improve the effectiveness of the training programs in the way we communicated with trainees. Because training is inherently a communication activity (Beebe, Mottet, & Roach, 2013), it makes sense that an understanding of the effectiveness of training should be rooted in an exploration of the quality of the communication processes that constitute the substance of organizational training itself. The Training and Development Division of the National Communication Association addresses the role that communication has on improving the quality of training in their list of 7 Best Practices. In the following chapter, I focus on Best Practice 6 – Demonstrate Effective and Appropriate Instructional Design. This best practice plays a pivotal role in improving the track record of success of training programs in general. As a trainer, it is likely that your work is assessed, in part, by the marked change in your trainees after they engage in your training class. Effective and appropriate instructional design (that is, Best Practice 6) will help improve the quality of your work by giving you tools to improve trainees' learning in the training environment and, subsequently, increasing the likelihood that trainees will implement the training as they return to their job. In addressing Best Practice 6, I provide you, the corporate trainer, with actionable and tested messaging methods to improve the effectiveness and appropriateness of instructional design. Specifically, I discuss how messages about a trainee's identity as a learner influence the training environment.

To provide more context about how a trainee's identity might influence the effectiveness and appropriateness of the training, imagine the following scenario: An employee at a call center has been identified as needing extra training in the area of improving soft skills. The training agenda includes topics such as establishing good rapport, empathizing, and building trust with customers. When the employee receives the directive to take the training class, she perceives the training mandate to be a threat to her public image. In an effort to protect her public image, she tells her trainer, "I'm just not a touchy-feely person." Notice this socially-acceptable excuse allows the employee to restore her public image by pointing to her so-called inherent abilities. By focusing on her "natural inability" to learn soft skills, the employee avoids taking responsibility for lacking the skills to communicate effectively in her job and, therefore, removes responsibility from needing to learn the soft skills. In other words, the employee's expectations about her own identity as "not a touchy-feely person" influence her likelihood to expend effort during the training session. This example illustrates that trainees' communication of identity influences learning in the training environment. Can you think of examples from your own experiences when your trainees' messages about their own identity stunted their learning in your training environment? How did you respond to your trainee's message?

Certainly, many trainers realize the threat to identity that training programs may cause trainees, and, in response, trainers may communicate in ways to restore the public images of the trainees. Envision that the trainer in the previous example realizes that the trainee may perceive the training as a threat to her public image. In response to this realization, the trainer may then start the training with comments to help reestablish the trainee's public image such as, "I know this information is not new to you" and "I'm sure you already know a lot of the information we'll be talking about." In this attempt to restore the employee's public image, the trainer's messages devalue the purpose of the training. This familiar predicament begs the question, How can trainers realize and address trainees' public images, while also motivating trainees to learn and grow in any training environment?

In short, the answer to the previous question is simple: As trainers, we can uphold trainees' public images and also motivate trainees to grow by implementing careful messages about our trainees' expectations of effort and ability. This focus on training communication offers a chance for all trainers to address Best Practice 6 by implementing effective and appropriate instructional design in any training program. The following chapter applies decades of research on Implicit Person Theory (IPT; see Dweck, 2006) to the context of training in order to offer a model for instructional design that is tested, workable, and contextually appropriate. The chapter begins with a brief description of IPT. The theoretical frame of IPT is followed by specific and actionable recommendations by which you can modify your current training programs. These recommendations offer you messaging methods for designing training programs that encourage your trainees to learn and grow, thus improving the likelihood of training transfer. These messaging methods include listening to trainees' comments about their own abilities, building a response repertoire, shifting trainees' assumptions about their own and others' ability, and providing growth mindset-oriented feedback.

Rationale

Implicit Person Theory

Much of the work regarding learners' assumptions and expectations about their own identity and learning is established in Dweck and colleagues' work on Implicit Person Theory (IPT; see Dweck, 2006). IPT theorizes that individuals fit into one of two groups regarding their assumptions about their own and others' ability: entity theorists (also known as learners with a fixed mindset) and incremental theorists (also referred to as learners with a growth mindset). Learners with a fixed mindset assume their own and others' abilities are permanent, inflexible, and constant, whereas learners with a growth mindset think of abilities as changeable, flexible, and subject to development. Research on IPT demonstrates that learners' assumptions about their own and others' abilities predict success in academics (Blackwell, Trzesniewski, & Dweck, 2007) and the workplace (Heslin & VandeWalle, 2011). More recent research indicates that learners' assumptions about abilities are shaped by their own and others' messages (Yeager et al., 2014). These research findings reveal the sweeping number of benefits enjoyed by individuals with growth mindsets in comparison with people with fixed mindsets (Dweck, 2006).

Fixed mindsets

Learners who hold a fixed mindset believe ability is a product of their natural born talents and traits. Because fixed mindset learners believe success should come naturally, they also view hard work as an indication of failure. When met with a setback, learners with a fixed mindset are likely to experience a decrease in motivation, performance, achievement, and engagement. Setbacks also cause learners with a fixed mindset to feel helpless and to make face-saving excuses for their poor performance.

Growth mindsets

Learners who have a growth mindset believe ability is the product of hard work and effort. Instead of viewing effort as a sign of weakness, learners with a growth mindset believe effort and ability are related, and more effort equals higher ability and performance. Growth mindset learners are less focused on looking smart and performing well, and more interested in learning. As such, learners with a growth mindset react to setbacks with increased effort, engagement, motivation, and performance. These learners also meet setbacks with the generation of new problem-solving strategies to improve performance in the future.

Mindset reflection

As you compare and contrast fixed and growth mindset learners, consider your own mindset. Think of contexts where you identify as a fixed mindset learner. For example, perhaps you identify as "not a computer person" or "naturally good at customer service." These messages about our own identity illustrate a fixed mindset in these contexts. You may also identify as a growth mindset learner in other contexts. For instance, you might identify as "good at math, but only because I work really hard." Dweck (2006) states that mindset is contextual. As trainers, it is important to reflect on our own mindset, and consider how context might change that mindset. By reflecting on your own mindsets, you will be better equipped to identify and shift the mindsets of your trainees.

Shifting learners' mindsets

Due to the vast number of benefits afforded to learners who hold a growth mindset in comparison with learners with a fixed mindset, researchers have explored how, if at all, mindsets can be shifted. Fortunately, research indicates that mindsets are malleable. Researchers have implemented communication strategies such as task framing (Wood & Bandura, 1989), self-persuasion (Pratkanis & Aronson, 2001), and feedback (Cimpian, Aree, Markman, & Dweck, 2007) to shift learners' mindsets from fixed to growth. These strategies are communicative in that they draw on messaging to intervene and shape learners' mindsets as a means of framing subsequent messages.

Taken together, the research on mindset provides a theoretical framework for creating more receptive and resilient learners in the training environment through strategic messaging. For example, instead of confirming a trainees' fixed mindset of "just not a touchy-feely person" with a comment that devalues training like, "I know this information is not new to you," the trainer might construct a more strategic message that points to the trainee's ability to grow and change by working through the training. In the following section, the research summarized here is applied to a set of messaging methods in order to provide you with a model for designing effective and appropriate training programs.

Messaging methods

The messaging methods presented here are designed to provide you, the corporate trainer, with communicative tools to apply to any training environment. While it is possible and worth consideration to create and implement a training program designed specifically to shift trainees' mindsets, the purpose of these messaging methods is to supplement and shape the design of existing training programs by identifying your trainees' mindsets and engaging in messages to shift those mindsets toward growth. Table 20.1 offers an overview of each messaging method and the corresponding messages that communicate fixed versus growth mindsets.

Messaging Method 1: Listen to trainees' messages

Trainees' messages about their own and others' abilities reveal their mindsets. Consider the messages you say about your own mindset: What do your messages about your own abilities say about the expectations you have for effort? Do your words ignore effort in favor of ability? That is, do you find yourself saying, "I'm naturally a great presenter"? See how that message devalues the effort you put into your presentations and favors a fixed ability? On the other hand, do your messages celebrate effort as an expectation for success? That is, do you hear yourself saying, "I worked hard on that presentation for several weeks, and I am proud of how well I did"? These messages provide others with insight about your assumptions about your own and others' abilities. Just as you hear mindset in your own words, you can listen for mindset messages in the words of your trainees as well.

Qualitative data from Blackwell, Trzesniewski, and Dweck's (2007) study on tracking students' mindsets and achievement over time demonstrates that learners communicate their mindsets in distinct ways. When asked to talk about goals for school,

Table 20.1 Examples of fixed and growth mindset messages for each messaging method

Messaging Method	Messaging Goals	Fixed Mindset Messages	Growth Mindset Messages
Messaging Method 1: Listen to Trainees' Messages	Listen for Messages about Effort	"I did well on that assessment without even trying." "I passed that training with my eyes closed."	"That activity was difficult and fun." "Let's try something harder next time."
	Listen for Responses to Feedback	"I'm never going to be able to do this." "I made that mistake because I'm tired." "The reason I didn't get that correct is because I'm not at my best today."	"I'll keep trying until I can do this." "I'm sure I'll learn from all my mistakes." "That was difficult, and I'll keep working until I get it right."
	Listen for Messages about Identity	"I'm not good with computers." "I'm a natural-born leader." "I'm not naturally good at public speaking."	"I'll get better with computers with more practice." "I work hard at being a strong leader." "I struggle with public speaking, and I look forward to the challenge."
Messaging Method 2: Build a Response Repertoire	Respond to Trainees' Messages	"It's okay if you're not good with technology. This will be easy." "You must be a natural. You completed the task so easily!" "Great job! You didn't make a single mistake."	"You might not be good with technology yet, but by the end of the training and with hard work, you'll be on your way." "Let's do something hard that you can learn from, not something easy and boring." "Did you make any interesting and fun mistakes?"
Messaging Method 3: Shift Trainees' Mindsets	Frame the Task	"The purpose of this activity is to demonstrate excellence." "Try not to make any mistakes."	"The purpose of this activity is to practice in order to get better over time." "If you're struggling with this activity, you're doing something right."
	Facilitate Self-Persuasion	"What is an area in which you were born with natural talent and do not have to work to be better." "Think of a person you identify as a strong leader. Name three natural talents they have that make them a great leader."	"What is an area in which you once had low ability, but improved over time by struggling and working hard." "Think of a person you identify as a strong leader. Name three ways they work hard to be a great leader."
Messaging Method 4: Provide Growth-Mindset Feedback	Praise Effort Instead of Ability	"You're a natural." "I'm impressed by your smarts." "You have so much talent for this type of work."	"Your hard work is paying off." "I'm impressed with how hard you're working." "You took a big challenge, and I admire that."
	Explain the Purpose of Feedback	"I'm giving you these comments so you have feedback on your performance." "Feedback is part of the training process."	"I'm giving you these comments because I have high expectations of you and I know you can reach them." "The reason I give you feedback is because I expect a lot of you, and I know you can reach these expectations."

fixed mindset students commented, "The main thing I want when I do my school work is to show how good I am at it," while growth mindset students responded, "It's much more important for me to learn things in my classes than it is to get the best grades." Similarly, when students were asked how they would respond to a disappointing score, fixed mindset students said, "I would spend less time on this assignment from now on" and "I would try not to take this subject ever again." Conversely, students with a growth mindset replied, "I would work harder in this class from now on" and "I would spend more time studying for the tests." These differences in messages illustrate how fixed and growth mindset beliefs manifest in talk about learning.

In application to the training environment, the way trainees speak about learning reveals their mindset. Think back to how your own mindset manifests in your messages. Do you talk about your abilities as fixed and unchanging, or do your messages reflect a belief that your abilities are a product of your effort? Listen for these same patterns in talk from your trainees. First, listen to the way trainees' talk about effort. Remember, learners who hold a fixed mindset believe the relationship between effort and success is inverse, such that more effort equals less success. When the trainees speak, listen for fixed mindset messages that devalue effort and suggest success should come easily. In comparison with trainees who hold a fixed mindset and devalue effort, trainees with a growth mindset value challenge and work. The contrast between the two types of messages discloses trainees' assumptions about the relationship between ability and effort.

Second, listen to the trainees' responses to feedback. Learners with a fixed mindset view negative or corrective feedback as threatening, and may also meet corrective feedback with face-saving excuses (Hong, Chiu, Dweck, Lin, & Wan, 1999). When presenting negative or corrective feedback to trainees, listen for general messages of helplessness and for face-saving excuses. In contrast to students who hold a fixed mindset and are threatened by negative and corrective feedback, students with a growth mindset are likely to meet corrective feedback with excitement and more effort (Hong et al., 1999). These responses to feedback reveal the learner's mindset.

Third, listen to the trainees' messages about identity in relation to assumptions about learning. The example offered in the opening paragraphs demonstrates how a trainee might communicate mindset in a simple statement. As a reminder, the trainee responded to a mandate to complete a soft skills training with the message, "I'm just not a touchy-feely person." The trainee's message about her own identity demonstrates her fixed mindset in relation to practicing and developing her soft skills. Such comments in response to training mandates point to trainees' beliefs that ability is fixed.

Trainees' messages about effort, feedback, and identity reveal assumptions about learning and allow the trainer to understand the assumptions that may influence the training process. Just as developing a growth mindset takes practice, so too does recognizing these messages. Once trainers identify these messages, it takes more practice to develop strategic messages to respond in a way that promotes a growth mindset.

Messaging Method 2: Build a response repertoire

Developing recognition for fixed mindset messages also requires building a response repertoire that addresses your trainee's fixed mindset and upholds the value of the training program. Consider how you might respond to a trainee's fixed mindset message in the opening example. The trainer responded to the trainee's message of "I'm just not a touchy-feely person" with "I know this information is not new to you" and "I'm sure you already know a lot of the information we'll be talking about." Although the trainer's response may help the trainee feel better, the messages reiterate fixed mindset beliefs by setting expectations that the training will not be challenging and will not require the trainee to learn new information. In trying to make the trainee feel more comfortable, the trainer's messages do not set expectations for growth, change, and development. How would you respond in a way that addresses the trainee's fixed mindset and also motivates the trainee to continue learning? Such exchanges can happen quickly, which require you to be equipped with a repertoire of responses to address these fixed mindset messages.

Dweck and colleagues (2006) offer several suggestions for creating messages that orient learners toward a growth mindset. First, consider the power of "yet." When a trainee explains his identity as a person who is "not good with computers," consider responding with, "you're just not good with computers … yet." The inclusion of "yet" at the end of the identity statement emphasizes that the trainee can become a person who is good with the computers. "Yet" accentuates an identity that can change, grow, and develop over time. By orienting trainees to a growth mindset with the power of "yet," you also communicate your own expectations for the trainee's effort during the training program. Such statements allow you, the trainer, to respond in kind to the trainee without reinforcing a harmful fixed mindset that is likely to devalue the purpose of the training.

A second way to build a response repertoire is to draft a list of statements directed to trainees that encourage effort, struggle, challenge, and devalues low-effort success. Drafting these responses in advance aids in your preparedness when met with a trainee's fixed mindset messages. By building a response repertoire that focuses on growth mindset values, you become more equipped to address the trainee's fixed mindset assumptions.

Messaging Method 3: Shift trainees' mindsets

Once you identify a trainee's fixed mindset and respond with a quick growth mindset message, your trainee will also benefit from more support and direction in shifting their mindset toward growth. As mentioned, mindsets are malleable, and research demonstrates that mindsets can shift with task-framing and self-persuasion. First, consider the role of task-framing on shaping learners' mindsets. Wood and Bandura (1989) manipulated participants' mindsets in the instructions of their managerial simulation task. Participants who were induced with a fixed mindset were told that skills reflect the basic cognitive capabilities that people possess. In order to induce growth mindsets, participants were told that skills are developed through practice. The simple message strategy of framing the task shifted participants' mindsets.

In application to the training context, the way you frame a task is likely to influence trainees' assumptions about their learning. Imagine a training program for new technology implemented in the organization. Instead of framing activities in the program as a way to measure a person's fixed traits and natural ability to handle computers, consider framing activities as practice to develop technology skills over time. Consider asking trainees to challenge themselves with the tasks, to be willing to make mistakes, and to continue learning from those mistakes as they engage in the activity. These messages frame the training environment as a safe place to make mistakes in order to grow and develop, thus creating trainees with growth mindsets.

Second, scholars also argue for the importance and effectiveness of self-persuasion as it applies to inducing growth mindsets. Pratkanis and Aronson (2001) explain how change in the beliefs and attitudes induced by direct persuasion from others are often small and temporary, while self-persuasion gives participants a chance to reflect on their own experiences. In order to get participants to persuade themselves into the thought-processes of a growth mindset, participants have been asked to engage in reflection questions (e.g., "What is an area in which you once had low ability, but now perform well?"); counterattitudinal idea generation (e.g., "As a manager, what are at least three reasons why it is important to realize that people can develop their abilities"); counterattitudinal advocacy (e.g., participants act like a mentor by writing an email offering advice); and cognitive dissonance induction (e.g., participants identify when they had observed another person learn to do something that they had been convinced that this person could never do). These self-persuasion techniques provide learners with an opportunity to convince themselves of the value of effort, work, and embracing challenges.

The training context offers an opportunity for you to shift trainees' mindsets with self-persuasion activities. You may choose to have trainees write their responses, share the story in a small group, or turn to their neighbor and share. Consider a training program to develop leadership skills. You may consider beginning the class with a reflection question designed to shift trainees' mindsets toward the work and effort necessary for a person to be identified as a great leader. Here, the focus of the reflection is how another person's identity is the result of hard work and effort.

Self-persuasion activities also work when the trainee is the subject of the reflection. As a trainer, one of my favorite questions to ask my trainees is, "Think of a time when you believed you did not have a natural talent to succeed at an activity. How did that belief influence your effort in that activity?" This reflection question asks trainees to consider how a belief in natural talent creates a mindset where failure is met with low effort and often results in giving up in the face of setbacks. These experiences from trainees become more salient when juxtaposed by the next question, "Next, think of an area in your life in which you have worked hard to succeed. How many hours of work have you spent on improving your success in this area?" This reflection question is designed to highlight that successes are the product of hard work and hours of concerted practice. Taken together, the questions offer trainees an opportunity to see that success does not come naturally but rather is the product of work, challenges, failures, and more work.

You may also consider self-persuasion activities at the completion of a training program. For example, at the end of a training class, consider asking trainees to offer advice for the next class. An example of a prompt is, "Write a short note to a person in the next training class. Identify a specific area of the training that challenged you. You may choose to write about mistakes you made, and how you overcame those mistakes. Offer the person three suggestions to be successful in this training program." In this example, trainees have the chance to reflect on the challenges they faced, the mistakes they made, and the ways they overcame these mistakes, therefore reminding the students of the value of a growth mindset. Collectively, these methods of shifting trainees' mindsets toward growth offer trainers ways to fold values of mindset in existing training programs.

Messaging Method 4: Provide growth-mindset feedback

Since fixed mindset learners are less resilient after setbacks than growth mindset learners, subtleties in the type of feedback learners receive have significant implications for receptiveness and actions (Mueller & Dweck, 1998). In order to provide growth mindset feedback, praise trainees for the process instead of ability, focus on the purpose of feedback, and create a training program that offers frequent and low-cost feedback opportunities.

First, researchers argue for the benefits of feedback that praise the process instead of ability and talent. For example, Cimpian et al. (2007) studied how subtle linguistic differences in feedback can influence learners' ideas about their abilities and their achievement motivation. In their design, participants were praised for either ability (e.g., "Wow. You must be smart!") or effort (e.g., "Wow. You must have worked hard!") after completing a task. The researchers found that students praised for effort were less affected by subsequent negative feedback and were more likely to continue the task than students praised for ability.

Such research has implications for trainers to communicate praise effectively. Avoid messages that praise trainees for their ability, talent, or traits. Instead, try praising trainees for the process and effort. Praising trainees for effort and process reinforces the expectation that success is the product of hard work and not a function of natural ability (Mueller & Dweck, 1998).

Second, Yeager and colleagues (2014) demonstrate the value of informing students about the purpose of the feedback. In the research study, students were asked to write essays, teachers collected and graded the essays as they typically would, then researchers attached one of two sticky notes to each student's paper. Half of the students received a bland message on the sticky note that read, "I'm giving you these comments so that you'll have feedback on your paper." The other half of students received a growth mindset message on their paper that said, "I'm giving you these comments because I have very high expectations and I know you can reach them." Finally, students were given a chance to revise their essay after receiving the feedback. The students who received the growth mindset message were significantly more likely to revise their paper than students who received the bland message. These findings demonstrate the value of focusing on the purpose of feedback as a commitment to students' growth.

As applied to the training environment, your explanations for the purpose of feedback might influence trainees to work harder, become more resilient to corrective feedback, and seek more opportunities for feedback in the future. Similar to the growth mindset sticky note in the research study, consider prefacing feedback with an explanation of high expectations and a general belief in the trainees' growth over time. This framing of feedback offers you an opportunity to uphold high expectations in the training environment without compromising trainee motivation.

Finally, because so much of messaging about ability occurs in the form of feedback, training programs should be designed with multiple chances for trainees to receive feedback. In this design, feedback should occur early and often in order to create opportunities for trainees to fail in a low-stakes environment. More chances to fail safely creates more opportunities for you to celebrate failures, capitalize on mistakes, and encourage persistence in trainees. As trainees continue to advance through the training, use previous feedback sessions as a way to inspire effort and praise change over time. This process mirrors the values of a growth mindset by demonstrating that success in the training environment is a product of struggles, effort, and development over time.

Conclusion

The opening example posed the following question: How can trainers realize and address trainees' public images, while also motivating trainees to learn and grow in the training environment? The chapter replies to this question by presenting an effective and appropriate model of instructional design that gives you, the corporate trainer, tools to provide trainees with growth mindset messaging. Such messaging are benchmarks in demonstrating effective and appropriate training design. Specifically, the chapter offers four messaging methods for talking to trainees, including listening to trainees' comments about their own abilities, building a response repertoire, shifting trainees' assumptions about their own and others' ability, and providing growth mindset-oriented feedback. These messaging methods provide actionable suggestions to increase trainee receptivity across a range of training situations.

As you implement these messaging methods in your existing training programs, I encourage you to continue to reflect on how your knowledge of mindset influences your communication with trainees and, in turn, how your trainees react to challenging training programs. When you tell a trainee, "you're just not good at it ... yet," do you see the trainee become more engaged in the material? How do stories of struggles open trainees' willingness to admit challenge in the training program? When you celebrate a trainee's failure as proof of her willingness to accept a challenge, how does that celebration create trainees who continue to grow, even after training? I challenge you to begin and continue to implement these messaging methods in your own training programs and, when you find it challenging, remember, you might not be excellent at identifying and shifting trainees' mindsets ... yet, but with more effort and practice, you will continue to improve and grow.

References

Beebe, S. A., Mottet, T. P., & Roach, K. D. (2013). *Training and development: Communicating for success* (2nd ed.). Boston, MA: Pearson.

Blackwell, L. S., Trzesniewski, K. H., & Dweck, C. S. (2007). Implicit theories of intelligence predict achievement across an adolescent transition: A longitudinal study and an intervention. *Child Development, 78*, 246–263. doi: 10.1111/j.1467–8624.2007.00995x

Cimpian, A., Aree, H. C., Markman, E. M., & Dweck, C. S. (2007). Short report: Subtle linguistic cues affect children's motivation. *Psychological Science, 18*, 314–318.

Dweck, C. S. (2006). *Mindset: The new psychology of success.* New York, NY: Random House.

Heslin, P. A., & VandeWalle, D. (2011). Performance appraisal procedural justice: The role of a manager's implicit person theory. *Journal of Management, 37*, 1694–1718. doi: 10.1177/0149206309342895

Hong, Y., Chiu, C., Dweck, C. S., Lin, D. M., & Wan, W. (1999). Implicit theories, attributions, and coping: A meaning system approach. *Journal of Personality and Social Psychology, 77*, 588–599. doi: 10.1037/0022–3514.77.3.588

Kalev, A., Kelly, E., & Dobbin, F. (2006). Best practices or best guesses? Assessing the efficacy of corporate affirmative action and diversity policies. *American Sociological Review, 71*, 589–617.

Mueller, C. M., & Dweck, C. S. (1998). Praise for intelligence can undermine children's motivation and performance. *Journal of Personality and Social Psychology, 75*, 33–52.

Pratkanis, A., & Aronson, E. (2001). *Age of propaganda: The everyday use and abuse of persuasion.* New York, NY: Freeman.

Tharenou, P., Saks, A., & Moore, C. (2007). A review and critique of research on training and organizational-level outcomes. *Human Resource Management Review, 17*, 251–273. doi: 10.1016/j.hrmr.2007.07.004

Wood, R. E., & Bandura, A. (1989). Impact of conception of ability on self-regulatory mechanisms and complex decision making. *Journal of Personality and Social Psychology, 56*, 407–415.

Yeager, D. S., Purdie-Vaughns, V., Garcia, J., Apfel, N., Brzustoski, P., Master, A., Hessert, W. T., Williams, M. E., & Cohen, G. L. (2014). Breaking the cycle of mistrust: Wise interventions to provide critical feedback across the racial divide. *Journal of Experimental Psychology, 143*, 804–824. doi: 10.1037/a0033906

Chapter 21

Belbin Team Roles

Assessing behavioral interaction to improve communication

DeeDee Smartt Lynch, Michael J. Lynch, and Cody M. Clemens

Abstract

This chapter will focus on Best Practice 6 – Demonstrate Effective and Appropriate Instructional Design, which requires communication coaches, consultants, teachers, and trainers (CCCTTs) to adopt approaches, tools, and practices which allow the impact of the training or coaching to be designed to meet specific needs with measurable goals and objectives assessed. We illuminate an assessment tool and methodology, Belbin Team Roles, which we use to achieve positive measurable outcomes.

Throughout the world, communication training represents a positive hope for individuals to master needed communication skills, perform and develop new functions, and be promoted into new situations (Beebe, 2007; Goldstein, 1989). The overarching goal of communication training and development is for employees or participants to master knowledge, hear insightful feedback, improve skills and behaviors emphasized in training programs, and apply it to improve their workplace environments or daily lives (Beebe, 2007; Beebe, Mottet, & Roach, 2004; Noe, 2010). As individuals, we have a strong desire to understand how we fit into a job, a team, a class, a division, or an organization. When we are clear about expectations, responsibilities, priorities, and goals, and possess the belief that we are equipped to meet all of these, then there exists a sense of purpose, belonging, and engagement. High levels of engagement yield higher levels of productivity (Belbin, 1981). Yet, for all of these elements to come together can be a monumental challenge, and effective communication of behavioral understanding is the cornerstone. The role of communication coaches, consultants, teachers, and trainers (CCCTTs) is to help individuals achieve these outcomes to improve ultimately their personal capacity and productivity.

Many times, one of the most effective ways to accomplish these desired outcomes is through the use of assessment tools. Accomplished CCCTTs are aware of and access a variety of useful assessment tools to meet the different needs of clients/students. Assessment tools provide insight and information for a broad range of areas, including personality, behavior, leadership, conflict, and more. As CCCTTs, part of our role is to understand the needs of our clients/students and the outcomes they are seeking, and to select a valuable assessment tool that matches those needs and enables them to achieve their goals. It is also part of our role as CCCTTs to be mindful of how our own abilities and approaches meet the needs and desired outcomes of our clients/students and agree to a means for evaluation and measurement of both how well the training meets agreed deliverables, and how well we satisfy expectations.

As CCCTTs, we are purveyors of assessable methods and tools, however, we are also learners and consumers. We find it is essential to benefit personally from an assessment tool in order to understand it fully and believe in its value on a personal level. For more than a decade, we have provided training and development using a plethora of useful, well-known assessments including Myers–Briggs Type Indicator (MBTI), DiSC Assessment, Blake Mouton Managerial Grid, and others. For this chapter, we have selected the Belbin Team Roles methodology and assessment tool as an exemplar of Best Practice 6 – Demonstrate Effective and Appropriate Instructional Design, because we have found it to be well-researched, provide insights for individuals and teams, and offer additional aspects of awareness not addressed with other assessments. We will show how we have been able to evaluate and measure improvements to both individual and team performances. In addition, we apply and integrate the tenets and philosophy of this methodology in our own business, experiences, and relationships and see the impact and results on an ongoing basis. The intent of this chapter is to provide you with a positive example of how an effective assessment tool, Belbin Team Roles, can be used to produce positive measurable and quantifiable results and outcomes when matched to the needs of your clients/students.

We hope through this example CCCTTs will benefit in the following ways: (1) understand the value of measuring and evaluating deliverable outcomes; (2) learn how and why using an assessment tool is one way to achieve preferred outcomes; (3) learn how a specific assessment and methodology is used effectively and applied to achieve the outcome of improved communication and interaction; and (4) gain knowledge, understanding, and ability to use the featured assessment tool, Belbin Team Roles. Through using, employing, and becoming more familiar with the Belbin methodology you will learn how to benefit and develop the recipients of your work. Also, you will find self-development and self-awareness for yourself as you discover how powerful the Belbin methodology is in relating to understanding the reason for the behavior of human beings. This discovery will significantly benefit you in the understanding of behavior and how it affects relationships for yourself and your students/client. Belbin Team Roles was selected as our example because it is based on years of research and its level of predictability as an evidence based tool enables us to use it confidently with our clients knowing it is grounded and validated with evidence (Aritzeta et al., 2007; Belbin et al., 1976, p. 26). Because the research, history, and evolution of Belbin helps establish its credibility, the following is a brief overview we believe will help CCCTTs understand how it has been developed over the years.

History and development of Belbin Team Roles

Henley Management College (United Kingdom) in 1969 was the place to send your high-potential managers for enhanced management training. Here, Henley regularly assigned maneuvers that simulated businesses to their student teams and measured how successful they were. In an effort to understand why some teams were successful and bonded, Henley commissioned a thorough and extensive study to better understand why some teams were successful and others could barely stand to be in the same room together. This research was carried out over a nine-year period, and it was overseen by Dr. R. Meredith Belbin at the Industrial Training Unit with assistance from Henley (Belbin et al., 1976; Dulewicz, 1995).

During these exercises, trained observers recorded the behavior of individuals during the team interaction every 30 seconds based upon criteria set out by Bales's (1950) analysis. From the analysis, there were eight clusters of behavior (or team roles) that emerged

(Belbin, 1981). Officially developed in 1981, there are years of scholarly literature that support the validity and effectiveness of the Belbin Team Roles assessment method, and it is a method that has demonstrated reasonable expectations of training transfer. In 1993, a ninth team role was recognized, and together they explain how each individual role exhibits a unique cluster of behaviors and specific contribution toward a team's success (Belbin, 1993a). These nine team roles revealed that there are distinct differences between successful and unsuccessful teams.

As the differences were uncovered, researchers found that the measure of success relied more on behavior than experience or intellect (Belbin, 1981, 2010a). Industrial psychologists and other scholars continue to work on keeping the Belbin methodology refreshed and essential with today's contemporary requirements (Belbin.com, 2017). It is widely used in practice and has been featured extensively on research into team roles and teams at work. For many organizations, consultants, and practitioners around the world, this is the "go to" methodology and has been translated into 17 languages. In addition, Belbin demonstrated that balanced teams (teams exhibiting all nine team roles) out-perform unbalanced teams over time (Belbin 1981, 2010b). Along with the specific contribution, each team role was found to include behaviors which did not contribute but were nonetheless associated with the team role. Belbin called these "allowable weaknesses" in that to fully gain the strength of the contribution, it may require some tolerance of the noncontributing behaviors. If this noncontributing behavior is an inconvenience, it is allowable; however, if the behavior negatively impacts the team, it is then considered "non-allowable" and needs to be managed. CCCTTs need to be aware of these weaknesses within their own behavior to understand how to manage or mitigate the harmful impact that these can have on their performance. Equally, CCCTTs also need to be aware of the behavior of student/clients to help them achieve self-awareness and improve performance.

Furthermore, a plethora of scholars have published literature continually evaluating and validating the nine Belbin Team Roles. Topics of scholarly conversation directly relating to Belbin Team Roles have included an evaluation of gender differences on the self-perception inventory (Anderson & Sleap, 2004); validity and structure of the Belbin Team Roles model (Aritzeta et al., 2007; Dulewicz, 1995; Fisher, Hunter, & Macrosson, 1998); the relationship between Belbin role diversity and team performance (Batenburg et al., 2013; Fisher, Hunter, & Macrosson, 2000); examination of the distribution of team roles among UK managers and non-managers, respectively (Fisher et al., 2000, 2001); a psychometric assessment of the Belbin Team Role self-perception inventory (Furnham, Steele, & Pendleton, 1993); the way in which emotional intelligence relates to Belbin Team Roles (Golonka & Mojsa-Kaja, 2013); Machiavellianism in Belbin (Macrosson & Hemphill, 2001); and a comparison of the self-perception inventory and observer's assessment as measures of individual's team roles (Senior & Swailes, 1998).

As this chapter continues, it will highlight the Belbin Team Roles assessment. It will also cover a detailed explanation of the nine team roles, how they are grouped into the three skill categories, self-perception versus observer reports, as well as balanced versus unbalanced teams. It is important to note that the methodology behind Belbin's work is used as a means for improving self-understanding and enhanced understanding of others, especially, but not exclusively in a team setting. Moreover, the chapter will help readers better understand how the Belbin Team Roles assessment is used to identify people's behavioral strengths and weaknesses in the workplace, build productive working relationships, select and develop high-performing teams, raise self-awareness and personal effectiveness, aid recruitment processes, and build mutual trust and understanding and how this can be harnessed by the CCCTT to best advantage (Belbin.com, 2017). Also, it will offer insight and knowledge from Smartt Strategies, a training and development firm that specializes in Belbin Team Roles, about how to apply and use it to improve performance for both individuals and teams. Finally, and most importantly, this chapter will connect to Best Practice 6 – Demonstrate Effective and Appropriate Instructional Design by showing how an assessment tool, such as Belbin, can be used by the CCCTTs in a way that will enable the effectiveness and impact of the training or coaching to be measured and assessed. Best Practice 6 establishes that your role as a CCCTT is to provide appropriate support and solutions that can be measured and quantified.

The Belbin Team Roles

Before furthering the discussion on Belbin's Nine Team Roles, it is important for the reader to establish an understanding of the team roles. In the following paragraphs, descriptions, functions, as well as allowable and non-allowable weaknesses of the nine Belbin Team Roles, will be acknowledged. Building from the work of Aritzeta et al. (2007), Batenburg et al. (2013), Belbin (1981, 1993a, 1993b, 2010, 2013b), Fisher et al. (1998), Haaf et al. (2002), van de Water, van de Water, and Bukman (2006), and van de Water and Bukman (2009), the following paragraphs outline the team roles. The definition of a team role, according to Belbin, is a person's "tendency to behave, contribute and interrelate with others at work in certain distinctive ways" (1993a, p. 24).

As CCCTTs, you will want to be familiar with these descriptions as they are the basic building blocks for the Belbin Team Role methodology. Although the Belbin Reports are easy to understand, we have found when students/clients are first exposed to their Belbin assessment profiles, having a knowledgeable facilitator of the methodology to help interpret the report data is useful to accelerate understanding and acceptance. As with any assessment, a lack of in-depth knowledge by the CCCTTs can be a barrier to the student/client accepting the report leading to loss of credibility for the methodology and/or the CCCTTs.

Plants (PL)

Known as the inventors, *plants (PL)* are highly imaginative and creative. They provide seeds and ideas from which major developments spring. Usually they prefer to operate by themselves and often work in an unorthodox way. They can solve difficult problems. They tend to react strongly to criticism and praise. Their ideas may often be radical, and may lack practical constraint. They are independent, clever, and original, and may be weak in communicating with people who are on a different wavelength, which is considered an allowable weakness as is ignoring incidentals. Non-allowable weaknesses include strong ownership of ideas when co-operation with others would yield better results or ignoring protocols.

Monitor Evaluators (ME)

Notorious for having a built-in immunity from being over-enthusiastic, *monitor evaluators (ME)* are serious-minded, prudent individuals. They are slow to make decisions, as they prefer to take their time as they think things over. Usually they have a high critical-thinking ability and a capacity for shrewd judgements that take all factors into account. A good ME is seldom wrong. Allowable weaknesses might include lack of drive and ability to inspire others along with being overly critical. Non-allowable weaknesses include cynicism without logic.

Specialists (SP)

Priding themselves on acquiring technical skills and specialized knowledge, *specialists (SP)* are known for their dedication to their work. Their priorities center on maintaining professional standards, and on furthering and defending their own field. While they show immense pride in their own subject, they usually lack interest in other people's interests. Eventually, the SP becomes the expert by sheer commitment along a narrow front of knowledge. They are self-driving and provide knowledge and skills in rare supply. There are few people who have either the single-mindedness or the aptitude to become a first-class SP. Contributing only on a narrow front, dwelling on technicalities, and being territorial are allowable weaknesses, while ignoring factors outside area of competence is non-allowable.

Shapers (SH)

Continually striving for achievement, *shapers (SH)* are highly motivated people with a lot of nervous energy. They are dynamic and challenging and thrive under pressure. Usually, they are assertive (sometimes aggressive) extroverts, and possess strong drive. SHs like to challenge others, and their concern is for the team to win. They like to lead, and to push others into action. If obstacles arise, they have the courage to find a way around. Headstrong and assertive, they tend to show strong emotional response to any form of disappointment or frustration. SHs are direct and argumentative, and may lack or are not concerned with interpersonal understanding. This is the most competitive team role. Allowable weaknesses include being prone to provocation and offending people's feelings, while non-allowable weaknesses are inability to recover situation with good humor or apology and over aggressive behavior.

Implementers (IMP)

Known for having practical common sense, *implementers (IMP)* agree upon plans and have a good deal of self-control and discipline. They favor hard work and tackle problems in a systematic fashion. On a wider front, the IMP is typically a person whose loyalty and interest lie with their organization, and who is less concerned with the pursuit of self-interest. However, IMPs may lack spontaneity and show signs of rigidity, both are allowable while obstructing change is non-allowable.

Completer-Finishers (CF)

Continually conscientious, *completer-finishers (CF)* have a great capacity for follow-through and attention to detail. They are uncomfortable starting anything they cannot finish to a high standard. They are motivated by internal anxiety, yet outwardly they may appear unruffled. Typically, they are introverted, and require little in the way of external stimulus or incentive. CFs can be intolerant of those with a casual disposition. They are not often keen on delegating; preferring to tackle all tasks themselves, which is allowable until it becomes obsessional behavior, which in non-allowable.

Co-ordinators (CO)

Known for their ability to clarify and encourage others to work toward shared goals, *co-ordinators (CO)* are important members of a team. They strive to keep everyone on board with decisions that are being made. Also, they are mature, trusting, and confident; they delegate readily; and they promote decision making. In interpersonal relations, they are quick to spot individual talents, and to use them in the pursuit of group objectives. They tend to understand the abilities of other team members. While COs are not necessarily the cleverest members of a team, they have a broad and worldly outlook, and generally command respect. The allowable weaknesses are they can be seen as manipulative and appear to offload their personal work. Non-allowable weaknesses are when they take credit for the ideas and efforts of others.

Team Workers (TW)

The most supportive members of a team are the *team workers (TW)*. They are mild, sociable, and concerned about others. They have a great capacity for flexibility, and adapting to different situations and people. TWs are perceptive and diplomatic. They are good listeners, and are generally popular members of a group. TWs operate with sensitivity at work, but they may be indecisive in crunch situations and avoid confrontation, both of which fall under allowable weaknesses. Avoiding confrontations and other pressure situations at all costs though is non-allowable.

Resource Investigators (RI)

Prone to be openly enthusiastic, *resource investigators (RI)* are the extroverts on a team. They are the "go to" networkers who are good at communicating with people both inside and outside the company. They are natural negotiators, and are adept at exploring new opportunities and developing contacts. Although not a great source of original ideas, the RI is effective when it comes to picking up other people's ideas and developing them. As the name suggests, they are skilled at finding out what is available, and what can be done. They usually receive a warm reception from others because of their outgoing nature. RIs have relaxed personalities with a strong inquisitive sense, and readiness to see the possibilities in anything new. However, unless they remain stimulated by others, their enthusiasm rapidly fades. The tendencies to be easily bored, over-talkative and over-optimistic are allowable weaknesses, while letting clients down by neglecting to follow up on arrangements is non-allowable.

Having read the descriptions above, consider which role(s) resonate with your own behavior. Also, of the people with whom you interact, can you see other roles emerging for them? You may identify two or three roles that are like you, others that could be you, and some that you think are definitely not you. These are described later as preferred, manageable, and least-preferred roles. Can you see areas of potential (or actual) conflict with the different approaches? As stated earlier, how we perceive ourselves and how we are perceived by others is very much based on behavior. By understanding behavioral tendencies as described by Belbin, you might better appreciate the interaction you have with others and modifications you might consider for improving relationships and communication. Remember the role(s) you identify with and think describe you is your self-perception only, and a benefit of Belbin is the opportunity to include a more robust assessment using observer 360-degree feedback and is highly encouraged.

Grouping team roles

Although there are nine different team roles, Belbin, and his team, provide further clarity to each role through grouping into three skill categories (Belbin 2012, 2013a). Each role was grouped into one of three different skill categories: 1) *Thinking*; 2) *Action*; and 3) *Social* (see Figure 21.1). These groupings are purposeful because they help to identify different approaches for how individuals mentally process information, get work done, and form working relationships as related to team roles. Furthermore, these classifications serve to differentiate what might seem like similar team roles and help people remember the different team roles. Although each team role brings its own unique contribution, it does manifest itself into one of these skill groups.

In addition to being familiar with the nine team roles, a CCCTT wanting to effectively use the Belbin methodology, would want to know the following key points:

- Belbin's research acknowledged the success a team achieved depended on how the nine team roles were represented within a team. Teams that failed to meet expectations were generally missing some of the team roles. Belbin (1981, 1993a, 2010a, 2010b, 2013b), along with other scholars (Benne & Sheats, 1948; Torrington, Weightman. & Johns, 1985), defends the idea that high-performing teams need to have a balanced representation of all team roles. CCCTTs should be able to speak to the balance of the team they are working with in order to point out potential unbalances and help the team formulate strategies and agreements to mitigate these imbalances.

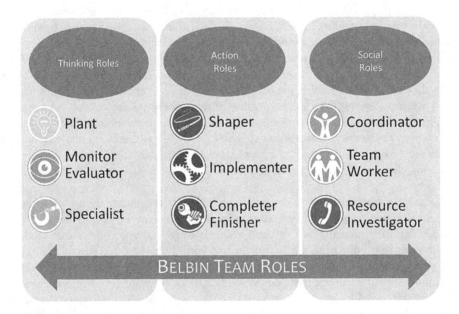

Figure 21.1 Belbin Team Roles chart.

- All nine team roles are not required at all times. Certain team roles will be more or less important, depending on the team situation, phase of a project, and current circumstances; however, a team needs access to all nine contributions (Belbin, 2010a, 2010b). For example, innovative ideas are required (RI, PL) at the outset of the task to ensure that new ideas and best practices are available to the team. In the next phase, a ME is useful to ensure the ideas are practicable. CCCTTs should be able to help the team identify the particular team situation and the team roles that are required to be dominant at the stage.
- Most people naturally contribute two or three of the team roles while struggling with others. Belbin (1981, 1993a, 2010a, 2010b, 2013b) put extensive work into analyzing an individual's preferred, manageable, and least-preferred team roles. The "preferred roles" are the roles, typically two to three, where people have a tendency to contribute to a team in a natural way requiring minimal effort and stress from the individual. Alternatively, individuals are known to struggle with two or three roles, called "least-preferred roles." With *least-preferred roles*, individuals require significant extra effort to contribute in these areas, whereas other people make it appear easy. The remaining team roles that fall in the middle are called "manageable roles"(see Figure 21.2). Belbin found people can do a fairly good job contributing the *manageable roles* for a limited amount of time. When individuals learn what their *preferred roles* are and how to use them in a way that aligns with the goals and desired outcomes of the team, this has a positive impact on the individual and the team. CCCTTs should coach individuals and teams on how to ensure that tasks are being managed by the most appropriate person from a behavioral perspective when

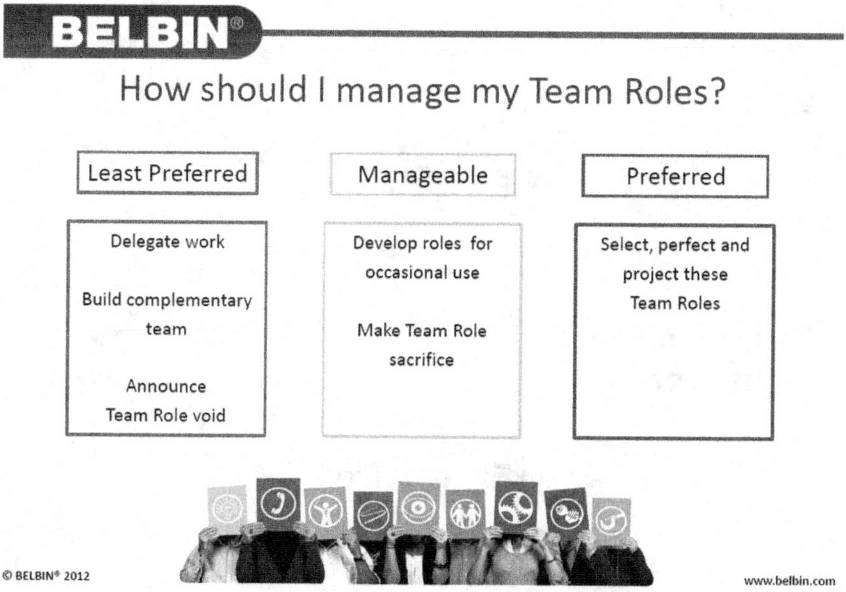

Figure 21.2 Preferred, manageable, and least preferred team roles.

Source: BELBIN logos and slides reproduced by kind permission of BELBIN, UK. All rights reserved and remain the intellectual property & copyright of BELBIN, UK – www.belbin.com. Belbin is a registered trademark.

possible, minimizing the situation where individuals are required to perform in a *least-manageable role*. Where this is not possible, the CCCTT would help individuals who find themselves contributing with *manageable* or *least-preferred roles* to expect that they might find this difficult and not to "beat themselves up" about how difficult they find the task.

- Along with the strengths and benefits associated with a preferred role, there comes a complementary set of behaviors that do not necessarily advance the cause of the team's progress. If the behavior does not hamper the team this behavior is known as an *allowable weakness*. However, if the behavior is having a dilatory or negative effect on performance within the team, it is known as a *non-allowable weakness* and the CCCTTs should help the team address this behavior with the team member to mutually agree how this will be handled.

- There are six factors that underpin team role behaviors and determine team role preferences (see Figure 21.3). Belbin's Team Role model found these six factors have significant impact on how the team roles manifest for an individual (Aritzeta et al., 2007, p. 99; van de Water et al., 2007, pp. 499–500). The first three factors or

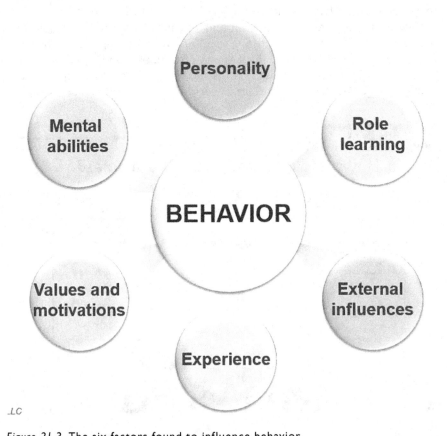

Figure 21.3 The six factors found to influence behavior.

predictors are *personality, mental ability*, and *values/motivations*. These were measured through a battery of tests during the Henley research and linked with distinct team roles types. Additionally, the three other factors found to have further influence on team role behaviors are *experience, field constraints*, and *role learning*.

- The Belbin Team Roles theory is unique (Belbin, 1993a; Broucek, Willard, & Randell, 1996), because the assessment of both the individual and observers are valued. This assessment model greatly differs from that of the Myers-Briggs Type Indicator (MBTI, 2017), for example, which only considers the individual's self-perception. Although there is a general presumption that individuals know themselves best, this is not always the case (Belbin, 2013b). Belbin and his team found self-perception and the perception of others are equally important to understanding behavior and led to the development and integration of Observer Assessments into the assessment methodology and reporting (Belbin, 1993b, 2010a, 2010b).

- It is important to remember that the team roles do not define the person, but rather the contribution that is being made, so it is important not to "label" someone as a "shaper," for example. Understanding these Belbin Team Roles, and the cluster of behaviors associated with each, allows the team to learn a new language or vocabulary to allow open communication in a non-defensive way. It is important, as a CCCTT, to continually emphasize the contribution that is discussed and not the person (Belbin, 1993a).

Measuring the impact

In order to meet Best Practice 6, it is imperative that CCCTTs establish up front what the client's expected outcome for the training is. Remember that the client is probably represented by a number of key stake holders, not all of whom will have the same expectations. All of these expectations need to be addressed. These objectives and outcomes need to be fully understood along with how to measure that the objectives have been successfully achieved. With these success criteria identified, the CCCTT should customize the training to ensure these objectives are being addressed to maximize the chance of success.

When we start working with a new client partner to provide training, our first concern is to make sure we fully understand the training needs and have agreed upon the desired outcomes with our client partners. As CCCTTs, you will want to ascertain who your training partners and stakeholders are and how best to determine training needs and desired training outcomes. The CCCTT that has agreed success criteria with their respective training partners and stakeholders is in a good position to assess the success following the completion of the training. While these initial steps can be complex, they tend to be considered standard practice. However, the discussion and agreement on how these training outcomes will be measured, along with how well the training needs of the participants have been met, is unfortunately not commonplace. According to a 2016 research study conducted by the Association of Talent Development, only 35 per cent of talent development professionals "reported that their organizations evaluated the business results of learning programs to any extent" (ATD Research, 2016).

If our purpose for providing training is to deliver improvements through learning and behavioral change as a result of instruction, we need to make sure our methods are effective (Mayer, 2010). But how can we measure changes in behavior that result from the learning experience of the training? This effort to provide valid and effective measurements of training impact has proven troublesome for many in this field for many years and probably explains why so many organizations forgo the effort altogether. However, we find and firmly believe that to be considered highly credible learning partners who provide valuable training programs, it is imperative we use tools and methods which can be measured against a set of deliverables, desired outcomes, and success criteria to determine the training effectiveness that reinforces the premise of Best Practice 6 – Demonstrate Effective and Appropriate Instructional Design.

One of the most well-known training evaluation models is *Kirkpatrick's Four Levels* (Kirkpatrick, 1998), although there are a plethora of lesser-known options. Using one of these formal programs for evaluation often ensures the proper steps and tools for evaluation are used. Kirkpatrick's Four Levels help to enforce the understanding that the impact of training should be seen as more than the immediate reaction to the actual training session or event (Level 1). Level 2 evaluation looks at what has been learned as a result of the training, while Level 3 explores behavioral change because of the training. These three levels are essential and important; however, it is only with Level 4 that we see the training impact on business results (Kirkpatrick, 1998; Kirkpatrick & Kirkpatrick, 2016). When we, as CCCTTs, are able show successful outcomes and make this link, our efforts become highly prized and valuable. Whether it is the formal evaluation program, like Kirkpatrick, or a means of evaluation and measurement you agree with your client, having an upfront and agreed method for how you will evaluate the success of the training is essential.

As consultants who specialize in team effectiveness, most of our client partners come to us with training needs that seek to improve team communication, cohesiveness, productivity, and interaction. As previously mentioned, it is important to use the appropriate tools and methods which will enable participants to achieve the desired learning and meet the desired training outcomes. For our particular area of expertise, we often use the Belbin Team Roles methodology, as it allows us to offer training that supports and tracks both individual and team performance.

While we customize the training experience for each client partner, common to all is the use of the Belbin Team Role individual assessment report. The data in this report along with an understanding of the methodology help individuals understand the impact of their behavior on those around them and they include observer feedback that explicitly informs them of how their behavior is perceived. This report offers information and insight about their strengths and weaknesses and how to use this knowledge to improve contributions toward team success. During the training event, and often in subsequent coaching sessions, individuals use the Belbin Report information as a catalyst for a performance improvement strategy.

For example, Mark is a client partner who we began working with almost two years ago and is a good representation of one of the ways we measure behavioral change. As head of a manufacturing company division, Mark and his team were tasked with overseeing the building of, and then managing of, a new bottling plant. Mark was part of a production leadership team selected to participate in a prototype training course to determine the merits of using Belbin Team Roles for improving inter- and intra-team cohesiveness for the organization. After the initial training course, attendees participated in individual coaching sessions to maximize the Belbin Report information. In the coaching session, we discussed how both Mark, and his observers, perceived him as a creative and imaginative problem solver ("Plant"). There was strong coherence with the "Plant" team role contribution, meaning Mark's self-perception matched his observers' perceptions.

Belbin determined that candidates who have coherent reports, meaning an individual self-perception is matched by the assessment of others, tend to have an initial advantage over non-coherent candidates, because it is easier to develop a mutual understanding of team expectations if one already has a good understanding of his/herself (Belbin 1993a, 2010a, 2010b).

However, there was little alignment with Mark's next three top-ranked team roles. His Belbin Report revealed he saw himself as someone who is hard-driving and pushing results with a sense of urgency; a challenging and "charge ahead" type of leader ("Shaper"). The feedback from his observers showed they perceived Mark to be conscious of priorities and goals, but in a collaborative style. He was also seen to be encouraging of others and an effective facilitator and delegator ("Coordinator"). The discrepancies between the self-perception versus the observer data were discussed in the coaching session. Mark believed the Coordinator contribution would be more effective for his current position and truer to his natural leadership style. When he understood the differences between the Coordinator and Shaper roles, we developed a strategy for improving his Coordinator contributions. In addition, he identified one of his team members whose natural Shaper tendencies would ensure that team role contribution was covered. To measure the effectiveness of this strategy, we agreed Mark would re-do the Belbin assessment in six months, with the goal of closing the 38-point gap (see Figure 21.4) between his self-perception percentile and observers' percentile on the comparison report analysis. Six months later, his new Belbin Report showed only a 9-point difference for the Coordinator Role, now in a strong second place to his still strong and most preferred Plant Role. Mark shared that verbal feedback from his team on the strategy to emphasize the Coordinator Role had been positive, and they believed that this had contributed significantly to the success of the new building and the ongoing success the team was experiencing.

In addition to measuring individual progress, we often are called upon to train, and therefore measure, a team's progress. Again, we customize the training based on the client partners' needs, but common to all team training is the analysis of the overall team role make up. Using the Belbin Team Report along with an examination of a comprehensive grid that includes the rank order of all team members' team roles, a vast amount of data can be collected on the team's current state. Depending on the outputs of the team data, we facilitate discussions that typically include the following: What is the impact when half the team or more has the same team role as a preferred role? This is known as a team role surplus. What is the impact when no one on a team has a particular team role as their preferred role? This is known as a team role void. Depending on the team's specific make up, we will analyze and discuss how this helps explain what the team is currently experiencing. Most significantly, using this information we facilitate and support discussions that lead to team agreements on how they intend to address these team issues. These team agreements include milestones and check points for making sure these team adjustments are effective and lead to improved performance. We encourage all CCCTTs to discuss these points with the students/clients.

Many times, we find that simply having a new way of understanding interaction and behavior in a team has a substantial impact on performance. It can also help clarify what has been happening in the team. For example, one team we worked with was several

Comparing Self and Observer Perceptions

The bar graph in this report shows how you perceive your Team Role contributions, in comparison to your Observers' views. The table below the graph shows the percentile scores for Self-Perception and Observers.

This report is based on your Self-Perception plus 6 Observer Assessments.

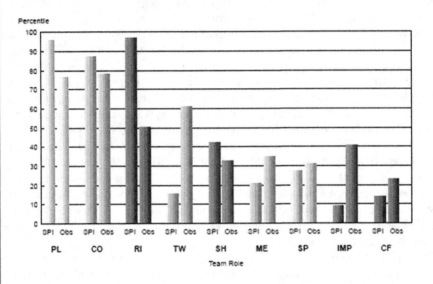

Key		Self-Perception (SPI) (Percentile)	Observations (Obs) (Percentile)
PL	Plant	96	76
CO	Co-ordinator	87	78
RI	Resource Investigator	97	50
TW	Teamworker	16	61
SH	Shaper	42	33
ME	Monitor Evaluator	21	35
SP	Specialist	27	31
IMP	Implementer	9	41
CF	Completer Finisher	14	23

Figure 21.4 Mark's Belbin Report page: Comparing self-perception with observer-perception. BELBIN Team Role report produced from Interplace 7 – reproduced by kind permission of BELBIN, UK. All rights reserved and remain the intellectual property & copyright of BELBIN, UK – www.belbin.com. Belbin is a registered trademark.

months behind deadline on critical materials they were developing for a major project. They were in jeopardy of losing the contract on this project, which would lead to substantial layoffs. When we analyzed the comprehensive team role make up of this small division of 12, we found there was an abundance of people with preferred roles (top three roles) in the Social-Oriented category (Coordinator, Team Worker, and Resource Investigator). This helped explain why everyone was so concerned about each other, got along really well, and why they were so frustrated that despite their congeniality toward each other, they were not meeting work product expectations.

During the first day of training, a woman we will call Janice came to us and declared that she had written her letter of resignation but decided to wait until she attended this training before submitting it. She said she was tired of being the office nag and frustrated because there was always a lot of talking about getting work done, but it never seemed to get done. She was fed up. She explained that after going through the Belbin training, she finally understood what had been happening in the team. It now made sense to her when she looked at the team grid and realized she was the only person with Shaper in the preferred roles. Every other person had Shaper in their bottom least-preferred roles. The next day the entire team began discussing that Janice, as the Shaper contributor, was a scarce resource and her driving, deadline-focused approach was exactly what they needed. They realized that because she was not as "people oriented" as most others, they had been ostracizing her and indeed had seen her as a "nag."

With this new understanding, they established team agreements that empowered Janice to play the Shaper role with the full support and appreciation of the team. They agreed Janice would be the time keeper at all meetings and they would all be accountable to agreed upon deliverables and schedules. Janice was supported and encouraged to play the Shaper role, keeping everyone focused on deadlines and no longer considered the "nag." The team set a three-month target to get back on track with their work product schedule. At our team coaching session three months later, the team reported that it was not only back on track with the material development, they were ahead of schedule on the next phase, Janice was now highly respected and on the executive team. All attributed this success to having a new team language with which to communicate and deal with team issues.

These are examples of how we use the Belbin methodology to measure individual and team performance. As CCCTTs, having a standard practice for evaluation allows you to compare how effective different sessions with different client partners has been. With most of our client partners we use a formal evaluation form, commonly called a "smile sheet," to collect the immediate response to the training session or event. We use a set of questions and statements that align with the objectives initially agreed upon to gage how well participants believe these have been met, or not. We use a scale of 1 to 5 where "1" represents "strongly disagree" and "5" represents "strongly agree." Through many years of using this scale, we find that training sessions which have an overall average of 4.3 or higher for each question or statement have a tendency to show greater learning and behavioral change as a result of the training. While this is subjective and difficult to track, we have had the chance with several client partners to do more in-depth analysis using their annual performance reviews to substantiate this theory.

One client partner uses an annual survey to their more than 45,000 employees to measure employee engagement, which they have linked with business performance. We were able to track that the managers who took part in particular training courses saw 7 to

15 per cent higher employee engagement scores than managers who had not had these training courses. Seeing this kind of positive business impact from the training validates that the training needs of the managers were properly analyzed and the objectives and success criteria were met meritoriously.

Conclusion

This chapter addresses the significance and importance of analyzing the training needs to determine the most appropriate and effective training or coaching to be provided, and a means for measuring the impact of the training for the benefit of all stakeholders and to examine how well you met the agreed success criteria. We hope as fellow CCCTTs you now have an enhanced recognition of the following:

1   Recognize the importance of fully understanding the current situation of you client/students and what they are seeking to achieve through the training or coaching you provide.
2   Understand the value of measuring and evaluating deliverable outcomes; in order to meet the expectations of Best Practice 6, we have offered advice as to how evaluating the effectiveness of the training using e.g. Kirkpatrick's evaluation adds both credibility and value to the training that has been delivered.
3   Learn how and why using an assessment tool is one way to achieve preferred outcomes; we have discussed the importance of agreeing desired outcomes, success criteria, and objectives with our client stakeholders in order that we have an objective way of measuring the value of the training delivered.
4   Realize how a specific assessment and methodology is used and applied to achieve the outcome of improved communication and interaction; we have spoken extensively to our exemplary Belbin Team Role methodology, and how that, for team situations where the desired result is better team cohesiveness, productivity, team awareness, and self-awareness, this methodology lends itself to be assessed for effectiveness against agreed success criteria.
5   Gain knowledge, understanding, and ability to use the featured assessment tool, Belbin Team Roles. Belbin Team Roles was selected as our example because it is based on years of research and its level of predictability as an evidence-based tool enables us to use it confidently with our clients; we have found that the methodology resonates with the trainee, especially with additional explanation and coaching through the CCCTT's insight and knowledge of the methodology.

Best Practice 6 – Demonstrate Effective and Appropriate Instructional Design, if followed faithfully will result in more-affective training, better enlightened trainees, and an increase in productivity to benefit the host shareholder. As CCCTTs, we should be providing a means of learning that optimally results in behavioral changes that positively impact individuals and organizations. When we are able to identify the gaps between the current state of a situation and the desired future state and then provide the most appropriate tool or method for reducing that gap to achieve the ideal outcomes in a way that can be measured and shown to be positive and productive, we have done our job.

References

Anderson, N., & Sleap, S. (2004). An evaluation of gender differences on the Belbin team role self-perception inventory. *Journal of Occupational and Organizational Psychology, 77*, 429–437.

Aritzeta, A., Swailes, S., & Senior, B. (2007). Belbin's team role model: Development, validity and applications for team building. *Journal of Management Studies, 44*(1), 96–118.

ATD Research (2016). Evaluating learning: Getting to measurements that matter. Retrieved from http://www.td.org/Publications/Research-Reports/2016/Evaluating-Learning

Bales, R. F. (1950). *Interaction process analysis: A method for the study of small groups.* Cambridge, MA: Addison-Wesley.

Batenburg, R., van Walbeek, W., & in der Maur, W. (2013). Belbin role diversity and team performance: Is there a relationship? *Journal of Management Development, 32*(8), 901–913. doi: 10.1108/JMD-08-2011-0098

Beebe, S. A. (2007). Raising the question #6: What do communication trainers do? *Communication Education, 56*(2), 249–254.

Beebe, S. A., Mottet, T. P., & Roach, K. D. (2004). *Training and development: Enhancing communication and leadership skills.* Boston, MA: Allyn & Bacon.

Belbin, R. M. (1981). *Management teams: Why they succeed or fail.* Oxford, UK: Butterworth-Heinemann.

Belbin, R. M. (1993a). *Team roles at work.* Oxford, UK: Butterworth-Heinemann.

Belbin, R. M. (1993b). A reply to the Belbin team-role self-perception inventory by Furnham, Steele and Pendleton. *Journal of Occupational and Organizational Psychology, 66*, 249–260.

Belbin, R. M. (2010a). *Management teams: Why they succeed or fail* (2nd ed.). Oxford, UK: Butterworth-Heinemann.

Belbin, R. M. (2010b). *Team roles at work* (2nd ed.). Oxford, UK: Butterworth-Heinemann.

Belbin, R. M. (2012). *Method, reliability and validity, statistics and research: A comprehensive review of Belbin team roles.* Cambridge, UK: Belbin Associates UK.

Belbin, R. M. (2013a). Belbin accreditation v7.3. Cambridge, UK: Belbin Associates UK.

Belbin, R. M. (2013b). *Management teams: Why they succeed or fail* (3rd ed.). New York, NY: Routledge.

Belbin.com (2017). Belbin Team Roles. Retrieved from http://www.belbin.com/about/belbin-team-roles/

Belbin, R. M., Aston, R. R., & Mottram, R. D. (1976). Building effective management teams. *Journal of General Management, 3*, 23–29.

Benne, K. D., & Sheats, P. (1948). Functional roles of group members. *Journal of Social Issues, 4*, 41–50.

Broucek, W. G., & Randell, G. (1996). An assessment of the construct validity of the Belbin Self-Perception Inventory and Observer's Assessment from the perspective of the five-factor model. *Journal of Occupational Psychology, 69*, 389–405.

Dulewicz, V. (1995). A validation of Belbin's team roles from 16PF and OPQ using bosses' rating of competence. *Journal of Occupational and Organizational Psychology, 68*, 81–99.

Fisher, S. G., Hunter, T. A., & Macrosson, W. D. K. (1998). The structure of Belbin's team roles. *Journal of Occupational and Organizational Psychology, 71*, 283–288.

Fisher, S. G., Hunter, T. A., & Macrosson, W. D. K. (2000). The distribution of Belbin team roles among UK managers. *Personnel Review, 29*(2), 124–140.

Fisher, S. G., Hunter, T. A., & Macrosson, W. D. K. (2001). Belbin's team role theory: For non-managers also? *Journal of Managerial Psychology, 17*(1), 14–20. doi: 10.1108/02683940210415906

Furnham, A., Steele, H., & Pendleton, D. (1993). A psychometric assessment of the Belbin team-role self-perception inventory. *Journal of Occupational and Organizational Psychology, 66*, 245–257.

Goldstein, I. L. (1989). *Training and development in organizations.* San Francisco, CA: Jossey-Bass.

Golonka, K., & Mojsa-Kaja, J. (2013). Emotional intelligence and team roles – analysis of interdependencies with regard to teamwork effectiveness. *International Journal of Contemporary Management, 12*(4), 32–44.

Haaf, W. ten, Bikker, H., & Adriaanse, D. J. with contributions from J. in 't Veld & P.Ch.-A. Malotaux (2002). *Fundamentals of business engineering and management. A systems approach to people and organisations.* Delft, The Netherlands: VSSD.

Kirkpatrick, D. L. (1998). *Evaluating training programs: The four levels.* San Francisco, CA: Berrett-Koehler Publishers.

Kirkpatrick, J. D., & Kirkpatrick, W. K. (2016). *Kirkpatrick's four levels of training evaluation.* Alexandria, VA: ATD Press.

Macrosson, W. D. K., & Hemphill, D. J. (2001). Machiavellianism in Belbin team roles. *Journal of Managerial Psychology, 16*(5), 355–363.

Mayer, R. (2010). *Applying the science of learning.* London: Pearson.

MBTI (2017). Myers-Briggs Type Indicator. Retrieved from http://www.myersbriggs.org/

Noe, R. A. (2010). *Employee training and development.* New York, NY: McGraw-Hill Irwin.

Senior, B., & Swailes, S. (1998). A comparison of the Belbin self-perception inventory and observer's assessment sheet as measures of an individual's team roles. *International Journal of Selection and Assessment, 6*(1), 1–7.

Smarttstrategies.com (2017). Smartt Strategies: Better teams, better business. Retrieved from https://www.smarttstrategies.com/

Torrington, D., Weightman, J., & Johns, K. (1985). *Management methods.* London: Personnel Management Institute.

van de Water, H., Ahaus, K., & Rozier, R. (2007). Team roles, team balance and performance. *Journal of Management Development, 27*(5), 499–512.

van de Water, H., & Bukman, C. (2009). A balanced team-generating model for teams with less than nine persons. *IMA Journal of Management Mathematics, 21*(3), 281–302.

van de Water, T., van de Water, H., & Bukman, C. (2006). A balanced team generating model. *European Journal of Operational Research, 180,* 885–906.

Chapter 22

Operationalizing Kolb's Experiential Learning Cycle

A user-friendly template for instructional design and self-assessment

Kristen A. McIntyre, Belynda Dix, and Marian L. Ward

Abstract

Grounded in Kolb's (1984) Experiential Learning Cycle, the Activities/Learning Mode Assessment (ALMA) aligns instructional methods with each of the four main learning preferences – diverging, assimilating, converging, and accommodating – simplifying the instructional design process for CCCTTS while improving the likelihood of participant learning. By using the ALMA, CCCTTs are able to document instructional strategies, self-assess the strength of each strategy to facilitate learning, as well as respond to guided self-reflection questions related to the training experience.

Training design can be a varied and individual process, often reflecting our assumptions about what it means to teach and to learn. Didactic approaches are common because that is how most of us were taught. We find this to be especially common in training situations, when a presenter is called on to do a training based on expert knowledge alone and perhaps little background on how to facilitate meaningful learning.

You may be saying to yourself, "Of course I facilitate learning. I carefully organize my key information, focus on my talking points, and create dynamic PowerPoint presentations. Besides, anything anybody misses will be on my (very thorough) handouts, I'm covered." And to that we say, "Excellent!" But if you have ever looked out at your participants and encountered closed eyes, confused faces, restless bodies, and/or private side conversations, we invite you to read this chapter.

In our efforts to improve our own training development and avoid having to ask ourselves the dreaded post-training question, "I wonder if they got it?" we developed a training design tool named *Activities/Learning Mode Assessment* (ALMA). First, the ALMA tool streamlines the instructional design process for you, allowing a style-flexing (Beebe, Mottet, & Roach, 2013) approach that aligns key learning preferences with instructional strategies. Second, the tool serves as instructional design self-assessment documentation by allowing you the ability to not only plan a training using the tool but also to go back after a session to reflect on how well the overall design and the individual instructional strategies worked to facilitate learning and meet the respective training outcomes.

In keeping with the seven best practices outlined by the National Communication Association's Training and Development Division, this chapter specifically works to help you be more intentional by using the ALMA tool to build your *instructional design* competencies. To do so, we move theory to practice by presenting this practical instrument, grounded in Kolb's (1984) Experiential Learning Theory (ELT), that meets the two key objectives of the *instructional design* best practice – the ability to recognize different learning styles and corresponding instructional methods and the ability to produce and design instructional documentation. Through this versatile tool, we hope you, our readers, will find exciting ways to support and enrich your efforts to communicate your ideas and promote meaningful learning in a variety of instructional contexts.

In order to understand how using the ALMA tool will serve you in keeping the learning process in the forefront of your training design, first it is necessary to begin with a brief synopsis of the key principles of the grounding framework, Kolb's (1984) Experiential Learning Theory. These principles will provide you with the philosophical approach to teaching and learning foundational to this chapter. We also spotlight Kolb's (1984) Experiential Learning Cycle (ELC), the key piece of ELT that guides our ALMA tool. We follow our discussion of Kolb's ELC with our description of the ALMA tool and how it can be used to intentionally include methods that align with different learning preferences. Finally, we present the implications of instructional design using the ALMA tool.

Theoretical frame

ELT (Kolb, 1984) is the supporting framework for the ELC, which guides the ALMA tool. ELT was influenced strongly by the work of John Dewey, Kurt Lewin, and Jean Piaget. Particularly concerned with the *quality* of experiences for the learner, Dewey (1938) contended that learners' experiences were not contained in the vacuum of the classroom alone; but, rather were on a continuum with experiencing the outside world. Specifically, Dewey argued that each learning experience opens up new avenues of subsequent learning: "Just as no man lives or dies to himself, so no experiences lives or dies to itself. Wholly independent of desire or intent, every experience lives on in further experiences" (Dewey, 1938, p. 27). Embracing this experiential approach, teachers (and trainers) become mentors and guides to quality experiences rather than simply conductors of rote knowledge (Dewey, 1938).

For Piaget (1977), the key to learning was in an individual's ability to accommodate and adjust their personal, existing frameworks about the world as they assimilate ongoing events and learning experiences (Kolb, 1984). The concept of deliberate connection to the learners' previous experiences is often executed through post-lesson discussion, providing learners with an opportunity for active reflection directly and immediately related to the subject(s) of the material. Learners are able to have new respective personal learning experiences while simultaneously sharing that experience with others through self-disclosure (Kolb, 1984). For Piaget (1977), there was a natural attempt at balance between the learner and adjusting their viewpoint to accommodate newly created knowledge through experiences with the world around them. The need to re-establish equilibrium makes active reflection a non-negotiable for experiential learning.

Reinforcing Dewey's (1938) contention that learning and experience are inextricably intertwined, Lewin (1951) explored the constant interplay between the learner and their environment. Lewin's (1951) interpretation of learning relies heavily on concrete experience and subsequent observation and reflection associated with that concrete experience. Every experience matters, both personal and educational, for the learner's continued growth. The concern was not only with outcomes of specific stimuli, but with what Lewin (1951) termed a "constellation of interdependent factors" which provide for inclusion of both the person and their psychological environment (p. 240). Lewin's work helped inform an examination of the learner as a unique individual and how that individual's experience and psychological makeup affect the learning process.

These three forefathers of Kolb's ELT do not compose an exhaustive history but do constitute the most major contributions. Dewey's, Piaget's, and Lewin's models attempt to examine the relationship between learning and knowledge and our understanding of the world as learners (Kolb, 1984).

Kolb's Experiential Learning Theory

Kolb (1984) describes learning as "the process whereby knowledge is created through the transformation of experience" (p. 38) and "*the* major process of human adaptation" (p. 32). In this model, experience and learning are so intertwined that they are inextricable, as experience creates knowledge along the way and knowledge begets new avenues of experiences in which to learn. Kolb (1984) describes the ELT in terms of six major principles: Learning is best viewed in terms of process and not outcome; process is grounded in experience; experience seeks to resolve conflicting modes of adaptation to the world; adaptation involves the whole person; learning involves the inner person and the outside environment working together; and learning creates knowledge. We now unpack these key principles to build our philosophical framework for the ALMA tool.

Learning is best conceived as a process, not in terms of outcome. Experiential learning stands in contrast to a behavioral approach to education in its emphasis on process. Unlike the behavioral approach, which relies on outcomes or "rewards", the experiential learning perspective most prizes the process of learning. In this context, learning is an organic, reiterative, and ongoing undertaking unmarked by timestamps and "a process whereby concepts are derived from and continuously modified by experience" (Kolb, 1984, pp. 26–27). Crucial to an experiential learning approach, then, is framing outcomes as far less valuable than the learning process itself. The learning journey becomes its own reward as knowledge is acquired along the way, not merely at the end of the experience. Consequently, failure becomes less intimidating and instead framed as an opportunity for deeper learning rather than a negative final experience for the learner in a challenging area.

Learning is a continuous process grounded in experience. Experiential learning begins to unfold as a cyclical process whereby "[k]nowledge is continuously derived from and tested out in the experiences of the learner" in this characteristic (Kolb, 1984, p. 27). It relies heavily on Dewey's emphasis on the contrast of continuity and breached expectations as essential to the learning process. This element of surprise and newness is where the learning happens, as it is not repetition of previous experience. This is commonly observed as new students enter college and begin their basic courses. Students are exposed to subjects previously unexplored, creating opportunities for choosing majors they had not previously considered.

The process of learning requires the resolution of conflicts between dialectically opposed modes of adaptation to the world. Drawing upon all three of Kolb's predecessors, this characteristic is concerned with the struggle within the learner between previous knowledge and new information about the world. The learner gets a sense with Kolb (1984) and Dewey (1938) that the goal is not resolution of these tensions, but rather, it is through continual balancing that learning is produced. As the learner alternates between new or surprising experiences and integrating those experiences into their existing body of knowledge, they can, in turn, learn from the very act of balancing those things. These dialectical tensions are not unlike Baxter's (2004) Relational Dialectics. Just like relationships benefit from the tension that causes subsequent balance between openness and closedness of partnerships, the learner stands to gain from their struggle with adjusting their viewpoint about the world around them (Baxter, 2004).

Learning is a holistic process of adaptation to the world. Learning as a holistic process of adaptation is closely related to the previous characteristic of resolving conflicting modes of adaptation, but is more concerned with how the learner adapts to their social and physical environment. It integrates aspects of the whole individual: thinking, feeling, perceiving, and behaving, helping build bridges between the classroom and real life situations as a part of a continuous process (Kolb, 1984). It views the psychological state as well as previous experiences of the learner as essential elements of learning (Dewey, 1938). This overlapping, multi-layered process is easily understood when we consider the way a child discovers new information about the world around her through touch, smell, taste, and sight, even as she grows and develops the motor skills for further discovery. Even as the baby crawls, she pulls up on furniture to explore, but the crawling and climbing build muscle memory and serve as a springboard for learning to walk.

Learning involves transactions between the person and the environment. A transactional environment incorporates the learner's internal and external environment and their relationship to each. Kolb expresses a strong preference for the word "transaction" over "interaction" as a more powerful and dimensional descriptor of the process. Interaction evokes a simple model – one entity affects one other entity in a back-and-forth, while a transaction can better encompass the synergy of all influencing factors. Some of those factors might be the psychology of the learners, the environment surrounding them, the time frame of that transaction, etc. Transaction also evokes the image of a financial or barter arrangement. In such an arrangement, parties might leave a transaction with something of even greater value to them than what they brought to that transaction.

Learning is the process of creating knowledge. Situating knowledge as the byproduct of the process makes knowledge not the destination, but the journey. Again, outcomes are not the objective, but are the natural result of experiential learning. Dewey's ideas come to the fore in this aspect as well since learning is far from being limited to the classroom experience. In fact, in-class, organized learning experiences and out-of-class, less organized or unplanned experiences feed one another as a part of the holistic learning cycle (Kolb, 1984).

Again, this more organic, self-directed learning is observable in a small child. A pre-schooler, for example, may be learning her colors during organized class time, but may also be discovering those colors with each new bird or butterfly she observes outdoors during recess or at home. Often, flashcards created for small children rely on images with which they are already familiar from daily play and observation to introduce newer concepts.

Kolb's Experiential Learning Cycle

Kolb's (1984) six characteristics are the philosophical framework that inform the four-stage Experiential Learning Cycle (ELC) (see Figure 22.1) that guides our ALMA tool. Those four stages are *Concrete Experience*, *Reflective Observation*, *Abstract Conceptualization*, and *Active Experimentation*.

Beginning at the top of the cycle, there is *Concrete Experience* (CE); this represents the present, the here and now, what's actually happening. *Reflective Observation* (RO) is the thinking, watching, and processing mode. The learner is sorting through previous experience, finding a way to accommodate new ideas, which may bring up conflicted

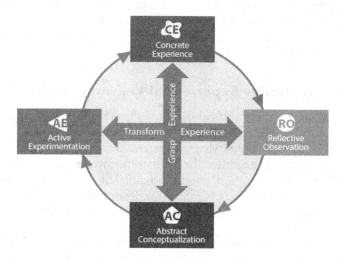

Figure 22.1 Kolb & Kolb's (2013) Experiential Learning Cycle (ELC).

feelings. *Abstract Conceptualization* (AC) is the consideration of new applications for practical action with respect to a learner's current experience, such as their job or personal relationship, to the material being learned (Frontczak, 1998; Kolb & Kolb, 2005). The fourth element is *Active Experimentation* (AE). This is the active doing phase of the cycle. This is a phase where the learner may feel particularly uncertain or uncomfortable because they are taking observable steps away from their previous ideas and beliefs (Kolb, 1984). As each stage of the ELC is addressed, a spiral of learning is created:

> When a concrete experience is enriched by reflection, given meaning by thinking, and transformed by action, the new experience created becomes richer, broader, and deeper. Further iterations of the cycle continue the exploration and transfer of experience in other contexts.
>
> (Passarelli & Kolb, 2011, p. 77)

The stages of learning in Kolb's ELC are not necessarily sequential. For example, a learner may enter into the cycle from any of the stages, but the cycle needs to be completed for learning to be most effective. The stages may overlap; for example, in response to a *Concrete Experience* such as a lecture, you may have a learner who leaps to *Abstract Conceptualization*, that is, they may already be thinking of ways in which the new information can be extended, built on, or a unique application. Some of your participants may absorb new knowledge through feelings, thinking, and observation at the same time. Will you know that? You may not, but when you get questions that seem out of left field, you might get a sense about where that individual is on the cycle.

Kolb's ELC is a dynamic illustration of an experiential learning process. Inherent in that process is the active participation of the learners and the attendant necessity for respect of the participant's ability to be responsible for her own learning. If you are fully aware of the practical applications of the stages of learning represented in the ELC, the learning space you create will naturally foster the safety and shared interaction necessary to support learning. Another way to view the ELC is as a blueprint or map for learning. Each stage/mode can be connected to specific activities, which is purposeful, and if you, as the facilitator, offer a variety of activities, you are acknowledging learning style preferences, which is respectful and flexible.

Instructional design and Kolb's Experiential Learning Cycle

Learning styles are "the unique ways that individuals spiral through the learning cycle based on their preference for the four different learning modes – CE, RO, AC, and AE" (Kolb & Kolb, 2009b, p. 314). Nine learning style preferences address the individual and unique ways in which human beings negotiate their environments and the development of new knowledge: Experiencing (CE), Reflection (RO), Thinking (AC), Acting (AE), Diverging (CE and RO), Assimilating (AC and RO), Converging (AC and AE), Accommodating (CE and AE), and Balancing (CE, RO, AC, and AE) (Kolb & Kolb, 2009a; see Figure 22.1).

Do you need to know your students' learning preferences? While it might be very helpful for you to understand each participant's preferred learning style, time constraints often make tailoring a training in such a way impossible; and, given the inherent need for tension in learning, arguably detrimental (Kolb, 1984). However, by incorporating the principles you are learning here and using the ALMA tool to guide your training design, it is possible to include all trainees' learning preferences, giving each a moment of comfort and familiarity during the learning process, through the intentional inclusion of a variety of instructional strategies that align with each preference stage of the ELC.

Activities/Learning Mode Assessment tool (ALMA)

We hope by now you understand how valuable we think Kolb's ELC can be to you during the instructional design phase of building a training. We believe it is important that you, as trainers, are intentional in your inclusion of the ELC, in order to best facilitate meaningful learning. To that end, choosing instructional methods that not only facilitate the achievement of your intended learning outcomes, but also ensure that each stage of the ELC is incorporated into your participants' training experience is key. To better help you develop training plans grounded in the ELC, we come now to the ALMA.

The ALMA tool was first developed and piloted to help professional trainers in a southern Early Childhood Mental Health Consultation program, Project Play. The organization's administrators were seeking an observational assessment of Project Play trainings, and we found that by tracking the activities selected and matching them to the ELC learning preferences, an effective assessment could be completed. Initially, the assessment was created to determine if the Project Play trainers included only some, or all four of the learning stages of Kolb's ELC. In an effort to streamline the instructional design process as well as provide guidance for the important practice of trainer self-reflection, the tool has since been adapted and modified for general training application. The ALMA tool contains three parts, Section 1: Aligning Instructional Activities, Section 2: ELC Inclusion and Quality, and Section 3: ELC Reflection (see Appendix A).

Section 1: Aligning Instructional Activities. Selecting appropriate and meaningful instructional activities is key to the success of any training, regardless of template design. However, it is even more so when using the ELC as an instructional template. To that end, you will want to be particularly mindful of how each activity selected and integrated facilitates a participant's movement through Kolb's (1984) ELC. Since Kolb (1984) asserts that any instructional design can be seen as "having degrees of orientation toward each of the four learning modes" (p.197), the instructional activities that you choose should be selected with the intent of best addressing each stage of the learning cycle through the inclusion of activities that align with each of the four learning preferences. A list of aligned instructional activities helps identify and connect instructional methods with the four ELC modes (see Table 22.1).

Table 22.1 ELC preferences and corresponding instructional activities (Kolb & Kolb, 2009a)

Learning Preference	Abilities	Instructional Activities	Trainee Experience
Diverging (CE/RO)	Considers experiences from many perspectives; likes to gather information and enjoys working in a group; Brainstorming sessions	teamwork; small groups; brainstorming sessions; personalized feedback; listening with an open mind, e.g. facilitated discussion	Feeling/ Watching
Assimilating (RO/AC)	Understands a wide range of information and the ability to put it in concise, logical form; enjoys abstract concepts	Reading; lectures; analysis and reflective activity, e.g. individual problem solving tasks; research based activities; activity instructions	Watching/ Thinking
Converging (AC/AE)	Best at finding practical uses for ideas & theories; problem solving; decision making; interested in technical tasks and problems	Experiment with new ideas; simulations and practical applications, e.g. role-plays; case studies from the real world	Thinking/ Doing
Accommodating (AE/CE)	Hands- experience; relies more on gut instinct Than on technical analysis; seeks information from people rather than research or analysis; prefers to work with other people to complete assignments	Groups; teams; role plays; experimenting, e.g. improvisational activities	Doing/ Feeling

Section 2: ELC Inclusion and Quality. Since the quality of learning is often only as powerful as the learning space created (Kolb & Kolb, 2005), how you manage or facilitate the selected instructional methods aligned with Kolb's (1984) ELC are just as important. While not always possible, recording your training and reflecting on the effectiveness of how the activity was integrated and facilitated (e.g. trainer behaviors and communication strategies) is often the best tool for assessing how well you have integrated the ELC in a training situation. Specifically, the ALMA tool uses a Likert-type scale of 1 to 4 (1 being weak, 2 being adequate, 3 being strong, and 4 being very strong) to assess the strength of individual instructional strategies to facilitate learning, the overall ELC competency strength of each stage, and the overall ELC inclusion competency.

For example, when assessing an individual instructional strategy, a 4 (very strong) could be assigned if the strategy worked in the training moment to engage learners in meaningful and complex ways (see Table 22.2.) Conversely, a strategy could be assessed as a 2 (adequate) if it met the objective, but participants needed significant amount of motivation or probing to engage. In terms of assessing each learning preference (e.g. diverging, assimilating, converging, and accommodating), you would take into consideration both the number (variety) of strategies used to help facilitate that particular part of the ELC as well as the strength of those strategies. Finally, a training ELC inclusion competency may be rated 1 (weak) if the training simply offers only one activity (stage 4/1) regardless of strength. A 2 (adequate) level may be given if the training offers activities that are related to the topic and have a purpose for learning, for example, a well ordered lecture (stage 2) followed by a group discussion (stage 1). A training may be rated a 3 (strong) if, for example the training included a lecture (stage 2), followed by small group (stage 1) discussion, followed by a larger transfer discussion (stage 3). Finally, a 4 (very strong) might describe a training that offers a lecture (stage 2), followed by a small group activity (stage 4) that asks the trainees to decide something related to problems posed (stage 3) in the lecture, which is then followed by a full de-briefing of the trainee experience (stage 1), choices, and speculations about the targeted problem (stage 3).

The use of the ratings is not meant to be extra work; but, instead, offer a way to empower you to engage in a guided, concrete self-assessment on your own perceived training effectiveness. It is in your best interest to be as objective as possible when self-assessing the use of instructional strategies, inclusion of each learning preference stage, as well as the overall ELC inclusion competency. Therefore, use of video and/or reflective journaling can help provide you with the necessary data to substantiate each respective self-assigned assessment.

Finally, in keeping with our overall goal of developing a tool that supports ELC learning, we added a third section for post-training reflection.

Section 3: ELC Reflection. This provides a space, structured after the EDIT (Experience, Describe, Infer, and Transfer) process (Beebe et al., 2013), for you to unpack your own training experience and the self-assessment in order to identify what worked or needs work for subsequent trainings. The *experience* step of the EDIT process is the activity itself. In this case, it is the actual training event. However, this could also be any instructional strategy used in the training. The second step, *describe*, asks learners (in the case of post- training reflection, the trainer) to use concrete language to paint a picture of their experience—what they saw, what they heard, what they felt, etc. The third step, *infer*, encourages you the trainer/learner to make direct connections between the experience and the instructional material being covered. The final step, *transfer*, pushes us as trainer/learners to consider ways we can apply and adapt those connections outside the immediate learning situation to a variety of contexts.

By combining these three sections – activities connected with the learning modes followed by a ratings plan for quality of trainer/participant engagement and then reflection—the assessment is intended to use Kolb's multi-layered ELC components of the experiential learning process to describe and hopefully improve the effectiveness of a professional training program. Specifically, using the ALMA offers you a framework that can facilitate alignment with the cycle, keeping a learner-centered training design in the forefront of your training plans. Kolb, Kolb, Passarelli, and Sharma (2014) assert, "Learning style is not a fixed personality trait, but more like a habit of learning shaped by experience and choices- that can be modified and changed" (p.215). The focus on and knowledge of the connection between preferred learning tasks and the stages of learning can offer you the means to increase the likelihood of more engaged and productively challenged learners. In the following section, we offer an example of a training plan that was assessed using the ALMA tool.

Example application of the ALMA tool

In the following paragraphs we apply the ALMA tool to our friend Marian's communication training on building civil discussion skills. What we find valuable about this particular example is that it emphasizes the importance of discussion as a stand-alone communication skill but also as a foundational vehicle for facilitating experiential learning. Additionally valuable is the illustration of how a relatively short training, through the use of ELC as an instructional design template, can provide powerful, useful communication skill-building for learners. Using the ALMA tool, we first analyze the civil discourse training and then offer Marian's self-assessment reflection.

Training design analysis. In this particular civil discourse training, Marian's aim was to help trainees strengthen the following positive communication skills: asking, disclosing, and listening in order to be able to actively and peacefully engage on difficult topics. Marian designed a training plan (see Appendix B) with the ELC in mind but did not apply the tool until after the training was facilitated. This situation provided an excellent opportunity to test the ALMA for its usefulness as an analytical and reflective guide.

Beginning with analysis, Marian opened the training by engaging the *accommodating* preference, which involves active experimentation and concrete experience (see Table 22.2). To do so, Marian used a warm-up activity, Human Bingo, designed to lightheartedly engage the participants – both to make them feel more comfortable with unfamiliar fellow participants as well as introduce them to the material. During Human Bingo, Marian invited participants to ask questions to discover not-so-easy-to-detect qualities or experiences of their fellow participants. The game introduced the skills of asking, listening, and disclosing that would be the focus of the training in a way that would be fun for participants as well as allow them to immediately dive into experiencing the material to be covered.

Table 22.2 Activity alignment application

Stage 4 Accommodating (AE/CE)	Stage 1 Diverging (CE/RO)
X Game: Human Bingo _____ Role-play _____ Skit _____ Group work X Other activity: Heard, Seen, Respected	_____ Video examples X Participant examples/stories relevant to topic _____ Facilitated discussion comparing and contrasting new concepts with past experiences _____ Guided journal reflections X Debriefing Stage 3 & Stage 4 activities (e.g. EDIT)
Stage 3 Converging (AC/AE)	**Stage 2 Assimilating (RO/AC)**
_____ Simulation _____ Case analysis _____ Practical application activity _____ Problem-solving task X Facilitated discussion focusing on learning transfer/direct application	X Ordered lecture X Definitions of concepts X Clear explanations of concepts X PowerPoint/Prezi X Opportunity for note-taking X Direct questions X Clear activity instructions

Instructional strategies related to the preferences of *diverging*, which involve concrete experience and reflective observation, and *assimilating*, which involves concrete reflective observation and abstract conceptualization, follow the lecture/discussion portion of the training (see Table 22.2). In this section, Marian used direct questions (*assimilating*) to ask participants to share their previous experiences (*diverging*) with being heard. Responses transitioned into Marian explaining definitions (*assimilating*) of the asking, disclosing, and listening concepts from the Model of Positive Communication (Mirivel, 2014) through the support of a PowerPoint presentation, providing a visual for the presented concepts (*assimilating*).

Marian invited participants to further engage in the *assimilating* and *accommodating* preferences of Kolb's (1984) ELC through the *Heard, Seen, & Respected* (McCandless & Lipanowicz, n.d.) activity designed to help learners practice the active listening skills discussed during the lecture/discussion portion of the training (see Table 22.2). For this activity, Marian asked participants to rotate through three different roles. One would interview another about a time in their life when they felt heard, seen, and respected. The interviewer was given a list of open-ended questions on a worksheet that he could use to guide the conversation. The third person in the group would serve as an observer and give the other two members of the group feedback on their engagement of the skills discussed in the lecture/discussion portion on active listening behaviors. The design of the activity provided participants the opportunity to enact the skills presented (*accommodating*) as well as observe and analyze the skills enacted by others (*assimilating*), thus achieving the learning objective of demonstrating active listening skills. The interaction of the activity itself also promoted the opportunity for participants to have fun engaging with one another for a deeper learning experience (Kolb, 1984).

Following the major activity portion, Marian facilitated a reflective discussion using the EDIT (Experience, Describe, Infer, and Transfer) method (see Appendix B), integrating the *diverging* and *converging* learning preferences. Marian asked debrief questions such as,

- How did it feel to tell your story?
- How about listening to another's story?
- What are some good ways to begin open-ended questions that helped you connect with the others in your group?
- How did it feel to focus on open-ended questions only?
- How did it feel giving feedback to others? Receiving immediate feedback?

focused on understanding the learners' experiences during the training (*diverging*). Marian used questions such as,

- How did paraphrasing affect the way you listened to others' stories?
- How might paraphrasing help in engaging in classroom discussions?
- Asking questions?

in order to assess to what extent participants could relate the experiential activities to the intended concepts and skills as well as the immediate context (workshop). Additionally, Marian asked the following debrief questions to invite participants to consider ways in which the learning could transfer the concepts outside the immediate classroom context (*converging*):

- How might using these types of questions help if you're discussing a sensitive topic?
- How might something we discussed today help you outside of this workshop?

Trainer self-assessment. After completing the ELC Inclusion and Quality chart and reflecting on the training, Marian identified two learning preference areas, diverging and assimilating, that she would strengthen if given the opportunity to facilitate the training again. Take a look at Table 22.2. You can see that Marian's training plan appears to include all four learning preferences. However, if you look at Table 22.3, you can see that Marian's self-assessment included 2s and even a 1 in those areas. Being able to compare the tables shows us that the problem is not with activity inclusion, but instead that Marian felt she could have managed the activities more successfully in those preference areas.

First, Marian decided she would find more opportunities to self-disclose (*diverging*) throughout the workshop. Specifically, she felt that in asking disclosure of her participants it is important for her to model more intentionally the kind of disclosure she's encouraging. Brookfield (2006) discusses this modeling as a form of instructor authenticity, which is crucial for creating an inviting space in the classroom for authentic discussion to follow. Marian also acknowledged that next time she would fill out the participant worksheet herself in order to demonstrate more directly the instructions for the activity (*assimilating*). Second, she found during the workshop she asked more questions regarding the role of observer in the *Heard, Seen, & Respected* (McCandless & Lipmanowicz, n.d.) activity than were included in her training plan. Marian concluded that it would be helpful to include a more robust list of observer questions in her formal debrief (*diverging*) so as to be better prepared during that segment of the training (see Appendix B). Like Marian, how might you use the ALMA tool to help you reflect more deeply on the strengths and weaknesses of your instructional strategy facilitation?

Table 22.3 ELC inclusion and quality

Overall ELC inclusion and quality training competency score: 3.1

Stage 4 Accommodating (AE/CE)	Stage 1 Diverging (CE/RO)
3 Game: Human Bingo 4 Other activity: Heard, Seen, Respected	2 Participant examples/stories relevant to topic 2 Debriefing Stage 3 & Stage 4 activities (e.g. EDIT)
3.5 Average Stage 4 Score	2 Average Stage 1 Score

Stage 3 Converging (AC/AE)	Stage 2 Assimilating (RO/AC)
4 Facilitated discussion focusing on learning transfer/direct application	4 Ordered lecture 3 Definitions of concepts 4 Clear explanations of concepts 4 PowerPoint/Prezi 2 Opportunity for note-taking 2 Direct questions 1 Clear activity instructions
4 Average Stage 3 Score	2.9 Average Stage 2 Score

Though Marian did not use the ALMA to design the training, she did intentionally work to integrate all four stages of the ELC. Through the use of the ALMA, she was able to visualize how well her intention was met by mapping each instructional strategy to the respective learning stages. The process of mapping instructional strategies provided not only excellent documentation of Marian's instructional design, as seen in Table 22.2, it also provided Marian with a clear visual of how well she integrated the ELC into her training, as seen in Table 22.3.

Implications

In the following section we offer key takeaways from the application of Kolb's (1984) Experiential Learning Cycle as a training instructional template. Specifically, we focus on the depth of learning the ELC works to facilitate and the flexibility of using the ELC as a training template.

First, trainings grounded in the ELC work to increase the likelihood of meaningful learning. When an individual with her unique experiences and beliefs confronts new ideas in a learning situation tension naturally occurs as the learner wrestles with letting go of old ways of knowing. This tension can be both internal as well as external. Passarelli and Kolb (2011) offer this description, "in the process of learning one is called on to move back and forth between opposing modes of reflection and action, and feeling and thinking" (p. 72). It is the way the learner resolves this tension that determines how much or what she learns (Kolb, 1984).

Through embracing the ELC, it is possible to promote tolerance for uncertainty and unique solutions, creating a learning space that values mistakes as well as successes, leading to the development of trust. As well-meaning teachers and trainers we all want to feel that we can engender the kind of trust in our learners that promotes the psychological safety needed to grapple with the dialectical tensions that exist between reflection and action, or between the feeling and thinking required for knowledge creation. However, experiential learning also places the focus on the faith and trust that you have in a participant's intrinsic desire and ability to learn, and to self-identify what she needs to learn in a given moment.

This belief and trust that human beings, i.e. students or participants, want to learn and are capable of taking responsibility for their own individual and personal learning process necessitates a profound shift in our attitude as teachers. The following quote from Carl Rogers (1969) succinctly illustrates this point,

> If I distrust the human being then I must cram him full of information of my own choosing, lest he go on his mistaken way. But if I trust the capacity of the human individual for developing his own potentiality, then I can provide him with many opportunities and permit him to choose his own way and his own direction in learning.
>
> (p.114)

The activities-learning mode assessment offers us a way to map these "many opportunities" for learning around Kolb's cycle, effectively grounded in ELT.

Our intentional focus on selecting activities that align with each of Kolb's learning preferences moves participants away from their habitual approach to learning tasks and encourages development of other learning preferences (Kolb et al., 2014). When participants are stretched and flexing across learning preferences they are not only more likely to retain the training content (Kahl & Venette, 2010) but they are also developing their ability to learn in a variety of contexts (Kolb & Kolb, 2009b).

Not only can intentional use of the ELC deepen learning, the use of the ELC as an instructional template translates well into a variety of contexts. In this chapter we shared the ALMA, a tool that was initially developed as an observational assessment to rate the trainings offered to Project Play's Early Childhood mental health consultants, whose goal is to support positive teacher/child interactions in at-risk preschool environments. We then offered Marian's example of using the ALMA to analyze and assess her intentional inclusion of the ELC as a template to build a training on civil discourse in a college-level communication class. Additionally, the ALMA has been introduced to a group of training and development (TD) experts at a southern medical university and research hospital, seeking to include ELC into their work. The response to the assessment was incredibly positive, with the TD experts expressing appreciation for the ease of using the tool to both design as well as assess their upcoming and already facilitated trainings and interventions. They also commented on the importance of being able to explain and document the theoretical grounding for their instructional strategy choices. These are just a few examples of the usefulness of the ELC as an instructional template. Regardless of the expert knowledge to be imparted or the context or reason for learning, facilitating learning can be structured successfully and easily with the ALMA tool.

The flexibility of when and how we choose to incorporate each preference into the learning situation makes the ELC an ideal template for instructional design. Since the

ELC is prescriptive only in the acknowledgment and inclusion of all learning preferences through specific types of training activities, the operationalization of the ELC through the ALMA tool offered in this chapter allows for high levels of individual creativity while still grounding that creativity in strong learning theory. For this reason, you, the instructional designer, are able to select the activities from each preference that best align with any needs assessment data as well as the intended learning outcomes. As long as each preference is addressed with an intentional inclusion of structured reflection (diverging), participants will not only be more active in their own learning, they are, consequently, more likely to meet the learning outcomes. Additionally, through the intentional use of the ELC, as well as the tools offered in this chapter, you are better able to reflect on the function and effectiveness of instructional strategies to better facilitate experiential learning.

Conclusion

Grounded in six principles that emphasize learning as an experiential process focused on resolving adaptation tensions (discomfort) between a learner and her environment through guided reflection, ELT can be operationalized through the Experiential Learning Cycle for a training framework that provides each learner their preferred way of learning (learning style), while at the same time creating the necessary discomfort for meaningful learning. The ELC invites learners to work through four specific stages when learning new knowledge and skills: concrete experience (CE), reflective observation (RO), abstract conceptualization (AC), and active experimentation (AE).

In this chapter we moved theory to praxis by providing a concrete explanation of the ELC as a user-friendly template for instructional design. Our operationalization of the ELC through the ALMA tool aligns specific instructional methods with each of the four learning preferences, simplifying not only the design process but also the self-assessment of an experiential learning training.

Using the ELC as a framework not only streamlines the instructional design process, it also allows you a style-flexing approach that can work in a variety of training/learning situations (Beebe et al., 2013). By intentionally including instructional activities that align with all four ELC preferences, learners are ensured moments of learning comfort when their preference is addressed; but, with the inclusion of all four learning preferences, they are also provided the discomfort of the other less favored learning modes, creating an experience necessary for meaningful, deep learning. Given all that we have covered, how will you use the Experiential Learning Cycle in your trainings to connect with your participants, to push them outside of their comfort zones in the interest of learning, and to increase your confidence that they have, indeed, gotten it?

References

Baxter, L. (2004). A tale of two voices: Relational dialectics theory. *The Journal of Family Communication, 4*(3&4), 181–192.

Beebe, S. A., Mottet, T. P., & Roach, K. D. (2013). *Training and development: Communicating for success* (2nd ed.). Upper Saddle River, NJ: Pearson.

Brookfield, S. D. (2006). The skillful teacher: On technique, trust and responsiveness in the classroom (2nd ed.). San Francisco, CA: Jossey-Bass.

Davenport University. (2010). Experiential learning, Kolb's Cycle Image. Retrieved May 30, 2017 from http://nonprofit.davenport.edu/explearning/model.html

Dewey, J. (1938). *Experience and education*. New York, NY: Touchstone.

Frontczak, N. T. (1998). A paradigm for the selection, use and development or experiential learning activities in marketing education. *Marketing Education Review, 8*(3), 25–33.

Kahl, D. H., & Venette, S. (2010). To lecture or let go: A comparative analysis of student speech outlines. *Communication Teacher, 24*(3), 178–186.

Kolb, A. Y., & Kolb, D. A. (2009a). Experiential learning theory: A dynamic, holistic approach to management learning, education and development. In S. J. Armstrong & C. V. Fukami (eds.), *The Sage handbook of management learning, education and development* (pp. 42–68). Thousand Oaks, CA: Sage Publications Inc.

Kolb, A. Y., & Kolb, D. A. (2009b). The learning way: Meta-cognitive aspects of experiential learning. *Simulation & Gaming, 40*(3), 297–327. doi: 10.1177/1046878108325713

Kolb, A. Y., & Kolb, D. A. (2013). *The experiential learning style inventory-version 4.0; A comprehensive guide to the theory, psychometrics, research on validity and educational approaches.* Experience Based Learning Systems, Inc.

Kolb, A. Y., Kolb D. A., Passarelli, A., & Sharma, G. (2014). On becoming an experiential educator: The educator role profile. *Simulation and Gaming, 45*(2), 204–234.

Kolb, D. A., (1984). Experiential learning: Experience as the source of learning and development. Englewood Cliffs, NJ: Prentice Hall.

Kolb, D. A., & Kolb, A. Y. (2005). Learning styles and learning spaces: Enhancing experiential learning. *Academy of Management Learning & Education, 4*(2), 193–212.

Lewin, K. (1951). Field theory in social science: Selected theoretical papers. New York, NY: Harper & Row.

McCandless, K., & Lipmanowicz, H. (n.d.). *Liberating structures: Including and unleashing everyone.* Retrieved June 28, 2017 from http://www.liberatingstructures.com/

Mirivel, J. C. (2014). The art of positive communication: Theory and practice. New York, NY: Peter Lang.

Passarelli, A. M., & Kolb, D. (2011). The learning way: Learning from experience as the path to lifelong learning and development. In M. London (ed.), *The Oxford handbook of lifelong learning* (pp. 70–90). Oxford, UK: Oxford University Press.

Piaget, J. (1977). *The development of thought*. New York, NY: Viking Penguin.

Rogers, C. R. (1969). *Freedom to learn*. Columbus, OH: Merrill Publishing Company.

Spiro, H. M. (1993). *Empathy and the practice of medicine: Beyond pills and the scalpel* (pp. 7–14). New Haven, CT: Yale University Press.

Weger, H., Castle, G., Paro, S., & Emmett, M., (2007). Active listening in peer interviews: The influence of paraphrasing on perceived understanding, conversational satisfaction, and social attractiveness. Unpublished conference paper. National Communication Association.

Weger, H., Castle, G., & Emmett M. (2010). Active listening in peer interviews: The influence of message paraphrasing on perceptions of listening skill. *The International Journal of Listening, 24*, 34–49.

Appendix A

Experiential Learning Cycle instructional design: Activities/ Learning Mode Assessment tool (ALMA)

Instructions: The goal of this tool is to identify to what extent a training aligns with the four learning modes of Kolb's (1984) Experiential Learning Cycle (ELC). Using the training plan, first check for instructional activity alignment with each of the four learning modes/preferences. Second, using the training video (if possible) or reflection, assess how well each instructional strategy supported the learning modes. Third, use the reflection questions to help you process how well the training integrated the ELC stages.

Section 1: Aligning Instructional Activities

Using the table below, identify the instructional strategies in your drafted training plan. If you do not see a listed activity do not place any mark beside it. Ideally, there should be, at minimum, one instructional strategy marked per stage to ensure the ELC is being fully integrated at least once during the training.

Stage 4 Accommodating (AE/CE)	Stage 1 Diverging (CE/RO)
_____ Game _____ Role-play _____ Skit _____ Group work _____ Other activity _____	_____ Video examples _____ Participant examples/stories relevant to topic _____ Facilitated discussion comparing and contrasting new concepts with past experiences _____ Guided journal reflections _____ Debriefing Stage 3 & Stage 4 activities (e.g. EDIT)*
Stage 3 Converging (AC/AE)	**Stage 2 Assimilating (RO/AC)**
_____ Simulation _____ Case analysis _____ Practical application activity _____ Problem-solving task _____ Facilitated discussion focusing on learning transfer/direct application	_____ Ordered lecture _____ Definitions of concepts _____ Clear explanations of concepts _____ PowerPoint/Prezi _____ Opportunity for note-taking _____ Direct questions _____ Clear activity instructions

*MUST be included regardless of other Stage 1 strategies.

Section 2: ELC Inclusion and Quality

Ideally, watch the video of the training (or, at least take a few minutes to journal about the strengths and weaknesses of the training). Using the worksheet below, identify and assess how the included instructional strategies supported and guided trainees around the ELC. If a strategy was not included, do not assess it. Additionally, just because a strategy might have been included does not mean that it worked successfully to support participant learning. The stages are meant to rate levels of your interactive behaviors that promote participants' movement through all stages of learning.

Use the following scale to evaluate A) the quality of the instructional strategy worked to facilitate learning, B) the overall successful inclusion of each stage, and C) the overall ELC training competency:

1 weak   2 adequate   3 strong   4 very strong

Overall ELC inclusion and quality training competency score: _____

Stage 4 Accommodating (AE/CE)	Stage 1 Diverging (CE/RO)
_____ Game _____ Role-play _____ Skit _____ Group work _____ Other activity _____	_____ Video examples _____ Participant examples/stories relevant to topic _____ Facilitated discussion comparing and contrasting new concepts with past experiences _____ Guided journal reflections _____ Debriefing Stage 3 & Stage 4 activities (e.g. EDIT)*
_____ Average Stage 4 Score	_____ Average Stage 1 Score
Stage 3 Converging (AC/AE)	**Stage 2 Assimilating (RO/AC)**
_____ Simulation _____ Case analysis _____ Practical application activity _____ Problem-solving task _____ Facilitated discussion focusing on learning transfer/direct application	_____ Ordered lecture _____ Definitions of concepts _____ Clear explanations of concepts _____ PowerPoint/Prezi _____ Opportunity for note-taking _____ Direct questions _____ Clear activity instructions
_____ Average Stage 3 Score	_____ Average Stage 2 Score

Section 3: ELC Reflection

After reviewing your work in Section 1 and Section 2, provide responses to the following reflection prompts to help you use this analysis for future trainings.

1. Which instructional strategies were particularly successful in the training? What, specifically, made them successful for this topic and this group?

_____

2. Which instructional strategies were not as successful? Based on the training experience, why might this be?

_____

3. Looking holistically, how well was each ELC stage integrated into the training?

_____

4. Which stages, if any, need more development if this training were offered again? Why?

_____

5. What specific steps can you take, based on this analysis, to strengthen the ELC design of your future trainings?

_____

6. What specific steps can you take, based on this analysis, to strengthen your facilitation and execution of the ELC in your future trainings?

_____

NOTES:

Appendix B

"Heard, Seen, & Respected": An Active Listening Activity
50 minutes/33 participants/laptop projection
(http://www.liberatingstructures.com/19-heard-seen-respected-hsr/)

Learning Objective 1: Students will, by the end of the workshop, have discussed and practiced asking open-ended questions of others as a component of active listening through a reflection activity and group discussion.

LO2: Students will, by the end of the workshop, discussed and practiced paraphrasing as a component of active listening through a reflection activity and group discussion.

INTRO (5 min game; 2 min rest--7 min total)

I   Attention getter/warm-up: Human Bingo (students warm up/practice asking and answering questions to "win") Accommodating http://www.flandersfamily.info/web/ice-breaker-bingo-free-printable/; Word Bingo template

II   Listener Relevance Link: We have all had times in which we felt we really needed or wanted to be heard, but for whatever reason, we were unable to accomplish that in an interaction. Based on the survey, many of you have some hesitation about participating in class discussion, perhaps based on experiences when it didn't go so well.

III Speaker Credibility: (*Based on your experience and/or formal education; varies by speaker*)

IV   Thesis: Today we're going to discuss and practice the skill of active listening through asking open-ended questions and paraphrasing others' answers.

V   Preview: To do that, we'll talk a bit about the active listening practices of open-ended questions and paraphrasing, we'll have a chance to practice them in groups, then we'll unpack everything together.

Transition: Now that I've given you a bit of an overview of what's happening today, let's discuss Asking as a positive communication behavior in classroom discussions.

I   Active listening Discussion (8 min)
(Listening transcends separateness, Mirivel, 2014, Ch. 7) (Asking to Discover the Unknown) (Mirivel, 2014, Ch. 3)

   a Necessary Qualities for Listening Converging

      1 Openness—ability to welcome new ideas, perspective; willingness to change
         "Listening openly is about letting people in." (p. 122)
      2 Unconditional positive regard—look at someone with affirmation and without conditions
      3 Empathy—"the feeling that 'I might be you' or 'I am you'" (Spiro, 1993); or envisioning the world of another person (Mirivel, 2014)
      4 Genuineness and authenticity—seeming vs. being; tending to act in incongruence—striving for congruence through honest moments of dialogue; "our best communication comes from our core" (p. 128)

b Asking Open-Ended Questions—What do you think it means? Assimilating

1 Avoid:
   a Strictly Yes/No
   b Closed (questions leading to a specific answer)
   c Did you?
   d Requests for an account (accusatory)

2 Do:
   a Be interested in others
   b Have a willingness to discover
   c Bring a sense of curiosity
   d Pause and think about the wording: Think like a reporter—Begin
      with these words for open-ended questions:
      1 How
      2 Tell me about
      3 Why/do you know why...?
      4 What/how do you feel...?

Transition: Since we've talked about the kinds of questions to ask, why don't we discuss listening to the answers to those questions?

c Paraphrasing Converging
   (Weger, H., Castle, G., Paro, S., & Emmett, M. (2007). Active listening in
   peer interviews: The influence of paraphrasing on perceived understanding,
   conversational satisfaction, and social attractiveness. *Conference Papers—
   National Communication Association.* pp. 1–27.)
   (Weger, H., Castle, G., & Emmett M. (2010). Active listening in peer
   interviews: The influence of message paraphrasing on perceptions of
   listening skill. *The International Journal of Listening, 24,* 34–49.)

   1 "Identified as an important behavior because it demonstrates that the lis-
      tener has understood what the speaker is trying to communicate, thereby,
      confirming the speaker's experience as valid and significant" (2007, p. 8).
   2 Makes the speaker feel more understood and listener more likeable (We-
      ger et al., 2007).
   3 "Paraphrasing a speaker's message is one element common to all treat-
      ments of active listening" (2010, p. 39).
   4 Steps of paraphrasing (Weger et al., 2010).
      a Reflect on speaker's words
      b Repeat back to them in your own: "I heard you say that..." "So, I
         understand (this) happened and you felt (this)."
      c Questions for clarification

II Activity: Heard, Seen, Respected (15min)
    (worksheet with questions and directions) Accommodating/Diverging
    (http://www.liberatingstructures.com/19-heard-seen-respected-hsr/)

A Divide into threes.

B Discuss with partner a time when you really felt you were heard, seen, or respected. A third person will act as an observer and give feedback to the two asking and listening immediately following their exchange (feedback worksheet).

C Avoid interruptions unless it's to encourage the story, like "What happened next?" or "What else?"

D When one partner finishes their story, the other partner should practice paraphrasing it back to them in their own words. "I heard you say that..." "So, I understand (this) happened and you felt (this)."

E Now, allow another team member to tell their story.

F Activity Debrief (4 min)
(Have students shout answers; volunteer write answers on the board):
Diverging/Converging
1 What are some things to avoid when asking questions?
2 What are some of the "dos" of asking questions?
3 What are some important qualities for a listener to have? Why might these be helpful?
4 What are the steps of paraphrasing we covered?
5 What are some benefits to paraphrasing?

III Debrief (10 min) Diverging/Assimilating

A How did it feel to tell your story?
B How about listening to another's story?
C What are some good ways to begin open-ended questions that helped you connect with the others in your group?
D How did it feel to focus on open-ended questions only?
E How did paraphrasing affect the way you listened to others' stories?
F How did it feel giving feedback to others? Receiving immediate feedback?
G How might paraphrasing help in engaging in classroom discussions? Asking questions?
H How might using these types of questions help if you're discussing a sensitive topic?
I How might something we discussed today help you outside of class?

Conclusion (2 min) Assimilating

I Restate thesis
II Review—Asking and listening, open-ended questions and paraphrasing, activity, unpacking
III Clincher: I hope today you've had the opportunity to feel heard, seen, and respected, at least for a little while ... may you take what we've done today to give others that opportunity as well.

Best practice 7

Demonstrate communication proficiency

- Executable communication proficiencies including, but not necessarily limited to presentations skills, interpersonal skills, organizational culture, and group techniques

Best Practice 7 – Demonstrate Communication Proficiency, requires that an effective communication coach, consultant, trainer, teacher (CCCTTs) be able to exhibit a level of skill in the delivery of the various techniques and enhancements being proposed. Whichever communication techniques are being delivered clients and trainees should easily discern a level of communication proficiency competence. That is, CCCTTs should demonstrate executable communication proficiencies including, but not limited to, such skills as listening, presentation, interpersonal skills, group techniques, coaching and training skills, and the previous Best Practices (Transparency, Assessment, Technology, Professional Development, Organizational Knowledge, and Instructional Design). This particular Best Practice requires the Communication Training professional to "walk the walk", "do what you teach others to do", and generally be a model of proficiency in the areas you are helping others to strengthen.

In this final section there are examples of foundational types of Communication proficiencies along with benchmarks regarding what such a proficiency entails. These include fundamental communication and presentation skills, persuasion techniques, humor and storytelling, group techniques, and intercultural and diversity skills.

Chapter 23

The communication skills of an effective trainer

Seth S. Frei and Steven A. Beebe

Abstract

As communication training and development professionals, we often train others on how to use essential communication skills. This chapter provides the reader with a combination of research and practical application for scholars and trainers alike. Focusing on presentational speaking skills, interpersonal communication techniques, and small group facilitation skills, trainers can improve their communication in training sessions.

Communication is at the heart of everything a trainer does, whether the context is an interpersonal relationship when establishing a contact with a client or working in a coaching session, collaborating in a group or team, or presenting to a large audience. Communication training and development professionals typically train others about *how* trainees can effectively use these important communication skills. However, before teaching others the skills of effective communication, it is critical to first take a look in the mirror and ask yourself, "Am I practicing these skills myself?"

The skills of effective communication have been taught for millennia. Indeed, Aristotle's classic, *The Art of Rhetoric*, written in 333 B.C.E., recognized the importance of learning rhetorical competencies. Though the study of communication has expanded and transformed over the decades, significant literature continues to emphasize the importance of teaching communication skills (Morreale, 2009; Waldeck & Seibold, 2016; Wardrope, 1999). Communication trainers teach the basic communication skills and incorporate them into workplace competencies. In an article entitled, "What do communication trainers do?" Beebe (2007) suggests that many of the skills presented in training seminars are the same competencies communication instructors present in introductory communication courses. While training individuals on these skills, it is important that the trainer also demonstrates mastery of these skills. Social learning theory suggests that the communicative behaviors of one individual are likely to lead another person to demonstrate similar behaviors (Richmond & McCroskey, 2000). Because of the importance of leading by example, trainers must be competent in using communication skills when presenting training seminars.

This book is inspired by the National Communication Association (NCA) list of the best practices for communication training and consulting. These best practice prescriptions represent a "multi-year effort involving thousands of possible topics and input from literature, government, practitioners, and scholars" (National Communication Association Training and Development Division, 2015, p. 1). Best practice seven states that communication trainers must "Demonstrate communication proficiency" (NCA, 2015, p. 2). The practice further states that trainers and consultants should have a variety of communication skills that help demonstrate their proficiency. While this chapter focuses largely on face-to-face training, many of the same principles apply to the ever-expanding area of online and web-based training. Although it takes a considerable number of communication skills to train workplace professionals, this review focuses on three core macro sets of trainer communication competencies—presentational, relational, and group facilitation skills.

Presentation skills

Presenting a training seminar in an unmediated context requires skilled presentation techniques. Although each phase of the preparation and delivery of a training session is important, Beebe and Beebe (2018) recommend an audience-centered speaking process in their widely adopted book on public speaking. This process, not unlike the Needs-Centered Training Model, presented in this volume and elsewhere, considers the needs and goals of trainees throughout all stages of preparation and delivery (Beebe, Mottet, & Roach, 2013). Thus, an effective trainer remains audience-centered/needs-centered, focusing on the trainee in the delivery of the presentation. Three essential dimensions include: verbal delivery, nonverbal delivery, and presentation aids.

Verbal delivery

Organizational training demands that the trainer engage trainees in different settings, each with their own unique audience. Regardless of the audience type, background, culture, or expectations, the trainer must adapt his or her language to effectively connect with a given audience (Beebe & Beebe, 2018). One way that trainers adapt their language is through the use of language (McArdle, 2015). Concrete words are those that we interact with using our five senses, compared with abstract terms which are words that do not. The linguistic theory of general semantics suggests more concrete words are related to clearer communication (Hayakawa & Hayakawa, 1990). These specific and generally understandable words increase the clarity of the trainer and help the trainee to more clearly grasp the subject.

As a trainer, you must also focus on using concise words that get to the point rather than overstating information. Often, trainers might feel the need to give all of the information on a topic, but research demonstrates that people who use fewer words are viewed as more credible (Ng & Bradac, 1993). When providing training on complex topics, it might be necessary to use complex words or vocabulary in the session. When this specialized language is necessary, trainers should always practice saying these words out loud. Mispronouncing words can lead to decreased perceptions of credibility and speaking ability (Beebe & Beebe, 2018).

Trainers must also strive to create memorable word structures to improve the potential for audience retention. When the goal of training is behavior change, it is crucial that the messages shared are remembered by the audience members. Marketing-communication experts have labeled this quality "ear appeal," which simply means a phrase that people hear and cannot get it out of their head (Klepper, 1994), much like an "ear worm," a musical phrase that we hum well after we hear a commercial jingle or advertisement. When you appeal to the ears of trainees, there is an increased possibility that the message will be recalled and applied.

In addition to focusing on memorability, research has confirmed that trainers who are verbally immediate are more likely to facilitate learning (Faylor, Beebe, Houser, & Mottet, 2008). Verbal immediacy is the ability to engender feelings of psychological closeness through the use of words and word choice (Mehrabian, 1967). Verbally immediate messages enhance liking and feelings of inclusion. Strategies for enhancing verbal immediacy include:

- Using inclusive words such as "us," "our," and "we" rather than "I," "me," and "mine."
- Calling trainees by name.
- Using personal examples.
- Disclosing personal experiences.
- Asking questions and making the training more like a conversation than a lecture.
- Asking questions that provoke interaction.

The best application of verbal immediacy is to interact spontaneously rather than with a scripted, pre-planned, or manuscript delivery style. In conjunction with verbal immediacy, a trainer should demonstrate verbal affinity-seeking cues with trainees. Affinity-seeking cues include those messages that result in increased liking or positive regard for the trainer and the training content (Frymier & Wanzer, 2006). Verbal affinity-seeking cues include:

- Assuming equality between trainer and trainee by talking about each other as having equal status and power.
- Maintaining culturally appropriate conversational rules by letting others interact and respond to trainer and encouraging trainee interaction.
- Customizing stories and anecdotes for the specific training audience.
- Self-disclosing and encouraging appropriate self-disclosure from trainees such as asking for personal examples to illustrate concepts and skills.
- Communicating that the trainer enjoys presenting the skills and concepts by using humor and other strategies to facilitate enjoyment of the training content.
- Remaining optimistic about the value and importance of the training content.

Being aware of one's verbal immediacy and affinity-seeking cues will improve the connection a trainer has with trainees. Overall, a spontaneous, extemporaneous, verbally immediate style is best.

Nonverbal delivery

Although it is important to focus on the verbal messages used in presenting training material to enhance learning and facilitate immediacy, nonverbal delivery also plays a significant role in enhancing presentation efficacy. In fact, nonverbal messages are more spontaneous than verbal messages, which makes them harder to fake, leading us to believe them more than verbal messages (Knapp, Hall, & Horgan, 2013). Nonverbal messages play a primary role in creating the emotional learning climate. Delivery is also crucial in how an audience reacts to a speaker's overall credibility (Adams & Cleck, 2005; Wagner, 2013). Trainees have expectations of how a trainer will act, thus it is the job of the trainer to make sure they are meeting those nonverbal expectations. During a training seminar, trainers must focus on several fundamental and classic nonverbal characteristics such as eye contact, facial expressions, gestures, movement, personal appearance, and immediacy.

Eye contact with the audience opens communication, and engages the trainees in the material being presented. This is especially important for trainers because they are often walking into a setting where they do not know the individuals to whom they are speaking. According to Beebe and Beebe (2018), "Eye contact nonverbally sends the message, 'I am interested in you; tune me in; I have something I want to share with you'" (p. 191). Trainers should practice giving intentional eye contact to encourage the audience to pay attention and tune in to the presentation.

Along with eye contact, strong facial expressions will help the audience determine if they will choose to pay attention. When trainees see the face of the trainer, they begin to create an understanding of the climate for the overall training session. Emotions displayed through the face are cross-cultural and nearly all people around the world agree on the general meaning of the primary emotional cues (Keltner, Eckman, Gonzaga, & Beer, 2003). By paying attention to the messages conveyed through eye contact and facial expressions, trainers will be able to better connect with their intended audience.

Gestures and movement are indicators of instructor immediacy, which has been show to produce higher levels of recall, motivation, and learning (Goodboy, Weber, & Bolkan, 2009; Pogue & Ahyun, 2006). Because the primary goals of training are often recall and motivation, skilled trainers will likely use gestures as well as movement around the physical room of the training seminar. Gestures are the movements made by the hands of the trainer to add meaning to the presentation. Beebe et al. (2013) suggest using natural gestures as if you were having an informal conversation. If gestures are overdone, they become distracting and they reduce the potential for benefits of immediacy.

Movement around the physical location of a training session adds to the immediacy benefits of gestures. If a trainer remains at a podium, they might be perceived as distant and detached. Rather, they must use proxemics to their advantage and adapt the distance between them and the trainees depending on the message being communicated. While conducting a training seminar, trainers must also focus on their personal appearance and what they choose to wear for a presentation. Generally, we consider attractive people more credible, happier, and popular than unattractive people (Beebe, Beebe, & Redmond, 2017; Kelly, 1969). The clothes a trainer wears are often the first impression made on group of trainees whom they have never met. While there is not a universal rule of dressing for success, the trainer must consider their audience and the types of clothing they will likely be wearing. Then the trainer will be able to adapt their clothing choices to be "one step nicer" than the rest of the audience.

Nonverbal immediacy includes using nonverbal behaviors that enhance the feeling of psychological closeness between trainer and trainee (Faylor et al., 2008). To be nonverbally immediate includes using many of the delivery strategies we have emphasized:

- Direct eye contact.
- Forward lean.
- Moving closer to trainees.
- Coming out from behind a lectern or table.
- Smiling.
- Using appropriate and natural gestures.

These strategies can also act as nonverbal affinity-seeking cues in the training seminar. Like verbal affinity-seeking cues, nonverbal cues also result in increased liking or positive regard for the trainer and content. Nonverbal affinity-seeking cues include:

- Communicating in ways that suggest the trainer is comfortable speaking to others through smiling, verbalizing comfortableness, being relaxed, and telling personal stories.
- Communicating dynamism through movement, gestures, facial expression, and vocal cues.

Considering nonverbal aspects of delivery will help trainers to improve their connection with trainees to improve the overall impact of the message.

Presentation aids

When considering the visual aspect of a training session, presentation aids are likely one of the methods used by trainers. It is often easy to immediately consider the ubiquitous PowerPoint as a presentation aid, but it is important to avoid overusing visual images. Contemporary research suggests that providing mind-numbing bulleted lists of words, terms, and phrases are likely to mostly accomplish death by PowerPoint! Using pictures and images appear to be the best application of PowerPoint (Cyphert, 2004; Kernbach, Bresciani, & Eppler, 2015; Mayer & Sims, 1994).

In their comprehensive book on training and development Beebe et al. (2013) remind readers that "presentation aids are not the presentation or the training content. Presentation aids can trigger training success or ruin a training session" (p. 174). While these aids can be beneficial to the audience for clarity and retention purposes, trainers must use them intentionally and strategically to support the message rather than replacing it (Bucher & Niemann, 2015). Always consider the needs of the audience before creating presentation aids that might otherwise be considered unnecessary. Because the most common type of aids used in training sessions are computer-generated slides, we discuss strategies for creating high quality slides.

Effective trainers must resist the temptation to put large amounts of information in slides in the hopes that trainees will be more likely to retain something (Kernbach et al., 2015). As a general guideline, use no more than seven lines of text on any visual aid slide—but fewer than seven lines is even better. When creating visual aids, less is more. It is also important to make the writing large enough to be seen by everyone in the room. Keeping visual aids simple with a polished look will help the audience recognize the important take-aways from the session. Our key suggestion: *Keep words to a minimum, and primarily use images that enhance the trainee understanding of a concept or skill.* Additionally, by choosing an easily readable font and using slides with high contrast, participants in the back of the room will be able to more easily read the information on the visual aids.

Considering the room where the training will be presented can also help you, as a trainer, to prepare for using visual aids. By talking to the contact within the organization, a trainer can determine if a projector will be supplied, or if they will need to bring one in. The organizational contact can also provide important information like the approximate dimensions of the room and the room set-up to determine if computer-generated aids will be useful. Allowing yourself plenty of time to prepare and set-up on the day of the training will help reduce the possibilities of technical difficulties (Beebe & Beebe, 2018). Above all, when working with technology, always have a backup copy and paper copies of the information in case of a malfunction. Keeping these strategies in mind will help you effectively use presentation aids that assist, rather than distract, from the presentation.

Relational skills

One might ask, "Why is the relationship between a trainer and a trainee important if it only lasts a few hours?" The answer lies in the importance of relationships and the impact they have on effective dissemination of training messages. In fact, the title of Mistry and Latoo's (2009) article puts it best: "The dysfunctional relationship between trainer and trainee: Mother of all problems" (p. 59). Relational skills, whether in a one-on-one coaching setting or in a larger speaker–audience context, are essential in communicating trust, credibility, and expressing interest. Ineffective communication skills are one of the prime reasons a trainee–trainer relationship may become dysfunctional (Mistry & Latoo, 2009). Many of the skills reviewed in the verbal and nonverbal presentational skills section of this chapter are also applicable to interpersonal relationships. Because of the often short-term nature of training/consulting relationships, it is of utmost importance that trainers use the skills already discussed, in addition to modeling effective listening when interacting with trainees.

Effective listening

Surveys seeking to identify the most important skills to master in business and organizational contexts typically list listening as one of the most important (Brunner, 2008; Purdy & Manning, 2015; Welch & Mickelson, 2013). Several chapters in this handbook have emphasized the importance of addressing the specific needs of the trainees. In addition to pre-training needs assessment methods, one of the most important strategies is listening to discern the goals and objectives of trainees during a training session.

Understanding your listening style and the listening style of trainees can help you adapt your training message to address specific trainee needs. Listening research has identified four primary listening styles: relational, analytical, critical, and task-oriented listening (Bodie, Gearhart, & Worthington, 2013; Bodie & Worthington, 2010).[1] Table 23.1 provides an overview of the primary listening styles, their definition, the characteristics of that type of listener, and the techniques trainers can use to accommodate that particular listening style.

Researchers caution that there is no single best listening style; but being able to adapt your listening style to different listening situations, is the ideal listening strategy. Watson, Barker, and Weaver (1995) found that about 40 per cent of listeners have a primary listening style. In addition, 40 per cent of listeners typically use more than one style. About 20 per cent of listeners do not have a single listening style preference. There is also evidence that females tend to have a preference for the relational listening style (Kiewitz, Weaver, Brosius, & Weimann, 1997). Most training audiences include individuals with different listening style preferences; some may tend to be more relational listeners whereas others may be critical listeners. An effective trainer ensures that he/she presents information that would appeal to all four listening style preferences. Using strategies identified in the third column in Table 23.1 will help a trainer appeal to different kinds of listeners. In addition, there is also evidence that listeners tend to adapt their listening style to achieve specific listening goals (Gearhart, Denham, & Bodie, 2014). Helping to clarify the listening goal for your trainees (which, in a training context, is usually task-oriented listening and sometimes analytical or critical listening), can help the trainer adapt his/her presentation style to trainee's listening styles. Identifying the listener style or styles of your trainee and then adapting to their listening style preference will help you successfully acquire and maintain effective relationships with them.

To enhance your listening skills when working with trainees, research suggests there are a number of best practices. These researchers (Acheson, 2008; Halone & Pecchioni, 2001) suggest that good listeners:

Table 23.1 Primary listening styles

Listening Style	Definition	Characteristics	Trainer Technique to Accommodate
Relational	Relational listeners focus on emotions and feelings communicated both verbally and nonverbally	Search for common interests, enjoy listening to stories and anecdotes, and are empathic with their listening partner.	Incorporate stories in lessons and try to demonstrate common interests with the trainees.
Analytical	Analytical listeners may often withhold judgment. Before reaching a conclusion they usually listen to all sides of an issue and want to hear the facts.	Like a judge in the courtroom, they tend to listen to the entire message before determining the accuracy and reliability of what they hear.	Provide detail in explanations to and seek to present information in an unbiased format.
Critical	Critical listeners prefer to listen for evidence, data, and facts to support key conclusions; they look for the underlying logic of a message and are attuned to listen for discrepancies, inconsistencies, and errors.	Appreciate facts and data, you should use ample details and well-documented evidence when presenting your session to a trainee.	Share facts and data with the trainees and do not leave out small details.
Task-Oriented	Task-Oriented listeners prefer to listen for evidence, data and facts to support key conclusions; they look for the underlying logic of a message and are attuned to listen for discrepancies, inconsistencies, and errors.	Look at the overall structure of a message when determining what needs to be done with the information. Task-oriented listeners also like brief, clear, and efficient messages.	Make clear action-steps that the trainee can take after learning the information. Don't be overly wordy, but make sure that you share the important information.

- Put aside their own thoughts and focus on the message of others.
- Mentally prepare to listen by consciously focusing on the other person even before the other person begins speaking.
- Are mindfully concentrated and try to listen.
- Take their time; they don't rush the speaker; they are patient; they pause and let the speaker finish.
- Don't interrupt the speaker.
- Appropriately contribute to the conversation.
- Provide nonverbal reinforcement by nodding and saying "yes" or "I understand" at appropriate times.

When studying professional settings, Ruyter and Wetzels (2000) found that customers preferred listeners who seemed focused and gave their full attention to them. This finding can be applied to training where the trainees are the customers receiving the service provided by the trainer. Effective listeners are perceived as effective because they enact observable behaviors that signal they are paying attention to their listening partner. Having direct yet natural eye contact (without a constant stare), nodding and appropriately responding, and having an interested facial expression are ways of communicating that you are listening. In addition, a slight forward lean as well as non-fidgeting, keeping your hands quiet communicates warmth and attention (Harrigan, 1985; Imhof, 2001).

While our discussion of relational skills has largely focused on listening, we hope this emphasizes the importance we place on this skill for trainers. Listening is the quintessential relationship-building skill (Beebe, Beebe, & Redmond, 2017). Because long-term relationship building skills do not apply to the often short-term nature of training, listening is of ultimate importance in this relationship. Using the techniques we suggest and outline to recognize listening styles and improve listening skills will help trainers connect with trainees on a relational level.

Group facilitation skills

Training for communication skills often requires small groups of trainees working on a specific training objective. To effectively facilitate a group training, trainers must help guide the conversations occurring in small groups. Group facilitation skills are especially beneficial whenever there are more than two people having a task-oriented conversation. The increased communication complexity breeds potential for uncertainty and misunderstanding. To help alleviate these possibilities, the conversation among participants needs a balance of two things: structure and interaction.[2] Strategies to manage group structure and facilitate group interaction can enhance both the efficiency and group collaborative climate (Beebe & Masterson, 2015).

Structure consists of providing the strategies and behaviors that guide a group toward achieving its task. For example, having a clear and appropriate agenda help a group stay on task. A group with appropriate structure has a more focused discussion and avoids hopping from topic to topic. An unstructured discussion is one in which participants don't listen to one another, are thinking about their own comments rather than what the group is discussing, and there are frequent interruptions and often confusion.

Interaction is the give-and-take conversation that occurs when people collaborate. Interaction is vital to achieve the goals of the group. A group with no interaction resembles a speech – one person talks and the others listen. In contrast, a group with too much interaction consists of people talking over one another, little connection between contributions, and conversation that doesn't stick to the topic at hand. The goal when facilitating a group or team discussion is to seek a balance of structure (focus) and interaction (talk).

How to provide structure for group discussion

Group communication researchers have found that groups, which have no planned structure or agenda, have more difficulty accomplishing the task (Kerr & Tindale, 2004). Specifically, without structure, groups are likely to do the following (SunWolf & Seibold, 1999):

- Take more time to achieve their goals, which increases organizational expenses.
- Prematurely focus on solutions, without recognizing the potential lack in effectiveness they might cause.
- Hop from one unconnected idea to the next.
- Be controlled by a dominating group member.
- Experience more conflict and are less likely to reach consensus.

In a corporate context, unstructured groups without a clear purpose or explicit agenda are more likely to waste time and money and be less effective in accomplishing the goal than in a more structured group conversation. Research has documented one important conclusion about the role of providing structure to group discussions: *Any method of structuring group discussion is better than no method at all* (Beebe & Masterson, 2015; Witte, 2007). Researchers have found that groups shift topics about once a minute (Berg, 1967; also see Poole, 1983) unless there is structure, such as an agenda and a facilitator to help the group stay on the agenda.

Groups benefit from an agenda and the employment of other methods and techniques to keep the discussion focused on the task. The primary tool for providing group structure is an agenda. Beebe and Masterson (2015) offer guidelines for creating and using agendas that trainers could follow in planning meetings with clients or facilitating group interactions as part of a training session. These suggestions include: (1) identifying the goal(s) of the meeting (to give information, discuss information) on the printed agenda; (2) organizing agenda items around three general functions – information items, discussion items, action items; (3) placing information items toward the end of the agenda so as to not take time away from discussion and action items; and (4) placing high priority agenda items early on the agenda. It is also important to ask for input about agenda items before the meeting and then distribute an agenda prior to the meeting so that meeting participants can be appropriately prepared for discussion.

Why is having an agenda so important for a communication trainer? If an organization is paying you well for your service as a trainer, it is to their advantage that they remain on task and not follow conversational trails "into the woods." Having an agenda models effective meeting management principles and also increases the likelihood that there is a common task that the trainees will accomplish.

How to facilitate group interaction

In addition to structure, groups need a counterbalance of synergistic interaction, talk, and dialogue (Pavitt, Philipp, & Johnson, 2004). It is through talk and dialogue that the group accomplishes the task. But the conversations should be managed effectively. To manage meeting interaction there are several key tasks.

First, be a gatekeeper. A gatekeeper is an individual in a group who manages the flow of conversation by encouraging less-talkative members to participate and who limits lengthy contributions of group members who may talk too much. The key skill of a gatekeeper is to listen, invite, and encourage those who contribute less frequently for ideas and those who over verbalize to hold their thoughts until others have spoken. This can be completed by the gatekeeper saying phrases like "That's a great idea, what do you think [Group Member]" or "We haven't heard your thoughts on this yet [Group Member], what do you think?" While these phrases do not seem very complex, they help ensure that all members have their voice heard in a group discussion.

Second, summarize frequently and focus the group on its mission. This helps remind the group where it is (and where it isn't). Ludwig and Geller (1997) found that the most experienced facilitators helped orient the group toward the goal, helped them adapt to what was happening in the group at any given moment, and involved the group in developing an agenda for the meeting. Simply reminding the group what the goal is can help a group stay on task.

A third essential facilitation skill is the use of metadiscussion. Metadiscussion literally means discussion about discussion. A metadiscussional statement focuses on the discussion process rather than on the specific topic under consideration (Beebe & Masterson, 2015). Examples of metadiscussion include "I'm not sure where we are on the agenda," or "I don't think we are addressing the key issues." They address the group's process, rather than the specific issue the group is discussing. Metadiscussional phrases help to keep the group on task. Research supports the importance of metadiscussion; simply having someone periodically reflect on where the group is on the agenda and review what has been accomplished helps the group remain aware of the topic and issues at hand (Gouran, 1969; Kline, 1972).

Group facilitation strategies

A skilled trainer knows how to clearly facilitate discussion in the training seminar and uses many of the aforementioned techniques. Additionally, the following strategies will help trainers as they prepare and facilitate discussion:

- Display known facts for all group members to see.
- Listen for group-oriented (we, us, our) rather than self-oriented (I, me, my) pronouns to provide clues about the group's sense of cohesiveness and identity.
- Seek to clarify misunderstandings by, when appropriate, summarizing what you hear others saying.
- Emphasize areas of agreement.
- Encourage differences of opinion if the group seems to agree too quickly (avoid groupthink).
- Monitor time to prevent exceeding set time limits by noting the amount of time left to achieve the goals on the agenda.
- Use the "write then speak" technique. For added productivity, selectively structure the conversation by having members provide written responses before they provide oral responses.

Through this process, it is important to keep the needs of the trainees at the center of all group discussions (Beebe et al., 2013). Some groups might require greater levels of structure, whereas others will require increased interaction. These are often not variables that are known before the training begins, but rather will require adaptation as you continue to evaluate their needs. Through preparation and practice of the skills discussed in this chapter, trainers will continue to improve the crucial skills of group facilitation.

Conclusion

Communication skills are among the most coveted skills on the planet. Warren Buffet has claimed, "If you improve your communication skills I guarantee you that you will earn 50 percent more money over your lifetime" (Buffet, 2010). Although Buffet did not explicitly claim that communication trainers would reap enhanced financial benefits because of enhanced communication skills, it is reasonable to conclude that enhanced trainer communication skills will result in an improved return on your investment (ROI). Our admonition that *communication is at the heart of everything a trainer does* is true. We believe that through practiced presentational, relational, and group facilitation skills, trainers are able to more clearly connect with their trainees and improve the quality of their training session. The skills are not inherently complex, but mastery requires motivation to improve, coupled with intentional practice and a dedicated focus.

If trainers fail to recognize the importance of using these skills in their sessions, trainees could become disinterested, unengaged, and removed from conversations. Through "leading by doing", training sessions focused on communication skills will improve if the trainer is demonstrating competent skills themselves. As the National Communication Association recognizes the importance of communication proficiency in their list of best practices, trainers must also embrace these essential skills in the successful presentation of their training sessions.

Notes

1 Our discussion of listening skills is based on a discussion in Beebe, S. A. (2016). Communication skills for consulting excellence. In J. H. Waldeck & D. R. Seibold (eds.), *Consulting that matters: A handbook for scholars & practitioners* (pp. 127–146). New York, NY: Peter Lang.
2 Our discussion of facilitation skills is based on a discussion in Beebe, S. A. (2016). Communication skills for consulting excellence. In J. H. Waldeck & D. R. Seibold (eds.), *Consulting that matters: A handbook for scholars & practitioners* (pp. 127–146). New York, NY: Peter Lang.

References

Acheson, K. (2008). Silence as gesture: Rethinking the nature of communicative silences. *Communication Theory, 18*, 535–555. doi:10.1111/j.1468–2885.2008.00333.x

Adams, R. B., & Cleck, R. E. (2005). Effects of direct and averted gaze on the perception of facially communicated emotion. *Emotion, 5*, 3–11. doi:10.1037/1528–3542.5.1.3

Beebe, S. A. (2007). What do communication trainers do? *Communication Education, 56*, 249–254. doi:10.1080/03634520601145266

Beebe, S. A., & Beebe, S. J. (2018). *Public speaking: An audience-centered approach* (10th ed.). Boston, MA: Pearson.

Beebe, S. A., Beebe, S. J., & Redmond, M. V. (2017). *Interpersonal communication: Relating to others* (6th ed.). Boston, MA: Allyn & Bacon.

Beebe, S. A., & Masterson, J. T. (2015). *Communicating in small groups: Principles and practices.* Boston, MA: Pearson.

Beebe, S. A., Mottet, T. P., & Roach, K. D. (2013). *Training and development: Communicating for success* (2nd ed.). Boston, MA: Pearson.

Berg, D. M. (1967). Descriptive analysis of the distribution and duration of themes discussed by task-oriented, small groups. *Speech Monographs, 34,* 172–175. doi:10.1080/03637756709375538

Bodie, G. D., Gearhart, C. C., & Worthington, D. L. (2013). The listening styles profile-revised (lsp-r): A scale revision and evidence for validity. *Communication Quarterly, 61,* 72–90. doi:10.1080/01463373.2012.720343

Bodie, G. D., & Worthington, D. L. (2010). Revisiting the listening styles profile (lsp-16): A confirmatory factor analytic approach to scale validation and reliability estimation. *International Journal of Listening, 24,* 69–88. doi:10.1080/10904011003744516

Brunner, B. R. (2008). Listening, communication, & trust: Practitioners' perspectives of business/organizational relationships. *The International Journal of Listening, 22,* 73–82. doi:10.1080/10904010701808482

Bucher, H. J., & Niemann, P. (2015). Visualizing science: The reception of PowerPoint presentations. *Visual Communication, 11,* 283–306. doi:10.1177/1470357212446409

Buffet, W. (2010). Warren Buffet on communication skills. *YouTube,* December 6. http://www.youtube.com/watch?v=tpgcEYpLzPO.

Cyphert, D. (2004). The problem of PowerPoint: Visual aid or visual rhetoric? *Business Communication Quarterly, 67,* 80–84.

Faylor, N. R., Beebe, S. A., Houser, M. L., & Mottet, T. P. (2008). Perceived differences in instructional communication behaviors between effective and ineffective corporate trainers. *Human Communication, 11,* 149–160.

Frymier, A. B., & Wanzer, M. B. (2006). Teacher and student affinity-seeking in the classroom. In T. P. Mottet, V. P. Richmond, & J. C. McCroskey (eds.), *Handbook of instructional communication: Rhetorical & relational perspectives* (pp. 195–211). Boston, MA: Allyn & Bacon.

Gearhart, C. C., Denham, J. F., & Bodie, G. D. (2014). Listening as a goal-directed activity. *Western Journal of Communication, 78,* 668–684.

Goodboy, A. K., Weber, K., & Bolkan, S. (2009). The effects of nonverbal and verbal immediacy on recall and multiple student learning indicators. *Journal of Classroom Interaction, 44,* 4–12.

Gouran, D. S. (1969). Variables related to consensus in group discussions of questions of policy. *Speech Monographs, 36,* 387–391. doi:10.1080/03637756909375631

Halone, K. K., & Pecchioni, L. L. (2001). Relational listening: A grounded theoretical model. *Communication Reports, 14,* 59–71. doi:10.1080/08934210109367737

Harrigan, J. A. (1985). Listeners' body movements and speaking turns. *Communication Research, 12,* 233–250. doi:10.1177/009365085012002004

Hayakawa, S. I., & Hayakawa, A. R. (1990). *Language in thought and action.* New York, NY: Harcourt, Brace, Jovanovich.

Imhof, M. (2001). How to listen more efficiently: Self-monitoring strategies in listening. *International Journal of Listening, 15,* 2–19. doi:10.1080/10904018.2001.10499042

Kelly, J. (1969). Dress as non-verbal communication. Paper presented at the American Association for Public Opinion Research.

Keltner, D., Eckman, P., Gonzaga, G. S., & Beer, J. (2003). Facial expression of emotion. In R. J. Davidson, K. R. Scherer, & H. H. Goldsmith (eds.), *Handbook of affective sciences* (pp. 415–432). New York, NY: Oxford University Press.

Kernbach, S., Bresciani, S., & Eppler, M. J. (2015). Slip-sliding-away: A review of the literature on the constraining qualities of PowerPoint. *Business and Professional Communication Quarterly, 78,* 292–313. doi:10.1177/2329490615595499

Kerr, N. L., & Tindale, R. S. (2004). Group performance and decision making. *Annual Review of Psychology, 55*, 623–655. doi:10.1146/annurev.psych.55.090902.142009

Kiewitz, C., Weaver, J. B., Brosius, H. B., & Weimann, G. (1997). Cultural differences in listening style preferences: A comparison of young adults in Germany, Israel, and the United States. *International Journal of Public Opinion Research, 9*, 233–246. doi:10.1093/ijpor/9.3.233

Klepper, M. M. (1994). *I'd rather die than give a speech.* New York, NY: Carol Publishing Group.

Kline, J. A. (1972). Orientation and group consensus. *Central States Speech Journal, 23*, 44–47. doi:10.1080/10510977209363091

Knapp, M. L., Hall, J. A., & Horgan, T. G. (2013). *Nonverbal communication in human interaction.* Boston, MA: Wadsworth.

Ludwig, T. D., & Geller, E. S. (1997). Assigned versus participative goal setting and response generalization: Managing injury control among professional pizza deliverers. *Journal of Applied Psychology, 82*, 253–261. doi:10.1037/0021–9010.82.2.253

Mayer, R. E., & Sims, V. K. (1994). For whom is a picture worth a thousand words? Extensions of a dual-coding theory of multimedia learning. *Journal of Educational Psychology, 68*, 389–401.

McArdle, G. E. H. (2015). *Training design and delivery: A guide for every trainer, training manager, and occasional trainer* (3rd ed.). Alexandria, VA: Association for Talent Development.

Mehrabian, A. (1967). Attitudes inferred from non–immediacy of verbal communications. *Journal of Verbal Learning & Verbal Behavior, 6*, 294–295. doi:10.1016/S0022–5371(67)80113-0

Mistry, M., & Latoo, J. (2009). The dysfunctional relationship between trainer and trainee: Mother of all problems. *British Journal of Medical Practitioners, 2*, 59–63.

Morreale, S. P. (2009). Competent and incompetent communication. In W. F. Eadie (ed.), *21st century communication: A reference handbook* (pp. 444–453). Los Angeles, CA: Sage.

National Communication Association Training and Development Division (2015). Best practices for communication training and consulting, communication best practices: Competency, accountability, and transparency. Retrieved from http://dev.natcom.org/uploadedFiles/More_Scholarly_Resources/Other/TnDBestPractices.pdf

Ng, S., & Bradac, J. J. (1993). *Power in language: Verbal communication and social influence.* Thousand Oaks, CA: Sage.

Pavitt, C., Philipp, M., & Johnson, K. K. (2004). Who owns a group's proposals: The initiator or the group as a whole? *Communication Research Reports, 21*, 221–230. doi:10.1080/08824090409359984

Pogue, L. L., & Ahyun, K. (2006). The effect of teacher nonverbal immediacy and credibility on student motivation and affective learning. *Communication Education, 55*, 331–344. doi:10.1080/03634520600748623

Poole, M. S. (1983). Decision development in small groups, III: A multiple sequence model of group decision development. *Communication Monographs, 50*, 321–341. doi:10.1080/03637758309390173

Purdy, M. W., & Manning, L. M. (2015). Listening in the multicultural workplace: A dialogue of theory and practice. *International Journal of Listening, 29*, 1–11. doi:10.1080/10904018.2014.942492

Richmond, V. P., & McCroskey, J. C. (2000). The impact of supervisor and subordinate immediacy on relational and organizational outcomes. *Communication Monographs, 67*, 85–95. doi:10.1080/03637750009376496

Ruyter, K., & Wetzels, M. G. M. (2000). The impact of perceived listening behavior in voice-to-voice service encounters. *Journal of Service Research, 2*, 276–284. doi:10.1177/109467050023005

SunWolf, & Seibold, D. R. (1999). The impact of formal procedures on group processes, members, and task outcomes. In L. Frey (ed.), *The handbook of group communication theory and research* (pp. 395–431). Thousand Oaks, CA: Sage.

Wagner, T. R. (2013). The effects of speaker eye contact and gender on receiver's assessments of the speaker and speech. *Ohio Communication Journal, 51*, 217–236.

Waldeck, J. H., & Seibold, D. R. (eds.). (2016). *Consulting that matters: A handbook for scholars & practitioners*. New York, NY: Peter Lang Publishing.

Wardrope, W. J. (1999). A curricular profile of U.S. communication departments. *Communication Education, 48*, 256–258. doi:10.1080/03634529909379173

Watson, K. W., Barker, L. L., & Weaver, J. B. (1995). The listening styles profile (lsp-16): Development and validation of an instrument to assess four listening styles. *International Journal of Listening, 9*, 1–13. doi:10.1080/10904018.1995.10499138

Welch, S. A., & Mickelson, W. T. (2013). A listening competence comparison of working professionals. *International Journal of Listening, 27*, 85–99. doi:10.1080/10904018.2013.783344

Witte, E. H. (2007). Toward a group facilitation technique for project teams. *Group Processes and Intergroup Relations, 10*, 299–309. doi:10.1177/1368430207078694

Chapter 24

Re-motivating Monroe, *Click-Whirr*

Social suasion and the motivated sequence

Jay Baldwin

Abstract

This chapter considers best practices in communication proficiency with a focus on persuasion utilizing Monroe's Motivated Sequence. Readers will discover not just how to arrange a message per the sequence but why the arrangement matters. The chapter begins with a rehabilitation of Monroe's early theories of persuasive speaking before concluding with a novel integration of contemporary theories, with particular emphasis on the work of social psychologist Robert Cialdini and his "Six-principles of Persuasion."

If you took an introductory speech course when in high school or college, you likely learned of Monroe's Motivated Sequence. First developed in 1935 by Purdue University Professor, Alan H. Monroe, the motivated sequence is a fixture in the literature of persuasive speech. One would be hard pressed to find a widely circulated text on public speaking that did not include a discussion of the five-step sequence as a simple organizational pattern, or systematic method for preparing persuasive messages. Its step-by-step simplicity may explain why it is so frequently used by account executives, nonprofit professionals, and political strategists to close sales, raise funds, and get votes. Further, the motivated sequence is widely adaptable beyond public speaking contexts, so it is often used to construct advertising, marketing, and public relations messages in print and video. Perhaps its popularity is explainable by the fact that it works. In his book, *The Art of Public Speaking* (2012), Stephen Lucas asserts so, writing, "One indication of its effectiveness is that it is widely used by people who make their living by persuasion—especially advertisers" (p. 316).

Together, all the above warrants the inclusion of a discussion of the motivated sequence in a training book of best practices in communication. A review of the extant literature supports the commonly held view that the motivated sequence is easy to teach, learn, and use. Moreover, there appears to be broad consensus that the method is effective – it works; and finally, the fact that it has stood the test of time suggests its use will continue well into the future. In short, the method is worth your time and effort to know because it is a fundamental practice that promises to enhance your communication proficiency (Best Practice 7) as it pertains to persuasion.

However, as the title of this chapter suggests, it is my view that the motivated sequence needs re-motivating. What I mean by this is that too often the method is uncritically presented in our teaching and learning texts, and with light regard for the underlying theory that motivates it. The sequence has, over time, been de-motivated in the literature on its use. There is form but little apparent function beyond routinizing persuasive message construction. To see what I mean, and to bring all readers up to speed on what the motivated sequence is before going further, let's do a quick summary review of the sequence as it is most commonly understood.

Monroe's Motivated Sequence

Each step in the sequence is commonly treated as a kind of paint-by-numbers square. Speakers are taught to just fill in the blanks (see Figure 24.1):

Step 1: Gain the audience's **Attention** and then direct it to the issue or problem at hand, making clear the relevancy of the circumstance to the lives of the individual audience members.

Step 2: Present the problem or **Need** in detail, complete with credible supporting evidence.

Step 3: Propose a plan or solution that leads to the **Satisfaction** of the need or problem.

Step 4: Describe a **Visualization** of the imagined future consequences of adopting or rejecting the proposed solution.

Step 5: Conclude with a call to **Action**, i.e. an explicit appeal to adopt the speaker's proposition. Tell the audience what to do next.

In many cases the above is about as far as the training goes. The motivated sequence is offered up as one method among others (e.g. problem-solution, problem-cause-solution) for organizing persuasive message content. The problem as I see it with this simplified model is that one could easily learn how to organize a persuasive message without ever knowing why the sequence matters. It breeds what philosopher Daniel Dennett has called in another context, "competence without comprehension" (2017, pp. 94–101). It's knowing *how to* but not *why to*. In such a condition, one is operating with only partial understanding and, I suspect, this unnecessarily limits persuasive effectiveness. I suppose an argument could be made for training novice speakers in this manner because it undoubtedly enhances their proficiency without over-burdening them with deep understanding, but I would disagree.

Here's why: If you don't know why you're doing something, regardless of your experience level, you can't know the full measure of your actions. Knowing the *why* of each moment in the sequence heightens our awareness to what it is we are actually doing, which is intentionally setting out to influence another human being's decisions – to persuade them. To persuade is to act on another, and it is a highly personal act. It involves their emotions and thoughts. As the adage about "winning hearts and minds" implies,

Step 1: Attention ⟶ Step 2: Need ⟶ Step 3: Satisfaction ⟶ Step 4: Visualization ⟶ Step 5: Action

Figure 24.1 Monroe's Motivated Sequence.
Image credit: Jay Baldwin and Remington Miller.

it is among the more intimate forms of our interpersonal communication. What other form of communication so explicitly seeks to alter the attitudes, beliefs, and behaviors of others? When one undertakes to persuade, they're assuming a certain degree of moral agency for their audience. In my view, the ethical duty to audiences is higher than in many other communicative acts because it's so personal and potentially consequential. It's our ethical duty to know what we're doing.

So, while novice trainees can perhaps achieve a higher level of communication proficiency quickly by following the above organizational model, those seeking advanced skills, or those conducting advanced training for communication professionals, require a deeper understanding of the theory that animates the sequence and guides the construction of message content. For example, former-president Barack Obama, in a 2012 re-election campaign ad dubbed the "Kitchen Table" ad (Public Broadcasting System [PBS], 2012), deftly demonstrates the expert use of the motivated sequence, informed by theory, at the highest levels of public discourse.[1] To achieve such a level of proficiency and/or teach it to others, you need to know better how and why the motivated sequence works. The first goal of this chapter is to explain just this.

Additionally, this chapter seeks to be a bit of a corrective to what is widely thought of the motivated sequence and its relation to applied theory. The five-step sequence as it is outlined above is far removed from Monroe's original vision of it being the framework for a comprehensive method of persuasion (Monroe, 1935/1962). The disjuncture is the result of subsequent research that overturned some of Monroe's early twentieth-century theorizing about human decision making. In short, Monroe got some things wrong, necessitating those ideas be discarded from the literature. The motivated sequence, in its above abbreviated form, is what is left after Monroe's original theories have been largely stripped out, leaving what I have called a de-motivated sequence. So, a second goal of this chapter is to re-motivate Monroe's sequence by introducing contemporary theory into the training literature on its use. Readers are encouraged to consider how applied theory might increase their own persuasive effectiveness.

The chapter will proceed in three sections. In the first, we'll consider what Monroe got right, some of which was subsequently lost in the shuffle and needs to be restored. For example, recent research indicates that the ordering of content matters to persuasive effectiveness and, in retrospect, Monroe seems to have gotten the order right. Further, Monroe was keenly aware of the role human emotion plays in motivating action, but this aspect is often downplayed or ignored in the current literature and warrants discussion. In the second section, I'll fill the void left by the removal of Monroe's theories – what Monroe got wrong – by introducing the well-supported work done or synthesized by social psychologist Robert Cialdini in his book, *Influence: Science and Practice* (2009), now in its 5th edition. Here I will summarize Cialdini's "Six-Principles of Persuasion" (alternatively, "Weapons of Influence"),[2] cognitive biases, or judgmental heuristics that play a powerful role in human decision making. The final section will conclude with a summary of what I call, "Monroe's Re-Motivated Sequence," complete with a well-supported rationale for strategically integrating Cialdini's theories into the discreet steps of the sequence. We'll see that each of Cialdini's six-principles has a kind of natural fit into one or more of Monroe's five steps. The result is a re-motivated sequence not intended as a one-best-way approach to persuasion but, instead, as one tool among others useful for enhancing your own persuasive proficiency. As we will see, the re-motivated sequence acknowledges the humanity of the audience as feeling, thinking, autonomous, individuals worthy of respectful rhetoric; concurrently, it acknowledges that we humans often make decisions uncritically, without really thinking at all. The ideas that follow provide a context useful for all readers to consider their ethical duties and responsibilities as communicators (and decent human beings) while engaging in persuasive discourse.

What Monroe got right

When Monroe first published his book, *Principles and Types of Speech* (1935/1962), he wasn't merely proposing the motivated sequence as an organizational pattern for persuasive speeches. In his own words, he was developing practical "methods of securing a particular audience response" (1962, p. v). It was a complete theory of persuasion designed "to impart knowledge and secure cooperative action" (p. 27). As noted above, he got some things wrong, and those have been rightly removed from the current literature. We'll come back to those in the next section. Also removed, however, were some things that subsequent research suggests he got right. Here I want to restore those to our current thinking. Particularly, I want to address what he got right about the sequencing of content and the roles of emotion and reason therein.

Monroe's method began with a five-step sequencing of ideas that in his words, "[followed] a normal process of human thinking" (p. 35). His was a common-sense approach. He observed that the normal process of human thought required that people first become consciously aware of an issue. Second, they consider the ways in which they are personally affected by that issue. Only then, Monroe argued, will they proceed to the third stage of thinking, which is to examine an issue in-depth. Current research suggests that he got this mostly right. People do think about things more carefully after being made aware of an issue's personal relevancy (O'Keefe, 2016, pp. 152–153; Cialdini, 2009, pp. 8–9); but Monroe went further:

> Although he uses his own and his listeners' thinking processes to give sensible direction to his proposals, it is his knowledge of emotion that he uses to give power and exhilaration to his own speaking and to elicit an active response from his audience.
>
> (1962, p. 35)

Monroe acknowledges here that there is little persuasive power in the sequence without an additional applied theory of emotion's role in persuasion. The sequence alone provides only a "sensible direction" to proposals. To motivate an audience, Monroe insists that one must elicit an emotional response. "You must," he wrote, "puncture a hole in their apathy … make them feel unsatisfied" (p. 170).

In Monroe's view, people are moved to consider a proposition carefully when the issue is made clearly relevant to their lives and feelings of dissatisfaction or dissonance are engendered. Subsequent research on personal relevance (aka, Involvement) and negative affective states confirms Monroe's observations. As Daniel O'Keefe notes in his book, *Persuasion: Theory and Research* (2016), the more relevant an issue is made to audience members' lives (pp. 152–153), combined with their feelings of actual or anticipated negative emotions (fear, guilt, anger, disgust, etc.) (p. 255), the higher degree of audience involvement; i.e., the more time and effort they will spend thinking about problems and proposed solutions. So, if you want to increase the odds that your audience will seriously consider your proposal, make the problem relevant and concerning to them.

This places the sequence of steps one and two, Attention and Need, on firm theoretical ground. Speakers must understand that by the end of step two, their audience should be well-informed on whatever the issue is and understand its personal relevance to their own lives, while also being made to feel uneasy regarding the circumstance. I often say that the audience should feel or anticipate feeling "sad, mad, or otherwise bad" (i.e. sorrow, anger, worry, empathy, etc.). Mnemonic devices notwithstanding, the audience should experience a lowered emotional state by the end of step two of the sequence because it properly prepares them – heightens their involvement – to carefully consider the speaker's proposition in step three, Satisfaction, just as Monroe had asserted and current research affirms.

I often encounter resistance from some learners on this point. They say, "It's manipulative;" or "It doesn't 'feel' right" to intentionally evoke negative emotions in an audience. Given, however, what we know about audience involvement, isn't it *our duty to elicit an emotional response?* Some may disagree, but think about it. Heightened audience involvement leads them to expend *more time and effort on proposals not less.* They're engaged. If your audience truly has a problem, and you really believe that you have the solution, aren't you obligated to use your knowledge of human decision making to help them to a well-considered decision?

The key, of course, is that it is done in keeping with the conventions of ethical argumentation. This is not a prescription for fallacious emotional appeals or blatant manipulation. Whatever the emotional response sought, it ought to be elicited by credibly sourced, empirical evidence, and solid reasoning. It is the speaker's further duty to provide the audience with accurate information about whatever the issue, thereby eliciting a legitimate emotional response. Indeed, shabby arguments can significantly weaken persuasive appeals because these have been shown to undermine the speaker's credibility (O'Keefe, 2016, pp. 156–157). In short, you should give your audience good reasons to feel bad. The overarching idea is to activate the high-involvement condition in your audience.

We have seen that steps one, two, and three are well supported by current research. What of steps four and five, Visualization and Action? Monroe seems to have those right, too.

Monroe's thinking included the notion that it is often best to make compliance requests of people when they are in a good mood. This hypothesis has found some support in recent research (O'Keefe, 2016; Forgas, 1998; Millberg & Clark, 1988), although more research may be needed.[3] Following Monroe's line of thought, however, the objective of the Visualization step is to create among the audience a heightened affective state just prior to making your compliance request in step five. Steven and Susan Beebe, in their classic textbook, *Public speaking: An audience centered approach* (2015), suggest this option as a "positive visualization approach … paint a picture with words," they write, "to communicate how wonderful the future will be if your solution is adopted" (p. 334), thus putting the audience in a positive affective state just prior to the call-to-act. To make this point more memorable, I tell my own students the audience should feel or anticipate feeling "relieved, eased, or otherwise pleased" (i.e. optimistic, proud, charitable, kind, important, etc.) by the end of the Visualization step (step four), because doing so prepares them emotionally for the compliance request to come in step five. The point here, as it was earlier in the sequence, is that you should be conscious of the audience's affective state, seeking to guide them emotionally to places where rational discourse can be persuasive. A clearer illustration of the motivated sequence than the earlier linear model tracks the steps according to the flow of information and emotion through the entire process (see Figure 24.2):

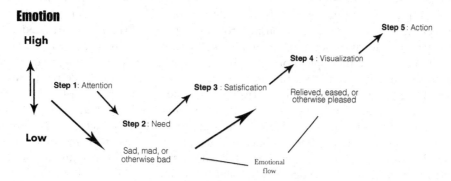

Figure 24.2 Tracking the emotional flow through the sequence.
Figure credit: Jay Baldwin and Remington Miller.

Can you better "see" what you are doing with your audience by visualizing the sequence in this way? Look at Figure 24.2 again. See how you first move (emotion = motion = moves) the audience to a place where reason can then fix them on a course of action. Why is this important? Because we know that logical appeals alone are often viewed more critically by audiences, i.e., they view logical claims with more skepticism. You can overcome this human tendency by moving your audience first with emotion, then fixing them with your well-reasoned arguments – in that order. First the one, then the other. Evoking a particular emotional response at particular moments within the sequence matters to the method's effectiveness; it's what motivates the sequence. So, aim to lower your audience's emotional state by the end of step two; then, in step three, offer them a way out of their discomfort. Use step four to heighten their good feelings before making your compliance request.

Obviously, the motivated sequence is more than merely an organizational pattern for constructing persuasive messages. It is a method grounded in theory for gaining assent. Its discrete sequential ordering of content and, importantly, its applied theories of emotion and logic are instrumental. To maximize your own effectiveness, it's imperative to attend to these details. There is, however, more to say in the next section about Monroe's ideas and the model presented above in Figure 24.2.

What Monroe got wrong

In the earlier quoted passage, Monroe presumes that audiences are passive. When he writes that a speaker must initially "puncture a hole in their apathy," he presents us with an ill-considered view of what we now know is an active audience. To proceed on the assumption that the initial emotional state of any given audience is apathetic invites unnecessary complications. In an audience-centered approach the speaker recognizes that an audience's initial disposition toward any topic can range from amenable to hostile or some point along a continuum, with apathy perhaps being at its center. The speaker should make every effort to ascertain by way of audience analysis the intended audience's position on a topic. Are they likely to be agreeable? Adversarial? Or do audience members hold a mix of views? The answer to the question influences how the speaker should proceed in preparing their message.

Taking another look at Figure 24.2, speakers should determine where their own audience's pre-existing emotional state would fall on the high–low emotional scale and meet them where they're at. Consider that the amount of time or effort needed to provoke an emotional response from an audience will vary per their existing attitudes and beliefs relative to the topic. For example, an amenable audience that is sympathetic to or already in agreement with the speaker's position on any given issue requires less time and effort to be made to feel dissatisfied than a hostile audience might; therefore, you should spend more time and effort arguing the plan of action and describing a vivid visualization to elevate their positive emotions prior to the call to action. The reverse is true of a hostile audience. With an adversarial audience, it may take you much more time and effort in steps one and two to elicit the desired emotional state and present sufficient data to activate audience involvement. Less time may be available for detailing solutions or describing vivid visualizations (Beebe & Beebe, 2015, p. 335). To be most effective using the motivated sequence one must accept that there is no one-size-fits-all approach. You need to know beforehand who your audience is and what their relevant attitudes and beliefs are relative to your topic. Ask: What will the initial emotional state of my audience most likely be? Then go from there.

More critically, Monroe was wrong in his view of human nature and decision making. He believed that "everything we do or think or feel is based upon some fundamental motive or urge or drive within us that has been set in motion by some event or condition in our immediate experience" (1962, p. 169). Humans, he argued, universally possess what he called "primary motives" and, crucially in his view, to be persuasive one must make tailored "motive appeals" to activate those "primary motives." In this way humans were somewhat like push-button controlled robots, to use Monroe's own analogy, speakers only needing to know which buttons to push (p. 168).

This bit of intellectual history aside, and without wading too deeply into the nature/nurture debate, I'll simply point out that we now know that much of human behavior and, specifically, decision-making behavior is not innate but learned; or, more accurate still, human behavior likely results from the complex interaction between our evolved human natures and our socially constructed cultures (Sapolsky, 2017; Pinker, 1999). Nevertheless, Monroe's essentialism, common to his era, as applied to human decision making was overly deterministic and needed to be extensively modified or pragmatically jettisoned. His thinking along these lines constitutes the bulk of what has over the years been stripped from the motivated sequence literature.

This brings us back to addressing the problem at hand; namely, the relative paucity of applied theory in much of the present-day literature on the motivated sequence. As noted earlier, stripping the sequence of theory left us with a de-motivated organizational pattern, "competence without comprehension." The foregoing discussion of content sequencing, emotion, and logic goes a long way in illustrating just what speakers are up to when employing the motivated sequence and, importantly, what we're up to when teaching this method to others. A clearer understanding of the *why dos* immediately calls us to reflect on our own philosophical commitments and/or professional and personal values (Are these different? Should they be?).

Hitherto, the sequence's persuasiveness has relied heavily on audience involvement, i.e., their close attention to a proposal out of concern for its relevancy to their lives. While the current research discussed above tells us that we can increase audience involvement by using the covered techniques, we also know that despite our best efforts many (most?) people frequently make decisions, even important decisions, in a condition of low involvement (O'Keefe, 2016; Cialdini, 2009). They don't really weigh the pros and cons, or otherwise consider proposals strictly on merit. Instead, they make decisions based on other, unrelated factors. Integrating theories of persuasion into the sequence that acknowledge this reality of human decision making completes the task of re-motivating Monroe and will increase persuasive effectiveness by including members of the audience who remain in the low-involvement condition. This is the task to which we now turn.

Cialdini and Click-Whirr persuasion

Interestingly, one additional way in which Monroe was right, even if for the wrong reasons, seems to be that, as it turns out, humans are a bit robotic when it comes to everyday decision making. "In fact," writes Robert Cialdini (2009), "automatic, stereotyped behavior is prevalent in much human action ..." due to the learned habit of using usually reliable mental shortcuts as a means to more efficient decision making (p. 7). Cialdini, echoing Monroe, confirms that there are indeed psychological "triggers" that speakers can activate to produce an (almost) automatic response in audiences. *Click* goes the trigger, *whirr* goes the behavioral response, Cialdini observes (pp. 2–6).

The critical difference between Cialdini and Monroe is where Monroe conjured innate "primary motives" Cialdini finds learned cognitive habits. The point here is not to compare and contrast the ideas of Monroe and Cialdini but simply to announce my intention to re-motivate the sequence, de-motivated by the removal of Monroe's thought, by turning to Cialdini. It's another interesting point of intellectual history (at least to me) that both scholars identified human automaticity as key in much of our decision making. Communication trainers may find, as I have in my own practice, that teaching and learning the two thinkers together enlivens both, making clearer the application of contemporary theory to modern practice.

Cialdini's work is meticulously researched, well-supported, and decidedly less deterministic than Monroe's (none of the triggers possesses an absolute power to persuade). Nevertheless, Cialdini argues that these triggers can be used to activate particular audience responses (p. 37). Integrating these triggers, or "principles of persuasion" into the motivated sequence is a relatively easy and effective way to further re-motivate Monroe, restoring purpose to its organizational structure. The six principles are:

1   Liking
2   Authority
3   Consistency
4   Consensus (aka, social proof)
5   Scarcity
6   Reciprocity

Each of these, I propose, recommends themselves to specific steps in the motivated sequence. Put another way, there is a theoretically supported 'natural' fit between particular principles and corresponding steps of the motivated sequence (see Table 24.1):

Table 24.1 Fitting Cialdini's principles into Monroe's sequence

Motivated Sequence	Principles of Persuasion
Step 1: Attention	Liking
Step 2: Need	Authority
Step 3: Satisfaction	Consistency
Step 4: Visualization	Consensus (i.e. social proof)
Step 5: Action	Scarcity and/or Reciprocity

Looking at Table 24.1, my suggestion is that Cialdini's "Liking" principle fits into Monroe's Step 1, Attention; Cialdini's "Authority" principle into Monroe's Step 2, Need; and so on. To understand how and why, it is necessary that I briefly summarize Cialdini's main thesis and describe each of the six principles and their relation to Monroe's sequence in a bit more detail.

According to Cialdini, humans have a tendency to make decisions based upon just one piece of information – information often unrelated to the proposition – instead of making a thorough analysis of all the relevant facts (p. 8). Citing a number of studies showing that people habitually use "mental shortcuts ... Termed *judgmental heuristics* ... that tell us what to believe or do what we are told" (p. 7), Cialdini argues that speakers can gain the assent of injudicious audience members, those who do not take the time to evaluate our well-considered arguments, by activating these heuristics. For example, Cialdini shows how a person's sense of social obligation can make them more likely to uncritically agree to a speaker's request (Reciprocity); or how a person is more likely to comply with a speaker's request without much thought because of their positive assessments of the speaker, rather than because of any factual merits of their proposal (Liking). As with Monroe's ideas about evoking emotional responses in audiences, Cialdini's work gives us reason to reflect on our own values. As you read on, be asking yourself, *Could I do that? Should I do that? Why or why not?* I think that best practices in communication proficiency demands we have clear answers to these questions for ourselves.

What follows is a brief description of each of Cialdini's Six-Principles of Persuasion, drawn from the 2009 edition of his book, *Influence: Science and Practice*. Included in each description is its implication for speakers and a recommendation for where you might fit these into the motivated sequence. Keep in mind, however, that these are suggestions not intended to be overly prescriptive. The application of theory to practice should be limited only by your own creativity, reason, ethics, and the assessment of results. It may not be practical or useful to include all six principles into every persuasive message. Use the following to stir your own thinking about how to apply theory to your practice of the motivated sequence:

1   Liking. According to Cialdini, we are more easily persuaded by people we personally like because of our tendency to use that one factor, our liking, in deciding whether to agree with someone or not (p. 142). In short, we can expect some audience members to agree with us simply because they like us, irrespective of the value of our proposal. The implication of this for speakers is clear: Be likeable. Given that people like others whom they see as similar to themselves, an effort should be made to highlight similarities between speaker and audience through speech and appearance. Speakers

should make reference to the common experiences, beliefs, and values that they share with their audience. Additionally, Cialdini notes, people are inclined to like those who offer them sincere compliments (pp. 148–150). Speakers should include in their audience analysis an effort to discover things for which their audience can be genuinely complimented. Finally, since research suggests that we make liking judgments of others early in our encounters with new people (Willis & Todorov, 2006), Liking fits well into step one, Attention, of the motivated sequence.

2   Authority. We tend to defer to the judgments of those we believe to be experts or authority figures (Cialdini, 2009, pp. 175–195). We will often comply with the requests or accept the assessments of those whom we believe to be especially knowledgeable. This heuristic can be readily activated by appearances only, through the use of symbols of authority such as titles, uniforms, and other trappings (pp. 184–190). In short, speakers can expect some audience members to agree with them to the degree they believe they are agreeing with experts. The implication is to incorporate *bono fide* titles and authentic symbols of authority into messages. The caveat being that these titles and symbols bear directly on the subject matter. A speaker should never misrepresent, exaggerate, or misuse symbols, or otherwise make fallacious appeals to authority. Since step two, Need, of the motivated sequence calls for the speaker to build a well-supported argument detailing the problem and its relevance to the audience – often citing experts – a special effort should be made to frame citations in such a way as to trigger the *click-whirr* Authority response during this step by injecting information that speaks to the expertise of sources. Additionally, your choices of visual aids ought to incorporate topic-relevant symbols of authority during the Need step.

3   Consistency. Humans possess a deep-seated desire to presently act in ways that appear consistent with our previous commitments; or, as Cialdini puts it, "Once we make a choice or take a stand, we will encounter personal and interpersonal pressures to behave consistently with that commitment" (p. 52). "Even preliminary leanings that occur before a final decision has to be made can bias us toward consistent subsequent behavior." Activating the trigger depends upon you getting the audience to make a commitment to some belief or course of action prior to the call-to-act (p. 59). The implication here is that speakers can move audiences closer to complying with a final call to action (step five) well before making it by reminding their audience of previous commitments. Doing so in step three, Satisfaction, where parallels between past commitments and the current proposal can be easily drawn, makes sense. For example, as a local United Way board member in my city, I was often asked to do group fundraising talks. As part of my audience analysis, I always wanted to know if the group had supported us in the past so I could be sure to remind them of their past commitment during this stage of my presentation. Reminding an audience of their past commitments in step three of the sequence sets the stage for an act of Consistency in step five's call-to-act.

4   Consensus (aka Social Proof). According to Cialdini, humans are copy-cats, by which he means that when people are unsure of how to act in a social situation they tend to do what others like themselves are doing in that setting (p. 99). It is a bias toward conformity. Anyone who has ever visited their state's motor vehicles bureau and endured an interminable wait only to discover that they have been standing in the wrong line because they simply followed the crowd knows the power of social proof. The implication for speakers is that they should demonstrate to their

audience through words and pictures how they are expected to behave. Social proof seems tailor made for step four of the motivated sequence – Visualization – which calls for a vivid description of the imagined state of affairs to come after enacting the proposed solution. Authentic testimonials and factual arguments demonstrating that people similar to the audience already support the proposed action should be incorporated; but perhaps the more powerful use of social proof is in activating this heuristic visually, through the use of images, visual aids depicting people enacting the desired behavior, and, importantly, emoting the desired positive affective state. In other words, speakers should in the Visualization step, whenever possible, use images of real people (not actors in simulated situations) acting and emoting in accordance with the plan proposed in the preceding Satisfaction step.

The fifth and final step of Monroe's sequence is the Action (aka: call-to-act) step. In this final stage of the sequence an explicit call-to-act on the proposal is made. According to Monroe, the call should be brief and unambiguous, the shortest and most direct part of the persuasive message (1962, p. 301). The two remaining of Cialdini's Six-Principles of Persuasion – Scarcity and Reciprocity – fit well into the Action step because they can both be effectively deployed quickly and unambiguously in conjunction with an explicit call-to-act.

5   Scarcity. According to Cialdini's research, when goods or time are in short supply, people are motivated to act. It is a fear of loss that most drives this impulse. The urgency to act out of a fear of loss is particularly acute when "opportunities become less available [and] we lose freedoms …we *hate* to lose freedoms we already have" (pp. 200–205). The implication of this heuristic is straightforward. For example, if the act is to purchase a product, and the product is truly limited in supply, just ask the audience to buy it noting the limited quantity. If the act is time-sensitive, if it must be done before some specific date to influence the issue, emphasizing the scarcity of time is an appropriate tactic. To fully realize the power of Scarcity, however, calls to act should be, whenever possible, framed within the context of a legitimate constraint on the audience's ability to exercise some freedom they already possess. According to Cialdini, this fear of the loss of choices (freedoms) seems to outweigh any other consideration. Speakers seeking to activate the Scarcity heuristic should frame their explicit calls to act in terms of what freedoms audience members would lose if they do not heed the call.

6   Reciprocity. The social norm of reciprocating favors, gifts, and even concessions in negotiations carries a sense of obligation that is a powerful influencer of human behavior arising out of our need to cooperate with others. Most interestingly, the obligation often extends equally to uninvited actions (Cialdini, 2009, pp. 19–37). In other words, if you wash my back, even if I don't ask you to, I'll wash yours. Like all of Cialdini's Six-principles of Persuasion, Reciprocity is only a tendency, albeit a strong one, to behave in a certain manner in response to particular stimuli. In this case, the heuristic implies that speakers increase their chance of gaining audience assent to their proposals when first providing the audience with a favor, or giving them a small gift, or by making some concession as in a negotiation. The key to triggering the click-whirr response is to activate the audience's sense of obligation *prior* to making the final call-to-act. If the purpose of the message is to sell a product, giving a free sample of

that product before asking them to buy would be an obvious thing to do. If samples are impractical or the communicative purpose is unrelated to a product purchase, gifts can still be effective, if done so creatively. I once had a student who wanted her audience to donate money to an organization which provided counseling services to young people dealing with anxiety (something she struggled with personally). During step four, Visualization, before asking them to donate in step five, she gave each audience member a very inexpensive soft rubber ball, called a stress ball, which one squeezes in the palm of their hand to release nervous energy, mitigating their anxiety. By doing so, she helped the audience visualize stress relief and established the reciprocal sense of obligation she would later rely upon in step five's call-to-act.

Still, giving each person in the audience a gift will be impractical in many situations. In lieu of a gift, Cialdini argues that the Reciprocity heuristic operates on a principle of compromise and can, therefore, be activated by making a concession prior to the call-to-act (p. 35). He suggests what he calls the "rejection-then-retreat" (aka: door-in-the-face)[4] technique that I would describe as a two-stage call-to-act (p. 37). In the first stage, the speaker makes an extreme version of their call-to-act that borders on the unreasonable but does not seem ridiculous, which would undermine its effect (p. 39). In the second stage, the speaker concedes that the first request would be a challenge for most in the audience to undertake and that rejecting it would be reasonable on their part. Then the speaker makes a compromise request, which is the action they wanted the audience to take all along.[5]

The advantages of synthesizing Monroe and Cialdini are clear. Doing so arms speakers with powerful tools for creating persuasive messages by, among other things, engaging audiences in both the high- and low-involvement condition. The questions raised, as we've discussed throughout, are ultimately ethical ones which deserve fuller consideration than I have space here to discuss. Ultimately, before integrating any of these ideas into your own work, you should situate them within the larger framework of professional standards and your personal conscience.

Before concluding, I want to provide a brief, clear, restatement of what I'm calling Monroe's Re-motivated Sequence for the reader, who should find it a quick reference—a "cheat sheet"—for constructing persuasive messages according to the foregoing discussion:

Step 1 – Attention: Activate the **Liking** response while gaining the **Attention** of your audience, and then direct their attention to the problem and its relevance to their lives.

Step 2 – Need: Activate the **Authority** response by presenting the **Need** in detail, citing empirical evidence from credible sources and utilizing appropriate symbols of authority. Give your audience good reasons to feel bad about the current state of affairs. The goal is to heighten audience involvement by initially lowering their affective state.

Step 3 – **Satisfaction**: Activate the **Consistency** response. Propose a plan or solution that leads to the **Satisfaction** of the need by appeal, whenever possible, to the past commitments of the audience, remembering that people seek present actions that are consistent with their past commitments.

Step 4 – Visualization: Activate the **Consensus** response by offering various social proofs consistent with a **Visualization** of the imagined consequences of adopting the proposed solution. Give your audience good reasons to feel good about the proposed plan of action. The goal is to heighten your audience's affective state to prepare them emotionally for the call-to-act.

Step 5 – Action: Activate the **Scarcity** and/or **Reciprocity** heuristic in your call to **Action** by unambiguously telling the audience what it is you want them to do next. The call-to-act should be the shortest and most direct part of the sequence.

That's it, Monroe's Re-motivated Sequence. It is a method of applied contemporary theory. Novice and professional communicators alike who employ it come face-to-face with the fact that we use our knowledge of human decision making to influence the attitudes, beliefs, and behaviors of others; and with that comes a great deal of responsibility to communicate ethically toward our fellows when engaging in persuasion. It demands that you remain mindful of your obligations to reason, full-disclosure, honesty, allowance for other viewpoints, and the Golden Rule.

Notes

1 Video of the two-minute ad can be easily found at numerous online sites, including the cited PBS site, or by a simple web search for "Obama kitchen table ad" or on YouTube.
2 This latter militaristic descriptor has been dropped for the more benign former for reasons that should be obvious.
3 See O'Keefe (2016, pp. 255–257) for discussion of conflicting data.
4 See O'Keefe (2016, p. 235) for elaboration.
5 One personal note of caution when teaching the rejection-then-retreat method: Sometimes people will say "yes" to the first request, even if it's not in their best interest. If a speaker's compensation is calculated on a commission basis, the temptation to allow people to over-pay, or buy more than they need so as to increase the speaker's own income can be overwhelming. Practitioners must prepare their students to guide prospects to the right decision, even if it lowers their own paycheck. The Golden Rule is instructive here.

References

Beebe, S. A., & Beebe. (2015). *Public speaking: An audience centered approach* (9th ed.). Boston, MA: Pearson.

Cialdini, R. B. (2009). *Influence: Science and practice* (5th ed.). Boston, MA: Pearson.

Dennett, D. (2017). *From bacteria to Bach and back: The evolution of minds.* New York, NY: W.W. Norton.

Forgas, J. P. (1998). Asking nicely? The effects of mood on responding to more or less polite requests. *Personality and Social Psychology Bulletin, 24*(2), 173–185.

Lucas, S. (2012). *The art of public speaking* (11th ed.). Boston, MA: McGraw-Hill.

Milberg, S., & Clark, M. S. (1988). Moods and compliance. *British Journal of Social Psychology, 27*(1), 79–90.

Monroe, A. H. (1935). *Principles and types of speech.* New York, NY: Scott, Foresman and Co.

Monroe, A. H. (1962). *Principles and types of speech* (5th ed.). New York, NY: Scott, Foresman and Co.

O'Keefe, D. J. (2016). *Persuasion: Theory and research* (3rd ed.). Thousand Oaks, CA: Sage.

Public Broadcasting System (2012). *Obama makes appeal to voters with 'Kitchen Table' ad.* Web.

Pinker, S. (1999). *How the mind works.* New York, NY: W.W. Norton.

Sapolsky, R. M. (2017). *Behave: The biology of humans at our best and worst.* New York, NY: Penguin Random House.

Willis, J., & Todorov, A. (2006). First impressions: Making up your mind after a 100-ms exposure to a face. *Psychological Science, 17*(7), 592–598.

Chapter 25

The use of humor and storytelling skills as a best practice in demonstrating communication proficiency

Dakota C. Horn and Robin Golinski

Abstract

This chapter provides a review of benefits of using humor and storytelling for communication instructors, trainers, and consultants. The chapter reviews why these two instructional variables are crucial to establishing communication proficiency. Humor and storytelling have a long list of potential benefits to help with engagement, participation, retention, demonstrating relevance, and other potential positive outcomes. This chapter discusses these connections and the essential nature of these two training elements.

Without doubt, a professional in the field of communication skill transfer must himself or herself be an effective communicator. The critical nature of this best practice cannot be overstated. This chapter will promote and provide evidence supportive of why the ability to demonstrate communication proficiency is an imperative skill. Demonstrating communication proficiency is a broad best practice but is *vital* to the success of a communication trainer or teacher. You must have a firm grasp of learning principles while creating a learning environment with competencies that include knowledge, skills, and attitudes (Barbazette, 2005). The foundation of successful communication teachers is found in mastered communicative behaviors such as humor, clarity, and immediacy (Seibold, Kudsi, & Rude, 1993; Worley, Titsworth, Worley, & Cornett-DeVito, 2007; also see Sidelinger, this volume). Understanding the significance and importance of these communication skills within the training and classroom setting is vital to your success as a communication trainer or teacher. Seibold, Kudsi, and Rude (1993) found that participants showed significant behavior changes including strong positive responses in retention and skill acquisition when involved in a training program with a teacher who had communication training themselves for presentation skills. Evans and Cleghorn (2010) argue that teachers cannot develop their learners' basic communicative skills or their cognitive ability unless they *themselves* have demonstrated communication proficiency.

Communication-teaching professionals work in complex communication environments that demand ability to adapt and adjust accordingly with hard and soft skills that are scattered across a continuum (Worley, Titsworth, Worley, & Cornett-DeVito, 2007). Instructional communication competency studies provide a static definition of what the proficiencies are but do not address the complexity of *accomplishing* these proficiencies while in the training environment (Worley et al., 2007). To best understand communication proficiency, it is important to understand the research that argues for its worth and examine how it is used in classroom and training environments. Accomplishing communication proficiency acts as a gateway to other training skills. A proficient communicator is viewed as competent by his or her audience and connects with them on a much deeper level, leading to positive outcomes.

Humor and storytelling

This chapter reviews humor and storytelling as two specific communication skills that are a valuable addition for instruction and training in order to *demonstrate your proficiency as a practitioner and create a comfortable, engaging, and productive learning environment.*

HUMOR: Any verbal or nonverbal behavior that elicits laughter, pleasure, and delight.
STORYTELLING: The telling or writing of a narrative, either true or fictitious.

Humor and storytelling are crucial elements to long-term retention, recall, and ability to generate interest in the content (Kaplan & Pascoe, 1977; Mandelbaum, 2003). The intent of this chapter is to have an opportunity for all trainers to assess the humor and/or storytelling use within his or her content and delivery and justify the reasoning behind the use or lack thereof. The chapter will identify humor and storytelling research separately and then address why these two skills are important in the training and education setting. The first is done by a cursory overview of prevailing literature. The second is done by identifying key findings from the literature and bringing in an accomplished practitioner's view of the same. The practitioner is a seasoned professional with deep roots in corporate training and professional experience as a humorist and storyteller. The result is a rare look at some of the consistencies in scholarly and pragmatic views of humor and storytelling.

These two skills can be used simultaneously or separately. This chapter identifies the common benefits from both of these best practices because of their similar positive outcomes. Using humor and storytelling is an interrelated skill and deserves examination in the same chapter because of

1   similar outcome benefits when the skills are utilized;
2   the skills are context, content, and audience specific;
3   necessary practice is required to be successful.

Humor is defined as any verbal or nonverbal behavior that elicits laughter, pleasure, and delight (Booth-Butterfield & Booth-Butterfield, 1991). Not all individuals are naturally humorous, however that does not mean that humor cannot be incorporated into instructional design and/or the learning environment. Similarly, storytelling for a purpose is another advanced communication skill for trainers to include. Storytelling can be defined as "extended units of talk in which past experience is recounted", variously referred to and defined (Mandelbaum, 2003, p. 597). However, storytelling is not limited to past experiences and may also be used to illustrate a possible future outcome. Storytelling may be true or fictitious and has been shown to increase not only learning but retention as well (Gray, 2009). Humor and storytelling create a connection between people often leading participants to consider the instructor to have better delivery and effectiveness as a trainer (Bryant, Comisky, & Zillmann, 1979; Frymier & Thompson, 1992).

Humor and storytelling use in the classroom and training setting has been "associated with a more interesting and relaxed learning environment, higher instructor evaluations, greater perceived motivation to learn, and enjoyment of the course" (Banas, Dunbar, Rodriguez, & Liu, 2011, p. 137). Gruner (1967) started the research examination of humor and its impact on heightening interest on potentially boring topics and increasing retention. Braverman and Petrini (1993) studied the positive impact of humor on employees of an organization and how it results in similar outcomes from that of classroom use. Barker and Gower (2010) found similar benefits while using storytelling to explain organizational narratives. Organizational training also sees an additional benefit of humor and storytelling as they can be used as a tension reliever, reducing self-consciousness of the adult learner thereby increasing full participation (Greene, 1996; Teslow, 1995). *Instructors that use humor and/or storytelling are found to be more competent than those who do not* (Sole & Wilson, 2002; Wanzer & Frymier, 1999).

Much of the research is focused around instructional literature; however, this has its natural extension in the training environment. Humans enjoy humor and storytelling, and both will help the learning process through connecting content with pleasure.

Humor research

Humor is not a training skill that everyone may have. Individual differences such as culture, gender, instructional experience, immediacy, and individual humor orientation can easily affect one's ability to implement humor in the training or classroom environment (Banas, Dunbar, Rodriguez, & Liu, 2011). You should evaluate several factors such as comfort using different types of humor, content, appropriateness, and audience acceptance of different types of humor (Wanzer, Frymier, Wojtaszczyk, & Smith, 2006) before using. Males use humor more frequently, but it is found that females benefit most in terms of overall perception and effectiveness when using humor (Decker & Rotondo, 2001). Humor is not something that is natural to everyone's communication repertoire. However, if you feel you are not naturally funny, you can still incorporate humor purposively into your education delivery (Fortson & Brown, 1998). Understanding the benefits, identifying different types, assessing appropriateness, and finding what fits into your personal style are the keys to success with humor.

Some might believe that humor is always inappropriate and unprofessional, nonetheless, it is an effective tool to enrich communication with subordinates in the professional atmosphere (Decker & Rotondo, 2001). Humor can reduce boredom and increase performance leading to several positive learning outcomes (Hackathorn, Garczynski, Blankmeyer, Tennial, & Solomon, 2012). For example, humor allows for divergent thinking that is not typical in learning or training situations (Korobkin, 1988).

Humor helps with group cohesion in instructional settings, allowing students to feel comfortable with both the instructor and peers (Booth-Butterfield, Booth-Butterfield, & Wanzer, 2007). This effective teaching tool can also improve perceptions individuals have of instructors leading to positive and constructive relationships, improving not only the students' learning experiences but also evaluations of the instructor (Claus, Booth-Butterfield, & Chory, 2012; Wanzer & Frymier, 1999).

Humor skills provide a greater deal of instructor influence as well as a coping mechanism for stress for both students and instructor (Sidelinger, 2014). A communication trainer or teacher who can utilize humor can establish a precedent that will allow that instructor to better deal with future transgressions, such as inappropriate conversations (Sidelinger, 2014). Sudol (1981) acknowledges that humor not only provides learning benefits but also an opportunity to diffuse embarrassing situations. Studies have shown that instructional settings that regularly use humor help create positive environments for learning (Ziv, 1979; Torok, McMorris, & Lin, 2004).

Participants report one of the most desirable qualities in an instructor is humor (Check, 1986; Powell & Andresen, 1985). Humor was one of the top ranked instructional variables identified as a desired characteristic of instructors. Bousfield (1940) had students list desired instructor skills and they listed humor *higher* than appearance, voice, poise, research success, and scholarly reputation. Could it be that they intuitively understand the benefits of learning when the instructor/trainer uses humor?

This list of ideal communication proficiencies must include humor as a part of that success. Rizzo, Wanzer, and Booth–Butterfield (1999) found that leaders who used humor to instruct often had participants who reported learning and job satisfaction. In organizational settings, people perceive managers who use humor as having more productive work environments, being more effective as leaders, and being more liked by their employees (Avolio, Howell, & Sosik, 1999; Rizzo, Wanzer, & Booth–Butterfield, 1999).

Why is humor effective for achieving the objectives listed above? One reason might be due to its wide spread nature. Certainly, humor is a link to our common humanity, allowing us to chuckle at our common experience. Physiological evidence also shows that when a person is laughing or amused, their brain processes change because of the release of endorphins (Bennett & Lengacher, 2008). The human smile is the only facial expression that has the same meaning across all cultures (Pluta, 2016). One of the first things babies use as a survival technique is the smile (Gastaldo, 2015). Most people do not realize the simple power they have in their smile (Wildrich, 2013). Smiling can also change the mindset of the person who forces a smile (Giang, 2015). When it comes to remembering material, most of us can recall the last time we laughed or something that was humorous. In fact, stop for a moment and think about your favorite teacher when you were a kid, do you remember them as humorous?

"Humor that engages listeners in such a process seems to create more persuasive effect than visual humor that can be more passively observed" (Lyttle, 2001, p. 213). There is a long list of potential humor methods that include: funny stories (Bryant, Comisky, & Zillmann, 1979), humor unrelated to class material (Frymier, Wanzer, & Wojtaszczyk, 2008), unplanned humor (Wanzer, Frymier, Wojtaszczyk, & Smith, 2006), ironic wisecracks and self-effacing humor (Lyttle, 2001), self-disparaging humor (Bryant & Zillmann, 1989), wordplay/puns (Bryant et al., 1979; Wanzer, Booth–Butterfield, & Booth-Butterfield., 2005), gestures, funny facial expressions, vocal tone, and impersonations (Wanzer et al., 2005). When you use humor, you must be aware of humor potential in specific situations, know the audience, know the setting, adapt humor to fit the medium, be authentic, recognize that the potential for humor changes over time, and be conscious of why humor is being used (Roth, Yap, & Short, 2006). All of these types of humor must be addressed individually by content, audience, skill and expertise of the communicator, and very importantly – relevancy. With all of that being said humor is always a risk, when it falls flat it can usually be fixed by using more humor! Make sure you incorporate this best practice into your repertoire.

Practitioner's take on humor

Humor is the discovering, expressing, or appreciating the ludicrous or absurdly incongruous, and also the ability to be funny or to be amused by things that are funny.

What can you do to make sure that the training experience has humor woven throughout? Some people find it easy to be humorous, however, it would be a mistake to act as an entertainer instead of a trainer or instructor, this can occur when there is too much humor and/or the humor is not particularly relevant to the training. Entertaining instead of training and teaching will have the opposite effect, distracting and/or detracting from the learning. Naturally humorous instructors and trainers can use their humor as a crutch to distract from their lack of confidence, preparation, and/or knowledge. It is easy to think you are doing well when everyone is smiling at you. Sometimes it is only after the fact that the anonymous survey will reveal the frustration or dissatisfaction of the learner. Being sensitive to everyone in the room is key when using humor. You should always be reflecting on whether the humor was relevant and helpful. If you feel you are not naturally humorous you can still insert humor into the training and apply this powerful tool as a best practice for communication training.

There are two types of opportunities for you to use humor in the training experience. The first is organic, unique events that occur unexpectedly, moments when there is a gaffe by the instructor, a problem with the room set up, a challenge with technology ... the list is infinite. Organic humor can bubble up at any time, sometimes the trainees contribute humor and it's a simple matter of allowing it, being amused ourselves. Organic humor is much riskier because in order to capitalize on it, you must seize the opportunity in the moment. Take care never to use humor that causes embarrassment to one of the trainees. An example may be someone who is falling asleep and you want to say, "Bob are we keeping you up?" Maybe Bob would think that it's funny, however, there may be others in the room who become terrified of being called out so in that case it's not worth the risk. On the flip side, humor can also alleviate existing embarrassment. If Bob wakes himself up with a loud snore, you might casually say "Bob just hang on to that thought and we will circle back." You may totally disagree with those two examples and that will just reinforce the point, it's risky and it's subjective. Just like a sharp knife, humor can either be a helpful tool or hurtful weapon, and this is a nuanced training skill. The best thing an instructor or trainer can do to increase their aptitude more quickly with organic humor is record themselves for review later. This is an effective way to review the impact of humorous attempts and continue to sharpen the skill by identifying better word choice, timing, inflection, etc., and also evaluating the humor that worked well and why.

The second opportunity is planned humor, which is much easier and less risky. When planning for humor in a learning experience, you can look for opportunities through the use of images, video clips, storytelling, and/or comments that are relevant to the training objective. Using humor can make the learning experience not only productive but pleasant too! We often see a cartoon or humorous image in a slide presentation used to underscore a point, change the subject, and/or lighten the mood. Trainers should take care to avoid humor that is controversial, political, religious, gender-related, or stereotypical. What's left you ask? Common human experiences or making fun of the human condition.

Practitioner's tip on using more humor: Put yourself in the shoes of the learner and articulate their most common inner thoughts. For example, after introducing a lengthy reading list that is required, you could say "You may be thinking 'what's the deadline for dropping a class?'" or "Am I going to have to give up personal hygiene to get this reading done?". If you get a big laugh, save it and use it again. The more original, the better, as we have all heard the canned lines way too often. For example, when drawing something on a flip chart, almost everyone makes a sarcastic joke about being "a great artist". This is tired and old, avoid clichés at all costs.

Humor examples

Example I

A female coaching-client working in a male dominated industry was having great difficulty joining in group conversations. One of her fundamental challenges was her volume of which she was aware. When working with her I said "If you increase your volume outside of your comfort zone, most likely, you will feel like you're yelling. One of your listeners *might* say 'I *think* I heard something.'" My point was to illustrate to her the lengths she will need to go to because of how soft-spoken she is. When I painted this picture, it caused her to laugh uncontrollably because of the truth it spoke, also I acted it out. Because she laughed so hard, she will not only remember the lesson (go outside her level of comfort with volume), she will also have the humor as a source of courage when she is in that situation again.

Example 2

Effective learning experiences will have humor that is relevant and universal. Self-deprecation can be especially appreciated by the trainees. For example, a trainer may share their personal experience of an embarrassing moment and how they overcame it or were able to move beyond it. The example below combines storytelling with humor.

A trainer tells the humorous story of leaning on the bathroom sink and accidentally getting the crotch area of his pants wet right before being introduced on stage.

Table 25.1 Possible benefits and detriments of humor

Possible Benefits	Possible Detriments
Increases long term retention of information	Distorts perception leading to incorrect information
Creates a physiological response of relaxation, which then generates more engagement and releases tension	Distracts from the content and implies permission for interruptive behavior
Helps listeners perceive instructors/ trainers as more competent	Results in instructors/trainers perceived as less competent or not serious enough when overdone
Removes defensiveness and opens minds to alternative views, increasing engagement	Leads to engagement that causes instructor/practitioner to lose control over time and/or group
Presents meaning in an alternative way triggering critical thinking	Opens up non-relevant topics leading to confusion, running over time, and/or losing engagement of the listeners
Helps to gain and maintain attention of participants	Emphasizes entertainment over quality content and skilled delivery
Builds a collaborative environment through shared amusement	Produces side conversations and distraction
Allows transgressor to 'save face' while involving the group through collective amusement	Ostracizes or publicly humiliates the transgressor
Increases productivity	Reduces productivity when distracting and inappropriate

He quickly got behind the podium to hide it, however, he made the situation worse by taking a folder in one hand and fanning the area rapidly to dry it behind the podium. When he looked into the faces of the crowd, he realized what that the rapid movement of his arm behind the podium looked like to the listeners. He had to quickly explain what happened in the bathroom and find the humor. He now uses this personal story when training public speakers to illustrate how to be resilient in an embarrassing situation and as a side note – don't lean against the sink!

Humor can increase the engagement and comfort level of the trainees as laughing creates a physiological response, generating endorphins (Dunbar et al., 2011). The use of humor is a nuanced skill and a best practice of effective communication training, beneficial to the sender and the receiver. Table 25.1 provides the practitioner's explanation of potential benefits and detriments that may be encountered with the use of humor.

Storytelling research

Similarly to humor, storytelling allows for a unique perspective that helps an instructor and trainer connect through personal dialogue (Mandelbaum, 2003; Morgan & Dennehy, 1997). Storytelling is not acting, memorization, or recitation. It is more and accomplishes much of what cannot be articulated without the rhythm of a story (Gray, 2009). Storytelling allows the audience to connect with you through envisioning situations and scenarios that are much more detailed than typical instruction. "The story is a familiar form of communication and one that resonates with most in daily life" (Gray, 2009, p. 269). Students and training participants will find comfort in a story that helps them not only see what is important to the instructor/trainer but also see how it relates to their own life. Emotional connection is the greatest benefit of storytelling and surpasses any practice that helps explain information (Sole & Wilson, 2002). Storytelling allows you, the teacher, to take ideas, concepts, and information and relate them to the audience and themselves on a personal level. Exposing ourselves through shared experiences allows people to relate because of our willingness to show our own vulnerability (Greene, 1996). When a person relates to both the storyteller and the story, the material is easier to recall (Sole & Wilson, 2002; Yang & Wu, 2012).

Storytelling is a powerful message strategy, communication medium, and educational tool (Gray, 2009). The use of stories conveys the importance of organizational norms and values. Those who train in organizational settings can articulate the values shared over time and how they have changed. This is important in teaching a class as well. Communication has developed over time, and understanding those principles is facilitated by examining changes through detailed and descriptive stories. Creating a vision about what has been and what might be helps learners feel connected to all of the material being delivered (Prusak, 2001; Denning, 2002; Brown, 1982). Communication that helps create order out of chaos, co-creation of meaning, revolution, and transmission of images and visions that change how one thinks of a situation is a factor of good storytelling (Greene, 1996). Students and participants can step outside the story and analyze and critique, while getting to know the details and revealing their interpretations (Gray, 2009; Swap, Leonard, Shields, & Abrams, 2001). This allows the instructor to have a sense of the students' knowledge and understanding.

Storytelling provides a platform to help people create and hold onto values, whether this is a student needing to understand the importance of studying or an individual in an organization who needs help understanding organizational change. Stories have the ability to spark tacit understanding in those listening (Whyte & Classen, 2012). Any knowledge or information that is difficult to transfer to another must be coupled with an exciting and emotionally connectable account. As a practitioner, this is an invaluable tool for illustrating the relevance of the skill you are training. A good story will answer the question of why this information is relevant and valuable.

Stories help communicate competence as well as communicate trust and commitment to the topic and audience (Sole & Wilson, 2002). Rapport is created through storytelling and often carries over to other aspects, including the act of leading an educational group. Listening is a critical component to learning. Storytelling encourages the art of listening through visualization, entertainment, and ultimately, education (Greene, 1996).

A considerable amount of the research on storytelling as a training and educational practice has been focused in educational settings. However, organizational research also justifies the use of storytelling in training. If implemented successfully, storytelling can help bring a sense of community to a group of individuals trying to learn new skills and information within an organization (Barker & Gower, 2010). Storytelling helps individuals find the narrative of the organization while providing a safe learning environment, encouraging creative thinking, and encouraging motivation to develop storylines that may or may not align with the narrative of the organization (Beigi, 2014). "Engaging in a process of re-storying enables participants to reflect on narrative order and experience story-disorder, thus creating opportunities for participants to understand, appreciate and take multiple perspectives on organizational life and decision-making" (Schedlitzki, Jarvis, & MacInnes, 2015, p. 423). Sharing personal experiences as well as organizational narratives help with transitions as well as jumpstarting collaboration and cohesiveness in professional development and training (Boje, 1991; Kahan, 2006).

Practitioner's take on storytelling

Storytelling is an account of imaginary or real people and events told for entertainment, illustration, persuasion, education, rapport, influence, etc. Why is storytelling effective for achieving these objectives? Stories answer the question "why?". Why is what you are teaching valuable? Can you not only articulate it, can you tell the story of why? Why and how does it apply to the learner? For example, let's say we are training participants to use PowerPoint (visual aid) more effectively by animating (build) the content (bullets) in the slides in order to have content synchronized with the verbal delivery during a presentation. As an instructor, you could take the opportunity to use data or statistics to demonstrate the effectiveness of retention with synchronized visuals vs non-synchronized … OR … you could use a story to illustrate the consequences of *not* synchronizing the content with the oral presentation. Case in point, below is a story used with clients when instructing on the importance of using the build feature of PowerPoint to synchronize visual and auditory content during a presentation.

Story example

"I had a client named Sally who was delivering an important presentation with PowerPoint to higher ups in a corporation. Sally had spent hours putting the slides together and practicing her delivery. This was a rare opportunity for her to demonstrate her leadership, knowledge, and presentation skills. When she landed on a slide with five bullets of important information, she was interrupted and barraged with questions for the fifth bullet when she was still presenting the first bullet. Sally became rattled as she knew that if she had the chance to deliver bullets two through four that she would not be getting these questions. Because she was caught off guard, she was no longer in control and was not only nervous, but in a defensive state. Needless to say, she did not make the impression she had hoped and the opportunity to demonstrate her skills was not only lost but she demonstrated incompetence and nervousness instead."

By using this story to illustrate a real-life example of the consequences of not applying this lesson, it is much easier for learners to accept the teaching and rationale. The power of story in this example is that it resonates to the common fear of being perceived as ineffective in a professional setting or even worse, public humiliation. Imagining this fear while listening to the story example helps the trainee retain the lesson. By feeling the emotion of fear by imagining themselves in Sally's shoes, the trainee understands *viscerally* why they should build their slides and synchronize their message, thereby increasing their retention of the lesson. Storytelling demonstrates communication proficiency because of its power to simultaneously demonstrate relevance, incite emotion, and illustrate consequences thereby increasing the value of the information. Instructors should consider designing lessons incorporating relevant storytelling as a best practice in order to make the training more effective. Table 25.2 provides the practitioner's explanation of potential benefits and detriments that may be encountered with the use of storytelling.

Practitioner's tip on using more storytelling: Often times in a training situation the participant will offer a story (example) illustrating the teaching point. Ask for permission to use the story in future training, alter it if necessary to be more universal and document it so you don't forget. Try to have multiple stories you can switch off of so your delivery does not sound canned or rote.

Table 25.2 Possible Benefits and Detriments of Storytelling

Possible Benefits	Possible Detriments
Increases long term retention of information	Distorts perception leading to incorrect information
Helps to gain and maintain attention of participants	Causes listeners to be distracted or confused
Listeners perceive instructors/trainers as more competent	Instructors/trainers perceived as less competent or not serious enough when overdone
Removes defensiveness and open minds to alternative views increasing engagement	Leads to engagement that causes instructor/practitioner to lose control over time and/or group
Presents meaning in an alternative way triggering critical thinking	Opens up non-relevant topics leading to confusion, running over time and/or losing engagement of the listeners
Builds a collaborative environment through shared narratives.	Could erupt in side conversations and distraction.

Humor and storytelling as skills demonstrating communication proficiency

Humor and storytelling research and usage outline several benefits. As can be seen from both research and practitioner views above, they share similar positive outcomes that should be noted for both scholars and trainers. These skills are examined together because they are often used together and share many of the same benefits.

First, storytelling and humor help an instructor and practitioner open minds and remove defensiveness, facilitating an environment that allows for comfortable exchanges of ideas as well as provides the instructor or practitioner with tools to deal with transgressions in the classroom or training environment (Claus, Booth-Butterfield, & Chory, 2012; Sidelinger, 2014; Sole & Wilson, 2002).

Second, humor and storytelling help increase retention. These two delivery methods present meaning in a different way, triggering critical thinking and improving recall, retention, and comprehension skills (Wanzer, Frymier, & Irwin, 2009; Hackathorn, Garczynski, Blankmeyer, Tennial, & Solomon, 2012; Yang & Wu, 2012). Humor and storytelling are unique in that they help gain and maintain attention, increasing the chance that learners are engaged and focused (Ziv, 1979). In the practitioner world, retention is measured as a return on investment and can translate into much more business.

Third, these skills encourage engagement easily from hesitant participants. Those who have not felt comfortable to speak in typical classes can find a sense of renewed energy in classes that use these two strategies (Banas, Dunbar, Rodriguez, & Liu, 2011; Korobkin, 1988). As a practitioner, it is essential to get everyone engaged and productively learning because "time is money"; being proficient with humor and storytelling allow you to accomplish engagement in less time.

Fourth, humor and storytelling can increase the comfort level of the participants. These two strategies are not communication practices that directly increase comprehension, but develop a comfortable environment that encourages participation, thus leading to better comprehension and learning (Neuliep, 1991; Ravichand, 2013).

Fifth, humor and storytelling can build a collaborative environment through shared laughter or amusement (Holmes, 2006; Booth-Butterfield, Booth-Butterfield, & Wanzer, 2007; Fletcher & Cambre, 2009). Often when laughing, people will look around to see who else "gets" the humor. Some of this checking on others' reactions also comes from a need to belong, to be sure that we are not being inappropriate, offensive, or rude. Many times, laughter is contagious and creates a positive shared emotion and shared experience which makes approachability and collaboration easier. This process is often referred to as: "breaking the ice". For practitioners, you become someone that management values as they see your "collaborative environment" as an added benefit of team building for the business.

In summary, humor and storytelling are essential skills for communication trainers who value openness, comfort, engagement, and retention in the learning environment. This chapter has outlined benefits and detriments that may be encountered. You should reflect on your existing aptitude and make an intention to hone these skills where possible. Although these skills complement each other, they can be used simultaneously or separately. Not everyone is naturally proficient in humor and/or storytelling. However, these skills are worth acquiring and practicing because of the many benefits outlined in this chapter. Both are worth incorporating with practice, preparation, and careful consideration. You, the practitioner, should assess the relevance, appropriateness, and effectiveness, then strive to improve and incorporate these skills naturally in your own training process. Besides, everyone looks better when they're smiling, including you!

References

Avolio, B. J., Howell, J. M., & Sosik, J. J. (1999). A funny thing happened on the way to the bottom line: Humor as a moderator of leadership style effects. *Academy of Management Journal, 42*, 219–227. doi:10.2307/257094

Banas, J. A., Dunbar, N., Rodriguez, D., & Liu, S. J. (2011). A review of humor in educational settings: Four decades of research. *Communication Education, 60*, 115–144. doi: 10.1080/0363 4523.2010.496867

Barbazette, J. (2005). The trainer's journey to competence: Tools, assessments, and models. San Francisco, CA: John Wiley & Sons.

Barker, R. T., & Gower, K. (2010). Strategic application of storytelling in organizations: Toward effective communication in a diverse world. *The Journal of Business Communication, 47*(3), 295–312. DOI: 10.1177/0021943610369782

Beigi, M. (2014). Using fictional stories to facilitate training and development. *Human Resource Development International, 17*(4), 491–496. doi:10.1080/13678868.2014.932083

Bennett, M. P., & Lengacher, C. (2008). Humor and laughter may influence health: III. Laughter and health outcomes. *Evidence-Based Complementary and Alternative Medicine, 5*(1), 37–40.

Boje, D. M. (1991). The storytelling organization: A study of story performance. *Administrative Science Quarterly, 36*, 106–126.

Booth-Butterfield, S., & Booth-Butterfield, M. (1991). Individual differences in the communication of humorous messages. *Southern Communication Journal, 56*, 205–217. doi: l0.1080/ 10417949109372831

Booth-Butterfield, M., Booth-Butterfield, S., & Wanzer, M. (2007). Funny students cope better: Patterns of humor enactment and coping effectiveness. *Communication Quarterly, 55*, 299–315. doi:10.1080/01463370701490232

Bousfield, W. A. (1940). Students' ratings of qualities considered desirable in college professors. *School & Society, 51*, 253–246.

Braverman, T., & Petrini, C. (1993). Enhance your sense of self-mirth. *Training & Development, 47*(7), 9–12.

Brown, M. H. (1982) *That reminds me of a story: Speech action on organizational socialization.* (Doctoral Dissertation). Available from ProQuest Dissertations and Theses database. (UMI No. 8217827)

Bryant, J., Comisky, P., & Zillmann, D. (1979). Teachers' humor in the college classroom. *Communication Education, 28*, 110–118. doi:10.1080/03634527909378339

Bryant, J., & Zillmann, D. (1989). Using humor to promote learning in the classroom. In P. E. McGhee (ed.), *Humor and children's development: A guide to practical applications* (pp. 49–78). New York, NY: Haworth Press.

Check, J. F. (1986). Positive traits of the effective teacher—negative traits of the ineffective one. *Education, 106*, 326–334.

Claus, C. J., Booth-Butterfield, M., & Chory, R. M. (2012). The relationship between instructor misbehaviors and student antisocial behavioral alteration techniques: The roles of instructor attractiveness, humor and relational closeness. *Communication Education, 62*, 161–183. doi: 10.1080/03634523.2011.647922

Decker, W. H., & Rotondo, D. M. (2001). Relationships among gender, type of humor, and perceived leader effectiveness. *Journal of Managerial Issues, 13*, 450–465.

Denning, S. (2002). Using stories to spark organizational change. *Systems Thinker, 13,* 2–6.

Dunbar, R. I., Baron, R., Frangou, A., Pearce, E., Van Leeuwin, E. J., Stow, J., Partridge, G., MacDonald, I., Barra, V., & Van Vugt, M. (2011). Social laughter is correlated with an elevated pain threshold. *Proceedings of the Royal Society of London B: Biological Sciences, 279,* 1–7. doi:10.1098/rspb.2011.1373

Evans, R., & Cleghorn, A. (2010). 'Look at the balloon blow up': Student teacher-talk in linguistically diverse foundation phase classrooms. *Southern African Linguistics and Applied Language Studies, 28,* 141–151. doi:10.2989/16073614.2010.519105

Fletcher, C., & Cambre, C. (2009). Digital storytelling and implicated scholarship in the classroom. *Journal of Canadian Studies, 43,* 109–130. doi:10.3138/jcs.43.1.109

Fortson, S. B., & Brown, W. E. (1998). Best and worst university instructors: The opinions of graduate students. *College Student Journal, 32,* 572–576.

Frymier, A. B., & Thompson, C. A. (1992). Perceived teacher affinity-seeking in relation to perceived teacher credibility. *Communication Education, 41,* 368–399. doi:10.1080/03634529209378900

Frymier, A. B., Wanzer, M. B., & Wojtaszczyk, A. M. (2008). Assessing students' perceptions of inappropriate and appropriate teacher humor. *Communication Education, 57,* 266–288.

Gastaldo, E. (2015, September 24). Researchers say they know why babies smile. [Web log post]. Retrieved from http://www.newser.com/story/213410/researchers-say-they-know-why-babies-smile.html

Giang, V. (2015, January 28). How smiling changes your brain. [Web log post]. Retrieved from https://www.fastcompany.com/3041438/how-smiling-changes-your-brain

Gray, J. B. (2009). The power of storytelling: Using narrative in the healthcare context. *Journal of Communication in Healthcare, 2,* 258–273. doi:10.1179/cih.2009.2.3.258

Greene, E. (1996). *Storytelling: Art and Technique: Art and Technique.* Westport, CT: Greenwood Publishing Group.

Gruner, C. R. (1967). Effect of humor on speaker ethos and audience information gain. *Journal of Communication, 17,* 228–233. doi:10.1111/j.1460–2466.1967.tb01181.x

Hackathorn, J., Garczynski, A. M., Blankmeyer, K., Tennial, R. D., & Solomon, E. D. (2012). All kidding aside: Humor increases learning at knowledge and comprehension levels. *Journal of the Scholarship of Teaching and Learning, 11*(4), 116–123.

Holmes, J. (2006). Sharing a laugh: Pragmatic aspects of humor and gender in the workplace. *Journal of Pragmatics, 38,* 26–50. doi: 10.1016/j.pragma.2005.06.007

Kahan, S. (2006). The power of storytelling to jumpstart collaboration. *Journal for Quality and Participation, 29,* 23–25.

Kaplan, R. M., & Pascoe, G. C. (1977). Humorous lectures and humorous examples: Some effects upon comprehension and retention. *Journal of Educational Psychology, 69,* 61–65.

Korobkin, D. (1988). Humor in the classroom: Considerations and strategies. *College Teaching, 36,* 154–158.

Lyttle, J. (2001). The effectiveness of humor in persuasion: The case of business ethics training. *The Journal of General Psychology, 128*(2), 206–216.

Mandelbaum, J. (2003). How to "do things" with narrative: A communication perspective on narrative skill. In J. Greene & B. Burleson (eds.), *Handbook of communication and social interaction skills* (pp. 595–633). Mahwah, NJ: Psychology Press.

Morgan, S., & Dennehy, R. F. (1997). The power of organizational storytelling: A management development perspective. *Journal of Management Development, 16*(7), 494–501.

Neuliep, J. W. (1991). An examination of the content of high school teachers' humor in the classroom and the development of an inductively derived taxonomy of classroom humor. *Communication Education, 40,* 343–355.

Pluta, P. (2016, September 20). The universality of smile and laughter. *Psychology of Humor.* [Web log post]. Retrieved from http://www.psychologyofhumor.com/2016/09/20/the-universality-of-smiles-and-laughter/

Powell, J. P., & Andresen, L. W. (1985). Humor and teaching in higher education. *Studies in Higher Education, 10,* 79–90.

Prusak, L. (2001). Storytelling in organizations. In J. S. Brown, S. Denning, K. Groh, & L. Prusak (eds.), *Storytelling in organizations: Why storytelling is transforming 21st century organizations and management* (pp. 15–48). New York, NY: Routledge.

Ravichand, M. (2013). Humor—An aid to learning and instruction. *Journal of Humanities and Social Science, 11*, 18–21.

Rizzo, B. J., Wanzer, M. B., & Booth-Butterfield, M. (1999). Individual differences in managers' use of humor. Subordinate perceptions of managers' humor. *Communication Research Reports, 16*(4), 360–369.

Roth, G., Yap, R., & Short, D. (2006). Examining humour in HRD from theoretical and practical perspectives. *Human Resource Development International, 9*(1), 121–127.

Schedlitzki, D., Jarvis, C., & MacInnes, J. (2015). Leadership development: A place for storytelling and Greek mythology? *Management Learning, 46*(4), 412–426. doi: 10.1177/1350507614560303

Seibold, D. R., Kudsi, S., & Rude, M. (1993). Does communication training make a difference? Evidence for the effectiveness of a presentation skills program. *Journal of Applied Communication Research, 21*, 111–131. doi:10.1080/00909889309365361

Sidelinger, R. J. (2014). Using relevant humor to moderate inappropriate conversations: Maintaining student communication satisfaction in the classroom. *Communication Research Reports, 31*, 292–301. doi: 10.1080/08824096.2014.924339

Sole, D., & Wilson, D. G. (2002). Storytelling in organizations: The power and traps of using stories to share knowledge in organizations. *LILA, Harvard, Graduate School of Education*, 1–12. http://www.providersedge.com/docs/km_articles/Storytelling_in_Organizations.pdf

Sudol, D. (1981). Dangers of classroom humor. *English Journal, 70*(6), 26–28.

Swap, W., Leonard, D., Shields, M., & Abrams, L. (2001). Using mentoring and storytelling to transfer knowledge in the workplace. *Journal of Management Information Systems, 18*(1), 95–114.

Teslow, J. L. (1995). Humor me: A call for research. *Educational Technology Research & Development, 43*, 6–28.

Torok, S. E., McMorris, R. F., & Lin, W. C. (2004). Is humor an appreciated teaching tool? Perceptions of professors' teaching styles and use of humor. *College Teaching, 52*(1), 14–20.

Wanzer, M. B., Booth-Butterfield, M., & Booth-Butterfield, S. (2005). "If we didn't use humor, we'd die": Humorous coping in health care settings. *Journal of Health Communication, 10*, 105–125.

Wanzer, M. B., & Frymier, A. B. (1999). The relationship between student perceptions of instructor humor and students' reports of learning. *Communication Education, 48*, 48–62. doi:10.1080/03634529909379152

Wanzer, M. B., Frymier, A. B., & Irwin, J (2009). An explanation of the relationship between instructor humor and student learning: Instructional humor processing theory. *Communication Education, 59*(1), 1–18. doi:10.1080/03634520903367238

Wanzer, M. B., Frymier, A. B., Wojtaszczyk, A. M., & Smith, T. (2006). Appropriate and inappropriate uses of humor by teachers. *Communication Education, 55*, 178–196.

Whyte, G., & Classen, S. (2012). Using storytelling to elicit tacit knowledge from SMEs. *Journal of Knowledge Management, 16*(6), 950–962. doi:10.1108/13673271211276218

Wildrich, L. (2013, April 9). The science of smiling: A guide to the world's most powerful gesture. [Web log post]. Retrieved from https://blog.bufferapp.com/the-science-of-smiling-a-guide-to-humans-most-powerful-gesture

Worley, D., Titsworth, S., Worley, D. W., & Cornett-DeVito, M. (2007). Instructional communication competence: Lessons learned from award-winning teachers. *Communication Studies, 58*, 207–222. doi:10.1080/10510970701341170

Yang, Y. T. C., & Wu, W. C. I. (2012). Digital storytelling for enhancing student academic achievement, critical thinking, and learning motivation: A year-long experimental study. *Computers & Education, 59*(2), 339–352.

Ziv, A. (1979). Sociometry of humor: Objectifying the subjective. *Perceptual and Motor Skills, 49*(1), 97–98.

Chapter 26

Effectively integrating group techniques to develop communication proficiency

Kristine M. Nicolini and DeAnne Priddis

Abstract

This chapter examines communication proficiency in relation to group communication by analyzing the stages of typical group communication processes to provide CCCTTs with effective techniques and strategies to help to maximize group performance. Gaining a deep understanding of the stages of group communication and developing effective methods to help groups at each stage of the process is a critical skillset for any CCCTT to continuously enhance throughout one's career.

Communication coaches, consultants, teachers, or trainers (CCCTTs) use best practices within the communication discipline to guide and to enhance the quality of services provided. Best practices serve as a benchmark for competence, accountability, and transparency within the discipline (NCA, 2017) and define the most important communication outcomes for clients. The National Communication Association's (NCA) Training and Development division (2017) has identified 12 best practices focused on seven areas. These best practices help shape how CCCTTs assist others in developing more effective communication skills.

Communication proficiency is one of the seven areas identified and is demonstrated by advanced skills in: (a) presentation techniques for a range of speaking contexts and experiences; (b) speaker credibility design and assessment; (c) interpersonal communication techniques and theories; (d) organizational culture; and (e) group communication techniques and strategies. This chapter will focus on communication proficiency, as it relates to group communication techniques and strategies by offering insights and tools for CCCTTs to help groups maximize performance. Gaining a deep understanding of group communication and developing effective techniques and strategies to help groups achieve desired outcomes is a critical skillset for any CCCTT.

Helping individuals understand how the small group process unfolds is essential to developing group communication proficiency. The five-stage small group process model (forming, storming, norming, performing, and adjourning) helps CCCTTs and individual team members develop a more robust understanding of the process groups must experience to achieve shared goals (Tuckman & Jensen, 1977). This chapter highlights the Tuckman model which has been lauded for both ease of use for practitioners and as a valuable resource for conversations between academia and the field (Bonebright, 2010; McMorris, Gottleib, & Sneden, 2005). Researchers have noted both educators and practitioners can learn from the model that has stood the test of time for over 45 years by "providing a simple, accessible starting point for conversations about key issues of group dynamics" (Bonebright, 2010, p. 119). Based on our experiences helping groups achieve optimal performance, we have found the Tuckman model to be a valuable asset in understanding the opportunities and challenges of the small group process. This chapter combines research and practical experience related to this model to share with CCCTTs strategies for success.

Before we delve into the Tuckman model further, it is important for CCCTTs to recognize the model's limitations. Specifically, Rickards and Moger (2000) contend the model must be extended to consider two key barriers (behavioral and performance) groups encounter. Only through the integration of a creative leadership style will groups overcome these two challenges and achieve optimal success. CCCTTs should be mindful of the limitations highlighted by Rickards and Moger's (2000) two compelling questions: "What if the storming stage never ends?" and "What is needed to exceed performance norms?" The first question is overcome through the creation of a shared standard of performance discussed later in the chapter. The second inquiry requires the integration of a creative leadership style centered on seven team factors (see Rickards & Moger, 2000). Therefore, if CCCTTs observe the fruition of one or both of the two compelling questions, they may seek out additional resources to help teams transition through these two barriers.

Once individuals have a strong sense of what each of the phases in the five-stage model entails, they can better identify which stage the group is experiencing, what challenges need to be addressed, and how to move the team forward. Furthermore, as group members become more adept at recognizing these stages, they develop stronger levels of small group communication proficiency, resulting in better team outcomes.

CCCTTs facilitate this process by clearly explaining and exploring each stage within the small group process model to ensure individuals know what to expect throughout their small group experience. The CCCTT ensures the group remains on task and facilitates differing viewpoints throughout the process (Beebe, Mottet, & Roach, 2013). Developing a clear roadmap where individuals can recognize each stage and adjust their communication behavior accordingly is paramount to navigating the small group process successfully.

While this chapter focuses on exploring the small group process model (Tuckman & Jensen, 1977), it is imperative that CCCTTs dedicate themselves to the continuous development of group strategies and techniques. Honing these abilities will allow CCCTTs to help others develop the necessary skills to succeed in a variety of group communication settings, which may or may not include the small group process model outlined within the chapter. Therefore, CCCTTs should focus on reflecting on their own knowledge and prowess with the many skills outlined throughout the chapter. As CCCTTs read the information presented, they should ask themselves how adept they are at each of the skills discussed and how comfortable they feel navigating the diverse situations presented throughout the chapter. Continuously cultivating both knowledge and expertise in group communication techniques and strategies is essential to building a CCCTT professional tool kit of best practices designed for success.

Advantages and disadvantages of working in groups

Small groups are defined as individuals that come together for a specific purpose, such as solving a complex problem. Each group member brings unique contributions to the group (i.e. skills, background, and access to resources) that will help the group be more productive. One group member may have experience working on this type of project at a previous employer, whereas another group member may have access to department policies and decision makers within the company. These interdependent group members will help the overall group be more productive as they work toward achieving their common goal. Interdependent groups achieve synergy when performance surpasses expectations due to increased motivation, effort, effective communication, and diversity of knowledge, skills, and abilities (Rothwell, 2016).

Companies and college classes often encourage the use of group work to create a learning community that produces more effective results. Successful groups are able to accomplish more and experience greater success in the workplace or classroom.

CCCTTs must recognize that individuals come to the group with preconceived notions about group work. Some individuals embrace the opportunity to work in a team environment whereas others may experience grouphate based on past negative group experiences (Adams & Galanes, 2015; Allan, 2016; Rothwell, 2016).

There are several reasons past experiences may cause some individuals to avoid working in groups including: differing levels of participation, unbalanced workloads, and interpersonal conflict. Individuals may have had a past negative work experience with an individual or group which created a hardship in completing the project. Although teams often self-manage and self-correct, this conflict can cause teams to be less productive and get stuck in one of the five stages of the small group process model (Tuckman & Jensen, 1977).

To create an environment for group success, CCCTTs should recognize that individuals have different positive and negative past experiences that may color their perspective as they join the group. Having candid conversations about these issues during the beginning stages (i.e. forming, storming, norming) of the small group process and developing strategies to help individuals work through these issues is essential to helping groups transition to the later stages of performing and adjourning (Rickards & Moger, 2000) and creating a cohesive, productive group experience.

Small group process model

The small group process model consists of five stages (forming, storming, norming, performing, and adjourning) that most groups experience throughout a project (Tuckman & Jensen, 1977). While some groups experience the stages in order, CCCTTs should recognize groups can transition through the stages out of order or get stuck in a specific stage. CCCTTs who understand and recognize each stage can provide tools and strategies to help group members navigate this process more smoothly. It is important to note that the CCCTT functions as guide or support system for the group but may not be an active member. In this role, the CCCTT provides knowledge and resources to help the group function more effectively. It is from this facilitation perspective the following recommendations in each stage of the model are provided.

Forming

During the first stage in the small group process, forming, CCCTTs play an important role in helping the team acclimate to working together by creating a shared vision to achieve the desired outcome. During this phase, individuals may feel heighten levels of uncertainty as they often meet for the first time, learn about the task at hand, and begin to become acquainted with one another (Edwards, Edwards, Wahl, & Myers, 2013).

CCCTTs help clients better facilitate this initial meeting by advising the creation of a structured agenda that includes opportunities for each individual team member to participate and to share his or her expertise with the group. Doing so prioritizes the development of a shared identity and focuses the team on a common goal. One way to start this conversation is to provide background information on why the team is coming together. This background discussion helps both set the tone for the group project and provides an opportunity to discuss why the team was formed, what problem the team is being asked to solve, and how that situation links back to organizational goals and objectives. The conversation helps establish the importance of the group's outcomes and ensures all group members understand the significance of accomplishing the assigned project.

Communication may be excessively polite and superficial (Maples, 1988) during this stage because group members are more focused on being accepted and included rather than the task at hand (Wheelan, 2014). Many different factors impact communication during this first phase of group development including past group experience and perceptions of group work. To help alleviate some of the initial uncertainty and demonstrate the level of expertise represented on the team, CCCTTs should advise building on the background discussion by asking each group member to share their expertise related to the project with the team. Providing time for each person to reflect on their background information and then share how they will contribute helps each group member determine his or her role within the group, initial perceptions of teammates, and the level of effort that will be required to complete the task at hand (Edwards et al., 2013).

At times, the group may experience challenges from individual team members who are reticent to participate. To effectively overcome these moments of uncertainty, CCCTTs must have extensive interpersonal communication skills and rely heavily on their ability to read the nonverbal communication cues being given. CCCTTs should take time to assess their interpersonal communication abilities using both assessments and research. Emotional intelligence assessments can be used to gauge understanding of oneself and others (Bar-on, 1997; Goleman, 1995). Specific interpersonal communication assessments can help CCCTTs assess their own competency levels related to key skills such as listening, identity, roles, power differentials, and conversational exchanges. The findings of interpersonal communication researchers (Sabee, 2015; Spitzberg, 1983) related to the efficacy and appropriateness of communication in different settings may also be beneficial to CCCTTs. Specifically, CCCTTs should understand the demonstration of effective interpersonal communication skills (i.e. listening, reading nonverbal cues) is intimately linked to a deeper level of communication illustrated through the appropriate use of those skills in a given situation. This vital link between appropriateness, effectiveness, and motivation is the key to mastering communication competence and will allow CCCTTs to leverage strategies to bring all group members into the conversation in a positive, productive manner.

As part of these opening conversations, the CCCTT should advise the group to take time to discuss the scope of the project. The scope should provide a clear, concise definition of project expectations, set parameters for successful project completion criteria, and provide justification for the work being undertaken. For shorter projects this discussion may be limited to the establishment of verbally agreed upon ground rules or formal agendas. For longer projects or projects in which team members are working together for the first time, the conversations may take place through the creation of a team charter, a document that is crafted to guide the group through the small group process (Natvig & Stark, 2016). A team charter is defined as "a formal document written by team members at the outset of a team's life cycle that specifies acceptable behaviors in the team" (Courtright, McCormick, Mistry, & Wang, 2017, p. 1). This tool assists individuals coming together as a team to establish group expectations for the life cycle of the project. Research has demonstrated a high-quality team charter can increase performance (Courtright et al., 2017) and provide a mechanism for individuals to begin immediately leading and influencing each other (Blanchard, 2006).

CCCTTs who suggest the implementation of a team charter may faces challenges from the group pertaining to the necessity of the tool. Often groups are unaware of the obstacles ahead and want to begin working on the task at hand rather than spend time coming up with strategies to overcome unforeseen obstacles. In such situations, CCCTTs may recognize that the use of the term "team charter" is the cause of resistance and may instead choose to incorporate a less provocative title such as "ground rules" or "group expectations". Conversely, the CCCTT that moves forward with the team charter concept must establish credibility as the expert on successful group work while also sharing observed past negative group experiences (Myers & Goodboy, 2005). If the CCCTT both establishes credibility and helps group members identify past negative group experiences, they will be better positioned to help the group understand the value of a team charter process. Alternatively, the CCCTT can also guide the group through the project by providing training throughout the group process to help team members maintain a clear picture of success.

Demonstrating project outcomes are both realistic and attainable is an important step to obtain buy-in from individual group members. Past research demonstrates group goals increase overall team performance by focusing attention toward the team and enhancing cooperation amongst members (Gardner, Kosemund, Hogg, Heymann, & Martinez, 2017; O'Leary-Kelly, Martocchio, & Frink, 1994). CCCTTs who provide tools to engage in candid conversations and set realistic goals and objectives based on available resources help groups prioritize outcomes and maintain project scope boundaries. Tools such as prioritization of outcomes mapped to available resources can help facilitate such fruitful discussions.

Roles and responsibilities. Successful groups ensure each individual member understands and embraces their roles within the team. CCCTTs facilitate this process by providing a robust opportunity to explore each team member's unique skill sets and knowledge in relation to the project scope. This can be accomplished in several stages including: (a) individual assessment of strengths, weaknesses, and roles; (b) discussion of the importance of balancing roles across work groups; and (c) clear responsibilities and role delineations (Galanes, Adams, & Brilhart, 2004).

Each team member must understand their individual contributions to the realization of the team goal. Unclear connections may cause individuals to pursue personal goals which may conflict with the team goals (Slater, 1955). Research on small groups currently and historically situates roles into three distinct categories based on behaviors used to help or hinder the group progress towards the goal: task, maintenance, and individual (Benne & Sheats, 1948). Individual group members will typically fulfill multiple task and maintenance roles during a project. Task roles assist the group in achieving the assigned task. These group members will contribute by reporting the current status of the project, completed stages of work, and future deliverables through roles such as initiator, summarizer, recorder, and orienter (Adams & Galanes, 2015). Maintenance roles help build and strengthen relational aspects of working in a team. These group members fulfill roles such as harmonizer, encourager, and gatekeeper. The maintenance group members help to improve overall group relational satisfaction and group communication throughout the project (Myers et al., 2010).

Group members that are unclear of group goals may instead assume roles that do not help the team achieve the assigned task. The emergence of individual roles, such as aggressor, recognition seeker, and dominator, distracts members from the work at hand and refocuses attention on individual members in a manner that detracts from overall group effectiveness.

To help individuals identify what roles they typically assume within a group environment, CCCTTs may provide an assessment activity where each group member has the opportunity to review the different roles within a small group and identify the roles in which they feel most comfortable. Comparing each member's preferred roles with both task and maintenance aspects of group work often leads to beneficial conversations about existing role gaps on the team and which members might be willing to assume those roles to help balance the overall team dynamic. CCCTTs should also take time to discuss the detrimental impact individual roles can have on the overall effectiveness of the group. Allowing individuals to identify if they assume these roles and having a robust conversation about how the group will address if any individual traits appear is a powerful preventative measure to reduce potential distractions from the goal throughout the small group process.

Other important considerations include: (a) what additional skills or expertise might be needed for project success; (b) are there other teams or individuals that must be consulted during the project duration; and (c) is additional training required to complete the project scope. Addressing these variables will help individual members better understand their own unique contributions to the team and identify and alleviate any gaps in talent, skill sets, or communication channels before they become a source of conflict. The CCCTT will be challenged to help the group not only understand each group member's skillset, but also to help each group member understand their role on the team, and individual contribution to the group's success. This clear connection helps team members remain engaged in achieving the overall group goal without the distraction of personal agendas (Slater, 1955).

To help facilitate this process, CCCTTs should assess their own prowess in the integration of different roles within group communication. This is accomplished by CCCTTs studying the different characteristics of each role and learning to recognize when members are exhibiting key indicators associated with assuming that role (Benne & Sheats, 1948). It is important for CCCTTs to be well versed in this area as there are a variety of roles that CCCTTs may be using including the classic ones mentioned earlier or others such as Belbin Team Roles (see Smartt Lynch, Lynch, & Clemens, this volume). Regardless of which type of roles are being implemented, it is important to take time to understand how they intersect and support successful group work. This will help CCCTTs promote individual and group commitment at the early stages of the project.

The integration of tools designed to help establish a sense of group identity and expectations are helpful to understand the group's purpose and for relational development. After group members have established an initial level of comfort with each other, they transition to the storming phase. CCCTTs ensure they are prepared for this next stage by monitoring the group's progress toward building a shared identity. Using plural pronouns such as "we" and "our" and demonstrating a common vision for success are two indicators that individuals within the group are beginning to develop a shared identity. The CCCTT helps the team get to this stage by modeling the use of these pronouns throughout the project.

Storming

During the storming phase, group members experience challenges associated with learning to work together. CCCTTs help groups better navigate this by acknowledging that conflict is a normal part of the group process and empowering groups to work through issues effectively. At this stage, team members have a heightened level of comfort with each other, resulting in the sharing of ideas, initial self-disclosure, and contributions to discussions. While these signs of progress indicate positive steps toward group identity, the team has not yet established the procedures necessary to accomplish the assigned task (Edwards et al., 2013) resulting in open disagreements about both the goal of the group and the task at hand (Wheelan, 2014). These points of contention, coupled with individuals struggling to reconcile their individual identity with their newly emerging group identity, often result in increased levels of communication and conflict.

The goal of a CCCTT is to appropriately help minimize the amount of time groups spend in the storming stage by helping them integrate strategies to handle these points of contention. A warning sign that a group is struggling with conflict is when individual team members use individual identity indicators instead of a group identity. The use of the pronoun "I" signals that the person is not feeling part of the group and may require individual consulting from the CCCTT to overcome the struggle (Burrell & Nicolini, 2017).

To effectively support individuals who are struggling with group identity, the CCCTT must assess his or her knowledge of interpersonal conflict management. Common barriers teams may have to overcome include: team dictators (West & Markiewicz, 2004), free riding (Wagner, 1995), social loafing (Karau & Williams, 1993; West, 2004), and a lack of team psychological safety (Edmondson, 1999).

Specifically, the CCCTT must be able to exhibit exceptional listening skills to identify the issue at play and provide the individual who is experiencing conflict with communication strategies to help address the issue. Individual members may share their perspective of what is causing the issue. A skilled CCCTT will be able to integrate this information with past observations of the group's and the individual's interactions to help formulate a plan for how the individual can successfully address the situation.

CCCTTs may also point out to the group the positive aspects of conflict. Having strategies to handle disagreements and see multiple perspectives on a situation will help teams grow together and increase relational satisfaction while creating greater cohesiveness within the group (Galanes et al., 2004; Myers et al., 2010). For example, a group that is moving forward with a decision without considering alternative options (i.e. groupthink) may need a group member to discuss the impact on other departments and projects to prevent tunnel vision (Janis, 1972).

Group members must work through important issues that may deter their effectiveness, including: group member participation, accountability, and deadlines. An individual group member can create hardship for the team through over-participating or under-participating. Over-participating group members can be challenging, make others feel less significant (West & Markiewicz, 2004), and limit equal participation. CCCTTs should observe groups to ensure equitable participation and schedule check-in meetings with each team member. During the check-in session, the CCCTT should discuss with individual members the positive and challenging aspects of their experiences working in a team and empower them to troubleshoot any issues. CCCTTs should then offer customized strategies, based on the situation, to help individuals work through their challenges. For example, if a team member is having an issue with a specific teammate not listening to their ideas, the CCCTT may serve as a sounding board for the issue and then suggest strategies to approach the teammate and resolve the problem.

Under-participating group members can also cause group conflict. Group members may not realize their importance to the group and allow others to carry the weight through social loafing (Lumsden & Lumsden, 2000; Galanes et al., 2004; Rothwell, 2016). Social loafing is defined as "the tendency for people to reduce their efforts and work less hard on a task when working in a group than when working individually" (Karau, 2010, pp. 809–811). Other group members may get frustrated with a social loafer missing meetings or not offering suggestions, and consider ways to correct the problem through reporting the person to a higher authority, removing the person from the team, or working around the problem.

One of the challenges for CCCTTs may be recognizing when it is time to step away from a group experiencing storming and let the team determine the best course of action. The CCCTT has provided the tools for the group to be successful and must allow the group to utilize the tools and to make adjustments to get through this stage in a productive manner. Giving groups time to work through their issues and formulate a plan to move forward often results in stronger group cohesion, a more unified vision, and a stronger outcome.

Norming

The norming phase is defined by the creation of shared norms to support positive group interactions. CCCTTs must utilize interpersonal communication strategies to help group members share expectations and build cohesiveness (Edwards et al., 2013.). Addressing prior issues of contention and defining expectations and procedures helps groups move past previous disagreements and refocus on how to accomplish the assigned task. For example, the use of status reports, work assignment processes, and clear reporting structures can be used to measure and report out on accountability and goal progression.

CCCTTs should encourage groups to discuss who will handle different aspects of the project in addition to how the workflow will be communicated. Establishing the overarching project timeline and working backwards to set deadlines for each assignment can create shared expectations regarding workload delineation, expertise, communication channels, and quality expectations (i.e. first draft or finalized item). Providing both a consistent process and clear procedures that all group members agree on ensures work is completed on time, moving the project forward toward completion. Several important aspects to address include: meeting protocol, decision-making guidelines, a conflict resolution process, communication procedures within and outside of the team, and progress updates. CCCTTs may provide the group with group development and team learning assessment tools (Raes, Kyndt, Decuyper, Van den Bossche, & Dochy, 2015; Smartt Lynch, Lynch, & Clemens, this volume) to help them examine best practices for success in these areas.

Meeting protocol, decision-making guidelines, and conflict resolution. CCCTTs provide training on meeting protocol standards including: setting a regular meeting schedule, creating an agenda, establishing action items, and providing communication guidelines. CCCTTs may also encourage a group discussion about decision-making guidelines (i.e. consensus, voting, or deferring to an expert) and conflict resolution. These steps will help the group have more focused meetings and understand how to effectively use the time they have together to complete the project. More importantly, encouraging the group to take time in preparing guidelines can help prevent regressing to an earlier stage of the Tuckman model (Rickards & Moger, 2000).

Communication procedures. Ensuring all group members have shared expectations about when and how the team will communicate about the status of the project is essential. To accomplish this, the group must determine the appropriate communication channels (i.e. Google docs, email, online meeting software) and the frequency with which they will interact both within the group and with key stakeholders (i.e. managers, resource administrators). CCCTTs play an integral role in this process by helping the group explore and work through which channels work best for communicating different aspects of the project. CCCTTs must also help guide the group in establishing regular communication practices to keep everyone informed of progress and any issues that may impact project deliverables. For example, group members may decide to use a shared Google docs document to notify groups of regular project updates but may decide to use email if there is a change in the budget or timeline that may have a more eminent impact on progress. The group will also need to decide how and when to communicate with stakeholders. For example, the group will need to decide who will serve as the contact person for the Human Resources department to provide a single point of contact and information. CCCTTs support this process by helping the group brainstorm and identify stakeholders who need to be informed and the rate of communication frequency.

Progress updates. CCCTTs should initiate a discussion on the importance of regularly scheduled progress updates and reports as a strategy for longer term projects or highly critical assignments. Progress reports help keep members on task and assess whether the group is functioning at an optimal level. Reports also allow individual members to share how each teammate is contributing and what challenges, if any, the group is experiencing. CCCTTs may share examples of progress report criteria including: status of the project, ranking of assessment items (i.e. quality of work, equal contributions, participation in team meetings), reflections on overall group functionality, and challenges experienced by the team and possible solutions. The CCCTT may feel challenged at times to respond to the progress updates with supportive, useful feedback. The direction must include honest feedback and encouragement, as well as how to correct the mistakes made by the team (Beebe et al., 2013). It is important for the CCCTT to recognize that the team will make and learn from mistakes. Gauging how to recognize when feedback is helpful and when it hinders the group process is another nuanced skill CCCTTs will utilize during this stage. At times, the team may need to provide internal feedback and self-correct in order to learn and grow as a group.

Team member motivation and performance is directly linked to clear expectations regarding how individual performance will be assessed, how frequently the assessments will occur, and how team performance will be measured. To leverage these benefits, the CCCTT should share tools to help individual members understand how they will assess others and be assessed upon project completion. Several important aspects for the team to consider in the assessment process include: assessment criteria and compensation, delineations between performance standards (i.e. meeting versus exceeding expectations), project contribution to overall performance-oriented goals, and skills gained during the project. After the group has successfully established norms for communication and workflow, they will transition into the performing stage of the small group process model.

Performing

The performing stage focuses on working collaboratively to achieve group goals. In this stage the group will overcome obstacles, combine efforts, and solve problems

(Hargie, 2017). Individual members have fully embraced their group identity and are, for the most part, working harmoniously together. Cooperation and collaboration lead to synchronized strategies on how to provide the best solution. However, the group must also evaluate the performance of individuals and the group to make sure relational and task-related obstacles do not prevent the group from reaching its goals (Edwards et al., 2013). Continuous monitoring of the group's progress and quick diffusion of any issues that arise are two mechanisms to help groups effectively complete the task assigned. After the group's work is complete, they transition to the final stage, adjourning.

Team member progress reports. Throughout the performing stage, the group may choose to provide the CCCTT with progress reports. The progress report will include: tasks completed since the last report, action item updates, and any obstacles the group is encountering. If the team perceives more resources may be necessary, they can communicate this need to decision makers to ensure outcome expectations are consistent amongst all organizational levels.

In this stage, the CCCTT is a resource to help the group both overcome obstacles and fulfill outcome deliverables. For example, the group may require the CCCTT to help with a barrier to project completion, such as not receiving a necessary report from a department. The CCCTT may reach out to remove the barrier or provide additional strategies to the team on how to address the issue. In addition, the CCCTT must determine if the project is still in scope. If a group is struggling in gaining consensus and moving forward effectively, the CCCTT should also request individual progress checks to help address and overcome issues early in the performing stage (see Table 26.1 for a summary of action steps and tools).

Table 26.1 Action steps and recommended tools for each stage of small group process

Stage	Action Steps	Recommended Tools
Forming	Create structured agenda Establish desired outcomes Identify roles	Meeting Agenda Team Charter Role Assessment Activity
Storming	Demonstrate effective small group and interpersonal communication strategies Refocus team on established outcomes	Communication strategies to address conflict Member accountability
Norming	Provide communication strategies related to workflow, decision making, and conflict resolution	Project timeline examples Meeting protocol and decision-making guidelines Team member expectations Inter-group communication resources Conflict resolution best practices Assessment tools
Performing	Continue receiving progress reports and providing timely feedback to group Act as resource for group members, and only intervene if requested	Group progress report templates Leverage resources to help the group overcome obstacles, when requested Request individual group member progress checks
Adjourning	Reflect and assess progress of individuals and groups	Individual reflection guidelines Evaluation and assessment tools

Adjourning

Team members depart from the group, or adjourn, once the goal has been realized (Frisby, Kaufmann, & Beck, 2016) and assessments have been completed. To help facilitate this closure, groups may utilize specific techniques to assess and evaluate their contributions and performance both individually and as a team. Providing robust opportunities to reflect on the group process from both an individual contribution and larger group perspective allows each group member to identify his or her successes and opportunities for growth. Utilizing the assessment tools introduced during the norming stage, CCCTTs refocus group members on evaluation and reflection of the group experience. The reflections should also include a self-reflection exercise by the CCCTT. To accomplish this task, the CCCTT must look at the individual challenges encountered during the group process, the approaches used to overcome the challenges, and the future improvements that could be made to help conquer these obstacles in future groups. These reflections can provide powerful insights to improve individual contributions in future team experiences.

Conclusion

The ability to effectively work in a team environment is one of the most desirable employee skills (National Association of Colleges and Employers, 2016). To help clients develop this critical skillset, CCCTTs must develop and utilize best practices within the communication discipline to guide and enhance the quality of services provided. The National Communication Association's (NCA) Training and Development Division (2017) has identified group communication techniques and strategies as one of the critical skills necessary for CCCTTs to demonstrate the best practice of communication proficiency.

As part of the ongoing process of developing a professional tool kit, CCCTTs must dedicate themselves to the continuous development of their own group strategies and techniques. As they complete this chapter, CCCTTs should reflect on their own knowledge and prowess with the many skills presented. Taking time to reflect on levels of adeptness and mastery for each of the strategies and techniques discussed is a critical aspect of developing a more robust professional tool kit. If CCCTTs discover a specific area of opportunity, they should take time to revisit the strategies and techniques outlined in the chapter that address that issue and reflect on how to further develop the necessary skills to strengthen this aspect of group communication. Continuously cultivating both knowledge and expertise in group communication techniques and strategies is an ongoing process for CCCTTs seeking to progressively build a professional tool kit for success.

References

Adams, K., & Galanes, G. J. (2015). *Communicating in groups: Application and skills.* New York, NY: McGraw-Hill.

Allan, E. G. (2016). "I hate group work!": Addressing students' concerns about small-group learning. *InSight: A Journal of Scholarly Teaching, 11,* 81–89.

Bar-On, R. (1997). *BarOn emotional quotient inventory A measure of emotional intelligence.* Toronto, ON: Multi-Health Systems, Inc.

Beebe, S. A., Mottet, T. P., & Roach, K. D. (2013). *Training and development: Communicating for success* (2nd ed.). Upper Saddle, NJ: Pearson Education.

Benne, K. D., & Sheats, P. (1948). Functional roles of group members. *Journal of Social Issues, 4*(2), 41–49. doi:10.1111/j.1540-4560.1948.tb01783.x

Blanchard, K. (2006). The critical role of teams. Retrieved from www.kenblanchard.com/img/pub/pdf_critical_role_teams.pdf

Bonebright, D. A. (2010). 40 years of storming: A historical review of Tuckman's model of small group development. *Human Resource Development International, 13*(1), 111–120. doi:10/1080/13678861003589099.

Burrell, N., & Nicolini, K. M. (2017). Pronomial use (solidarity). In M. Allen (ed.), *The Sage encyclopedia of communication research*. Thousand Oaks, CA: Sage Publications

Courtright, S. H., McCormick, B. W., Mistry, S., & Wang, J. (2017). Quality charters or quality members? A control theory perspective on team charters and team performance. *Journal of Applied Psychology*, doi:http://dx.doi.org/10.1037/apl0000229

Edmondson, A. (1999). Psychological safety and learning behavior in work teams. *Administrative Science Quarterly, 44*, 350–383. doi:10.2307/2666999

Edwards, A., Edwards, C., Wahl, S. T., & Myers, S. A. (2013). *The communication age: Connecting and engaging*. Thousand Oaks, CA: Sage Publications.

Frisby, B. N., Kaufmann, R., & Beck, A.-C. (2016). Mediated group development and dynamics: an examination of video chatting, Twitter, and Facebook in group assignments. *Communication Teacher, 30*(4), 215–227. doi:10.1080/17404622.2016.1219038

Galanes, G. J., Adams, K., & Brilhart, J. K. (2004). *Effective group discussion: Theory and practice* (11th ed.). New York, NY: McGraw Hill.

Gardner, A. K., Kosemund, M., Hogg, D., Heymann, A., & Martinez, J. (2017). Setting goals, not just roles: Improving teamwork through goal-focused debriefing. *The American Journal of Surgery, 213*(2), 249–252. doi:10.1016/j.amjsurg.2016.09.040

Goleman, D. (1995). *Emotional intelligence*. New York, NY: Bantam Books.

Hargie, O. (2017). *Skilled interpersonal communication: Research, theory and practice*. New York, NY: Routledge.

Janis, I. L. (1972). *Victims of groupthink*. Boston, MA: Houghton Mifflin.

Karau, S. (2010) Social loafing. In J. M. Levine & M. A. Hogg (eds.), *Encyclopedia of group processes & intergroup relations*. doi: http://dx.doi.org/10.4135/9781412972017.n249

Karau, S., & Williams, K. (1993). Social loafing: A meta-analytic review and theoretical integration. *Journal of Personality and Social Psychology, 65*(4), 681–706. doi:10.1037/0022-3514.65.4.681

O'Leary-Kelly, A. M., Martocchio, J. J., & Frink, D. D. (1994). A review of the influence of group goals on group performance. *Academy of Management Journal, 37*(5), 1285–1301. doi:10.2307/256673

Lumsden, G., & Lumsden, D. (2000). *Communicating in groups and teams: Sharing leadership* (3rd ed.). Belmont, CA: Wadsworth/Thomson Learning.

Maples, M. F. (1988). Group development: Extending Tuckman's theory. *The Journal for Specialists in Group Work, 13*(1), 17–23. doi: https://doi.org/10.1080/01933928808411771

McMorris, L. E., Gottlieb, N. H., & Sneden, G. G. (2005). Developmental stages in public health partnerships: A practical perspective. *Health Promotion Practice, 6*(2), 219–226. doi:10.1177/1524839903260647

Myers, S. A., & Goodboy, A. K. (2005). A study of grouphate in a course on small group communication. *Psychological Reports, 97*(2), 381–386. doi:10.2466/pr0.97.2.381-386

Myers, S. A., Shimotsu, S., Byrnes, K., Frisby, B N., Durbin, J., & Loy, B. N. (2010). Assessing the role of peer relationships in the small group communication course. *Communication Teacher, 24*, 43–57. doi:10.1080/17404620903468214

National Association of Colleges and Employers (2016). *Job Outlook 2016: Attributes employers want to see on new college graduates' resumes*. Retrieved from: http://www.naceweb.org/s11182015/employers-look-for-in-new-hires.aspx

Natvig, D., & Stark, N. L. (2016). A project team analysis using Tuckman's model of small-group development. *Journal of Nursing Education, 55*(12), 675–681. doi:10.3928/01484834-20161114-03

NCA (2017). NCA's Training and Development Division's Best Practices for Communication Training and Consulting. Retrieved 2017, July 4 from: http://ncatraininganddevelopment. com/training-best-practices/best-practices-for-communication-training-and-consulting/

Raes, E., Kyndt, E., Decuyper, S., Van den Bossche, P., & Dochy, F. (2015). An exploratory study of group development and team learning. *Human Resource Development Quarterly, 26,* 5–30. doi: 10.1002/hrdq.21201

Rickards, T., & Moger, S. (2000). Creative leadership processes in project team development: an alternative to Tuckman's stage model. *British journal of Management, 11*(4), 273–283. doi: https://doi.org/10.1111/1467-8551.00173

Rothwell, J. D. (2016). *In mixed company: Communicating in small groups and teams* (9th ed.). Boston, MA: Cengage Learning.

Sabee, C. M. (2015). Interpersonal communication skill/competence. In C. R. Berger, M. E. Roloff, S. R. Wilson, J. P. Dillard, J. Caughlin & D. Solomon (eds.), *The international encyclopedia of interpersonal communication* (pp. 1–9). Hoboken, NJ: John Wiley & Sons. doi:10.1002/9781118540190. wbeic080

Slater, P. E. (1955). Role differentiation in small groups. *American Sociological Review, 20*(3), 300–310. doi:10.2307/2087389

Spitzberg, B. H. (1983). Communication competence as knowledge, skill, and impression. *Communication Education, 32*(3), 323–329. doi:10.1080/03634528309378550

Tuckman, B. W., & Jensen, M.A. (1977). Stages of small-group development revisited. *Group & Organization Management, 2*(4), 419–427. doi:10.1177/105960117700200404

Wagner, J. A. (1995). Studies of individualism-collectivism: Effects on cooperation in groups. *Academy of Management Journal, 38*(1), 152–172. doi:10.2307/256731.

West, M. (2004). Do teams work? In M. A. West, *Effective teamwork: Practical lessons from organizational research* (2nd ed., pp. 7–26). Oxford: Blackwell Publishing.

West, M. A., & Markiewicz, L. (2004). *Building team-based working: A practical guide to organizational transformation.* Oxford: Blackwell Publishing.

Wheelan, S. A. (2014). *Creating effective teams: A guide for members and leaders.* New York, NY: Sage Publications.

Chapter 27

Incorporating Cosmopolitan Communication into diverse teaching and training contexts

Considerations from our work with military students and veterans

Susan Steen, Lauren Mackenzie, and Barton Buechner

Abstract

This chapter describes Cosmopolitan Communication (Pearce, 1989) as a "Best Practice in Demonstrating Communication Proficiency" for Communication coaches, consultants, teachers, and trainers working with and among diverse populations. Based upon our work with military members and veterans, we present perspectives and strategies of Cosmopolitan Communication as means of cultivating intercultural competence, along with practical applications designed to facilitate sense-making and perspective-taking within complex social situations that involve unfamiliar contexts, divergent worldviews, or uncertain outcomes.

With the recent increase of non-traditional learners in U.S. colleges and universities, contributions from scholars and practitioners of Communication are more relevant now than ever – not only in classrooms, but in the campus culture at large, in post-educational preparation, and in other professional contexts such as coaching, social work, counseling, training, or advising. Communication educators are well-poised to support adult learners by offering ways to incorporate and make meaning of the diverse "lived experience" they bring to the learning environment – especially those who are experiencing life or career transitions that involve ambiguous outcomes, expose them to others with worldviews radically different from their own, and at times, challenge their sense of identity. Such circumstances present a myriad of challenges – not only for the individuals experiencing them, but for those who work with them, in the classroom and beyond. To ameliorate these challenges, we propose incorporation of principles and strategies of "Cosmopolitan Communication" (Pearce, 1989) as novel approaches in diverse instructional and training contexts, and offer some current examples of their usage from our work with military members and veterans.

This chapter describes theoretical underpinnings and major premises of Cosmopolitan Communication, explains its utility as a framework for understanding the socially-constructed nature of interactions and developing intercultural competence, and discusses practices employed by Communication scholars who teach and train military students and veterans – and who have taught and trained other populations, in different settings. The strategies described here are applicable to contexts that extend well beyond the traditional academic classroom. Indeed, we believe that proficiency in cultivating and enacting cosmopolitan communication is important to *any* accomplished Communication coach, consultant, teacher, or trainer, and may be usefully viewed as a scaffold reinforcing other best practices examined in this handbook. This is because Cosmopolitan Communication provides a framework for bridging our highly connected worlds, for "communicating as critical global citizens and for building community, intercultural dialogue and solidarity across... cultural differences" (Sobré-Denton & Bardhan, 2013, p. 14). While our discussion and examples are informed by the military and veteran contexts in which we primarily teach and train, the model we present and the methods we offer are adaptable to other settings and should be helpful to practitioners working with many diverse populations.

Cosmopolitan Communication as a "best practice" in developing intercultural competence

"Cosmopolitan Communication" is a potentially liberating theoretical branch of social construction, one worthy of inclusion as a best practice for developing intercultural competence in academic and training settings. It derives from the Coordinated Management of Meaning (CMM) theory advanced by W. Barnett Pearce and Vernon Cronen, which offers principles and heuristic tools to reveal the dynamics of communication by which our social reality is constructed – and therefore may be engaged and changed. It is a "liberating" practice in the sense that it helps restore communicative agency to individuals in managing outcomes in complex social situations that might otherwise appear out of their control, because CMM theory views communication as *constitutive*, or shaping our social reality, not merely as a way of transmitting information from a sender to a receiver within a fixed system. It is, therefore, a particularly useful concept to be taught to populations where diversity and complexity of experience – and potential for conflicting worldviews – are considerations, and features prominently in our work with military members and veterans. Understanding the constitutive nature of communication between and among learners with diverse backgrounds is essential to applying the principles of Cosmopolitan Communication that we describe throughout this chapter. We will first illustrate how these principles work around military and veteran cultures, and then extrapolate to other populations and settings.

Coherence and coordination

Members of the military services operate frequently at the spaces between cultures, where ineffectiveness in communication, or misinterpretation of intent, can have life-or-death consequences. Two principal dynamics of Cosmopolitan Communication are useful in addressing the complexity of such interactions: *Coherence* and *Coordination*. Coherence speaks to the shared ability to make collective sense of what is going on in the moment. Maintaining *coherence* between intent and the way it is communicated is not easy in the best of circumstances; less so when the context is tense and emotionally charged; and even less still when events appear to be spinning out of control, or unfolding too rapidly for deliberate decision-making. Coordination enables collective action, or the ability to respond in constructive ways even when intent and context are not apparent. Within military culture, *coordination* of actions is often achieved by symbolism and deeply shared values and experience. While these qualities work very well within the service culture, they do not always translate well to those who do not share them.

Each branch of the United States military services – Army, Navy, Air Force, Marines and Coast Guard – represents a closed society, with its own language, symbolism, values, code of conduct, and ethics. Despite best intentions, and the "citizen-soldier" concept of a military closely linked to the general population it serves and protects, the services have come to embody characteristics of exclusiveness and insularity. While these strong service cultures impart many desirable shared values, such as loyalty, fraternity, and dedication to duty, they may also contribute to problems in communicating effectively with outside groups, including the propensity to communicate in shorthand terms (through slang or acronyms), distrust of "outsiders" who have not been tested and accepted, and the sense of not being understood or accepted by those outside the group.

These characteristics, and the challenges associated with them, are not unique to the military. Indeed, many professional organizations – police, firefighters, first responders, health care workers, and so on – may likewise realize coherence and coordination through a shared "esprit de corps," tight bonds of connection, and patterns of communication (i.e., jargon) that could similarly interfere with their capacity to relate to outsiders. Extrapolating outwards, we can imagine how these communicative gaps might play out in other situations, as well. In an era when our social worlds are paradoxically more closely interlinked and more fragmented, society is rife with examples of groups talking past each other, instead of seeking a common understanding. Whether the divide is over religious values, political beliefs, or economic opportunity, these divisions are deeply felt, and can take on dimensions of existential moral and ethical imperatives, resulting in repeating patterns of polarization, conflict, and division. Pearce (2008) refers to these as "Unwanted Repetitive Patterns" (URPs), and CMM theory offers some heuristic tools to help detect – and hopefully change – these patterns. Specifically, Cosmopolitan Communication, as a form of best practice based upon CMM theory, embodies concepts and strategies for enacting coherence and coordination between and among diverse cultures.

The importance of developing intercultural competence

To make sense of situations in which cultural differences affect the quality of communication, it is helpful to understand intercultural competence as a function of personal development of perspective, or social capacity, rather than simply a learnable skillset. We draw from Wiseman's (2002, p. 203) definition of intercultural competence as "the knowledge, motivation, and skills to interact effectively and appropriately with members of different cultures." With the overarching goal of intercultural competence in mind, this chapter advances the best practice of Cosmopolitan Communication (Pearce, 1989) which depicts stages of the evolution of communication in a multicultural society. As a key dimension of intercultural competence, Cosmopolitan Communication offers a processual approach for considering and articulating alternative perspectives in intercultural interaction.

Pearce (1989) described communication as developing progressively over four levels: (1) monocultural communication; (2) ethnocentric communication; (3) modernistic communication; and finally (4) cosmopolitan communication. Each level has its own schema for making meaning of encounters with others, and its own "action logic" for responding in various situations. In recent years, Kazuma Matoba, a professor at the German Defense University, has expanded upon these concepts. Matoba views cosmopolitan communication as helping persons and organizations shift upward towards a more complete human and societal dimension of experience (Matoba, 2013). A central feature of this involves the way others outside one's group are viewed and treated, as shown in Figure 27.1:

		Acculturation Attitude	
		Not open to be integrated	Open to be integrated
Treat others as	similar	**Monocultural Communication** (Treat everyone as similar)	**Cosmopolitan Communication** (Treat everyone as similar and different)
	different	**Ethnocentric Communication** (Treat own group as similar and others as different)	**Modernistic Communication** (Treat everyone as different)

Figure 27.1 Forms of communication: Acculturation attitudes and how others are treated. Source: Matoba (2013).

In this model, monocultural communication is a comfortable space where we all know and understand each other at a deep level (such as in a family, or a highly integrated military unit). Others outside the group are viewed in an ethnocentric way, which creates separation between ourselves and even well-meaning "others" as persons who don't (or can't) share our experience – and therefore don't understand us. Modernistic communication is a step forward from this level of engagement in that it recognizes and respects differences, but it still presents some challenges around cohesiveness. That is, we recognize and accept that others are different from us, but we don't have enough common ground to build upon our similarities. To do that, we must move towards a cosmopolitan sensibility. Cosmopolitan communication transcends many of these barriers by acknowledging – and respecting – that everyone is both similar *and* different. It widens the social sphere to include (and value) not only those who are considered part of the inside group, but those who are not. Being "different" is not assumed to mean "inferior," and important group differences are taken into account, not ignored or discounted (Matoba, 2013).

Within each stage, we see distinct differences in the way the communication dynamics of conflict are treated, and why this can be problematic. A *monocultural* perspective sees everyone as essentially similar and regards disagreement as a lack of either proper training or common sense. Great importance is placed upon *coherence*, or a shared sense of meaning and values. At the next stage, *ethnocentric* communication, members of the in-group value and understand their own members, and feel superior to members of other groups. Consequently, they may "ignore, devalue or dismiss crucial aspects of others" (Matoba, 2013, p. 4), leading to blind spots and miscalculation in social interactions, and perhaps ultimately to polarization or social isolation. *Modernistic* communicators treat everyone as different, and view disagreements largely as problems to be solved, possibly through compromise or negotiation. For highly integrated culture groups, this presents a conundrum, requiring them to set aside closely held beliefs and values in order to negotiate with the "other." In the Cosmopolitan Communication frame of reference, however, disagreement through difference can be seen as positive, because cosmopolitan communicators "would see disagreement as an opportunity for learning of (a) different reality" and interpret it as a resource, as long as coordination was not completely blocked (Matoba, 2013, p. 5). In fact, within this perspective, differences are not necessarily seen as requiring resolution. This allows for the capacity to achieve *coordination* among all, preserving a sense of integrity and identity by all parties.

Emergence and mystery

In addition to the communication dynamics of coherence and coordination, the Cosmopolitan Communication model accounts for the emergence of *Mystery*, things we can neither predict nor control. This is a useful construct for addressing areas of individual and shared responsibility, of vital interest to many experiencing major life changes, such as veterans in transition from the strong collective identity of the military to a more individually-oriented citizen role. That is, military culture inculcates a strong sense of personal responsibility by individuals to both the group, and other members. This is a healthy thing, until we encounter forces beyond our control. Allowing for *Mystery* provides space for those things that can otherwise not be accounted for, and should not be considered as a personal responsibility.

We will say more about how the Cosmopolitan Communication dynamics of coherence, coordination, and mystery can be broadly applied in experiential learning situations later in this chapter, when we introduce the practice of "circular questioning" as a way for instructors or group leaders to focus learners' attention on systemic forces, instead of qualities and constraints of personal identity or individual roles in events. Before doing so, we offer an overview of intercultural competence strategies from our own teaching and training that incorporate Cosmopolitan Communication approaches.

Intercultural competence teaching and training for adult professional populations

The interconnected nature of the twenty-first century has prompted growing recognition of the importance of developing "intercultural" and "cross-cultural" competence across an array of disciplines and professions, including business, health care, human resources, international education, teaching, and others (Deardorff, 2009). The Department of Defense (DOD) is no exception, in 2005 approving the *Defense Language Transformation Roadmap* that characterized language, regional expertise, and culture skills as critical for "sustaining coalitions, pursuing regional stability, and conducting multi-national missions" including post-conflict and humanitarian operations (DOD, 2005, p. 3). The U.S. military has introduced cross-cultural training and education throughout numerous Professional Military Education (PME) contexts and, though each branch uses different terminology and takes slightly different approaches in related research, teaching, and training, the overall goal is for military members to understand the process of acquiring and understanding cultural knowledge in order to interact appropriately and effectively regardless of cultural context (Mackenzie & Miller, 2017).

Consequently, our teaching and training is designed, in part, to challenge learners to examine intersections of culture, communication, and conflict in a world whose borders are increasingly porous and in which issues such as cybercrime, security, global disease, and natural disasters don't adhere to boundary lines drawn on a map. In such an environment, where military members may be operating in geographic (and figurative) "borderlands," preparation requires not only a deep understanding of cultural constraints and complexities, but also the development of interpersonal skills to forge effective relationships across cultural divides. Ultimately, our goal is to prepare learners for successful intercultural interaction and provide them with tools for cultural sense-making, within a cosmopolitan framework.

Regardless of whether the audience is military or civilian, and whether the professional context is in-residence or online, we view the model of Cosmopolitan Communication as a helpful tool in fostering respect for diversity of worldviews and perspectives, and in cultivating intercultural competence. Matoba (2013) asserts that the cosmopolitan communicator "recognizes others as both different and similar... different in that they have their own worldviews and resources for dealing with the world... similar in that their focus and habits of attention provide similar functions for them as ours do for us" (pp. 4–5). Skrbiš (2014, p. 6) suggests Cosmopolitan Communication involves "an open disposition towards others" with a "strong and inclusive ethic which emphasizes... other-directedness, hospitality to strangers and an all-embracing communitarian concern." One element of cosmopolitan pedagogy described by Sobré-Denton and Bardhan (2013, p. 166) involves "engagement with the cultural Other," self-reflexivity, and perspective-taking.

Perspective-taking is, quite simply, the ability to see things from another point of view. It is often referred to as a foundational intercultural skill simply because it begins the *process* of recognizing and articulating how a situation could appear from someone else's standpoint. This recognition, in turn, sets the stage for a conversation that is open to alternative perspectives and finding common ground where it may not have been immediately obvious (Myers & Hodges, 2011).

Indeed, Kurusawa (2011, p. 279) suggests that cosmopolitanism involves the capacity for "multiperspectivism." By introducing approaches and tools to help learners focus on the constitutive nature of social interactions, and on perspective-taking as a means of understanding and affirming the ways people are at once similar and different, the authors of this chapter aim to approach intercultural competence holistically. That is, we suggest its teaching and training should involve not only the cognitive domain (e.g., understanding how cultural values are reflected in communication styles) and skills-based behaviors (effective cross-cultural negotiation skills), but also an affective appreciation for the "both/and"-ness of intercultural communicative space – the recognition of *everyone* (ourselves and others) as both insider and outsider, and a certain openness to the world, as well as to diverse perspectives.

Adult learning and the Cosmopolitan Communication perspective

An important consideration for us – and for others working with adult populations – is the significant professional experience students bring to the "learning table." Thus, our teaching and training are guided by principles of andragogical design. A theory of adult learning advanced by Malcolm Knowles (1968), andragogy's tenets include: Adults have a need-to-know about the teaching/training (what material will be covered; how so; and why it's important); adult learners are largely self-directed; they bring a reservoir of prior experience that can aid or inhibit their future learning; adults typically become ready to learn when confronted with a specific need; they are likely to prefer problem-solving learning approaches with immediate applicability to their own concerns; and adults are generally motivated to learn based on internal, rather than external, factors (Knowles, Holton, & Swanson, 2015).

Scholars of andragogy acknowledge that these principles are not exclusive to adults (indeed, Wingate [2010] suggests that giving middle school students an active role in decision-making likewise encourages their ownership of learning), and caution against viewing adult learners as a monolithic group all having the same needs (Long, 2004). However, Knowles' focus on learner-centeredness and adult self-direction represent important contributions to the education profession. Hence, in our own teaching and training, we deliberately frame the content in a professionally-relevant and cosmopolitan context, and whenever possible involve participants in goal-setting, decision-making, and leading activities or group discussion. We also infuse our instruction with participant case studies, critical incident methodology, and circular questioning to bolster perspective-taking and focus attention on the co-constructed, constitutive nature of communication in shaping social reality. In doing so, we encourage learners to examine and integrate their own lived experience as it relates to the lesson content and discussion. These simple strategies have proved effective for us, and we offer them as easily adaptable and potentially useful in your own work with diverse professional populations.

Incorporating experiential learning techniques in teaching and training

According to Knowles et al. (2015), adult learners typically prefer problem-solving learning approaches, preferably when the learning is anchored in real-world contexts. The experiential learning model developed by David Kolb (1984) reflects this orientation. The model includes a four-stage learning cycle of participants engaging in concrete experiences (e.g., a field trip, a case study, a simulation); making observations and reflecting on the experience; absorbing and distilling these into abstract concepts; and finally, actively experimenting through applying the new concepts in making decisions and solving problems (Kolb, Boyatzis, & Mainemelis, 2001). It is considered particularly effective in adult learning as it engages the cognitive, emotional, and physical aspects of learning (Conlan, Grabowski, & Smith, 2003); central to its success is the integration of knowledge, activity/experience, and reflection.

Participant case studies. Experiential learning events are interwoven throughout many of our teaching and training events. One that has worked well for us is the participant case study. Case studies are useful in that they "bridge the gap between theory and practice and between the academy and the workplace" (Barkley, Cross, & Major, 2005, p. 182). Our case studies are typically embedded in lessons that incorporate conceptual texts along with professionally-relevant readings, examples, and scenarios to forge concrete connections between the subject material and the real-world situations learners are likely to encounter. For example, participants may review an article on conflict styles, a reading on military approaches to conflict negotiation, and a story featuring a conflict scenario. In the spirit of cultivating Cosmopolitan Communication, guided discussions include themes of co-constructed meaning; interpretation of the issue(s) from the perspectives of all parties; impressions about what went wrong (and right); how the conflict might be framed (as negative, positive, both, or neither); and how the scenario might play out differently under different circumstances. Then, as a capstone exercise, learners present a case study incident from their own professional experience (a conflict or major misunderstanding, for example) that involves important concepts covered in the lesson. Participants analyze the case, using questions such as: What is the nature of the problem? What is the context in which it's occurring? What key factors bear consideration? What worked well/what did not? How might other parties involved interpret the situation? How might this have been handled or resolved differently? How might the outcome(s) have differed as a result?

This case study strategy facilitates cosmopolitan approaches of perspective-taking in considering the point of view of "Others" that might conflict with one's own. It likewise evokes andragogical principles of taking into account prior experiences of participants, and the notion that adults are best motivated to learn when they perceive the content will help them manage problems relevant to their lives. By relating the subject matter(s) to their professional contexts and enabling them to draw on their own lived experience, we encourage learners to make meaningful connections between the subject matter and their personal and professional lives. You can readily adapt this method for use in your own work, for a classroom of college students (by involving readings and scenarios related to "the student experience," for example); in a coaching or group therapy session; in a professional workplace environment; and so on.

Critical incident methodology. Critical incident methodology is described by Storti (2015, p. 136) as:

> the use of critical incidents in an education or training setting to enable participants to practice resolving culture-based conflicts. Critical incidents are also used outside the intercultural field, but within the field they are distinguished by the fact that the core problem or conflict, the heart of the incident is the result of one or more cultural differences.

Critical incident approaches have been used by intercultural communication scholars and practitioners for over 60 years and typically include the following elements (Snow, 2015):

1   A story involving two or more well-intentioned individuals from different cultures which results in surprise/confusion;
2   Questions which ask students to consider the cause of misunderstanding;
3   Discussion of preferred interpretations of the incident by persons from the other culture.

Fowler and Blohm (2004) note that critical incident exercises are an effective means for using narrative to develop more accurate expectations, self-reflection, preparing for future interactions, and generating multiple explanations for a misunderstanding. Conducting critical incident exercises in face-to-face settings is advantageous since this offers the potential to generate a large number of explanations and interpretations of behavior; just as focus groups can facilitate a different kind of discussion than a one-on-one interview, due to the variety of perspectives brought into the conversation, a real-time critical incident interaction increases the possibility of creative results. Nevertheless, critical incident methodology also lends itself well to online, asynchronous culture education in cultivating intercultural competence that is professionally relevant, culture-specific, and communication-focused (Mackenzie & Wallace, 2015). Many of the benefits of using critical incidents for in-person training carry over to distance education, and critical incident methodology is a useful practice for trainers, coaches, and instructors wishing to illuminate strategies for managing cultural complexity in *context.*

The example below demonstrates how Cosmopolitan Communication can be *applied* in an online training or education context, using a template developed to create new scenario-based culture content for military students (and which can be easily adjusted to various contexts involving learners with diverse skillsets, as it was designed primarily to apply intercultural communication skills via critical incident exercises). The template, used to guide a team of writers charged with creating critical incidents, featured a variety of educational objectives, including this one: "Provide multiple explanations for the outcome of a successful or failed intercultural interaction" (with the following Knowledge, Skills and Abilities, or KSAs):

1   Distinguish between linguistic & communication competence;
2   Describe the implications of identity in intercultural interactions;
3   Practice the skills of perspective-taking & perception-checking.

The educational objective and accompanying KSAs exemplify key tenets of Cosmopolitan Communication in emphasizing communication, identity, and perception, thus offering learners resources for considering cultural difference and potential alternatives for making sense of confusing behavior. Decades of work in intercultural training suggest that the process of learning culture/region-specific content is enhanced by a foundational overview grounded in culture-general communication concepts and skills (Brislin & Pedersen, 1976). The scenario template was created for guiding the writers to develop critical incidents as follows:

1   *Background*: Provide a one-paragraph description of the setting/scene and the mission that the military member is involved with leading up to the critical incident. If possible provide a graphic or map that depicts the location.
2   *Critical incident*: This section provides a detailed description of a military member who is engaged in a culturally complex interaction. At the point where frustration or confusion sets in, pause the narrative to emphasize the importance of taking multiple explanations into consideration before responding.
3   *Context considerations*: What should the military member keep in mind before s/he prepares a response? What concepts or background knowledge might help him/her make sense of this situation?
4   *Alternative viewpoints/elaboration of concepts*: Provide at least two possible explanations for the confusing cultural behavior. Use the KSA explanation provided to you to help make sense of the interaction. Picture yourself as an advisor talking the military member through the situation and the potential consequences of his/her response.
5   *For further consideration*: Reiterate the KSA and expand on it in at least one other area of the region. The point here is to emphasize the vast cultural variation within a particular region (for example, in Africa, taking the time to share a cup of coffee when you are a guest in someone's home may have a different prominence in Ethiopia than it does in Kenya).

We offer this template as a model that can be modified, with appropriate customization, for your own purposes and needs. Not only can it be used in a variety of training contexts to develop critical incidents for a wide range of professions and learning levels, it illustrates several elements of Cosmopolitan Communication in its acknowledgement of operational communication and consideration of alternative perspectives as opportunities to manage and coordinate learners' expectations of intercultural interactions.

Circular questioning: Modeling a systems view of Cosmopolitan Communication. The practice of circular questioning (Rossmann, 1995) embodies the social construction of reality in communication, in that it encourages us to look beneath the surface at how we are; in effect, constantly co-constructing our experiences together in processes of communication. It is a relatively simple process in which participants in a group can engage with each other in ways that facilitate taking multiple perspectives, depersonalizing positions and conflicts, and seeing the impact of communicative forces in creating multiple versions of reality. It begins with the group leader or instructor taking a communication perspective of the learning process, and acts into conversations in a way that changes participant perceptions of their own identities and positions. The term "circular" refers to consideration of a full spectrum of human experience, which has many dimensions. This multi-dimensional phenomenon is also part of a dynamic process, and like all "living systems" it is subject to change based upon inputs and adjustment of variables. It may look entirely different from various points within the circle, paving the way to understanding multiple perspectives and the potential validity of multiple versions of reality.

To create an environment where circular questioning is a part of the learning process, we must be aware of two types of questions, descriptive and reflexive, and mindful of when and how to employ them. *Descriptive* questions elicit information from learners/participants and are used to bring their personal stories and "lived experiences" into the learning space, as well as what they know or believe about the system or problem under study. Such questions can also be used to draw connections, enabling learners to see how things may be systemically linked. *Reflexive* questions bring out factors that could result in changes to the system under study or reveal how changes have taken place over time. The historical perspective is a particularly useful lens for viewing social change and social justice, allowing learners to construct common ground. For example, in our own teaching and training, we have found that when talking about the treatment and roles of women, LGBT persons, and minorities in the military, some learners may harbor resentment which emerges in the discussion, while others may feel unfairly blamed by this. In situations like this, instructors can use descriptive questions that encourage learners to share multiple personal perspectives, and reflexive questions that expand the timeline and context – such as aspects of military culture that place shared values and common cause over individual differences, and progress over time to increase full acceptance and opportunities for marginalized groups. In this way, divergent lived experiences are honored, while envisioning changes towards an agreed-upon, more desirable future state by the entire group.

In our experience, this circular (systemic) approach is useful for defusing conflicts among persons with differing racial, gender, ethnic, and social backgrounds, allowing the group to arrive at a shared perspective – even if not agreement. Moreover, an important aspect of circular questioning is the development of ability to move from the subjective to the objective, requiring the group leaders to intentionally shift the viewpoints of learners from first and second person perspectives to the third person (objective). In a classroom or group therapy discussion (or an online forum) this can be done by inviting certain participants, at certain times, to take on different conversational roles, in the presence of other learners or in small groups, and then directing attention to the systemic nature of the issues – away from the argument itself, and the personalities of those involved. An example from our work involves a scenario in which, after some heated debate concerning the incorporation of women into combat roles in the military, two female learners with opposing views were invited to create a joint presentation that included both of their experiences and beliefs – but also challenged current practice. This exercise applied several techniques of promoting circular thinking, including shifting the time frame in which the phenomenon is considered; balancing objectivity and subjectivity; making new systemic connections; and exploring underlying logics that learners individually used to make meaning, while creating new ones based on shared understanding. The result was a systemic analysis that went beyond the prevalent arguments based upon physiology and historically masculine soldier roles and training and envisioned a service culture in which women could have equal, yet different, status and presence in forward-deployed units. The two learners engaged the project with good humor and ended up supporting each other in many ways for the remainder of the course.

This is a useful illustration of how cosmopolitan approaches can be incorporated in different ways into a wide range of professional contexts. In your own work as a Communication consultant, coach, teacher or trainer, perhaps you have encountered – or can envision – situations in which the use of circular questioning, with its capacity for shifting perspectives from the subjective (and personal) to the objective (and more distant), may help broaden a difficult conversation among groups with disparate perspectives, and thereby defuse interpersonal tension or conflict. While the examples we have provided throughout this chapter are grounded in the military and veteran milieus of our own teaching and training, the strategies we describe can be used by Communication professionals working with diverse populations in many different contexts. Whomever the audience, and whatever the setting, the lasting personal impact of learners becoming more aware of the socially constructed nature of the multiple social worlds in which they (and we) live, interact, and communicate, cannot be overlooked. Acquiring such capacity for contemplative awareness, and the integrative tools and skills to collaboratively "make better social worlds" through more intentional forms of communication, can be a profoundly transformative act (Rehorick & Bentz, 2008). This is an area in which the Communication discipline can make substantial and much-needed contributions. Indeed, given our increasingly complex social world in which communication plays an essential role – and yet with examples of failed or inadequate communication visible everywhere – we may have an obligation to do so.

Conclusion

The model of Cosmopolitan Communication represents a helpful tool to those engaged in Communication coaching, consulting, teaching, and training, especially when undertaken in a collaborative space, incorporating andragogical principles to support adult learners in making meaning of personal and collective experience. This chapter offers specific approaches – including participant case studies, critical incident methodology, and circular questioning – that readers can incorporate to deliberately infuse a Cosmopolitan Communication mindset into their work, along with templates for application in a myriad of contexts. We offer these perspectives and tools in hopes that they may aid you in your work with and among diverse populations, in developing an enriched capacity for perspective-taking, attention to the social construction of meaning, and de-personalization and defusing of conflict. This nuanced cosmopolitan approach to meeting the demands of increasingly complex and unpredictable teaching and training contexts offers a window through which we can see ourselves – military, civilian, faculty, students, trainers, coaches, citizens of different countries, citizens of the world – as part of a more integrated and inclusive "us." Perhaps this is the most hopeful reason for teaching and developing the capacity for this type of communication as a new standard of this still emerging "best practice."

References

Barkley, E., Cross, K., & Major, C. (2005). *Collaborative learning techniques: A handbook for college faculty.* San Francisco, CA: Jossey-Bass.

Brislin, R., & Pedersen, P. (1976). *Cross-cultural orientation programs.* New York, NY: Gardner.

Conlan, J., Grabowski, S., & Smith, K. (2003). Adult learning. In M. Orey (ed.), *Emerging perspectives on learning, teaching, and technology.* Retrieved June 2017 from from http://epltt.coe.uga.edu/

Deardorff, D. (2009). Preface. In D. Deardorff (ed.), *The Sage handbook of intercultural competence* (pp. xi–xiv). Thousand Oaks, CA: Sage.

Department of Defense (2005). *Defense language transformation roadmap.* Washington D.C. Retrieved from http://www.dtic.mil/dtic/tr/fulltext/u2/b313370.pdf

Fowler, S., & Blohm, J. (2004). An analysis of methods for intercultural training. In D. Landis & J. Bennett (eds.), *Handbook of intercultural training* (pp. 37–84). Thousand Oaks, CA: Sage.

Knowles, M. (1968). Andragogy, not pedagogy. *Adult Leadership, 16*(10), 350–352, 386.

Knowles, M., Holton, E. F. III, & Swanson, R. (2015). *The adult learner* (8th ed.). New York, NY: Routledge.

Kolb, D. (1984). *Experiential learning: Experience as the source of learning and development.* Englewood Cliffs, NJ: Prentice-Hall.

Kolb, D., Boyatzis, R., & Mainemelis, M. (2001). Experiential learning theory: Previous research and new directions. In R. Sternberg & L. Zhang (eds.), *Perspectives on cognitive, learning, and thinking styles* (pp. 227–247). Mahwah, NJ: Lawrence-Erlbaum.

Kurusawa, F. (2011). Critical cosmopolitanism. In M. Rovisco & M. Nowicka (eds.), *The Ashgate research companion to cosmopolitanism* (pp. 279–293). Burlington, VT: Ashgate Publishing Company.

Long, H. (2004). Understanding adult learners. In M. Galbraith (ed.), *Adult learning methods: A guide for effective instruction* (pp. 23–37). Malabar, FL: Krieger.

Mackenzie, L., & Miller, J. (2017). Intercultural training in the military. In Y. Kim (ed.), *International encyclopedia of intercultural communication.* Maiden, MA: Wiley Blackwell.

Mackenzie, L., & Wallace, M. (2015). Intentional design: Using iterative modification to enhance online learning for professional cohorts. In T. Milburn (ed.), *Communicating user experience: Applying local strategies research to digital media design.* Lanham, MD: Lexington.

Matoba, K. (2013). *Global integral competence for Cosmopolitan Communication.* CMM Institute Fellows Paper. Retrieved from: http://www.cmminstitute.net/sites/default/files/2013%20Fellow%20-Matoba%20final%20paper.pdf

Myers, M., & Hodges, S. (2011). The structure of self-other overlap and its relationship to perspective-taking. *Personal Relationships, 19*(4), 663–679. DOI: 10.1111/j.1475-6811.2011.01382.x

Pearce, W. B. (1989). *Communication and the human condition.* Carbondale, IL: Southern Illinois University Press.

Pearce, W. B. (2008). *Making social worlds: A communication perspective* (1st ed.). Hoboken, NJ: Wiley-Blackwell.

Rehorick, D. A., & Bentz, V. M. (2008). *Transformative phenomenology: Changing ourselves, lifeworlds, and professional practice.* Lanham, MD: Lexington Books.

Rossmann, L. (1995). What if we asked circular questions instead of "rhetorical questions?": Possibilities for the classroom and daily interactions. Retrieved from https://eric.ed.gov/?id= ED391191

Skrbiš, Z. (2014). Coming to terms with cosmopolitanism, global citizenship & global competence. [Presentation]. Paper presented at the International Education Association of Australia's Global Citizenship Forum, *Fostering Global Citizenship and Global Competence: A National Symposium*. Retrieved from https://www.ieaa.org.au/documents/item/294

Snow, D. (2015). English teaching, intercultural competence, and critical incident exercises. *Language and Intercultural Communication, 15*(2), 285–299.

Sobré-Denton, M., & Bardhan, N. (2013). *Cultivating cosmopolitanism for intercultural communication*. New York, NY: Routledge.

Storti, C. (2015). Critical incident methodology. In J. Bennett (ed.), *Sage encyclopedia of intercultural competence* (pp. 136–138). Thousand Oaks, CA: Sage.

Wingate, J. (2010). Using online student polling for continuous improvement planning (Doctoral Dissertation). Retrieved from https://etd.auburn.edu/bitstream/handle/10415/2237/July9 resubmissiondissertation.pdf?sequence=2&isAllowed=y

Wiseman, R. (2002). Intercultural communication competence. In W. Gudykunst & B. Mody (eds.), *Handbook of intercultural and international communication* (pp. 207–224). Thousand Oaks, CA: Sage.

Chapter 28

Social and cultural diversity in training and group facilitation

Sara DeTurk

Abstract

An essential element of communication proficiency and training is responsiveness to social and cultural difference. Trainers should be prepared to accommodate differences in learning styles, cognitive styles, communication styles, and other cultural norms, and to manage power dynamics and mitigate the effects of stereotypes and prejudice through group facilitation processes. This chapter will guide trainers in developing programs that are culturally sensitive and inclusive, and that foster full participation, equity, and voice among group members.

What does it mean to demonstrate communication proficiency? In my mind, the concept is problematic. "Proficiency," for one thing, seems to imply standards of evaluation that are objective and context-free. If the outcome of an interaction is satisfactory to me but not you (perhaps because I have used my knowledge or power to take advantage of you), who is to judge whether my communication has been "proficient"? Communication, moreover, is inherently paradoxical. On one hand, of course, it connotes sharing and commonality. On the other hand, though, it implies bridging across difference. This is especially true to the extent that communicators reflect different social groups or cultural backgrounds. This chapter, then, aims to sensitize readers to ways in which difference is of central relevance to training and group facilitation as communication processes, and to equip trainers and facilitators with strategies for applying this sensitivity in various group contexts.

Like all communication, training is most effective when carefully tailored to its target audience and cultural context. We need to be aware of the norms and other cultural characteristics of client organizations and must be mindful of the demographic makeup of each trainee group. Trainees represent wide varieties of learning styles, cognitive styles, and communication styles, and it behooves us to understand these differences and be able to adjust instructional methods accordingly. Equally important, though, is sensitivity to social and cultural diversity within training groups. As trainers, we should be prepared not only to accommodate differences, but also to manage power dynamics and mitigate the effects of stereotypes and prejudice through group facilitation processes. This helps to ensure comfort and safety for participants and to draw out ideas from diverse perspectives; it is also important for promoting an equitable learning environment and modeling/promoting communication processes that contribute to social justice. This chapter will guide you in developing training programs that are culturally sensitive and inclusive, and that foster full participation and voice among group members.

It will address cultural differences in learning styles, cognitive styles, and communication styles; approaches to training that accommodate difference; challenges of social diversity to group facilitation, and best practices for facilitating diverse groups.

The recommendations presented in this chapter are rooted in an understanding of training as a form of communication, and of communication as inherently intercultural in the broadest sense of the term. Communication inevitably implies interaction with others, and since no two of us are the same, that means striving for understanding across difference. For trainers, essential skills include not only needs assessment, curriculum design, oral presentation, and knowledge of group dynamics, but also communication proficiencies at interpersonal, small group, and organizational levels, with an awareness of, and appreciation for, culture.

Learning styles, cognitive styles, communication styles, culture, and identity

Our first task as trainers is to understand ourselves and our trainees. Beyond "audience analysis," a successful trainer – and, indeed, a successful communicator in general – is aware not only of the cultural characteristics of the training group, but also of one's own social/cultural identities, assumptions, preferences, and styles of thinking, learning, and communicating.

In terms of cultural patterns, researchers from a variety of disciplines have catalogued national and ethnic differences in value orientations (e.g. Hofstede, 1980), cognitive styles (Anderson, 1988; Jonassen & Grabowski, 1993), and communication styles (Scollon & Wong-Scollon, 1991). Value orientations, in brief, reflect cultural worldviews and involve concepts such as individualism, power distance, and tolerance for ambiguity. As Hofstede (1986) has explained, these have important implications for teaching and training in group settings; individualists, for example, may enjoy competitive activities, whereas their collectivistic counterparts may prefer collaboration. In terms of power distance (i.e. the appropriateness of social differentiation by status), trainers attempting to encourage informal, egalitarian group norms may face resistance from trainees who prefer high degrees of formality and clear lines of authority. Creative, open-ended tasks, similarly, can be uncomfortable for people with high levels of uncertainty avoidance.

Cognitive styles refer to individuals' ways of thinking: interacting with their environments, gathering information from them, and constructing, organizing, and applying knowledge (Jonassen & Grabowski, 1993). Anderson (1988) reviewed research indicating apparent racial/ethnic differences between students who thrived in the abstract, field-independent learning expected by most school settings and those who preferred more holistic (and social) cognitive approaches.

Communication styles are also important to be cognizant of, as they can have significant impacts on group processes. Scollon and Wong-Scollon (1991), for example, observed ethnic differences between native (Athabaskan) Canadians and Anglo-Canadians in how much they talked, how they presented themselves, how status was expressed, and in terms of norms of turn-taking and narrative organization. In meetings, these differences led not only to problems of synchrony, but also of stereotyping (of Athabaskans as ignorant and reticent, and of Anglos as arrogant and pushy). They led, moreover, to dynamics in which Anglos tended to dominate conversation and control agendas. Educators and facilitators, in order to foster harmonious, equitable, and productive communication, should be sensitive to the existence of such differences and their potential impacts on group processes.

Within the training literature, considerable attention has been devoted to variation in learning styles. Beebe, Mottet, and Roach (2013) describe, for example, differences between "reflective" and "impulsive" learners; differences among visual, aural, and kinesthetic learners; and Gardner's (1983) seven types of intelligence. One of the most well-established models is that of David Kolb (1984), who differentiated among "assimilators" (people who prefer to learn via lectures by expert sources), "divergers" (who prefer learning through observation), "convergers" (who prefer to learn by doing and thinking through problems logically), and "accommodators" (who prefer to solve problems through instinct, trial-and-error, and cooperation with others). Joy and Kolb (2009), moreover, have found cultural differences in learning styles. In a meta-analysis of teacher adaptation of educational content, Lovelace (2005) found that accommodation for student learning styles led to better attitudes and significantly higher test scores. It stands to reason that training programs would experience similar benefits of responsiveness to difference.

Regardless of whether or not they are a function of nationality or ethnicity, differences in styles will exist within any training group. As trainers, we can try to accommodate the styles of particular cultures where appropriate, but most important is to check the tendency to privilege our own preferences and taken-for-granted assumptions. Ask yourself: What are my cultural assumptions and worldviews? What characterizes my communication style, cognitive style, and learning style, and how might they differ from those of other people? We should be reflexive about these predispositions, and cautious about designing training programs that reflect them too heavily. Differences in styles and preferences can – and should – be accommodated in training through variety.

Andragogy and the Experiential Learning Cycle

Two features of training (in contrast to traditional classroom teaching) make it easily responsive to difference. The first is that it tends to be learner-centered, and the second is that it tends to be experiential. A learner-centered approach to education is a hallmark of what Malcolm Knowles (1990; Knowles, Holton, & Swanson, 2001) called *andragogy*, or the education of adults. Rather than being based on a mandated, standardized curriculum, adult education (and training in particular) should be responsive to the needs and concerns of the particular learners.

Adults, typically, engage in education either because they are intrinsically motivated or because it is specifically required for their jobs. In the former case, trainees know what it is they want to learn, and in the latter case, training can be tailored to their professional needs. In either case, effective training is designed and implemented in ways that center the trainees' various interests and real-life experiences.

The second way in which andragogy is experiential is that it follows what Kolb (1984) described as the Experiential Learning Cycle, which by definition incorporates all four learning styles. The first part of the cycle is *concrete experience*, where learners have exposure to direct experience with a phenomenon. This can either be through their own life or on-the-job experiences, or through a structured activity such as a role-play, simulation, video, or case study. The second part of the cycle is *reflective observation*, where trainees consider what they have experienced or witnessed, and reflect on its significance. The third phase is *abstract conceptualization*, or theorizing about the experience and observations. The fourth and final phase is *active experimentation*, where they practice, test, or apply what they have learned. Kolb's learning cycle is not only effective in integrating and consolidating knowledge and skills; it also responds to all four learning styles.

In order to reach *all* training participants, then, we should (1) be aware of wide ranges of cultural and individual patterns of learning, cognition, and communication; (2) be prepared to learn about their trainees and accommodate their needs; (3) expect differences *within* each training group; and (4) accommodate difference through (among other things) the use of the experiential learning cycle. Such sensitivity to difference is a central component of communication proficiency within training contexts.

Social diversity and group dynamics

To accommodate difference in all of its forms, training should be inclusive in terms of the styles and orientations addressed above. In terms of learning styles, this means building the experiential learning cycle into training plans and varying the types of activities. Otherwise, it requires awareness of cultural variation, knowledge of the training participants, and reflexivity about our own assumptions and preferences. Beyond accommodating difference, though, effective and ethical training requires sensitivity to group dynamics and intercultural communication.

Social diversity complicates group dynamics because it heightens the likelihood of problems such as misunderstandings, stereotypes, prejudice, uncertainty, anxiety, and marginalization. Research in psychology and communication has identified a variety of intercultural challenges. Perhaps the most obvious is difficulty with encoding and decoding messages (Kim, 1991). Others include attribution errors (Pettigrew, 1979), intergroup posturing (Brewer & Miller, 1984; Brown & Turner, 1981), and depersonalization and distancing of the "other" (Lee & Boster, 1991). For communication trainers and group facilitators, then, we must be able to minimize these problems through interpersonal communication (especially metacommunication) and group techniques.

Collier (1990) reviewed research on group processes indicating that ethnic and racial minority groups such as Asians (Collier & Powell, 1990), Mexican Americans, and Native Americans (Shen, Sanchez, & Huang, 1984) experienced anxiety and verbal reticence vis-à-vis white Americans in mixed groups. While some of these findings related to linguistic confidence in English-speaking contexts, Collier also proposed sociocultural power as an explanation.

Communicating training inevitably occurs within contexts where some people have more authority, social privilege, and cultural capital than others. Sometimes this relative power is formal, as in cases where supervisors are in training sessions with their subordinates. In other cases it reflects cultural systems of oppression that privilege some groups by virtue of their gender, race, social class, or other identities. People with more social power tend to find themselves in institutional environments whose spoken and unspoken norms reflect them, and where they feel not only more comfortable but also more entitled to speak and drive decisions than their more marginalized counterparts. Members of muted groups, in contrast, find that even when they do speak, their ideas are often misunderstood, ignored, or co-opted (Ardener, 1978; Essed, 1991; Kramarae, 1981; Orbe, 1998; Parker, 2002). Learners whose identities or cultural patterns do not reflect the expectations of the institution are often victims of silencing (muting), exclusion, and even microaggressions.

Educators sometimes feed into this marginalization through discourse that centers dominant groups as "normal" and renders subordinate (minority) group members as "other" (DeTurk, 2018). In a recent analysis of U.S. public speaking classes, Boromisza-Habashi, Hughes, and Malkowski (2016) observed that the curricula tended to reproduce Anglo-American assumptions and ideals. The implied goals of public speaking skills, for example, typically involved individual upward mobility within entrepreneurial contexts. Speakers and audiences, furthermore, were expected to share a direct, egalitarian relationship. The study also identified other culturally-specific norms such as those relating to argument structures and emotional expression.

In order to inhibit this tendency, we can consciously reflect on who our intended or imagined audience is. We can also strive to use inclusive language, stereotype-free materials, and examples that speak to a wide range of experiences. To the extent possible, too, we should get to know each of our trainees as individuals.

Effective facilitators can also manage dysfunctional power relations by drawing attention to them, inviting and honoring contributions of those who are silenced, and enforcing ground rules (discussed further below). We can also promote inclusion through techniques like paraphrasing and active listening. Another strategy is to minimize reliance on large-group discussion, which is especially prone to muting, especially where language fluency is a barrier for some participants. Turning instead to small-group activities and those that rely on visual, rather than verbal, expression can empower and draw out participants who might otherwise be silenced.

In many cases the most important gap is between the trainee group and the trainer (DeTurk, 1992). Not only is the trainer often an outsider to an otherwise cohesive group, but s/he is often of a very different educational level and represents a "training" culture that has its own idiosyncrasies. Collier (1990), for example, noted that group facilitation as a process tends to be highly reflective of U.S American cultural norms, especially low power distance. (I am mindful of the irony here in advocating a very egalitarian approach in the interest of cultural sensitivity!) Collier recommended encouraging groups to establish their own rules and norms and enabling an emergent group culture to evolve. Casse (1981), similarly, offered guidance for trainers working outside of their own cultures: When taking approaches that are unfamiliar to the trainees, we should explain the reasons for those approaches, seek information and feedback from the trainees, and negotiate a "third culture" within the training environment. In doing so, Casse advised, we should keep the goals of the training clearly in mind.

Responsiveness to diversity and power dynamics requires high-level communication skills. Techniques like deep listening, solicitation of feedback, and perspective-taking are especially important in contexts of social and cultural difference. We must also be prepared for the facilitation of dialogue and sensitive conversations which may involve conflict. Cognitively, communication with culturally different others demands flexibility, tolerance for ambiguity, nonjudgmentalness, complex thinking, and cultural self-awareness (DeTurk, 1992).

Sensitive, inclusive, and effective group facilitation

Troublesome intercultural dynamics can be mitigated by careful training design and mindful group facilitation. When culture and identity are addressed directly as fundamental elements of communication, this signals to trainees that we are open to addressing and interrogating difference. By being explicit about how culture and identity are reflected in the training program, we can minimize trainees' uncertainty and encourage open discussion of difference.

Trainees' anxiety may be largely driven by their uncertainty about each other; giving them opportunities to get to know each other through non-threatening activities can help to alleviate it. Such activities can include icebreakers, openers, and small-group (or paired) exercises. High-risk topics (such as conflict or racism) should be addressed using low-risk activities (such as lectures, videos, or private reflection) until participants are comfortable with one another. Riskier activities such as roleplays or large-group dialogue, on the other hand, are best reserved for less threatening topics.

Tools for lessening misunderstanding include active listening, paraphrasing, perception checking, and metacommunication. When the training is not in participants' first language, we should also avoid using slang, and should ensure that oral messages are supplemented with clear visual aids.

To reduce stereotypes, trainees should be provided chances to learn about one another simultaneously as individuals and as members of their social/cultural groups. Encourage them to talk both about their social identities *and* their idiosyncrasies as they relate to the training topic, and put them in heterogeneous teams for group tasks.

When it comes to group discussion, the greatest threat to full participation is muting. When this occurs, you can represent voices not being heard by playing the "devil's advocate." Other strategies are to explicitly invite the thoughts of those who have not spoken. Depending on the goals of the training, too, it may be beneficial to ask participants to notice who is (not) speaking, or make other observations about the communication dynamics in the room.

Muting can also be managed by plenty of structure that counteracts that tendency of more vocal participants to dominate conversation. Such structure can take a variety of forms: communication (and justification) of expectations, ground rules, and facilitator intervention. Regarding expectations, I always point out at the beginning of a program that we all have different styles of thinking, learning, and communicating, and that speaking and listening are equally valuable. I explain the importance of making room for each participant to do both, and I tell trainees that I may intervene if I find some people dominating discussion or others being silenced. Ground rules are critical; a typical list includes things like listening to understand, avoiding debate, showing respect for others, speaking only for oneself, listening actively, maintaining confidentiality, and balancing speaking and listening. It is important to give participants a chance to edit and ratify the ground rules as a group. Once this has been achieved, the trainer has relative freedom to intervene to manage participation.

Conclusions

Fully engaging the social and cultural diversity in any training group is imperative for the program to reflect real-world communication. It also validates learners and helps them to develop intercultural awareness and skills. One of the most fundamental ways to do this is to vary the training methods and activities, not only because this accommodates the experiential learning cycle and a variety of learning styles, but because observation, individual reflection, and small-group activities are less prone to muting than large-group discussion. When engaging trainees in large-group conversation, structured facilitation and ground rules are essential.

It is also important to consider the cultural appropriateness of training activities for any given group, and to be responsive to difference. Culturally sensitive trainers demonstrate reflexivity, too, about our own identities and the cultural norms being reflected and reinscribed through the program; to ignore the position of the trainer is to obscure the power dynamics in the training situation. When the educator's identity is made explicit, "then the power dynamics in the group can be linked more consciously to the wider power relations in which our work is situated" (Arnold, Burke, James, Martin, & Thomas, 1991, p. 12). We must also be mindful of how we are perceived by others. As a white, middle-aged, U.S. American woman, for example, I strive to reflect both on how my perceptions and communication patterns are culturally situated *and* how I might be perceived by trainees who do not share my identities (including how I present myself through dress, verbal and nonverbal communication styles, use of humor, etc.). Depending on the training topic, it may be important to share the training task with a colleague who represents other identities; this can facilitate both trust and understanding within the training group.

Many of these tips are especially important for training *on* culture and diversity. Because culture and difference are central to communication, though, they should be part of any communication-related curriculum. Regardless of the topic, sensitivity to difference is a key element of communication proficiency, and of the necessary skill set for communication coaches, trainers, teachers, and consultants.

References

Anderson, J. A. (1988). Cognitive styles and multicultural populations. *Journal of Teacher Education, 39*(1), 2–9. DOI: 10.1177/002248718803900102

Ardener, E. (1978). Some outstanding problems in the analysis of events. In G. Schwinner (ed.), *The yearbook of symbolic anthropology* (pp. 103–121). London: C. Hurst.

Arnold, R., Burke, B., James, C., Martin, D., & Thomas, B. (1991). *Educating for a change.* Toronto: Between the Lines.

Beebe, S. A., Mottet, T. P., & Roach, K. D. (2013). *Training and development: Communicating for success.* Boston, MA: Pearson.

Boromisza-Habashi, D., Hughes, J. M. F., & Malkowski, J. A. (2016). Public speaking as cultural ideal: Internationalizing the public speaking curriculum. *Journal of International and Intercultural Communication, 9*(1), 20–34. DOI: 10.1080/17513057.2016.1120847

Brewer, M., & Miller, N. (1984). Beyond the contact hypothesis: Theoretical perspectives on desegregation. In N. Miller & M. Brewer (eds.), *Groups in contact: The psychology of desegregation* (pp. 281–302). New York, NY: Academic Press.

Brown, R., & Turner, J. (1981). Interpersonal and intergroup behavior. In J. Turner & H. Giles (eds.), *Intergroup behavior* (pp. 33–65). Chicago, IL: University of Chicago Press.

Casse, P. (1981). *Training for the cross-cultural mind.* Washington, DC: SIETAR.

Collier, M. J. (November, 1990). The role of culture in group facilitation processes. Paper presented at the Speech Communication Association, Chicago, IL.

Collier, M. J., & Powell, R. (1990). Ethnicity, instructional communication and classroom systems. *Communication Quarterly, 38,* 334–349.

DeTurk, S. (2018). All students are special (though some are more special than others). In A. Atay & D. Trebing (eds.), *Rearticulating the discourse of "special populations": Critical intercultural communication pedagogy approach* (pp. 11–22). New York, NY: Routledge.

DeTurk, S. (1992). Training trainers to work with culturally diverse groups. Unpublished M.Ed. thesis, University of Massachusetts, Amherst, MA.

Essed, P. (1991). *Understanding everyday racism: An interdisciplinary theory.* Newbury Park, CA: Sage Publications.

Gardner, H. (1983). *Frames of mind: The theory of multiple intelligences.* New York, NY: Basic Books.

Hofstede, G. (1980). *Culture's consequences: International differences in work-related values.* Beverly Hills, CA: Sage Publications.

Hofstede, G. (1986). Cultural differences in teaching and learning. *International Journal of Intercultural Relations, 10,* 301–320.

Jonassen, D. H., & Grabowski, B. L. (1993). *Handbook of individual differences, learning, and instruction.* Hillsdale, NJ: Lawrence Erlbaum.

Joy, S., & Kolb, K. A. (2009). Are there cultural differences in learning style? *International Journal of Intercultural Relations, 33,* 60–85. DOI: 10.1016/j.ijintrel.2008.11.002

Kim, Y. Y. (1991). Intercultural competence: A systems-theoretic view. In S. Ting-Toomey & F. Korzenny (eds.), *Cross-cultural interpersonal communication* (pp. 259–275). Newbury Park, CA: Sage Publications.

Knowles, M. (1990). *The adult learner: A neglected species.* Houston, TX: Gulf.

Knowles, M. S., Holton, E. F., & Swanson, R. A. (2001). *The adult learner: The definitive classic in adult education and human resource development.* Woburn, MA: Butterworth-Heinemann.

Kolb, D. A. (1984). *Experiential learning: Experience as the source of learning and development.* Englewood Cliffs, NJ: Prentice-Hall.

Kramarae, C. (1981). *Women and men speaking.* Rowley, MA: Newbury House.

Lee, H. O., & Boster, F. J. (1991). Social information for uncertainty reduction during initial interactions. In S. Ting-Toomey & F. Korzenny (eds.), *Cross-cultural interpersonal communication* (pp. 189–212). Newbury Park, CA: Sage Publications.

Lovelace, M. K. (2005). A meta-analysis of experimental research based on the Dunn and Dunn learning-style model, 1980–2000. *Journal of Educational Research, 98*(3), 176–183.

Orbe, M. P. (1998). *Constructing co-cultural theory.* Thousand Oaks, CA: Sage Publications.

Parker, P. S. (2002). Negotiating identity in raced and gendered workplace interactions: The use of strategic communication by African American women senior executives within dominant culture organizations. *Communication Quarterly, 50,* 251–268.

Pettigrew, T. (1979). The ultimate attribution error: Extending Allport's cognitive analysis of prejudice. *Personality and Social Psychology Bulletin, 5,* 461–476.

Scollon, R., & Wong-Scollon, S. (1991). Athabaskan-English interethnic communication. In D. Carbaugh (ed.), *Cultural communication and intercultural contact* (pp. 259–286). Hillsdale, NJ: Lawrence Erlbaum Associates.

Shen, W. W., Sanchez, A. M., & Huang, T. (1984). Verbal participation in group therapy: A comparative study on New Mexico ethnic groups. *Hispanic Journal of Behavioral Sciences, 6,* 277–284.

Author index

Aakhus, M. 22
Aboutanous, M. 88
Abrams, L. 381
Acheson, K. 354
Adams, K. 390, 392, 394–5
Adams, Linda 214
Adams, R.B. 350
Addison, R.M. 220, 222
Adriaanse, D.J. 311
Adrian, A.D. 53–5, 62
Afifi, T.D. 39–40
Aggarwal, R. 88–9
Agnew, B. 241, 249–50
Aguinis, H. 26, 69, 81
Ahaus, K. 316
Ahyun, K. 264, 351
Alexander, B. 149
Allan, E.G. 390
Allen, J. 182
Allen, M. 263–4, 287
Allen, T.H. 15
Alley, M. 137–41
Altschuld, J.W. 65–7
Ambrose, S.A. 274
Amoroso, L.M. 53, 58
Andersen, J.F. 287
Anderson, A.O. 290
Anderson, D.L. 51
Anderson, J.A. 415
Anderson, M. 279
Anderson, N. 310
Anderson, R.B. 135, 137
Anderson, T. 129
Andresen, L.W. 378
Andrews, C.M. 272
Andrews, D.H. 255
Andrews, M. 243
Anson, R. 146
Antion, T. 212
Apfel, N. 300, 306
Apperson, J.M. 263

Ardener, E. 417
Aree, H.C. 301, 306
Aritzeta, A. 309–11, 316
Armellini, A. 113
Armstrong, S.J. 109, 113
Arnold, R. 420
Aronson, E. 301, 304
Arthur, W., Jr. 65–6, 75
Asen, R. 30
Ashcraft, K.L. 38–9
Aston, R.R. 309
Atkinson, C. 138, 141
Atkinson, J. 290
Augestein, J. 88
Avolio, B.J. 378
Aziz, H. 255

Babbie, E. 54
Babin, B.J. 180, 183, 185
Backlund, P. 194
Baddeley, A. 136
Baker, T. 182, 186
Balandin, S. 75
Baldwin, Jay 363, 367
Baldwin, T. 74, 78, 272
Bales, R.F. 309
Ball, H. 290
Ball-Rokeach, S.J. 149
Banas, J.A. 284–5, 377, 384
Bandura, A. 301, 304
Barbazette, J. 375
Bardhan, N. 402, 406
Barge, J.K. 243
Barker, L.L. 353
Barker, R.T. 377, 382
Barkley, E. 407
Baron, R. 381
Bar-On, R. 391
Barra, V. 381
Barrett, F.J. 187
Barroquillo, K. 26

Subject index

Note: Page citations in **bold** indicate text contained within tables, and page citations in *italics* indicate text contained within figures.

data collection methods 54–55, 69–71, **72,** 73
debriefing 270–80: content 273; definition
of best practices 272–9; effective
communication skills 275–9; importance of
271–2; location 274; overview of 279–80;
participants involved 273; planning the
debrief 273–4, 279; rationale 274; strategic
structuring of debrief 274–5, 279; time
frame 273
deliberate practice activities 194–208: access to
resources 196–7, **203**; audience connection
197–8, **203**; audience-centered mindset
205–6; authenticity 206; commitment
206; community 196–7, **203**; definition
of deliberate practice 195; description and
methods of study 195–6; effort ratings
of 202–7; experience 200, **203**; feedback
201–2, **203**; focused attention to detail 207;
frequency of 202–7; implications for training
and consulting 205–7; learning 198–200,
203; limitations of 205; overview of 207–8;
reading 207; reflection, opportunities for
206–7; rehearsal 200, **203**; rehearsal 207;
relevance of 202–7; self-development
198–200, **203**; self-monitoring 201–2, **203**;
studying 207; themes and activities 196–202;
video critique 206–7; writing 207
diagnosis of organizational needs 50–63:
anonymity 58; benefits of 60–1;
Burke-Litwin model 56; client lessons 60;
confidentiality 58; context 50–1; credibility
59; critical incidents 55; data interpretation
57–8; definition of diagnosis 51; diagnosis
as an intervention 59; diagnosis, disruption
of 59; diagnostic methods 53–5; diagnostic
models 55–7; diagnostics professionals 51;
executive support 58; external consultants
60; faculty and academic tenure 60–1; field
notes 58–60; focus groups 53–4; force
field analysis 56; form and function 59;
foundations 51; general consulting process
52; human process issues 57; human resource
issues 58; ICA Communication Audit 52;
internal consultants 60; interpersonal lessons
58–9; interviews 53–4; Johari Window 56;
leadership support 58; learning and skill
development 59; limitations 59; mixed
methodology 59; network analysis 54–5;
OD consulting process 52–3; old data 60;
ownership for problems and solutions 60;
personal lessons 59; poor communication
60; process lessons 59; processes for 52–3;
reflective questions 62; standardized
instruments 54; summary of 62; surveys 54;
SWOT 57; techno-structural issues 57–8;
town hall meetings 53–4; training 61; trust,

impact of 58; utility 59; validity 59; voice to
others 58–9
distraction 110, 124, 130, 140, 150, 154, 157,
214, 285, **380, 383**, 393
diversity *see* social and cultural diversity

EDIT technique 41,42, 262, 275, 332, 335
effectiveness: communication 93, 98, 197;
slide design 135, 139; group 393–394;
performance *222*; persuasion 367, 369;
training 16, 61, 75, 113, 116, 233, 234, 256,
259, 272, 286–288, 318, 332
emotional appeals 366
ethics 3, 5, 370, 262, 403
evaluation *see* training evaluation
experiential learning cycle *see* Kolb's
Experiential Learning Cycle
experiential learning techniques 407–11:
alternative viewpoints 409; application 409;
background 409; circular questioning 410;
context considerations 409; critical incident
methodology 408–10; cultural consideration
409; descriptive questions 410; elaboration of
concepts 409; participant case studies 407–8;
see also Cosmopolitan Communication
experiential learning theory *see* Kolb's
Experiential Learning Theory
expertise *see* organizational expertise

facilitation *see* group facilitation skills
feedback 201–3, 234–5, 305–6
feminism 37, 39, 41, 43–5; *see also* transparent
practice
focus 95: attention to detail 207; exposure
experiences 166–7, 170–2; groups 53–4, 256;
questions 223–5
frames: civic 21–33; theoretical 326–38

group communication 388–98: overview of
398; pros and cons of group work 389–90;
see also small group process model
group dynamics 417–18
group facilitation skills 355–8: group
facilitation strategies 357–8; group
interaction 356–7; structure for group
discussion 356; *see also* communication skills
group techniques 216–17
group work 389–90
growth mindset 300, **302**, 305–6; *see also*
Implicit Person Theory (IPT)

heutagogical learning 129; *see also*
mobile devices
higher education context 129, 238–42, 249–50
holistic approach *see* Human Performance
Technology (HPT) framework

93; instructions for coders 93; instructions for use 94; interpersonal noise 97; inter-rater agreement 94; key terms 93–4; noise management 96–7; nonverbal communication 94; organization 95; social talk 96; structure 95; team emergent leadership 97–8; team emotional control 95; team flow 95; team listening 97; team noise 96; team relationships 95–6; team space negotiation 96; trustworthy behavior 96; verbal communication 94; *see also* observational assessment

verbal immediacy 265, 267, 350–1: nonverbal 10, 31, 264, 276, 278, 284, 287–8, 291–3
veterans 401–12

webinar development 150–7: adult learning theory **153**; evaluation 155–7; follow-up 155–7; follow-up evaluation, responses on **156**; participation during delivery 152–5; post-work **153**, 155–7; pre-work 151–2
webinar training 145–58: adult learners 146–8; characteristics of a good story **150**; learning challenges 145–6; learning outcomes 146–8; overview of 157–8; storytelling as a training method 148–50
written training proposals 263; See also requests for proposals RFPs

Zoeller, Hope 150–2, 154–6

Printed in the United States
by Baker & Taylor Publisher Services